The Mammoth Book of
True Crime

Real Stories of Bad Behavior

By

Jim Fisher

ISBN: 1502496496
ISBN-13: 978-1502496492

The beauty of being a true crime writer is that every day there are fifty new stories.
Jim Fisher

Life's tough...it's even tougher if you're stupid.
John Wayne

If you want to know who your friends are, get yourself a jail sentence.
Charles Bukowski

Also by Jim Fisher

Security for Business and Industry

The Lindbergh Case

Fall Guys:
False Confessions and the Politics Of Murder

The Ghosts of Hopewell:
Setting the Record Straight in the Lindbergh Case

Crimson Stain (mass market paperback)

Ten Percent of Nothing:
The Literary Agent From Hell

The Writer's Quotebook:
500 Authors on Creativity, Craft, and the Writing Life

Forensics Under Fire:
Are Bad Science and Dueling Experts Corrupting Criminal Justice?

SWAT Madness and The Militarization of the American Police:
A National Dilemma

Crimson Stain (trade paper edition with Epilogue)

The GE Mound Case:
The Archaeological Disaster and Criminal Persecution of Art Gerber

The Mammoth Book of Murder:
True Stories of Violent Death

CONTENTS

ACKNOWLEDGEMENTS

Veronica Fisher designed and prepared this book for publication. I am grateful for her invaluable contribution to this project.

1 MISSING PERSONS

The Florida Millionaire

Guma Aguiar's parents immigrated to the United States from Brazil in 1979 when he was two-years-old. The family, from Rio de Janeiro, settled in Pompano Beach, Florida. After college, Guma, a born-again Christian, moved to Texas where, working with his uncle in the oil and gas business, he made a fortune.

In 2012, the 35-year-old millionaire lived in Fort Lauderdale with his wife Jamie and their four children. The family resided in a $5 million, six-bedroom mansion located in the exclusive oceanside neighborhood called Rio Vista.

Aguiar, after converting to Orthodox Judaism, began donating millions of dollars to charitable causes in Jerusalem where he was considered a hero philanthropist. Others considered Aguiar a rich, eccentric man who was losing touch with reality. (Aguiar, according to reports, had spent some time in mental wards. I do not know the extent or nature of his mental health problem.) His marriage to Jamie, whom he'd met in high school, had become a tumultuous relationship. On one occasion he had sued Jamie for divorce, then later withdrew the petition. In April 2012, Jamie Aguiar's attorney challenged the prenuptial agreement she had signed. The following month, Guma transferred guardianship of his $100 million estate ("in the event of my incapacity") from his wife Jamie to his mother, Ellen Aguiar. Jamie's legal representatives challenged this as well.

On June 18, 2012, Jamie Aguiar informed Guma that she intended to file for divorce. An hour later, at 8:30 in the evening, Guma was seen driving his twin-engine, fiberglass powerboat "T.T. Zion" through Port Everglades toward the Atlantic Ocean. Just after midnight, employees of a beachfront bar called Elbo Room spotted a boat in rough seas drifting toward the beach. The craft came to rest on shore with its navigation lights still on, the shifter in gear, and the keys in the ignition. Guma Aguiar was not in the boat.

That morning, while investigators searched Aguiar's boat, the Coast Guard launched a search-and-rescue operation. Inside the abandoned craft, officers recovered the owner's wallet, his iPhone, a black T-shirt, and a pair of flip-flops. According to the boat's GPS system, Aguilar had traveled at high speeds two miles northeast of his house before the craft turned around and started drifting back to the shore. Aguiar had left his wedding ring at home.

After three days, the Coast Guard called off the search-and-rescue mission. Several weeks after Guma's disappearance, Jamie, engaged in a battle against her mother-in-law for control of the $100 million estate, fired her missing husband's chief financial officer. At this point in the case, everybody had a lawyer that was costing the family $1 million a month in legal fees. (In big money disputes like this, the lawyers are always the big winners. When they're finished with the case, there usually isn't much left for anyone else.) The Rio Vista mansion was put on the market along with Aguiar's 75-foot yacht, and his twin-engine powerboat.

Unless Aguiar was found alive, the distribution of his assets would remain in limbo. Under Florida law, it takes five years before a missing person can be declared legally dead.

So, what happened to Guma Aguiar? Did he go out for a quick swim and drown? (Did taking an evening swim in the ocean conform to past behavior?) Did mental illness and a hatred for his wife drive Guma to suicide? Assuming he went into the sea, is it unusual that the Coast Guard searchers didn't find his body? Why hasn't his corpse washed up on shore somewhere in this populated area? Could he be alive?

Jamie Aguiar's attorney told reporters that he believed Guma, after faking his own death, fled to the Netherlands where he was hiding out, or living under a false identity. The attorney suspected Guma was in the Netherlands because a close business associate of his had recently relocated there. Still, it was hard to believe that Aguiar would actually go to that much trouble to avoid the cost of divorce and the loss of some of his wealth.

I think it's unlikely that Guma Aguiar faked his own death, then disappeared into thin air. It seems to me the money trail would lead investigators right to him. I think he either downed accidentally or committed suicide. The history of mental illness points to suicide, but statistics suggest a downing accident. (Eighty percent of all drowning cases are accidental.) I'm sure some people believe this Florida millionaire was murdered. There doesn't seem to be evidence of foul play in this case - blood in the boat and so on - but I guess anything is possible when this much money is involved.

Gavin Smith: 20th Century Fox Executive

A native of the San Fernando Valley in Los Angeles County, Gavin Smith, in 1973, graduated from Van Nuys High where the six-foot-six basketball player caught the attention of UCLA's legendary coach, John Wooden. Two years later, Smith played on the UCLA team that won the NCAA college basketball championship.

In 1994, following a lackluster career as a television and theatrical film actor, Smith became a film distribution executive for 20th Century Fox. He worked out of an office in Calabasas, California, and resided with his wife Lisa and their three sons in the West Hills area of the San Fernando Valley.

In recent years, Gavin Smith had been plagued with financial and marital problems. His marriage had gone sour after Lisa became devoutly religious. After her conversion, Gavin began having affairs. He and Lisa had purchased their West Hills home when the Los Angeles area real estate market was booming. After the 2008 recession, the market value of the dwelling declined significantly. The Smiths ended up owing more on the house than it was worth. They were, as they say, underwater. The couple wanted to sell the place but couldn't afford the loss.

Because of the marital disharmony, Gavin, in the spring of 2012, was living with a friend in Oak Park, a community not far from his house in West Hills. At ten at night on May 1, 2012, Gavin drove off in his black 2000 Mercedes-Benz 500E. He hasn't been seen since.

At the Oak Park residence, Smith left behind his cellphone, credit cards, a shaving kit, and other personal belongings. To investigators, this indicated his intention to return to his friend's house. The next day, when he didn't show up for work, the Los Angeles County Sheriff's Office opened a missing persons investigation. As the days passed without a sign of Smith or his vehicle, volunteers began handing out flyers. Friends and family also posted a $20,000 reward. The Sheriff's office created a special hotline number for tipsters. None of these efforts bore fruit.

Investigators learned that Smith had been having an affair with Chandrika Creech, the wife of convicted drug dealer John Creech. On June 8, 2012, deputies searched the Creech home and were seen leaving the dwelling carrying several boxes and a computer. A few days later, a judge sentenced John Creech to eight years in prison for selling drugs.

On March 14, 2013, Lieutenant Dave Dolson of the Sheriff's Homicide Bureau, held a press conference to announce that the authorities had located Smith's missing Mercedes. The vehicle had been found on February 21 at a storage facility in the Porter Ranch area of San Fernando Valley. Detectives had linked the storage place to a person with close ties to John Creech.

Lieutenant Dolson said, "We believe Gavin Smith was murdered." The detective also named John Creech as a person of interest in the case. Investigators were still looking for Gavin Smith's body. Detective Dolson refused to say if Smith's Mercedes contained physical evidence of foul play.

In May 2014, a Los Angeles County Judge ruled Mr. Smith legally deceased. Law enforcement authorities had not located his body.

A Bad Ending to a Tragic Case

Twenty-four-year-old Mandy Matula lived with her parents in Eden Prairie, Minnesota, a town of 60,000 12 miles southwest of Minneapolis. A graduate of the University of Minnesota at Duluth, she worked for the Eden Prairie Public Works Department. In high school, Mandy had been a standout softball player.

In September 2012, Mandy ended her relationship with David Roe, a 24-year-old from Victoria, Minnesota who had been a classmate of Matula's at Eden Prairie High School. From 2007 to 2009 Roe had attended the University of St. Thomas where he played football. After the break-up, he and Mandy remained friends.

On the night of Wednesday, May 1, 2013, Roe showed up at the Matula house and asked to speak with Mandy. Leaving her cellphone and purse in the dwelling, she and Roe sat outside the house in his black, 2013 Ford Escape SUV. Around eleven-thirty that night, Roe drove off with Mandy in the vehicle.

Mandy didn't return home that night, and didn't show up for work in the morning. This prompted her worried mother to call David Roe to find out what happened to her. According to Roe, they had continued their discussion in Miller Park near the Matula house. Following an argument, Mandy got out of his vehicle. He presumed she had walked home. Mrs. Matula, at eight-thirty that morning, called the Eden Prairie Police Department and reported her daughter missing.

As the last person seen with Mandy Matula, David Roe was the obvious person of interest in her disappearance. For that reason, a detective with the Eden Prairie Police Department, on Thursday, May 2, asked him to come to the police station for questioning. That afternoon, after getting out of his SUV in the police department's parking lot, Roe put a handgun to his head and shot himself.

Paramedics rushed David Roe to the Hennepin County Medical Center. At three the next morning, he died from his self-inflicted head wound. He had stains of Mandy's blood on his jacket.

As a result of David Roe's suicide, investigators lost the best lead they had regarding Mandy Matula's whereabouts and status. A search of Roe's vehicle produced a note that, according to the police, contained "limited writing."

On Saturday, May 4, 300 volunteers searched Miller Park for Matula's body. Not far from the Victory Lutheran Church, a searcher found a bullet.

In October 2013, Mindy Matula's body was found in a shallow grave at Mississippi River Park in Rice, eighty miles from her home. Someone, presumably her boyfriend, shot her in the head with a single bullet.

Alive But Legally Dead

In 2002, forty-three-year-old Brenda Heist and her husband Lee were going through an amicable divorce. The couple had two children, a daughter who was eight, and a twelve-year-old son. They lived in Lititz Borough, a small Lancaster County town in southeastern Pennsylvania. Brenda worked as a bookkeeper at a local car dealership.

In an effort to finance her own apartment, Brenda applied for state housing assistance. The agency denied her request. Depressed, overwhelmed, and distraught, Brenda, after driving the children to school one day in February 2002, drove to a nearby town and parked her car in a bus station lot. From there she walked to a park where she sat on a bench and cried.

Brenda did not go back to her car and drive home that day. To her family and friends, and to the local police, she became a missing person.

Four days after Brenda dropped her children off at school, police found her car parked in the bus station lot. When a mother takes her kids to school and doesn't return home, the police assume that she has been abducted. As days went by without anyone hearing from or seeing Brenda Heist, detectives began to think that she might have had been murdered. At this point the missing persons case turned into a homicide investigation. As in most missing wife cases, the suspicion in Brenda's disappearance fell on her husband.

As psychic detectives and other whack-job callers flooded the Heist missing person investigators with false leads, homicide investigators focused on Lee Heist as their primary murder suspect. Mr. Heist had to quit his job. He ran into financial difficulties, and eventually lost his home. After several years as a suspect in his wife's disappearance and murder, investigators, after a series of polygraph tests cleared Lee Heist of wrongdoing in the case. His wife remained missing, however, and was presumed dead.

In 2008, the Lancaster County Major Crimes Unit began investigating the Brenda Heist disappearance as a cold-case murder. Two years later, Lee Heist petitioned a Lancaster County Court to declare his wife legally dead.

With Brenda officially declared "missing and possibly deceased", Mr. Heist was able to marry another woman.

As it turned out, while Lee Heist was put through hell as a suspect in his wife's murder, Brenda was alive in south Florida. On the day of her disappearance, two men approached the crying woman on the park bench. After she related her tale of woe, they invited her to join them on a hitchhiking trip to Florida. She accepted their offer.

Brenda Heist spent her first two years in Key Largo, Florida living under bridges and eating restaurant garbage. She entered a new phase in her life when she moved into a camp trailer with a man she met on the street. For the next seven years Brenda lived with this man in Key West. They both worked as day laborers cleaning boats and doing odd jobs for cash.

In 2011, after her relationship with her trailer roommate soured, Brenda was back on the street. She worked odd jobs and hung out on the beach. In December 2012, under her alias Kelsie Lyanne Smith, Brenda got a job as a live-in housekeeper for a family in Tampa Bay. (According to her employer she had good references.)

A few months after landing the housekeepers job, a police pulled Brenda over for driving with an expired license plate. The officer found drugs in her car. She served two months in Pensacola County Jail on the drug possession offense. Following her release from jail, she spent a few weeks behind bars in Santa Rosa County on an identify theft charge. At one point she lived in a tent community run by a Florida social service agency.

On Friday, April 26, 2013, Brenda Heist surrendered herself to the Monroe County Sheriff's Office. Thinking that there were warrants for her arrest out of Pinellas County, the 54-yar-old told the Monroe County deputies that she was at the end of her rope, and tired of running. She informed the officers that eleven years ago she had walked out on her family in Lititz Borough, Pennsylvania.

The Florida authorities called Lititz Borough Sergeant John Schofield with the news that Brenda Heist was not dead, and no longer missing. Her children, now college students, still had a mother.

On May 3, 2013, Brenda was sent back to the Santa Rosa County Jail on various theft-related charges. Morgan Heist, her 19-year-old daughter, has told reporters that she has no interest in reuniting with her mother.

On June 11, 2013 a judge in Pensacola, Florida sentenced Heist, known in the Santa Rose court system as Kelsie Smith, to one year in jail in connection a probation violation. She pleaded no contest to failing to check in with authorities after leaving the Pensacola area following her release from jail in April. She'd been on probation for using someone else's identification during a traffic stop.

Six Skeletons in the Lake

There's no telling how many murder victims lay on the bottom of America's lakes, rivers, and ponds. Most people don't realize that these boating, swimming, and fishing sites are also the unmarked graves of people who have gone missing and might never be found. It's a sobering thought.

Whenever a lake goes dry or is drained, law enforcement officers often gather to recover guns, knives, cars, safes, cellphones, computers, wallets, and other potential indicia of foul play. Occasionally, the remains of missing persons are exposed as well. When that happens, one mystery is solved and another is created.

On September 10, 2013, Oklahoma Highway Patrol officer George Hoyle, while testing a sonar detection device from a boat on Foss Lake 110 miles west of Oklahoma City, discovered a pair of vehicles sitting under twelve feet of murky water.

A week after the vehicles were detected, Darrell Splawn, a member of the state's underwater search and rescue team, dove into the lake for a closer look. At this point, officers believed they had found a pair of stolen cars.

When officer Splawn opened the door to one of the vehicles and probed its interior, his hand came in contact with a shoe. He also discovered, near the car, a human skull. The diver surfaced to report his finds. When the diver slipped back into the muddy water to check on the other vehicle, he saw skeletal remains inside the second car.

Once the heavily corroded cars--a 1952 Chevrolet and a 1969 Chevy Camaro--were pulled out of the reservoir, they revealed their gruesome secrets. Each vehicle contained the skeletal remains of three people. Officers also recovered, among other items, a muddy wallet and a purse.

On April 8, 1969, 69-year-old John Alva Porter, the owner of a 1952 green Chevy, went missing. In the car with him that night were his brother Arlie and 58-year-old Nora Marie Duncan. These three residents of nearby Elk City, along with the Chevy, disappeared without a trace. No one had any idea what had happened to the three of them.

Jimmy Williams, a 16-year-old from Sayre, Oklahoma, a town of 4,000 a few miles from the lake, owned a 1969 Chevrolet Camaro. On the night of November 20, 1970, he and two friends--Thomas Michael Rios and Leah Gail Johnson--both 18, were riding in Williams' car. Instead of going to the high school football game in Elk City, the trio had gone hunting on Turkey Creek Road. The teenagers and the Camaro were never seen again.

While the six skeletal remains are presumed to match the two sets of missing persons, it will take months to scientifically confirm their identities. Forensic scientists in the Oklahoma Medical Examiner's Office will compare DNA from the bones with DNA samples from surviving family members. Dr. Angela Berg, the state forensic anthropologist, will determine the gender, general stature, and approximate ages of the people pulled out of the lake. She will do this by analyzing leg and pelvic bones along with the skulls. This data will be compared with information contained in the missing person reports.

The 44-year-old remains did not tell investigators how and why they died. While the six people presumably drowned, they could have been murdered by gun, knife, or blunt instrument then dumped into the lake. To rule out foul play, the forensic pathologist and the anthropologist will look for signs of trauma such as bullet holes, knife wounds, and smashed or broken bones. The forensic scientists will also attempt to determine if the fates of the people inside the two cars are somehow connected. Assuming they were murdered, identifying the killer or killers, after all of these years, will not be easy.

Custer County Sheriff Bruce Peoples told an Associated Press reporter that it was possible these underwater victims had been driven accidentally into the lake where they had drowned. "We know that to happen even if you know your way around," he said. "It can happen that quick." While that is certainly possible, until murder is ruled out, it should be presumed.

Girls Missing Since 1971

On May 29, 1971, Cheryl Miller and Pamella Jackson, high school juniors from Vermillion, South Dakota, were in a 1960 Studebaker Lark en route to a party held at a gravel pit near Elk Point, a town near the Iowa border thirty miles east of their hometown. Along the way, the girls asked a car full of boys for directions to the party site. According to the boys, while leading the girls to the gravel pit, they looked in their rearview mirror and didn't see the Studebaker.

The Vermillion High School Students did not arrive at the party, and did not return home. The Studebaker went missing as well. (The youths who gave Miller and Jackson directions were never suspects in their disappearance.) The missing persons investigation led nowhere, and died on the vine. Decades after they went missing, no one had a clue regarding what had happened to the Vermillion students. It seemed they had just vanished off the face of the earth.

Early in 2007, Aloysius Black Crow, a South Dakota prison inmate, told the authorities that he had secretly audiotaped a fellow prisoner who had confessed to him that he had raped and murdered the Vermillion girls. David Lykken, the 54-year-old man Black Crow he'd taped, was a convicted rapist and kidnapper who was serving a 227-year prison sentence. In 2004, the police had found human bones, articles of female clothing, and a purse on Lykken's farm. (In 1971, Lykken would have been 18-years-old.)

A Union County Grand Jury based upon the jailhouse snitch's audiotape, indicted Lykken on two counts of murder, kidnapping, and rape. As it turned out, Black Crow's taped confession was a fake. The charges against Lykken were dropped, and in 2008, the jailhouse informant pleaded guilty to perjury.

On Tuesday, September 24, 2013, a fisherman on Brule Creek near Elk Point spotted the wheels of a car sitting on its roof in the drought-shallow creek. Several hours later, the authorities pulled a 1960 Studebaker Lark out of the water and mud. Inside the rusted vehicle, police officers discovered what appeared to be the skeletons of two people, remains presumed to be those of Cheryl Miller and Pamella Jackson.

On April 15, 2014, South Dakota Attorney General Marty Jackley told reporters that forensic scientists had confirmed the identities of the remains as being Miller and Jackson. Investigators and forensic experts determined that the vehicle's ignition and headlights were on when the car went into the water. The car was also in the third gear. Given the absence of gunshot or knife wounds, and no signs of alcohol consumption, the deaths went into the books as accidental.

The attorney general said the families could collect the remains. As a missing persons case, this 42-year-old mystery has been solved. While the case is officially closed, family members will never know the exact circumstances of the crash, or how quickly the girls had died.

If the lakes, rivers, creeks, and ponds in the United States suddenly went dry, there wouldn't be enough forensic scientists to analyze all of the remains. America's waterways function as graves for the missing among us, people whose stories will never be told.

The Missing College Woman

In 2011, Lauren Spierer, a 20-year-old fashion merchandising major from Edgemont, New York, attended Indiana University at Bloomington. She resided in the Smallwood Apartment complex located in downtown Bloomington. The university sophomore disappeared on June 3, 2011, and despite the efforts of the Bloomington Police Department and the FBI, she remains a missing person.

The Spierer case has attracted a lot of attention from the national media that has provided investigators with thousands of investigative tips and leads that have not produced results. The following narrative of Spierer's activities and associations before she disappeared are based on surveillance camera footage and the accounts of two male students who, at various times, were with her that night.

Around midnight, Spierer and a friend showed up at a party hosted by an Indiana student named Jay Rosenbaum. At 1:46 in the morning, Spierer left Rosenbaum's apartment with another student, Corey Rossman. A short time later, Rossman and Spierer were seen entering Kilroy's Sports Bar in downtown Bloomington. A surveillance camera, at 2:27 AM, caught Rossman and Spierer leaving the bar together. She was visibly inebriated to the point of being severely incapacitated. (There is the possibility that Spierer, who suffered from an irregular heartbeat condition called Q T Syndrome, had been given Xanax or cocaine at Rosenbaum's party, or at the bar.)

Shortly after entering the Smallwood Apartment complex with Rossman, the two students ran into Zachary Oakes, also a student at Indiana University. Oakes didn't like what he saw, and following an angry exchange of words between the two men, Oakes punched Rossman to the floor. Following the altercation, Rossman was seen carrying the incapacitated Spierer to his apartment building. (Rossman, when questioned by detectives, claimed he had no memory whatsoever of the night in question. He said he didn't recall his fight with Oakes.)

Corey Rossman's roommate, Mike Beth, later told detectives that after Rossman arrived at the apartment with the girl that night, Beth helped Rossman to his bed. According to Beth, he next walked Spierer down the hall to Jay Rosenbaum's apartment, the site of that night's party.

When questioned by investigators, Rosenbaum said he had non-student guests staying with him that weekend. He claimed to have offered to put Spierer up for the night on his couch. According to Rosenbaum, the girl refused his hospitality. At 4:30 AM, Rosenbaum said he stood on his balcony and watched Spierer begin the six-minute walk to her apartment at the Smallwood complex.

Jesse Wolff, Lauren Spierer's boyfriend, told detectives that sometime that morning, he sent Spierer a text message. The reply to his message came from an employee of Kilroy's who said the girl had hours earlier left the bar without her cellphone. Wolff called 911 and reported her missing.

Two years after the mysterious and suspicious disappearance of the University of Indiana student, detectives with the Bloomington Police Department were still investigating the case as a missing persons matter rather than a homicide. Rob and Charlene Spierer, the missing girl's parents, wanted the authorities to keep pressuring Jay Rosenbaum, Mike Beth, Corey Rossman, and Jesse Wolff - so-called persons of interest in the case - for more details regarding their activities that night. The parents also wanted the four students to stop "hiding behind their attorneys" and submit to polygraph tests.

In speaking to a reporter with the Westchester, New York *Journal-News*, Rob Spierer said, "I feel if she [his daughter] never met Corey Rossman, she'd be alive today." (From this it is obvious that the missing girl's father thinks she was murdered and her body disposed of.) Later, Mr. Spierer said this to a reporter: "We still believe that [Lauren] may not have left Corey [Rossman's] and Mike [Beth's] or Jay [Rosenbaum's] apartment."

A month after Spierer went missing someone attacked a woman not far from where she was last seen walking to her apartment. That assailant has not been identified. While stranger abductions are rare, detectives on the case have not ruled out that possibility.

In May 2013, Robert and Charlene Spierer filed a civil suit against Corey Rossman, Mike Beth, and Jay Rosenbaum. The plaintiffs, through Indianapolis attorney Larry A. Mackey, a former federal prosecutor who has been involved in several high-profile cases, allege that their daughter's status is the result of the defendants' negligence which included having supplied the underage Lauren with drugs and alcohol. By forcing the defendants to testify in a civil trial, the parents hoped to learn more about what happened to Lauren that night.

In July 2013, attorneys representing Mr. Beth, Rosenbaum, and Rossman asked a federal judge in Indianapolis to dismiss the wrongful death suit against their clients. According to these lawyers, Lauren Spierer's two-year disappearance wasn't enough evidence to legally presume she was dead. Under Indiana law, for a missing person to be declared legally deceased, this person must have been "inexplicably absent for a continuous period of seven years."

The missing woman's mother, Charlene Spierer, in September 2013, in an effort to keep interest in her daughter's case alive, posted a new letter on Facebook. In the letter, the distraught and frustrated parent discussed the family's struggle and urged anyone with information to come forward.

Charlene Spierer, in addressing the people she believed were responsible for Lauren's disappearance and presumed death, wrote: "You know the answers to our questions. You are responsible for the tragedy surrounding Lauren's disappearance. What can be said that hasn't already been said? At times I think if I could make you feel some compassion, maybe, just maybe, you would send Lauren's location to the P. O. Box...."

"We have tried and tried to get answers. There have been awareness events, concerts, and interviews [the Spierers have appeared on the TV show "Katie" and have been interviewed for *People Magazine*]. We have handed out fliers, distributed thousands of bracelets, searched and searched with the help of hundreds of volunteers, throughout Bloomington and surrounding areas, without success. We have received and followed countless leads all of which have led disappointingly nowhere. What did you do as we waited, only to receive the crushing news that a lead had come up short? Has it given you pleasure or have you been relieved? Have we come close or are we still far from the truth?"

In late October 2013, Charlene Spierer learned that city officials had decided to take down the faded, outdoor missing person signs that had been posted around Bloomington since June 2011. According to a statement released by the city communications director, "For the many people who have felt the signs should have been taken down long ago, it's long overdue. For those who believe they should remain in place, no time was the right time to remove them...Posters about the case remain up throughout the campus and community, including in city government buildings, and police agencies continue to actively investigate."

In December 2013, federal judge Tanya Walton Pratt allowed Robert and Charlene Spierer's civil lawsuit against Jason Rosenbaum and Corey Rossman to go forward. The plaintiffs alleged that Rosenbaum and Rossman negligently provided Lauren with alcohol. Earlier in the month the judge dropped the suit against Michael Beth who was not seen with Lauren the night she disappeared.

In June 2014, media outlets in Indiana reported that Jesse Wolff, Spierer's boyfriend at the time of her disappearance, passed a polygraph test administered by a private examiner. According to his parents, Wolff refused to take a police polygraph test because he did not trust the authorities.

The Missing Hospital Patient

On September 19, 2013, Lynne Spalding checked herself into the San Francisco General Hospital. The 57-year-old native of Peterlee, England worked in San Francisco's tourist industry. She suffered from a bladder infection. The divorced mother of two, thin and frail, seemed confused and disoriented from her medication. Members of the hospital staff assigned to her care were under orders to look in on Spalding every fifteen minutes.

When one of Spalding's friends showed up at the hospital on September 21 for a visit, Spalding was not in her room. Hospital employees, in a search of the immediate area, couldn't find her. Perhaps she had checked herself out. The friend went to Spalding's apartment and found it vacant. When Spalding didn't return to her dwelling, the friend filed a missing persons report with the police.

Over the next few days, the missing woman's friends and members of her family looked for her at various places in the city. One of her friends created a "Find Lynne" Facebook page. Friends posted missing persons flyers around the city. Deputies with the sheriff's office, the agency in charge of hospital security, searched the giant medical complex. It seemed this woman had vanished into thin air.

At ten in the morning of October 8, 2013, seventeen days after Lynne Spalding went missing from her hospital room, a hospital employee discovered the body of a middle-aged woman lying dead in a stairwell used as a fire escape. Todd May, the chief hospital medical officer tentatively identified the dead woman as Lynne Spalding. (I presume she was wearing a hospital identification bracelet.)

The job of determining when, where, and exactly how this woman had died rested in the hands of the San Francisco Medical Examiner's Office. The principal determination involved Spalding's manner of death. While it was not unreasonable to presume that this hospital patient's death occurred naturally, the forensic pathologist looked for signs of physical trauma that suggested a struggle. The pathologist who performed the autopsy also looked for physical evidence of a sexual assault.

Assuming the absence of foul play in this unusual death, the Spalding case presented investigators with questions that demanded answers. The most obvious question was how this sick woman got from her room to the stairwell without being observed by hospital staff? (I don't know exactly when on September 21 Spalding went missing. I presume it was during the middle of the night.) Moreover, why didn't the hospital searchers find this woman sooner? And finally, was there surveillance camera footage that shed light on this mystery?

Unless the stairwell where Spalding's body was found was located in an extremely remote section of the hospital, someone should have detected the odor of decomposition.

San Francisco General Hospital spokesperson Todd May, at a press conference held on October 8, 2013, said, "What happened at our hospital is horrible. We are here to take care of patients, to heal them, to keep them safe. This has shaken us to our core. Our staff is devastated."

David Perry, Lynne Spalding's friend and the family spokesperson told reporters that, "We need to know what Lynne's condition was. We need to know what she was being treated for and frankly we need to know what medications she was on and what state of mind she was in. We're not trying to place blame. We're trying to find answers."

On Thursday, October 10, San Francisco General Hospital Chief Operating Officer Roland Pickens announced that pursuant to the medical examiner's office report, the corpse in the stairwell was Lynne Spalding's body. A second hospital spokesperson revealed that the stairwell in question was located several hundred feet from the unit where Spalding was being treated. According to this spokesperson, Spalding was being treated in a unit where patients are not watched closely. This contradicted previous information regarding the fifteen-minute patient check-ups.

In a private ceremony held on October 21, Spalding's body was cremated. (This means, of course, that there will be no second autopsy if one was needed.)

On October 22, 2013, the *San Francisco Chronicle* reported that four days before sheriff's deputies responded to the dead woman found in the city-owned hospital's stairwell, an orderly had twice stepped over her body thinking she was a homeless person. To reporters, Haig Harris, the attorney representing Spalding's children, said, "This is a hospital. Why didn't somebody put their hand on the body to see if there was a pulse?"

David Perry, a Spalding family spokesperson said this to reporters: "The family is angry and frustrated and out of patience. While we understand the need for a thorough investigation, it has now been one month and three days since Lynne Spalding went missing...The time for answers and real solutions that will protect lives of future patients is long past due."

A woman who had been visiting her son at the hospital in June said she had been locked in the same stairwell. She had taken the stairs instead of the elevator, entering the fifth-floor stairwell without realizing it was an emergency exit. The woman walked down to the ground level, but the door sounded an alarm when she opened it. She slammed the door shut and went back upstairs where she pounded on the door window to attract someone's attention. A nurse let her back inside. No one had responded to the exit alarm.

Investigators and hospital authorities have not revealed if Spalding had changed into her street clothes before leaving her room. (The fact the orderly presumed she was a homeless person suggests that she had.) While the coroner has not revealed Spalding's cause of death, the family has been assured that she had not been the victim of foul play.

Dan Cunningham with the San Francisco Police homicide unit announced on October 28, 2013 that four days before Spalding's body was discovered, an Asian man in his thirties wearing a hospital name tag told a hospital supervisor that he had seen a person lying in the stairwell. The supervisor checked out the stairwell but didn't see anyone there. Homicide investigators were trying to identify this man for questioning. (It's not clear if the Asian man was the orderly who stepped over the body on October 4, 2013.)

On December 15, 2013, the medical examiner's office released the results of Spalding's autopsy. According to the San Francisco medical examiner, Spalding had died of "probable electrolyte imbalance with delirium...clinical sepsis." In other words, she had died from a chemical imbalance related to chronic alcoholism. According to Dr. Thomas Shaughnessey, the electrolyte imbalances, in combination with a liver whose inability to compensate from the imbalance, resulted in a collapse of

Spalding's heart or her brain resulting in her demise. The forensic pathologist who performed the autopsy did not state a time of death.

Members of Spalding's family immediately disputed the allegation that she was an alcoholic. They were therefore outraged by the contents of the medical examiner's report.

The Vanishing Family

Joseph McStay, a 40-year-old owner of a company that installed home water fountains, resided with his wife and their two boys in Fallbrook, a suburban community 55 miles north of San Diego, California. On Monday, February 8, 2010, the McStays were reported missing after a security guard in Ysidro, a town across the border from Tijuana, Mexico, discovered the locked and apparently abandoned Isuzu Trooper parked in a mini-mall parking lot two blocks from the border.

A surveillance camera on a neighbor's house in Fallbrook showed the couple and their boys, ages three and four, pulling out of their driveway in their SUV at 7:45 in the morning of February 4, 2010.

Poor quality surveillance camera footage on the Ysidro/Tijuana border revealed a family resembling the McStays walking into Mexico four days after they were video-recorded leaving their home in Fallbrook.

On February 14, 2010, police officers entered the McStay's cul-de-sac home in Fallbrook. The house had not been forcibly entered. Moreover, officers found no evidence of a struggle or the theft of household property. Police officers found bowls of popcorn in the living room and eggs on the kitchen counter. The family's two dogs were in the backyard, an indication the McStays hadn't planned for an extended trip.

Investigators found no recent activity on the McStay's credit cards or bank account. An examination of their home computer revealed an Internet search that read: "What documents do children need for traveling to Mexico." Friends and relatives, however, had no knowledge that the McStays had planned a short trip into Mexico. After leaving Fallbrook that morning, the family simply disappeared.

At ten in the morning of November 11, 2013, an off-road motorcyclist near a dirt road in the desert outside the San Bernardino County town of Victorville, came across what appeared to be human bones. At that location, 100 miles north of Fallbrook, detectives discovered two shallow graves each containing two sets of skeletal remains. A few of the bones had been scattered by animals. Items of clothing were also recovered from the scene. The remains were not far from Interstate 15 that connects that part of California to Las Vegas.

Forensic scientists, through dental records, identified Joseph McStay and his 43-year-old wife as the two adults found in one of the desert graves. The other two sets of skeletons presumably belong to their children. (DNA tests were underway.) According to San Bernardino County Sheriff John McMahon, the McStays and their children were murdered. The Sheriff did not reveal how they had been killed. There were no suspects. The FBI took over the investigation of the murder case.

In speaking to reporters, Joseph McStay's father said he did not believe the people in the Ysidro surveillance footage seen walking into Mexico depicted his son and his family. "My son doesn't walk that way," he said. "They didn't walk into Mexico. They would never do that." The father explained that his son and his wife were aware of the Mexican drug gangs and would not have exposed the children to that risk.

As of July 2014, the McStay family remained missing. What happened to them was still a mystery.

The Missing Amish Family

In Ohio, doctors at Akron Children's Hospital, in April 2013, diagnosed 10-year-old Sarah Hershberger with lymphoblastic lymphoma, an aggressive form of non-Hodgkin lymphoma. The Amish girl's parents, Andy and Anna Hershberger, when told that 85 percent of the patients treated for this illness survive, agreed to a two-year chemotherapy program. After the first round of the chemotherapy, the tumors on Sarah's neck, chest and kidneys were diminished.

In June 2013, after a second round of chemotherapy treatment made their daughter extremely ill, the parents decided to stop the treatment. They took this action against the advice of cancer doctors who warned them that without the chemotherapy, Sarah would die.

The hospital authorities, believing they were morally and legally bound to continue treating the girl, went to court to take away the parents' right to make medical decisions on their daughter's behalf.

Andy and Anna Hershberger, in September 2013, took Sarah to an alternative cancer treatment center in Central America where doctors put the girl on a regimen of herbs and vitamins. When the family returned to the United States, hospital scans showed no signs of the lymphoma.

On October 13, 2013, an Ohio appellate court judge granted Maria Schimer, an attorney and licensed nurse, limited guardianship over Sarah Hershberger. The guardianship included the power to make medical decisions on her behalf over the objections of her parents.

Shortly after the court ruling, the guardian sent a taxi out to the family farm near the village of Spencer, Ohio to fetch Sarah and take her to the hospital in Akron for additional chemotherapy. When the cab arrived at the Medina County home located 35 miles southwest of the Cleveland metropolitan area, the family was gone.

A few weeks later, pursuant to a welfare check on Sarah, deputy sheriffs went to the farm to find the place unoccupied. No one in the Amish community seemed to know where the parents were hiding out. If members of this Amish enclave knew the family's whereabouts, they weren't cooperating with the authorities. Attorneys for the Hershberger family have appealed the guardianship ruling to the Ohio Supreme Court on issues related to religious freedom.

If Sarah Hershberger's fate remains in her parents' hands, and she dies from the cancer, Mr. and Mrs. Hershberger could face negligent homicide charges. Moreover, people who helped them avoid the authorities could be charged as accomplices to the crime. The right of religious freedom does not match the right of a child to receive life-saving healthcare. Being given vitamins and herbs as a cancer cure, while less painful than the immediate aftermath of chemotherapy, does not qualify as adequate healthcare.

On December 6, 2013, according to media reports, the court-appointed guardian decided not to force Sarah Hershberger to undergo further chemotherapy treatments.

Missing and Murdered

To get away from her estranged husband against whom she had been granted a restraining order, 28-year-old Elsa Oliver and her three children moved from their home in Fitchburg, Massachusetts to Florida where they lived with her mother. Early in 2013, Elsa, still married to Jose Oliver, returned to Fitchburg, a town of 40,000 in the north central part of the state. She came home with 5-year-old Jeremiah, his 7-year-old sister, and his older brother who was nine.

In Fitchburg, Elsa began a relationship with Albert Sierra, a local man six years younger than her.

In June 2013, a social worker with the Massachusetts Department of Children and Families (DCF), during a monthly visit to the Oliver home, noticed that Jeremiah wasn't in the house. In response to the social worker's inquiry regarding the boy's whereabouts, Elsa said he was in Florida living with her mother. The social worker took Elsa for her word and didn't verify the story.

Five months later, the social worker left a DFC card at Elsa's house with the message there would be no further monthly visits from the agency.

Jeremiah's sister, on December 2, 2013, told her elementary school counselor that her mother's boyfriend, Alberto Sierra, had abused her. The

7-year-old and her 9-year-old brother were taken out of Elsa's custody and placed into protective care. Jeremiah still wasn't around, and his siblings had no idea what happened to him. When detectives asked Elsa about Jeremiah, she stuck to her Florida story.

After Jeremiah could not be located in Florida, a state juvenile court judge brought Elsa into court and asked her to account for her missing son. She refused to answer the judge's questions. The judge gave Elsa 72 hours to produce the boy. At the hearing, officials noticed physical signs that Elsa had been recently abused.

Shortly after the judge's deadline passed without proof that Jeremiah was alive, a Worcester County prosecutor charged Elsa with two counts of reckless endangerment of a child and two counts of accessory after the fact of a felony. These charges related to the alleged physical abuse of Jeremiah's sister. Police officers booked Elsa into the Worcester County Jail where she was held under a $5,000 cash bond.

Police officers also arrested 22-year-old Albert Sierra on charges of assault and battery with a dangerous weapon (a knife) and two counts of assault and battery on a child causing bodily injury. A judge denied Sierra bail. Both of the accused pleaded not guilty to all charges.

A party made up of Fitchburg police officers, K-9 units, and 100 volunteers searched the vicinity of the Oliver house without finding the missing boy. Detectives and others involved in the case believed that he had been murdered and that Elsa, out of fear, was covering up for her boyfriend.

While the police tried to find Jeremiah's body, a bureaucratic fight broke out within the Massachusetts Department of Children and Families over what person in the agency bore the most blame for the delayed reaction to Jeremiah Oliver's disappearance. The head of the public union that represents DCF employees protested the firing of Jeremiah's social worker and her supervisor. The union leader accused the department's commissioner of deflecting blame by scapegoating the social worker and her boss. In the meantime, the 5-year-old was still missing and presumed dead.

Duval Patrick, the governor of Massachusetts, promised an investigation into DCF's handling of Jeremiah Oliver's case. He asked the Child Welfare League of America to review the workings of the agency. Several local politicians wanted more--they called for the governor to fire the agency's commissioner, Olga Roche.

In March 2014, the Child Welfare League of America reported that state social workers missed nearly one in five home visits during a recent 12-month period.

A Worcester County grand jury, in March 2014, indicted Elsa Oliver and Alberto Sierra on charges of kidnapping, assault and battery with a dangerous weapon, and reckless endangerment. Oliver was held on $125,000 bail and Sierra on $100,000. Three other people were indicted for interfering with a criminal investigation and misleading the police.

On April 18, 2014, Worcester County District Attorney Joe Early announced that Jeremiah Oliver's body had been found at nine that morning. The remains were wrapped in a blanket inside a suitcase discovered in a grassy area 40 feet off Interstate 190's southbound lane not far from Exit 6 in Sterling, Massachusetts. Found 12 miles from his home, the boy, according to the district attorney, was a victim of criminal homicide.

The day after the missing boy's discovery, DCF Commissioner Olga Roche assured the public that the "DCF continues to focus on Jeremiah's siblings to ensure they are receiving the support they need during this very difficult time." The commissioner admitted that the boy's killing reflects a "serious failure" on the part of the child protection agency.

On April 19, Jose Oliver, the murdered boy's father, in a cell phone call to a reporter from the spot where his son's body was found, said, "I know the body has not been here for six months. I believe the body was thrown here Thursday morning [April 17]. Anybody that drives through here, you could see it. There are more people involved in this besides my wife and Alberto Sierria. A couple of people know what happened. My question is who did it and why they did it. I want answers."

The Murder of an Autistic Boy

Avonte Oquendo, an autistic 14-year-old who didn't speak, attended school in Long Island City, Queens New York. The black, five-foot-three, 120 pound student was enrolled in the school's special needs program. He lived with his mother, Vanessa Fontaine, a social services case manager, and his four older brothers aged 19 to 29. Avonte's school sits on a busy street across from a playground, a dog run, and a jogging path that overlooks the East River.

At 12:40 PM on October 4, 2013, a school surveillance camera caught Avonte coming out of the building with other school kids. He hasn't been seen since. Reacting to the missing persons report filed by his mother, dozens of New York City police officers from the 102 Precinct, aided by two helicopters, conducted a thorough search of the neighborhood.

Following the initial surge of police activity on the case, Avonte's mother Vanessa, working out of a donated recreational vehicle parked in front of the school, oversaw the deployment of volunteer searchers and the distribution of missing person fliers.

Vanessa Fontaine also organized candlelight vigils and rallies, raised $95,000 in reward money from anonymous donors, and appeared on several nationally broadcast television programs. While the police received hundreds of tips, nothing panned out.

Two months after her son's disappearance, Vanessa moved her operation out of the RV and set up shop in a rented office. Thirty days after that, with still no leads on Avonte's whereabouts, activity on the case waned. There were fewer tips coming in, and only a handful of volunteers showed up each day at Vanessa's missing persons headquarters.

The missing boy's mother recently filed a lawsuit against New York City's Board of Education. The plaintiff accuses the staff at Avonte's school of failing to protect him.

On Thursday night, January 16, 2014, body parts and items of clothing found near the Queens shoreline. The remains were believed to be the missing boy's. The search was over and a new phase of the case, determining Oquendo's cause and manner of death, was underway.

Dr. Teleka Patrick: The Woman in the Lake

Raised in New York City, Teleka Patrick graduated from the Bronx High School of Science before earning her Bachelor of Science Degree at Oakwood University in Huntsville, Alabama. Three months after graduating from medical school at Loma Linda University in southern California, Teleka, in June 2013, began her four-year residency at Western Michigan University. She moved into the Gull Run apartment complex in Kalamazoo.

At seven o'clock in the evening of December 5, 2013, Teleka was caught on a parking lot surveillance camera at the Borgess Medical Center where she worked. She had just finished her shift. From the hospital a male co-worker gave Teleka a lift to the Radisson Hotel in downtown Kalamazoo. A hotel surveillance camera recorded Teleka entering the lobby dressed in a black hoodie and dark slacks.

According to a Radisson employee, the woman in the hoodie tried to rent a room using cash. Because she did not show any identification, the person on the front desk refused to register her.

At eight o'clock, Teleka got a ride back to her car at the Borgess Medical Center in a hotel shuttle van. The shuttle driver later described her behavior as nervous. He said she ducked between cars to avoid being spotted. From the medical center parking lot that night, Teleka Patrick went missing.

Two hours after Teleka returned to the medical center, an Indiana State Trooper 100 miles from Kalamazoo came across, off Interstate 94 in

Portage, an abandoned light-gold 1997 Lexus ES 300. The vehicle, registered to the missing woman, had a flat tire.

Inside the Lexus, officers found a wallet containing Teleka's driver's license and credit cards. The car also contained pieces of the missing woman's clothing and a small amount of cash. The car keys were gone along with Teleka's cellphone.

A bloodhound later traced Teleka's steps from the abandoned vehicle to the freeway where her trail went cold. A search of the area surrounding the car failed to produce any clues to her whereabouts.

According to Carl Clatterbuck, a Kalamazoo private investigator hired to find Patrick, the missing woman's ex-husband and a former boyfriend were not suspects in the disappearance.

In late December 2013, several YouTube videos made by Teleka surfaced. Unfortunately, they raised more questions than answers. One of the videos, produced in early November 2013, features a table in Teleka's apartment containing an elaborate breakfast spread. The narrator, identified as Teleka, says, "I just wanted to show you what I made. If you were here this would be on your plate." In another video, she addressed an unknown person as "baby," and "love."

On January 1, 2014, Ismael Calderon, married to the missing woman from 2000 to 2011, told a Grand Rapids, Michigan television reporter that his ex-wife suffered from a serious mental problem. The illness led her to believe she was being followed. "This is a tragedy," he said. "I don't think she's hiding somewhere. I think she's being held against her will or the worst. I think that Teleka had this fear of first, being branded with a mental illness. Second, the practical fear of losing her career."

The next day, a 46-year-old Grammy-nominated gospel singer and Grand Rapids, Michigan pastor named Marvin Sapp said he had filed a protection order against Teleka three months before she disappeared. According to Reverend Sapp, she had sent him 400 love letters, joined his congregation, and contacted his children.

On April 6, 2014, a man fishing on Lake Charles in the northern part of Indiana saw something floating in the water. It turned out to be a body, and the corpse was Teleka Patrick. The lake had been frozen over during the winter. According to a family member, Patrick had been on her way to Chicago to visit a relative.

Finding The Body

Heather Elvis, a 20-year-old employee of a bar and restaurant in Myrtle Beach, South Carolina, lived with a female roommate at the River Oaks Apartments in the city. Her parents, Terry and Debbie Elvis, lived nearby.

At three in the morning of Wednesday, December 18, 2013, Heather called her roommate from her cellphone about 45 minutes after being dropped off at River Oaks by her date. She called to report how the evening with the young man had worked out.

On December 19, 2013, Heather's abandoned 2001 Dodge Intrepid was found parked at the Peachtree Landing along the Waccamaw River in the town of Socastee just outside of Myrtle Beach. The dark green vehicle had not been involved in an accident. Parked about nine miles from the River Oak Apartments, the car did not contain Heather's purse or her cellphone.

On Friday, December 20, after Heather failed to show up for her scheduled shift at the Tilted Kilt Pub and Eatery, her parents, Terry and Debbi Elvis, reported their 5-foot-1 inch, 118-pound daughter missing.

The next day, under the supervision of the Horry County Police Department, 300 people spent ten hours combing the woods and ponds in the vicinity of the abandoned car.

On January 3, 2014 another search party made up of law enforcement officers and volunteers, aided by several K-9 units and searchers riding horses and ATVs, continued the hunt for the missing young woman.

Lieutenant Robert Kegler with the Horry County Police Department, on January 6, told a Fox News reporter that detectives had questioned several people in connection with the disappearance. While the young man who had dropped Heather off at her apartment after the date in the early morning hours of December 18 was not a suspect, some of the uncooperative men interviewed by detectives were being scrutinized.

At 8 PM on Monday, January 6, 2014, television crime host Nancy Grace devoted a segment of her show to the Heather Elvis missing persons case. A $25,000 reward was posted for information leading to the discovery of the missing young woman.

At seven o'clock on the morning of Friday, February 21, 2014, officers with the Horry County Police Department, South Carolina State Police, and U.S. Marshal's Office, executed a search warrant at a house in Myrtle Beach occupied by 37-year-old Sidney Moorer and his 41-year-old wife Tammy. Officers spent eleven hours at the dwelling. Cadaver dogs searched the property without result. Two pickup trucks were towed from the house and officers were seen placing several boxes into a white police van.

A prosecutor, following the search of the Moorer house, charged Sidney and Tammy with indecent exposure and obstruction of justice. (It was reported that Tammy, angry at Heather because she and Sidney had been involved in a sexual relationship, sent her nude pictures of herself and Sidney. In January 2014, Tammy told a reporter that Sidney had sex with Heather Elvis in his car "a total of three times." According to Tammy, Sidney ended the relationship when he realized that "something wasn't right about her.")

On February 24, 2014, a Horry County prosecutor charged the couple with Heather Elvis' kidnapping and murder. They were held without bail. As of August 2014, Elvis' body had not been found.

The Wall Street Reporter

David Bird, a 55-year-old journalist with the *Wall Street Journal* who covered the world's energy markets--OPEC and such--lived with his wife Nancy and their two children in central New Jersey's Long Hill Township. Although he underwent a liver transplant operation in 2005, Mr. Bird was an avid hiker, biker, and camper. The Boy Scout troop leader, in 2013, ran in the New York City Marathon. His children are ages 12 and 15.

On Saturday, January 11, 2014, after he and his wife had put away their Christmas decorations, David said he wanted to take a walk and get some fresh air before it started to rain. At 4:30 PM, dressed in a red rain jacket, sneakers, and a pair of jeans, the six-foot-one, 200 pound, gray-haired reporter walked out of his house. Shortly thereafter it began to rain, and rain hard.

Two hours after David Bird started his walk in the neighborhood, his wife became worried. He hadn't returned home, and it was still raining. To make matters worse, Dave had been suffering from a gastrointestinal virus. Nancy Bird called the Long Hill Township Police Department to report her husband missing.

Over the next three days police officers and hundreds of volunteers searched the neighborhood and nearby wooded areas for the missing journalist. Dogs, a helicopter, people riding all-terrain vehicles, and horses assisted in the search. Volunteers also distributed hundreds of missing person flyers.

Notwithstanding the effort to locate Mr. Bird, he is nowhere to be found. It seems he has disappeared without a trace.

The fact the missing man left his house without the anti-rejection medication he takes twice a day in connection with his liver transplant makes finding him all the more urgent. Without that medicine he will surely become ill.

On January 16, 2014, police officers learned (but have not confirmed) that someone in Mexico, the night before, had used one of David Bird's credit cards. The card was supposedly used four days after Bird's disappearance. Investigators, without a clue as to where David Bird is, or why he went missing, considered the possibility that his disappearance had something to do with his reporting on recent Middle East crude oil price changes.

As of August 2014, the missing reporter's body had not been found.

The Missing New Jersey Couple

Jorge Rodriguez, 24, and his girlfriend Melissa Pereira, one year older, had been in a relationship for more than two years. She worked as a production assistant with Fox News in New York City and was also the assistant director of the Boys and Girls Club of Paterson, New Jersey. Melissa resided with her mother at the Wayne Village apartment complex in Wayne, New Jersey. Jorge, the manager of a photography studio, lived in Garfield, New Jersey.

On Friday night, December 27, 2013, the couple told Melissa's mother they were taking a short drive in Jorge's white Honda Prelude. She left the apartment with her cellphone but left behind her jacket and wallet. People saw the couple that night buying candles at a local K-Mart store.

The next morning, Melissa was not back in her apartment and Jorge did not show up for work at the photography studio. On Monday, December 30, family members reported Jorge and Melissa missing. The couple had made New Year's Eve reservations at the Cherry Valley Manor in Stroudsburg, Pennsylvania. They did not show up at the bed and breakfast, and had not called for a refund of their reservation deposit.

At 10:30 on the morning of January 19, 2014, after a wireless company determined the location of Melissa Pereira's cellphone, police officers entered the Pereira rented garage behind the Wayne Village apartment complex. Inside the garage officers found the white Honda with the frozen couple inside the car. They had been dead for some time.

According to a police spokesperson, the bodies did not show outward signs of trauma. The Honda's fuel tank was bone-dry, and the car battery was dead.

While detectives would have to wait for the autopsy results to know the estimated times of death, a resident of the apartment complex provided information that suggested that the couple had died the night they left the Wayne Village apartment in Rodriguez's car.

The apartment resident told investigators she had seen a young couple in a white Honda pull up to the garage at eleven o'clock on the night of December 27. The man got out of the car, unlocked the door, and backed the vehicle into the garage. The witness said the young man and his companion were smiling and appeared to be happy.

The Suicide

In 1999, Leanne Hecht from Roswell, Georgia graduated from the University of Georgia. With her degree in marketing, she moved to Denver, Colorado after being offered a job there. In 2008, Leanne began dating Josh Bearden, a Denver resident from Garden Ridge, Texas. Bearden had graduated from Texas A & M and possessed a degree in marketing as well. The couple got married in 2009.

Leanne and Josh, in March 2012, left their home in Denver to embark on a trip around the world. Twenty-two months later, after visiting 56 countries and blogging about their adventures, they returned to the United States.

In December 2013, following a short stay with Leanne's family in Roswell, Georgia, the pair traveled to Garden Ridge, Texas to visit his folks. They had scheduled a flight back to Denver for January 21, 2014.

Early Friday afternoon, on January 17, 2014, Leanne left the Garden Ridge house to hike in the rugged west Texas terrain northeast of San Antonio. The five-foot, 100-pound woman with two piercings on her left ear wore hiking shoes and a pair of jeans. She did not take her cellphone, but was in possession of $60 and a couple of credit cards.

At 5:30 PM that Friday, when Leanne didn't return home from her outing, Josh reported his wife missing. At eight the next morning, officers with the Garden Ridge Police Department and the Comal County Sheriff's Office, accompanied by 150 volunteer civilians, a contingent of Texas National Guard members, Texas Rangers and a search and rescue team, launched a massive search for the missing 33-year-old. A pair of helicopters, for three hours, flew over a 23-mile-square patch of landscape that features boulders, cliffs, and caves. The search produced no clues as to what happened to Leanne Bearden.

Leanne had been missing a week when a group in Denver held a fundraiser to solicit money to hire a private missing persons investigator named Charles Parker.

Assuming Leanne wasn't abducted or murdered, she either ran off, got lost, or suffered an injury. She could have twisted an ankle or fallen off a cliff. It seems rather odd, however, that given the hostile terrain, and the possibility of getting injured or lost, she did not leave the house with her cellphone.

On January 29, 2014, a member of the missing woman's family posted the following message on Facebook: "The pressure of transitioning from her two-year trip back into what we consider "normal" life seems to have left Leanne very anxious and stressed. As a result there is evidence that Leanne may have voluntarily left the area. We initially believed that she was somewhere in the local area. However, after much searching…no evidence has been found of her presence. If Leanne has indeed fled this area, she is extremely vulnerable. She left with only a few assets and is traveling very light. Although she is athletic, she is small in stature. Her mental and physical status is uncertain. We fear for her greatly."

On Thursday, February 13, 2014, a Garden Ridge police spokesperson announced that Leanne Bearden's body was found in a wooded area not far from her in-law's house. Jewelry and identification cards were with the body.

According to media reports, Bearden's body was discovered hanging from a tree. The area where she was found had been searched several times by members of her family. As a result, it was not included in the search conducted by law enforcement agencies, volunteers, and search and rescue crews.

On Friday, February 14, 2014, Garden Ridge Police Chief Donna O'Conner announced that the autopsy results revealed that Leanne Bearden had committed suicide. The case was closed.

Was The Boy Murdered?

In 2000, 26-year-old Kaine Andrew Horman, an engineer in Portland, Oregon, married Desiree Young. The marriage did not work out. Within a year the couple discussed separating. But in January 2002, when Desiree learned that she was pregnant, she and Kaine decided to give their marriage a second chance. But it still didn't work. In August 2002, Desiree filed for divorce and moved in with her parents in Medford, Oregon.

A month after the separation, Desiree gave birth to Kyron. The divorce became final in 2003, and a year after that, Desiree moved to Canada where she received treatment for a kidney ailment. When she returned to the U.S. two months later, she relinquished custody of 2-year-old Kyron to Kaine.

The toddler, in 2004, began living with his father in a house on Sheltered Nook Road in a rural section of northwest Portland. Because of Kaine's demanding job at the Intel Jones Farm Campus in Hillsboro, the father arranged day care for Kyron. For that job, he hired a friend of his ex-wife's named Terri Moulton.

Terri Moulton grew up in Roseburg, Oregon, a town three hours from Portland. After graduating from high school in 1988, she attended Umpqua Community College where she met Ron Tarver. Terri and Ron were married in 1991, and three years later had a son named James. A year after the birth of their son, Terri and Ron divorced.

In 1996, Terri married Richard Ecker in Springfield, Oregon. Four years later she graduated from Northwest Christian University with a bachelor's degree in education. From March 2001 to June 2002, Terri worked as a substitute teacher in the Hillsboro School District. In 2002 she divorced Richard Ecker.

In 2004, Terri moved into the home on Sheltered Nook Road with Kaine and his 2-year-old son. She had been taking care of the boy for more than a year. Kaine's divorce from Desiree Young had been finalized a year earlier.

In April 2007, Kaine and Terri were married. Their daughter Kiara Horman was born in 2009.

Kyron, in 2010, attended second grade at Portland's Skyline Elementary School two miles from his home. On most days he rode the bus to school, but on June 4, 2010, Terri drove her stepson to class. That day Kyron wanted to set up his Red-Eyed Tree Frog exhibit at the school's science fair.

Terri and the boy arrived at the elementary school at eight in the morning. They were last seen together fifteen minutes later near Kyron's science exhibit. That day Kyron's teacher marked him absent. At 3:45 in the afternoon of June 4, 2010, Terri Horman reported Kyron missing after he didn't come home from school.

Students and teachers at the school told detectives that no one had seen Kyron after the 8:45 AM bell. According to Terri, she left the school just before the morning bell. She told detectives that Kyron told her he was leaving the exhibit site en route to his classroom. That's the last time she saw him.

Teachers and staff described the three-foot, eight-inch 50 pound boy as too timid to have left the school on his own. That morning he was dressed in a black T-shirt with "CSI" in green lettering and an image of a handprint. The boy with the metal rimmed eyeglasses wore cargo pants and sneakers trimmed in orange.

In the week following Kyron's disappearance, police officers and others searched the school building, its grounds, and the surrounding neighborhood. It seemed the 7-year-old had vanished into thin air.

From the start, detectives, operating on the theory that Kyron had not been abducted by a stranger focused on Terri Horman's activities on the morning of the disappearance. The police became particularly suspicious when a search of her cellular phone records revealed that she wasn't where she said she was that morning. In fact, her cellphone showed she had been on Sauvie Island five miles from the school. This led to a massive search of the island for the missing boy. Searchers found no trace of Kyron.

Interrogated by detectives as a suspect in the case, Terri maintained her innocence. She reportedly took and failed two polygraph tests. Detectives, looking for physical evidence of foul play, seized and searched her car. They found nothing incriminating.

On June 26, 2010, 22 days after Kyron's disappearance, detectives approached the boy's father with startling information about his wife Terri. According to these investigators, Terri, five months before Kyron went missing, asked a landscaper named Rodolfo Sanchez to kill her husband.

Sanchez, in reporting the murder solicitation, claimed that Terri told him that Kaine Horman physically and mentally abused her. The would-be hit man's compensation was supposed to be the $10,000 in cash Kaine always carried on his person. To help facilitate the murder-for-hire scheme, Terri allegedly provided Sanchez details regarding her husband's daily routine. She suggested that Sanchez make the hit look like a mugging.

On the day he learned of the alleged plot against his life, Kaine kicked Terri out of the house. Two days later he filed for divorce and served his estranged wife with a restraining order. Terri moved back into her parents' house in Roseburg, Oregon.

In 2011, with her son still missing and no charges filed in the case, Desiree Young posted missing person's fliers around a strip mall in Roseburg not far from Terri's residence. She also asked the reclusive suspect's neighbors to grill Terri about Kyron's disappearance. Desiree told the Roseburg neighbors that Terri had blamed her failing marriage on Kyron, that she had grown to hate her stepson.

On June 1, 2012, Desiree Young filed a lawsuit against Terri Horman claiming that the defendant was "responsible for the disappearance of Kyron." The plaintiff sought $10,000,000 in damages. On July 30, 2013, Young dropped the lawsuit. She said she didn't want the civil action to jeopardize the continuing police investigation into her son's case.

Desiree and a small group of supporters, in November 2013, staged a demonstration outside of Terri Horman's house in Roseburg. Terri's mother called the police who came and disrupted the demonstration.

On December 31, 2013, a Multnomah County judge finalized the divorce of Kaine and Terri Horman. The couple still had to resolve the issue of who would get legal custody of their daughter Kiara who was now 5-years-old.

As of February 2014, Kyron Horman is still missing. No charges have been filed and there have been no arrests. The police say they have not closed the case. Desiree Young still organizes searches for her son.

According to Terri Horman's attorneys, she was not the last person to see Kyron alive. Moreover, they believe the murder-for-hire allegation against their client is bogus. According to her neighbors, Terri seldom leaves the house in Roseburg. A lot of people revile this woman and a few support her. But for most people familiar with this case, it's hard not to suspect that Terri Horman is somehow responsible for her stepson's disappearance and presumed death.

In June 2014, the missing boy's mother told reporters that Horman, when asked by a polygraph examiner if she had knowledge of the disappearance, failed three lie detector tests.

Presumed Dead But Missing

On March 7, 2011, 25-year-old Tiffany Michelle Whitton, a resident of Marietta, Georgia within the Atlanta metropolitan region, showed up in

Dalton, Georgia with two other women and a man named Matthew Stone. That night, Tiffany, Tracy chambers, Casey Renee Cantrell, and Matthew Stone broke into a woman's house and terrorized her with a tire iron. The victim managed to lock herself into the bathroom and call 911. Before fleeing the dwelling, Tiffany and her crew stole the woman's purse that had been lying on the couch. It contained $60.

When questioned by detectives, Tiffany claimed the owner of the purse owed her money. She and her friends had gone to the house to collect what was hers. Investigators suspected that the victim and the four intruders had been in a drug deal. Tiffany, a user of illicit drugs, had paid the woman for pills, and when the supplier didn't deliver the goods, Tiffany and her friends raided the house to get her money back.

A prosecutor charged Tiffany and her accomplices with armed robbery, burglary, and possession and use of drug-related objects. Following her guilty plea, the judge gave Tiffany a probated sentence.

Tiffany, a former Hooter's waitress in Kennesaw, a suburban community north of Atlanta, disappeared on September 13, 2013. The mother of a 6-year-old daughter was last seen at two in the morning in the parking lot of a Walmart store not far from her home. Since that night she has not made contact with family members or friends. Her mother has created a Facebook page called "Find Tiffany Whitton."

On February 20, 2014, Marietta police officer David Baldwin, in referring to the multi-tattooed, five-foot-two-inch, 100-pound missing woman, said, "What really worries use is that she literally vanished without a trace."

So, what could have happened to Tiffany Whitton? She could have run off to start a new life. However, because of her daughter, that doesn't seem likely. It's also unlikely that some abductor is holding her captive. If she is dead, she could have killed herself in some remote location, or accidentally overdosed on drugs. If neither of these events took place, someone may have murdered her. As a drug abuser, Tiffany rubbed shoulders with unsavory and dangerous people. Did she fail to pay a drug dealer? Did her criminal associates come to believe that she was a snitch?

If Tiffany Whitton was murdered, her case will not move forward until someone who knows something about her disappearance calls the police, or someone stumbles upon her body. Finding a person who is dead is a lot more difficult than finding someone who is alive. Where do you even begin to look for a corpse?

The Relisha Rudd Case

In 2014, eight-year-old Relisha Tanau Rudd resided in the D.C. General homeless shelter in Washington with her mother, stepfather, and three brothers. The family had lived in the shelter a year when Relisha's mother, on March 1, 2014, arranged to have 51-year-old Kahlil Malik Tatum and his wife Andrea take the girl in and care for her. Kahlil Tatum worked at the homeless shelter as a janitor where he had a reputation of paying a lot of attention to the young girls who lived there.

On March 19, 2014, after Relisha missed several days of school, the authorities launched a missing persons investigation. Mr. Tatum had also vanished. The janitor and the girl were caught on a D.C. area Holiday Inn Express surveillance camera walking down a hallway on February 26, 2014, a few days before the girl's mother gave her up.

Detectives learned that Tatum, on March 2, had purchased a carton of black, 42-gallon contractor trash bags.

Police officers, on March 20, 2014, found Andrea Denise Tatum's body in a motel room at an Oxon Hill, Maryland Red Roof Inn. She had been killed by a gunshot to the head. Her husband and Relisha Rudd were nowhere to be found. Homicide detectives uncovered evidence linking the dead woman's husband, Kahlil Tatum, to the homicide.

A Prince George's County prosecutor charged Kahlil Tatum with first-degree murder. On March 26, 2014, the FBI added the fugitive homicide suspect to its "Most Wanted List" and offered a $70,000 reward for information regarding his whereabouts. The Prince George's County Police Department posted a $25,000 reward for information leading to his arrest.

On March 27, 2014, shortly after a witness reported having seen a man meeting Tatum's description with a girl in Kenilworth Park and Aquatic Gardens in northeast D.C., a party of more than 100 officers searched the 700-acre park. Four days later, a searcher came across Mr. Tatum's body. He had committed suicide by shooting himself in the head with the gun used in the murder his wife. Searchers found no signs of Relisha Rudd. On April 3, 2014, the park search was called off.

The D.C. City Council Committee of Human Services, in the course of reviewing the hiring policy at D.C. General, found that Kahlil Tatum possessed an extensive criminal record. He had been convicted in 1983, 1986, 1987, 1991, and 1993 of various crimes including breaking and entering and grand larceny. He was last convicted of a crime in 2004. In those days he went under his birth name, Karl Lee Tatum.

According to the administrator in charge of hiring at the D.C. homeless shelter, Tatum, because his last conviction was ten years old, was eligible for employment at the facility. Had any of his offenses involved children, he would have been automatically excluded regardless of the date of the conviction.

Relisha Rudd's whereabouts are not known. Detectives presumed that Tatum murdered the girl and disposed of her body.

Missing College Students: Two Cases

Hye Min Choi

From Greensboro, North Carolina, 19-year-old Hye Min Choi attended the University of Illinois at Urbana-Champaign as a full-scholarship mechanical engineering major. The five-foot-six, 100- pound junior, who went by the first name Joseph, had earned high grades at the university.

At three in the afternoon of Saturday, May 17, 2014, Choi checked his luggage at Chicago's O'Hare International Airport in advance of a 7:40 PM United Airlines flight to Greensboro. Two hours later, the student called and spoke to his father from the airport. During their brief conversation, the father told his son to make sure he got something to eat before boarding the plane. At seven that evening, forty minutes before the flight's scheduled departure, someone swiped Hye Choi's Wells Fargo credit card at an airport McDonalds.

Hye Min Choi did not board the plane or re-book another flight. His mother, waiting for him at the airport in Greensboro, went home without him.

Three days later, on Tuesday, May 20, Chicago police superintendent Gary McCarthy announced that the college student had been found, safe and sound. "The young man," he said, "was apparently having some problem in school. It appears that he may not have wanted to go home." According to reports, Choi had been upset over his final exams. The police have not released information regarding what Choi was doing, or where he was, while the police in Chicago wasted their time looking for him. He was back in North Carolina with his family.

Brogan Dulle

Brogan Dulle, a 21-year-old student at the University of Cincinnati, resided in an apartment building in the Mount Auburn Historic District of the city. At two in the morning of Sunday, May 18, 2014, Dulle walked out of his apartment carrying a flashlight in an effort to find his missing cell phone by retracing his steps. He believed he had left the phone at the St.

Clair, a bar, or at Mac's Pizza near campus. He left behind his keys, wallet, and jacket. He did not return to his apartment.

Over the next eight days, hundreds of volunteers searched for the missing student. Dulle's friends and family posted missing persons posters around the city, and a $30,000 reward was offered for information regarding his whereabouts.

At 9:00 PM on Monday, May 26, 2014, the landlord of the building adjacent to Dulle's apartment, called 911 to report a possible break-in. At the time, the building was under renovation. Police officers investigating the landlord's complaint found Brogan Dulle's body hanging from a cord in the basement. Dulle had apparently gained entry by climbing up a fire escape and using a crowbar to break an upper floor window. The building was unoccupied at the time.

The Hamilton County Coroner listed Brogan Dulle's cause of death as "asphyxiation by strangulation," and his manner of death as suicide. A police spokesperson told reporters that the student had not left a suicide note. Near his body officers found a wine bottle. The police official said there is no suspicion of foul play in this case.

In the social media, there were some who disagreed with the coroner's ruling of suicide in Brogan Dulle's death.

2 ARSON

Arson Motives

The identification of the fire setter's motive can help establish if the fire was a single event of fire setting or a series of fire setting behavior. Repetitive fire setting is broken down into three classifications: serial arson, spree arson and mass arson. Serial arson is as many as three fires set at different locations with a cooling off period in between. Spree arson is as many as three fires at different location with no cooling off period between fire sets. Mass arson is many fires set at the same time at the same location.

There are six motive classifications for arson:

1. Vandalism [includes many school fires]
2. Excitement [which includes sexual gratification]
3. Revenge [also referred to as anger fires]
4. Crime concealment [murder, embezzlement]
5. Profit [usually insurance fraud]
6. Extremism [environmental extremists who set fire to saw mills]

Robert Disbrow Jr., *Firehouse Magazine*, December 13, 2010

Human Spontaneous Combustion: Fact or Myth?

Soak a rag in linseed oil, ball it up and throw it into a bucket. This rag, as a result of a chemical reaction that creates heat, will eventually catch on fire and burn. Fire scientists call this reaction spontaneous combustion. Under the right conditions, all kinds of material will self-combust. So, can the human body, under the right conditions, catch on fire from within? Those who believe that people can self-generate ignition temperature heat, call this phenomenon human spontaneous combustion.

For decades, fire investigators around the world have been baffled by fire death scenes involving badly burned bodies lying in beds or sitting in a stuffed chairs. In these cases the middle section of the body has been almost completely consumed by fire suggesting high, localized temperatures. In the immediate vicinity of the body, and in the room, there is very little burning. This fire pattern seems out of joint with normal fire spreading behavior. To add to this cause of origin mystery, investigators at these sites--encountered mostly in Great Briton--find no traces of flammable liquids such as gasoline. Are these fires accidental, arson/murder, or something else altogether?

In December 2010, fire fighters in Ireland discovered a 76-year-old man dead in his sitting room. It looked as though someone had lit him up, but there seemed to be no source of heat other than the blaze in the fireplace. Except for some charring on the ceiling above his chair, the room did not burn. Although the man's body was almost completely consumed by the fire, investigators found no evidence that an accelerant had been used to jack-up the heat.

The Irish coroner, having ruled out accident and arson as the manner of death, declared the cause as spontaneous human combustion.

In the 1980s, the American fire scientist, Dr. John de Haan, conducted an experiment in which he set fire to a pig wrapped in cloth. The low-heat, long-burning fire almost completely consumed the hog without creating high ambient temperatures. Dr. de Haan called this the "wick effect." The cloth held the flame like a wick while vapors from the pig's heated fat slowly burned like candle wax.

As it turns out, most so-called spontaneous human combustion fire scenes have involved people who had been drinking in bed or in their chairs while smoking. They fell asleep and their clothing catches on fire. In the Irish case, a spark from the fireplace had probably ignited the man's clothing.

In May 2012, Rajeshwari Kamen, a 23-year-old farm worker, gave birth to a son named Rahul. The mother and her 26-year-old husband, Karnan Perumal, already had a 2-year-old girl. The couple resided in a village in the Indian state of Tamil Nadu.

The baby was a month old when his parents rushed him to the hospital. According to their account of what happened, they were outside their hut when they heard Rahul scream. They ran to him and found the baby on fire. They saw flames on his belly and right knee. The father put out the fire with a towel.

After being treated at the local hospital and released, Baby Rahul, during the next two months, caught on fire at least three more times. The child was badly burned but survived. The couple's neighbors, believing that the baby was haunted by an evil spirit that caused the combustion, and that the fire could spread to their huts, forced Rajeshwari and her husband to move to a nearby village where Rahul caught on fire again.

Dr. Naarayan Babu, the head of pediatrics at the Kilpaul Medical Hospital in the city of Chennai, told a reporter with *The New York Times* that "We are in a dilemma and haven't come to any conclusion [regarding the cause of the fires]. The parents have said that the child burned instantaneously without any provocation. We are carrying out numerous tests. We are not saying it was spontaneous human combustion until all investigations are complete."

On August 20, 2013, the *Times of India* reported that upon completion of the hospital tests, doctors found no evidence of spontaneous human combustion in Baby Rahul's case. Dr. Jagan Mohan, head of the burn unit at the Kilpauk Hospital, told reporters that, "There is no such thing as spontaneous human combustion. The possibility of child abuse exists and needs to be explored."

Baby Rahul's parents have denied setting fire to their baby. The boy's father, in speaking to a reporter with *The New York Times*, said, "Some people don't believe us, and I am scared to return to my village and am hoping for some government protection. There is also the fear that our child could burn once again."

Since Baby Rahul was not the victim of spontaneous human combustion, he was either burned accidentally or on purpose. It's hard to image how a baby could be accidentally burned on four or more occasions. Moreover, if there was something in the home that caused the fires, why wasn't the baby's sister also burned?

This child should be separated from his family and placed under close observation. As long as the child is beyond the reach of his parents, there is no chance he will catch on fire again. The parents, pursuant to an aggressive investigation, should be asked to take polygraph tests.

Notwithstanding forensic evidence to the contrary, there are those who still believe spontaneous human combustion is real. This is not surprising since strong opinions are not always based on what people know, but what they want to believe.

How Arsonists Set Fires

Arsonists hardly ever simply strike a match to light a fire, using any combustible material at hand such as a piece of paper or a curtain. Such a course of action is too uncertain, since a fire lit in this way may burn itself out very quickly. Usually, an accelerant is used. A flammable liquid such as kerosene [or gasoline] is poured over a wide area of carpets and furnishings, before the match is applied. This ensures that a hot fire will follow and that the building be ablaze long before any firefighters arrive. However, what most arsonists do no know is that traces of such accelerants can be detected, even after the fire has destroyed the building. Small amounts of accelerant will seep into carpets, floorboards, plaster, brickwork and other materials and will not be consumed by the fire. The cooling effect of the water used to extinguish the fire will slow down the rate of evaporation of the accelerant and enough will usually remain to be detected.

Dr. Zakaria Erzinclioglu, *Forensics*, 2012

Burning Hollywood

Robbers and thieves commit their crimes for financial gain. Arsonists, on the other hand, set fires for a variety of reasons. As a result, motive and criminal profiling is an important lead in arson investigations. Regarding motive, unlawful fire setting generally falls into one of two categories: rational and irrational. The rational arsonists can be put into two groups: people who set fires for direct gain, and those who do it for indirect benefit or gain. Direct gain arsonists torch their homes, cars, and businesses for the insurance money. (January is usually a busy month for these people.) The indirect gain fire is set, for example, as retaliation, revenge, competitor elimination, or to cover-up another crime such as homicide. People who set fires for reasons that make sense are usually not repeat offenders. If they do repeat their crimes, it's rarely more than twice.

Arsonists who are irrationally or pathologically motivated are almost always young men. They are powerless losers who are mad at the world. They set fires to get even with society, to experience feelings of power, to play the role of hero, and in a small percentage of cases, for sexual gratification. Many of them have had problems at school, with their parents and with the police. Some are mildly retarded. Others have mental health problems. Older pathological fire setters often have drug and/or alcohol addictions.

Because the vast majority of serial arsonists are pathological fire setters who have no regard for human life, they are the most dangerous. Unlike rational fire setters, they tend to hang around the fire scenes soaking up the excitement they have created. When taken into custody, trained and experienced arson investigators should question these suspects. For the pathological arsonist, the bigger the fire, the bigger the rush. Serial arsonists have been know to set several fires in one night.

In California, a serial arsonist set 15 fires in Hollywood and 4 fires in neighboring West Hollywood during the early morning hours of Friday, December 30, 2011. Dozens of residents were rousted from their homes. The only injury involved a firefighter who fell while battling one of the blazes. Many of the structural fires were started when the arsonist set fire to vehicles parked nearby. All of the fires were set in an area of four square miles.

In 2008 and 2009, in and around Coatesville, Pennsylvania in the eastern part of the state, a group of arsonists set 23 fires. One of the arsons killed an 83-year-old woman. Dozens of homes were destroyed, and many residents were displaced. In 2009 the police arrested five arsonists. The oldest, a 25-year-old volunteer firefighter, had responded to fires he had set. The rest were young, unemployed men with histories of mental illness and problems with the law. One of the fire setters, a 19-year-old misfit, matched the classic profile of a pathological arsonist. He set a number of copycat house fires simply for the excitement. The fact these dwelling were occupied at the time only enhanced his experience.

In the California case, authorities, on January 2, charged 24-year-old Harry Burkhart with setting more than 50 fires in Hollywood, West Hollywood and in the San Fernando Valley. From Frankfurt, Germany, Burkhart had been upset over his mother's immigration problems. He had recently attended her hearing in immigration court. When taken into custody, Burkhart reportedly said, "I hate America." He was held in the Los Angeles County Jail without bail. Since his arrest, there have been no further arson fires.

Burkhart and his 53-year-old mother Dorothee came to the United States from Neukirchen, Germany in October 2011. Just before leaving Germany their house went up in flames. Arson investigators, after locating to separate points of origin, suspect the fire had been intentionally set to defraud the insurance company. In Germany, Dorothee Burkhart has been charged with 19 counts of fraud, crimes unrelated to the house fire. One of the counts involves defrauding the surgeon who had enlarged her breasts.

In early December 2011, police in Los Angeles pulled Dorothee Burkhart over for a traffic violation. The traffic stop led to her recent appearance in immigration court. The prospect of being deported apparently set off Harry Burkhart's fire setting spree. Dorothee and her son had been living in an apartment in Hollywood.

Before coming to the U.S., Burkhart and his mother resided for a time in Vancouver, Canada. In March 2010, a Vancouver team of psychiatrists, in connection with a civil court case, examined Harry Burkhart. The battery of shrinks diagnosed him as suffering from autism, severe anxiety, post-traumatic stress disorder, and depression. The police in Vancouver, in the wake of the LA fires, were looking into the possibility that he set a series of fires in that city. A German national, Burkhart was born in Chechnya.

In January 2012, Burkhart pleaded not guilty to felony charges related to the commission of 100 arson fires. A federal judge, in May 2012, ordered his mother Dorothee back to Germany to face a host of fraud charges.

As of August 2014, Burkhart had not been brought to trial.

Majoring in Arson

At West Virginia University (WVU), a well-known party school, there is a really stupid and dangerous student tradition that dates back to the late 1970s. When the football team, the Mountaineers, win or lose a big game, students either celebrate, or vent their anger, by getting drunk, and setting what the local authorities call "street fires." The boozed-up kids pour gasoline into dumpsters, onto stuffed furniture (sometimes purchased for that purpose), and onto piles of rubbish, then set these highly flammable combustibles on fire. Most of the arson (legally called malicious burning because structures are not involved) takes place in the student-dominated, low-rent part of town called Sunnyside, or as the students call the neighborhood, "Scummyside."

Between 1997 and 2003, Morgantown, the site of more than 1,200 street fires, had the highest per capita incendiary fire rate in the country. After the Mountaineer's win in November 2002 over Virginia Tech, celebrating WVU students set 90 large street fires, and dozens of less spectacular blazes. The police charged 20 students with malicious burning, a misdemeanor that usually involves a fine of up to $1,000. A few of the fire setters were expelled, but most were merely disciplined. In this fire-setting spree, a police officer was punched, and a car went up in flames. This was just another big weekend in Fire City, West Virginia.

In 2005, city officials, in anticipation of another flame-filled football weekend, ordered Sunnyside residents to remove all stuffed chairs, couches, and flammable debris from their porches and yards. (This is asking a lot from a West Virginian.) There were street fires that weekend, but no one's house burned to the ground.

In May 2011, WVU students, celebrating the completion of exam week, blew off steam by getting drunk and lighting-up 18 dumpsters and 11 couches. One of the drunken idiots received facial burns after pouring two gallons of gasoline into a dumpster then hanging around to admire his work. The low-grade explosion took off his eyebrows and knocked him on his butt. A week earlier, WVU students, drinking to the death of Osama Bin Laden, set 22 more dumpsters and sofas on fire. By the end of 2011,

Morgantown was the site of more than 200 street fires. Drunken fire setting has become a college tradition.

After WVU defeated the Clemson Tigers in the Discovery Orange Bowl in January 2012, the streets of Morgantown were once again lit up by dumpster, furniture and loose rubbish fires. A couple months later, over the St. Patrick's Day weekend (a big holiday of booze on campuses across the country), the West Virginia kids really got fired-up. They ignited 35 dumpster and couch fires, then outdid themselves by torching a semi. The police arrested five students for malicious burning. On April 2, 2012, several more Morgantown dumpsters and pieces of overstuffed furniture went up in flames.

If *U.S. News & World Report* ever published a list of the nation's top ten universities where students are most likely to get busted for public intoxication, disorderly conduct, *and* criminal fire setting, West Virginia University would be number one. That, of course, would provide the young scholars at WVU a good excuse to break out the booze, and the $4 a gallon gas.

Michael Marin's Court Room Suicide

Former Wall Street trader Michael Marin lived alone in a $3.5 million, 10,000 square-foot-mansion in Biltmore Estates, an high-end neighborhood in Phoenix. The attorney and art collector, who owned original Picasso sketches among other valuable paintings, had scaled six of the world's seven tallest mountains. In May 2009, he had reached the summit of Mr. Everest. The 51-year-old had four grown children.

While Michael Marin had been able to climb Mr. Everest, he had not been able to climb out of debt. Besides falling behind in his Biltmore Estates mortgage, Marin couldn't keep up the $2,500-a-month payments on a second home, and owned $34,000 in back taxes. He had amassed numerous other debts as well.

During the early morning hours of July 5, 2009, flames broke out in Marin's Biltmore Estates mansion. Wearing scuba gear to protect himself from the smoke and toxic gases, he escaped through a second-story window by climbing down an emergency rope ladder.

The fire insurance payout to a policyholder who was in deep financial trouble raised suspicion that the blaze had been intentionally set, and motivated by insurance fraud. Marin's convenient, well-prepared, and bizarre escape from a dwelling engulfed in flames added to the suspicion he had torched the place. (There aren't too many inhabitants in houses consumed by flames who manage to escape down a rope ladder wearing scuba gear.) This financially strapped man was very lucky, extremely prepared for a fast-developing fire, or an arsonist.

After fire scene investigators found several points of origin and traces of accelerants at these separate fire starts, the arson investigators declared the fire incendiary. Since Michael Marin was the last person in the dwelling before the blaze, and had a rather obvious motive for burning the place down, the Maricopa County prosecutor charged him with arson of an occupied structure, a felony that carries a 10 to 20 year sentence. When taken into custody in August 2009, the former high roller and adventurer said he was "shocked" that anyone would accuse him of such a crime.

On Thursday, June 28, 2012, a Maricopa County jury found the 53-year-old defendant guilty of arson. Just seconds after the verdict was read, Michael Marin popped something into his mouth, then took a swig from a sports bottle. His face turned red, he started to cough, then convulsed and collapsed to the floor. Fire personnel who happened to be in the courtroom rushed him to a local hospital where he died a few hours later.

The quickness of Marin's demise after putting something into his mouth has led to speculation he took some kind of poison pill. If Michael Marin had poisoned himself, what was the toxic substance? Where did he acquire the deadly pill? And how did the defendant get it into the Maricopa courthouse?

In July 2012, the medical examiner reported that Mr. Marin had swallowed a cyanide pill that took his life.

In the annals of crime, there is rarely anything new. It's all been done before. But Michael Marin, upon hearing his fate from the arson jury then dispatching himself with a poison pill like a captured cold war spy, added a new line to the history of crime.

Vehicle Arson

Automobiles *seem* to be very combustible…they contain flammable liquids, have many electrical circuits, and their interiors are made of combustible material. Combine that with a careless smoker and you have a vehicle fire, or so you would think. But actually, with new technology, most interiors are fire resistant--a cigarette will seldom ignite a seat cover or a floor mat, the fuel systems are designed with safety in mind, and the electrical circuits are shut off by fuses and other interrupt devices.

Accidental vehicle fires do occur, but the fire generally remains in one compartment, i.e. engine, trunk, glove compartment or interior….

There are two types of vehicle arsonist: amateur and professional. An amateur is usually behind on his car payments and desperate to rid himself of the car. He knows that the vehicle must be declared totaled by his insurance company, so he will go for mass destruction. The professional criminal uses vehicle arson to conceal other crimes: stolen cars used during the commission of a crime, or a homicide, for example.

In general, after driving a car to a remote location, the arsonist will completely dowse the interior and exterior of the vehicle with a combustible material such as gasoline and set the fire. A one- to five-gallon gas can is generally found at the scene. Using five gallons is quite dangerous, and the arsonist may end up like the car if the flammable vapors have saturated the area.

The arsonist might make what are known as *trailers* by pouring a stream of gasoline from the vehicle to a location he feels is far enough away from the vehicle to ignite it safely. These types of fires are easily tagged as arson because of the evidence left behind....

Mauro V. Corvasce and Joseph R. Paglino, *Modus Operandi*, 1995

The Carlos Diaz Blowtorch Case

Carlos Diaz and Cathy Zappata were married in 2007. He worked at W. D. Auto Repair at Tenth Avenue and 207th Street in Harlem, New York. A year later, the couple had a son. In 2010, Diaz lost his job at the body shop, and shortly after that his marriage fell apart. He became homeless, moving from one parking lot to another where he slept in his van.

Although estranged from his wife, Diaz refused to accept the fact they were finished as a couple. He resented it when Cathy, to improve her looks, had cosmetic breast surgery and liposuction. She also made him jealous by going out with other men.

On January 15, 2013, Diaz flew into a rage when he discovered that Cathy had sent a nude photograph of herself by cellphone to another man. This was the straw that broke the camel's back. The next morning, at eight o'clock, Diaz asked Cathy to meet him at a Pathmark parking lot on Ninth Avenue at 207th Street where he had spent the night in his van. The lot was a block from the auto body shop where he had once worked.

As Cathy sat behind the wheel of her car, Diaz sprayed the 38-year-old's face, head, and neck with lighter fluid then ignited the accelerant with a blowtorch. With her entire head engulfed in flames, Cathy managed to exit the vehicle and extinguish the fire by rolling in a puddle of water. (The victim was rushed to Harlem Hospital's burn unit with second-degree burns on her lips, eyelids, nose, cheeks, and neck. Her hair had been burned off to the scalp. Doctors listed her condition as critical.)

After setting his estranged wife on fire, Diaz, in possession of a can of gasoline, walked to W. D. Auto Repair. He found the owner, Helson

Marachena, the man who had fired him, in his office. Diaz doused the room with the accelerant, but when he tried to ignite the place, his lighter wouldn't fire. The malfunctioning lighter gave Mr. Marachena the opportunity to escape.

Later in the day, the 35-year-old arsonist turned himself in to the New York City police. When questioned by detectives, Diaz said, "I had to teach her a lesson, give her a little pain. Now she can worry about our kid and get serious instead of focusing on going out with other men." In relating how he felt when he discovered the nude photograph on his wife's cellphone, Diaz said, "I couldn't think straight. I wanted to pass out. I had to do something. I had to be a man about it. She hurt my pride." Diaz described his perception of his marriage this way: "She was my right arm. I did everything for her. I forgot all about my own life. I just worked to support her and to pay the rent. And this is what she does."

Charged with attempted murder, arson, assault, and attempted assault, Diaz is in jail at Riker's Island. A magistrate has denied him bail.

In September 2013, a judge ordered a psychiatric examination for Diaz. As of July 2014 his case had not come to trial.

Jealous boyfriends, discarded husbands, and rejected suitors can be dangerous. In the annals of crime, men like Carlos Diaz have done terrible things with fire, including mass murder. It's extremely difficult for women to protect themselves from these angry, sociopathic losers who feel justified in their acts of depraved violence.

Man Sets Himself on Fire in Front of Wife

At noon on Sunday, March 24, 2013, a 46-year-old Vietnamese man walked into the Creative Nails & Spa salon in the Orange County town of Costa Mesa, California. He carried a bucket and began screaming at his estranged wife Lina who worked in the shop as a nail technician.

Five months earlier, Lina had moved out of the house with the couple's three sons. She had filed a restraining order against her spouse after he had threatened and harassed her with phone calls.

The angry, drug-addled husband sat cross-legged in the center of the salon. He lifted the bucket and soaked his body in gasoline. Using a lighter, he set himself on fire. As he sat on the floor engulfed in flames, one of the horrified onlookers threw towels on him. A bystander doused the burning man with a fire extinguisher. Another employee dialed 911.

Paramedics rushed the charred man to the Western Medical Center where he was treated for third degree burns over 70 percent of his body. He was listed in critical condition.

In the United States, self-immolation by fire is a rare form of suicide. Most of these cases involved Asian males.

Serial Arson in Virginia

The incendiary fires started on November 12, 2012 in Hopeton, a town 100 miles east of Richmond on Virginia's Eastern Shore, a peninsula along the Chesapeake Bay. Over the next four months, volunteer firefighters in the county responded to 77 intentionally set fires involving abandoned houses, barns, camper trailers, and various outbuildings that included a chicken coop.

Arson investigators with the Virginia State Police and the Accomack County Sheriff's Office suspected that the serial fire-setter was either a disgruntled firefighter, a teenage boy sexually aroused by flames, or a young man committing arson simply for the thrill and excitement of causing havoc. Given the nature of the places burned, financial gain was not a motive. These were pathologically motivated arsons.

Since the vast majority of arsonists are men, the fire investigators were not looking for a woman. Female arsonists usually have histories of mental illness, and set fire to their own property. A vast majority of the fires set by women are motivated by the need for sympathy and attention.

On April 2, 2013, forty-five minutes after midnight, a Virginia State Trooper near the Eastern Shore community of Melfa, pulled over a vehicle with an expired inspection sticker. (This was probably not the real reason for the stop.) The traffic stop occurred shortly after a nearby abandoned house had been torched. Later that morning, a local prosecutor charged the occupants of the car, 38-year-old Charles Smith III and Tonya Bundick, his 40-year-old girlfriend, with setting the Melfa house fire.

Smith (also known as Charlie Applegate) and Bundick were held without bail at the Accomack County Jail. They are both from Accomac, Virginia. Smith, the owner of a body shop, was once captain of the Tasley Volunteer Fire Company. Smith and Bundick had planned to get married within a month.

A Virginia State Police spokesperson, at a press conference on April 2, 2013 said, "We are confident that Bundick and Smith are guilty of the majority of the fires." According to reports, arson investigators watched Smith set the Melfa house fire. He started the blaze with a towel soaked in gasoline.

Tonya Bundick resided in a dwelling that sat next door to a shed that had been set on fire in December 2012. The authorities did not identify the motive behind the arson spree. Since the couple received no monetary gain from the fires, their motives must have been pathological. Perhaps they were bored, or angry at the world.

In October 2013, Smith pleaded guilty to 67 counts of arson. He faced life in prison, and $5.6 million in fines. As part of the plea deal, Smith agreed to testify against Tonya Bundick.

Bundick's arson trial got underway in Virginia Beach in January 2014. Smith took the stand against the defendant as the prosecution's star witness. Following his testimony, Bundick entered an Alford plea to one count of arson. (She faced dozens of other arson charges.) By this plea, the defendant did not admit guilt, but acknowledged that the prosecution had enough evidence to convict. As of July 2014, the cases against these two serial arsonists had not been completely resolved.

The Homeless Arsonist

Thirty-eight-year-old Raymond Sean Clark, a homeless panhandler, regularly loitered outside the 7-eleven store on the Pacific Coast Highway in Long Beach, California. Clark made a habit of hassling customers who patronized the convenience store by begging them for money and cigarettes. He had become an unwelcome fixture in the neighborhood. (A pain-in-the-neck like Clark is a store manager's nightmare.)

At five in the afternoon of April 12, 2013, as Jerry Payne sat outside the 7-eleven store in his Toyota 4-Runner, the 62-year-old was approached by Clark who asked him for money. (If Mr. Payne was a regular customer of the store, he probably had been hit-up for money by Clark before.)

When Mr. Payne refused to give Clark a handout, the transient poured a bottle of gasoline into the SUV then tossed in a match. The vehicle and its occupant were immediately engulfed in flames. (The fire produced so much heat customers and employees were trapped inside the store before escaping through a back door.)

After bystanders pulled Mr. Payne out of the burning vehicle, paramedics rushed him to Torrance Memorial Hospital, a medical facility that specializes in burn patients. With third-degree burns on his chest and face, the victim is in critical condition.

Police officers arrested Raymond Clark around the corner from the fire. Charged with attempted murder, he is in the Los Angeles Inmate Reception Center under $502,200 bail.

There is no way to protect oneself from people like Raymond Clark. That is the sad truth of this case. As a result of his senseless assault on this totally innocent and unsuspecting victim, Clark will spend the rest of his life being fed, housed, and otherwise cared for by the already overburdened taxpayers of California.

Potato Chips as Fire Starters

Crime laboratories do not always detect accelerants that were used in an incendiary fire. Accelerant-sniffing dogs, whose sniffers are more sensitive than even the most sophisticated laboratory equipment, don't always, either. If it is believed that an accelerant was used in the fire, it might be that the accelerant itself is undetectable. One such accelerant could be a bag of potato chips. It is possible to set a bag of chips on fire and throw it on a couch, creating an accelerant-like effect. The fat in the chips make them extremely volatile when ignited (think of a kitchen grease fire). An accelerant-sniffing dog won't even detect the chips, and the labs won't be testing for them, either. The crime scene investigator should always question finding a couch with too many crumbs in the cushions.

Jarrett Hallcox and Amy Welch, *Bodies We've Buried,* 2006

The Marcel Melanson Case

In 1998, 22-year-old Marcel Melanson joined the fire department in Los Angeles County's Compton, California. While the ambitious and popular firefighter succeeded at his job, he wasn't good at managing his financial affairs. In 2005, the state of California filed a $29,000 tax lien against him. Two years later, the IRS hit him with a $80,240 tax lien.

Melanson became a minor celebrity in 2009 as a regular participant in a BET Network reality TV series called "First In." A TV crew followed the fire battalion chief as he led a rescue team that came to the aid of victims of traffic accidents and street crime. About this time, *Inked* Magazine featured Melanson's elaborate tattoos on his back, arms and neck.

The crime-ridden city of Compton, like its celebrity firefighter, had run into financial problems. The municipality, due to a revenue shortfall and bloated budgets, had disbanded its police department. In June 2010, members of the Compton City Council, in anticipation of bringing back the police force, authorized the purchase of $1.7 million in communications equipment from the Motorola Corporation. Melanson an emergency communications expert sat on a three-person technology committee that oversaw the purchase of this equipment.

By 2011, the city of Compton was on the verge of insolvency. As a result, the police department was not coming back, and the city was stuck with hundreds of radios that cost $2,500 a piece. The city stored the excess communications equipment at the Compton Fire Department.

In December 2011, a fire broke out and quickly spread at the Compton Fire Department in the area housing the surplus radio equipment. Arson investigators determined that the fire had been intentionally set, and that Marcel Melanson was the only person in the station at the time of the fire. Detectives with the Los Angeles Sheriff's Office discovered that prior to the blaze, someone had stolen thousands of dollars worth of the radios. Further investigation revealed that over the past several months the thief had been selling the stolen property, one radio at a time, on Internet sites like eBay. Theft detectives, by 2013, had recovered fifty of the stolen communication units.

In February 2013, Melanson, the prime suspect in the thefts and the arson, was fired. Deputies with the Los Angeles Sheriff's Office, at eleven o'clock on the morning of May 15, 2013, arrested the 37-year-old at his home in Torrance, California. Los Angeles County Deputy District Attorney Renee Rose charged the former celebrity firefighter with arson, grand theft, and embezzlement. A judge set his bail at $350,000.

Investigators believe that Melanson set the fire to cover his radio equipment thefts. The suspect's attorney, Robert Rico, publicly insisted that his client was innocent. According to the defense attorney, a Long Beach Fire Department arson investigator had initially reported that the Compton fire was *not* arson then later changed his mind.

While a firefighter committing arson is not that unusual, this type of arsonist rarely torches a fire station. Due to the celebrity element in this particular case, Melanson's arrest has attracted a lot of southern California media attention. People who know him and have worked with the former high-ranking firefighter had a difficult time believing he was guilty as charged.

In April 2014, Melanson pleaded no contest to felony arson of property and embezzlement by a public official. The judge sentenced him to three years and four months in prison. The judge also ordered the ex-firefighter to pay $517,477 in restitution.

The Professor's Revenge

Rainer Klaus Reinscheid was an Associate Professor in the Department of Pharmaceutical Sciences at the University of California, Irvine. The 48-year-old lived in the Orange County city of 223,000, thirty miles southeast of Los Angeles, with his second wife, two stepchildren, and his 14-year-old son from his first marriage.

In March 2012, Reinscheid's son, Claus Stubbe, a student at Irvine's University High School, got in trouble for stealing something from the student store. As punishment, the assistant principal assigned the boy trash pick-up duties during the school's lunch hour. Shortly after this mild disciplinary action, a worker at the Mason Park Preserve adjoining the high school campus, found the boy hanging from a tree in a wooded area of the park.

Professor Reinscheid blamed his son's suicide on the assistant principal who had disciplined the boy. On April 26, 2012, the distraught father, on his cellphone, emailed his wife details of his intention to take out revenge on his son's death. His plan, in general, included shooting 200 students at University High School, murdering the assistant principal, and raping as many high school girls as he could. Once he had accomplished his mission, he'd kill himself.

In one of two emails to his wife that day, the revenge-minded professor wrote: "I need a gun, many guns, and then I have the ride of my life. I will give myself a wonderful ending with Klaus very soon. I like this plan, finally a good idea." Two days later, in another email, Reinscheid said that while he was casing out the high school campus, he had fantasized about having sex with every girl he had seen.

On July 4 and 19, 2012, a series of small fires broke out in Mason Park Preserve. Fire fighters also responded to a fire someone had set outside the house of University High School's assistant principal. Following the two fires in the park, the Irvine police beefed up patrols of the preserve. At 12:45 in the morning of July 24, police officers patrolling the park caught Professor Reinscheid igniting newspapers soaked in lighter fluid. He was starting the fire not far from where his son had committed suicide. The officers arrested him on the spot. The next day, charged with arson, Professor Reinscheid posted his $50,000 bond, and was released from custody.

Police investigators, after linking Reinscheid to three incendiary fires at the high school, and the one at the assistant principal's house, charged the professor with four additional counts of arson, and a count of attempted murder. By now, detectives had discovered the emails Reinscheid had sent to his wife detailing his intent to seek revenge for his son's suicide. Although the content of these emails--private musings rather than threats sent to targeted individuals--were not considered chargeable criminal offenses, police re-arrested the professor on the additional arson and attempted murder charges. (Whether or not the professor's very specific revenge communications constitutes a crime poses an interesting legal question. Had the emails suggested a conspiracy, and he had acted upon that plan by buying a gun, it would have been an offense. Had there been an agreement with a fellow conspirator to carry out the crimes, the fires would have been acts in furtherance of that conspiracy.)

The Orange County prosecutor, using the revenge emails as evidence that Rainer Reinscheid was a danger to society, asked that he be held in custody without bail. The judge agreed, and denied the professor bond.

On July 27, the Irvine police re-arrested Professor Reinscheid in his office at the University of California. When they took him into custody, he was drafting a document on his computer giving his wife power of attorney over his finances. When searching his car, officers found a red folder containing a newly drafted and signed last will and testament.

Reinscheid pleaded guilty in July 2013 to six counts of arson, three counts of attempted arson, and resisting or obstructing an officer. Reinscheid faced a maximum sentence of 18 years behind bars. The Orange County prosecutor had dropped the attempted murder charge. A month later, on the first day of his sentencing hearing, Reinscheid said, "I lost my son, and then I lost myself. Now, I am asking you, your honor, and many other people, to forgive me and show mercy." Reinscheid said he wanted to return to his native Germany where he could find work to support his family. The ex-professor acknowledged that his career in academia was over.

School superintendent Tracy L. Walker, in a statement read aloud at the hearing, wrote: "That tragedy [the boy's suicide] cannot serve as justification for terrorizing a school community and staff members who have dedicated their lives to helping others."

On the second day of Reinscheid's sentence hearing, the judge heard from the University High School assistant principal whose house Reinscheid tried to burn down. The school administrator said that as a result of the fire, his life has been changed.

In an effort to mitigate his client's criminal rampage, defense attorney Joshua Glotzer noted that his client had been "self-medicating" with drugs he had ordered online. The professor had also been drinking cheap wine. The drugs and the wine, according to the attorney, had led to a "perfect storm" that provoked the arsons.

On August 22, 2013, the judge sentenced the former professor to 14 years and 4 months in prison.

3 RAPE

Problems in New Orleans

The head of the New Orleans Police Department's sex-crimes unit was replaced in June 2010 after an audit by the Louisiana Commission on Law Enforcement found that 32 percent of the rape complaints filed in 2009 ended up in the books as "miscellaneous incident" cases. This study followed a 2009 *Times-Picayune* report revealing that in 2008, 60 percent of rape complaints in the city had been written-up as so-called Signal 21 cases. Police superintendent Ronal Serpas, in response to the scandal, announced that the city planned to hire two DNA specialists to work on rape cases in the Louisiana State Crime Laboratory.

In March 2011, a review of the New Orleans Police Department's sex-crime unit by the U.S. Department of Justice revealed that detectives rarely interrogated rape suspects, and while questioning rape accusers, suggested they were to blame for their attacks. Investigators, in questioning victims' credibility, often emphasized inconsistent statements, gaps in memory, and various motives for false accusations. This approach encouraged victims to become less cooperative with the police that in turn justified the filing of cases as Signal 21s rather than rapes.

The head of the New Orleans Police Department's criminal investigations division, in October 2011, announced a backlog consisting of 800 untested rape kits dating back to the late 1980s. These kits contain DNA evidence that had been collected by nurses following reports of sexual assault. The hiring of the two additional DNA analysts had not cleared the backlog at the Louisiana State Crime Laboratory. DNA experts at Marshall University in Huntington, West Virginia would conduct some rape kit testing for the New Orleans Police Department.

While law enforcement agencies across the country are adding expensive and unnecessary SWAT vehicles to their crime-fighting arsenals, crime labs are struggling with DNA backlogs that allow rapists to remain on the loose.

A Rape Case in India

The gang-rape of a Danish woman in one of New Delhi's most popular tourist districts is prompting concern for the safety of foreign travelers and raising questions over how much progress has been made in India after a year in which considerable attention has been focused on the prevalence of rape.

Indian police said that a 51-year-old Danish tourist was gang-raped [on January 14, 2014] in the popular Paharganj district after asking a group of men for directions to her hotel. Police have arrested two people in connection with the rape....

The incident came a year after the rape and death of a 23-year-old student in a bus in New Delhi that sparked mass protests across the country and a national dialogue on the position of women in society and the pervasiveness of rape.

Chelesa Sheasley, *The Christian Science Monitor,* January 15, 2014

In India a Victimless Crime

Because of the country's high rate of infanticide, child marriage, and slavery, India is one of the worst places in the world to be a female. Moreover, girls and woman who have been raped are routinely blamed for their victimization, and discouraged from reporting these assaults to the police. If they do, the victims and their families are subjected to public ridicule and humiliation.

Police officers in this male-dominated society often refused to accept rape complaints. And when they did register rape complaints, the crimes weren't professionally investigated. In those occasional instances where rape cases were taken seriously, crime lab delays slowed down the process of identifying the rapists. In India's Forensic Science Laboratory in Rohini, it took 75 days for a DNA report to come back to the investigating officer. These delays were caused by a work backlog created by a serious shortage of qualified lab personnel. (There are many crime labs in the U.S. that have worse backlogs.) In the rare instance of an Indian rape prosecution, the case will drag on for years, and almost always end with an acquittal. In India, rape is treated as a victimless crime.

Among India's major cities, New Delhi, the nation's capital and home to 16 million people, had the country's highest number of reported rapes. Because such a small percentage of these assaults were reported, crime statistics did not come close to reflecting India's extremely high sex crime rate. If just half of India's rapes were reported and investigated, the nation's crime lab system, unable to cope with the workload, would completely break down.

On the evening of December 16, 2012, in New Delhi, a 28-year-old software engineer and his 23-year-old female companion boarded a city bus after attending a movie. The woman, from an urban, middle-class family, had recently qualified as a trainee physiotherapist in a private New Delhi hospital. The bus driver and five men from the city's slums were the only other people on the bus. The passengers began taunting the woman's friend, then knocked him unconscious with an iron rod. Five of the men then beat and gang-raped the woman. At some point, the bus driver turned the wheel over to one of the rapists, walked to the back of the bus, and had sex with the beaten and bloodied woman. Before the one-hour ordeal came to an end, one of the attackers inserted the iron rod into the female victim's body. The men undressed both victims then threw their nude bodies off the moving bus.

The unidentified woman (In India, journalists do not have the kind of access given to American reporters.) was taken to the Safdarjung Hospital in New Delhi with serious brain trauma and severe injuries to her intestines and abdomen. The police, with the help of the rape victim's friend, quickly identified the bus driver and the five other rapists. Shortly after the suspects were taken into custody, the men confessed, telling the police they had tortured and raped the woman "to teach her a lesson."

On December 26, following three operations and a heart attack, the authorities flew the victim to Mount Elizabeth's Hospital in Singapore.

This brutal beating and gang rape on a city bus (operated by a private company) sent thousands of protesters into the streets in several Indian cities. The irate protestors demonstrated against the government's lax attitude toward crimes against women. In New Delhi, demonstrators clashed with riot police.

Indian Prime Minister Manmohan Singh, facing serious civil unrest, promised police and legislative reforms. But the public demonstrations continued throughout the country, growing in strength daily.

On December 29, 2012, at 4:45 in the morning, the female victim of the brutal bus attack died in the Singapore hospital. Her body was flown back to India for cremation. (In the United States, there would be an autopsy.) The rape victim's cause of death was listed as brain injury complicated by a lung infection. The six men responsible for her torture, rape, and death were charged with murder, which in India can lead to the death penalty.

(The Indian media did not provide any information regarding the identities of the rapists, or of their male victim.)

The fact that Ban Ki-moon, the head of the United Nations voiced "deep sorrow" over this young woman's ordeal and death reveals how this case had focused international attention on India's rape problem.

On the day following the 23-year-old's passing, a human rights organization called on the Indian government to ban the so-called "finger test," a medical procedure routinely given to rape victims. This unscientific and irrelevant measure involved testing the laxity of a rape victim's vagina to determine if she had been "habitual to sexual intercourse." The obvious purpose of this procedure was to humiliate victims and to discourage them from reporting their rapes.

Amid the women's rights protests, a legislator from the state of Rajasthan, in proposing his own rape prevention measure, suggested replacing girls' school uniform skirts with pants. While many ridiculed this politician and his idea, it reflected how most men in India blame rape on the rape victim. If the five slum degenerates and the bus driver hadn't beaten and murdered this young woman, she would be alive, and they would still be out in public raping women with impunity.

City politicians in New Delhi, facing a wave of public anger, offered the rape victim's family monetary compensation. Officials also offered one of the victim's unemployed relatives a government job. I'm sure they were doing this out of the goodness of their hearts.

I don't know enough about India to venture a guess as to whether or not this case will be the catalyst for change. But given the nature of government, and how difficult it is to alter deeply ingrained cultural traditions, it's hard to be optimistic. There was one good sign, however. At least half of the anti-rape protestors had been men. (The women held candles for the victim while the men called for the perpetrators to be quickly hanged.)

On January 3, 2013, five of the suspects were charged with, among other crimes, rape, kidnapping, and murder. The defendants were Ram Singh, the 33-year-old bus driver; his brother Mukesh, 26 who cleaned buses for the company; Pavan Gupta, 19, a fruit vendor; Akshay Singh, 24, a bus washer; and Vinay Sharma, 20, a fitness trainer. The sixth suspect, a juvenile, had not yet been charged.

The male friend assaulted by the men on the bus, in his first public statement about the case, said that he and his friend were lying nude and bleeding on the street for an hour while pedestrians passed by without stopping to help them.

On January 6, 2013, a popular Indian spiritual guru who calls himself godman Asharam, in a video circulated in the Internet, said, "This tragedy would not have happened if she [the murder victim] had chanted God's name and fallen at the feet of the attackers. The error was not committed by just one side."

A defense attorney representing three of the accused rapist/murderers announced on January 9, 2013 that his clients intended to plead not guilty. The attorney had also claimed that the police had beaten the suspects.

A second gang rape involving an Indian bus passenger occurred in a village in the northern state of Punjab. On January 11, 2013, the bus driver and his conductor drove the 29-year-old victim, the only passenger on the bus, to a vacant building where they and five other men raped the woman. The timing of this crime makes one wonder if these rapists were making a political statement.

On March 11, 2013, one of the men in custody for the New Delhi bus rape was found dead in his cell. Police say Ram Singh had hanged himself. The suspect's father claimed that he had been murdered.

Rapist Collaborators

My first lesson about sex-crimes prosecution was that perpetrators were not the only enemy. There is a large, more or less hidden population of what I later came to call collaborators within the criminal justice system. Whether if comes from a police officer or a defense attorney, a judge or a court clerk or a prosecutor, there seems to be a residuum of empathy for rapists that crosses all gender, class, and professional barriers. It gets expressed in different ways, from victim bashing to jokes in poor taste, and too often it results in giving the rapist a break.

Alice Vachss, *Sex Crimes,* 1993

Juvenile Rapists

In August 2011 in Louisville, Kentucky, 16-year-old Savannah Dietrich, while drinking with two teenage boys she knew, passed out drunk. The boys took advantage of her condition by having sex with her. This, in most states, including Kentucky, is rape. If that wasn't bad enough, the rapists photographed each other committing the crime, and put the photographs on the Internet.

When Dietrich learned of the humiliating photographs, and the fact they had been published, she and her parents reported the crime to the Louisville Metro Police Department. The two minors were charged with first-degree sexual abuse, a felony. Since the juveniles had photographed each other in the act, they had no choice to plead guilty. But for some reason, the prosecutor, in return for the pleas, promised a lenient sentence.

Following the defendant's June 26, 2012 plea hearing before Jefferson County District Judge Dee McDonald, Savannah Dietrich posted several tweets on her Twitter account in which she named the two boys who had pleaded guilty to her sexual assaults. By doing this, she had violated the judges' order not to reveal information about the case, especially the identities of the assaulting juveniles.

The judge sentenced the boys to 50 hours community service. If they stayed out of trouble until they reached the age of 19, their criminal records would be expunged.

The attorneys representing the two minors, asked Judge McDonald to hold Dietrich in contempt of court. If held in contempt of court, the judge could sentence Dietrich to 180 days in jail. And the judge could also fine her $500.

Dietrich, in speaking to a Louisville reporter with *The Courier-Journal*, said, "So many of my rights have been taken away by these boys. I'm at a point that if I have to go to jail for my rights, I will do it. If they really feel it's necessary to throw me in jail for talking about what happened to me-- then I don't understand justice."

On Monday, July 23, 2012, the lawyers representing the juveniles awaiting their sentences, withdrew their motion to have Dietrich held in contempt of court. In a single day, an online petition on change.org had brought 62,000 signatures in support of Dietrich's decision to publicize the identities of her assaulters.

Turkish Victim Turns the Tables

Nevin Yildirim lived with her husband and two children, ages two and six, in a village in southwestern Turkey. In January 2012, her husband left home to work at a seasonal job in another town. Shortly after Mr. Yildirim began working in the other place, a 35-year-old member of the village named Nurettin came to Nevin's house and raped her. This married father of two threatened to shoot Nevin's children if she reported the crime to anyone.

By August 2012, after months of being raped on a regular basis by Nurettin, Nevin was five months pregnant with his child. When she visited a clinic regarding an abortion, a health care worker informed her that her pregnancy was too far along for that option. In Turkey, abortions are illegal after the first ten weeks of pregnancy.

On August 28, 2012, when Nurettin came to Nevin's house to rape her again, she pulled her father-in-law's rifle off a wall rack and shot him. As the wounded Nurettin reached for his handgun, Nevin shot him again. Hit with her second slug, he tired to run, but stumbled and fell. As he lay on the ground cursing her, Nevin fired a third bullet, this one into his genitals. The rapist went silent, and a few seconds later, died where he lay in a pool of his own blood.

After killing the man who for months had been raping her, Nevin laid down her rifle. She picked up a kitchen knife and used that to decapitate him. Nevin then picked up the detached head by the hair, and carried it triumphantly to the village square. To a group of men sitting around a coffee house, Nevin, still gripping her rapist's head as it continued to drip blood from the base of the severed neck, said, "Here is the head of the man who played with my honor."

As the coffee house drinkers looked on in horror, Nevin Yildirim tossed her blood trophy. The head rolled along the ground and came to rest in the public square. A short time later, a local police officer took the blood-splattered woman into custody.

A few days after the killing, in speaking to her court-appointed lawyer who came to the local lock-up, Nevin reportedly said, "I thought of reporting [Nurettin] to the military police and to the district attorney, but this was going to make me a scorned woman. Since I was going to get a bad reputation, I decided to clean my honor, and acted on killing him. I thought of suicide a lot, but couldn't do it. Now no one can call my children bastards. Everyone will call them the children of the woman who cleaned her honor."

On August 30, 2012, at the preliminary hearing on the charge of murder, Yildirim told the magistrate she didn't want to keep her rapist's baby, and that she wished to die. The public prosecutor advised the court he had ordered psychiatric evaluations of the defendant.

Because I'm not familiar with the Turkish criminal justice system, I have no idea what will happen to this murder defendant. I do know that in the Middle East, citizens found guilty of criminal homicide can be treated harshly. Recently in Saudi Arabia, a stunt driver who accidentally ran over and killed two bystanders was sentenced to death. Unless murder defendants in Turkey have access to the insanity defense, or there is international pressure to spare this rape victim's life, Nevin Yildirim could be executed. The fact she had killed the man who had repeatedly raped her might not mitigate her sentence. In Turkey, and other Middle Eastern countries, women and men are not always treated equally under the law. In the United States, a case like this would at least bring the defendant a stint in a mental institution. At worst she could spend the rest of her life in prison.

As of August 2014, Nevin Yildirim has not been brought to trial for murder.

A Mass Rape in Paradise

Acapulco, the famous vacation mecca in the Mexican state of Guerrero on the country's Pacific Coast, had become increasingly more dangerous. Once an oasis amid rampant drug gang violence, the crime had filtered into the city. The violence came from rival drug cartels fighting for control of drug routes from South America.

In 2010, 20 million Americans visited Acapulco. Today, following travel warnings issued by authorities in the United States and Great Britain, hotel occupancy rates in the city had fallen to 46 percent. It was the threat of crime that was killing Acapulco's tourist industry.

On February 1, 2013, a pair of Mexican tourists returning from a beach east of Acapulco were shot and wounded by members of a masked self-defense squad at an improvised roadblock. To defend their neighborhoods against drug gang violence, citizen self-protection units have sprung up throughout the region. The tourists were fired upon because they failed to stop at the roadblock. (The tourists probably thought the men blocking the road were drug criminals.)

At two in the morning of Monday, February 4, 2013, five men wearing facemasks broke into a beach bungalow on the outskirts of Acapulco. A Mexican woman, six Spanish women, and seven Spanish men had rented the picturesque house. The armed intruders, motivated by robbery and "to have some fun," tied-up the seven men with phone cords and bikini straps. Over the next five hours, the robbers raped the six Spanish women. The rapists spared the Mexican woman because of her nationality.

According to the Guerrero state attorney general, if investigators determined that the crime was related to drug cartel activity, the case would be turned over to the federal authorities. Military checkpoints were set up in an attempt to quickly identify and arrest these violent intruders. The crime had attracted international media attention, and presented a nightmare for Acapulco's tourism business, an industry already suffering from Mexican drug violence.

To a large extent, Mexico's out-of-control crime problem, and the corruption of its government, was caused by America's insatiable appetite for drugs.

The Bail Jumper

In 1978, a jury in Norfolk County, Massachusetts found 18-year-old Gary Irving guilty of three counts of rape with force, unnatural acts, and kidnapping. Irving had knocked one of his victims off her bike, dragged her to a secluded area, and viciously raped her. He had threatened a second rape victim with a knife. The convicted rapist faced up to life in prison.

Immediately following Irving's guilty verdict and sentencing, the rapist's attorney asked Judge Robert Prince to extend his client's bail a couple of days so Irving could make final arrangements before being packed off to prison.

The prosecutor in the case, Louis Sabadini, pointed out that if the authorities did not send Irving straight to prison, he would flee. Extending bail to a convicted rapist who was facing 35 years in prison was simply out of the question. This young man was a violent, sexual predator.

Judge Prince shocked the prosecutor and the rape victims' families by granting Irving the weekend to settle his affairs before his incarceration. Irving took this opportunity to flee the state. Except perhaps for Judge Prince, Irving's bail jumping surprised no one.

If there was anything surprising in the Irving case, it was how long it took the authorities to find this rapist and put him behind bars where he should have been living since 1978.

In trying to find this fugitive, the police received plenty of help from reality television. The Irving bail-jumping case was featured on "America's Most Wanted," "Unsolved Mysteries," and "Real Stories of the Highway Patrol." It seemed that Gary Irving had somehow left the planet.

On Wednesday, March 27, 2013, 35 years after Judge Prince set the rapist free, local police and FBI agents arrested Irving at his home in Gorham, Maine where the 52-year-old had been living under the name Gregg Irving. (He hadn't even bothered to change his last name.)

Gary Irving is currently behind bars in Portland, Maine awaiting extradition back to Massachusetts.

What can you say about a judge who made such a reckless decision? What was he thinking? Could he have been that stupid, or were his motives more complicated, and perhaps pathological? One can only hope that Mr. Irving, during his 35 years of freedom, didn't rape more victims. If he did, Judge Prince was his accomplice. (The judge has since died.)

Rape by Prison Guards

New data suggested that inmates had just as much to fear from their guards than they did from each other: Nearly half of all sexual assaults in U.S. jails and prisons were committed by corrections officers and staff. That statistic actually represented an uptick in reported cases of sexual assault. Accusations of rape against prison guards and staff rose 18 percent between 2006 and 2011--the most recent year for which data was available-- according to the Bureau of Justice Statistics....

According to the statistics, in cases where the accusation was found credible, 77.1 percent of the victims--and 80 percent of the perpetrators--were male. More than a third of the victims were 24-years-old or younger....

Some experts think rape between guards and prisoners was occurring at an even higher frequency than the number of accusations suggest....

Robby Soave, The Daily Caller, January 24, 2014

A Mishandled Case

In the summer of 2013, Mary (not her real name), a 15-year-old with Down syndrome, worked a few hours a week at a coffee shop in southwest Detroit called Cafe Con Leche. On July 17, Mary did not show up for her two-hour shift that began at 3:30 PM. The shop's owner, Jordi Carbonell, at 3:35, called Mary's legal guardian who lived a few blocks away. (Mary's mother had died of cancer in 2006.) The legal guardian informed Carbonell that Mary had left the house on time for her four-block walk through the Hubbard Farms neighborhood to her place of employment. Not long after Mr. Carbonell made the call, Mary walked into the shop. When asked why she was late, Mary said she had been with a friend.

That evening, Mary shocked her legal guardian by telling her that she had been raped that afternoon by a neighborhood man named Bill (not his real name) who invited her to his apartment. According to Mary, Bill had kissed her, told her to undress, and raped her. She said he used his cellphone to take photographs of her in the nude.

Bill, who referred to himself as Super Fly and an Aztec Warrior, was known in the neighborhood for his strange and often confrontational behavior. The 43-year-old, generally disliked by residents of the area, was considered an oddball. He had big, puffy hair and walked around in shorts and high socks. In January 2012, a judge had committed Bill to a mental health facility. According to a psychiatrist who treated him there, Bill was severely depressed. The doctor had written: "He feels hopeless and helpless. He plans to kill himself by hanging."

Mary's guardian reported Mary's claim of rape to the Detroit Police Department on the day the girl reported the crime to her, July 17, 2013. A member of the sex crimes unit asked a medical technician to gather physical evidence from Mary for possible DNA analysis. (I'm not sure when this evidence was gathered.) Because of the complainant's limited communication skills, a detective, *five days after the complaint,* brought in a specialist to question her.

Mary's guardian became concerned when twelve days passed without anything happening in the case. Finally, on July 29, police officers took Bill into custody for investigation. When they questioned him at the police department he refused to cooperate. Before booking him into the Wayne County Jail, an officer swabbed his cheek for a DNA sample.

The lead investigator on Mary's case asked the Wayne County Prosecutor's Office to charge Bill with rape. An assistant prosecutor in the office, in denying the request, asked for more evidence. The prosecutor recommended that detectives search Bill's apartment. (Apparently the police didn't search the apartment when they took Bill into custody.)

On July 31, 48 hours after taking the rape suspect into custody, the police, without a criminal charge, had no choice but to release Bill back into the community. Two days later, 16 days after the rape report, police officers searched Bill's apartment. They seized a bed sheet, a blanket, and a cellphone.

On August 5, 2013, Mary's guardian and members of the community who were following the case with great interest were surprised to learn that the officer in charge of the investigation, 19 days after the rape report, had just sent Mary's rape kit to the Michigan State Police Laboratory for analysis. At this point in the investigation, detectives couldn't even prove that the complainant had engaged in sex.

In response to criticism and neighborhood outrage over the way the case was being handled, a Detroit police administrator blamed the rape kit submission delay on the fact that during this crucial period in the case, the sex crime unit moved its offices to a new headquarters. When it became obvious that this excuse only created more anger and frustration in the community, the police administrator promised an internal investigation. This did not silence critics of the police department. As far as neighborhood residents were concerned, a rapist was living among them and the police, instead of doing something about it, were fooling around with an office move. It was obvious what the police considered important.

On August 11, 2013, 24 days after Mary's rape report, a man on a bicycle carrying a baseball bat rode up to Bill as he walked along the street not far from his apartment building. "You like raping little girls?" the man asked as he began whacking Bill in the legs with the bat. A witness to the assault called 911. After the beating, Bill, as he limped along the sidewalk back to his apartment, was attacked by five men who, as a group, punched and kicked him. By the time the Detroit Police rolled up to the scene, Bill was on the ground and his assailants were gone. An officer called for an ambulance that took Bill to a nearby hospital.

Bill did not return to his dwelling. On the night of his beatings, someone broke into his apartment. It was this person who spray-painted "rapist" on the outside wall near the windows to his residence. The next day the building owner hired an armed security guard to make his nervous tenants feel safer.

The police did not arrest anyone in connection with the assaults on the neighborhood rape suspect.

This Detroit rape case split the neighborhood into two camps. One group was in support of the vigilantism while the other faction deplored the idea of citizens taking the law into their own hands. One thing they all agreed on was that the Detroit Police Department, by bungling the investigation, created the environment for vigilantism.

Falsely Accused

Dr. Jon Norberg, an orthopedic surgeon in Fargo, North Dakota who specialized in hands, elbows, and upper extremities, was estranged from his wife Alonna, a former pediatrician who suffered from Sjogren's syndrome, a rare immune system disorder. In 2011 the couple, in their early 40s, were in the midst of a contentious divorce and child custody battle. In June of that year, Dr. Alonna Norberg filed a complaint with the Fargo Police Department in which she accused her estranged husband of endangering her life by repeatedly, and without her consent, injecting her with the powerful anesthetic drug propofol. (This drug gained notoriety after Michael Jackson overdosed on it in 2009.) According to Alonna, Dr. Norberg had injected her with the drug thirty times between September 2010 and June 2011. The complainant also accused her husband of rape. She told detectives that on the morning of June 17, 2011, she awoke to discover physical evidence that her husband, while she was under the influence of the drug, had forced her to have oral sex. She found, on the nightstand next to the bed, a bottle of Diprivan (a propofol brand).

On August 2, 2011, a prosecutor with the Cass County State Attorney's Office charged Dr. Jon Norberg with gross sexual imposition, a class AA felony that carries a maximum sentence of life. For injecting his wife with propofol, the surgeon was also charged with reckless endangerment, a class C felony that could put him in prison for up to five years. As a result of these criminal charges, Dr. Norberg took a leave of absence from his medical practice. (The State Board of Medical Examiners would later suspend his medical license indefinitely.) Following his arrest, arraignment, and release from custody on bail, Dr. Norberg pleaded not guilty to both charges.

On November 7, 2012, Cass County prosecutor Reid Brady, in his opening remarks to the jury, said, "At the end of this case you will know that the defendant defied dangerous risks by unsafely using propofol on his wife. You will know that he obsessed with sex so much that he perpetrated sex acts on her when he knew she was unaware."

Defense attorney Robert Hoy, in his opening address to the jury, said that Alonna Norberg had concocted the drug and rape allegations to get the upper hand in the couple's divorce and child custody battles. The defendant had injected his wife with the drug three times to alleviate her pain from Sjogren's syndrome, and to help her sleep.

Two days into the trial, Dr. Alonna Norberg took the stand as the prosecution's principal witness. For two days she gave, in a breathless manner, graphic and dramatic testimony of being constantly drugged, and on the one occasion, raped under its influence. "I remember," she said, "looking around thinking I've got to get up and I got to get away...It was just true true horror because I was choking and I couldn't get his mouth away, I couldn't get my body away."

Following her testimony, Alonna Norberg walked out of the courtroom and did not return to the trial. On November 14, Robert Knorr, Alonna's father, took the stand and testified about an October 28, 2012 meeting he had with Dr. Norberg, at the defendant's request. At this meeting in a Fargo restaurant, Dr. Norberg suggested, for the benefit of all parties, that his estranged wife recant her accusations. According to this witness, the defendant had said, "She could either say that it was a dream, or that she was lying, or that she didn't remember." Mr. Knorr believed the defendant thought it would be in the best interest of the entire family if this matter did not go to trial. The witness said, "I told him there was no way that was going to happen." Following Robert Knorr's testimony, the state rested its case.

Under defense attorney Robert Hoy's direct questioning, Dr. Harjinder Virdee, a Fargo psychiatrist with 35 years experience, painted a psychiatric portrait of the defendant's accuser that undermined her credibility. Dr. Virdee had spent more than 100 hours reviewing Alonna Norberg's extensive medical history comprised of hundreds of documents. The psychiatrist had also conducted a five-hour interview with the former pediatrician. According to the witness, Alonna was a compulsive, nonstop talker who dominated the session.

Regarding Alonna Norberg's accusations against her husband, it was Dr. Virdee's expert opinion that they were false. The accuser's description of what happened to her was simply too detailed and graphic to ring true. A person under the influence of the drug propofol could not recall what had happened to them is such detail.

According to Alonna Norberg's medical file, she had been diagnosed with more than fifteen mental illnesses and disorders including obsessive-compulsive disorder; anxiety; narcissistic personality traits; depression; violent mood swings; and chemical dependency. At no time in the past decade had Alonna Norberg been taking fewer than twenty medications. Occasionally during this period she was ingesting more than fifty different drugs at one time. Many of these prescriptions involved opioid medication such as the addictive oxycodone. "She's got everything," Dr. Virdee said. "If you go through her medical notes there are umpteen diagnoses in the records. It jumps from one thing to another, one [doctor's] visit to the next. She is ill, she is psychiatrically ill."

Based upon her review of Alonna Norberg's vast psychiatric history, Dr. Virdee added a new diagnosis. In Dr. Virdee's medical opinion, Alonna Norberg suffered from what the psychiatrist called fictitious disorder, a condition or personality trait in which people either fabricate symptoms or intentionally produce symptoms to gain attention and sympathy. (This sounds a lot like the Munchausen Syndrome Disorder.)

On cross-examination, prosecutor Reid Brady pointed out that Dr. Virdee was the first doctor to diagnosis Alonna Norberg with the syndrome called fictitious disorder. "I'm the only doctor," she replied, "that has reviewed all the records as well. It's hard to wonder how she became a physician if she can't tell the difference between all these drugs. Her credibility is very low."

Kori Norberg, the defendant's sister-in-law, took the stand and testified that Alonna's accusations were motivated by her fear that because of her drug addiction, she would lose custody of the couple's two children.

In his closing argument to the jury, defense attorney Hoy said, "There is not one shred of physical evidence to support their [the state's] case. Everything else...originates with Alonna Norberg. Desperate people do desperate things."

On November 21, 2012, the day before Thanksgiving, the jury, after a quick deliberation, found Dr. Jon Norberg not guilty of both charges. Given the circumstances surrounding these accusations, the charges should never have been filed in the first place. This case, in my view, reflects a gross lack of prosecutorial discretion.

In March 2013, a Fargo judge granted Norberg primary custody of his children. Five months later an official with the North Dakota Board of Medical Examiners reinstated his medical license with conditions. For an unstated period of time the physician will undergo "professional monitoring" which will include working with a mentor.

An Unsolved Case

Shortly before midnight on Tuesday, February 5, 2013, moviegoers leaving a theater in Cypress, Texas, a Houston bedroom community in northwest Harris County, saw a teenage girl walking aimlessly about the Cinemark

Cypress parking lot. The nude, unnamed 16-year-old was drenched in blood from a severe head wound. The theater security guard called 911 while several of the theater patrons attended to the dazed girl. Paramedics transported the Cypress Woods High School student by helicopter to a Houston hospital where she remained in critical but stable condition.

According to the victim, she left her home around eleven that night after an argument with a family member. While walking along Spring Cypress Road not far from the high school, a man knocked her to the ground with a hatchet. He dragged her into the woods where he raped her while she played dead. She described the man who ambushed her as a white male in his early twenties who was thin, muscular and between five-foot-seven and five-foot-ten inches tall. He wore dark-colored clothing. After the assault, the victim walked half a mile to the theater parking lot.

K-9 officers with the Harris County Sheriff's Office searched the rape site for the suspect. If the deputies came across physical evidence pertaining to the rape or the attacker, they did not reveal this information to the media.

A woman told the police she had seen a suspicious man that night at a grocery store. The witnesses said that this man's knuckles were bloody. "Not overly bloody," she said, "but you could tell he'd been in a scuffle." Presumably, detectives followed up on this lead.

A second witness reported seeing a sweaty man in the area that night. Described as thin and wearing a gray shirt, he walked with his head down. The witness, before she learned of the rape, assumed this man had come out of a nearby 24-hour fitness center.

A third witness claimed to have seen a man in bloody clothes enter a gas station restroom. According to this witness, when the man came out of the restroom he was wearing a clean set of clothing. It is not known if detectives were able to identify this man.

On February 10, 2013, the Harris County Sheriff's Office released a composite sketch of the rapist. This was not good news because it indicated that the police, five days into the investigation, did not have a suspect.

Eight months have passed since the moviegoers saw the bloody teen walking about in the parking lot. There has been no arrest in the case, or a sign that detectives have a suspect. Moreover, there has been nothing in the papers or on television about the status of the investigation. This apparent lack of police progress and media silence has created frustration and fear in the community. Could there be a serial rapist on the loose?

The lack of information in the Cypress rape case has also fueled speculation about a possible cover-up, and rumors that the rapist was a football player who is enrolled at Cypress Woods or Cypress Ranch High School.

Residents of the Cypress community, in the absence of an arrest, would at least like to know if investigators have recovered the hatchet. Did they find the girl's bloody clothing in the woods where she said she had been raped? Did the rapist leave behind trace evidence to confirm sexual intercourse, evidence that would link him to the assault through DNA? Did the police employ a rape kit? Is there any chance the victim knew the person who assaulted her? And finally, with whom did she have the argument that night, and what was it about?

The lack of information and apparent progress in this case could mean several things, all of them bad. If the few pieces of information known about this crime are true, the rapist should have been caught by now. The rapist must have been covered in physical evidence that would link him to the victim. Someone would have noticed this, and notified the authorities. DNA analysis would then confirm or not confirm the suspect's guilt.

As of August 2014, this Cypress, Texas rape case remained unsolved. It's hard not to suspect that the police have bungled this investigation.

A Serial Rapist in The Neighborhood

In 1969, when Christopher Hubbart attended high school in Los Angeles, he reached out and touched a woman's breast as she walked by him on the street. He did this to several woman until he quickly evolved into a rapist. In the early 1970s the sexual predator drove around Los Angeles in the morning hours looking for women to rape.

Hubbart's criminal M.O. was simple: in residential neighborhoods he'd look for open garage doors that revealed that the man of the house had left for work. If Hubbart saw toys in the yard or in the garage he saw an opportunity. Hubbart believed that mothers protective of their children were more likely to submit without a struggle. As a calculating sexual predator, Christopher Hubbart represented one of society's worst nightmares.

Once inside the carefully chosen victim's house, Hubbart bound the woman's hands, and while he raped her, held a pillow over her face. In 1972 the so-called "pillowcase rapist" sexually assaulted 26 women in Los Angeles County.

Detectives identified and arrested Hubbart in 1973. He pleaded guilty, and instead of being sent to prison for at least fifty years, the judge sent him for sex offender treatment at the Atascadero State Hospital. (Criminal justice practitioners in California thought they could rehabilitate anyone. Perhaps that's why the state has become a haven for sex offenders.)

In 1979, after a team of therapists, counselors, psychologists, and psychiatrists proudly proclaimed that the pillowcase rapist had been cured and was no longer a danger to society, these mental health experts decided to treat him as an outpatient. Hubbart must have been grateful for his clean bill of health and the chance to continue his career as a serial rapist.

Within months of walking out of the state hospital Hubbart raped several women in northern California. Convicted in 1980, the judge sentenced him to prison instead of putting him back into the hands of counselors and therapists. But this is California, and in 1990, corrections experts released him on parole. As could be expected by anyone who knows anything about serial sex offenders, Hubbart re-offended. He raped a female jogger shortly after his release from prison.

For the pillowcase rapist it was back to prison. One would think that as a habitual rapist Mr. Hubbart was finally behind bars for good. The parole authorities, obviously with warm spots in their hearts for rapists, released Hubbart back into society after three years behind bars.

In 1996, while living in the Santa Clara County town of Claremont, California, Hubbart told his parole officer that he felt he was losing control of himself. Later that year, pursuant to a new California law called the Sexual Predator Act, a judge committed Hubbart to the Coalings State Hospital. The new law applied to serial sex offenders like Hubbart who were likely to re-offend. (I guess politicians in the state had grown tired of correction officials and mental health experts putting serial sex offenders back into society.)

In May 2013 history repeated itself when a judge in Santa Clara County ordered Christopher Hubbart released from the state hospital. Once free, he would come under the supervision of bureaucrats running the Forensic Conditional Release Program. Under this program, administered by the California Department of State Hospitals, Hubbart will receive free housing, continued psychological assessment, group and individual therapy, and regular home visits.

Serial rapist Hubbart, under the release program, will be required to wear a GPS monitoring device. He will also be subjected to random drug testing, regular polygraph examinations, and house searches. A security guard will be posted at his place of residence. Because it will take at least six months for the Forensic Conditional Release Program bureaucrats to find this rapist a suitable home, his release from the state hospital is not imminent.

In July 2013 District Attorney Jackie Lacey petitioned a state judge to block Hubbart's release on the grounds of public safety. The judge denied the request, and the government appealed that decision. On August 25, 2013, the California Supreme Court affirmed the lower court's denial of the prosecutor's request. The high court justices did not accompany their ruling with a written decision.

Prosecutor Lacey, in speaking to reporters after losing the appeal, said, "We are now committed to working with law enforcement partners to ensure that all terms of conditions of release are strictly enforced. We will do everything in our power to keep all members of our community safe from harm."

Here was the obvious problem: Prosecutor Lacey has no power that will guarantee that this serial rapist will not take off his GPS ankle bracelet and slip into the night only to re-surface after he has raped more women. The prosecutor knew this, the police knew it, and so did the bureaucrats in charge of Hubbart's supervision.

Sixty-two-year-old Christopher Hubbart was being kicked out of the state hospital to make room for younger rapists. The state was simply overrun with sexual predators. Christopher Hubbart's release has nothing to do with rehabilitation.

In May 2014, Judge Gilbert Brown ruled that upon Hubbart's July release, he must take up residence in Palmdale, California. According to the terms of the release, the rapist must also wear a GPS ankle bracelet.

Victim Anonymity in Scotland

Rape is dealt with differently under the Scottish legal system from the way it is treated in England, particularly in how the crime is reported in the media. Up here, we are extremely careful about preserving the anonymity of the victim--another example of the superiority of Scots Law over the English version.

Anonymity is vital--rape often results in victims of the crime being mentally scarred for life and the last thing they need is the added distress of having their names appear in the media. Even the successful conviction of an offender can be of little consolation to a woman violated in this manner, something that the psychologists have been examining for years. In some respects, being a rape victim is like no other type of victim: the ramifications run deep into the subconscious for years, perhaps for a lifetime. It cannot be shrugged off in the way some other crimes are ultimately forgotten, buried under the pressure of getting on with life. For the victim and the family concerned, the anguish is horrific.

Les Brown and Robert Jeffery, *Real Hard Cases,* 2006

The Rape of a Nun

On Friday, December 13, 2013 at eleven-thirty in the morning, a nun in the Order of St. Joseph named Sister Mary Pellegrino encountered a young man in the parking lot behind St. Titus Church in Aliquippa, a western Pennsylvania town 25 miles north of Pittsburgh. The six-foot teenager, wearing a black-hooded sweatshirt, dark pants, and work boots, came up behind the retired 85-year-old nun, tapped her on the shoulder and asked if he could be of help. When Sister Pellegrino declined the smiling youth's offer he exposed himself, choked her, punched her in the jaw, and then raped the nun as she lay injured in the snow.

Rushed to Allegheny General Hospital in Pittsburgh, Sister Pellegrino underwent surgery to repair her dislocated lower jaw. Although the nun was unable speak to detectives, she described the attack and her attacker in writing.

At the scene of the crime, investigators photographed a series of boot impressions in the snow. Detectives also questioned people who had seen an 18-year-old named Andrew Clarence Bullock near the church just before the assault. Bullock had been wearing clothing that matched the victim's description of her attacker's sweatshirt, pants, and shoes.

A few hours after the assault behind St. Titus Church, Aliquippa police officers questioned Andrew Bullock. The suspect, after initially denying the assault, confessed. Officers noticed that Bullock wore work boots that matched, in size and tread pattern, the shoe impressions in the snow behind the church.

Police officers booked Bullock into the Beaver County Jail on charges of rape, aggravated assault, and several lesser offenses. The District Judge set his bail at $50,000.

On Sunday, December 15, 2013, doctors released Sister Mary from the hospital in Pittsburgh. It's hard to believe she survived such a vicious attack. Had she not, Mr. Bullock would have faced charges of first-degree murder.

Killer Rapists

Although the murder of a rape victim certainly may indicate hostile motivation, at least some such murders may be due to the simple fact that killing the victim greatly increases the rapist's chances of escaping punishment by removing the only witness to the rape...Rape-murders, however, are a very small percentage of all murders. In the United States, over the period 1976 to 1994, in no year was the percentage of murders that included rape or other sexual assault higher than 2 and an unknown portion of that small percentage involved *male* murder victims....

Young women, highly overrepresented as rape victims, are also at the greatest risk of being killed by their assailants...Young women appear to resist rape more than females in other age groups. The strong sexual motivation of the rapist to rape a young victim, in combination with her greater resistance, may account for young women's overrepresentation in homicides with sexual assault.

Randy Thornhill and Craig T. Palmer, *Rape*, 2000

A False Charge

In 2013, Mitch Ford, his 25-year-old fiancée Melinda Muniz, and his 3-year-old daughter Grace from a previous marriage, lived in Plano, Texas, the sprawling suburban community north of Dallas. Ford and his ex-wife Emily Ward were engaged in a custody battle over Grace Ford, their daughter.

Mitch and Melinda's relationship ran into trouble in late December 2013 when she revealed that she had been cheating on him.

Early in the morning of January 9, 2014, before he left for work, Mitch told Melinda that within the next few days she would have to move out of the apartment. The engagement was over. Melinda did not take this news very well.

Later that day, Mitch Ford, concerned about how Melinda was reacting to the break-up, called the Plano Police Department and asked that officers check on Melinda and his daughter. At one-forty that afternoon, when officers made the welfare call, they didn't get a response when they knocked on the door. This prompted the officers to open the unlocked door and enter the apartment.

In the master bedroom, officers found Melinda with her pants down with duct-tape over her mouth. In the toddler's room, they found Grace Ford unconscious in her crib. Someone had placed tape across her mouth as well.

The child was taken by ambulance to the Children's Medical Center in Dallas where doctors pronounced her brain-dead. Physicians put the 3-year-old on life support until her organs could be harvested.

Melinda Muniz told detectives that an intruder had forced his way into the apartment and raped her. The rapist had covered her mouth, and the child's, with the tape. Melinda said the intruder was a complete stranger.

Melinda's story quickly unraveled. A medical examination revealed that she had not been sexually assaulted. Moreover, a surveillance camera at a nearby store showed Melinda buying duct-tape, zip ties, cotton balls, and a pair of scissors. Confronted with the inconsistencies in her statement as well as the recent surveillance camera evidence, Muniz confessed to suffocating the toddler and staging the rape.

The Dallas County Medical Examiner ruled Grace Ford's death criminal homicide by asphyxiation.

Police officers, on January 28, 2014, booked Melinda Muniz into the Collins County Jail on the charge of capital murder. A judge set her bond at $1 million. If convicted as charged, a judge could sentence her to life without parole.

The Massage Parlor Rapes

In 2011, 47-year-old Danford Grant and his wife Jennifer lived in the Seattle suburb of Auburn, Washington with their 5-year-old son, 8-year-old daughter, and a 16-year-old boy from Mr. Grant's former marriage. A graduate of the University of Washington School of Law, Danford was a litigation partner at Bailey Grant and Onsanger, a prestigious Seattle law firm. Grant had handled appeals before the Washington State Supreme Court and before the federal 9th Circuit Court of Appeals in San Francisco. Years earlier he had been a King County prosecutor.

Grants 38-year-old wife Jennifer, an attorney herself, worked in the Seattle City Attorney's Office as a supervisor. She had worked in that office since the mid-1990s. To the casual observer these successful attorneys living in the big, fancy house with their beautiful children represented the American dream come true.

As it often the case, superficial appearances can be misleading. It seemed that Danford Grant had a problem controlling his sexual urges around women. Because of his unwanted sexual advances, female paralegal employees at the law firm had nicknamed him "Dirty Dan." And this wasn't the worst of it.

Early in 2011, using the last name Hunter, Grant allegedly received a massage from a 45-year-old Asian masseuse in Bellevue, Washington. After the massage, he grabbed the woman and told her to remove her pants. When she refused and broke down in tears, Grant left the parlor.

Grant allegedly purchased a massage in June 2011 at the Carnation Chinese Massage Clinic in Greenwood, Washington. He grabbed the masseuse and had a condom in his hand when a noise from the hallway outside the room ended the assault. The victim of the attempted rape quit her job at the Greenwood parlor and opened a massage operation out of her home in Shoreline, Washington.

On August 19, 2012, Grant allegedly had an appointment under the name Pete with the Asian masseuse he had tried to rape in Greenwood. When she cracked her front door in response to his knock, she immediately recognized him as the man who had tried to rape her at her previous place of employment. Before the masseuse could close the door, he pushed his way into her house and raped her.

On August 28, 2012, the attorney allegedly returned to the massage clinic in Bellevue where he raped the 45-year-old masseuse at knifepoint. After the assault the victim realized this was the Mr. Hunter who had tried to rape her in early 2011.

Not long after the Bellevue attack, Grant allegedly raped a massage clinic cashier in Seattle. He attacked the woman in his car after identifying himself as a police officer.

Danford Grant, at 9:30 on the night of Monday, September 24, 2012, allegedly returned to the massage clinic in Greenwood where, after the massage, he pulled out a pocketknife and demanded sex with the Asian masseuse. She said she'd go along if he put away the knife then informed him that she had HIV. To that he replied, "Me too." He then slipped on a condom and raped the victim.

After the sexual assault, employees of the massage parlor called the police. Later that night, the rapist returned to the clinic. When employees tried to detain him, he fled on foot. Just after midnight on September 25, 2012, police officers arrested Grant and booked him into the King County Jail.

King County prosecutor Valiant L. Richey, on September 28, 2012, formally charged the prominent Seattle attorney with four counts of first-degree rape and several lesser offenses. The judge set Grant's bail at $3 million.

In October 2012, Grant posted his reduced bail and was confined to house arrest. Four weeks after the Greenwood massage clinic rape detectives located the suspect's Honda Pilot parked in the garage of Jennifer Grant's aunt.

The day after her husband's arrest, Jennifer Grant and her aunt moved Danford's SUV from where it had been parked near the massage parlor to the aunt's house in Auburn. (Jennifer insisted that she had moved the vehicle at the direction of her husband's attorney, David Allen. She denied intentionally hiding potential evidence against her husband from the police.)

Inside the rape suspect's SUV, searchers found a realistic looking pellet gun, a cell phone, an iPad, a laptop computer, a black stocking cap, and a bottle of Cialis.

In November 2012, Jennifer Grant filed a petition for legal separation from her husband. The couple would remain married, but divide their assets and debts. Danford Grant, under the terms of the separation, would be liable for child support. After six months, either spouse could ask the family court judge to convert the separation into a divorce.

On March 6, 2013, *The Seattle Times* reported that investigators had recovered the September 24, 2012 rape victim's DNA from Grant's underwear. One of Grant's attorneys, Richard Hasen, told the reporter that, "Much of the DNA evidence actually favors the defense." The defense attorney acknowledged that his client had been a regular customer at several Asian massage parlors where he had been a problem client. "But that doesn't mean he was raping everyone there," said Hasen. Investigators have not found the pocketknife used by the rapist.

On June 2013, Jennifer Grant resigned from her position in the Seattle City Attorney's Office. The Danford Grant rape trial is scheduled for the spring of 2014. If convicted as charged, the once prominent attorney could be sent to prison for up to 45 years.

4 THEFT

Pickpockets

To avoid having your pocket or purse picked while Christmas shopping at the local mall, crime prevention experts recommend that men carry their cash and credit cards in front-pocket wallets and that women tote their handbags diagonally across their bodies. While there's nothing wrong with that advice, is it really necessary? In America, are there any pickpockets left?

Today, when people say they've had their pockets picked, they're usually referring to politicians, not those dexterous thieves who actually pick pockets and lift wallets from handbags. You don't hear much any more about those street larcenists with the educated fingers and nerves of steel. In the old days, as-told-to memoirs featuring the exploits of these soft-touch artists had a small niche in the true crime genre. But as far as I know, there hasn't been a book like this published for decades. Are these guys still around plying their sticky-fingered trade? Has pickpocketing become a lost art?

In Europe, particularly Rome, Italy and Barcelona, Spain, pickpockets still mingle with the tourists. Most of them are from Bulgaria and Romania. But even in those cities, criminals that snatch purses vastly outnumber their more talented criminal cousins. In America, street thugs have supplanted the practitioners of this lost art. The FBI, through its uniform crime reporting system, no longer keeps track of reported pickpocketing cases nationwide.

New York City has always been paradise for pickpockets. But even in the Big Apple, pickpocketing has been a dying criminal trade. In 1990, there were 23,000 reported cases, but in 2000, less than 5,000. Up until the 1970s, the city was home to organized pickpocket schools where students lifted wallets from mannequins outfitted with bells that would ring if the trainee lacked the required finesse. These academies are gone, and no one is passing the torch to a new generation of wallet-lifting thieves.

The beginning of the end for professional pickpocketing came when people started carrying credit cards instead of cash. About the only people still practicing this ancient trade are a handful of professional magicians whose motives are entertainment rather than theft. These entertainers have the skill, but without the threat of detection, arrest, and jail, they don't possess nerves of steel.

Inside Jobs: Four Cases

While it's impossible for a normal person to understand why, for example, a 14-year-old boy sets a building on fire for a sexual thrill, we all know why people steal. We understand because either as children, adolescents, or adults, we have taken something that didn't belong to us. The motive for theft is simple and direct, to get something for nothing. Theft is immoral, and of course, illegal. As a matter of morality, and certainly in law, the more one steals, the more serious the crime.

In criminal law, there are several forms of theft, or illegal taking. Customers who steal merchandise from stores are retail thieves. People who slip out of restaurants without paying their bills commit theft of service. Employees who steal from their employers are larcenists security professionals call internal thieves. Criminals that threaten to expose victims' secrets if not paid money to remain silent are blackmailers. A thug threatening future physical harm if the victim doesn't pay up is called an extortionist. (If you don't pay me $1,000 a month I'll burn down your business, is not how fire insurance is supposed to work.) Robbers are thieves who take money and valuables through the use of force or threat of immediate physical force; and burglars steal (and commit other crimes) by unlawful intrusion into homes and buildings. Swindlers and con artists acquire their loot through deception and fraud. And don't forget the passers of bad checks, forged money orders, and stolen and fake credit cards. While there is only one way to be honest, there are many ways to steal.

Except for major armored truck ambush jobs, big time jewelry heists, and massive credit card cases, the thieves who hit their victims the hardest financially, are the embezzlers. (The average bank robbery haul, for example, is just a few thousand dollars.) An embezzler is a person who's in what is called a fiduciary relationship with the victim, a position of trust. The embezzler--accountants, company and organization treasurers, financial managers, and various financial institution employees--steal from private and government employers and clients who have entrusted them with their money. While an embezzler can make a big, one-time haul, most steal smaller amounts over extended periods of time. To accomplish these illegal diversions of funds, embezzlers often alter financial documents, and commit the separate crimes of forgery and false swearing. Quite often, embezzlers, to get away with their thefts, have accomplices within the victim companies and organizations. Detectives and federal agents who investigate these cases (particularly when they involve sophisticated computer crimes) should be specialists in the investigation of financial offenses and criminal conspiracies.

Ligonier Township, Pennsylvania

A recent audit of the personal finances of 95-year-old Dr. Robert Monsour led to criminal charges against 58-year-old Maureen A. Becker who was hired in 2000 to take around-the-clock care of the doctor, and to look after his money. She has been charged with diverting to her own use, between January 2008 and March 2010, $340,000 of the old man's money. Becker stood accused of depositing, into her own bank account, $167,000 from the sale of 67 acres of the doctor's estate. When asked why she had diverted these funds to her own bank account, Becker claimed the money had been a gift from her employer. (This, apparently, was news to Dr. Monsour.) Becker also told investigators that the doctor had raised her salary from $300 a week to $800. Detectives also found that the suspect deposited a number of her employer's CDs into her account, money she claimed the doctor wanted her to have.

The judge, following Becker's guilty plea, sentenced her in June 2012 to three years in prison.

New York City

Anita Collins, in 1986 and 1999, pleaded guilty to fraud in connection with the theft of funds from a pair of her New York City employers. In return for her pleas, she avoided prison. In 2010, Collins, at age 65, worked in the finance office of the Roman Catholic Archdiocese of New York. She had been hired without a background investigation. In an article published in the archdiocese newspaper, *Catholic New York*, she received praise for volunteering at St. Patrick's Cathedral when Archbishop Timothy Dolan presided over a mass welcoming 600 people to Catholicism. Described as an "unassuming" person, Collins told the author of the piece that "My faith has always been a steadfast part of my life."

An outside auditor, in November 2011, discovered $350,000 of the church's money missing. Following a criminal investigation by the Manhattan District Attorney's Office, Collins was charged with siphoning $1 million in church donations. Over a period of seven years Collins sent fake invoices to the archdiocese then issued some 450 checks to accounts she controlled. All of the transactions were in sums just under the $2,500 threshold that required a supervisor's approval.

The church fired Anita Collins in December 2011. According to the chief investigator on the case, the suspect spent the $1 million on mortgage payments and on "a lifestyle that was not extravagant but was far from her lawful means."

Collins pleaded guilty to grand larceny in the first degree in September 2012. In October 2012, the Manhattan judge sentenced her to 4 to 9 years in prison. The judge also ordered her to pay back the church.

Belgrade, Montana

In November 2010, police were called in when members of the Belgrade Little League Baseball Association couldn't figure out why outstanding bills for uniforms and supplies had not been paid. During a period of four years, league board members had signed blank checks, and given them to the treasurer, Amy Jo Erickson, to pay the bills.

In January 2011, after the police discovered that $92,000 from the organization had vanished, they confronted Erickson. The little league treasurer admitted that she had made the blank checks out to herself in "cash," and to her husband's plumbing company. She started embezzling in 2007 because, according to court records, she "needed help financially."

Anita Collins took money from the church and Amy Jo Erickson stole from the parents and sponsors of little league baseball players. These thieves weren't starving, they didn't use the money for life saving surgery, and they didn't play Robin Hood by giving it to the poor. They simply redistributed a little wealth to themselves.

In October 2012, after Erickson pleaded guilty, the judge sentenced her to 180 days in the Gallatin County Jail. The judge ordered her to pay full restitution.

Lakewood, Washington

On November 29, 2009, a police assassin named Maurice Clemmons walked into a coffee shop in Parkland, Washington and shot four Lakewood police officers to death. Two days later, a police officer in Seattle killed Clemmons in a gun battle. Following the mass murder, the police department formed a charity to help the families of the slain officers called the Lakewood Police Independent Guild (LPIG). Officer Timothy Manos became the treasurer of the fund.

Although the 34-year-old treasurer received a police salary of $93,347 a year, Manos had serious financial problems. In June 2006, Ford Motor

Credit Company sued him for $12,000 he owned in car payments. He had been sued for unpaid medical expenses, and owed a lot of money to credit card companies. He and his wife also enjoyed what some would consider an extravagant lifestyle.

In 2010 and 2011, citizens in the Lakewood community donated $3.2 million to the fund from which Manos allegedly skimmed $150,000. During the period the FBI believed he was embezzling the money, this debt-ridden cop took his wife to Las Vegas to enjoy the Cirque du Soleil, and several nights of gambling. Also during this period, Manos spent $1,700 on snowboarding and other outdoor gear. He bought a high-definition video camera; a computer; a stainless-steel refrigerator; and a high-definition television set. Between February 12, 2010 and February 20, 2011 Manos withdrew $50,000 from ATMs.

In March 2011, FBI agents arrested Manos on 10 counts of wire fraud. LPIG officials placed Officer Manos on paid administrative leave pending the completion of the federal investigation.

A federal judge in Tacoma, following Manos' guilty plea, sentenced him to 33 months in prison and ordered him to pay $159,000 in restitution.

Stealing from the Catholic Church and the little league is bad enough, but the ripping-off of a charity for the families of slain police officers by a fellow officer is perhaps as bad as it gets.

Car Theft

Car theft accounts for one of the most significant and least-discussed crimes in America. While narcotics and hit men and gang shoot-outs monopolize the headlines of the nation's press, the car thief is quietly stealing your beautiful new car. Then he sells that car to a higher-up in the crime world, who in turn puts it into a professionally organized car face-lifter. When it comes out, it is a car of different color, perhaps with different accessories, and almost certainly with altered serial numbers.

Thomas Plate, *Crime Pays!* 1975

A Theft Victim's Ordeal

Fredrick Brennan, a 19-year-old with a disability commonly known as brittle bone disease, while confined to a motorized wheelchair that operates by a joystick, lives on his own in an apartment in Brooklyn, New York. He makes his living working at home creating code for new websites.

Late in 2013, an acquaintance withdrew money from Brennan's account by using, without authorization, his debit card.

Brennan, before traveling to Atlantic City, New Jersey to visit his mother on December 1, 2013, pulled $4,850 out of his account before the possibility of a second unauthorized withdrawal. When he boarded the bus for Atlantic City, the cash was in his wallet packed inside his luggage.

On January 1, 2014, at the conclusion of his New Jersey visit, Brennan headed home to Brooklyn. Upon arrival at the Port Authority transportation complex in mid-town Manhattan, Mr. Brennan wheeled himself toward a MetroCard machine. It was there he encountered a homeless man who offered to help him find his way through the massive Port Authority building. The man asked Brennan for a dollar. When Brennan removed a dollar bill from his wallet, the man said, "Come on, I can't even buy a hotdog with this." Brennan handed the panhandler another buck. The man took the money and walked off.

With his cash-filled wallet sitting on his lap, Brennan started the process of buying a MetroCard. The homeless guy, having returned to the scene, grabbed Brennan's wallet and fled. "He took my wallet," the victim screamed.

A bystander overheard Brennan and ran after the thief who bolted up the stairs that led to Eighth Avenue. A short time later the witness, accompanied by a police officer, returned to the victim. The thief had escaped into the hubbub of Eighth Avenue. The police officer, however, had retrieved Brennan's wallet. The cash was gone.

Although Brennan's description of the thief was vague, the crime had been caught on a Port Authority surveillance camera. The next day, January 2, a New York City detective called Mr. Brennan with the news that officers had made an arrest in the case. Could the victim come back to Manhattan and pick the suspect out of a line-up at the police station?

On January 2 Brennan traveled by bus and subway to the police station in Greenwich Village. The fact the city was expecting a massive snow storm that day caused Brennan to worry about how he would get back to his home in Brooklyn.

At the police station, Brennan had no trouble identifying the man who had stolen his wallet. The man he picked out of the line-up was Chris Sanchez. The 49-year-old suspect had been arrested near the Port Authority earlier that morning with $4,073 in his pocket. Police also found, on his person, small quantities of crack and marijuana.

A Manhattan assistant prosecutor charged Chris Sanchez with grand larceny. Until the matter was resolved in the slow-moving criminal justice system, the authorities would have to hold onto the victim's stolen cash.

Following the line-up identification, Brennan was asked to spend some time at the station filling out police forms and writing up a statement of the crime. By the time he left the police building it was late in the evening and snowing heavily. Worried that his wheelchair--he had been saving up for a new one--would short out in the snow, the cooperating crime victim asked a police officer if he could arrange for a ride back to Brooklyn. The officer said the station didn't have access to a van with a wheelchair lift. The theft victim would have to find his own way home.

A detective pushed Brennan through the snow to the Union Square subway station, then left. It was eleven o'clock at night and snowing hard.

Frederick Brennan boarded a subway train en route to the Atlantic Avenue Station where he got on another train that took him to 86th Street and Bay Parkway in the Bensonhurst section of Brooklyn. There he waited for the bus that would take him on the final leg of his trip home. Problem was, the bus didn't come and the snow kept falling.

After waiting at the bus stop for more than an hour, Brennan's hands and feet were starting to numb. Since his wheelchair couldn't plow through the snow, he used his cellphone to call 911 for help. A short time later an ambulance pulled up and carried him to a nearby medical center. The next day the hospital discharged him.

A few days after Mr. Brennan's ordeal, he returned to Manhattan to testify before the grand jury considering the case. Based on the surveillance video and the victim's testimony, Mr. Sanchez was indicted on the charge of grand larceny. If the matter involves a trial, that will require his testimony as well. In the meantime, the theft victim will have to live without his money until the case is resolved.

The Bone Smuggler

A dinosaur smuggler turned informant will spend only a few months in prison, about two years after Mongolian authorities realized Tyrannosaurus fossils had been pilfered from the Gobi Desert. Eric Prokopi, 29, pleaded guilty last year [2013] to three counts related to the smuggling of dinosaur fossils into the U.S. His biggest find was a 2-ton *Tyrannosaurus Bataar*, about 8 feet tall, 24 feet long, and 70 million years old. Prokopi enlisted a New York auction house to put the dinosaur up for bid, but the quirky offering caught the eye of paleontologists, including an advisor to the Mongolian president.

The fossils had a grayish-sand hue, which indicated they could have only come from Mongolia. Officials there worked with U.S. authorities to halt the million-dollar sale and prosecute Prokopi. Mongolian authorities even uncovered photographs of Prokopi working at an excavation site in the Gobi Desert.

But prosecutors eventually requested leniency for him because Prokopi shared details about the fossil smuggling world that helped them recover several other items...Every fossil-smuggling investigation since Prokopi's arrest has been made possible in part by information he provided....

Prokopi had faced up to 17 years in prison, but a federal judge on June 3, 2014 sentenced him to three months in prison and about a year of probation. Still, Prokopi had sought to avoid prison altogether because his reputation as a professional fossils dealer already has been tarnished, according to his attorney. He must turn himself in by September 2014. Prosecutors said Mongolia plans to open a natural history museum, beginning with the fossils recovered from the Prokopi case.

Paresh Dave, Nation Now, June 4, 2014

The Bread Truck Heist

The act of taking something that isn't yours, while against the law and anti-social, is hardly considered outlandish behavior. Nor is it commonly driven by mental illness. (For years psychologists and criminologists have debated among themselves over whether so-called kleptomaniacs were sick or simply criminal. I'm in the simply criminal camp.) Theft is a specific intent crime committed in cold-blood, as it were. Schizophrenics don't go around swindling people, or stealing cars for chop shops. Moreover, people accused of theft rarely plead insanity. But in the case of a 30-year-old New York City man named David Bastar, the insanity plea may arise.

On Monday, May 19, 2014, at three in the morning on Second Avenue near East 99th Street on Manhattan's Upper East Side, the driver of a Grimaldi's Home of Bread truck left the vehicle running in front of a pizzeria. When the deliveryman exited the pizza joint, his truck was gone.

David Bastar, dressed only in a pair of briefs, had jumped into the $60,000 truck and driven off with $8,000 worth of baguettes, whole-wheat rolls, loaves of sourdough, and other baked products. Instead of meeting up with a baked goods fence, Bastar, working off a set of instructions and a map left on the truck's front seat, delivered product to at least three restaurants.

Later that morning, while driving the bread truck south on Lexington Avenue, Bastar began throwing loaves of bread out the window. As he crossed the 59th Street Bridge into Queens, Bastar became fixated on a Cadillac Escalade limousine driven by 43-year-old Armondo Sigcha. Sigcha was headed to La Guardia Airport to pick up customers.

Once the stolen bread truck and the limo crossed the bridge, Sigcha realized that some nut in a delivery truck was following him too closely.

The limo driver made several quick, evasive turns but couldn't get the truck off his tail. At this point, Sigcha asked his dispatcher to arrange to have an officer with the Port Authority meet him at the airport.

When Bastar pulled the bread truck to a stop behind the limousine near La Guardia's Central Terminal, a Port Authority officer greeted him. The cop took one look at the underwear-clad bread truck driver and called for an ambulance to deliver him to a mental ward.

After being evaluated at Elmhurst Hospital's Psychiatric Ward, officers escorted Mr. Bastar to the Queens Criminal Court where he was charged with criminal possession of a stolen vehicle, and driving without a license. The judge released the suspect to the custody of his baffled parents.

Diana Bastar's, the accused truck thief's mother, told a reporter with *The New York Post* that she had no idea why her son had been bent on delivering bread. "I'm speechless," she said. "He's been estranged from us, so I really can't tell you want's going on."

Following his arrest, Bastar told police officers that he had tailed the limousine into Queens because, "I thought I had to follow him to make the deliveries."

Stealing a Taxi Ride

A Massachusetts woman was arrested after allegedly racking up a taxi fare so high she couldn't afford to pay it. Thirty-one-year old Denise Rebelato was arrested on February 5, 2014 after hailing a cab at New York's JFK Airport and getting a ride all the way to the Boston area...The cabby told Rebelato it would cost nearly $1,000 to get to Framingham from New York and she agreed to pay it when they left the airport. But after the roughly 200-mile journey...Rebelato couldn't get the money to pay for the trip-- meaning the driver still hadn't gotten paid. He says he spent $75 on gas and $40 in tolls in addition to the $150 he spent to rent the cab for a shift...Rebelato was charged with larceny....

Collin Ruane, *The Atlanta Journal Constitution*, February 8, 2014

The Santa Monica Art Heist

A burglar broke into investment fund manager Jeffrey Gundlach's Santa Monica mansion sometime between 3 PM September 12 and 8 PM September 14, 2012. The intruder made off with $10 million worth of art as well as bottles of rare wine and several expensive watches. The burglar returned to the scene a few hours after the initial break-in to steal Mr. Gundlach's red 2010 Porsche Carrera 4S.

Investigators did not reveal how the burglar gained entry, or how he circumvented the home intrusion alarm system. Moreover, there was no information released regarding how the thief knew the art was in Gundlach's dwelling. The house burglar also knew to strike when Gundlach was on a business trip.

Following the heist, Jeffrey Gundlach offered a $1 million reward for one of the paintings as well as a separate $500,000 for information leading to the recovery of another piece of art.

On September 26, 2012, detectives in Pasadena called the Santa Monica burglary squad regarding a tip they had received about the location of some of the stolen paintings. According to the tipster, most of the stolen art was being held at Al and Ed's Autosound Store in Pasadena. Detectives executed a search warrant at the store that led to the recovery of several of Mr. Gundlach's paintings.

Following the Pasadena search, officers arrested the store's 45-year-old manager, Jay Nieto. A Los Angeles County prosecutor charged Nieto with receiving stolen property and possession of stolen items.

Shortly after Nieto's arrest, detectives recovered four of the stolen paintings from a house in San Gabriel owned by 40-year-old Wilmer Cadiz. Cadiz was charged with the possession and receipt of stolen property.

Nieto and Cadiz's cooperation with investigators led to the arrest, on January 4, 2013, of a known burglar named Darren Agee Merager. Charged with first-degree residential burglary and receiving stolen property, the 43-year-old Merager faced up to nine years in prison.

The Los Angeles prosecutor also charged Merager's 68-year-old mother, Brenda Merager, and his two brothers, Wanis and Ely Wahba, with receiving stolen property. According to detectives, Merager's mother and his brothers had tried to sell some of the loot. Eventually the prosecutor dropped the charges against the mother.

On January 22, 2014, Jay Nieto and Wilmer Codiz each pleaded no contest to one count of receiving stolen property. In return for their guilty pleas, the judge sentenced the men to three years probation. The Wahba brothers also pleaded no contest to receiving stolen property. A judge will sentence them in March 2014. But according to the terms of their plea deals, they will be given probated sentences as well.

The burglar and car thief, Darren Agee Merager, pleaded guilty on January 22, 2014 to first-degree residential burglary and receiving stolen property. The judge sentenced him to four years in prison.

All of the wealthy financier's paintings, as well as his Porsche, were recovered in good condition. (I don't know about the watches and the wine.) Breaking into houses is usually not that difficult. But high-end burglaries like this case often unravel when thieves try to convert the stolen merchandise into cash. Also, when there are several thieves involved in the caper, chances are someone will talk too much, and when brought in for questioning, snitch on the others.

The Cookie Heist

A 15-year-old boy has been arrested by Fort Lauderdale police on charges of stealing a Girl Scout's cellphone while she was selling cookies outside a grocery store. Police said Thursday, February 13, 2014 they identified the ninth-grader from previous police encounters by viewing the Winn-Dixie store's video surveillance. The Samsung Galaxy S3 phone was stolen from the girl during a cookie sale Sunday night, February 9. Police said one person distracted the group while his accomplice took the phone that was lying on a table....

In 2008, thieves in Palm Beach County stole $168 from a Girl Scout selling cookies outside a supermarket...

CBS News, February 13, 2014

Stealing Mental Patients' Brains

While most collectors acquire everyday objects such as coins, stamps, and books, a few collectors specialize in things that are odd and to most people disgusting. There is even a reality television series devoted to the acquisition of bizarre objects. The show is called "Oddities" and is presented on the Discovery Channel. Viewers follow the operation of a retail shop in Manhattan, New York called Obscura Antiques and Oddities. Items bought and sold on the show have included a mummified cat, various animal teeth, a dead four-legged chicken, and a shrunken head.

The "Oddities" television series has helped establish a market for unusual items and "conversation pieces" most of us would consider too disgusting to possess. It has also created an opportunity for thieves who specialize in these collectibles.

In early October 2013, a thief in Indianapolis, Indiana walked off with sixty jars of brain and other tissue from dead mental patients. The specimens were kept, among thousands of other such containers, in warehouse space on the campus of the Indiana Medical History Museum. The brains and other specimens had come from clinical autopsies performed at the Central Indiana Hospital for the Insane, an institution that opened its doors in 1848 and closed in 1994. According to the director of the museum, the stolen jars were valued at $4,800. (Is there a bluebook for the pickled brains of dead mental patients?)

In early December 2013, the director of the Indiana Medical History Museum received a call from a collector in California who said he had purchased, through an eBay auction site, six jars of brain matter. He had paid $600 for the specimens. According to the oddities buyer, he became suspicious when the jars he acquired appeared similar to the ones pictured on the museum's website.

The tip from the California collector led to the identification of David Charles as the seller of the stolen brains.

On December 16, 2013, an undercover Indianapolis police officer posing as an oddities collector interested in jarred brains met Mr. Charles in the parking lot of a Dairy Queen. When the 21-year-old suspected thief offered to sell the officer the stolen property, the cop took him into custody.

A Marion County prosecutor charged David Charles with felony theft. He was accused of possessing marijuana and drug paraphernalia. (If the suspect broke into the museum to steal the specimens he could also be charged with burglary.)

The Toll Thief

Rodolfo Sanchez, 69, is accused of stealing from the Metropolitan Transit Authority (MTA) by crossing the Robert F. Kennedy Bridge and entering the Midtown Tunnel without making a toll payment on more than four thousand occasions by "piggybacking" on cars directly in front of his cab....

In order to pass the toll plaza before the gates closed, Sanchez tailgated other paying drivers while they entered the bridge...From August 2012 to April 2014 Sanchez snuck onto the bridge and ducked a total of more than $28,000 in toll payments...Sanchez said he did this to save money for his family....

Sanchez was caught with the help of an expired E-ZPass transmitter in his cab. Investigators matched the tracking data from the transmitter to video footage of taxicabs ducking tolls and to cab company records of when Sanchez was on duty. He was charged with grand larceny, theft of services and criminal possession of stolen property. If convicted, he faced up to seven years in prison....

Rida Ahmed, *The New York Times,* April 19, 2014

Stealing Human Skin

Gary Dudek, a resident of Wallingford, a suburban community outside of Philadelphia, from September 2006 to September 2013, worked for a Massachusetts based company called Organogenesis. As a sales representative and "tissue-regeneration specialist," Mr. Dudek had allegedly been given a so-called "open purchase order" that authorized him to acquire human skin grafts from Mercy Philadelphia Hospital.

During the period November 2011 to July 2013, Gary Dudek ordered 219 human skin grafts from Mercy Philadelphia Hospital. According to hospital administrators, each graft is worth $1,700, money the medical facility has not been paid.

On Monday, May 26, 2014, detectives with the Philadelphia Police Department took the 54-year-old suspected skin thief into custody. According to reports, Mr. Dudek had been caught twice on a surveillance camera taking skin grafts from Mercy Philadelphia Hospital to his car. Officers booked him into the city jail on charges of theft, receiving stolen property, and tampering with records. He quickly posted his $10,000 bond, and was released.

Following the accusations in this unusual theft case, a spokesperson for the suspect's former employer, Organogenesis, told reporters that the firm is not in the business of buying or selling human skin grafts. (Skin grafts or patches are used mainly as replacements for serious infections, burns, or wounds.) According to this corporate spokesperson, the company has developed a product called Apligraf, an organic material made of collagen and skin cells that is designed to mimic human skin.

Mr. Dudek's attorney, Eugene Tinari, in speaking to a television reporter with a local NBC affiliate, said, "If Mercy Hospital has suffered losses they deem to be a result of Mr. Dudek's actions, then perhaps a civil suit could have been initiated. But to take this case into the criminal arena against a man who has been nothing but hard working and law abiding his entire life is a bit draconian, in my view."

A preliminary hearing in the Dudek case was scheduled for June 10, 2014. Law enforcement authorities had not revealed what the suspect did with the 219 skin grafts.

The Tiffany Jewelry Theft

On July 1, 2013, at 8:45 PM, three men walked into the jewelry store inside the Borgata Hotel in Atlantic City, smashed a glass jewelry display case, scooped up $200,000 in Rolex watches then ran out of the hotel. As of this writing the thieves have not been identified.

While the Atlantic City smash-and-grab theft is considered a fairly big haul, it is nothing compared to what a jewelry thief working from the inside can steal.

On Tuesday, July 2, the day after the Borgata Hotel smash-and-grab, FBI agents arrested Ingrid Lederhaas-Okun at her fancy home in Darien, Connecticut. A federal prosecutor charged the 46-year-old vice president in charge of product development at the Tiffany flagship location on Manhattan's Fifth Avenue with stealing $1.3 million worth of jewelry from the famed store.

FBI agents working the case believed that between November 2012 and February 2013, the executive checked out more than 165 pieces of jewelry that were not returned to the store. The missing merchandise included diamond bracelets, platinum and gold diamond drop and loop earrings, platinum and diamond rings, and platinum and diamond pendants. Lederhaas-Okun stood accused of selling the checked-out pieces of jewelry to another company. Federal investigators believed the suspect used her husband and a friend as sales intermediaries.

In February 2013, after Tiffany & Company auditors couldn't find the 165-plus pieces of merchandise in the store's inventory, the firm fired Lederhaas-Okun. She held the position of vice president since January of 2011. Lederhaas-Okun began working for the company in 1991 following her graduation from Georgetown University.

Lederhaas-Okun's husband had not been charged in connection with the case.

On December 23, 2013, U.S. District Court Judge Paul G. Gardenphe, following Lederhaas-Okun's guilty plea, sentenced the former executive to one year and one day in prison. Her lawyer had asked for a sentence of six months while the prosecutor sought at least three years behind bars.

In terms of stolen merchandise and cash, retail employees steal three times more than shoplifters and robbers combined. Quite often the most trusted and longtime employees were the thieves who did the most damage. Most of them are eventually caught. A few of these so-called internal thieves avoid prosecution by agreeing to pay restitution. Occasionally, a retailer will decline to prosecute a dishonest employee because such an action would create unwanted publicity. Most of the time, however, inside retail thieves who have stolen large amounts of cash or merchandise end up in prison.

It's hard to understand why a trusted, high-paid executive would risk everything by stealing from his or her employer. Some prominent, high-end thieves steal because they are living beyond their means, have large medical expenses, are compulsive gamblers, or addicted to drugs. Some employees simply enjoy the thrill of enriching themselves at the expense of their employers. Forget the Robin Hood Syndrome, rich people often steal from other rich people.

Stealing Gasoline

Two Texas men allegedly manipulated gas pumps at local 7-Eleven stores in the Austin area to allow gas to flow freely, charging drivers a discounted rate for the fuel....Guilibaldo Gonzales Puente, 48, and Alejandro Conteno Alvarez, 33, would create a rally point, and, at times, spend between one to three hours at the pumps filling up cars....

"A lot of the vehicles were large trucks with big bladders in the back, which could hold between 200 and 400 gallons," Detective Rickey Jones, said. Puente and Alvarez were arrested at a gas pump Monday, April 14, 2014.

Fox News, April 16, 2014

The Painkiller Thief

David Kwiatkowski traveled around the country working as a hospital temp in cardiac catheterization labs as a radiology technician. From January 2007 to September of that year, the 29-year-old worked at the Oakwood Annapolis Hospital in Wayne, Michigan, his home state. From November 2007 to March 2010, Kwiatowski was employed in six hospitals in Poughkeepsie, New York, Pittsburgh, Pennsylvania, Baltimore, Maryland, and Clinton, Maryland.

On April 1, 2010, the roving lab technician landed a job in Phoenix at Arizona Heart Hospital. Eleven days later, a fellow employee found him out cold in the men's locker room. After testing positive for cocaine and marijuana, the hospital fired him. Less than a week later, Kwiatkowski was in Philadelphia working at Temple University Hospital. That job lasted less than a month. That May the roving temp was employed at a hospital in Hays, Kansas. A month after taking the job in Kansas Kwiatkowski's drug usage caught up with him. He was diagnosed with hepatitis C. After a month or so at the Hays Hospital, the infected temp was in Warner Robins, Georgia at the Houston Medical Center. (There must be a shortage of radiology technicians. And wasn't anyone keeping track of this guy?)

Two years after Kwiatkowski was fired from the Arizona Heart Hospital in Phoenix, he began work in the cardiac catheterization unit at the Exeter Hospital in Exeter, New Hampshire. On May 12, 2012, six weeks after the temp started work at Exeter, the hospital experienced an hepatitis C breakout involving 32 patients and former patients.

Because the infected patients had all received cardiac catheterization procedures at Exeter, David Kwiatkowski came under suspicion. Investigators began looking into his bizarre work history, and learned he had been diagnosed with hepatitis C in June 2010. Fellow hospital employees, based on the temp's erratic behavior, and the fresh needle tracks on his arms, suspected he was a drug addict. (Why didn't any of these people speak up? What kind of zombies do we have working in our hospitals?) Kwiatkowski's roommate told investigators that he had found needles in their apartment. When confronted by his roommate, Kwiatkowski said he had cancer. The hospital fired the radiology temp on May 24, 2012.

Following a month-long investigation, FBI agents determined that Kwiatkowski had injected himself with syringes meant for patients. These syringes were filled with Fentanyl, a painkiller more potent than morphine. Patients were then infected with syringes Kwiatkowski had refilled with a saline solution. Patients had not only been denied relief from pain, the temp had given them hepatitis C. (Kwiatkowski managed to get his hands on the syringes even though this drug-addicted temp wasn't authorized to handle medication. Who was watching the store?)

On July 13, police in Marlborough, Massachusetts responded to a call from a Holiday Inn regarding a guest who may have overdosed on drugs. Officers found David Kwiatkowski in a stupor amid pills scattered about the hotel room. He had also written a suicide note. Medics transported him to a nearby hospital.

A federal grand jury sitting in New Hampshire, on July 19, 2012 indicted Kwiatkowski for acquiring controlled substances by fraud, and for tampering with a consumer product (the hospital syringes). If convicted of these offenses, he could face up to 24 years in prison. On the day of his indictment, FBI agents arrested Kwiatkowski at the Marlborough hospital where he was recovering from his drug and alcohol overdose.

When interrogated by the FBI, Kwiatkowski denied stealing the syringes and switching out their contents. He said he didn't use drugs. When asked how the 32 patients at the Exeter Hospital had contracted hepatitis C, the suspect said, "You know, I'm more concerned about myself, my own well-being. I've learned here to just worry about myself. And that's all I care about now." Spoken like a true sociopath.

David Kwiatkowski is being held in the Strafford County Jail in New Hampshire. In that state alone, he came into contact with more than 3,000 patients, people who have yet to be tested for hepatitis C.

In August 2013, Kwiatkowski, pursuant to a plea agreement, admitted that he had been stealing drugs for more than a decade and was "killing a lot of people." He pleaded guilty to fourteen federal drug theft and tampering charges.

On December 3, 2013, the judge sentenced this thief to thirty-nine years in prison.

The Cost of Shoplifting

Shoplifting incurs remarkable real-life costs for retailers and consumers. The "crime tax"--the amount every American family loses to shoplifting-related price inflation--is more than $400 a year. [This does not include the cost of retail security to combat it.] Shoplifting cost American retailers $11.7 billion in 2009. The theft of one $5 item from Whole Foods can require sales of hundreds of dollars to break even.

Rachel Shteir, *The Steal*, 2009

Flash Mobs

In the summers of 2011 and 2012, gangs of teenage black kids invaded, for the purpose of retail theft, stores in downtown Los Angeles, New York, Chicago, Philadelphia, Washington, D.C., and Norfolk, Virginia. (These are not the only cities where this has happened.) Groups of 20 or more males and females overwhelmed store security in order to steal expensive merchandise--usually clothing--for resale. These mobs were assembled, mobilized, and coordinated through social media networking.

These gangs of retail thieves commit a brand of unlawful taking that falls between team shoplifting and robbery (taking by force). It's essentially looting, and reflects a group entitlement mentality as well as total disrespect for the rule of law. This form of urban anarchy is a serious social problem. If it's not brought under control, this civil disorder will drive retailers and other businesses out of downtown America.

In Chicago, Luke Cho, the owner of a Wicker Park clothing store, became alarmed at 6:40 PM on Saturday, August 14, 2012. Twenty or more black teenagers entered his place of business as a coordinated group. Mr. Cho knew what this meant he was about to be looted by a flash mob.

The gang moved purposefully toward the section of the story that housed the display of Nudie brand jeans. At $200 a pair, these jeans have been in demand since some rap singer was seen wearing them on TV. Mr. Cho, to keep a second wave of looters out of his store, locked the front door, and asked an employee to call 911.

As the thieves scooped up armloads of jeans in front of alarmed store employees and customers, members of the second wave of looters, who were locked out of the store, banged angrily on the glass. Once the inside thieves had gathered up all the jeans they could carry, they moved toward the front of the establishment, stopping along the way to put other stolen items into their backpacks. After fumbling with the door, one of the looters figured how to unlock it. The door opened, the pack rushed onto the street, and dispersed with more than $3,000 worth of Mr. Cho's merchandise. By the time the first police officer arrived at the scene, it was all over.

Mr. Cho, when he reviewed the store's surveillance tape, recognized several of the looters as previous shoplifters. He posted the video online, and asked the public to help identify as many thieves as possible. (Victims of flash mobs, aware that the police are indifferent to crimes like this, essentially have to conduct their own investigations.)

Scott Paulson, a CBS news commentator, wrote an article about these retail marauders. Paulson criticized the media, police administrators, and politicians for not calling these mob heists what they really are--race riots. According to Mr. Paulson, "The Media, the politicians, and the bulk of the commentators on social issues need to quit being afraid of people like Rev. Al Sharpton." Pointing out that these mobs are comprised of black kids, and that their victims are white, Paulson wrote: "If a story is about race, it must be reported as a racial story for the good of the people who could easily be subjected to the next flash mob attack...Protecting a community's image or a segment of society's image should not override the public's need to know and be protected."

While Scott Paulson makes a valid point, I'm sure he realizes that because of political correctness, and the abject cowardice of politicians and people in the media, no one will treat these raids as race riots. And the police will shy away from these cases as well. Politicians, cops, and media hacks *are* afraid of race hustlers like Al Sharpton, and will never characterize these alarming acts of anarchy as race riots.

While we all pay the price for this form of cowardice and political correctness bordering on corruption, the true victims are retailers who try to make a living in urban America.

The History of Kleptomania

The birth of criminal anthropology codified scientists' ideas that kleptomaniacs, mostly women, were born to steal. In *The Female Offender* (1893) Cesare Lombroso wrote: "Shoplifting, which has become so fashionable since the establishment of huge department stores, is a form of occasional crime in which women specialize. The temptation stems from the immense number of articles on display. We saw that fine things are not articles of luxury for women but articles of necessity since they equip them for conquest." This, according to Lombroso, resulted in "women's organic inability to resist stealing."

The idea that kleptomania arises out of female sexual repression was made popular around 1906 by Freud's disciples, who attached the Oedipal myth to the disease, attributing it to infantile revenge fantasies and the castration complex. The affliction was also equated with sex. Best known as a charismatic anarchist, free-love advocate, and cocaine addict who influenced expressionism and Franz Kafka [a novelist], Otto Gross was the first psychoanalyst to champion kleptomania as sexual release.

Rachel Shteir, *The Steal*, 2011

The Mountain Man Burglar

In 1986, when he was 28, Troy James Knapp went to prison in Kalamazoo, Michigan for burglary and related offenses. Knapp pleaded guilty to destroying property in 1994 while living in Salt Lake City. Two years later police in Seattle arrested him on the charge of stalking and harassment. In 2002, after serving two years in a California prison for burglary, Knapp left the state in violation of his parole.

In 2007, the wilderness survivalist (he survived on other people's stuff) lived in the mountains of southern Utah. In the summers he stole food and gear from cabins in Iron, Kane, and Garfield Counties, and moved from one campsite to the next. During the winter months Knapp lived in the cabins he burglarized in the summer. The owners would return to their seasonal dwellings to find bullet holes in the walls and doors. Knapp also left notes with messages like: "Pack up and leave. Get off my mountain." (If everyone had packed up and left, Knapp would have starved.)

Between 2007 and 2013, prosecutors in Iron, Kane, and Garfield Counties charged Knapp with 13 felony burglary crimes and 5 misdemeanor offenses. Because of the remoteness of Knapp's break-ins and the fact he kept on the move, he had eluded capture for more than five years.

In late February 2013, a man hunting with his son in Sanpete County crossed paths with Knapp about 125 miles southeast of Salt Lake City. Aware they had conversed with the mountain man burglar, the father notified the authorities.

A few days after speaking with the hunters 9,000 feet up on a mountain near Ferron Reservoir in the central part of the state, forty police officers and a law enforcement helicopter closed in on the fugitive as he trudged through three feet of snow. After firing fifteen rifle shots at the helicopter, Knapp surrendered to the small army of approaching lawmen.

When taken into custody, Knapp possessed an assault rifle and a handgun. He was booked into the Sanpete County Jail without bond. An Assistant United States Attorney in Utah charged Knapp with several federal firearms offenses.

In April 2014, pursuant to an arranged plea bargain, Knapp pleaded guilty in U.S. District Court to the use of a firearm during a crime of violence. At his sentence hearing on June 9, 2014, federal court judge Ted Stewart handed down the mandatory minimum sentence of ten years in federal prison.

Knapp's attorney, in addressing the court, said, "There's an admiration for somebody who chooses to live off the land, because he does it while the rest of us wouldn't. Even if he needs a little help from some cabin owners."

Sanpete County prosecutor Brody Keisel had a different take on the case. He told reporters after the federal sentencing that Knapp was nothing more than a "common crook." Knapp had also agreed to plead guilty to the burglary charges filed against him in the seven Utah counties. According to that plea deal, he will be sentenced to fifteen years on each of the state felony counts, the sentences to run concurrent with each other and the federal sentence. That means that Mr. Knapp will live behind bars for the next fifteen years, first in a federal institution, then in a Utah prison.

Burglars

Burglars are the cowards of the underworld. They sneak around hotels, apartment houses and homes in the suburbs like cockroaches in the night, nibbling quietly at private wealth, and scattering into the dark at the slightest disturbance. They are the bugs of the underworld, ever fearful of being snuffed out by the police officer's service pistol or the homeowner's unregistered shotgun.

But this cowardice pays off. It puts the criminal on the very cautious side of the crime business and reduces the possibility of eyewitnesses to the crime. The one drawback is that the burglar must later deal with a fence, since most burglaries yield merchandise rather than currency. But it is a price that burglars are prepared to pay in return for the practice of what they regard as a trade considerably less risky than armed robbery, where the yield is usually cash. Most burglars do *not* carry a dangerous weapon.

Thomas Plate, *Crime Pays*, 1975

A Bump in the Night

Ross Wilson, a man in his mid-forties with six children who didn't live with him, resided in a rental house in a crime-ridden neighborhood in Fairfield, a suburb of Hamilton on New Zealand's Northern Island. Mr. Wilson, who worked at a sales job in Hamilton, had, within the past year, moved to Fairfield from Porirua, Wellington, New Zealand. He recently told his relatives that he hated living among drug dealers and other criminals but couldn't afford a safer neighborhood.

In March 2013, after someone broke into his house, Mr. Wilson posted the following on his Facebook page: "To the scumbag who burgled my house--I hope I'm there to watch when Karma comes and [screws] you up."

Just after midnight on June 19, 2013, Tom Smith [not his real name], broke into Ross Wilson's house. As the 21-year-old burglar crept through the dark, he bumped into Mr. Wilson's corpse as it hung from the end of a rope. The thief screamed so loud, several of Mr. Wilson's neighbors called 911 to report a domestic disturbance. The terrified burglar ran out of the house. When he arrived at his own place of residence, Smith called the police and reported what he had encountered at the scene of his crime.

The Hamilton County police believed that Mr. Wilson had hanged himself a couple of days before Smith's criminal intrusion. A few of Mr. Wilson's relatives urged the local prosecutor to charge Smith with burglary. Because Smith had been scared witless, the authorities decided not to bring charges against him even though he had been in trouble with the law. The local police hoped this burglar had been scared straight by his deceased burglary victim.

The Art of Safecracking

The first and easiest way to gain entry into a safe is, if the safe is small enough, to remove it from the premises where it can be worked on without worry of detection....

The safe door is the strongest point of a small safe. By turning a small safe upside down, you can often use a sledgehammer and chisel or a pick and axe and, by brute force, smash a hole into the bottom of the safe.

If you drill a small hole in one corner of the safe door, thereby missing all of the extra anti-theft protection, you may be able to peel back the layer of steel [covering the safe insulation material] exposing any locking mechanism. This peeling is accomplished with a pry bar, chisel and hammer. [It's a matter of popping the spot welds.]

To make certain that the safe contains valuable items you may first want to go on a scouting expedition. Drill a small hole into one of the four walls of the safe and insert a small video camera with a light unit to illuminate the contents of the safe...

Mauro J. Corvasce and Joseph R. Paglino, *Modus Operandi,* 1995

The North Pond Hermit Case

In 1986, a year after Christopher T. Knight graduated from Lawrence High School in Fairfield, Maine he took to the woods where he lived as a hermit for 27 years. From his Kennebec County campsite in the central part of the state, the so-called North Pond Hermit managed to survive in the wilderness without hunting, fishing, or foraging for food, clothing, or shelter. He stole what he needed from camps and cottages around the town of Rome. To avoid detection, Knight never started a fire. He stole propane to cook and keep warm on stolen propane stoves.

Christopher Knight lived in a tent covered by tarps suspended between two trees. He slept in a LL Bean sleeping bag on a raised, homemade bed. In addition to his propane heating and cooking stoves, he had a battery-operated radio with an antenna that ran up a tree. Over the years the hermit burglar had stolen shovels, rakes, Nintendo Game Boys, a battery-operated TV set, coolers, coffee pots, and all of his clothing. He didn't even buy his own toilet paper.

On April 4, 2013, Knight stole $283 worth of food from the Pine Tree Camp for Children with Disabilities located near the village of Rome. Knight had broken into this camp fifty times. On this occasion, however, he got caught when he activated a surveillance camera sensor that had been installed by a game warden. State troopers arrested Knight later that day at his campsite.

Charged with one count of burglary and a single count of theft, Knight is in the Kennebec County Jail under $5,000 cash bond. Police officers have dismantled and hauled-off the hermit's campsite. The job required two pickup trucks, and will probably lead to more burglary charges.

While Knight's long suffering burglary victims should be happy he's in custody, the North Pond Hermit will probably become, in the eyes of many, some kind of folk hero. You know, a real-life Robin Hood who steals from the rich and gives to himself.

In this unusual case, I'm having trouble figuring out how a man in the woods got away with 1,000 burglaries over a period of 27 years. One would think that hunters and game wardens had stumbled upon his campsite many times. Others must have seen him walking on roads around Rome. In the world of crime, I can't image any burglar not getting caught well before his 1000th break-in. I'm guessing that Mr. Knight's activities and location were known by a number people who chose not to turn him in to the authorities.

On April 13, 2013, a man who didn't know the hermit burglar showed up at the Kennebec County Jail and offered to pay his $5,000 bond. (Charged with additional burglaries, the authorities have raised Knight's bail to $250,000.) A woman called the jail with a marriage proposal.

On October 28, 2013, Christopher Knight pleaded guilty to 13 counts of burglary and theft. In return for his plea, the authorities admitted the North Pond Hermit into a special court program. A week after his plea the burglar walked out of the Kennebec County Jail. He would spend the seven months under the supervision of corrections official appointed by the court.

The Strong Man Case

Police in Weymouth, Massachusetts are looking for a strong thief who managed to carry a 250-pound safe out of a restaurant…The burglar walked out of the restaurant on Sunday night, December 29, 2013 lugging the vault that was wrapped in a trash bag. Images from a security camera showed the man entering a side door at the rear of the restaurant, heading down the stairs, and then back up the stairs hauling the safe.

KWTX, January 1, 2014

5 PEDOPHILIA

The Pedophile Problem

Anyone who follows the news regularly comes across stories about boys who have been repeatedly sexually molested by relatives, neighbors, mothers' boyfriends, teachers, priests, ministers, Boy Scout Leaders, coaches, and youth counselors. These accounts tend to have the same narrative arc: following years of suspicious behavior and rumors of molestation, someone finally comes forward to report the crimes. After a plea bargained sentence, families of the victims sue the pedophile's school, church or institution, and if the offender is a public employee, the city or the state. Following this, local politicians and others call for measures that will protect future victims. But it never shops. Why?

While we are familiar with the general profile of the adult male who preys on boys under thirteen, we have no idea how many of them are out there working in our schools, juvenile facilities, churches, and day care centers. Dr. Gene Abel, an expert in this field, has estimated that between 1 and 5 percent of our adult population sexually molests children. If this is true, there are hundreds of thousands of them among us victimizing millions of youngsters. Because pedophiles are serial offenders who cannot be cured or rehabilitated, the victimization rates for this type of offense are through the roof. According to studies, before being caught for the first time, the average pedophile assaults 120 boys. Once released from prison, a vast majority of them reoffend. Since only a small percentage of pedophiles end up in prison, who knows how many children are victimized during the sex life of just one of these criminals?

Although conscientious parents teach their children to be wary of strangers, most cases of pedophilia involve predators who are either related to or acquainted with the boy. The most vulnerable targets are "at-risk" youths from dysfunctional families.

Pedophiles flourish in our society because, in matters of criminal justice, we are taught to be careful with our accusations. No one wants to be part of a "witch hunt." Moreover, if you make a false accusation, you can be sued. Besides pedophiles, America is home to a lot of lawyers. According to the FBI, only between 1 to 5 percent of child molestation crimes are reported to the police. I believe it's more like one percent. According to one study of 255 cases involving students sexually molested by their teachers, in only one percent of these cases did the school district superintendent attempt to revoke the offenders' teaching licenses.

Pedophilia is a crime of stealth, single-minded and clever offenders, frightened victims, and, on the part of people who should intercede on the child's behalf, denial. Pedophiles are often charming, hard-working employees who have ingratiated themselves into the community. Notwithstanding the increased awareness of this crisis, it will not go away. Unfortunately, there are certain social problems that cannot be fixed by a criminal justice system.

No Cure for Pedophilia

Everything I read said that pedophiles weren't treatable--they never stopped being pedophiles no matter what was done for them, or to them. There'd been fads where they'd tried everything from brain surgery to chemical castration to "aversion" therapy in which after he's been "cured," the pedophile is supposed to snap a rubber band against his wrist every time he wants to rape a child. [The rubber band under this so-called cure was on the wrong organ.] Occasionally there have even been cases in which physical castration has been considered--as if removing a body part could change what someone is, as if they wouldn't just use Coke bottles or broomsticks instead. None of it has worked. The worst part is the way the experimenters have found out they failed: at the expense of children. [Notwithstanding the universal realization that pedophiles are incurable serial offenders, they are never sentenced to life in prison.]

Alice Vachss, *Sex Crimes*, 1994

Pedophilia in Hollywood: Two Cases

While child sexual molestation takes place behind closed doors, pedophiles groom their potential victims in plain sight. They do this in classrooms, churches, gymnasiums, and day care centers--anywhere vulnerable children are subjected to the influence and control of adults. They also do it in Hollywood where parents eagerly offer up young, aspiring actors and entertainers to pedophiles working as talent managers, agents, acting coaches, and casting directors. For a pedophile in the entertainment industry, it's like shooting fish in a barrel.

Former child star Corey Feldman openly discussed his own Hollywood molestations in an interview with the British tabloid, "The Sun:" "When I was 14 and 15 things were happening to me. These older men were hovering around like vultures...It was basically me laying there pretending I was asleep and them going about their business."

State legislators in California have proposed a bill that will require all entertainment personnel working closely with children to undergo stringent background checks. Unless the politicians can create a law that will put an end to America's obsession with celebrity and fame, and turn stage-struck parents from entertainment pimps into protectors, fame-seeking children will continue to be sexually abused by Hollywood dream merchants.

Jason James Murphy

In Edmonds, Washington, 19-year-old Jason James Murphy, an aspiring actor working as a camp counselor, met and began grooming a 5-year-old boy for sexual encounters. In December 1995, an employee of the Hazelwood Elementary School in Lynnwood, Washington, saw Murphy kissing this boy who was now 7. The teacher notified the police who took Murphy into custody on a child molestation charge. Murphy's family posted his bail, and shortly after his arrest, he was released.

In January 1996, Murphy's fixation on this child was so intense, he disguised himself as a woman and lured the boy from the elementary school. Murphy and the abducted child flew to New York City and checked into a hotel. After a massive police hunt for the missing victim followed by a segment featuring the case on "America's Most Wanted," a New York City hotel clerk recognized Murphy and the boy, and notified the authorities. A short time later, FBI agents rescued the child, and arrested Murphy. Eight months later, a federal jury found Murphy guilty of kidnapping and child molestation. He served 5 of his 7-year sentence behind bars.

Four years after getting out of federal prison, Murphy moved to West Hollywood, California where he registered as a sex offender under his legal name, Jason James Murphy. Under California law, there are strict rules regarding the circumstances under which a registered sex offender can work with children under 16. The law also requires registered sex offenders to notify law enforcement if they change their names or use aliases.

Murphy, under the professional name Jason James, became a successful freelance casting director. He worked on films such as "Bad News Bears," "The School of Rock," and "Cheaper by the Dozen 2." Director and co-producer J. J. Abrams hired him as a freelancer on "Super 8." And more recently, Murphy cast child actors in the upcoming feature, "The Three Stooges."

On November 17, 2011, J. J. Abrams, having been tipped off by his manager David Lonner who had just learned of Jason James' true identity, informed Paramount Pictures, the studio that released "Super 8." Someone at Paramount called the police.

Officers with the Los Angeles Police Department, on December 9, 2011, arrested Murphy on charges he had violated California's sex offender registry regulations. Violations of these laws are felonies that carry sentences of up to three years in prison. Murphy's attorney blamed the arrest, and the attention it drew from the media, on the highly publicized Penn State child molestation story that was breaking at the time. The lawyer also claimed that the people who had hired Murphy as a casting director knew his full, legal name. Murphy was not accused of molesting any of the children he worked with professionally.

Martin Weiss

Less than two weeks after producer J. J. Abrams notified Paramount Pictures of who Jason James really was, Los Angeles detectives with the Topanga Division's Sexual Assault Unit arrested 47-year-old Martin Weiss, a Hollywood manager who specialized in child actors. Weiss stood accused of committing 30 to 40 sexual crimes against an aspiring singer and musician he represented from 2005 to 2008. The sexual encounters allegedly took place at Weiss' apartment/business office in Santa Monica, and at his home in Woodland Hills. After being taken to the Los Angeles County Jail, a judge set his bond at $300,000.

According to the alleged victim, now 18-years-old, the molesting stopped when he turned 15. After that, he and Weiss parted ways. The victim didn't report the abuse then because he didn't think anyone would believe his story. But after the Penn State scandal became big news, the victim decided to report his abuser, and come forward with evidence that backed up his story.

On November 15, 2011, the victim confronted Weiss at his apartment in Santa Monica, and secretly taped their conversation. (In the Penn State case, the victim's mother taped her confrontation with former football coach Jerry Sandusky.) In discussing their past relationship, Weiss did not deny having sexual relations with his accuser. When the victim compared their situation with that of Jerry Sandusky and his boys, Weiss reportedly said, "Those kids didn't want it." Weiss' accuser pointed out that their sexual encounters, when he was 11 and 12, had also not been with his consent.

Martin Weiss, at a December 15 pretrial hearing, entered a plea of not guilty. If convicted of the felonies he is charged with, the owner of Martin Weiss Management could serve up to 34 years in prison.

Paula Dorn, the co-founder of the non-profit child talent support organization BizParentz Foundation, reportedly said that, over the years, she and members of her group have heard rumors of Weiss' sexual relationships with some of his clients. But without any hard evidence of sexual abuse, no one reported this to law enforcement.

On June 1, 2012, Martin Weiss pleaded no contest to two counts of a lewd act with an 11-year-old client. The judge, Leslie Dunn, sentenced Weiss to one year in the Los Angeles County Jail. He also received five years probation, had to register as a sex offender, and stay away with people under 18. In return for the plea, the prosecutor dropped 6 other sex offense charges against him. Martin Weiss got off easy.

Using HIV as a Weapon

When 27-year-old Adam Lee Brown was discharged from the Marine Corps in 1990, he was HIV positive. The married military computer technician, while serving in southern California, had picked-up the virus after having affairs with homosexual men. Furious that he had contracted the disease, Brown told his estranged wife that he would somehow get revenge. He didn't say how, or who would be the target of his fury.

In 1992, Brown was living in the logging town of Roseburg, Oregon. The son of a pastor, Brown became the lay preacher at the Fair Oaks Community Church in nearby Sutherlin. That year, over a six-month period, Adam Brown sexually molested, and tried to infect, dozens of 5 to 10-year-old boys he met through friends and a women he knew who babysat in his neighborhood. Once he had lured a boy to his home, Brown would either drug the child or force him to drink alcohol. He also showed his victims pornographic videos, and after raping them, promised to stab them with knives and scissors if they told anyone. He also assured the boys that if they informed their parents what he had done to them, they would burn in hell. A 5-year-old boy told his parents, and then the police, that Brown had smeared semen into a scratch on the victim's arm. (The boy obviously didn't use the term semen.)

In the fall of 1993, Douglas County District Attorney William Marshall charged Adam Brown with 49 counts of rape and attempted murder. This was the first case in the country involving a pedophile that tried to kill his victims by infecting them with HIV.

For some reason, District Attorney Marshall allowed Brown to plead no contest to only 4 of the 49 counts. After Brown pleaded no contest to 3 counts of sodomy, and 1 count of child endangerment, the judge, in December 1993, sentenced him to 16 years in prison.

On October 5, 2004, after serving 11 years of his prison sentence, Oregon's corrections authorities released Adam Brown on parole. The freed pedophile was ordered to register as a sex offender, and was barred from frequenting places where children regularly congregate. His parole will expire in 2020.

At two in the afternoon of Sunday, July 1, 2012, Adam Brown, now 49 and still a pedophile, was loitering around the entrance to the men's room at a Wendy's in Portland, Oregon. When an unaccompanied 10-year-old boy approached the restroom, Brown grabbed the child, pulled him inside, and locked the door. As the abductor stabbed the struggling boy, the victim's father heard his screams and ran to help him. But the frantic parent couldn't save his boy because Brown had locked the door. When a supervisor at Wendy's unlocked the men's room, Brown pushed the wounded boy out of the restroom and locked himself inside. A group of employees held the door closed so Brown couldn't escape until the police arrived.

As paramedics rushed the badly injured boy to a nearby hospital, patrol officers with the Portland Police Department spoke to Brown through the men's room door. Brown refused to come out, and claimed to possess a gun. A hostage negotiator, following a two-hour standoff, coaxed Brown out of the restaurant. When taken into custody, the pedophile had a knife, but no firearm.

The district attorney in Multnomah County charged Adam Lee Brown with attempted murder, sexual abuse, kidnapping, and assault. The subject is being held in the Multnomah County Jail on $2 million bond. The injured child underwent emergency surgery, and is expected to recover.

It's hard to understand why a pedophile that had raped and tried to infect his victims with the HIV virus was allowed, in 1992, to plead *no contest* to such a small number of reduced charges. Prosecutors are put in office to protect the public, not to go soft on sexual predators.

In October 2012, Brown entered a guilty plea to ten counts related to the Wendy's offenses. The judge sentenced him to 33 years in prison.

The Puppeteer

In 1992, puppeteer Ronald Wilson Brown started his entertainment enterprise, Puppets Plus. (It's the "plus" part of his act that turned out to be disturbing.) Since then, Brown has performed with his hand puppets for thousands of kids at shopping malls, schools, churches, and birthday parties throughout the Tampa Bay area. (Serial killer John Wayne Gacy entertained children with his clown act.) During the past 15 years, through his so-called Kid Zone Ministry, Brown has hosted weekly gatherings at the Gulf Coast Church in his hometown of Largo, Florida. Ronald Brown also worked for the Christian Television Network, using his puppets to warn kids against viewing pornography. (Here's a simple rule: When some clown or guy with puppets wants to talk to your kid about pornography, even if it's in a church, get the hell out of there. If it's on TV, turn it off.)

The outgoing puppeteer, a resident of the Whispering Pines mobile home park in Largo, regularly invited neighborhood boys and girls between the ages 5 and 12 to his trailer for pizza and candy. (Brown lived in an area populated by young families as evidenced by all the playgrounds near his home.) He was also connected through Facebook with several of the local kids who knew him as the "cotton candy man." This neighborhood comprised an excellent hunting ground for a pedophile. For a sexual predator hiding behind goofy puppets, it was paradise.

In 1998, when a police officer pulled Brown over for a traffic violation, the cop noticed several pairs of boys' underwear in the car. When asked why he had children's undergarments in his vehicle, Brown explained that the clothing belonged to his puppets. (Puppets need underwear?) Whether or not the officer bought Brown's story, nothing came of the traffic cop's observation.

In 2012, agents with the Department of Homeland Security were conducting an international child pornography investigation that had led to 40 arrests in six countries. The child pornography ring, headquartered in Massachusetts, centered on an online chat room where sexual degenerates from around the world could communicate with each other. Ronald Brown, the 57-year-old puppeteer from Largo, Florida, was a regular presence on the pedophile site.

In one conversation with a man from Kansas named Michael Arnett, Brown wrote that he wanted to kidnap a child, tie him up, lock him in a closet then eat him for Easter dinner. "I imagine him wiggling and then going still," he wrote. Brown also mentioned a female toddler he knew who made his mouth water, describing how human flesh tastes when prepared in various ways. Michael Arnett sent Brown a photograph of a strangled 3-year-old girl. Turned on by the sight of a dead toddler, Brown replied that this was how he'd "do" the young boy he wanted to kill and consume.

On July 19, 2012, Homeland Security agents, pursuant to a search of the puppeteer's Largo mobile home, seized CDs, DVDs, thumb drives, micro disks, and VHS tapes containing images of nude children in bondage positions. Some of the youngsters had been posed as though they were dead.

The day following the search, the federal officers took Ronald Brown into custody. When interrogated, he identified the boy he said he wanted to kidnap and eat as a 10-year-old he knew from church. Brown referred to his Internet musings as being "in the realm of fantasy."

On July 24, 2012, at Ronald Brown's arraignment, the assistant United States attorney informed the defendant he had been charged with conspiracy to kidnap a child, and possession of child pornography. The judge set a date in August for Brown's bond hearing. Two days later, federal agents and deputies with the Pinellas County Sheriff's Office returned to Brown's mobile home where they removed more evidence from the dwelling. Agents and deputies were seen walking out of the place carrying seized boxes and bags containing who knows what.

In July 2013, following his guilty plea in federal court, the judge sentenced Brown to twenty years behind bars. The sentence also included probation for life if and when this pedophile ever left prison.

The Female Pedophile

Female pedophiles can be placed into three general categories: women who target children under six; those who molest adolescents; and women who assault children with a male partner. Female pedophiles who were victimized tend to target their own children. So-called self-made female offenders tend to prey upon victims outside the home. These pedophiles acquire access to children as trusted daycare workers, relatives, schoolteachers and coaches.

Female pedophiles most likely to grab headlines are schoolteachers who fall in love with and have affairs with adolescent males. According to criminologists who study these women, they lack self-esteem, are co-dependent, and are afraid of rejection. They tend to romanticize their victims as ideal partners who truly understand them.

Many female pedophiles avoid prison because prosecutors believe they are more difficult to convict than their male counterparts. Prosecutors worry that jurors won't believe that women are capable of such crimes. Even journalists, when referring to women accused of pedophilia, use words like "had sex with," or "affair," instead of "rape," or "molestation."

Tabatha Partsch, a chubby, round-faced 39-year-old with cat-lady eyeglasses and acne, lived in Claysburg, a town of 1,500 in central

Pennsylvania about 35 miles south of Altoona. In September 2011, a 14-year-old boy who had been to Partsch's house, told police he'd seen her take a girl his age into her bedroom and lock the door.

The Greenfield Township Police, pursuant to their investigation of Partsch (also known as Tabatha Sossong) as a suspected pedophile, acquired, in March 2012, a daylong exchange of text messages between her and a 12-year-old boy. Partsch instructed the kid to skip school and come to her house, noting that if his parents found out, she'd hide him. Partsch also suggested they exchange nude photographs of each other.

Detectives learned that Partsch had been involved in several conversations like this one with other boys she was possibly grooming for sex. In one of her texts, she wrote, "We can do stuff, maybe touch each other."

Shortly after midnight on March 29, 2012, police officers from several local jurisdictions arrived at Partsch's house with a search warrant. Among other items, they seized nine cellphones, two computers, and a PlayStation 3 video game console. Officers found nude photographs of children on several of the recovered cellphones.

Over the next few weeks, detectives questioned several children who had spent time at Tabatha Partsch's dwelling. If their stories are to be believed, the suspect had showed her young guests Internet pornography, supplied them with cigarettes and alcohol, and sexually molested them. According to an 11-year-old boy, Partsch forced him to sexually assault a 5-year-old girl.

On July 13, 2012, a detective, accompanied by a Blair County social worker, questioned the suspect at her home. Partsch said she didn't put the sexually explicit photographs on her cellphones, and denied sexually molesting anyone. All of the children were making things up and lying, she said.

Ten days following the interview, police officers took Tabatha Partsch into custody. Charged with 18 felonies related to child sexual abuse, she was placed into the Blair County Jail on $150,000 bond. Richard Consiglio, the Blair County District Attorney, charged Partsch with child rape, statutory indecent assault, disseminating explicit material to minors, and corrupting minors. Questioned by a local reporter, Consiglio noted that convictions in trials involving young witnesses are not sure things.

In November 2013, following her guilty plea, a Blair County Judge sentenced Tabatha Partsch to 15 to 30 years in prison.

Sex Offenders And Facebook

Constitutional law in America could be described as an ongoing struggle between the interests of society and the rights of individuals and groups. In this battle, most citizens, unless their individual rights are threatened, come down in favor of the government. This is particularly true when the individuals complaining about their rights being violated are convicted sex offenders.

The Indiana legislature, in 2008, passed a bill barring most registered sex offenders in the state from using social networking sites that allow access to youngsters under eighteen. The law, passed without a single opposing vote in the state house and senate, and signed by Governor Mitch Daniels, made it a crime for registered sex offenders to access Facebook and sites like it.

While the vast majority of Indiana's citizens embraced the new legislation, the American Civil Liberties Union (ACLU) filed a class-action suit on behalf of the state's registered sex offenders challenging the constitutionality of the law. According to the ACLU, the law violated its clients' First Amendment rights to free speech.

In June 2012, U.S. District Court Judge Tanya Walton Pratt upheld the social networking ban as constitutional on the grounds the state has a strong interest in protecting children from pedophiles. Judge Pratt, in her opinion, described Internet sites like Facebook as "virtual playgrounds for sexual predators."

The ACLU appealed the U.S. District Court ruling to the Seventh U.S. Circuit Court of Appeals in Chicago. In January 2013, the three-judge panel handed down its decision. The Indiana law denying registered sex offenders the right to avail themselves of Facebook and the other networking sites violated their right to free speech.

As a result of the federal appeals court decision, registered sex offenders in Indiana who have been found guilty of violating the 2008 law, can petition state courts to have their convictions vacated. If they don't, their convictions will stand.

It's not surprising that the appeals court decision to strike down this law was extremely unpopular in Indiana. Very few people have sympathy for sex offenders, even after they have "paid for their crimes." That's because most of them re-offend. That is particularly true of serial rapists and pedophiles. If alcoholics are prohibited from flying airplanes, why should convicted sex offenders be allowed to use Facebook to network with each other and prowl for victims? A lawyer for the ACLU would answer that the people don't have a constitutional right to fly a plane.

Chemical Castration

In 1984, a Kalamazoo, Michigan man was found guilty of sexually assaulting his underage stepdaughter over a period of seven years, until she ran away. Rather than serve prison time, the judge ordered that he undergo chemical castration, a drug therapy that would diminish his sex drive.

The craziest part is this: The Upjohn pharmaceutical company manufactured the drug, a firm founded by the grandfather of the accused. That made him the heir to the fortune. He'd go on to get rich off the company, but not before being forced to sample his own products.

Neil Patrick Steward, *Headlines! Headlines!* 2012

The Unrepentant Child Molester

In 2011, Ethel Anderson, a 29-year-old teacher at the Mango Elementary School in suburban Seffner, Florida outside of Tampa, resided in Riverside with her husband and 5-year-old daughter. Anderson had recently been named the Diversity School Teacher of the Year.

In December 2011, Teacher of the Year Anderson began tutoring a 12-year-old math student in her home. Over the next three months, she and the boy exchanged 230 pages of text messages in which she described, in vivid language, her lust for the kid. Anderson also expressed her anxiety over feeling unattractive because of her weight. In these exchanges, the boy used the name Dirty Dan. No one reading this material would have guessed that Dirty Dan was a 12-year-old kid communicating with one of his public school teachers. The online exchange between teacher and student, while a bit puerile, was pretty raunchy.

In February 2012, the teacher-student affair ended following a lover's spat. The angry kid got his revenge by telling his mom everything. It's hard to imagine what was going through the mother's mind when her son described receiving oral sex from a woman paid to teach him math. The couple, according to the kid, also simulated various sexual acts while fully clothed. The boy's tutor also fondled him.

The mother, perhaps worried that school officials and police officers would take the teacher's word over her son's, confronted Anderson before alerting the authorities. During that meeting, the teacher admitted having an inappropriate relationship with the boy. The student's mom, having clandestinely audio-taped the conversation, went to the police with the evidence. (The mother may also have seen the texted messages between her son and Anderson.)

Hillsborough County Assistant State Attorney Rita Peters, in March 2012, charged Ethel Anderson with nine counts of lewd and lascivious conduct with a child. Each count carried a maximum sentence of 15 years in prison. Following the teacher's arrest, the school suspended her without pay. Eight months later, Anderson resigned.

The child molestation trial got underway in Tampa on September 18, 2013. The boy, now 14, took the stand for the prosecution. "I felt she was like my real girlfriend," he said. "She said I was her boyfriend and she loved me. I was thinking, 'I'm living a guy's dream...dating my teacher.' "

According to the young prosecution witness, Anderson told him she planned to leave her husband because he wasn't a good father, and didn't communicate with her. As time went on, however, the student began having doubts about the relationship. "I'm dating a girl I'm in love with and she thinks of me as a kid. It didn't feel right."

On the third and final day of the trial, defense attorney William Knight, in a bold move, put his client on the stand. Rather than plead some kind of emotional breakdown, drinking problem or addiction to drugs, the former schoolteacher denied having physical contact with the boy, essentially calling him a liar. Claiming that the 12-year-old had tried to instigate a sexual relationship, Anderson said, "He attempted, at one point, to grab me in an inappropriate manner. He attempted to kiss me and I pushed him off."

Regarding her sexually vivid text messages, the defendant said they were nothing more than "sexual therapy" tools to get the boy to focus on his studies. "I recognize it was explicit and inappropriate, but it was all fantasy," she said. "He was going through puberty. He couldn't connect with his family. He was always thinking sexually. My purpose was to get his attention."

Prosecutor Peters, in a blistering cross-examination of the defendant, asked, "You want the jury to believe that you were in fantasyland to help the boy? Was that part of your training as a teacher? So by giving in to these sexual fantasies he did better in school?"

"Sometimes, yes," Anderson replied.

Defense attorney Knight, in his closing remarks to the jury, pointed out that the prosecution had not presented one piece of physical evidence proving any kind of sexual contact between his client and the student.

When it came her turn to address the jury, the prosecutor called the former teacher's attempt to explain herself "remarkable," and "amazing in its audacity." The state attorney told jurors "everything the defendant told you defies logic and common sense."

On September 19, 2013, the jury, after a two-hour deliberation, found Ethel Anderson guilty of all charges.

On December 9, 2013, Hillsborough County Judge Chet Tharpe asked Anderson, before he handed down her sentence, if she had anything to say to the court. "I am not a sexual predator," she said.

"You groomed the child," replied the judge. Judge Tharpe sentenced Anderson to 38 years in prison.

Running Free in California

There is a lot to dislike about California. The state is broke, taxes are too high, politicians live like kings and queens, and the public school system is one of the worst in the country. California is home to so many street gangsters, drug dealers, carjackers, drug abusers, wife beaters, rapists, burglars, and armed robbers, there is not enough room in its jails and prisons for the vast number of pedophiles who live and offend in the state. California is not a good place to raise children who are not from upper-middle-class or rich families.

In 2006, citizens of the Golden state, aware that they were living in the pedophilia capital of America, got behind a law that required all "high-risk sex offenders" (pedophiles) who had served their time or had been released early on parole, to be tracked for life with GPS monitors. These fiber-optic cables that transmit signals to private contract monitoring centers, are attached to sex offenders' ankles with rubber straps. Whenever a GPS-monitored pedophile enters a forbidden area such as a school zone or a playground, the ankle device is activated. Monitoring personnel, upon receiving an alarm signal, alert the appropriate parole authority through text message or email. The ankle device will also go off if tampered with or removed.

GPS monitored pedophiles and other sex offenders out on parole who were arrested for violating the terms of their conditional releases, used to sit in jail for months awaiting their parole revocation hearings. If found guilty of breaking the terms of their parole, judges sent these violators back to prison for up to a year. The system, designed to deter sexual deviates from reoffending, didn't work because there were so many of them they, along with all of the other criminals in California, overwhelmed the state's prisons and jails.

In 2011, justices on the California Supreme Court ordered state correctional bureaucrats to significantly reduce prison overcrowding. Many judges on the county level issued similar mandates to reduce local jail populations. In October of 2011, Governor Jerry Brown and the state legislature, to carry out the judicial decree, initiated the so-called "realignment program". Pursuant to this new corrections policy, prison inmates across the state were released on parole early. If those being shown the door prematurely were pedophiles and other high-risk sex offenders, they were fitted with the GPS tracking devices.

Under the realignment program, sex offenders who were incarcerated to await their parole hearings could not be held in jail for more than 180 days. Following the implementation of the new policy, many jails simply refused to take sex offenders arrested for breaking parole. Most parole violators were released from custody within hours of their parole violation arrests.

As a result of California's realignment program, tens of thousands of paroled, GPS-monitored pedophiles were serving their sentences out of the jail and prison system. Because these offenders knew they could break parole and not be incarcerated because jailers and prison wardens didn't want them, parolees started removing their GPS ankle devices. Alarms went off, parole violation warrants were issued (3,400 since October 2011), but no one was put back behind bars.

While California's jails and prisons are no longer crowded, pedophiles and sex offenders who have shed their tracking devices are re-offending.

Government, almost by definition, is dysfunctional. But criminal justice dysfunction that comes to the aid of child molesters and rapists is unforgivable. At some point in California's corrections field, inmate comfort trumped the welfare of children.

A Degenerate Dungeon Master

In 2009, a Milford Massachusetts hotel manager named Robert Diduca mistakenly sent an Internet image of a sexually abused 18-month-old boy to a federal investigator. This led to a federal child pornography and abuse sting operation called Operation Holitna. By 2013, the worldwide investigation resulted in 51 arrests and the rescue of 160 sexually abused children. Operations like this expose the massive scope and depth of child abuse in the United States and abroad.

In 2010, shortly after the launching of Operation Holitna, state and federal investigators intercepted online communications between 39-year-old Geoffrey Portway and Michael Arnett, a fellow sexual deviate and child pornographer from Kansas. Portway, a computer operator and British citizen, through a variety of online forums, sent Arnett 4,500 pornographic images of young boys that had been injured, mutilated, or murdered.

Using the Internet name "Fatlongpig" (cannibal-fetish site slang for human flesh cooked for human consumption), Portway sent thousands of messages that revealed his fevered desire to rape, murder, and eat young boys. To his pornographic pen pal in Kansas, Portway wrote: "I want to eat...the two boys you will bring me. Perhaps not today, but it will happen.

That is all I live for....I am serious. It is the only thing that gets me up in the morning."

On July 27, 2012, when state and federal officers raided Geoffrey Portway's house in Worcester, Massachusetts, the officers discovered a carefully designed and equipped rape/cannibal/murder dungeon in the suspect's basement. What officers found in this place left no room for imagination or interpretation. This pervert obviously planned to imprison, murder, dismember, and eat his young abductees. With this in mind, Portway had constructed a metal, four-foot-long, three-foot-wide, two-foot-high cage that contained locking hardware and an opening for food delivery. Officers also found a box of latex rings used for castrating calves, a set of butcher's knives, various restraining devices, a bottle of bleach, a child-sized coffin, and two small freezers.

Mr. Portway's extensive DVD collection featured titles like "Cannibal," "Criminal Lovers," and "Hansel and Grettel." One of the films in his possession, "Cannibal Ferox," contained a tagline that read: "Make them die slowly." Portway also possessed books such as *Cannibal Sacrifice* by Garry Hogg. The Englishman's computer contained child pornographic images of tens of thousands of boys. (In cases like this there seems to be no limit to the size of a pervert's collection of child pornography.)

Assistant United States Attorney Stacy Dawson Belf charged Portway with the federal crimes of solicitation to kidnap a child, and the distribution and possession of child pornography. In May 2013, faced with an overwhelming amount of evidence against him, the wannabe child rapist/killer/cannibal signed a plea agreement that could result in a prison sentence of 18 to 27 years.

At his sentencing hearing on September 17, 2013, Portway's attorney, Richard Sweeney, in arguing for a sentence of 20 years or less, said his client had never "laid a hand on any minors." According to the defense attorney, "There's pornography, there's a fantasy world. There's no child. Geoffrey lived in a fantasy world where he did live-action role-playing, did things online unrelated to child porn and cannibalism. A lot of the chats that he had were, in his mind, fantasy."

Attorney Sweeney, in an obvious attempt to garner sympathy for Mr. Portway, said his client had a history of mental problems dating back to middle school when he expressed his own desire to be eaten. The attorney informed the court that his client realized he was gay at age eight but was afraid to tell his father who was homophobic.

Prosecutor Belf pointed out that Portway "can only claim fantasy because he hadn't done it yet."

After hearing the prosecutor and the defense attorney make their sentencing arguments and recommendations, U. S. District Court Judge Timothy Hillman sentenced Geoffrey Portway to 26 years and 8 months in prison. After serving his time in the United States, Portway will be deported to England. Federal corrections authorities will register him as a Level 3 Sex Offender. (Sex criminals in this category are believed the most likely to re-offend.)

Florida Pedophile Gets Beating

In Daytona Beach, Florida, a father punched and kicked an 18-year-old man unconscious after finding him sexually abusing his 11-year-old son early Friday, July 18, 2014. The father walked in on the abuse at one in the morning. When the officers arrived, they found Raymond Frolander motionless on the living room floor. He had several knots on his face and was bleeding from the mouth.

"He is nice and knocked out on the floor for you," the father said. "I drug him out to the living room."… When asked if any weapons were in involved, the father said, "my foot and my fist."

Daytona Beach Chief of Police Mike Chitwood, in speaking to reporters said, "Dad was acting like a dad. I don't see anything we should charge him with. You have an 18-year-old who had clearly picked his target, groomed his target and had sex with the victim multiple times."

Frolander was charged with sexual battery on a child under 12. He was being held without bail. According to the arrest affidavit, Frolander admitted the abuse.

Associated Press, July 21, 2014

A Pedophile in Ohio

On January 12, 2014, Alliance Ohio police arrested a Cuyahoga Falls man after he tried to purchase a 10-year-old girl for sex from an undercover police officer. Robert W. Thomas Jr., 36, was arrested…following a weeklong investigation…Thomas requested a child in the 5-to-8-year range, offering to pay $400 in cash for her. The man told the undercover officer that he wished to keep the child permanently at his home to engage in sexual conduct and, police say, to "train her to please him."…

Alliance detectives also executed a search warrant at Thomas' home. They found a computer, electronic storage devices, sexual paraphernalia, videos and several firearms…He has been charged with trafficking in persons, attempted kidnapping, attempted rape and possessing criminal tools. He was held in the Stark County Jail on $2 million bond.
WKTC News Cleveland, January 12, 2014

The Golf Coach

In 2006, 24-year-old Andrew Michael Nisbet began working as a golf instructor at the Las Positas Country Club in Livermore, California, a suburban community 45 miles east of San Francisco. He quickly became a popular and well-known golf coach. Within a few years Nisbet was promoted to Director of Instruction. During this period he not only trained young golfers in the bay area, he taught students in Michigan, North Carolina, Mississippi, and Alabama.

On December 7, 2013, the day before Nisbet was to receive the PGA's Northern California Section 2013 Junior Golf Leader Award, police officers showed up at the country club and took him into custody. An Alameda County prosecutor had charged Nisbet with 65 counts of child molestation that included lewd acts and oral sex with three of his former golf students during the period 2009 to 2012. The boys were between the ages twelve and sixteen.

The alleged sex offenses took place in Nisbet's parked car at the country club, at his home, and on out-of-town golfing trips. According to the criminal complaints, the coach bought his victims expensive golf equipment, took them to restaurants, and showed them pornography on his computer. Whenever one of the boys rebuffed his advances, the gifts and other perks would stop.

Following his arrest, Nisbet reportedly confessed to the commission of lewd acts. He was booked into the Santa Rita Jail in Dublin, California. The judge denied him bond.

In late February 2014, from his jail cell, Nisbet began exchanging letters with a man Nisbet hoped would murder his three accusers. In the correspondence, Nisbet and the potential hit man discussed how much it would cost to kill the three murder-for-hire targets. He said he wanted them "taken care of."

The solicited triggerman took Nisbet's letters to the Alameda County Sheriff's Office. Shortly thereafter, a undercover officer posing as a hit man, visited Nisbet at the Santa Rita Jail. During these tape-recorded conversations, Nisbet provided the undercover cop with personal information about the targets of his homicidal wrath. The phony hit man told Nisbet he would make the murders look like robberies gone wrong.

In April 2014, the Alameda District Attorney's Office charged the 32-year-old golf coach with three counts of solicitation of murder.

While it is not uncommon to find pedophiles among the ranks of teachers and coaches, it is unusual when these type offenders turn into murder-for-hire masterminds.

Rounding Them Up in the UK

Police in the United Kingdom arrested 660 alleged pedophiles following a six-month investigation. The suspects included doctors, teachers, scout leaders, care workers, and former police officers. On July 16, 2014, the United Kingdom's Crime Agency reported that the operation occurred across the UK and included 45 police forces...

The operation, kept secret until the arrests, involved targeting those accessing online images of pedophilia. Thirty-nine of those arrested were registered sex offenders. The rest of the suspects had been unknown to the police. The charges ranged from possessing indecent images of children to serious sexual abuse...

These arrests followed a series of pedophilia scandals that have dogged the UK. In July 2014, the authorities revealed that in the 1980s, politicians in the UK routinely abused vulnerable children....

Mirren Gidda, "UK Police Arrest 660 Suspected Pedophiles," time.com, July 17, 2014

Teachers Who Molest
An Underreported Crime

Sexual abuse of children by teachers and other public school employees is likely underestimated because of a patchwork reporting system and involvement of numerous local, state and federal agencies in investigating such claims, according to a new government report...The report by the Government Accountability Office (GAO) raises numerous questions about how closely public schools are following federal requirements for mandatory reporting of child sexual abuse allegations or suspicions involving the public school employees who oversee the 50 million children enrolled in the nation's public K-12 schools. The report also raises doubts about the accuracy of the data on the scope of the problem....

Even when state law requires reports to be made to outside agencies, sometimes the information never goes beyond a school district--whether because of uncertainty about whether a report is necessary, delays in reporting or outright failure to report allegations or suspicions of abuse....

GAO investigators said they found that most states do not require training of educators on sexual abuse, even though experts say it's critical to preventing abuse. The report said such training might keep school officers from discounting their own suspicions or observations....

Gil Aegerter and Joel Seidman, NBC News, January 30, 2014

Coaches: Masters of Their Universe

Pedophilia has been a hidden aspect of boy's athletics. The problem has been brought to the surface by the coaching scandals at Penn State, the Citadel, and Syracuse University. Are these rare cases, or is this a major social and criminal problem? Just how many of these sexual predators are coaching our children?

As reported in the *Pittsburgh Post-Gazette*, Michael Soto, a clinical psychologist at the University of Toronto, estimated that between 1 and 3 percent of men are sexually attracted to children 12 and under. Dr. Soto believed pedophilia is not a learned behavior but the result of something different in the brains of men sexually attracted to children. Studies have shown that about a third of these men were abused sexually as children. Dr. Soto was of the opinion this childhood abuse triggered a physiological predisposition.

Dr. Thomas Plante, a psychology professor at Santa Clara University who studied and treated pedophiles (including hundreds of priests), estimated that 5 percent of all men have a predilection to be sexually attracted to children. According to an interview the professor gave to *New York Times* reporter Lynn Zinser, not all of these men act on their deviant attraction. But still, any way you figured it, our country was crawling with sexual predators who worked in jobs that brought them into contact with children. And what better position could there be for such men than coaching sports?

Pedophiles who sold insurance, drove trucks, or worked in factories, unless they were involved in organizations like the Boy Scouts, YMCA or Big Brother, will draw suspicion when they engage in any of the behavior associated with pedophilia. This included excessive interest in boys under 12, buying them gifts, taking them places overnight, and laying hands on them. Athletic coaches do these things as a matter of routine.

Pedophile coaches get away with their crimes because of the nature of the offense and the psychological make up of their victims. Boys who play sports serve at the pleasure of their coaches who they desperately want to please. These victims are reluctant to report being abused because they not only fear their coaches, they don't think anyone will believe them. Moreover, they're worried that the other players will think they are homosexuals. These boys are powerless in a culture dominated by sports fans and ex-jocks where coaches are kings. Even victims' fathers are afraid to offend coaches for fear of hurting their sons' athletic futures.

In Pennsylvania, the way state authorities handled the 1998 sexual molestation allegations against Penn State coach Jerry Sandusky illustrated why pedophile coaches are rarely brought to justice. Under Pennsylvania's Child Protective Services Law, Department of Public Welfare (DPW) social workers had the authority to "indicate" someone as a child molester. This determination is not made public, and is outside the criminal justice system. An employer of such a designee is informed of his status and that person is barred from contact with children. A criminal background check is then initiated.

In the 1998 Sandusky case, the DPW worker was informed that the coach had been accused of sexually abusing an 11-year-old boy in a locker room shower. On June 1, the DPW official and a detective with the university police department questioned Sandusky in the Penn State weight room. The coach admitted showering with the boy and said he felt bad about that. Whether he admitted hugging the boy at that time is not clear. The DPW investigator later declined the opportunity to monitor an electronically eavesdropped conversation between coach Sandusky and the alleged victim's mother. In that confrontation, the coach admitted hugging the boy in the shower.

The DPW social worker did not find "substantial evidence" of sexual abuse in this case. Had he done so, Coach Sandusky would have been barred from any contact with children through his charity, The Second Mile. His superiors at Penn State, including coach Joe Paterno, would have been alerted to the potential problem. The DPW official's decision, as well as Centre County District Attorney Ray Gricar's refusal to prosecute the case, allowed coach Jerry Sandusky continued access to children.

Looking back at the 1998 allegations, many child protection workers believed there was substantial evidence of sexual abuse, and that Coach Sandusky should have been kept away from young boys.

Because of our national obsession with athletics, we are sacrificing our children to the gods of sports--the coaches. New laws and greater awareness, in the face of this obsession, will not protect young athletes. Pedophiles do not believe that what they do to kids is wrong. Therefore they can't be shamed or humiliated. They respond to their accusers with anger and defiance. And whether these men are coaches, elementary school teachers, or priests, they know how to use and abuse their power. And as long as they have this authority, they will continue to molest children under their control.

The RICO Suit

The Poly Prep Country Day School is an elite, nursery to 12th grade private boy's academy located on two campuses in Brooklyn, New York. Poly Prep's middle and high school buildings are located in the Dyker Heights section of Brooklyn while the lower grades are on the Park Slope campus.

As is often the case in schools where the sports program plays an important if not vital role in the institution, faculty member and renowned football coach Philip Foglietta enjoyed icon status during the years 1966 to 1991.

In 1966, Coach Foglietta's first year at Poly Prep, a male student accused him of sexual molestation. A school administrator informed the boy's parents that an internal investigation revealed the accusation to be false. Moreover, if this student continued to make slanderous claims of this nature, the boy would face "severe consequences." The administration's handling of this case not only silenced the accuser, it became the school's future *modus operandi* in such matters.

After 25 years as Poly Prep's most successful football coach, Foglietta unexpectedly retired in 1991. In honor of his legendary coaching career, and important contributions to the institution, the school hosted a gala celebration held at the Manhattan Athletic Club. Members of the Poly Prep community, and the public at large, were not told of the real reason behind the coach's "retirement." He had been forced to quit as a result of accusations of "sexual misconduct."

Following Coach Foglietta's death in 1998, Poly Prep established a memorial fund and solicited donations in his name. Four years later, in a letter to all alumni, the Poly Prep administration revealed that for years Coach Foglietta had been suspected of sexually abusing his students. According to this 2002 letter, administrators had "recently received credible allegations that sexual abuse had occurred at Poly Prep more than 20 years ago by a faculty member/coach who is now deceased." Everyone familiar with the school knew that coach was Philip Foglietta. The author of this revealing letter promised a thorough internal investigation of the accusations. (If the school actually conducted such an inquiry, no report of it surfaced. Moreover there was no indication that these "credible" accusations were ever passed onto the police.)

In 2004, a Poly Prep alumnus named John Paggioli, alleging that Coach Foglietta had molested him, filed a lawsuit against the school. A year later, a judge, citing New York State's statute of limitations on such claims, dismissed the action. (In New York, a sexual abuse claimant must file suit within five years of his or her eighteenth birthday.)

On October 26, 2009, twelve Poly Prep alumni, claiming sexual abuse by Coach Philip Foglietta, filed a Racketeer Influenced and Corrupt Organizations Act (RICO) suit against the school in the Brooklyn District Federal Court. The plaintiffs alleged a 40-year criminal conspiracy to quash and cover-up student complains of sexual abuse allegedly committed by Poly Prep's greatest football coach.

According to court documents, current and former Poly Prep headmasters knew that Coach Foglietta had sexually abused "dozens if not hundreds of boys." The plaintiffs alleged, "Poly Prep administrators had...knowledge of Foglietta's sexual abuse of numerous boys at or near the school, but condoned and facilitated Foglietta's criminal behavior because he was a highly successful football coach, and instrumental in raising substantial revenue for the school."

In filing a RICO action, a technique the FBI used to cripple the Mafia, the Poly Prep plaintiffs were using this federal law as a way around the statute of limitations. These lawyers were asking the court to consider a sexual abuse defendant's repeated misrepresentations and deceitful conduct as a legal justification to override the application of the statute of limitations. These attorneys were attempting to create a legal exception to the doctrine that bars legal relief in older cases.

On August 28, 2012, in a 40-page decision, Judge Frederic Block of the Brooklyn District Federal Court allowed two of the twelve plaintiffs to go forward with their RICO claims against current and former Poly Prep administrators. If these plaintiffs prevailed under the RICO statute, other institutions like universities and churches could be faced with a flood of sexual abuse lawsuits previously blocked by statutes of limitations. For this reason future sexual abuse plaintiffs and their potential defendants were following this RICO case very closely.

On December 26, 2012, the school settled the landmark lawsuit out of court. As a result, there would be no legal precedent for other victims in old cases. In February 2014, the school issued a formal apology to all of the students sexually abused by the iconic coach and serial child molester.

The Teacher From Hell

People without sexual perversions are normal in generally the same way. Sexual perverts, on the other hand, are deviant in disturbingly diverse ways. Adults who use innocent children to satisfy their perverse sexual compulsions are not mentally ill in the sense they are detached from reality. To other adults, even to people they work with every day they seem normal. Sexually perverse elementary teachers are hard to detect because they victimize kids who are under their control. Sometimes the children don't even know they are being victimized. Teachers like this can get away with sexually abusive behavior for decades. Most of them probably die before they are caught. This is something to worry about. Short of launching McCarthy-like witch-hunts, how can these sexual predators be identified and stopped?

Mark Berndt, a 61-year-old third grade teacher at the Miramonte Elementary School in Florence Firestone, an unincorporated community in Los Angeles County, began teaching at the school in 1979. Miramonte, situated in a Hispanic neighborhood, is in the Los Angeles Unified School

District that is comprised of hundreds of campuses and 650,000 students. During his tenure at Miramonte, Berndt, according to his personnel file, had performed up to school standards without a single disciplinary action taken against him. Moreover, he had never been arrested for anything more serious than a traffic ticket.

In October 2010, a technician at a CVS drugstore in the South Bay area of Los Angeles came across a set of disturbing photographs of grade school boys and girls depicted in situations suggesting a bizarre form of sexual bondage. The film processor, as mandated by state law, notified the Redondo Beach Police Department. On December 2, 2010, the Redondo police turned the 40 photographs over to the Los Angeles County Sheriff's Office.

In some of the photographs, Mark Berndt either has his arm around a third grade boy or girl, or his hand covering their mouths. Some photographs show children with live bugs crawling on their faces. Other kids are either blindfolded, or have their mouths covered with clear tape. Some of the girls are depicted holding spoons containing a white liquid up to their mouths. Children are also pictured about to eat cookies topped with the teacher's semen. (In Berndt's classroom trashcan, police recovered a blue, plastic spoon containing traces of his semen.)

Detectives with the sheriff's office's Special Victims Unit started identifying the students in the photographs for interview. On January 3, 2011, a detective showed up at Miramonte to question Berndt. The teacher refused to speak to the investigator without first consulting with an attorney. To this day, the police have not interrogated the suspect.

A former fourth grade student of Berndt's, a woman now 30, told detectives that in 1990, she and two other girls spoke to a school counselor about their teacher's odd, inappropriate behavior. They had seen him, seated at his desk at the front of the classroom fondling his genitals. The counselor accused the girls of making up the story. As a result, nothing came of their complaint. (In 1993, police investigators looked into similar complaints against Berndt. The Los Angeles District Attorney's Office, on grounds the police had not gathered sufficient evidence against the teacher, decided not to pursue the case. Presumably, school officials knew of the investigation.)

Shortly after Berndt refused to be interviewed by the police, school administrators removed him from the classroom. A month later, February 2011, they fired him. (Actually, he wasn't fired. School officials induced him to retire by offering him $40,000 which he accepted. Firing a public school teacher is no small feat.) While the parents of the children depicted in the photographs were told of the investigation, the police kept the public in the dark. (Placed under police surveillance, Berndt, between the time of his discharge and arrest, was not in contact with children.)

On January 30, 2012, following a 13 month investigation, the case went public with Berndt's arrest at his home in Torrance. A search of his dwelling resulted in the discovery of 400 photographs similar to the ones seen by the CVS employee. (A normal person, knowing that he was under police investigation, would have destroyed these photographs. The fact that Brendt didn't reveals how important these photos were to him. The police have recommended that the children in the photographs be tested for sexually transmitted diseases.) Charged with 23 counts of lewd acts against minors, Brendt was hauled off to jail where he is being held on $23 million bond. The criminal charges against him pertain to his contact with children ages 6 to 10 from 2008 to 2010.

On February 3, 2012, the police arrested a second Miramonte teacher on charges unrelated to the Berndt case. Martin B. Springer, 49, is charged with three counts of committing lewd acts in connection with the alleged fondling an 8-year-old girl in one of his classes. He has been fired, and is being held on $300,000 bail. From Alhambra, Springer has been teaching at the school since 1986. The judge who set bail has decreed that if Springer makes his bond, he is to wear an ankle monitoring device, and stay 250 feet away from schools and parks. On February 7, one of the two girls who accused Springer of fondling her recanted her story.

A lawyer representing "Jane Doe 1," one of Berndt's victims who ate a sugar cookie laced with the teacher's semen, has announced plans to sue the Los Angeles Unified School District. The plaintiff will claim that the school district did not take adequate steps to prevent Berndt from repeatedly abusing his students after numerous complaints had been filed against him. (Since Berndt's arrest, seven more students have come forward with allegations of abuse.)

On February 6, 2013, perhaps in response to allegations of an institutional cover-up, and to regain parent's trust, the 88 teachers and 40 staff employees at Miramonte were suspended with pay. Angry parents protested outside the school.

The Miramonte situation continued to worsen on February 7, 2013 when the mother of a former fourth grader told the "Los Angeles Times" that in 2009, a 50-year-old female teacher's aide wrote three love letters to her then 11-year-old son. One of the letters read, "...when you get close to me, even if you give me the chills, I like that. Don't tell nobody (oh boy) about this!"

Berndt has pleaded not guilty to all charges. He was booked into the Los Angeles County Jail in lieu of $23 million bail.

The Miramonte schoolteacher had been the target of a 1993 criminal investigation triggered by a female student's claim that he had fondled her. Investigators dropped the case due to insufficient evidence.

On March 12, 2013, a spokesperson for the Los Angeles United School District announced it plans to pay $30 million to settle the claims filed by the Miramonte parents of Berndt's violated students.

In November 2013, Berndt pleaded guilty to 23 counts of committing lewd acts on children. Under his plea arrangement, Superior Court Judge George Lomeli immediately sentenced him to 25 years in prison.

The Missing Prosecutor

In Bellefonte, Pennsylvania, at 11:30 in the morning of Friday, April 15, 2005, Ray Gricar, the 59-year-old district attorney of Centre County, the home of Penn State University, called his live-in girlfriend to inform her he was on a pleasure drive through an area in the region called Penns Valley. Twelve hours later, his girlfriend, Patty Fornicola, called 911 and reported him missing.

The next day, Gricar's red mini cooper was found parked near an antique mall in Lewisburg, Pennsylvania, 55 miles east of Bellefonte. The interior of the vehicle reeked of cigarettes. Gricar, who didn't smoke, didn't like that smell. The car had been locked, and Gricar's cellphone was inside. According to a Lewisburg shop owner whose antique store Gricar had patronized in the past, the district attorney, on the day he left Bellefonte, was walking in the mall with a tall, dark-haired woman in her late 30s or early 40s. Investigators made no effort to identify and question this woman. Because this information wasn't published until 13 months after Gricar's disappearance, the police received no help from the public in identifying this woman. By the time the story came out, the case had grown cold.

In July 2005, three months after Ray Gricar drove off in his Cooper and didn't return, his county-issued laptop was found in the Susquehanna River not far from the abandoned car. Three months after that, the hard drive turned up in the same area of the river. Water had damaged it to the point that no data could be retrieved.

Following the recoveries from the river, the investigation of Gricar's disappearance, conducted by the Bellefonte Police Department (the Pennsylvania State Police didn't want the case, and the FBI wasn't involved), ground to a halt. In the summer of 2008, with Ray Gricar still missing, and no clues as to what happened to him or where he was, two of his colleagues, Bob Buehner, Jr., the district attorney of Montour County, and prosecutor Ted McKnight of Clinton County, held a press conference in Lewisburg where Gricar's vehicle had been found. Both men were highly critical of the Gricar missing person's investigation. The neighboring prosecutors said they couldn't understand why the information about

Gricar and the mystery woman at the mall hadn't been made public until May 2006.

On April 14, 2009, four years after Ray Gricar's disappearance, investigators discovered that someone using the missing man's home computer had, shortly before he went missing, searched the Internet on "how to fry a hard drive," and "water damage to a notebook computer." Assuming Gricar had made these inquiries, one of the more innocent explanations behind the Internet search is that Gricar, in contemplation of his retirement in 9 months, wanted to clear his computer before handing it back to the county. This doesn't explain, however, why the computer and hard drive ended up in the river. A more ominous motive is that before killing himself, Gricar wanted to destroy data he didn't want anyone to see. Once you start speculating like this, there's no end to the possibilities and scenarios.

On July 25, 2011, at the request of Ray Gricar's daughter, a Centre County judge declared him legally deceased.

There are three schools of thought regarding what happened to Ray Gricar. He could have been murdered, committed suicide, or had walked off to start a new life under a different identity. The two most popular murder theories feature a mistress who lured him to the Susquehanna River where her husband murdered him. The second murder scenario involves a criminal killing the district attorney out of revenge. Since prosecutors are rarely murdered by people they have prosecuted, or planned to put behind bars, the latter theory is the most improbable. However, the first possibility is far fetched as well.

Suicide seems more likely than murder in this case. Ray Gricar's brother, Roy J. Gricar, committed suicide in May 1996 by jumping off a bridge over the Great Miami River near West Chester, Ohio. If Ray had jumped from a bridge across the Susquehanna River, what are the chances his body would have been found? Some believe the odds are great that his body would have been recovered. Others disagree. To have an opinion on this question, one would have to know the ins and outs of the Susquehanna River.

The so-called "walkaway" theory, that Gricar walked-off to start a new life under a new identity, while quite intriguing, doesn't make much sense. For one thing, he hadn't cleaned out his bank account, and drove off without tying up a lot of loose-ends. Since his disappearance, there have been more than 300 false sightings of him. Those who subscribe to the walkaway theory point out that Ray had been fascinated by the 1985 disappearance of an Ohio police chief. Inside the chief's car, parked near Lake Erie, searchers found his wallet and his badge. They never found the chief's body. Some of those who believe Gricar is still alive think he could be hiding out in the federal government's witness protection program. This possibility is out of the question because prosecutors are not eligible for the program.

Ray Frank Gricar was born on October 9, 1945 in Cleveland, Ohio. He attended Gilmour, a prestigious Catholic high school in Gates Mills, Ohio. In 1966, while attending the University of Dayton, he met his future wife, Barbara Gray. They were married in 1969. After graduating from Case Western Law School in Cleveland, Gricar started his career as a prosecutor in northwest Ohio's Cuyahoga, County.

In 1980, the couple and their daughter Lara moved to Bellefonte, Pennsylvania when Barbara landed a job at Penn State University in nearby State College. Shortly after that, David Grine, the district attorney of Centre County, hired Ray as an assistant prosecutor. Five years later, Gricar ran for the office of district attorney and won.

Barbara and Ray divorced in 1991, and five years later, Ray married his second wife, Emma. Following a tumultuous marriage, he and Emma divorced in 2001. Two years later Ray moved in with Patty Fornicola, an employee of the Centre County District Attorney's Office who lived in a section of Bellefonte called Halfmoon Hill. By April 2005, having served several terms as district attorney, Ray Gricar was planning to retire in nine months.

Although a private, somewhat distant person, Ray's colleagues considered him an outstanding career prosecutor with high ethical standards. Because he never had political ambitions beyond the district attorney's office, Gricar was not, according to his legal colleagues, subject to political pressure or influence. On a personal level, he was known as a bit of a ladies' man.

In May 1998, when Jerry Sandusky was still an assistant football coach under Joe Paterno, and active in his organization for troubled youth called The Second Mile, two 11-year-old boys told their parents that Sandusky had fondled them in the Penn State locker room showers. The mother of one of the accusers contacted Detective Ronald Schreffler with the University Police Department. Shortly after receiving the complaint, Schreffler, on a pretext, got Sandusky to meet the mother at her house where she confronted him about being nude in the shower with her son. With the detective in the next room recording the conversation, the boy's mother asked the coach if he had been sexually aroused by his physical contact with her son, and if his "private parts" had touched the boy. Sandusky did not deny showering with her son. Regarding the arousal question, he said, "I don't think so--maybe. I was wrong. I wish I could get forgiveness. I know I won't get it from you. I wish I were dead."

A child psychologist who interviewed this boy concluded that his account, and Sandusky's response to the mother's interrogation, indicated to him that the coach was "likely a pedophile." A second psychologist, Dr.

John Seasock, after analyzing the same information, came to a different conclusion.

On June 2, 1998, District Attorney Ray Gricar decided not to prosecute the Penn State football coach. Four years later, the boy, referred to as victim # 6, took the stand at Sandusky's trail and described how the coach had lathered him up with soap then said, "I'm going to squeeze your guts out." Ronald Schreffler, now with the Department of Homeland Security, testified in June 2012 that he had wanted Ray Gricar to prosecute Sandusky in 1998, but was overruled.

Had Ray Gricar prosecuted Jerry Sandusky for indecent assault, corruption of a minor, and child endangerment, more victims, ones Sandusky had raped, might have come forward. Even if they hadn't, Gricar would have exposed a pedophile within the Penn State system, and have possibly acquired a conviction on these lesser charges. Assuming Sandusky would have been imprisoned, his sentence may have been light enough for him to get out and continue molesting boys.

In 1999, Jerry Sandusky retired from Penn State. He was awarded the title professor emeritus, and given an office in the football building. He had full access to all of the sports facilities, and used this access and his youth organization to attract and molest young boys.

It's unlikely that Ray Gricar was murdered, or that he's still alive. That leaves suicide. The question is, did Gricar's decision not to prosecute Jerry Sandusky weigh on his conscience, and play a role in his suicide? Between the time the prosecutor closed the case on Sandusky and his disappearance, Gricar must have been aware that accusations against the coach were still being made. Did he have regrets? Was Gricar second-guessing himself?

People who have had access to Ray Gricar's papers say there is virtually no reference in them to Jerry Sandusky. If this is true, we will never know if Jerry Sandusky's pedophilia and Ray Gricar's disappearance are in any way connected. All we are left with is speculation.

Pedophiles and Teachers Unions

Because of the influence of the California Teachers Association (CTA) and other education unions in the state, school administrators have an extremely difficult time firing anyone including teachers accused of pedophilia. Teachers so rotten they manage to get dismissed from their jobs in other states can always find a home in the California system. The pay is outstanding, benefits are out of this world, and it doesn't matter if you are no good. And for pedophiles, California's classrooms are heaven on earth.

In 2012, a group called Democrats for Educational Reform, introduced legislation in the state senate (S.B. 1530) that would make it easier to dismiss teachers accused of sex, violence, or drug offenses against children. That bill, with vast public support, passed the Senate on a 33-4 bipartisan vote.

In the California Assembly, when the Senate-passed legislation came before the Assembly Education Committee, committee members, by refusing to vote on the bill, killed the proposed law in committee. (These politicians didn't have the courage to vote "no.") That meant the bill did not reach the Assembly floor for a vote. If it had, it would have passed by a wide majority.

The committee members who killed this child protection legislation had bowed to the state's powerful teacher's unions, including the CTA. The politicians who killed the bill through their abstentions had been beneficiaries of large CTA political contributions. The fact the CTA could stop legislation favored by a vast majority shows that teachers unions are in control. Moreover, the undermining of this needed legislation revealed what most citizens of the state already know--that in California, it's the unions first, teachers second, and students, parents, and education third--and a bad third at that. It's not surprising that the state has one of the worst public education systems in the country. For a sexually perverted schoolteacher, except perhaps for West Virginia, there is no friendlier place in education than California.

In California, the CTA, backed by an army of 325,000 teachers, and plenty of money to bribe and control state politicians, is in reality the fourth branch of government. As the biggest political spender in the state, its influence dwarfs other special interest groups. From 2000 through 2009, the CTA alone shelled out more than $211 million in political contributions and lobbying expenses. That is twice the amount given to politicians by the second largest bribery machine, the Service Employees International Union (SEIU). Since 2009, the CTA has pumped another $40 million into the state's political community. The union also played a major role in putting Governor Jerry Brown into office. So the teacher's unions own him as well.

That teacher's unions in California and other states are destroying the quality of public education in the country is bad enough. Even worse, they are enabling and protecting classroom child abusers. If school administrators can't protect students from pedophiles, classrooms are not safe for children. I can see no better argument for home schooling, or moving to a state where education is a higher priority than protecting teachers from being fired for cause.

If the California's zookeepers belonged to the CTA, all of the animals would be starving in their cages while their custodians sat around gorging themselves, complaining about their jobs, and threatening to strike.

Reporting Pedophilia

On October 2011, a mother and her 8-year-old daughter met with the principal of the girl's elementary school regarding the behavior of a teacher named Craig Chandler. The 35-year-old taught second grade at the O.B. Whaley Elementary School in San Jose, California. According to principal Lyn Vijayendran's notes of the meeting, the student--identified as Jane Doe--was summoned from recess to Chandler's empty classroom. Pursuant to a lesson plan he called "The Helen Keller Unit," Chandler blindfolded the student and instructed her to lie down on the floor and part her legs. After the teacher removed the girl's shoes, she sensed something "gooey" on her feet that felt like his tongue. Chandler placed something into the student's mouth, and with his hands moved her head back and forth. The girl tasted something salty that dripped onto her jacket. Before Jane Doe left Chandler's classroom, he put a piece of hard candy into her mouth.

Instead of passing this information on to the police for further investigation, Vijayendran questioned Craig Chandler herself. The teacher explained that he had been doing his Helen Keller (a deaf and blind woman who rose to fame as an early twentieth century author) lesson plan for years. He said his "instructional goal" was to deprive students of sight so they could experience what it's like to be blind. The gooey sensation felt by the student on her feet had been caused by a wet sponge, and the taste in her mouth from a bottle of salt water. The teacher offered to meet personally with the girl's parents to clear up any misunderstanding.

Satisfied with Chandler's explanation, the principal told him to discontinue the Helen Keller business, transferred the student to another class, and reported the incident to the Evergreen School District's human resources department. Someone from that department also questioned Chandler, and the matter, institutionally, went no further than that. Craig Chandler continued teaching at the O. B. Whaley Elementary School.

Although principal Vijayendran had closed the book on the case, parents of other girls in his class were going straight to the police with complaints about Chandler's Helen Keller ploy. Following an investigation by detectives with the San Jose Police Department, a Santa Clara County prosecutor, on January 10, 2012, charged Chandler with the crime of lewd and lascivious acts performed on a child under fourteen. Seven months later, additional charges were filed against the teacher involving four other students who were, between the period August 2010 and May 2011, exposed to Chandler's Helen Keller experiment.

Incarcerated in the Santa Clara County Jail, Chandler faced up to 75 years in prison if convicted of these crimes. He pleaded not guilty to all charges.

On October 19, 2012, with Chandler still in custody awaiting his trial, Jane Doe's parents filed a civil suit against the Evergreen School District, the O. B. Whaley Elementary School, and principal Vijayendran.

Santa Clara County prosecutor Alison Filo, in July 2012, charged principal Vijayendran under a relatively new California law that made the failure of an educator to report the suspected sexual abuse of a student a crime. If convicted of the misdemeanor, a judge could sentence the principal up to six months in jail.

The Vijayendran trial got underway on October 31, 2012. Prosecutor Filo, in her opening statement to the jury said that any reasonable person under the circumstances of this case would have suspected sexual abuse on the part of this teacher. Defense attorney Eric Geffon argued that his client had no reason to suspect foul play on Mr. Chandler's part. Geffon described the teacher's Helen Keller cover as "a detailed, devious, well thought out, well prepared story he concocted that explained everything."

On November 2, Lyn Vijayendran took the stand on her own behalf in an effort to convince the jury that there was nothing in the student's story or her demeanor that suggested sexual impropriety on the part of the teacher. Referring to the 8-year-old girl, Vijayendran said, "She had a big smile on her face. She was her normal self, very talkative...." The witness said that at no point in the meeting with the student and her mother did the subject of sexual abuse come up.

On cross-examination, the defendant admitted that when she learned that Mr. Chandler had asked the student to "open her two legs," the idea of sexual impropriety crossed her mind. Prosecutor Filo asked, "If someone said that to you in a grocery story line, you'd slap him, wouldn't you?" (In today's society, I wouldn't recommend that.)

"You'd have to be crazy not to think it was sexual," the defendant answered.

On November 5, 2012, the jury found Lyn Vijayendran guilty of failing to report Craig Chandler's sexually suspicious behavior to the police. Judge Deborah Ryan sentenced the principal to two years probation, $602 in fines, and 100 hours of community service.

It's a shame that educators, to protect the children under their care, have to be induced to do the right thing by making it a crime not to. In a perfect society, there should be no need for crimes of omission.

On November 22, 2013, a judge in San Jose sentenced the former elementary school teacher to 75 years to life in prison.

Pedophile-Supporting Educators

In the spring of 2013, Neal Erickson, an eighth grade science and computer education teacher at the Rose City Middle School in northern Michigan, pleaded guilty to one count of sexual criminal conduct with a male student.

Back in 2006, Erickson had ten sexual encounters with the eighth grader at the teacher's house. (The authorities learned of these sex offenses several years later when an anonymous tipster sent the police an old photograph of the student that in some fashion incriminated the teacher. The victim is now in college, and Mr. Erickson is out of teaching.)

In anticipation of the former teacher's sentencing, six current Rose City educators, and two of their retired colleagues, wrote letters to the judge on Neal Erickson's behalf asking for leniency. Amy Huber Eagan wrote: "I am asking that Neal be given the absolute minimum sentence, considering all of the circumstances surrounding the case." (What circumstances could possibly mitigate this crime?)

Rose City teacher Sally Campbell, in her letter to the judge, wrote: "Neal made a mistake. [Losing your wallet is a mistake. Stealing someone's wallet is not.] He allowed a mutual friendship to develop into much more. He realized his mistake [again the mistake] and ended it years before someone sent something to the authorities which began the legal process."

Middle school teacher Harriett Coe wrote this on Erickson's behalf: "Neal has pleaded guilty his one criminal offense but he's not a predator. [One could argue that any time a teacher has sex with a student, the teacher, by definition, is a predator.] He understands the severity of his action and is sincere in his desire to make amends."

On July 15, 2013, Neal Erickson's sentencing day, Judge Michael Baumgartner looked out over his courtroom and noticed that the defendant's teaching supporters were sitting with members of his family. Speaking directly to Erickson, Judge Baumgartner said, "I'm appalled and ashamed that the community would rally around, in this case, you. What you did was a jab in the eye with a sharp stick to every parent who trusts a teacher."

Judge Baumgartner sentenced Neal Erickson to fifteen years to thirty years in prison. The former teacher's courtroom cheerleaders reacted with shock and disgust.

Following the sentencing hearing, one of Erickson's supporters told a reporter with *The Detroit News* that Judge Baumgartner had socked it to the teacher because he was a man who molested a boy. Had the defendant in this case been a woman, she may have gotten off light. (This may be true, but it doesn't mitigate Erickson's crime.)

Not long after Judge Baumgartner handed down the big sentence, someone burned down the garage owned by the victim's parents, John and Lori Janczewski. An unknown person also spray-painted a threatening message on their house.

Overall, citizens of this rural community agreed with Judge Baumgartner's hardline approach to pedophilia in the local school. Many have asked the school superintendent to fire Erickson's teacher friends.

Several parents have said that if these sex offense cheerleaders aren't sacked, they are taking their children out of the school system.

As could be expected, the embattled Erickson supporters responded to the public's outrage by making threats of their own. If anyone tried to fire them they would sue the cash-strapped school district. These pedophile-supporting educators were not going down without a fight.

A Teacher on the Move

Born in 1982, Eric Toth grew up near Indianapolis, Indiana. He earned good grades in high school where he was considered self-centered, eccentric, and when he wanted to be, charming and manipulating. Abused as a child, he suffered bouts of depression and engaged in compulsive lying.

The lanky young man enrolled at Cornell University in New York State. A year later he transferred to Purdue University at Calumet (Indiana) where he graduated with a Bachelor's degree in elementary education. During his college years he told several people he was an agent with the CIA.

Upon his graduation in 2002, Toth volunteered at an elementary school in Indianapolis where he worked as a teacher's aide. His intense interest in boys between the ages 8 and 11 led to parental complaints and concerns. The principal, suspecting that Toth was a pedophile, terminated his association with the school. A lot of parents were glad to see him go.

In 2003, Toth drifted around the mid west, always inserting himself into environments that put him in proximity to young boys. In 2004 and part of 2005 Toth worked as a counselor at a boy's camp in Madison, Wisconsin. It was at this camp he made videotapes of himself engaging in various sexual activities with several boys. When his behavior began to raise suspicion, he moved on. Moving on, that's what pedophiles do when too many people get suspicious.

In the fall of 2005, administrators at the Beauvior Elementary School attached to the National Cathedral in Washington, D.C. hired Toth to teach third grade. Many of the students in this small prestigious Catholic School came from families of wealth and political power.

Toth's enthusiasm for his job included tutoring children for free and even babysitting them at their homes. His gung-ho work attitude made him a popular teacher at the school. But his excessive familiarity with his male students including having boys sit on his lap, raised eyebrows and suspicions.

In 2008, a fellow Beauvior employee found disturbing photographs on a school camera assigned to Toth. The pornographic pictures featured the teacher and several boys. The school's principal confronted Toth and fired him. After a security officer escorted Toth out of the building and off the campus, the principal called the police. The delay gave Toth the head start he needed to get out of town and disappear.

Based upon the photographs recovered from Toth's camera, a federal prosecutor charged him with producing and possessing child pornography. This made Toth a fugitive from the law.

A month after the Beauvior principal kicked Toth out of Beauvior Elementary, a car that had been rented under the name Jay Kellor turned up at the Minneapolis-St. Paul Airport. Inside the Honda, FBI agents found child pornography linked to Toth's tenure as a boy's camp counselor in Wisconsin.

In the rented vehicle, agents also discovered a suicide note signed by Toth. According to the handwritten document, the authorities would find his body on the bottom of a nearby lake. A search of that lake failed to turn up Toth's remains. The FBI considered the suicide note a fake, a ploy to throw agents off his trail.

Toth, going by the name David Bussone, showed up in January 2009 at the Lodestar Day Rescue Center in Phoenix, Arizona. Toth volunteered to help homeless man complete their 12-step alcohol and drug addiction treatments. He told his colleagues at the rescue center that he had been an educator at an elite east coast school, and that the experience had turned him against wealth and the materialistic lifestyle. He said he had taken a five-year oath of poverty, and had re-dedicated his life to helping the downtrodden.

In the meantime, FBI agents across the country were still searching for Toth. The federal manhunt received a boost when the Toth case appeared on the television show, "America's Most Wanted." One of the homeless men at Lodestar saw the segment and recognized David Bussone as Eric Toth. The next day, realizing that he had been identified, the fugitive pedophile disappeared again.

In July 2009, under a another pseudonym supported by stolen identification documents, Toth turned up at a hippie commune in Austin, Texas. One of the members of the community found Toth a job at an Austin computer repair shop called P.C. Guru. Toth worked at the store two and a half years during which time he tutored grade school boys for free. He also gave the mother of two of his students financial aid.

The FBI, on April 10, 2012, replaced Osama bin Laden on the Bureau's Top Ten Most Wanted List with Eric Toth. In October of that year Toth used a fake passport, under the name Robert Shaw Walker, to flee to Nicaragua. He took up residence in a house in Esteli, a town 90 miles north of the capital, Managua. Toth told people he met that he had come to Nicaragua to write a book.

On April 18, 2013, while attending a social function, Toth ran into an American tourist who recognized him. Two days later, Nicaraguan police officers surrounded his house in Esteli. Following the arrest, officers found 1,100 images of child pornography Toth had downloaded from the Internet onto his personal computer.

Four days after his capture in Nicaragua, Toth was back in Washington, D.C. sitting in jail awaiting his trial.

On December 13, 2013, Toth pleaded guilty before a federal judge to three counts of child pornography and two counts of identify theft. He faced up to 30 years in prison.

On March 11, 2014, the judge sentenced the 32-year-old pedophile to 25 years in federal prison. At his sentencing Toth said, "I don't pretend that anything I could say here today would ever make up for what I did. Everything the prosecutor said about me is true."

The International Pedophile

In 1970, 20-year-old William James Vahey pleaded guilty in California to child molestation. Notwithstanding the sex crime conviction, he graduated from college in 1972 with a degree in education. Facing arrest for not registering as a sex offender, the pedophile fled to Tehran, Iran where he landed a job teaching eighth grade history at a private school attended by American and European children.

From 1973 to 1975, Vahey taught at the American Community School in Beirut, Lebanon. A year later he was in Madrid, Spain teaching at another private American school. After working one year in Spain, Vahey returned to Iran, this time teaching at the Passararod School in the city of Ahwal.

In 1978, the itinerate pedophile taught eighth grade students at the American Community School in Athens, Greece. Two years later Vahey turned up in Saudi Arabia at the Saudi Aramco School in Dhahran. After teaching in Saudi Arabia, Vahey moved to Jakarta, Indonesia where he taught at the Jakarta International School for ten years. After a decade in Indonesia, Vahey ended up in Caracas, Venezuela working at the Escuela Campo School.

Vahey's wife Jean (yes, many pedophiles are married), the former superintendent of the Esceula Campo School, was, in 2009, the executive director of the European Council of International Studies. This may explain why he had been able to land so many private school teaching jobs around the world.

After a year in Venezuela, Vahey was in London, England teaching at the Southbank International School. He taught English to boys ages eleven to sixteen, most of whom were offspring of foreign business executives and diplomats. During his three-year tenure at Southbank, Vahey took students on numerous overnight field trips.

In August 2013, administrators at the American Nicaraguan School in Managua hired Vahey to teach ninth grade history. Two months later, Vahey accused his housemaid of theft and fired her. In February 2014, the maid went to the principal of the American Nicaraguan School with a thumb drive she had taken from Vahey's computer. The memory stick contained at least 90 images of boys between the ages 12 to 14 who were either asleep or unconscious.

William Vahey, when confronted by school authorities in possession of this evidence, confessed to drugging and sexually assaulting male students. Fired on the spot, the traveling teacher fled the country to avoid being arrested by Nicaraguan police.

A federal judge in Houston, Texas, on March 11, 2014, ruled that FBI agents could lawfully search Vahey's thumb drive. Two days later, in a Luverne, Minnesota hotel room, the 64-year-old pedophile committed suicide. During his tenure as a middle school teacher, Vahey had taught at ten private schools in nine countries. He also coached boy's basketball and took students on hundreds of overnight field trips.

At the time of Vahey's death, he owned a home in London, England and a house in Hilton Head, South Carolina. (I do not know if he was still married or if he had any children of his own.)

On April 23, 2014, a FBI spokesperson issued a statement that read: "This is one of the most prolific and heinous sexual predator cases we have seen. It appears Vahey was able to perfect his crimes in such a way that his victims were unable to report them. He has been teaching overseas the entire time. We strongly believe there are more victims. (I image that most of his former employers will not be eager to admit the commission of his sex crimes under their noses. As is so often the case, when suspicions arise, education administrators simply pass the trash to another school.)

Priests Who Molest Children

The Catholic Church

Contrary to most state laws, which criminalize sex with adolescents under 16 or 18, the Catholic Church considered [in the 1980s] the age of consent to be as young as 12. This provided a convenient rationale for the Milwaukee archbishop Rembert Weakland, who shifted the blame onto teenage victims in a 1988 article for *The Catholic Herald*. "Sometimes not all adolescent victims are so innocent," he opined. "Some can be sexually very active and aggressive and often quite streetwise."

Janet Reitman, *The New York Times Book Review*, March 2, 2014

Victim John Doe

In 2008, a 31-year-old major in the U. S. Air Force Reserves brought a sexual molestation suit against Father Michael Kelly, the 58-year-old pastor of St. Joachim's Catholic Church in Lockeford, California. The plaintiff, referred to as John TZ Doe pursuant to a court order not to reveal his identify, didn't remember being molested by Father Kelly until 2006. Although the statute of limitations ruled out criminal charges, a civil suit could be brought against the priest and the church.

In the lawsuit, John Doe accuses Father Kelly of molesting him in the 1980s when he was a 10-year-old altar boy at the Cathedral of the Annunciation in Stockton, California. In September 2007 following the recovery of his "repressed memory," John Doe had filed a complaint with Bishop Stephen Blaine of the Stockton Diocese. Father Kelly, placed on administrative leave, denied the allegations. Following an internal investigation by diocesan officials, Father Kelly, in March 2008, was re-instated at St. Joachim's Catholic Church.

The civil trial got underway on February 29, 2012 in the San Joaquin County Superior Court. Judge Bob McNatt had ruled that the jury could not be told that Father Kelly was the subject of a pending sexual molestation investigation being conducted by the Calaveras County Sheriff's Office. According to the criminal complaint, Father Kelly had molested a boy during the period 2000-2002 while he was pastor of St. Andrew's Parish in San Andreas, California. (In 2004, Father Kelly was transferred to St. Joachim's in Stockton. Prior to his tenure in San Andreas, Father Kelly had been pastor at churches in Sonora, Tracy, Modesto, and Ceres, California.)

Plaintiff's attorney John Manly put on several witnesses who, as boys in the defendant's churches, had been repeatedly tickled and wrestled with by the priest. According to this testimony, Father Kelly had sexually touched and fondled them during these bouts of roughhousing.

John Doe took the stand and spoke of being molested by the defendant on a walking trail outside of Stockton, in a motel room, and in the priest's living quarters. In the motel room, the plaintiff said he had fallen asleep, and when he awoke, he and the priest were in bed naked. At the defendant's living quarters, Father Kelly had removed the witness' clothing. John Doe said he then fell asleep, and when he awoke, he was fully dressed. (From this testimony, the plaintiff was asking jurors to infer that he had been drugged.) Pointing at Father Kelly, the witness yelled, "You raped me, I was just a kid!"

On March 20, San Francisco psychiatrist Anlee Kuo testified that she, in evaluating the reliability of John Doe's recovered memories of events that had occurred when he was 10-years-old, gave him several tests that measured the validity of his accounts. The results of these tests convinced her that these memories were accurate. Dr. Kuo pointed out that the American Psychiatric Association and the American Psychological Association recognized the repressed memory phenomenon. Moreover, she said that repressed memory is included in the Diagnostic and Statistical Manual of Mental Disorders. According to the psychiatrist, Father Kelly's sexual molestation caused the plaintiff, as a 35-year-old adult, to suffer from depression and alcohol abuse.

The next day, defense attorney Thomas Beatty put Father Kelly on the stand. The priest told the jury that he had *not* sexually molested the plaintiff. On cross-examination, John Manly, the plaintiff's attorney, asked Father Kelly this: "At any time did you get under a blanket with [the plaintiff]?"

"Of course not," came the reply.

"Did you ever take him into the bathroom to disrobe?"

"I absolutely deny it."

"Did you ever take the [plaintiff] on a hike?"

"I did not," answered the priest.

Dr. J. Alexander Bodkin of Harvard University took the stand for the defense. Dr. Bodkin told the jury that repressed memories--also known as dissociative memory--is not a scientifically proven phenomenon. "Peoples' memories don't get better with time," he said. "They get worse. The plaintiff's story is difficult to believe."

Following the lunch break on Friday, April 6, 2012, the case went to the jury of 10 women and 2 men. Because this was a civil trial, only 9 votes were required for the jury to reach a verdict. Moreover, the standard of proof in a civil trial is less rigorous than in a criminal proceeding that requires guilt beyond a reasonable doubt. In a civil trial, a plaintiff merely has to establish his case by a "preponderance of the evidence." That is, the plaintiff's allegations against the defendant are more likely to be true than not true.

After deliberating a day, the jury found Father Michael Kelly liable for three of the sexual molestation allegations. The second phase of the trial, with the same jury, focused on the dioceses' handling of child abuse allegations against Father Kelly and other priests. One of the other priests was Father Oliver O'Grady who was convicted of child molestation and possession of child pornography. The O'Grady case had cost the Diocese of Stockton millions of dollars in civil case settlements in more than 20 lawsuits.

In the John Doe case, the jury awarded the plaintiff $3.57 in damages. This, along with settlements, plunged the diocese into bankruptcy.

Immediately after the verdict, the Bishop removed Father Kelly from the ministry. Three hours later, speaking to 100 of his parishioners at St. Joachim's Church in Lockeford, the ex-priest said, "The charges against me are untrue." When Michael Kelly reminded his supporters that he had passed two polygraph tests, they cheered. Because polygraph test results are not admissible in court, the jury did not know this. But the jurors didn't know about the ongoing sexual molestation investigation involving Michael Kelly in Calaveras County. Under the laws of evidence, jurors, in making their decisions, are kept in the dark about a lot of things.

Michael Kelly, on April 15, flew to his native Ireland for what he described as needed medical treatment. He was under subpoena to testify the next day in the second phase of the lawsuit in Stockton. John Manly, the plaintiff's attorney, said that he believed the ex-priest received help in leaving the country. Kelly's attorney, Tom Beatty, said that he was "saddened by Father Kelly's illness and his devastation brought on by the finding of the repressed memory claim of abuse. I believe it is important for Father Kelly to be present during the damages phase of the case, but he feels he has lost everything already. I hope to talk to him shortly." John Manly said that whoever helped Kelly to escape out of the country could be arrested for aiding and abetting.

In January 2014, a California grand jury indicted the defrocked priest on several counts of child molestation. The prosecutor began the extradition process to get the ex-priest back from Ireland. As of August 2014, Father Kelly is still in Ireland.

A Franciscan Priest

In 1994, Robert Van Handel, a 48-year-old Franciscan priest and former rector at St. Anthony's Seminary School in Santa Barbara, California, pleaded guilty to sexually molesting an 8-year-old student. He had been accused of molesting 15 other boys between the ages 8 to 11, but those cases were too old to prosecute. In preparation for his sentencing hearing, the psychiatrist who evaluated Van Handel at the Pacific Treatment Associates in Santa Cruz, asked him to write a history of his sexual life. Van Handel complied, producing a detailed, 27-page memoir of a life devoted to sexually abusing boys.

Van Handel's revealing description of his perverted thoughts and behavior provides a rare look into the twisted mind and life of a sexual predator. The document didn't come to light until 2006, the year the Franciscans, in a civil court settlement, paid 25 clergy abuse victims $28 million in damages. The church, in an attempt to keep Van Handel's revelations from the public, fought several newspaper organizations all the way to the California Supreme Court. The church lost. What follows is Van Handel's account of his life as a priest, teacher, and pedophile.

In 1956, at age 10, Van Hendel and his family of seven settled in Orange County, California. Three years later, the 13-year-old, to escape his strict, demanding father who forced him to read a sex education manual that scared the hell out of him, enrolled in the Franciscan run St. Anthony's Seminary School in Santa Barbara. Two years later, while in the infirmary with a fever, a priest sexually molested him. According to the seminarian pedophile who attacked him, this activity would, by making the sick boy sweat, draw the fever out of him.

Over the next nine years, while at St Anthony's, Van Handel collected magazines featuring child pornography, and used a telephoto lens to take clandestine photographs of children. While he fantasized about having sex with young boys, Van Handel did not actually molest anyone during this period.

In 1970, at age 24, Van Handel moved to Berkeley, California to pursue his master's degree at the University of California. While there, he formed a neighborhood boy's choir and molested a 7-year-old choir member. He also, during this period, raped his 5-year-old nephew.

Robert Van Handel, as an ordained Franciscan priest, returned to St. Anthony's in 1975 where he taught English. He also became the director of the school choir. In his sexual memoir, the priest acknowledged that the school choir provided him with a steady supply of victims. An 11-year-old boy, a student he had been abusing since the child was 7, resisted for the first time after four years of molestation. In his memoir, Van Handel said that he was shocked by the rejection. He wrote, "He started to cry and that snapped something in my head. For the first time, I was seeing signs that he really did not like this." In another passage, the priest wrote: "There is something about me that is happier when accompanied by a small boy. Perhaps besides the sexual element, the child in me wants a playmate."

Van Handel's relationships with students and his choirboys exemplified typical pedophile behavior. The priest rubbed their backs, photographed them tied-up in ropes, wrestled with them, and invented tickling games. (The Penn State pedophile, Jerry Sandusky referred to himself the "tickle monster.") In his memoir of perversion, Van Handel, noted that the fact the boys couldn't stop him from doing what he wanted, turned him on. He wrote, "It was though I could do anything with them that I wanted."

In 1983, Robert Van Handel became rector of St. Anthony's. As head of this enclave of pedophilia, he was asked to investigate another priest who had been accused of molesting two boys who were brothers. As it turned out, Van Handel had also sexually assaulted these students.

Van Handel's tenure at St. Anthony's came to an end in 1992 when the parents of one of his victims wrote a letter to the head of the Franciscan order. Within months of this letter, Van Handel was removed from the ministry.

After the defrocked pedophile's guilty plea in 1994, the judge sentenced him to eight years in prison. The 67-year-old, now a registered sex offender, lives in Santa Cruz, California.

Assaulting Your Molester

More than 16,000 Americans have been sexually molested by Catholic clerics. These victims represent the tip of the iceberg of pedophilia in the Catholic Church. According to a study conducted by researchers at John Jay College in New York City, between 1950 and 2002, 4,392 Catholic priests have been accused of sexual abuse.

Jerold Lindner, accepted into Jesuit training in June 1964, was, at 24, sent to the Sacred Heart novitiate in Los Gatos, California for two years of study. Six years later he was in San Francisco teaching English at St. Ignatius High School. In 1973, after sexually assaulting a number of boys at St. Ignatius, Lindner enrolled at the Jesuit School of Theology in Berkeley, California.

In the summer of 1975, while still at the Berkeley theology school, Lindner, as a "spiritual advisor" for the lay organization Christian Family Movement, accompanied a group of young boys on a church-sponsored camping trip to the Santa Cruz Mountains. During that weekend Lindner shared a tent with 7-year-old William Lynch and his 4-year-old brother Buddy. The spiritual advisor sodomized both boys, forced them to give him oral sex, then threatened to kill their sister if they told anyone what he had done to them. Lindner also promised the boys an eternity in hell if they squealed.

By 1976, the year the 36-year-old was ordained as a Jesuit priest, Father Jerry, as he was called, had molested dozens of boys. That year Father Jerry returned to St. Ignatius High School where he continued his career as an English teacher and a practicing pedophile. In 1982, the Catholic Church transferred Father Lindner to Loyola High School, a private prep school near downtown Los Angeles. Ten years later, while teaching at Loyola and molesting more of his students, Lindner's mother, aware that her son was a pedophile, spoke to Father Jerry's supervisor at his order--the Society of Jesus--and told him that Lindner had been a child molester long before he entered Jesuit training in 1964. Mrs. Lindner informed the supervising priest that her son had molested several members of his family, including a younger sibling.

In response to accusations of child molestation by the priest's own mother, the Jesuits took Father Lindner out of the classroom and sent him to a psychiatric facility for evaluation. Whatever the results of that psychiatric analysis, the Jesuit brass declared that Mrs. Lindner's allegations were not credible, and sent their pedophile teacher back into the classroom where he could continue preying on vulnerable victims. (This was not be the first time the Jesuits had Father Jerry psychiatrically tested, then declared suitable for classroom work.)

In 1995, twenty years after the weekend of sexual abuse in the spiritual advisor's tent on the Santa Cruz Mountain camping trip, William Lynch's younger brother, for the first time since their ordeal, revealed their secret. He told his parents what happened to them in Father Lindner's tent. Two years later, the Lynch brothers sued Lindner and the Society of Jesus. (Criminal prosecution, because of the statute of limitations, was no longer an option. The 6-year-stautue of limitations in California had protected Lindner from being criminally charged by dozens of his victims.)

To avoid an embarrassing and revealing civil trial, the Jesuits settled the lawsuit for $625,000. (After legal costs, William and his brother ended up with $187,000 a piece.) Following the settlement, the Society of Jesus removed the 58-year-old priest from active ministry. But Lindner still had access to children, and the complaints kept rolling in.

In September 2002, the Jesuits at the Society of Jesus sent Father Lindner to a Catholic retirement home and medical center for priests in Los Gatos called the Scared Heart Jesuit Center. Several of the priests in this place had been sent there because they were known pedophiles. Father Lindner was one of the residents placed on the institution's child molester register. However, he still had access to young people, and continued to offend.

It was not surprising, that in a facility where pedophiles are housed, there was a sex scandal. In 2002, it came to light that two developmentally disabled men who lived at the Sacred Heart Jesuit Center for 30 years had been regularly molested by priests they considered their friends. Two years after the scandal broke, a priest at the Los Gatos facility committed suicide after being raped by a gang of Jesuits. The order avoided an even bigger scandal by paying off several civil suit plaintiffs with million-dollar settlement.

William Lynch, the man Father Lindner had sexually abused as a 7-year-old in 1975, had not gotten over his ordeal. As a fourth grader in Los Altos, California, Lynch started smoking marijuana. By the seventh grade he was dealing in pot, and drinking heavily. At age 15, Lynch tried to kill himself by slashing his wrists, and as a adult, the victim of Father Lindner's sexual assault suffered severe depression. In his thirties, Lynch once again attempted suicide. Aware that the man who had ruined his life back in 1975 continued to abuse children under the protection of the church, Lynch could barely control his frustration and rage. By 2010, at age 42, Lynch decided to turn the tables on Father Jerry by becoming the predator.

On May 10, 2010, William Lynch used a false name and the pretense of notifying Father Lindner of a death in the priest's family, to meet with him in the guest parlor at Sacred Heart Jesuit Center in Los Gatos. When the two men came fact-to-face after all of these years, Lynch told the 65-year-old to take off his glasses. As he punched the priest in the head and body, Lynch asked him, "Do you recognize me?" After the beating that included several attempts to kick Lindner in the groin, Lynch said, "Turn yourself in or I'll come back and kill you."

After the attack, William Lynch made no attempt to conceal what he had done. The Santa Clara County prosecutor had no choice but to charge him with one count of assault, and one count of elder abuse. If convicted of both felonies, Lynch faced up to four years in prison.

After turning down a plea bargain in which he would serve no more than a year in jail, Lynch told reporters, "I want to take responsibility for what I've done. I don't think I'm above the law like the church and Father Jerry." Lynch said he looked forward to a trial in which the pedophile priest would be publicly exposed for what he was.

William Lynch's assault trial got under way on Wednesday, June 20, 2012 in the Santa Clara County Superior Court in San Jose. Prosecutor Vicki Genetti, in her opening statement to the jury of 9 men and 3 women, said she was prosecuting this defendant under the assumption that Father Jerold Lindner, the victim in the assault case, had in fact sexually molested Lindner and his brother back in 1975. And in an even more unusual remark for a prosecutor to make about one of her own witnesses, Genetti warned jurors that Father Lindner, in denying the allegations, would be not be telling the truth. The prosecutor labeled the assault in this case a "revenge attack." Defendant Lynch, Genetti said, had acted like a "vigilante."

On the first day of the trial, following the opening statements, Genetti put the prosecution's chief witness, Father Jerold Lindner, on the stand. As expected, the 67-year-old priest, overweight and wearing old-fashioned horn-rimmed glasses, denied sexually molesting the defendant and his brother. The witness said he had done nothing in 1975 to justify his beating at the hands of Mr. Lynch.

After the jurors were dismissed for the day, William Lynch's attorney, Pat Harris, said this to Judge David A. Cena: "He [Father Lindner] has chosen to perjure himself. He should be advised of his right to counsel." The judge said he would take the request under advisement.

The next day, before the defense attorney's cross-examination of Lindner, the priest took the Fifth, and refused to testify further. At this point attorney Harris moved for a mistrial on the grounds he had been denied his right to question his client's accuser. Judge Cena denied the motion, and the trial continued. Judge Cena also ruled that the jury would not hear from three witnesses prepared to testify regarding their childhood molestations by Jerold Lindner. The judge ordered the jury to disregard Lindner's testimony altogether.

The next day, prosecutor Genetti put a Sacred Heart Jesuit Center health care worker on the stand that had witnessed the assault. Mary Eden testified that she heard William Lynch scream that Lindner had raped him and his brother, and had ruined their lives. When it came time for the defense to present its case, William Lynch took the stand, and in great detail, told the jurors what the priest had done to him and his brother, and how the sexual assaults had affected their lives. According to the defendant, when he went to the Sacred Heart Jesuit Center that day, his intention was to get Lindner to take responsibility for what he had done by signing a written confession. When Lindner refused, and looked as though he might become aggressive, Lynch resorted to violence. (With this testimony, the defense was giving the jurors an opportunity, an excuse if you will, to nullify the evidence, and find Lynch not guilty.)

Following William Lynch's compelling testimony, the defense rested its case. Prosecutor Genetti, in her closing remarks to the jury, said that what Lindner had done to the defendant and his brother 37 years ago did not legally justify the assault. The prosecutor also accused the defense of encouraging the jurors to return a "nullified" verdict, one that ignored the evidence against the defendant.

On Thursday, July 5, the jury, in this difficult and unusual case, found William Lynch not guilty of felony assault and elder abuse. By this verdict, the jury sent a clear message to priests who get away with molesting b

oys. If as adults their victims hunt them down and beat them up, tough luck.

Pedophile Priests in Chicago

After a 13-year-old boy reported in 1979 that a priest raped and threatened him at gunpoint to keep quiet, the Archdiocese of Chicago assured the boy's parents that, although the cleric avoided prosecution, he would receive treatment and have no further contact with minors.

But the Reverend William Cloutier, who already had been accused of molesting other children, was returned to the ministry a year later and went on to abuse again before he resigned in 1993, two years after the boy's parents filed a lawsuit. Officials took no action against Cloutier over his earlier transgressions because he "sounded repentant," according to internal archdiocese documents released January 21, 2014 that show how the archdiocese tried to contain a mounting scandal over child sexual abuse.

For decades, those at the highest levels of the nation's third largest archdiocese moved accused priests from parish to parish while hiding the clerics' histories from the public.

The Associated Press, January 21, 2014

6 POLICE SHOOTINGS

Police Shooting Statistics: 2011

In 2011, according to data I collected from news reports, police officers in the United States shot 1,146 people, killing 607 of them. Between January 1, 2011 and January 1, 2012 I used the Internet to compile a national database of police involved shootings. The term "police involved shooting" pertains to law enforcement officers who, in the line of duty, discharge their guns. When journalists and police administrators use the term, they include the shooting of animals and shots that miss their targets. My case files only included instances in which a person was either killed or wounded by police gunfire. My data also included off-duty officers who discharged their weapons in law enforcement situations. They didn't include, for example, officers using their firearms to resolve personal disputes.

I collected this data myself because the U.S. Government doesn't. There is no national database dedicated to police involved shootings. Alan Maimon, in his article, "National Data on Shootings by Police Not Collected," published on November 28, 2011 in the *Las Vegas Review-Journal* wrote "The nation's leading law enforcement agency [FBI] collects vast amounts of information on crime nationwide, but missing from this clearinghouse are statistics on where, how often, and under what circumstances police use deadly force. In fact, no one anywhere comprehensively tracks the most significant act police can do in the line of duty: take a life."

Since the government keeps statistics on just about everything, why no national stats on something this important? The answer is simple: they don't want us to know. Why? Because police shoot a lot more people than we think, and the government, while good at statistics, is also good at secrecy.

The government does maintain records on how many police officers are killed every year in the line of duty. In 2010, 59 officers were shot to death among 122 killed while on the job. This marked a 20 percent jump from 2009 when 49 officers were killed by gunfire. In 2011, 173 officers died, from all causes, in the line of duty. The fact police officers feel they are increasingly under attack from the public may help explain why they are shooting so many citizens.

A vast majority of the people shot by the police in 2011 were men between the ages 25 and 40 who had histories of crime. Overall, people shot by the police were much older than the typical first-time arrestee. A significant number of the people wounded and killed by the authorities were over fifty and a few were eighty or older. In 2011, the police shot two 15-year-olds and a girl who was 16.

The police shot, in 2011, about 50 women, most of who were armed with knives and had histories of emotional distress. Overall, about a quarter of those shot were either mentally ill and/or suicidal. Many of these were "suicide-by-cop" cases.

Most police shooting victims were armed with handguns. The next most common weapon involved vehicles (used as weapons), followed by knives (and other sharp objects), shotguns, and rifles. Very few of these people carried assault weapons, and a small percentage were unarmed. About 50 subjects were armed with BB-guns, pellet guns or replica firearms.

The situations that brought police shooters and their targets together included domestic and other disturbances; crimes in progress such as robbery, assault and carjacking; the execution of arrest warrants; drug raids; gang activities; routine traffic stops; car chases; and standoff and hostage events.

Women make up about 15 percent of the nation's uniformed police services. During 2011, about 25 female police officers wounded or killed civilians. None of these officers had shot anyone in the past. While the vast majority of police officers never fire their guns in the line of duty, 15 officers who did shoot someone in 2011, had shot at least one person before. (This figure is probably low because police departments don't like to report such statistics.) Most police shootings involved members of police departments followed by sheriff's deputies, the state police, and federal officers. These shootings took place in big cities, suburban areas, towns, and in rural areas. Big city shootings comprised about half of these violent confrontations in 2011.

Almost all police-involved shootings, investigated by special units, prosecutors' offices and outside police agencies are investigated by government law enforcement personnel. It is perhaps not surprising that more than 95 percent of all police involved shootings were ruled administratively and legally justified. A handful of cases led to wrongful death lawsuits. Even fewer will result in the criminal prosecution of officers.

Critics of the system have called for the establishment of completely independent investigative agencies in cases of police involved shootings.

Most Deadly States

California 183 total (102 fatal)
Florida 96 (49)
Illinois 64 (26)
Texas 58 (26)
New York 49 (23)
Pennsylvania 49 (23)
Ohio 45 (28)
Arizona 45 (27)
Maryland 41 (16)
Washington 39 (29)

Least Deadly States

Delaware 0
Vermont 0
North Dakota 1
Wyoming 2 (1)
Alaska 2 (2)
Montana 3 (2)
South Dakota 3 (3)
Hawaii 4 (3)
Connecticut 6 (1)
West Virginia 6 (5)
New Hampshire 6 (5)
Idaho 7 (2)
Kansas 7 (5)

Most Deadly Cities

Chicago 46 total (10 fatal)
Los Angeles 22 (14)
Philadelphia 17 (7)
Las Vegas 17 (15)
New York City 16 (6)
Phoenix 15 (10)
Baltimore 15 (5)
Columbus, OH 14 (8)
Atlanta 12 (4)

St. Louis 11 (3)
Cleveland 10 (7)
Miami 10 (6)
Houston 10 (3)

Least Deadly Cities

Boston 1
New Orleans 1 (1)
Portland, ME 1
Buffalo 2
Detroit 2 (1)
Seattle 2 (1)
Denver 2 (2)
Pittsburgh 3 (1)

Cities with High Per Capita Shooting Rates

Fresno, CA 9 total (4 fatal)
Tucson, AZ 8 (6)
Aurora, CO 7 (6)
Oakland, CA 7 (6)
San Jose, CA 7 (3)
Albuquerque, NM 6 (5)
Mesa, AZ 6 (2)
Jacksonville, FL 5 (4)
Syracuse, NY 5 (3)
Orlando, FL 5 (2)
N. Miami Beach, FL 5 (2)
Little Rock, Ark. 5 (1)
Yakima, WA 4 (1)
Bakersfield, CA 4 (3)
Long Beach, CA 4 (2)
Garden Grove, CA 4 (3)
Redding, CA 4 (2)

Extra Rights For Police Officers

After a police-involved shooting, the Santa Barbara Police Department policy states that the officer must request a supervisor, additional units and medical personnel, handcuff the suspect, preserve the scene and identify witnesses. Officers cannot discuss the shooting with one another or write about the incident. Instead, the supervisor asks the officer for a description of the outstanding suspects, where the evidence is and what direction shots were fired. Among other duties, the supervisor is there to secure the crime scene and determine whether other suspects are at large and witnesses are being interviewed. He or she is not authorized to inquire about the involved officer's tactics and state of mind, according to the police manual. The police chief is the only one authorized to release the officer's identify.

To the question of who holds police accountable, in Santa Barbara, California, an officer-involved investigation is done internally....

An administrative investigation follows the [internal] investigation to ensure all department policies were met and to evaluate the officer's civil liability and examine training procedures. At this point, the investigation becomes a human resources issue with information gathered not permissible in court. The administrative investigation is considered a *"confidential peace officer personnel file,"* according to the manual....

Some bigger cities do have independent [police-involved shooting] oversight. Los Angeles, Oakland, Berkeley and San Francisco have implemented police commissions that include citizen oversight of police matters, especially deadly force issues. Smaller cities with fewer officer-involved incidents, such as Santa Barbara, generally don't....

Alex Kacik, missionandstate.org, January 8, 2014

Killing an Unarmed Woman

In June 2010, police in Brunswick, Georgia approached 35-year-old Carolyn M. Small who was sitting in her 1991 Buick smoking dope. When the suspect spotted the approaching officers she drove off. During the low-speed pursuit with Carolyn Small driving erratically on and off the road, officers flattened her front tires with stop sticks then forced her off the street into a telephone pole where she sat trapped inside her car. As a pair of Glynn County officers walked toward her car with their guns drawn, Small began rocking the car back and forth to get free. At that point the officers fired eight bullets at the unarmed woman. One of the slugs hit her in the face.

An ambulance rushed Carolyn Small to the hospital where a week later, while on life-support, she died. In response to the question of why these officers had shot at this woman, the answer was predictable: because she was using her car as a deadly weapon, they feared for their lives.

An internal police review of the shootings found that the officers, in using deadly force, had acted within departmental guidelines. A Glynn County grand jury heard the case and returned a no bill. No criminal wrongdoing here. The Georgia Bureau of Investigation took up the case and agreed with the county police that the officers had been justified in killing this woman.

In response to an open records request filed by The Florida Times-Union (Jacksonville), the Georgia Bureau of Investigation released the dashboard-camera video of the chase and the shooting. After shooting Small, neither officer rushed to check if she was alive. One of the officers said, "I hit her in the face...Right on the bridge of the nose."

"I think I fired twice," said the other officer.

A wrongful death lawsuit was filed against the officers and Glynn County by Carolyn Small's daughters aged five and twelve.

Police officers rarely shoot women, and when they do, it is usually because they are threatened with a knife wielded by someone mentally ill. What isn't rare is the justification for the Carolyn Small shooting. The vehicle, as a deadly weapon against the police, is more frequently cited as the justification for deadly force than the possession of knives, shotguns, rifles, and blunt objects added together.

In August 2011, a Glynn County Grand Jury cleared the officers of wrongdoing in the Carolyn Small case. A year later, members of Small's family filed a federal wrongful death suit against the county. The civil case is pending.

A Tragic Accident

At three in the morning of August 30, 2009, 45-year-old James Lee Whitehead, a well-known female impersonator in San Antonio, Texas, was walking home from his waiter's job in the city. Wearing men's clothing at the time, Whitehead was set upon by three assailants who demanded money and knocked him to the ground. Witnesses called 911 and within minutes San Antonia patrol officer William Karman arrived at the scene. Two of the muggers jumped into a nearby car and fled.

The third mugger, 22-year-old Jesse Ramon, intoxicated and high on marijuana, remained behind and pistol-whipped Whitehead. Officer Karman repeatedly ordered Ramon to drop his weapon. Instead, Ramon approached the officer with his handgun drawn. When Ramon ignored Karman's demands to drop the gun, the officer fired two shots, both bullets striking, but not stopping the subject. Karman fired three more times. Two of those bullets hit Ramon the third went into and killed the victim, Mr. Whitehead.

Shot four times, Ramon remained in a coma for more than a month but survived.

In September 2011, Ramon went on trial for criminally causing Mr.

Whitehead's death under the felony-murder doctrine that criminally holds a felon responsible for any death related directly to his felony. In this case, Mr. Whitehead had been killed as a result of Ramon's robbery and his threatening behavior toward the police officer. On October 29, the jury, after deliberating thirty minutes, found Ramon guilty of murder. A few days later the jury sentenced Ramon to forty years in prison.

Officer Karman, to save his own life, had no choice but to use deadly force. The shooting of Mr. Whitehead was a tragic accident. The fact the victim died from a single bullet and Ramon, his assailant, survived four, shows just how unfair life can be. While Ramon may regret the incident because he got caught, the police officer will struggle a long time with the outcome of his justifiable act.

Victimized by Crooks and Cops

David Sturdivant, a 64-year-old ex-Marine (Purple Heart/Vietnam) was doing okay in Atlanta, Georgia. He lived alone in a two-story house, and worked in his own engine repair shop attached to his dwelling. Mr. Sturdivant had recently been the victim of neighborhood burglars who had broken into his shop and swiped his HAM radio, various electronic items, a couple of riding mowers, and his tools. Things had gotten worse when thieves stole his two antique Thunderbirds.

After awakening from a nap at one o'clock in the afternoon on April 8, 2011, Mr. Sturdivant looked out his second-story window and saw a pickup owned by Dennis Alexander, its tailgate open, parked near a riding mower in the shop for repair. To Mr. Sturdivant, it looked like Mr. Alexander, a man with a criminal history of burglary and theft, was about to steal the mower. David Sturdivant stepped out onto his balcony and yelled, "Get off my property and stop stealing my stuff!" When Alexander mocked the property owner, Sturdivant entered his house and returned with a commercial grade M-14 rifle. From the balcony he fired one bullet into the ground to frighten Alexander off the property.

Close by, Atlanta police officers working with a television crew filming a segment for the reality TV show "Bait Car" heard the shot. In less than two minutes they were on the scene shouting at Sturdivant to drop his rifle. Without taking the time to fully comprehend the situation, three officers fired fourteen shots at Mr. Sturdivant. One of the bullets tore into his stomach. Mr. Sturdivant had not shot at the officers, and had not pointed his rifle at them.

A week after the shooting, hospital personnel discharged Mr. Sturdivant. He rolled out of the hospital in a wheelchair less one kidney and missing several inches of his colon. Police officers immediately took him into custody and hauled him off to the Fulton County Jail in his wheelchair. The district attorney charged Sturdivant with four counts of aggravated assault for pointing his gun at the police officers. He also stood accused of aggravated assault for shooting at the suspected thief, and for possession of a weapon in the commission of a crime. If convicted of all charges Mr. Sturdivant faced up to 105 years in prison.

While Mr. Sturdivant recovered from his bullet wound in the jail's hospital ward, looters cleaned out his house and business then burned the dwelling and shop to the ground.

At a preliminary hearing on October 27, 2011, Sturdivant turned down the district attorney's offer of a probated sentence in return for a misdemeanor plea. Claiming total innocence, the defendant rejected the plea bargain. On November 11, a judge tossed out the prosecutor's case against Mr. Sturdivant. After serving seven months in the county slammer, Mr. Sturdivant was free. But he had nowhere to go except the local VA hospital.

Mr. Sturdivant lost his house, his business, his household belongings, his antique cars, his tools, his kidney, and a piece of his colon. The man had no family, poor health, and no future.

Shooting Kids: Three Cases

January 4, 2011
Chicago, Illinois

Officers patrolling a west side neighborhood for gang and drug activity spotted a car that matched the description of a vehicle believed to be carrying guns and narcotics. As one of the officers approached the pulled-over car, the driver put it in reverse and rammed the police cruiser. The officer behind the wheel fired his gun as the suspect lurched forward and brushed the other officer. When the passenger in the suspect car pulled a gun, the officer on foot shot him and the driver.

The wounded suspects turned out to be a pair of 15-year-old boys. After a couple of days in the hospital, the teenagers were charged with aggravated battery and sent to a juvenile detention center. Given the circumstances of the case, no one objected when the authorities ruled this police involved shooting justified.

March 14, 2011
Lansing, Michigan

When the intrusion alarm at the Bank of America went off at 3:30 in the morning, five police officers responded to the scene. After discovering the place where the burglar had broken in, three of the officers entered the bank. Two of the officers encountered the intruder hiding in a small storage room. The cornered bank burglar turned out to be 17-year-old Derrinesha Clay. The five foot four, 120-pound girl, wearing a black winter coat with a fur-trimmed hood, black sweatpants over jeans, and a multicolored backpack, brandished a pair of scissors.

Lansing police officer Brian Rendon ordered Clay to drop the weapon. When she didn't, he grabbed her by the wrist. The girl put up a fight, and she, Rendon, and another officer ended up on the floor. As the officers tried to handcuff the burglar, she pulled out a serrated steak knife and took a swipe at Rendon, cutting the front of his coat. From a foot away, Rendon pulled his .45-caliber Glock and fired twice, hitting the black girl in the head and stomach as she knelt in front of him. The girl died at the scene.

In 2005, Officer Rendon shot and killed a pit bull, and three years later, shot and wounded a man who came at him with a knife. He was cleared on both shootings. Investigators with the Michigan State Police found that in the Clay shooting, Officer Rendon's deadly force was a "justifiable act of self-defense." The prosecutor's office agreed, therefore no criminal charges have been filed against Officer Rendon.

Derrinesha Clay had been in trouble with the law before. Police had recently arrested her for committing a pair of home invasions. She had also been diagnosed with attention-deficit hyperactivity disorder, and may have been bipolar.

Critics of the police shooting believed the girl's death could have been avoided. The officer, they said, could have backed off without risking his life. Why didn't he use a Taser gun to subdue her? In September 2011, the dead girl's mother, Mary Rush, filed a federal lawsuit in the U. S. District Court in Grand Rapids against Officer Rendon and the city of Lansing. The plaintiff accused the defendants of gross negligence, battery, and civil rights violations. Regardless of the outcome of this case, the incident strained relations between the police department and the city's minority community.

January 4, 2012
Brownsville, Texas

At eight in the morning, a school administrator at the Cummings Middle School, spotted a student who possessed what looked like a handgun partially concealed under his shirt. The boy stood in the hallway outside of the main office. A few days earlier, 15-year-old Jaime Gonzales had been in a fight with another boy. The concerned school official dialed 911.

Gonzales, when approached by several police officers, drew his gun. One of the officers yelled, "Take him out!" When the kid refused to lower his weapon, the police, armed with automatic rifles, shot him in the chest and in the back of the head, killing him instantly.

The weapon Gonzales pointed at the police turned out to be a pellet gun that looked like the real thing. The dead student's parents protested the shooting, and called for an independent investigation. But in the light of school shootings that have resulted in the deaths of so many students and teachers, it's hard to fault the police in this case. Hindsight is one thing, but these officers had to make a split-second shoot/don't shoot decision. Based on news reportage of this case, it seems justified even though the boy was fifteen, and armed with just a pellet gun.

Arming Teachers

What's easier--turning a law enforcement officer into a schoolteacher, or converting an educator into a cop? In the wake of the Newtown elementary school mass murder, a few politicians and a handful of education administrators have proposed that the police provide schoolteachers with firearms training. These teachers, under this proposal, would not be packing heat primarily for self-protection. They would be carrying guns to protect students against armed killers. This responsibility would essentially turn them into peace officers. That's a bad idea because there's a lot more to law enforcement that knowing how to fire a gun. Criminals and homicidal nut cases know how to fire guns. That doesn't make them cops.

Teaching a person how to shoot a gun more or less accurately is not that difficult. But finding the right person to arm, then training that individual when to use deadly force, requires more than a few shooting lessons. Every year, trained and experienced law enforcement officers shoot unarmed people. If police officers can make use-of-force mistakes, one can only image how many teacher cops would shoot the wrong person. Shoot or don't shoot situations often require spit-second decision-making under extremely difficult circumstances.

Just being a competent teacher in today's environment of difficult parents and troublesome students is tough enough. The added life and death responsibility of protecting kids from armed intruders would turn some of these cops-with-a-gun into mental cases. Empowering teachers who are not allowed to lay a hand on unruly students to blow away armed intruders is a formula for insanity. An insane teacher who is armed to the teeth is not my idea of how to make schools safer.

Every year, hundreds of gun owners shoot themselves, and people close to them, accidentally. Guns have a way of going off when they're not supposed to. Even trained police officers unintentionally shoot themselves when cleaning their weapons, or when practicing at firing ranges. In law enforcement, they refer to these embarrassing incidents as accidental discharges. Inside a school building, an accidental discharge could result in the death of a student.

Those who propose putting guns into the hands of schoolteachers haven't said how many educators should be issued weapons. There are about 100,000 schools in the U.S. So if just five teachers in any given school carry guns, that's 500,000 armed teachers. With a half million amateur cops walking around our schools with loaded weapons, these places, still safe havens for children, would become a lot less secure. (Studies have repeatedly shown than children are safer in schools than at home.)

I would argue that any schoolteacher willing to volunteer to be the front-line defense against a heavily armed intruder intent on mass murder, should quit teaching and join a SWAT team. Teacher-cops will not only make schools more dangerous, they'll make public education worse than it already is. (I'm also against placing armed security guards into schools. If these people were capable of professional law enforcement work, they would be cops. But at least school guards don't have to protect *and* teach.)

Bad ideas--so-called solutions that make the problem worse--often arise in the wake of disasters like the one in Newtown. Arming teachers is a bad idea.

The Trigger-Happy Constable

On November 2, 2011, at 3:30 in the afternoon, Jefferson County Constable David Whitlock, while shopping in a Louisville, Kentucky Walmart where he worked off-duty as a retail security officer, received a call on his cellphone regarding a possible shoplifter. Constable Whitlock approached the suspect Tammy Lee Jamian, aka Tammy Ortiz, as she sat in her car in the parking lot. When Whitlock reached the vehicle, the suspect started to drive away. Her car ran over Whitlock's foot so he shot her in the arm and hand.

In Kentucky, constables were elected under the state constitution that gave them powers of arrest in the enforcement of traffic laws. They also served certain types of warrants. Whitlock, in 2000 and 2002, had been charged in a couple of theft cases. Other law enforcement officers had criticized him for carrying a gun without the proper firearms training. In Kentucky, constables were not required to undergo special law enforcement instruction. Whitlock claimed, however, to have taken 122 hours of deadly force classes. According to a Jefferson County Sheriff's Deputy, Whitlock failed the shooting portion of the course and was sent home.

In a newspaper interview following the Walmart shooting, Whitlock told the reporter he spent 20 to 25 hours a week writing citations for illegal parking in fire lanes and handicapped spots. He also patrolled Louisville making sure addresses were visible on buildings as required by law.

Tammy Lee Jamian, who has an arrest record for burglary, theft, and prostitution, claimed she was not shoplifting in the store and that Constable Whitlock, when he confronted her in the parking lot, did not identify himself as a police officer. She drove off because she thought she was being mugged. Referring to Whitlock, Jamian's attorney told a reporter "This cowboy shot an unarmed woman for shoplifting. He didn't know if she was Bonnie from Bonnie and Clyde or Sister Teresa. He just shot her."

On November 11, Louisville Councilman Rick Blackwell called for the state legislature to remove Whitlock as a Jefferson County Constable. According to the councilman, Whitlock violated three state laws: deputizing staff members, failing to file monthly reports to the county clerk, and using oscillating blue lights on his car.

In October 2012, pursuant to his guilty plea to charges of wanton endangerment and second-degree assault, Whitlock agreed never to work in law enforcement again. After he completed a diversion program, the prosecutor dropped the charges against the former constable.

In Louisville, on January 27, 2014, David Whitlock announced his plan to run for a seat on the Metro Council.

Cops Shooting Cops: Two Cases

Santa Monica, California

Albert Covarrabias, Jr., a high school graduate, joined the Santa Maria Police Department in 2007. The Santa Barbara County town of 100,000, 170 miles northwest of Los Angeles, is home to 70,000 Hispanics. In 2011, Covarrabias' wife committed suicide. The 29-year-old patrolman, in mid-January of this year, married again.

A couple of weeks following his wedding, officer Covarrabias learned that members of his own department were investigating him for having sexual relations with a minor. (In California, the age of consent is 18, unless the parties are within 3 years of each other in age.) The alleged victim, a 17-year-old girl, was a member of the police department's Explorer program. (A police cadet.)

On January 27, 2012, after intercepting and recording a 15-minute phone conversation between Covarrabias and the 17-year-old, Santa Maria investigators decided to take their fellow officer into custody. According to police accounts of the intercepted conversation, Covarrabias told the girl to deny their relationship, and to implicate someone else. He said he'd kill himself before he went to jail, and threatened her if she revealed their secret.

At one o'clock the next morning, as officer Covarrabias was dismantling a DUI check-point in anticipation of going off duty, he was approached by his cousin Chris Nartatez, a Santa Maria sergeant, and officer Matt Kline, his best-friend on the force who had been his best man at the January wedding. When informed he was under arrest in connection with his alleged sexual relationship with the minor, Covarrabias backed away and reached for his gun.

The arresting officers charged Covarrabias, and as they wrestled on the ground, the arrestee managed to draw his weapon and fire four shots. Officer Kline pulled his gun and shot Covarrabias in the chest. The wounded officer died a few hours later while undergoing emergency surgery.

Santa Maria police chief Danny Macagni placed officers Kline and Nartatez on paid administrative leave as investigators with the Santa Barbara Sheriff's Office looked into the case.

The fatal shooting of officer Covarrabias by one of his own, outraged a large segment of the community. Santa Maria police officers have received death threats, and critics of the shooting have called for the chief of police to step down. On February 15, the Santa Maria Officers Association (a police union), called for a "vote of no confidence" against Chief Macagni who has insisted that the actions of officers Kline and Nartatez were morally, administratively, and legally justified. (These officers were not welcome at Covarrabias' funeral.)

The results of the no confidence vote have, as of this writing, not been made public. If a chief of police loses the support and confidence of the rank and file, he cannot effectively run the department. Based upon what has been reported in the media, the shooting of officer Covarrabias seems perfectly justified. However, if the chief loses support of his department and the community, he will have to go. At this point, the Covarrabias shooting case seemed more about identity politics than the use of deadly force.

Long Beach, California

The Los Angeles area's Immigration and Customs Enforcement (ICE) office is housed on the 7th floor of the federal building in Long Beach, a town 20 miles south of Los Angeles. As one of the federal agencies that make up the Department of Homeland Security, ICE came into existence in 2003 when two existing organizations--the Department of Justice's Immigrations and Naturalization Service (INS), and the Treasury Department's Customs Bureau--merged. Agents in the combined agencies had to be cross-trained to do the other bureaus' work. Agents, however, remained loyal to their old bureaus, and this has created internal rivalries and resentments that have been difficult to resolve. Administratively speaking, it was not a good marriage.

Late Thursday afternoon, February 16, 2012, 51-year-old Kevin Kozak, the Deputy Special Agent in charge of ICE's Los Angeles office, a former

Customs Bureau agent, was meeting with 45-year-old special agent Ezequiel Garcia. The purpose of the meeting involved the former INS agent's job performance. Kozak had earlier denied Garcia's request for an office transfer that had created animosity on his part. (In 2005, Garcia and another ICE agent had sued the Los Angeles Police Department after they had been roughed-up when working undercover. The plaintiffs lost the suit.)

The office job performance meeting, at 5:30 PM, turned violent when Agent Garcia pulled his service weapon. Agent Kozak grabbed the gun, and as the two men struggled for control of the weapon, Kozak was shot in the upper torso, legs, and hands--six times in all. Agent Perry Woo, who happened to be in the vicinity, shot and killed Agent Garcia. Paramedics rushed Kevin Kozak, severely wounded but alive, to a nearby hospital where, as of this writing, he remains in stable condition.

T. J. Bonner, a retired U.S. Border Patrol Agent who has worked with ICE, has described the agency's formation as a hostile takeover. Since its creation, the agency has seen several scandals involving agents arrested for drug dealing, obstruction of justice, embezzlement, and other crimes. ICE agents have also been accused of having improper sexual relations with informants.

Dangerous Cops

A narcotics officer with the North Little Rock (Arkansas) Police Department received information on December 20, 2007 that a woman known only as Kate was selling methamphetamine out of the house at 400 East 21st Street. The confidential informant who said he'd purchased meth there, didn't know who owned the dwelling, if other people lived there, how much drug activity was going on at that location, or anything about Kate other than she usually carried a gun. A judge, relying entirely on this sketchy report from a confidential informant, issued a nighttime no-knock warrant to search the house.

At 7:40 PM, 17 days after the judge issued the warrant, Tracy Ingle, a 40-year-old former stonemason with a bad back, was asleep in his first floor bedroom in the back of the house at 400 East 21st Street. Mr. Ingle awoke with a start at the sound of a SWAT battering ram breaking down his front door. He instinctively reached for his pistol, the unloaded and broken handgun he kept at his bedside to scare off intruders. This would not be the first time burglars had broken into his home. Suddenly, a flash bang grenade came though the window near his bed, filling the room with blinding light. The SWAT officer who climbed into the bedroom through the broken window yelled, "He's got a gun!" That's when the shooting started. The first bullet, fired from a .223-caliber semiautomatic rifle, tore into Ingle's left leg just above the knee. As he dropped to the floor, SWAT officers outside the window fired 20 more shots, hitting Ingle in the arm, calf, hip, and chest. Moments later, several officers were in the room. One of the officers kept referring to Ingle as Michael or Mike. Before being rushed to the Baptist Health Hospital, Ingle said, "My name is not Mike."

The police did not find methamphetamine or any other illegal drug at Tracy Ingle's house. They didn't find Kate, whoever she was, or any incriminating evidence in Ingle's car. They did seize a digital scale and a few small, plastic bags, common household items they designated as drug paraphernalia. Ingle's sister, a surgical nurse who made jewelry as a hobby, told the police the scale and little bags belonged to her.

Because the police had broken into Ingle's house and shot him five times, then failed to find the drugs they had raided the house for, they had to charge him with something. And they did: two counts of aggravated assault for picking up the handgun in self- defense, and felony possession of drug paraphernalia. The North Little Rock police, in a botched drug raid, had almost killed a citizen who had never been convicted of a felony. Instead of apologizing for their shoddy, reckless work, and overaggressive tactics, they wanted to send Tracy Ingle to prison.

Ten days after the shooting, the hospital discharged Ingle from the intensive care unit. Police officers immediately picked him up and drove him to the police station. For the next six hours, detectives grilled Ingle without an attorney present. From the interrogation room, they hauled him to the Pulaski County Jail, where they booked him, still in his hospital-issued clothing. When they released Ingle four days later (he had sold his car to make bail), his wounds had become infected because he had been unable to change his bandages every six hours.

The internal affairs investigation of the shooting cleared the two SWAT officers who had shot Ingle of wrongdoing. Seeing the gun in Ingle's hand, they had responded appropriately. Responsibility for this drug enforcement fiasco rested on the shoulders of the case detective and the judge who has signed the no-knock search warrant. Ingle, who couldn't afford to hire a lawyer, finally caught a break in May when John Wesley Hall, a well-known Arkansas defense attorney, agreed to represent him.

In an April 2008 interview conducted by a reporter with the *Arkansas Times*, North Little Rock Chief of Police Danny Bradley spoke about the department's SWAT team, officer safety, and police militarism. Because North Little Rock is a small city of 50,000, the SWAT team was made up of 12 to 15 regular-duty patrolmen and detectives assigned to the squad part time. These officers trained for the position twice a month. The chief said he deployed the unit only in high-risk situations. "If we have any doubts about detectives and uniformed officers being able to execute the warrant safely we're going to use the SWAT team. I would rather spend the extra money that it takes to get the SWAT team together than risk someone getting injured." (By "someone," the chief was obviously not thinking of a civilian. In modern police work, officer safety trumps citizen safety. That's just the way it is.)

Chief Bradley, regarding nighttime no-knock home invasions such as the one that got Tracy Ingle shot and almost killed, said, "How do you weigh a situation where executing a warrant safely means exploiting the element of surprise, versus the natural reaction of a person when someone is intruding into his house? It's a dangerous business." (Yes, but for whom? Body-armored cops with assault rifles, or innocent people who are taken by surprise because they were not violating the law?) The chief allowed that he didn't like the phrase "war on drugs" because he didn't want his officers thinking they were soldiers, and drug suspects their enemy. In that regard, he had worked to eliminate some of the militaristic trappings of the force. For example, he had switched his regular patrol officers out of their "fatigue-looking" uniforms. (This suggests there must have been citizen complains along these lines.)

Tracy Ingle's attorney, on September 8, 2008, filed a motion to suppress the evidence against his client. John Wesley Hall argued that owing to the vagueness of the informant's report, the warrant authorizing the raid lacked sufficient probable cause, which rendered the evidence against Ingle inadmissible. Moreover, had there been sufficient probable cause in the first place, it had been severely attenuated by the 17-day delay in the warrant's execution. In other words, the evidence had grown stale. (Under Arkansas law, search warrants must be served within a reasonable time, but not more than 60 days after issue.)

The judge denied attorney Hall's motion, and in March 2009, a jury found Tracy Ingle guilty of maintaining a drug house, and of felony assault. The judge sentenced him to 18 years in prison, and fined him $18,000. Tracy Ingle took his case to the Arkansas Court of Appeals, which, on May 12, 2010, affirmed his conviction.

Shooting People in Wheelchairs: Two Cases

San Francisco

On January 4, 2011, Randal Dunkin, a 55-year-old mentally ill man who had been born with polio and was confined to a wheelchair, was creating a disturbance in the street outside San Francisco's Department of Public Health building. That morning at ten o'clock, Dunkin started slashing tires with a knife, and throwing pieces of concrete at passersby. Someone called 911.

An officer in plainclothes arrived at the scene first, and when he approached the agitated subject to disarm him, Dunkin, from his wheelchair, slashed the officer in the arm with the knife. (The wound, which was not life threatening, required 21 stitches.) Following the assault, uniformed officers squirted Dunkin with pepper spray, and shot him with a beanbag gun. These nonlethal modes of force did not calm the subject down. As the erratic behaving Dunkin tossed the knife onto the street, Sergeant Noah Mallinger, from a range of ten feet, shot him twice in the groin as he sat in his wheelchair.

Following Dunkin's discharge from the hospital, the police transferred him to the city jail on charges of police assault, resisting arrest, vandalism, and brandishing a knife. San Francisco Police Chief George Gascon, in speaking to the media about the incident, said, "I believe from a legal stance, this shooting will be deemed an appropriate, lawful shooting."

In reaction to public outrage over the shooting of a crazy man armed with a knife in a wheelchair, the police chief, a few weeks later, announced the proposed formation of a specialized crisis intervention team to deal with mentally ill subjects. (Cops have to be trained not to shoot people in wheelchairs?)

On March 2011, Randal Dunkin filed a civil rights suit against the city of San Francisco and its police department. Two months later, the department announced that following an internal investigation officer Noah Mallinger had been cleared of any wrongdoing. In other words, the shooting, in the eyes of the police, was justified.

Randal Dunkin, in November 2011, went on trial for his alleged police assault and the lesser charges. Although convicted of vandalism and brandishing a knife, the jury inexplicably acquitted Dunkin of slashing the officer. (The defendant had claimed self-defense, that the officer in plainclothes had not identified himself.) The jurors split on the resisting arrest charge.

Use of force experts who studied this case voiced criticism of the shooting. A man in a wheelchair should not have been given the opportunity to inflict a knife wound on an officer. Once Dunkin had tossed the knife, he was no longer a deadly threat to the police. And even if he hadn't dropped the weapon, the police could have prevented, without the use of deadly force, a man in a wheelchair from hurting anyone. (In downtown Pittsburgh recently, police negotiators talked a mentally ill man, who was in possession of a knife and holding a hostage, into surrendering. The stand off lasted five hours and no one was hurt. In Pittsburgh last year, the police shot three people, killing one. In San Francisco, officers in 2011 shot eight, killing three.)

Houston, Texas

In Houston, Texas, at two in the morning on September 22, 2012, Brian Claunch, a resident of the Healing Hands group home, created a disturbance when a caregiver refused to give him a cigarette and a can of soda. In his mid-40s, and diagnosed with schizophrenia and bipolar disorder, Claunch was confided to a wheelchair after having lost an arm and a leg in a train accident.

Officer Matt Marin, a 5-year-veteran of the Houston Police Department, arrived at the group home with another officer. Shortly after responding to the call, officer Marin shot Brian Claunch in the head as he sat in his wheelchair, killing him instantly. According to a police spokesperson, "He [Claunch] was approaching them [the officers] aggressively. He was attempting to stab them with what is now found to be a felt-tip pen." This statement begs the question: just how aggressive can a pen-wielding man in a wheelchair be?

In October 2009, officer Matt Marin shot and killed a knife-wielding man who had stabbed his girlfriend and a neighbor. In 2011, officers with the Houston Police Department shot ten people, killing three.

For the city of Houston, the police killing of an unarmed man in a wheelchair is going to be costly. For example, a jury in Los Angeles just awarded a known gang member who was shot by the police in September 2005, $5.7 million. In 2009, 24-year-old Robert Contreras pleaded no contest to his role in the drive-by shooting that led to the police wounding and paralyzing him. After being released from prison in 2011, Contreras filed the excessive force suit against the city and the police department. In Los Angeles, police officers put a violent criminal into a wheelchair, and the taxpayers of that city will foot the bill. In Houston, where the officer killed an unarmed man *in* a wheelchair, taxpayers can expect a lawsuit, and a forthcoming multi-million dollar court settlement.

Shooting the Mentally Ill

According to a series of guidelines published by the U.S. Department of Justice, individuals suffering from some form of mental illness are 4 times as likely to be killed in confrontations with police officers than the general population....

Many officers simply are not equipped to deal with the mentally ill. There are strategies that work though, peaceful strategies. First, generalist police officers need more basic training in the plights and issues surrounding the mentally ill. Second, law enforcement agencies should place greater restrictions on deadly force tactics. Shoot first is not a viable solution. Officers reacting out of fear or choose to use physical force do more harm than good. Third, law enforcement departments need mental health specialists. They need police officers trained specifically for mental health related situations.

David Arroyo, Liberty Voice, October 8, 2013

Dirty Harry

What would you say about a police officer, who, in a span of nine years, shot and killed, in separate shooting incidences, six people? In 2011, the entire police forces of Delaware, North Dakota, Vermont, Wyoming, and Alaska, combined, shot less than six people.

During the period November 2002 through February 2012, Scottsdale, Arizona police officer James Peters shot at seven people, killing six of them. From this, one might conclude that Scottsdale, the Phoenix area suburb of 220,000, is the site of daily shootouts between the police and a large population of violent criminals. But this isn't the case. In 2011, the Scottsdale Police only shot one person, and it wasn't fatal. By comparison, the police in Phoenix that year shot 16, killing 9.

How could one member of a police department made up of 435 sworn officers, shoot so many people in a relatively low crime city? After say, the third shooting incident, why wasn't this man psychologically evaluated, and at the very least, put behind a desk? Moreover, didn't the officer himself ask himself why he was the only guy on the force doing all of the killing?

On November 3, 2002, roughly two years after joining the police department, Peters, as a member of the SWAT team, responded to a domestic violence call at the home of a man named Albert Redford. Following a 4-hour standoff, Peters and two other SWAT officers fired seven shots at the suspect, hitting him three times. Mr. Redford died a few hours later in the emergency room. As it turned out, none of the fatal bullets had been fired from Peter's rifle. An investigation by the Maricopa County Sheriff's Office cleared all three officers of wrongdoing.

Officer Peters, on March 25, 2003, responded to a call regarding shotgun blasts coming from the home of a distraught, disbarred attorney named Brent Bradshaw. Three hours later, Peters and his follow officers encountered the 47-year-old suspect wandering along the Arizona Canal carrying a shotgun. When Mr. Bradshaw refused to drop his weapon, Peters dropped him with a shot to the head. This shooting was declared justified.

On October 10, 2005, Officer Peters shot and killed Mark Wesley Smith. High on methamphetamine, Smith was smashing car windows with a pipe outside an auto-body shop. In justifying his use of deadly force in this case, Peters said the subject had threatened a fellow officer with the pipe.

Brian Daniel Brown, 28, took a Safeway grocery store employee hostage on April 23, 2006 after he had hijacked a Krispy Kreme delivery truck. After killing this hostage taker, the department awarded Officer Peters a medal of valor.

Peters and Scottsdale officer Tom Myers were in Mesa, Arizona on August 30, 2006 hoping to question Kevin Hutchings, a suspect in an assault committed earlier that evening in Scottsdale. After Mr. Hutchings fired a shot from inside his house, the officers had the power cut to the dwelling. When the armed man came out of his house to investigate the power outage, Peters shot him to death. The city, in this case, ended up paying the Hutchings family an out of court settlement of $75,000. Even so, the department declared this shooting justified, and Officer Peters kept his assignment as a street cop even though he had killed two people in one year.

On February 17, 2010, Officer Peters and Detective Scott Gailbraith confronted 46-year-old Jimmy Hammack, a suspect in five Phoenix and Scottsdale bank robberies. When Hammack drove his pickup truck toward the detective, Peters shot him. A few days later, Hammack died in the hospital. This shooting, on the grounds the subject was using his vehicle as a deadly weapon, went into the books as justified.

John Loxas, 50, lived alone in a trash-littered house near Vista De Camino Park in Scottsdale. In 2010 police arrested him for displaying a handgun in public. On February 14, 2012, Officer Peters and five other cops responded to a 911 call concerning Loxas who reportedly was threatening his neighbors with a firearm. To complicate matters, Loxas, who regularly babysat his 9-month-old grandson, had the child in his arms while intimidating the neighbors.

When Peters and the other officers arrived at the scene, Mr. Loxas and the baby were back inside the house. When ordered to exit the dwelling, Loxas, still holding the child, appeared in the doorway. As the subject turned to reenter the house, and lowered the baby exposing his upper torso and head, Peters, thinking he saw a black object in Loxas' hand, shot him in the head from 18 feet. The subject, killed instantly by the bullet from Peter's rifle, collapsed to the ground still holding the baby. Fortunately, and perhaps miraculously, the infant was not injured.

As it turned out, at the time Officer Peters killed Mr. Loxas, the subject was not armed, or within reach of a weapon. Police did find, in the dead man's living room, a loaded handgun hidden between the arm and cushion of a stuffed chair. Farther into the dwelling, searchers discovered a shotgun, several "Airsoft"-type rifles and pistols, and a "functional improvised explosive device."

In explaining why he had shot Mr. Loxas, Officer Peters said he had been concerned for the safety of the baby. Peters was placed on paid administrative leave pending yet another police involved shooting investigation by the Maricopa County Sheriff's Office. Critics of the shooting, including some of Loxas' neighbors, protested the incident outside the police department.

Except for the Safeway hostage case in April 2006, most police officers, faced with the choices presented to Officer Peters, probably would *not* have exercised deadly force. This doesn't mean Peters committed criminal acts, or that his shootings were even administratively unjustified. It's just that most officers wouldn't have been so quick on the trigger. If it were otherwise, every year thousands, not hundreds, of people would die at the hands of the police.

Because Mr. Loxas had been armed shortly before the police arrived at the scene, and Officer Peters thought the subject was holding a handgun when he shot him, this case was ruled a justifiable homicide. Whether or not, under the circumstances, the killing of Mr. Loxas was the right thing to do, is another question altogether.

On June 22, 2012, the Scottsdale police board for the Public Safety Retirement System approved Officer Peters' application for early retirement based on some unnamed disability. He received a pension of $4,500 a month for life. Not bad for 12 years of work.

In September 2012, the American Civil Liberties Union of Arizona, on behalf of John Loxas' relatives, sued the city of Scottsdale. The Scottsdale City Council, in June 2013, approved a court settlement of $4.25 million. The Loxas family had originally sought $7.5 million in damages. The city of Scottsdale, in this case, was self-insured up to $2 million, a sum that will have to be paid by municipal taxpayers.

Armed and Naked

Police officers in the United States do not shoot many women, and when they do, the women are usually suicidal and/or mentally ill, and armed with knives. It is rare for a police officer to shoot a woman who at the time is committing a crime, or armed with a gun. The public has gotten used to cops using deadly force on men, but when they shoot and kill a women, it's a bit more disturbing, and newsworthy. This is particularly true when the woman has no criminal record, or medical history of mental illness.

A few minutes past noon on Saturday, October 20, 2012, two men in a car traveling on a dirt road in the rural El Pico neighborhood of Spring Hill, Florida, came upon a nude woman walking along the side of the road. They pulled up to her and asked if she needed help. Sounding perfectly rational, she said everything was okay, and continued on her way. A short time later, the men saw this woman, still naked, in front of a mobile home on Orchard

Way. She held a large, sliver cross, and was waving it over her head while muttering something about the antichrist. The men did not report what they saw to the police.

The nude lady with the big, silver cross was 42-year-old Marie Swanson who lived in a mobile home on Orchard Way with her boyfriend.

Marie and her family moved to Tampa from Connecticut in 1979 when she was 9-years-old. After graduating from Gaither High School in Tampa, she attended community college on and off, but never earned an associates' degree. Her family left the state, but Marie, on her own since she was eighteen, paid for her apartment and car by working as a waitress around the Tampa Bay area. She worked several years at a place called Laker Cafe in Land O'Lakes. The restaurant closed in 2008.

About a year later, Marie met David Simpson, and eventually moved into his mobile home on Orchard Way in Spring Hill. According to Simpson, Swanson's principal interest in life centered on her religious beliefs. She attended the Holy Trinity Lutheran Church, led a bible study group, and listened to Christian radio. Swanson was also extremely shy, modest and conservative. Other than over-the-counter sleeping pills and occasionally smoking marijuana, she did not use drugs.

Ricky Howard, a 31-year-old Hernando County sheriff's deputy, on Saturday October 20, was attending a family gathering hosted by his wife's parents at their home on Orchard Way down the road from where the two men had seen the naked woman. William Mechler, a 26-year-old officer with the Tampa Police Department, was also a guest at the get-together on Orchard Way.

At 1:30 that afternoon, Marie Swanson, still naked, showed up at the party attended by the two off-duty police officers. Since no one had invited her, and she was obviously unbalanced, Deputy Howard asked her to leave. Following her departure, officer Howard called the sheriff's office to report the incident.

When Marie returned to the gathering a short time later, the nude woman carried an antique, single-shot firearm that wasn't loaded. (The gun once belonged to her boyfriend's father.) One or both of the off-duty police officers, when confronted with the nude woman with a gun, shot her dead.

Deputy Howard and officer Mechler were placed on paid administrative leave pending an investigation of the shooting by the Florida Department of Law Enforcement.

David Simpson, in speaking to a reporter with the *Tampa Bay Times*, said this about Marie Swanson: "She believed she was coming to an end...She always told me she was going home. She always told me she was dying of cancer. She had difficulty sleeping and would wake up to scribble lines from the Bible. I could tell it in her eyes, she wasn't the Marie that I knew." According to Simpson, Marie kept saying, "My brain won't shut off." Well it's shut off now, for good.

Both officers were eventually cleared on any wrongdoing in the shooting death of the unarmed, naked woman.

Officer Cleared

Just before eleven o'clock on the night of January 2, 2012 in Anaheim, California, police officers responded to several 911 calls regarding a man with a shotgun at an apartment complex. SWAT officers at the scene ran down a 200-foot alleyway, and as they rounded a corner, saw Bernie Villegas holding a rifle. Anaheim police officer Nicholas Bennallack shot Villegas who was pronounced dead at the scene. The 36-year-old immigrant from the Philippines had been holding his son's BB gun. Villegas, an alleged drug dealer, had a 14-year-old daughter, and a son who was twelve.

The Orange County District Attorney's office, following an investigation of the shooting, cleared Officer Bennallack of criminal wrongdoing. Villegas' family has filed a wrongful death suit against the city.

On July 21, 2012, about six months after the Villegas shooting, Officer Bennallack and his partner Brett Heitmann were patrolling an Anaheim neighborhood considered a hotbed of gang activity. The officers spotted a car parked in an alley surrounded by several men. Officer Heitmann recognized the man standing on the vehicle's passenger side as 25-year-old Manuel Diaz. Diaz, a known gang member, had prior gun possession convictions.

When officers Heitmann and Bennallack got out of the unmarked police car, Diaz ran down an alley leading to an apartment complex. As he fled, Diaz used both hands to hold up his trousers. The fleeing suspect ignored the officers' orders to stop. The officers caught up to Diaz at a wrought-iron fence. As they approached the suspect Diaz had his back to them. When he started to turn toward the officers, Bennallack, thinking that Diaz might have a gun, fired twice. One bullet hit Diaz in the buttocks, the other in the head. He died shortly after the shooting. Diaz had not been armed.

A toxicology report revealed that Diaz, at the time of the shooting, had in his system methamphetamine, amphetamine, and a prescription medicine to prevent seizures.

Following the Diaz shooting, Dana Douglas, the attorney who represented Bernie Villegas' relatives, filed a $50 million suit against the city on behalf of the Diaz family. Following Diaz's death, the Orange County District Attorney's Office opened an investigation of Officer Nicholas Bennallack. The officer had been an Anaheim police officer for five years.

On March 20, 2013, Assistant District Attorney Dan Wagner announced that Officer Bennallack had been cleared of any criminal wrongdoing in the

Diaz shooting. According to the Orange County prosecutor, at the time of the fatal incident, the officer "believed he was in imminent danger. In such a scenario, one can have only a split-second to decide how to proceed."

The Diaz family attorney, Dana Douglas, has a different take on the shooting. "This is like a rape case," she said. "Let's blame the victim."

When a police officer, within a period of five years, shot and killed two people, both of them unarmed, some would call this officer trigger-happy. Given the circumstances of these two police involved shootings, I don't think the term applied to Officer Bennallack.

A Justified Shooting in Connecticut

John Valluzzo, a wealthy, 75-year-old entrepreneur, businessman, and philanthropist, lived in a 9,000-square foot mansion in the historic town of Ridgefield, Connecticut. In 1995, the Army veteran funded and helped finance the Military Museum of Southern New England located in Danbury, Connecticut. Valluzzo made his fortune in manufacturing and real estate. He owned a world-class rare book collection as well as a home in Palm Springs, Florida.

On Friday, May 24, 2013, Valluzzo's 53-year-old girlfriend, Anna Parille, had come to the estate to pick up some clothing for a wedding she planned to attend. Although Parille owned a house in Danbury, she occasionally resided with Valluzzo in Ridgefield. Parille also owned an award-winning video production company called Inside Look, TV. Before becoming a successful real estate agent, she had operated, for 18 years, a nursery school called Kenosia Kids. Parille hosted a television show, and had published a children's book.

According to reportage in *The New York Times*, at five-thirty that Friday evening, Anna Parille phoned a friend in Florida. During that call, Parille reported that she and Valluzzo were fighting and that he was drunk and was brandishing a gun. The friend, on her own without Parille's knowledge, called the Ridgefield Police Department and reported a domestic disturbance at the Valluzzo estate.

When officers rolled up to the mansion they were greeted by Valluzzo who stood in his yard armed with a handgun. Officer Jorge Romero, a seven-year veteran of the force with the Bridgeport Police Department, ordered Valluzzo to drop the weapon. Instead of complying with that command, Valluzzo raised his gun. Officer Romero responded by shooting the armed man several times. Valluzzo died later that night at a hospital in Danbury.

The New York Times, relying on information provided by a friend of Anna Parille's who witnessed the incident, published a narrative at odds with the police version of the shooting. *The New York Times* version involved the police entering the Valluzzo house through a back portico off the kitchen. One of the officers yelled, "Freeze! Freeze!" before he shot Mr. Valluzzo as he stood in his kitchen. Immediately after the shooting, Officer Romero reportedly said, "What did I do?" as other officers tried to console him.

By all accounts, Jorge Romero, a good-natured, low-key man, had been an excellent police officer. In April 2013, he received a commendation for his May 2012 investigation of 26 car burglaries. The Ridgefield chief of police placed Romero on desk duty pending the investigation of the shooting by the New York State Police.

It didn't matter where Mr. Valluzzo stood when Officer Romero shot him as long as Mr. Valluzzo possessed a handgun and raised it in a manner that threatened the officer. Simply because Officer Romero expressed remorse over the shooting did not necessarily render the lethal force unjustified.

In July 2014, State Attorney Stephen J. Sedensky announced that under Connecticut law, officer Romero had been justified in shooting Mr. Valluzzo.

Police Kill 107-Year-Old Man

Police officers in Pine Bluff, Arkansas, a town of 48,000 forty-five miles south of Little Rock, responded to a call on September 7, 2013 regarding an elderly man who had pointed a gun at two people in his house. Shortly after arriving at the scene at 4:30 that Saturday afternoon, officers managed to get the endangered people safely out of the dwelling. The man with the gun, 107-year-old Monroe Isadore, locked himself into his bedroom and refused to come out.

Police officers who surrounded the house had the legally blind, dementia-confused old man contained. Although Mr. Isadore wasn't holding hostages or posing a threat to the general public, the officer in charge of the situation called for a SWAT team, law enforcement's heavy artillery.

By inserting a camera into Monroe's room, SWAT team officers were able to confirm that he still possessed the handgun. After a couple of hours of trying to talk the old man out of the house, a SWAT officer tossed a teargas canister through a bedroom window in an effort to flush the subject out of the dwelling. When the teargas didn't work, SWAT officers entered the home and destroyed the bedroom door with a battering ram. The second the door went down, a SWAT officer rolled in a concussion grenade that produced a loud noise and a disorienting flash of light.

As SWAT officers charged into the bedroom, Monroe fired his handgun. Several officers shot back, killing Monroe Isadore on the spot. The county coroner pronounced the bullet-ridden old man dead at 7:30 that evening. Just three hours had passed since the initial police call. In Pine Bluff, Arkansas, the cops don't mess around. You can come out of the house *now* or be shot to death a couple of hours later.

While the police-involved killing of Monroe Isadore was legally justified, was it absolutely necessary? Were innocent lives at risk? The police had the 107-year-old trapped in the house. Had the half-blind, confused old man stumbled out the front door holding the gun, a healthy 80-year-old woman could have disarmed him.

With the police camera in the bedroom, officers could have watched and waited until Monroe either passed out, fell asleep, or set the handgun aside. At the opportune moment, SWAT officers could have stormed the house and taken this man into custody. But in an era where police officer safety trumps civilian safety, this is not how they do it. It's kill the armed son-of-a-bitch, then go home to your family.

The Monroe Isadore shooting reflects, perhaps in the extreme, the effects of a highly militarized style of law enforcement where citizens are either treated like enemy combatants or potential enemy combatants.

What is truly concerning here is the stupendous lack of good judgment and police discretion. Also, where was the public outrage over the unnecessary killing of a confused, legally blind 107-year-old man? People demonstrate and wring their hands over the execution of a cold-blooded serial killer, but often shrug their shoulders when the police use unnecessary deadly force.

Stray Bullets in Manhattan

On September 14, 2013, a mentally ill man from Brooklyn, New York named Glenn Broadnax created a disturbance at 42nd Street and Eighth Avenue near Times Square in Manhattan. The 250-pound 35-year-old disrupted traffic by putting himself in the path of passing vehicles. Broadnax escalated his public disturbance when he resisted attempts by officers to pull him out of harms way. During the encounter, Broadnax reached into his pants pocket for his wallet. Fearing that he was going for a gun, two police officers shot at the mentally disturbed and distraught citizen. The bullets missed Mr. Broadnax but wounded two female pedestrians. As it turned out, Mr. Broadnax was reaching for his wallet. He was unarmed. A police sergeant, not wanting to fire his gun in a place crowded with people, subdued the subject with a Taser.

At Bellevue Hospital Center where he was taken for psychiatric observation, Mr. Broadnax told a detective that he had been "talking to dead relatives in his head." The obviously mentally ill man said that by putting himself into the path of moving vehicles he was trying to kill himself.

As the authorities booked Mr. Broadnax into jail on the misdemeanor charges of menacing, drug possession, and resisting arrest, the two officers who shot at him were placed on administrative duty pending an internal inquiry. The women who had been shot were treated for their gunshot wounds at a nearby hospital. They were both expected to survive.

A Manhattan prosecutor, perhaps worried about the public relations ramifications of this police involved shooting, decided to upgrade the charges against Mr. Broadnax. Pursuant to the truism that a prosecutor has the power and discretion to indict a ham sandwich, the assistant district attorney talked a Manhattan grand jury into indicting the mentally ill man, in relation to the two wounded women, with felony assault. Mr. Broadnax, according to the wording of his indictment, had recklessly engaged in conduct which created a grave risk of death." Further, "the defendant was the one who created the situation that injured the innocent bystanders." If convicted of the assault, Mr. Broadnax faced a maximum sentence of 25 years in prison.

The Broadnax grand jury, instead of looking into the actions of an unarmed, mentally unstable man trying to kill himself, should have been contemplating the conduct of the two hair-trigger police officers that fired into a crowd.

On January 8, 2014, Sahar Khoshakhlagh, one of the women who took a police bullet, wrote an open letter about the incident to New York mayor de Blasio. She called for better police training in the handling of mentally ill people. Officers should not she wrote shoot at people "indiscriminately." The 38-year-old Iranian-born mental health care worker said the following about Mr. Broadnax: "This man could possibly go to jail. That weighed heavily on my conscience. He didn't do anything to me. He needs help."

The Broadnax case illustrates a major shift in priority over the past thirty years in American law enforcement. During an earlier era, a time when crime rates were much higher, citizen safety came first, officer safety second. Today, in our highly militarized policing, the cop/warrior's safety is priority. Citizens suspected of crimes are treated as enemy combatants rather than people merely under suspicion. Moreover, police officers now presume that everyone is armed and dangerous. One furtive move and a person will be shot.

The Boy With the Toy AK-47

On the afternoon of Tuesday, October 22, 2013, in Santa Rosa, a city of 170,000 in California's wine country fifty miles northwest of San Francisco, 13-year-old Andy Lopez walked to his friend's house. The popular boy, dressed in a blue hooded sweatshirt, carried a brown plastic pellet gun with a black banana magazine that looked like an AK-47 assault rifle. The replica weapon did not come equipped with the required orange-tipped barrel. Tucked into his waistband, the boy also carried a toy handgun that did feature the orange tip.

At three in the afternoon that day, two Sonoma County sheriff's deputies in a marked patrol car spotted Andy Lopez walking in the field not far from his house. The officer behind the wheel, a sheriff's office trainee, pulled the cruiser to the curb, turned on the emergency lights, and chirped the siren. Deputy Erick Gelhaus radioed in a suspicious person report.

Positioned behind an open car door, deputy Gelhaus shouted to the boy faced away from him. Twice the officer yelled, "Drop the gun!" As the Andy Lopez turned, the barrel of his pellet gun rose up. That's when Gelhaus, a 24-year veteran of the force who had served with the Army in Iraq, fired eight shots. Seven of the bullets entered the boy who died on the spot.

The shooting occurred just ten seconds after officer Gelhaus called in the suspicious person report. Sixteen seconds after the boy went down the trainee called for medical assistance.

The next day, a hundred or so people marched on city hall in protest of the shooting of "an innocent boy."

Across the country, over the past few years the police have shot more than a dozen people armed with replica guns. In a few places realistic toy guns are banned. In several jurisdictions laws of this nature are moving though legislative pipelines.

On Friday, October 25, 2013, the sheriff of Sonoma County announced that his office would probe the shooting. The county district attorney said her office had opened an investigation into the incident. In the meantime, the sheriff placed the deputies on paid administrative leave. Deputy Gelhaus, a certified training officer, had been mentoring the other officer in the car.

On October 30, 2013, Santa Rosa resident Jeffrey Westbrook told a local television correspondent that on August 21, at eight-thirty in the morning, deputy Gelhaus had stopped him on Highway 101 for failing to use his blinker. Westbrook pulled his black BMW onto a narrow shoulder above a steep hillside. As the deputy approached the car, Westbrook moved the vehicle toward a wider spot on the shoulder. Officer Gelhaus yelled, "Turn off the car!" then pulled his gun and pointed the weapon at

Westbrook.

Deputy Gelhaus, his gun still aimed at Westbrook, ordered the motorist out of the vehicle. The deputy asked the motorist if he possessed a weapon. Westbrook did not have a gun in the car. Deputy Gelhaus did not issue a ticket to the upset motorist. Mr. Westbook said he intended to file a formal complaint against the deputy.

In defending the officer, a sheriff's office spokesperson pointed out that Westbrook's car matched the description of a vehicle that was on the "be on the lookout" sheet.

In July 2014, Sonoma County District Attorney Jill Ravitch announced that her officer would not file criminal charges against Deputy Gelhaus in connection with the Lopez shooting. A member of the community protesting this decision, in speaking to a local newspaper reporter, said, "The district attorney is giving permission to the deputies to kill our children. They get a paid vacation and there are no repercussions."

7 SCAMS, CONS, AND SWINDLES

The Confidence Man

Confidence men trade upon certain weaknesses in human nature. Until human nature changes perceptibly there is little possibility that there will be a shortage of marks for con games. So long as there are marks with money, the law will find great difficulty in suppressing confidence games, even assuming that local government officers are sincerely interested. Increased legal obstacles have, in the past, had little ultimate effect upon confidence men, except perhaps to make them more wary and to force them to develop their technique to a very high level of perfection. As long as the political boss, whether he be local, state, or national, fosters a machine wherein graft and bribery are looked upon as a normal phase of government, as long as juries, judges and law enforcement officers can be had for a price, the confidence man will live and thrive in our society.

David W. Maurer, *The Big Con*, 1940

A Cold Blooded Con Man

In 2002, Samuel Cohen, a 44-year-old San Francisco con man, talked the founders of a nonprofit foundation called Vanguard into investing millions into his company, Ecast. Vanguard, created in 1972 by actors Danny Glover and Harry Belafonte, issued grants that helped support environmental, anti-war, and other liberal causes.

Cohen told his investors that Ecast, the manufacturer of electronic jukeboxes for bars, was about to be acquired by Microsoft, and that the acquisition would make Vanguard and its donors a lot of money. Relying on Cohen's word, the foundation's founders, and a hundred other investors, gave Cohen, over a six-year period, more than $30 million. Cohen kept the scam going by telling his marks that regulators in the U.S. and Europe were holding up the acquisition. He needed the money to pay the fees and bonds needed to get the deal approved. His victims bought his spiel, and the money kept rolling in. In typical con man fashion, the product Cohen was selling himself. And the marks went along because they thought they were going to make a killing.

Confidence games cannot go on forever, and in 2008, Cohen's swindle fell apart. A federal prosecutor in San Francisco charged him with wire fraud, money laundering, and tax evasion. His victims were devastated, and the Vanguard Foundation collapsed.

Samuel Cohen had pulled off what criminologists call the "long con" by using his ill-gotten money to create a facade of enormous wealth that impressed and influenced his marks. He rented a $50,000 a month mansion in Belvedere, the exclusive enclave just north of San Francisco. The fake financier hung fake art on the walls of his rented palace, and bought his wife a $1.4 million diamond ring with money he had lifted from his investors. In his rented garage sat a $372,000 Rolls Royce, and a $260,000 Aston Martin. Cohen spent $6 million flying around in a rented jet he boasted that he owned. (Two of his celebrity passengers were Elton John and Jennifer Lopez. While they were not marks, they were props.)

Con man Cohen lured his victims to the mansion where he held lavish parties in their honor while separating them from their money. It was easy. The scam artist even bilked his father-in-law out of his retirement savings. For the con man, it's not the money so much as the thrill of making suckers out of trusting people. It's economic lust killing.

The federal prosecutor, after a San Francisco jury found Samuel Cohen guilty in November 2011 of 15 counts of wire fraud, 11 counts of money laundering, and 3 counts of tax evasion, asked Judge Charles Breyer to send this con artist to prison for 30 years, order him to pay $60 million in restitution, and fine him $250,000. In justifying what would be the stiffest penalty in the history of white collar crime (Jeff Skilling at Enron got 24 years, 4 months), the prosecutor pointed out that Cohen, instead of experiencing remorse for his on-going, cold-blooded swindle, has blamed everyone but himself for the harm he has caused so many victims. (When con men are caught, in their minds, *they* are the victims.)

Cohen's attorney, in arguing for a more lenient penalty, requested a prison sentence of less than 7 years. The defense lawyer told the judge that 30 years behind bars is excessive punishment for a 53-year-old first time offender. Moreover, Mr. Cohen had given $2 million to charity. (Yes, but with stolen money. Samuel Cohen as Robin Hood.)

Judge Breyer, in May 2012, sentenced Cohen to 22 years in prison, and ordered him to pay $31.4 million in restitution. Calling the con man "nearly sociopathic," (nearly?) the judge said the sentence would have been more severe, but the sentencing guidelines held him back. If Cohen serves his full sentence, he'll be 75 when he gets out. Many of his victims will be dead, and the ones who are not, might still be broke.

The Con Game Mark

A confidence man prospers only because of the fundamental dishonesty of his victims. First, he inspires a firm belief in his own integrity. Second, he brings into play powerful and well-nigh irresistible forces to excite the cupidity of the mark. Then he allows the victim to make large sums of money by means of dealings which are explained to him as being dishonest--and hence a "sure thing." As the lust for large and easy profits is fanned into a hot flame, the mark puts all his scruples behind him. He closes out his bank account, liquidates his property, borrows money from friends, and embezzles from his employer or his clients. In the mad frenzy of cheating someone else, he is unaware of the fact that he is the real victim, carefully selected and fattened for the kill. Thus arises the trite but none-the-less sage maxim: "You can't cheat an honest man." [Actually, you can't work a con game on an honest man. Honest people are *cheated* all the time.]

David W. Maurer, *The Big Con*, 1940

New York City's Biggest Psychic Swindler

Mrs. Frances Friedman of Manhattan's Upper West Side had been a widow for eight years. In September 1956 she visited a psychic parlor on Madison Avenue run by Volga Adams, a self-appointed gypsy princess. Adams advertised her services in the form of a large drawing painted on her storefront window of a hand, palm facing out. Mrs. Friedman hoped the psychic--"Madam Lillian"--would read her horoscope and reveal what caused her depression.

Volga Adams, a gypsy psychic well known to detectives on the NYPD Pickpocket and Confidence Squad, quickly diagnosed Mrs. Friedman's problem. "There is evil in you," she proclaimed with great authority. Adams instructed her client to go home and wrap an egg in a handkerchief that had belonged to her husband then put these two items into a shoe made for a left foot. The psychic instructed Mrs. Friedman to return to the parlor the next day with the handkerchief and the egg. At this point, Mrs. Friedman should have had the good sense to walk out of the shop and not return.

As instructed, the prospective mark returned to the gypsy psychic's place of fraud. Adams opened up an egg she had switched with the real one. The phony egg contained a small plastic head. The greenish-yellow head featured a pair of horns, pointed eyebrows, and a black goatee. According to Adams, the presence of the devil's head in the egg was a bad sign. It meant that Mrs. Friedman was cursed. But why was she cursed?

Phase two of Volga Adam's psychic confidence game involved handing the victim a dollar bill that had a rip in it. Friedman was to take the currency home, put it in a handkerchief, and wear it near her breast for two days.

Upon her return to Volga Adam's scam parlor, Madam Lillian, following a prayer in a foreign tongue, opened the handkerchief to find a mended dollar bill. This "miracle" supposedly revealed the source of Mrs. Friedman's curse. The money her husband had left her upon his death was the problem. Money, the root of evil had cursed the widow. If Mrs. Friedman wanted to rid herself of the monetary curse, she would have to give Madam Lillian all of that money, cash she would ritualistically burn. Once that was done, the widow's happiness would return. Divesting herself of the filthy lucre would also clear up her troublesome skin rash. Who would have guessed that this gypsy princess was also a skin doctor?

A few days after the miracle of the mended dollar, bill, Mrs. Friedman withdrew money from six bank accounts and cashed in all of her government bonds. She delivered the $108,273 in cash, stuffed in a paper bag, to another Madison Avenue psychic parlor. (In 1956, that was a lot of dough.)

Volga Adams suggested that Mrs. Friedman, now that she had unburdened herself of her money, leave the city for a few days to enjoy some "clean air." This is called cooling the mark. The next day, as Madam Lillian left town herself, her mark headed for the Catskill Mountains in eastern Pennsylvania. This looked like a perfect score.

For a period of a year after Volga Adams bilked Mrs. Friedman out of her life's savings, she cooled the mark with regular phone calls, made collect, from various places around the country. Back in Manhattan in the fall of 1957, Adams informed Mrs. Friedman that she needed another $10,000 to remove traces of the lingering evil underlying the victim's curse. Mrs. Friedman, obviously unaware that she had been swindled, gave Adams the cash. She turned over the money on the condition that the psychic would not destroy it, and later returned it to her. After she gave the cold-blooded swindler $108, 273, Mrs. Friedman barely had enough money to support herself. A couple months after walking off with the $10,000, Volga Adams called the victim and announced that she could only return $2,000 of the $10,000. The psychic said she was in Florida and would be returning to New York City soon.

The con game had run its course. Volga Adams did not return to Manhattan, and she quit calling the victim. Thanks to Madam Lillian, Mrs.

Friedman not only remained cursed with depression, she was now broke. Finally, she picked up the telephone and called the police. When detectives with the Pickpocket and Confidence Squad heard Mrs. Friedman's story, they recognized the M.O., and knew that Madam Lillian was Volga Adams, one of the city's most notorious con artists.

Following her indictment in New York City for grand larceny, the 42-year-old defendant went on trial in February 1962. Five weeks later, the jury of five women and seven men informed the judge that they were deadlocked and could not reach an unanimous verdict. The judge had no choice but to declare a mistrial.

The Manhattan prosecutor scheduled a second trial for May 1963. Volga Adams avoided that proceeding by pleading guilty to a lesser theft charge. After the judge handed the defendant a suspended sentence, she left the city. But before she departed for Florida, Adams placed a curse on the prosecutor. "No woman will ever love him," she predicted.

Volga Adams continued preying on vulnerable women. A few years after Madam Lillian left Manhattan, Frances Friedman died. At the time of her death, she was lonely, humiliated, and depressed. Thanks to the gypsy princess, Mrs. Friedman died broke.

Psychics and the Fools Who Consult Them

Many people are no longer satisfied that conventional religious institutions can meet their spiritual needs. So they visit psychics and other New Age types...People are paying psychics to predict the future, and they're just not getting what they paid for....

[As a journalist] I went undercover to visit ten psychics, looking for predictions about my future. The disparity between what each told me was quite telling. Each psychic began by asking me to cut a deck of cards or close my eyes and think about my problems. But beyond that, the similarities among them ended. Each psychic had a different prediction for me. The first nine psychics I saw suggested that I become a car salesman, a builder, a politician, a psychic, an actor, a businessman dealing with resorts, and finally, a bricklayer. The tenth told me to prepare to retire with the money I was going to inherit....

One psychic predicted that I would have a sex change operation. He was the same one who told me that I had a secret enemy, and suggested that I urinate in a milk carton, write the names of anyone who might be angry with me on the outside of the carton with a felt-tip pen, then place the full carton in my refrigerator to ward off danger.

Chuck Whitlock, *Chuck Whitlock's Scam School,* 1997

Sylvia Mitchell: Cleaning Out Bank Accounts

In October 2007, 33-year-old Lee Choong, a native of Singapore who worked 80 hours a week at a Manhattan investment-banking firm, walked into the Zena Clairvoyant Psychic parlor on Seventh Avenue South in Greenwich Village. Ms. Choong had sought help from psychics before. In 2006, she had paid $10,000 to a fortune- teller doing business in New York's So Ho district. Choong came away from that experience feeling cheated. This distraught and lonely woman had obviously not learned the obvious truth that psychics are not only fakes, they are thieves who prey mostly on gullible, desperate women.

In her opulent Greenwich Village storefront parlor, 34-year-old Sylvia Mitchell, a resident of Mystic, Connecticut (no kidding) offered to give people who walked into her cheesy shop an introductory "reading" for the bargain price of $75. The first session was in reality a combination sales pitch and hook designed to sucker the customer into subsequent psychic sessions that cost $1,000 each. Since only believers availed themselves of psychics, it didn't take much for one of these phony practitioners to close the deal. If these naive and troubled women had any money when they walked into Zena Clairvoyant's shop of financial horrors, they eventually walked out broke and broken. (It's amazing that cops raid whorehouses but let these joints operate.)

As a prologue to Lee Choong's first reading, she unburdened herself to the psychic. Choong said she had fallen in love with a co-worker at the investment-banking firm who did not feel the same way about her. Could Zena help? Of course Zena could help. Here was the problem: in one of Choong's past lives a member of her family had hurt the co-worker. This had created "bad spirits" that had carried forward to the present. But Zena told the victim not to worry. Because Choong and this man at the investment-banking firm were meant for each other, psychic Mitchell would bring them together by ridding Choong of the bad spirits that had kept him away.

During their first meeting, psychic Mitchell cautioned Lee Choong that cleansing her of those evil spirits would not be easy. It would take a lot of time, and as we all know, time is money.

Over the next year and a half, Lee Choong paid Sylvia Mitchell more than $120,000. The psychic said she needed the money to pay for evil spirit removal supplies. If the bad spirits were not vanquished, and Choong's life didn't get better, Mitchell promised to return the money.

In 2008, notwithstanding psychic Mitchell's efforts, Lee Choong lost her job at the investment-banking firm. When the unemployed woman, in April 2009, asked for a psychic refund, Sylvia Mitchell told her that within a period of four months Choong would get a new job, one that paid $95,000 a year. That, of course, didn't happen. Choong did not get her refund, either.

In September 2012, Lee Choong went to the police.

In August 2008, while Sylvia Mitchell was separating Lee Choong from her savings, Debra Saalfield, a single mother of three entered the psychic shop on Seventh Avenue South. The former competitive ballroom dancer from Naples, Florida, an employee of a Manhattan dance company, had lived in the West Village with her boyfriend, a man she wanted to marry. They broke up, she moved out, and a short time later, she lost her job at the dance company. With her life in shambles, Debra experienced what she called an emotional "meltdown." Rather than seek professional help, and perhaps medication, Saalfield turned to a psychic.

From psychic Mitchell, Debra Saalfield learned that in one of her past lives she had been an Egyptian princess. (Haven't we all.) As part of the ruling class, Saalfield had enjoyed great wealth. As a result, in her present life, she had become too attached to money. Yes, it was that filthy lucre that was ruining her life. To prove her diagnosis, Mitchell asked Saalfield to write her a check for $27,000. Without that wealth, Saafield's life would improve. If it didn't, Mitchell would return every penny. Saalfield took out a loan on her house.

After Saalfield realized she had been the victim of a confidence scam, she asked the psychic to return the $27,000. Mitchel, over a period of months, gave back about half of what she had taken.

In 2011, while running a psychic shop in her hometown, Mystic, Connecticut, the authorities accused Mitchell of bilking a Catskills woman out of $9,000. This prompted Zena Clairvoyant to leave the state. A short time later, while running a game in Florida, the police arrested her for stealing $27,000 from a woman who had paid for "consultations" by Zena Clairvoyant. (I do not know the status of these cases.)

In New York City, detectives working out of the 6th precinct arrested Sylvia Mitchell in February 2013 on charges of fortune telling, scheme to defraud, and grand larceny. On the grand larceny charge alone Mitchell faced up to 15 years in prison. The psychic made bail and went back to work in Greenwich Village as Zena Clairvoyant. No doubt she was predicting an acquittal.

The Mitchell trial commenced on September 30, 2013 in a Manhattan criminal courtroom. During the jury selection process, Assistant District Attorney James Bergamo asked members of the panel this question: "Does anyone believe that psychics are real?" (I'm not sure, from the prosecutor's point of view, if you want believers or nonbelievers on the jury. Nonbelievers might condemn the victims as willing suckers who got what they deserved. Believers might see the case as nothing more that a consumer's rights conflict.) In response to Bergamo's question, several members of the jury panel raised their hands as believers. One of these prospective jurors said, "I'm curious about the future." Another said she had a friend who visited a psychic as "a happy-hour thing." A third member of the panel said she had a friend who read palms.

In his opening statement to the twelve people who ended up on the jury, prosecutor Bergamo revealed his strategy of portraying Choong and Saalfield as vulnerable women taken advantage of by a cold-blooded con artist. "The defendant," he said, "is not in the business of cleansing spirits. She's in the business of cleaning out bank accounts."

When it came time for defense attorney William I. Aronwald to address the jury, he said, "You will not hear any evidence in this case that she [Sylvia Mitchell] did not provide the services that she was contracted to provide them." In other words, Choong and Saalfield had gotten what they had paid for--they paid for nonsense and that's what they got.

On Thursday, October 3, 2013, following the direct testimony of prosecution witnesses Saalfield and Choong, defense attorney Aronwald, carefully trying not to come off as a bully, put these pathetic women under cross-examination. Regarding the psychic's so-called "readings," Aronwald asked Debra Saalfield to explain what a reading was. "A reading of what?" he asked. "Palms? Tarot cards? You paid $75 for a reading, but what was read?"

"I don't know," replied the witness.

"When she told you that you had been an Egyptian princess, did you believe her?"

"No."

"Did you laugh?"

"No."

To Lee Choong, attorney Aronwald asked, "What led you to see a psychic instead of a licensed therapist?"

"I needed answers," Choong replied.

"In the eighteen months you were involved with Sylvia, there was no improvement in any of these areas, correct?"

"Yes."

"You continued to give her this money?"

"Yes."

On Monday, October 7, a prosecution witness named Rob Millet took the stand and testified that he sought the defendant's help after he learned that his boyfriend was moving back to Texas. To make matters worse, Millet's mother took ill. The psychic, after gaining Millet's confidence, said she had to have $10,000 to give him the quality of help he required. Millet, after borrowing $7,000 from his father, paid Mitchell her fee. He got nothing in return.

Attorney Aronwald, after resting his case without putting his client on the stand, gave his closing statement to the jury. He said that Sylvia Mitchell had done what her clients had paid her to do--try to help them. Yes, her methods were "unconventional," but so what?

Prosecutor Bergamo, in his final statement to the jury, said, "The defendant finds people's weaknesses and she exploits them to her advantage."

On Friday, October 11, 2013, the jury found Sylvia Mitchell guilty as charged. Two weeks later the judge sentenced the con artist to 5 to 15 years in prison.

What this case and others like it reveal about modern society is disturbing. In an era in which we are overwhelmed with information, Americans are losing the ability to draw logical conclusions, apply common sense, and to distinguish what is real from what isn't. We live in a culture of magical thinking devoid of objective truth. The loss of common sense and logic is a great danger facing our country. A nation that can't think straight, make rational decisions, and apply common sense solutions to its problems, is doomed.

Easy Money: Three New York City Cases

Case 1

A man and a woman, both well dressed approached an 86-year-old woman at a busy intersection in the Forest Hills section of Queens. The man showed the elderly woman a wallet fat with cash. "We just found it," the man said. "Look at all the money that's in it. Hundred dollar bills."

Having interested the victim in the money, the man proposed they take the lost wallet to the local police precinct house. If the wallet was not claimed in 30 days, the three of them could divide up the cash. They could deposit the lost wallet with the police in the old woman's name. At the end of the waiting period, the police would release the wallet and its contents to her.

But wait. How could the couple trust that a complete stranger will give them their share of the money? How about this? The woman could withdraw $10,000 from her bank account, money the couple could hold until the police release the wallet. If the wallet is claimed within the 30-day period, the couple will return the woman's good faith money.

After the victim took $10,000 out of her bank account and handed it to the con artists, they asked her to wait on the street until they returned with the receipt from the police station. They of course disappeared with the scam victim's cash.

Case 2

An 82-year-old man received a disturbing phone call regarding one of his grandsons. According to the caller, who said he was an officer with the New Jersey State Police, the young man had been arrested and needed $3,500 to get out of jail.

To spare his grandson the horrors of criminal incarceration, the old man, from a Western Union Office, sent $3,500 to the con man. The good news, of course, was that the kid was not in jail. The bad news: the victim ended up $3,500 poorer and was left feeling like a sucker.

Case 3

A con man impersonating an IRS agent informed a 35-year-old woman by telephone that she owed the government $2,000 in taxes. According to the faker, her problem was this: if she didn't pay up *immediately*, agents would come to her home and haul her off to prison.

The terrified victim ran to a 7-Eleven convenience store where she purchased four $500 prepaid debit cards. The con man withdrew the $2,000 after the victim, using her cellphone at the store, read him the card numbers. With one phone call this scam artist stole $2,000. Easy money.

Jeffrey Jarrett's Last Night Out

In the 1989 comedy, "Weekend at Bernie's," a couple of low-level insurance agency employees are invited to spend the weekend at a beach house owned by their boss--Bernie. They show up at the summerhouse and find Bernie dead, and for the next two days, carry on as though he were alive. In one scene, these guys drive around in Bernie's convertible with the dead man propped up in the back seat. When people wave at Bernie, the guy sitting next to him grabs the dead man's arm and waves back. It's that kind of movie, kind of funny in spots, but really stupid because in real life no one would do something like this. That is until a couple of clowns in Glendale, Colorado bar hopped one night accompanied by a dead man who picked up the tab.

Jeffrey Jarrett, a 43-year-old real estate agent, had a problem with drugs and alcohol. In the summer of 2011, he called a friend from his days at Colorado State University. Jarrett asked his old buddy to room with him until he got his life straightened out. Shortly after his cry for help, 43-year-old Robert J. Young moved into his friend's house.

On August 27, 2011, when Young came home from work, he found Jarrett sprawled on the floor, and obviously dead. The look of the death scene suggested a drug overdose. (A toxicology report confirmed this. According to the medical examiner, Jarrett had overdosed on Xanax and

Subutex--a drug addicts take to get off opiates). Robert Young, instead of calling 911, phoned a 25-year-old drinking buddy named Mark Rubinson.

That evening, a Saturday, Young and Rubinson stuffed Jeffrey Jarrett's lifeless body into the backseat of Rubinson's Lincoln Navigator, and took off for a night on the town. They started off with drinks at a joint called Teddy T's Bar and Grill. The corpse remained in the SUV as Young and his friend used Jarrett's credit card to pay for their booze. From Teddy T's, the pair visited Sam's No. 3 where they continued to imbibe on the dead man's dime.

Perhaps realizing that for Jarrett's credit card to work, his body didn't have to be sitting outside in Rubinson's SUV, they decided to take him home. After lugging the corpse back into the house, Young and Rubinson enjoyed a meal, at Jarrett's expense, at an eatery called Viva Burrito. (An appropriate pre-meal toast would have been, "Viva Jarrett's credit card.")

The party animals finished off the night at a strip club called Shotgun Willie's where Robert Young used the dead man's credit card to withdraw $400 from the ATM. After the joint closed at four in the morning, Young contacted the Glendale Police Department to report his housemate's death.

The local prosecutor charged Young and Rubinson with abuse of corpse, identify theft, and criminal impersonation. After first denying any wrongdoing, both suspects agreed to plead guilty to all charges.

On March 6, 2012, a judge sentenced Robert J. Young to two years probation, and ordered that he undergo "mental health evaluation and treatment; substance abuse assessment and treatment; and cognitive behavioral therapy." ("Cognitive behavioral therapy"? I guess that meant that some therapist or shrink would explain to Mr. Young that hauling a corpse from bar to bar while using the dead man's credit card was inappropriate behavior.) Pursuant to his sentence, if Mr. Young can behave himself for two years, his record of shameless behavior will be expunged.

Mr. Rubinson got off with a couple of years of probation as well. For some reason the judge didn't think he needed any cognitive behavioral therapy. He had just helped Young carry the corpse to and from the car, then drove his two companions, one dead and one alive, around town. The man drove a Lincoln Navigator, yet had to mooch drinks off a dead man.

Embezzling Federal Money

The former director of the Blackfeet Tribe's Temporary Assistance for Needy Families (TANF) program in Great Falls, Montana, has pleaded guilty to embezzlement and fraud after stealing nearly $300,000 from the federally funded program. Between 2006, when Sandra Marie Sanderville became director, to her dismissal in 2010, she devised schemes in which she would overpay TANF beneficiaries, who would then cash the illicit checks and give a portion back to Sanderville. She would also provide checks to people who were not eligible for the program and received portions back from that as well. She later told investigators that she misled the beneficiaries by telling them that the extra money was from a grant or another fund and that the money they gave to her was going back to TANF.

Sanderville was able to keep her activities under wraps for four years because she was able to "restrict" access to the records. However, when the Blackfeet Tribe's Internal Affairs Office began an investigation, Sanderville attempted to destroy the documents dealing with the fraud scheme. Investigators were still able to identify the scheme through a back up computer located out of state....

Sanderville pleaded guilty in February 2014 before Untied States Magistrate Judge Keith Strong...In interviews with investigators, Sanderville...explained that she had developed a gambling habit which cost her hundreds of dollars a week...She faces up to 10 years in prison....

Caroline May, The Daily Caller, March 7, 2014

Priest Accused of Embezzling from Church

Reverend Edward Belczak, the pastor of the 2,500-member St. Thomas More Catholic Church in the Detroit suburb of Troy, Michigan, lived extremely well for a priest who made less than $30,000 a year. In 2005, the well-known and popular 60-year-old man of the cloth purchased, with a $109,578 down payment, a luxury condo from his longtime church administrator, Janice Verschuren.

In late 2012, an internal audit of Reverend Belczak's church commissioned by the Archdiocese of Detroit, led the auditors to suspect the priest, during the period 2004 to 2012, of embezzling at least $429,000 from the parish. The archdiocese reported the audit results to the local police who turned the case over to the FBI.

Archbishop Allen Vigneron of Detroit, in January 2013, suspended Reverend Belczak. Church administrator Verschuren, suspected of helping the pastor divert church money, resigned.

Father Belczak's suspension did not sideline him altogether. With advanced permission from the archdiocese, he was allowed to conduct church services at other parishes throughout the Detroit area. He also continued to draw his salary.

On April 23, 2014, a U.S. Department of Justice spokesperson announced that a federal grand jury sitting in Detroit had indicted Reverend

Belczak and Janice Verschuren of conspiracy to commit mail fraud and wire fraud. According to the indictment, Belczak had purchased the Palm Beach condo with funds he had diverted from a parish bank account.

Another act of theft alleged in the grand jury true bill involved the unlawful taking of $420,204, money bequeathed to the church following the death of a parishioner. That money, according to FBI investigators, had ended up in a secret money-market account in Belczak's name. Forensic accountants with the FBI reported that the 69-year-old priest and his 67-year-old former manager diverted more than $700,000 of the church's money, then filed false financial reports to the archdiocese in Detroit in an attempt to cover the embezzlements. If convicted as charged, the defendants could be imprisoned up to twenty years.

Shortly after the indictments came down, Father Belczak's attorney, Jerome Sabbota, in speaking to reporters said, "My client is innocent. He is not happy. Nobody who gets indicted is happy. He looks forward to doing what he has to do."

Following the priest's suspension in January 2013, many of his parishioners expressed their belief in his innocence. One of his supporters created a website called, "Friends of Father B." The Internet site features photographs of a smiling Father Belczak conducting a variety of church related activities. Supporters are also encouraged to write letters of support to Archbishop Vigneron and even to Pope Francis. (The pope has his own problems with Vatican related embezzlements involving huge sums of money.) Believers in Father Belczak are asked to donate money to his legal defense fund.

The "Father B" website also includes a statement from the accused priest written after his suspension from St. Thomas More Church. Father Belczak writes: "I would have never expected a year like this, yet I am at peace with all that has happened. Losing my job, home, and good reputation has brought me to my knees and here I found God awaiting me. His grace has never left me and His assurance continues to direct me. I sense his presence every day working on my behalf and I struggle to align myself to His time frame and not my own. I am reminded daily that faith is the assurance of things hoped for, perceiving as real what is not yet revealed to the senses."

Faith is good, but in the world of criminal justice, a ruthlessly good lawyer is even better. Imagine, if you will, a teenager confessing to Father Belczak that he had shoplifted something from Walmart. There is petty theft and there is grand theft. If FBI agents and the federal prosecutor are right about Father Belczak, he is not a petty thief, and the parishioners who support him are victims of his crimes.

A Haven for Fall Down Artists

Liability law generally holds that property owners must warn people about dangers and pitfalls that aren't readily noticeable. It does not, however, require property owners to line their stores and houses with pillows, guarding against every conceivable injury.

The West Virginia Supreme Court of Appeals recently said otherwise. The plaintiff in the case was a man who walked with a cane and was accustomed to frequent tumbles. Yet he chose to descend a flight of stairs in a store parking lot, even though there were no guardrails. (The owner had removed the guardrails due to his concern that skateboarders who frequented them were going to break their necks, and was scheduled to have new rails installed in weeks.)

The court ruled 3-2 that the owner was at fault for the man's injuries. Writing for the dissent, Justice Allen Loughry II wrote that the unfortunate decision would, "saddle property owners with the impossible burden of making their premises 'injury proof' for persons who either refuse or are inexplicably incapable of taking personal responsibility for their own safety." [Tort law needs to be reformed to bring back the concept of contributory negligence. This case is just another example of the deep-pockets doctrine at work.]

Robby Soave, The Daily Caller, December 18, 2013

The Winner of a Giant Banana

In April 2013, 30-year-old Henry Gribbohm from Epsom, New Hampshire, took his toddler son to a carnival in nearby Manchester. Lured by the prospect of winning a Xbox Kinect (a motion-sensing accessory worth $100), Gribbohm began playing a game called Tubs of Fun operated by an independent contractor with an arrangement with the carnival's owner, Fiesta Shows.

When Tubs of Fun contestants make free practice throws, the balls land where they are supposed to land. But when playing for money, the balls don't stay in the tubs. That means the player doesn't win a prize. (Welcome to the carnival world where nothing is on the level, and all the food is bad for you.)

As hard as he tried, Mr. Gribbohm couldn't get the balls into the right tubs. It wasn't long before he had squandered $300 on the game. Instead of cutting his loses and walking away poorer but wiser, Gribbohm drove home for more cash. Determined to win his money back, he returned to Tubs of Fun with his entire life's savings, $2,300. (Like P. T. Barnum said, "There's a sucker born every day.")

In a desperate effort to win back his money, Mr. Gribbohm played double or nothing until he was broke. He had dropped a total of $2,600 on the Tubs of Fun Game. (These particular tubs were not much fun for Mr. Gribbohm.)

The next day, Gribbohm returned to the carnival where he accused the Tubs of Fun operator of running a rigged game. To show his good faith, the operator gave Gribbohm $600 in cash and a "Rasta Banana"--a six-foot stuffed banana with a happy face and dreadlocks.

The disgruntled owner of a Rasta Banana filed a complaint with the Manchester Police Department. Pending the results of the game-rigging investigation, Fiesta Shows has put Tubs of Fun on the shelf.

To a local television reporter, Gribbohm said, "You just get caught up in the whole 'I've got to win my money back thing.' "

Generally I have contempt for suckers. But when I saw a news photograph of this father pushing a stroller with the Rasta Banana over his shoulder, I couldn't help feeling sorry for the guy. I don't know if it's because he has a child, or looked pathetic carrying around that giant banana. Maybe the story got to me because I don't like carnivals. I guess all of us, at some time in our lives, have doubled down. Sometimes you win and sometimes you lose. But when the game is rigged, you always lose.

Living With a Corpse

In November 2012, 72-year-old Ann Marquis died of natural causes in the trailer house she rented in Long's Mobile Home Court in Redford Township just west of Detroit. At the time of her death Marquis resided with Dennis McCauley. The 64-year-old had been living with Marquis for two and a half years.

Mr. McCauley, instead of notifying the appropriate authorities of Ann Marquis' death, told her friends and neighbors that she had moved out of the trailer park. In reality, the dead woman, laid out on a living room sofa bed, hadn't gone anywhere.

Over the next six months, as Dennis McCouley cashed Marquis' social security checks and used her credit cards, she decomposed on the sofa bed.

Mr. McCauley should have used some of his dead roommate's money to pay the monthly trailer rent. On April 22, 2013, Redford Township police officers, accompanied by the landlord, showed up at the trailer with an eviction notice. When the landlord opened the front door, she and the officers were assaulted by the smell of death. The gruesome discovery terminated McCouley's six-month postmortem relationship with Ann Marquis.

A Wayne County prosecutor charged Dennis McCouley with nine felony offenses related to his macabre relationship with a dead woman. These crimes include larceny, social security fraud, illegal possession of a credit card, failure to report a death, and mutilation of corpse. The latter charge related to the discovery that the dead woman's right arm was separated from her body. (The arm may have come off when McCouley, months after Marquis' death, moved the corpse.)

Dennis McCouley was incarcerated in the Wayne County Jail under $250,000 bond. He faced up to ten years in prison if found guilty as charged.

In November 2013, the judge sentenced Mr. McCouley to probation.

Religious Scams

History is full of religious and spiritual scams and scandals. Religious scams can be found anywhere, but they are a particular problem in the United States. Here, the ideal of freedom of religion ends up allowing all kinds of con artists to get away with their scams. Gurus, cult leaders, swamis, ministers, televangelists--they come in all guises, seeking power and money. The most important piece of advice I can give you: Be aware and wary, especially when you're in an emotionally vulnerable state. That's when you're most likely to fall for a religious con....

Con artists are often exceptionally charming, and religious con artists are no exception. Of course, they have an advantage--most people have a built-in sense of trust toward clergy. A mistaken trust, it sometimes turns out....

Genuine religious leaders, including swamis, ministers, rabbis, and other spiritual leaders, are primarily interested in saving souls and persuading people to follow their teachings. A con artist pretending to be interested in your spiritual wellbeing, however, will insist on proof of your faith in the form of large gifts to him or her.

Chuck Whitlock, *Scam School,* 1997

Travis Scott's Fake Suicide

In 2006, Travis Magdalena Scott owned a computer company in Crystal, Minnesota that provided software to the U.S. Military and the private sector. That year, the 29-year-old scam artist filed a false insurance claim with Lloyd's of London based on a phony lightening strike he said had wiped out his computers and ruined his business. The insurance company paid him $3 million.

Two years later, Scott was living in a 15-room, 5,300-square foot $1 million mansion in the Twin Cities area town of Eden Prairie. He owned a new computer company and had filed another false insurance claim. This time, to indemnify him for another computer destroying lightening strike, the insurer paid him $9.5 million.

The FBI opened an investigation of Scott in 2010, and in early 2011, a federal grand jury sitting in Minneapolis indicted him for wire fraud, money laundering, and insurance fraud. If convicted of all charged, the crooked businessman faced up to thirty years in prison. FBI agents seized three of Scott's airplanes, a boat, three vehicles, and $5 million from various bank accounts in his name. Scott's mansion, taken over by the bank and put on the market, was now worth $600,000.

In May 2011, pursuant to a plea deal involving a sentence of between five to ten years in prison, Travis Scott pleaded guilty to all charges. His sentencing hearing before a U.S. District Court judge was scheduled for mid-September 2011.

A week before his sentencing, Scott staged a suicide by leaving his kayak on the west shore of Lake Mille Lacs. Inside the overturned kayak, Scott left a suicide note in which he wrote that he had drowned himself by jumping into the middle of the lake wearing heavy weights. (Had this been true, it would have been one odd suicide.)

Following the staged suicide, Scott flew his Piper airplane from the Flying Cloud Airport near Eden Prairie Scott to the St. Andrew's Airport in Winnipeg, Canada. The aircraft bore fake Canadian registration decals. Three days later, Mille Lacs County Sheriff's deputies found the kayak and the phony suicide note. The local authorities listed Scott as a missing person, and various law enforcement agencies in the region searched for his body.

In Winnipeg, under the name Paul Decker, Scott set up residence in a downtown apartment. He purchased a Jeep, and lived with a cat. Things were going smoothly for the missing businessman until December 22, 2011. The Canadian authorities caught up to him 82 days after his staged suicide when, at a Winnipeg pharmacy, he used a forged prescription slip to acquire pills for his anxiety disorder.

Police officers searching Scott's apartment seized $35,000 in U.S. and Canadian currency. The Winnipeg officers also recovered $85,000 in gold and silver coins. In Scott's Jeep, searchers found a loaded .45-caliber handgun. The officers also took Scott's Jeep and Piper aircraft.

On February 11, 2013, Scott, now 37, pleaded guilty in a Winnipeg court to possession of a firearm and a customs act charge for failing to report to border officials. Lest Scott stage a second suicide along the shore of a Canadian lake, the judge sentenced him on the spot to three years and three months in a Canadian prison.

When Travis Scott gets out of prison in Canada, he will face the federal fraud charges in Minneapolis. If he wants to plead guilty again, I'm sure the old plea deal is no longer on the table. The state of Minnesota could also charge Scott with crimes related to his fake suicide, and all of the manpower wasted in looking for him.

The Fake Cop Scam

Police were cautioning senior citizens who live in Chicago's Streeterville neighborhood after two men posed as police officers to con residents out of large amounts of money. In the two reported incidents, a man posing as an officer called elderly persons and told them a relative of theirs was under arrest...The man claimed that, to help in the investigation, the elderly people had to withdraw a large sum of money from their banks. Then, a second phony cop met the victims outside their banks to pick up the money.

The two con men told their victims that no one can be told about the money in order not to jeopardize their investigation....

The two suspects were described as black men between the ages 40 and 55.

CBS News, January 19, 2014

Raymond Roth's Fake Death

On July 28, 2012, Jonathan Roth reported his 48-year-old father, Raymond Roth, missing. Raymond, his wife Evana, and their 22-year-old son lived on Long Island in Massapequa, New York. According to Jonathan, his father, while swimming off Nassau County's Jones Beach, was swept out into the Atlantic Ocean.

As officers from the U. S. Coast Guard and various law enforcement agencies searched for Raymond Roth, he was relaxing in Orlando, Florida at his timeshare condo. A couple of days into the search for Raymond's body, his 43-year-old wife Evana came across emails between her missing husband and their son that laid out their plan to defraud the life insurance company of $410,000.

According the scheme, Evana would receive the life insurance payout, and Raymond would start a new life in Florida. Evana Roth, not a party to the fraud, called the Nassau County Police.

On August 2, 2012, Raymond was driving back to New York. He had agreed to meet with law enforcement authorities in Massapequa. In Santee, South Carolina, a cop pulled him over for driving 90 mph. After Roth failed to show up for his meeting with the police, a Nassau County prosecutor charged him with insurance fraud, conspiracy, and filing a false report.

Police officers, on August 6, 2012, took Raymond Roth and his son into custody. Both men made bail, and entered not guilty pleas to the criminal charges.

On March 22, 2013, Raymond Roth and a Nassau County prosecutor agreed on a plea deal. In return for his guilty plea, Roth was sentenced to 90 days in jail and five years of probation. The judge also ordered Roth to pay $27,000 in restitution to the U. S. Coast Guard and $9,000 to the Nassau Police Department.

People who fake their own deaths as a method of defrauding an insurance company rarely succeed. The most common technique in crimes like this involves staging phony drowning. Whenever a heavily insured person goes swimming or boating and doesn't come back, and the body is not recovered, alarm bells go of in the insurance company's office. In a world in which we are under constant video and computer surveillance, it's hard for insurance scam artists to remain dead very long.

Shortly after agreeing on the plea deal, Roth was in trouble again with the law. On March 22, 2013, in Freeport, New York, he identified himself to a woman as a police officer, and ordered her into his van. She fled into a nearby store and called the police. Instead of jail, the authorities took Roth to a psychiatric ward where he tried to commit suicide.

Raymond Roth is a troubled man who obviously wanted to be someone else.

Insurance Fraud

The great irony is that while insurance fraud is widely perceived as a victimless crime, it is far from victimless. The average burglary results in the theft of about $1,000 in property. The average arson results in damage of more than $100,000. While everybody believes that burglary is a serious crime that must be prevented and prosecuted, the same cannot be said for the perception of insurance-related fraud cases. While the typical burglary may have one, victim the typical insurance fraud case makes us all as victims. It is estimated that more than 20 percent of the premiums we all pay for insurance in this country goes to fraudulent claims. In some areas of the country, the numbers are even higher. So all of us pay for insurance fraud whenever we pay our insurance premiums. We are all victims of insurance fraud.

Jack Morgan, *SIU*, 2012

The Stripper Gang Credit Card Case

Dr. Zyadk Younan, a cardiologist from Homdel, New Jersey, refused to accept responsibility for $135,000 in credit card debt he had supposedly incurred in early 2014 at a strip club in Manhattan, New York called Scores. Dr. Younan claimed that strippers at Scores had spiked his drinks with drugs to incapacitate him while they swiped his credit card without his authorization or knowledge. Had the physician's credit card tab not been so outrageously high, his claim of victimhood may have fallen on deaf ears.

In the spring of 2014, DEA agents and officers with the NYPD launched an undercover investigation into Dr. Younan's allegations. As it turns out, the doctor and several other club patrons may indeed have been drugged and ripped-off.

According to the results of the joint investigation, strippers from Scores and the RoadHouse Gentleman's Club in Queens conducted fishing expeditions at bars in Manhattan and Long Island looking for potential credit card victims. They began looking for patrons they could drug and rip-off in September 2013. The suspects allegedly set up club dates with these men, encounters that led to spiked drinks and credit card fraud. Once the suspects dropped the stimulant methylone, commonly known as molly, or the tranquilizer ketamine into their targets' drinks, they were able to take advantage of their drug-addled customers. (I presume strippers earn commissions based on bar tabs.)

According to investigators, the suspects believed that if challenged, their victims could be blackmailed into silence. According to reports, the scheming strippers did in fact blackmail some of credit card victims.

On June 11, 2014, police officers and federal agents arrested four strippers and the manager of Scores on charges of grand larceny, assault, and forgery. At their arraignments in Manhattan, all of the suspects, including club manager Carmine Vitolo, and the suspected ringleader, Samantha Barbash, pleaded not guilty to the charges.

8 POISONING

The Birth of Poison

In the early twentieth century industrial innovation flooded the United States with a wealth of modern poisons, creating new opportunities for the clever poisoner and new challenges for the country's early forensic detectives. Morphine went into teething medicines for infants; opium into routinely prescribed sedatives; arsenic was an ingredient in everything from pesticides to cosmetics. Mercury, cyanide, strychnine, chloral hydrate, chloroform, sulfates of iron, sugar of lead, carbolic acid, and more, the products of the new chemistry stocked the shelves of doctors' offices, businesses, homes, pharmacies, and grocery stores. During the Great War poison was established as a weapon of warfare, earning World War I the name "The Chemist's War." And with the onset of Prohibition a new Chemist's War raged between bootleggers and government chemists working to make moonshine a lethal concoction. In New York's smoky jazz clubs, each round of cocktails became a game of Russian roulette.

There was no way for the barely invented science of toxicology to keep up with the deluge. Though a few dogged researchers were putting out manuals and compiling textbooks on the subject, too many novel compounds had yet to be analyzed and most doctors had little or no training in the subject.

Deborah Blum, *The Poisoner's Handbook*, 2010

Murder by Poison

Most of those who die from poisoning do so accidentally. As a mode of criminal homicide, poisoning, compared to guns, knives, blunt objects, and ligatures, is rare. According to FBI statistics, out of the 187,000 criminal homicides committed from 1990 to 2000, only 346 involved poison. During the period 2001 to 2006, the figure rose to 523. But forensic toxicologists, the experts educated and trained to detect and identify substances harmful to the human body, believe that homicidal poisoning is more common than crime statistics suggest. For example, in 2002, 26,435 people died of poisoning. While only 63 of these deaths were ruled as murder, 3,336 were listed, under manner of death, as "undetermined." In other words, forensic pathologists considered these poisoning deaths as suspicious.

Nobody knows how many people have been murdered by poison because most of these deaths were classified as naturally caused fatalities. In most of these cases, there were no outward signs of homicide. There were no bullet holes, stab wounds, cuts, bruises, or marks around the neck that signify that these deaths were not natural. In most instances, because these deaths were not outwardly suspicious, no autopsies were conducted. These victims were embalmed, buried, or cremated. Occasionally, when an estranged spouse received a large life insurance payment and a week later remarried, police became suspicious.

Money and sex are common motives for murder, but motive is not evidence. The evidence of a homicidal poisoning is the poison. If the toxic substance is not detected and identified in the course of an autopsy, the killer will get away with murder. Exhumations are rare.

Poisons are seldom detected through clinical (rather than criminal) autopsies that are performed by regular hospital pathologists. This is because the pathologist is not thinking homicide, or looking for poison. Unless a specific poison is suspected, the chance of random discovery is unlikely. Arsenic, because it is readily available, tasteless, and can be administered in a series of small doses that causes a period of illness before death, is the weapon of choice among those who murder by poison. Within 24 hours of ingestion, arsenic moves from the blood into the victim's liver, kidneys, spleen, lungs and GI tract. In two to four weeks, traces can be found in the victim's hair, nails, and skin. From there, traces of the poison settle in the bone. Thirty minutes after ingesting a small dose of arsenic, the victim will experience a metallic taste, garlic smelling breath, headaches, muscle cramping, vertigo, vomiting, abdominal pain, and diarrhea. If the victim doesn't die within a few hours from shock, the poisoned person may die a few days later from kidney problems. If the victim survives two to four weeks, in addition to horrible suffering, he will start losing his hair. When death finally comes, the likely cause will be identified as renal failure.

Other common poisons used in the commission of homicide include strychnine (rat poison), morphine, and Demerol. Antifreeze (ethylene glycol) has become a relatively popular weapon in murder-by-poison cases.

Angel of Death Cases

Deaths by homicidal poisonings that commonly do not raise suspicion, and are therefore misdiagnosed as natural fatalities, involve hospital patients who are elderly, or already ill. The death of an old or gravely ill patient, almost by definition, is a natural death. This is why physicians, nurses, and other healthcare workers who kill--so-called "angels of death"--have gotten away with murdering so many people.

Normally, homicide by poison is not an impulsive crime. But in the hospital, or home for the elderly, it is a crime of opportunity. The angel of death has easy access to the poison, and to the victim. There is no need for extensive preparation and planning. Moreover, there is no apparent or obvious motive for the homicide because these killers do not receive any direct personal gain out of the crime. The homicidal motives associated with angels of death are therefore pathological, and hidden. This type of serial killer is difficult to spot because angels of death are not manifestly insane. They possess personality disorders that compel them to murder out of generalized rage, boredom, or the impulse to play God.

As murderers, angels of death are cold-blooded, careful, and vain. This makes them hard to catch. Quite often, in their employment histories, they have been terminated from previous healthcare jobs. When too many patients die on a nurse or orderly's watch, and the employee comes under suspicion, he or she is fired. Healthcare workers suspected of murdering patients often quit, and get a similar job somewhere else. The tendency, among healthcare administrators, is to deny the obvious, and pass the problem on to the next employer. Over the years, dozens of angels of death have been caught, but only after large numbers of patients have been murdered. Given the nature of the crime, and the limited role forensic science plays in these cases, it is reasonable to assume that the small number of angel of death convictions represents the mere tip of a rather large homicidal iceberg.

Donald Harvey

In 1975, after working briefly as a hospital orderly in London, Kentucky, 23-year-old Donald Harvey took a job with the Veteran's Hospital in Cincinnati, Ohio. As the years passed, a pattern emerged. When Harvey was on duty, patients died. Finally, after ten years, and the deaths of more than

100 patients on his watch, the orderly was fired. He was terminated because several hospital workers suspected he was poisoning his patients. After Harvey left the facility, the death rate plummeted. Terminating Donald Harvey turned out to be good medicine, at least at the VA hospital.

Shortly after his firing, Harvey was hired across town at Drake Memorial Hospital where the death rate began to soar. As he had done at the VA facility, Harvey murdered patients by either lacing their food with arsenic, or injecting cyanide into their gastric tubes. The deaths at Drake, like those at the VA hospital, were ruled as naturally caused fatalities. While suspicions were aroused, it was hard to imagine that this friendly, helpful little man who was so charming and popular with members of his victims' families, could be a stone-cold serial killer.

As clever and careful as Harvey was, he made a mistake when he poisoned John Powell, a patient recovering from a motorcycle accident. Under Ohio law, victims of fatal traffic accidents must be autopsied. At Powell's autopsy, an assistant detected the odor of almonds, the telltale sign of cyanide. This was fortunate because most people are unable to detect this scent. The forensic pathologist ordered toxicological tests that revealed that John Powell had died from a lethal dose of cyanide. Harvey had been the last person to see Mr. Powell alive, and John Powell would be the last person he would kill.

The Cincinnati police arrested Harvey, and searched his apartment where they found jars filled with arsenic and cyanide, and books on poisoning. However, the Hamilton County prosecutor believed that without a confession, there might not be enough evidence to convince a jury of Harvey's guilt. The suspect, on the other hand, was worried that if convicted, he would be sentenced to death. So Harvey and the prosecutor struck a deal. In return for a life sentence, Donald Harvey would confess to all of the murders he could remember. Over a period of several days, he confessed to killing, in Kentucky and Ohio, 130 patients. When asked why he had killed all of those helpless victims, the best answer Harvey could muster was that he must have a "screw loose." Forensic pathologists familiar with the case speculated that the murders had given Harvey, an otherwise ordinary and insignificant person, a sense of power over the lives of others. Harvey pleaded guilty to several murders and was sentenced to life in prison.

The old saying that "murder will out" does not apply when the weapon of choice is poison.

The Ideal Murder Weapon

Poisoning is a method of murdering a person without leaving any inconvenient and incriminating clues like bloodstains, knife-wounds, strangulation marks or crude bludgeoning. With luck, the murder might even be put down to death from natural causes. That, quite simply, is the reason why poisoning was the favorite method of murder for thousands of years: because it was virtually undetectable, its effects indistinguishable from hear attack or a stroke....

Ancient Rome is the first society on record where rulers, as a matter of policy, used poison on a large scale, almost indiscriminately. But we know that the Greeks used poison much earlier, referring to aconite [a toxin derived from the aconitum plant] as the "queen of poisons", for example. And certainly poison was known and widely used in the East, the Arabs and the Indians in particular being great practitioners in the deadly uses of venom.

Brian Marriner, *On Death's Bloody Trail*, 1991

The Stepping Hill Case

Greater Manchester is a heavily populated metropolitan county in northwest England. Stockport, a city of 136,000, is one of the municipalities within the county. Between June 1, 2011 and July 15, 2011, three patients at Stepping Hill Hospital in Stockport died after being given saline ampoules or drips laced with insulin.

Detectives with the Greater Manchester Police Department (GMP) determined that at least eight other patients had suffered from insulin poisoning. (Insulin is used as a treatment for diabetes, but for people without an insulin deficiency, the substance can be toxic.)

Following the determination of how these three patients had died, armed police guards were stationed at the hospital in the event the poisoner was an outsider. To protect patients from a hospital employee, members of the staff were required to work in pairs.

On July 20, 2011, GMP detectives arrested a 27-year-old Stepping Hill nurse named Rebecca Jane Leighton. The Chief Crown prosecutor for the region charged Leighton with three counts of criminal damage with intent to endanger life. Nurse Leighton pleaded not guilty to the charges.

The Crown Prosecution Service, on September 2, 2011, dropped the charges against the nurse. Notwithstanding the dismissal of the case against her, the hospital fired Leighton on December 2, 2011. She appealed the discharge, but following a hearing in February 2012, she lost her case.

On January 5, 2012, detectives with the GMP arrested 46-year-old Victorino Chua, a male nurse originally from the Philippines. Chua has been a registered nurse since 2003. He has two children and claims to be a devout Roman Catholic. Police officers took him into custody at his home just outside of Stockport.

Arrested as a suspect in the Stepping Hill Poisonings, but not charged, Chua was interrogated then released on bail. Pursuant to the terms of his release, he was barred from approaching any potential witnesses in the case. He also lost his right to work in healthcare.

On March 29, 2014, the Chief Crown prosecutor charged Victorino Chua with poisoning to death 44-year-old Tracey Arden, 71-year-old Arnold Lancaster, and Alfred Weaver, 83. The murder suspect was also charged with 31 counts of causing grievous bodily harm, 22 counts of attempting to cause grievous bodily harm, and 8 counts of attempting to administer poison. Chua pleaded not guilty to all charges.

As the poison investigation progressed, GMP detectives identified eight other Stepping Hill patients killed by the insulin-contaminated saline. Dozens of patients who were poisoned got sick but survived. Mr. Chua was in custody awaiting his trial. The angel of death investigation in Stepping Hill, England continues.

Norway's Angel of Death

Arnfinn Nesset managed the Oakdale Valley Nursing Home in Norway, and between 1977 and 1980 he murdered 22 of his elderly patients by the administration of the drug curacit (a derivative of curare, which is used by the natives of South America to tip their arrows). During a preliminary interrogation Nesset confessed to the killings, adding, "I've killed so many I can't remember them all." At various times he gave different reasons for the murders, including euthanasia, pleasure killing, schizophrenia and a morbid need to take life.

By the time Nesset came to trial, he had retracted his confessions and pleaded not guilty. He was eventually convicted of 22 out of a final 25 counts of murder, plus charges of forgery related to the embezzlement of the deceased patients' money--not for his own use, he was quick to emphasize, but to swell the funds of missionary charities. Nesset was sentenced to 21 years' imprisonment, the maximum permitted under Norwegian law.

Brian Lane, Chronicle of 20th Century Murder, 1995

Canada's Black Widow

In 1988, in Ontario, Canada, the then 52-year-old Melissa Ann, married to a man named Russell Shephard, met Gordon Stewart, a factory worker with two children whose wife had passed away. They had an affair. Melissa then divorced Mr. Shepard and became Mrs. Stewart.

On April 22, 1991, after drugging Gordon Stewart with benzodiazepine (valium and restoril), Melissa drove him to a remote stretch of highway near the Halifax airport, pulled his body out of the car, and ran over him twice. (Mr. Stewart was probably dead from the lethal dose of drugs before she dumped him onto the road.) Three hours later, Melissa reported the incident to the police, claiming she had killed her husband while he was attempting to rape her.

Melissa's account of her second husband's death, in the context of an attempted rape, made no sense. Moreover, Mr. Stewart, before his death, had written a letter in which he chronicled how Melissa had cheated on him, repeatedly lied, and drained his bank account. The authorities also found traces of the deadly drug in the victim's system.

In the spring of 1992, a jury in Kingston, Ontario, found Melissa Stewart guilty of manslaughter. The judge sentenced her to six years in prison. While incarcerated, Melissa formed a support group for wives who had been abused by their husbands. (She should have formed a class on how to find husbands to murder for their bank accounts and inheritance.) After serving just two years of the manslaughter sentence, the homicidal sociopath became a nationally known spokesperson for the battered wife syndrome.

In April 2001, while looking for a husband to kill at a Christian retreat in Ontario, Melissa Stewart met 83-year-old Robert Edmund Friedrich. The next day, the 66-year-old black widow sent him a letter in which she wrote: "God wants us to be married." Within days of that letter, the couple tied the knot.

When Mr. Friedrich died of cardiac arrest one year after marrying Melissa, she emptied his bank account of $400,000, and continued to receive his social security checks. The happy widow arranged to have Mr. Friedrich hastily cremated before his body could be autopsied. Because of his age, and the quick cremation, notwithstanding some suspicion of foul play, Melissa was not charged in connection with this the old man's death.

In March 2004, about two years after Mr. Friedrich's passing, Melissa hooked up with a Florida man through an Internet dating site. A few days after the online meeting, she flew to 73-year-old Alexander Strategos' home in Pinellas Park. The next day, the Canadian moved into the recently divorced man's house. Not long after that, they were married.

During the next eight months, Mr. Strategos, feeling weak, kept falling and hitting his head, injuries that required eight hospitalizations. His doctors couldn't figure out what was ailing him. During his residence at a rest home, just before he died in January 2005, Mr. Strategos signed over power of attorney to his wife.

Mr. Strategos' son became suspicious when he discovered, in his father's medical papers, that he had died with the drug benzodiazepine in his system. Melissa had also withdrawn $20,000 from her deceased husband's bank account. On January 6, 2005, police arrested Melissa Friedrich on charges of grand theft and forgery. She pleaded guilty to these offenses, and was sentenced to five years. On April 4, 2009, upon her release from the Florida prison, the authorities deported her back to Canada. Melissa never faced charges in connection with the mysterious death of Alexander Strategos.

On September 28, 2012, Melissa Friedrich, now 77, married Fred Weeks, a 75-year-old from New Glasgow, New Brunswick. While honeymooning a few days later on Cape Breton, Nova Scotia, Mr. Weeks fell ill at their bed and breakfast, and had to be hospitalized. After nurses noticed signs that the patient had been injected with something, hospital personnel alerted the police. On October 1, Fred Weeks left the hospital a weaker but wiser man.

The day after her husband walked out of the hospital, the police arrested Melissa on the charge of administering a noxious substance. No doubt her criminal record, and the fates of her former husbands influenced the decision to take her into custody. The judge, at her October 5, 2012 bail hearing, denied her bond.

In June 2013, Melissa pleaded guilty to administering a noxious drug and failing the necessaries of life. The judge sentenced the 78-year-old woman to three and a half years in prison. The Crown, without success, had argued that the defendant's age should not be a factor in her sentencing.

The Poisoned Smoothie Case

Selena Irene York and her teenage daughter had fallen on hard times. A 79-year-old man named Ed Zurbuchen invited them to live in his Vernal, Utah home. On September 29, 2008, his 33-year-old houseguest gave him a peach smoothie. Shortly after drinking it, the old man was taken to the hospital complaining of dizziness, numbness of the face, and speech difficulties. At first, doctors thought he had suffered a stroke. After four days in the hospital, Mr. Zurbuchen underwent a series of liver and kidney tests that revealed he had ingested ethylene glycol, the main ingredient in anti-freeze.

Although Selena York had given Mr. Zurbuchen the drink that had made him sick, had made herself the beneficiary of his life insurance policy, and had taken control of his bank account, he didn't want to press charges against her. Without the victim's cooperation and testimony, the Uintah County prosecutor didn't have a case. In 2009, the suspect and her daughter moved to Eugene, Oregon. Although the authorities in Utah believed York had tried to murder the old man, the investigation went cold.

On April 2011, the poisoning case came back to life when the Uintah County prosecutor received a letter from Joseph Dominic Ferraro, Selena York's former boyfriend, and the father of her child. Ferraro, who was in jail for sexual assault, had been living with York and his daughter in Eugene, Oregon. According to Ferraro, York had bragged to him about poisoning an old man in Utah in an effort to kill him so she could take over his estate. Since York had drained Ferraro's bank account, and sold both of his cars while he sat in jail, he believed her story. And so did the authorities in Utah.

In June, police arrested York in Eugene on the charge of attempted murder. After being extradited back to Utah, York, in exchange for the reduced charges of aggravated assault and forgery, confessed to poisoning Mr. Zurbuchen. She said she had purchased the smoothie at a nearby store, dumped out half of its contents then poured in the antifreeze. After his death, she planned to gain power of attorney over his estate. Before she had left Utah after the failed homicide, York forged a check on the victim's bank account for $10,000.

In December 2011, Selena York was allowed to plead no contest to the reduced charges of aggravated assault and forgery. Two months later, the judge sentenced her to three consecutive five-year prison terms. (It's doubtful she will serve 15 years behind bars.) Had Mr. Zurbuchen died of poisoning, York would have been eligible for the death sentence. Had she not ripped-off Mr. Ferraro (who was convicted of sexual abuse), she would have gotten away with attempted murder. This woman was a cold-blooded killer, a sociopath who should never get out of prison.

The Happy Poisoner

In 1917, on trial for his life, accused of double murder, Dr. Arthur Warren Waite laughed at the law. It was, he agreed, all true. He had indeed murdered his mother-in-law by mixing germs in her food. He had also killed his wealthy father-in-law, but when germs failed, and the arsenic too, Waite had used chloroform, suffocating the old man with a pillow to finish him off. Why? "For the money," said Waite.

Waite's trial was the New York City sensation of its day. The debonair young dentist cheerfully explained how he had poisoned his mother-in-law mixing pneumonia, diphtheria and influenza germs into her meals.

Dr. Waite's father-in-law had been a hardier soul, resisting tuberculosis bacteria sprayed up his nose, chlorine gas, and various attempts to give him pneumonia, including dampening his bed sheets. Science caught up with Dr. Waite when arsenic he'd poured into the old man's soup was detected at autopsy. [Waite was found guilty and hanged.]

Roger Wilkes, The Mammoth Book of Murder & Science, 2000

The Urooj Kahn Case

Urooj Khan emigrated to the U. S. from India when he was twenty-three. He worked hard, saved his money, and by 2012, the 46-year-old owned three dry cleaning shops on Chicago's North Side where he lived with his wife Shabana Ansari and his 17-year-old stepdaughter, Jasmeen.

In June 2012, after returning from his hajj pilgrimage to Saudi Arabia where Mr. Khan promised himself he would live a better life--and quit buying lottery tickets--he paid $60 at a 7-Eleven store near his house for two instant scratch-off cards. After scratching off the second ticket, Mr. Khan yelled, "I hit a million!"

On June 26, 2012, at the Illinois Lottery Ceremony, Mr. Khan, with is wife, stepdaughter, and a few friends looking on, accepted the oversized mock check for $425,000. (After opting for the lump sum payment, this is what was left of the $1 million after taxes.) Khan said he'd donate some money to St. Jude's Children's Hospital in Chicago, and use the rest of his winnings to pay bills and grow his business.

On July 20, 2012, the day after the Illinois Comptroller's Office issued Mr. Khan his $425,000 check, and before he had an opportunity to cash it, the lottery winner had dinner in his modest West Roger's Park neighborhood home with his wife Shabana Ansari and his stepdaughter, Jasmeen. After dinner, Mr. Khan said he didn't feel well and went to bed. A short time later, he screamed that he was suffocating. Ambulance personnel rushed Mr. Khan to a nearby hospital where doctors pronounced him dead.

After a routine toxicological testing of Mr. Khan's blood for narcotics, alcohol, and carbon monoxide poisoning (his skin had turned pink) that produced negative results, the Cook County Medical Examiner's Office determined his cause of his death to be heart disease. The manner of Mr. Khan's death went into the books as natural. Pursuant to an internal medical examiner's office rule that dead people over the age of 45 who do not show signs of trauma are not autopsied, Mr. Khan was buried without a post-mortem examination. (The age limit has been since raised to 50.)

On August 15, 2012, Mr. Khan's widow cashed the $425,000 lottery check.

Five months after Urooj Khan's sudden and unexpected passing, one of his relatives called the Cook County Medical Examiner's Office. According to this unidentified family member, Mr. Khan had been poisoned to death.

Acting on what must have been a credible tip, Medical Examiner Dr. Stephen Cina ordered further toxicological testing of Mr. Khan's blood. This led to a rather shocking discovery: Mr. Khan had died from a lethal dose of cyanide. As a result of this finding, the medical examiner's office changed Mr. Khan's cause of death to cyanide poisoning. His manner of death, however, will be determined by the outcome of a homicide investigation conducted by detectives with the Chicago Police Department. (According to reports, investigators grilled Mr. Khan's widow for four hours.)

Cyanide is an extremely toxic white powder that has a variety of industrial applications. It can also be found in some pesticides and in rat poison. Small doses of cyanide swallowed, inhaled (gas chambers used it), or injected, denies the body's blood cells oxygen. Death from this poison, a form of asphyxia called histoxic hypoxia, while agonizing, is quick. To disguise its bitter taste, a cyanide poisoner would be wise to mix a small amount into a plate of spicy food.

Poisoning, as a mode of criminal homicide, was popular in the 19th Century before the dawn of pharmacology. Because there was no way to scientifically identify abnormal quantities of toxic substances in the body, no one knows how many wives, prior to 1900, poisoned their husbands to death. (In the era before forensic toxicology, homicide cops called cyanide "inheritance powder.")

In modern times, murder and suicide cases involving cyanide and other poisons are rare. In June 2012, the month Mr. Khan won his lottery money, millionaire Michael Markin, moments after a jury found him guilty of arson, swallowed a cyanide pill. Minutes later he died while sitting at the defense table. Markin's death was so unusual it received nationwide publicity.

On January 8, 2013, the day Medical Examiner Stephen Cina announced the planned exhumation of Urooj Khan's remains, his wife, Shabana Ansari, told an Associated Press reporter that she wasn't the relative who had requested the more sophisticated toxicological test. She said she had no idea who that person was, and that she "...didn't think anyone had a bad eye for [her husband], or that he had an enemy." The widow refused to provide details of the circumstances surrounding Mr. Khan's death. She said talking about his passing was too painful.

Chicago homicide detectives had the job of determining if Mr. Khan had been murdered, committed suicide, or had been exposed accidentally to the deadly substance. Given the timing of his death, and the unlikeliness of accident or suicide in this case, the most plausible explanation was criminal homicide.

In late January 2013, information surfaced that after Mr. Khan won the lottery, his 32-year-old wife and his siblings, a daughter from a previous marriage and his stepdaughter Jasmeen, began fighting over the money. According to Mr. Khan's brother Imtiaz and his sister Meraj, after his death, Shabana Ansari tried to cash the lottery check to avoid giving Khan's daughter her fair share. Last November, homicide detectives searched the West Roger's Park home for traces of the cyanide. The five-month period between Mr. Khan's death and the criminal investigation made solving this case difficult.

In early February 2013, the authorities exhumed Urooj Khan's 5-foot-5, 198-pound body from a Chicago cemetery and transported it to the Cook County Medical Examiner's office. Forensic pathologists collected samples of his hair, fingernails, stomach contents, and tissue from his major organs for tests to determine if he had been poisoned to death. Medical Examiner Dr. Stephen Cina told reporters that given the length of time Mr. Khan's body was in the ground, it was not certain that toxicological tests would produce positive results. According to Dr. Cina, "cyanide over the postmortem period can evaporate from the tissues." Dr. Cina said he remained convinced, however, that Mr. Khan had been the victim of a criminal homicide.

A few weeks after the exhumation, Dr. Cina, at a press conference, said that while earlier toxicological tests revealed a lethal dose of cyanide in Mr. Khan's blood, the poison was not detected in his tissues or digestive system. "In this case," the forensic pathologist said, "due to advanced putrefaction of the tissues, no cyanide was detected."

In December 2013, a Cook County Probate Judge ruled that Urooj Khan's wife was entitled to two-thirds of the lottery winnings. The widow also inherited the business and the other family assets. The homicide investigation continues. No one has been arrested.

The Eye-Drop Poisoning Case

Dr. Harry Johnston, since June 2009, had been treating Thurman Nesbitt for a mysterious illness. The 45-year-old patient complained of nausea, low blood pressure, and breathing difficulties. Dr. Johnston, suspecting that his patient was being poisoned, had his blood analyzed. On July 27, 2012, the serology tests revealed the presence of tetrahydrozolin, a chemical found in over-the-counter eye-drops.

On August 10, 2012, troopers with the Pennsylvania State Police arrested Nesbitt's girlfriend, Vickie Jo Mills. The 33-year-old McConnellsburg woman, on probation for forgery, admitted putting Visine drops into her boyfriend's drinking water. Mills told her interrogators that she had been making Nesbitt sick since June 2009. She said it had never been her intention to poison her boyfriend to death. To the obvious question of why she had done this, Mills explained that she had made Nesbitt sick in an effort to get him to pay more attention to her.

Most women who use illness to attract attention make themselves sick pursuant to a syndrome called Munchausen. In Munchausen Syndrome by Proxy, these women make their children sick. It's not clear why Mills thought poisoning her boyfriend would improve their relationship.

The Fulton County prosecutor charged Vickie Jo Mills with ten counts of aggravated assault that carried a combined maximum sentence of 240 years in prison and a $300,000 fine. Shortly after her arrest, the authorities released Mills on a $75,000 surety bond.

On October 16, 2002, the district attorney dropped nine of the ten counts in return for the defendant's guilty plea. A Fulton County judge, on February 14, 2013, sentenced Mills to two to four years in prison.

It's odd that something you put into your eyes will make you sick if you put it into your stomach.

The St. Andrews Poisoning Case

In 2011, Alexander Hilton, a 20-year-old rich kid from Princeton, Massachusetts, attended St. Andrews University in Fife, Scotland. The sophomore prep school graduate (St. Johns) had moved to United Kingdom to study economics at this ancient and prestigious institution of higher learning.

On March 5, 2011, on the eve of the annual St. Andrews ball, Hilton and a group of his fellow students were participating in a dormitory drinking game. One of the drinkers, Robert Forbes, an American from Virginia, after gulping down a bottle of red wine given to him by Hilton, became seriously ill. The 19-year-old suffered loss of balance, severe nausea, had trouble breathing, and temporarily lost his eyesight. He spent a week in the hospital. Doctors said that had Forbes not received medical treatment, he could have died.

A few days after the dormitory drinking game, local investigators questioned Hilton about the incident. The authorities suspected that Hilton, known around the school as an anti-social oddball, had intentionally poisoned Robert Forbes. Hilton denied mixing anything into the wine. The Scottish authorities didn't have enough evidence to charge the American with a crime, but urged him to leave the country. He was also kicked out of St. Andrews. On March 18, 2011, Alexander Hilton returned to his parents' home in Princeton, Massachusetts.

Back in Scotland, toxicological tests revealed that the red wine that had made Robert Forbes so sick had been spiked with methanol, an ingredient found in antifreeze. The sweet-smelling liquid, also known as wood alcohol, is colorless, highly flammable, and deadly. A search of Hilton's computer determined that he had investigated the toxicological effects of combining red wine and methanol. In Hilton's dormitory room, investigators found a funnel.

After Hilton returned to the United States, he enrolled in a college in New Mexico. About a year after the St. Andrews drinking party, Hilton learned that the authorities in Scotland planned to charge him with the attempted murder of Robert Forbes. Upon learning this, Hilton dropped out of the college in New Mexico and returned to his parents' house in Princeton, Massachusetts. Seven months later, in the fall of 2012, the prosecutor in charge of the case in Scotland charged Hilton with attempted murder.

On February 4, 2013, under an extradition treaty the United States has with the United Kingdom, United States Marshals took Alexander Hilton into custody. The federal authorities hauled the former St. Andrews student to the Central Falls, Rhode Island Detention Center where he was placed under suicide watch.

Hilton, on February 21, 2013, appeared at his bail hearing in federal court in Boston before a U. S. magistrate judge. Assistant United States Attorney David J. D'Addio, in arguing against bail for this defendant, said, "This is an attempted murder case, a serious case, and we can't lose sight of that. The evidence before us is that Mr. Hilton deliberately poisoned a student at St. Andrews."

Hilton's defense attorney, Norman S. Zalkind, argued that because his client was seriously mentally ill, bail should be granted in order that the defendant could continue taking his medication, and not be denied psychiatric therapy. According to the defense attorney, if Hilton remained in custody, he was "...going to get sicker and sicker and sicker." Zalkind described Hilton as an extremely intelligent person with the socialization skills of a 14-year-old. The defense lawyer wondered why someone at the university didn't notice Hilton's mental problem after he started flunking his classes.

The U. S. magistrate judge withheld his bail decision pending the outcome of Hilton's extradition hearing. As of August 2014, Hilton, still in the U.S., continued his fight to avoid extradition to Scotland.

Poisoned by Hand Sanitizer

A Louisiana woman has been charged with first-degree murder after police say she injected alcohol-based hand sanitizer into the feeding tube of her 17-month-old son who was afflicted with Down syndrome. Erika Wigstrom, 20 was being held without bond on March 12, 2014. Police say she told them she wanted to end Lucas Ruiz's suffering...Lucas died on January 21, 2014.

Plaquemines Parish Sheriff's Commander Eric Becnel said the child also had been poisoned with alcohol in October 2012 while hospitalized for treatment of a heart defect. The child's father, Cesar Ruiz, allegedly confessed in that instance, but Becnel said Wigstrom has now confessed to poisoning the child in both cases.

Associated Press, March 13, 2014

Daycare Worker Sedates Kids

In college, it doesn't take much to put students to sleep. A good number of them come to class half-drunk or drugged, and a lot of professors are really *boring*. In preschool, however, kids tend to be awake, and in many cases, pains-in-the-neck. So what can a daycare worker do to calm these little buggers down?

Recently, at the Morgan Hill Kiddie Academy (sounds prestigious) in Morgan Hill, California, a 59-year-old daycare worker named Debbie Gratz came up with a solution to the hyper-kid problem. A colleague saw her spiking kids' cups with the sleep aid Sominex. She must have figured that if you lace their little drinks with sleeping pills, they will drop like flies.

Apparently Morgan Hill Kiddie Academy administrators did not approve of Gratz's behavior altering methodology because they called the police. Following a search of the daycare worker's dwelling, officers took her into custody. Charged with felony child endangerment, Gratz waited for her arraignment in the Santa Clara County Jail. According to reports, she confessed to spiking the kiddie drinks with Sominex.

In May 2013, Gratz pleaded no contest to five counts of attempted child endangerment. Four months later, Superior Court Judge Kenneth Shapero sentenced the former daycare worker to six months in jail.

The Power of Poison

In 2012, 62-year-old Mark Staudte resided with his wife Diane and their four children in a modest neighborhood in Springfield, Missouri. The couple had met years ago at a small Lutheran College in Kansas. While active in the church, Diane and Mark kept to themselves. A man with strong political opinions who regularly wrote letters to the editor, Mr. Staudte had never been very good at holding down a steady job. He eventually stopped trying and devoted most of his time to family matters and playing in a band he had formed called "Messing With Destiny."

Mark Staudte's 51-year-old wife Diane played the organ at church and unlike her husband, never had much to say. The couple's oldest child, 26-year-old Shaun suffered from a mild form of autism. Sarah Staudte, 24, was having a hard time finding a good job. Rachel Staudte, two years younger than Sarah, was a dean's list student at Missouri State University. (At least according to her Facebook page.) She played the flute at church. The youngest member of the family was an eleven-year-old girl. (She has not been identified in the media.)

On April 8, 2012, Easter Sunday, Mark Staudte died suddenly at home. To the emergency personnel who rushed to the house, Diane explained that her husband hadn't been feeling well. He had recently experienced three seizures. When asked if her husband had a history of this kind of thing, she said he did not.

The Greene County Medical Examiner, Dr. Douglas Anderson, without conducting an autopsy or ordering toxicological tests, ruled that Mark Staudte's manner of death was natural. The forensic pathologist did not identify specifically what had caused this man to die. Pursuant to Diane Staudte's instructions, her husband's body was cremated. At his memorial service, friends and family couldn't help noticing that Diane's demeanor bordered on jubilant.

On September 2, 2012, almost five months after Mark Staudte's sudden and mysterious passing, tragedy once again raised its ugly head at the Staudte house. This time it was Diane's oldest child Shaun who became ill and suddenly died at the age of 26. Once again, Dr. Douglas Anderson, without the aid of an autopsy or toxicological tests, ruled the death as natural. The medical examiner did not, however, identify the disease that had taken the young man's life. Diane made sure that Shaun's body, like his father's, was consumed by fire. For a woman who, within a period of five months had lost her husband and her oldest child, Diane seemed unfazed by the unexpected deaths. Indeed, her spirits seemed to have been lifted.

On the day after Shaun's passing, the Springfield police received an anonymous tip from a man who said he was a friend of the Staudte family. According to the caller, Diane poisoned Mark and Shaun Staudte to death.

The police did not act on this tip. According to the medical examiner, both men had died natural deaths. Without a finding of homicide, there was nothing to investigate.

Sarah Staudte fell ill on June 10, 2013. Paramedics came to the house and rushed her to a nearby hospital. The next day, as the 24-year-old fought for her life, the Springfield police received a second anonymous tip in which the caller accused Diane Staudte of poisoning the third member of her family. This time the Springfield police sent a detective to the hospital to question doctors and nurses.

According to hospital personnel who were caring for the young woman, her mother had visited the patient briefly during which time she joked around with the medical staff. One of the nurses informed the detective that Diane Staudte told hospital personnel that she wasn't going to let her daughter's illness ruin a Florida vacation she planned to take in the near future. A physician described Sarah's condition as "very suspicious." The doctor told the investigator that in his opinion, this patient had been poisoned.

On June 20, 2013, after being asked to appear at the Springfield Police Department for questioning, Diane Staudte, following a short interrogation, confessed to poisoning all three members of her family. Over a period of days before the deaths of her husband and son, she had spiked their drinks with the sweet taste of antifreeze. Diane had poisoned her husband's Gatorade simply because she "hated" him. She had laced Shaun's Coke with the poison because she considered him "worse than a pest." Diane told her interrogators that she had poisoned her oldest daughter Sarah because the girl "would not get a job and had student loans that had to be paid." Diane insisted that in murdering Mark and Shaun, and attempting to kill Sarah, she had acted alone.

When detectives questioned Rachel Staudte, the 22-year-old college student, she admitted that she had helped her mother commit the crimes. The two of them had used the Internet to research how to administer antifreeze as a poisoning agent.

On June 21, 2013, a Greene County assistant prosecutor charged Diane and Rachel Staudte each with two counts of first- degree murder and one count of first-degree assault. The judge denied both women bail.

According to doctors, while Sarah Staudte will survive her poisoning, she will suffer the neurological effects of the antifreeze for the rest of her life. The eleven-year-old Staudte girl was sent to live with relatives. With her father and brother dead, her mother and one of her sisters on the way to prison for murder and assault, and the other sister permanently disabled, this girl's family no longer existed. That is the power of poison.

In April 2014, Greene County prosecutor Dan Patterson filed a notice of intent to seek the death penalty against Diane Staudte. As of August 2014, the case had not come to trial.

The Dr. Ferrante Murder Case

In 2013, Dr. Robert Ferrante and his wife, Dr. Autumn Klein, lived with their 6-year-old daughter in the Oakland section of Pittsburgh Pennsylvania. Dr. Ferrante held the positions of co-director of the Center of ALS Research, and visiting professor of neurology at the University of Pittsburgh Medical School. Dr. Klein, with offices in Magee-Woman's Hospital in the Kaufman Medical Building, was chief of women's neurology at the University of Pittsburgh Medical Center (UPMC) and an assistant professor of neurology, obstetrics, gynecology and reproductive services at the University of Pittsburgh.

Dr. Ferrante, twenty-three years older than his wife, met her in 2000 when they lived in Boston where she was a medical student and he worked at a hospital for veterans. They were married a year later. In 2010, Dr. Ferrante left his job at Harvard Medical School and Massachusetts General Hospital to join the University of Pittsburgh's neurological surgery team. Dr. Klein moved to Pittsburgh with him.

Dr. Klein, who was forty-one, was having difficulty getting pregnant with her second child. Her 64-year-old husband had been encouraging her to take a nutritional supplement to help her conceive. On April 17, 2013, Dr. Ferrante sent Autumn a text message in which he inquired if she had taken the supplement. She wrote back: "Will it stimulate egg production, too?" Nine hours after Dr. Klein sent that message, she collapsed in the kitchen of the couple's Schenley Farms home.

Emergency personnel rushed Dr. Klein to the UPMC Presbyterian Hospital in Oakland. On the kitchen floor next to her body paramedics notices a bag of white powder later identified as creatine, a nutritional supplement. Shortly after the patient was admitted into the hospital, a UPMC doctor ordered tests of her blood. When a preliminary serological analysis revealed a high level of acid, the doctor ordered toxicology tests for cyanide poisoning.

Dr. Klein died on April 20, 2013. Three days later, at Dr. Ferrante's insistence, her body was cremated. As a result, there was no autopsy. (I do not know if Dr. Klein, between the time she drank the poison and died, was conscious and talking to the police.)

Dr. Karl Williams, the Allegheny County Medical Examiner, based on the toxicology reports, determined that Dr. Klein had died of cyanide poisoning. The forensic pathologist ruled her death a homicide.

Cyanide kills by starving the cells of oxygen. A lethal dose for a human can be as small as 200 milligrams--1/25th the size of a nickel. The poison acts fast, and metabolizes quickly. The toxic substance can be undetectable from one minute to three hours after ingestion. Had samples of Dr. Klein's blood not been taken upon her admission to UPMC, there would have been no physical evidence of poisoning beyond the contents of the bag of white powder found lying on the victim's kitchen floor.

Two weeks after Dr. Klein's death, detectives with the Pittsburgh Police Department launched a homicide investigation with Dr. Ferrante as the prime suspect. Officials at UPMC placed the neurologist on leave, and denied him access to his laboratory. A police search of the lab resulted in the discovery that 8.3 grams from a bottle of cyanide was missing. Detectives learned that Dr. Ferrante had purchased a half-pound of the poison on April 15, 2013, two days before his wife collapsed in their home. Dr. Ferrante had used a UPMC credit card to buy the cyanide, and had asked the vendor to ship it to his lab overnight. Detectives believed the suspect, in his laboratory, mixed the cyanide--a substance not related to his work--into the dietary supplement.

According to friends of the victim, Dr. Ferrante had been a controlling husband who was jealous of his wife's fast-rising career. Moreover, he suspected that she was having an affair with a man from Boston. Dr. Klein had told friends she was planning to leave the doctor. Another possible motive involved the fact Dr. Ferrante did not want his wife to have another child.

On April 13, four days before she fell ill, Dr. Klein sent one of her friends a text message regarding a trip she planned to take to Boston by herself. In that message she wrote: "Change of plans. Husband is coming to Boston. Told me 'to keep me out of trouble.'"

"Oh, dear," replied the friend. "Did you know you were in trouble?"

"I feel like I have been in trouble for a long time now," Dr. Klein answered.

On July 24, 2013, an Allegheny County prosecutor charged Dr. Robert Ferrante with first-degree murder. The next day, as Dr. Ferrante drove back to Pittsburgh from St. Augustine, Florida, a West Virginia state patrol officer arrested him on I-77 near Beckley. According to the doctor's attorney, William Difenderfer, his client was on his way to surrender to the Pittsburgh police.

Dr. Ferrante's arrest for the murder of his wife has caused him serious financial problems. Except for $280,000 the suspect can use for legal expenses and a possible fine, a judge has frozen his assets. In August 2013, his 6-year-old daughter's maternal grandmother who was caring for the girl in Maryland, petitioned a family court judge for child support.

As of August 2014, the Ferrante case had not come to trial.

Kiddie Poisoners

Two Brooklyn, New York elementary school students have been arrested on suspicion of putting rat poison in a teacher's water bottle. The children, who are 9 and 12 and attend Public School 315 on Glenwood Road in Flatbush, were charged with reckless endangerment and assault. The teacher, who drank from the poisoned water bottle, is recovering….

The incident occurred on Monday, May 19, 2014 and was brought to light by a parent whose child reported witnessing other students putting something in the teacher's drink. The mother called the school and reported the episode. But by then, the teacher had already ingested the tainted water.

After being alerted, the teacher took the water bottle to the principal's office and went to see a private doctor, reporting mild nausea….

Al Baker, *The New York Times,* May 21, 2014

The Dr. Gonzales-Angulo Murder Case

Dr. Ana Maria Gonzales-Angulo and her colleague (and lover) Dr. George Blumenschein were on the staff at the University of Texas M. D. Anderson Cancer Center in Houston, Texas. Dr. Gonzales-Angulo, a breast cancer oncologist had attended medical school at the University of Cauca in Columbia, completed her residency in Internal Medicine at the Mount Sinai Medical center in Miami, then finished her training at the University of Texas Medical School. She had been with the M. D. Anderson Cancer Center since 2003. Dr. Blumenschein graduated from Vanderbilt University and the University of Texas Medical School. As a specialist in lung, heart and neck cancers, he had been on the cancer center staff since 2000.

On May 29, 2013, a prosecutor in the Harris County District Attorney's Office, based upon information received from investigators with the University of Texas Police Department, charged Dr. Gonzales-Angulo with aggravated assault. The doctor stood accused of poisoning Dr. Blumenschein's coffee with ethylene glycol, a chemical used in antifreeze and medical research.

According to the criminal complaint, the poisoning took place in Dr. Gonzales-Angulo's Houston apartment. Dr. Blumenschein, after sipping a cup of coffee made by Dr. Gonzales-Angulo, complained of its sweet taste. Dr. Gonzales-Angulo allegedly informed him that she had added Splenda to his drink, and urged him to finish it. After drinking a second cup of Dr. Gonzales-Angulo's coffee that evening, Dr. Blumenschein began slurring his speech.

Sixteen hours after drinking the two cups of coffee, paramedics rushed Dr. Blumenschein to a nearby emergency room where doctors diagnosed him with central nervous system damage, cardiopulmonary problems, and renal (kidney) failure. (The doctor would subsequently undergo dialysis treatment.)

Three toxicological tests of Dr. Blumenschein's urine revealed the presence of crystals consistent with ethylene glycol poisoning. (By the time the toxicological analysis, the ethylene glycol had been metabolized.)

Police officers booked Dr. Gonzales-Angulo into the Harris County Jail on May 30, 2013. Shortly thereafter she posted her $50,000 bond and was released. Officials at the M. D. Anderson Cancer Center placed the doctor on administrative leave. Her attorney, Derek Hollingsworth, told reporters that his client "is completely innocent. She is a distinguished citizen and scientist," he said, "and these allegations are totally inconsistent with her personal and professional life."

In September 2013, a Harris County Grand Jury indicted Dr. Gonzales-Angulo on one count of aggravated assault. As of August 2014 the case had not come to trial.

A Strange and Mysterious Death

According to Katee Dias, in early 2010 while residing in London, England, she received a package in the mail. The parcel bore the correct address but was intended for someone else, a former resident perhaps. Thinking that this person might claim the item, Katee held the package for six months before opening it. When she did, she found a bottle that, according to its label, contained a fruit drink. Katee kept the bottle and threw away the packaging.

At some point (here the story gets vague) Katee gave her father, a resident of Impington, a Cambridgeshire village in southeast England, the presumed fruit drink. In October 2013, 55-year-old Romano Dias opened the three and a half-year-old bottle and consumed half of its contents. (Based upon news reportage, Katee was present when her father gulped down some of the drink.)

After a couple of mouthfuls, Mr. Dias reportedly said that the liquid tasted "awful." Shortly thereafter he complained of a burning throat then said, "I am in trouble here. I am dying. I am dead." Mr. Dias collapsed and died, presumably from the contents of the outdated fruit juice bottle.

A laboratory analysis of the mystery bottle's contents revealed that it contained liquid methamphetamine. (Dealers in meth frequently transport the drug in liquid form.) In speaking to a reporter with the *Cambridge News*, pathologist Dr. John Grant said that Mr. Dias had consumed well above the lethal dose. He said that while meth use in the United Kingdom has been traditionally light, the American television show "Breaking Bad" has popularized the drug. ("Breaking Bad" was a series about a former high school chemistry teacher named Walter White who becomes an accomplished meth cook.)

Following a coroner's hearing, Cambridgeshire coroner William Morris ruled the manner of Mr. Dias' death "accidental." The coroner based his ruling on the fact there was no evidence that the sender of the lethal package had intended to harm the victim or anyone else.

In the United States, the sender of the liquid meth could have been charged with felony-murder. Under the felony-murder doctrine, the perpetrator of a felony that directly results in an unintended death is criminally culpable for the killing of that person. Mailing $34,000 worth of methamphetamine must be a felony in England. Mr. Dias died as a direct result of that crime. The sender, therefore, is guilty of criminal homicide.

By classifying Mr. Dias' death as accidental, the Cambridgeshire coroner shut the door to a criminal investigation. As a result, the public will never know who sent the bottle of meth to Katee Dias' house in London. (Did the police process the bottle for latent fingerprints?) Other questions that will remain unanswered include: Why did Katee keep the bottle so long? Exactly when did she give it to her father? Why did she give it to him? And did he know he was consuming a three and a half-year-old drink?

Arsenic Poisoning

A person can be accidentally poisoned by arsenic through inhalation, absorption through the skin or mucous membranes, skin contact, and ingestion. People have died by breathing arsenic fumes, licking paintbrushes to make a fine point, or wearing inadequate clothing when applying arsenic-based products. The effects of mild poisoning from inhalation include loss of appetite, nausea and diarrhea. Effects of more severe chronic or acute exposure include skin lesions, chronic headaches, apathy, a garlic odor on the breath, a metallic taste in the mouth, a bronzing pigment of the skin resembling "raindrops on a dusty road" and possible damage to the liver. In addition, arsenic and arsenic compounds are known cancer-causing agents and have been implicated in lung and skin cancer and associated with birth defects.

Michael Baden, M.D. and Marion Roach, *Dead Reckoning*, 2011

A Closed Case

Brittany Murphy's father, a man named Angelo Bertolotti who had served three stretches in the federal penitentiary in Atlanta for various racketeering offenses, had never been a factor in Murphy's life. But after her death, he became involved by filing a lawsuit against the Los Angeles Coroner's Office and the Los Angeles Police Department.

Bertolotti brought the legal action in an effort to force the coroner's office to test his daughter's hair for traces of heavy metal poisons. Bertolotti believed that additional toxicological testing would prove that she had *not* died from pneumonia, anemia, and a lethal mix of cold medications.

The Los Angeles Coroner's Office defended its decision not to test Murphy's hair follicles for traces of heavy metal poison on the grounds there was no indication that she had died from arsenic poisoning. (Professional death investigators, rather than basing their conclusions on personal assumptions, apply forensic science to unravel the mystery of sudden, unexplained deaths.)

In July 2012 a judge dismissed Angelo Bertolotti's lawsuit. However, as a consolation, Bertolotti acquired, from the coroner's office, samples of his daughter's hair, blood and tissue for independent toxicological testing. He promptly sent the samples to a private lab in Colorado for analysis.

The private laboratory, in November 2013, reported high levels of ten heavy metal poisons in the submitted Brittany Murphy samples. According to the toxicological report, Murphy's system contained, among other poisons, aluminum, manganese, and Barium, poisons found in rat poison, pesticides, and insecticides. (These are not substances Murphy would have voluntarily consumed.) According to the private crime lab, presence of these poisons strongly suggested the possibility of a homicidal poisoning.

Armed with the private toxicological findings, Angelo Bertolotti demanded that the Los Angeles Police Department re-open its investigation into Brittany Murphy's death. He also wanted the Los Angeles Coroner's Office to change its manner and cause of death rulings to homicidal poisoning. (This will have to take place before the LAPD will re-open the case.)

Speaking to reporters after the release of the private toxicological report, Bertolotti said, "Vicious rumors, spread by tabloids, unfairly smeared Brittany's reputation. My daughter was neither anorexic or a drug addict."

A few days after the new revelations in the case, Bertolotti appeared on the TV show "Good Morning America." Bertolotti said, "I have a feeling that there was a definite murder situation here. It's poison, yes, I know that." Bertolotti pointed out that the Colorado forensic lab was an accredited facility that "cannot be ignored."

Los Angeles Chief Coroner's investigator Craig R. Harvey, in response to the private laboratory's toxicological findings, said this to reporters: "The Los Angeles Coroner's Office has no plans to reopen our inquiry into the [Murphy] death. We stand by our original reports."

In speaking to a reporter with Fox News on November 20, 2013, addiction specialist Dr. Damon Raskin said the private toxicology results made him suspicious of foul play. Moreover, "other than lab error, there is no other good medical explanation for these abnormal levels of heavy metals. Therefore, some type of poisoning is clearly a possibility."

Fox reporter Hollie McKay also questioned Dr. Shilpi Agarwal, a Los Angeles based physician who said it was extremely unlikely that Murphy had elevated levels of the heavy metals in her system without being given supplements or unintentionally ingesting them.

Dr. Michael Baden, the famed forensic pathologist, had a different interpretation of the new toxicological findings. He said this to a Fox News reporter: "The grouping of heavy metals is more suggestive of hair product use--dyes, soaps, heat, etc. than of rat poison...When hair samples are stored for so long, the increased sensitivity of new chemical tests will pick up whatever was in the hair's container. Was the container tested?"

Rather than defend a premature conclusion, the Los Angeles Coroner's Office should have acknowledged the new toxicological evidence and reopened the case.

A Sick and Dangerous Woman

Adam and Connie Villa were married in 2005. She had a 5-year-old daughter from a previous marriage. He was a member of the Arizona National Guard. The couple and the child, Aniarael Macias, resided in Casa Grande, a suburban community 50 miles south of Phoenix. In 2006 Adam Villa served a year in Iraq with his National Guard unit. By 2010 the couple had three children of their own.

Adam and Connie Villa were divorced in 2012. Following the break-up, the battle over legal custody of the children began.

On Christmas day, 2013, Adam Villa called 911 to report that his wife had stabbed him in the chest and that he was driving himself to the hospital. Police officers rushed to the Villa residence where they encountered Connie Villa holding a knife to her chest. Officers subdued the distraught 35-year-old woman and called for an ambulance.

The three younger Villa children, ages 3, 5, and 8, were in the house when the police arrived. The youngsters informed the officers that their mother had forced them to consume what turned out to be a narcotics-based prescription drug.

In the bathroom, officers discovered the body of 13-year-old Aniarael Macias. Because there were no marks on her body, officers assumed that Connie Villa had poisoned the girl with prescription drugs.

While 33-year-old Adam Villa remained in stable condition at the Casa Grande Regional Medical Center, physicians at the Maricopa Medical Center in Phoenix treated Connie Villa for superficial, self-inflicted knife wounds. The three children, although there were traces of opiates in their bodies, were fine. The siblings were placed into the custody of relatives.

On Sunday, December 29, 2013, upon her release from the hospital, detectives took Connie into custody. When questioned at the police station, she admitted stabbing her husband and poisoning the three children. In the bathroom, after being unable to force Aniarael to ingest the prescription drug, Connie suffocated her to death with her bare hands.

Detectives asked Connie why she had killed her oldest child, stabbed her husband, and tried to poison the little ones to death. She said she was afraid the judge would grant custody of the children to her ex-husband. (This explains why she tried to kill Adam. But why did she want to murder her four children?)

On January 8, 2014, Pinal County Attorney Lando Voyles charged Villa with premeditated first-degree murder, four counts of attempted murder, kidnapping, and four counts of child abuse. Four months later, a Pinal County Superior Court judge approved the prosecution's request to seek the death penalty in this case.

The Child Bride Poisoner

A child bride forced into marriage in Nigeria killed a groom and three of his friends with a poisoned meal on April 7, 2014. Fourteen-year-old Wasila Umaru was married a week earlier to 35-year-old Umaru Sani…Over the weekend, the groom invited a dozen friends to his Ungwar Yansoro village, about 60 miles from the northern city of Majia.

The teenager told police she bought rat poison at a village market and used it to prepare a dish of rice. According to a police official, "The suspect confessed to committing the crime and said she did it because she was forced to marry a man she did not love…The groom and a friend died the same day, and two other victims died later in the hospital. Umaru is cooperating with police and likely will be charged with culpable homicide….

Child marriage is common in Nigeria and especially in the mainly Muslim and impoverished north, where the numbers increase in times of drought because a bride price is paid and it means one less mouth to feed. Fifty percent of Nigerian girls living in rural areas are married before they turn 18, according to the U.N. children's agency. That's a lot of child brides in a country of some 170 million....

Child brides often suffer difficult pregnancies--the leading cause of death worldwide for girls aged 15 to 19--and are much more likely to contract AIDS and be subjected to domestic violence, according to the International Center for Research on Women....

No one in Nigeria has been prosecuted for marrying a child, including Sen. Sani Ahmed Yerima, infamous for divorcing a 17-year-old that he married when she was 15 so he could marry a 14-year-old Egyptian girl in 2010, when he was 49. He had to divorce one of his child brides because Islamic law allows a maximum of four wives at a time.

Many child brides are divorced for that reason and because of incontinence and other medical problems caused by difficult pregnancies, according to local child rights advocates who say such girls are put out on the street.

Associated Press, April 10, 2014

Inheritance Powder

Until the early nineteenth century few tools existed to detect a toxic substance in a corpse. Sometimes investigators deduced poison from the violent sickness that preceded death, or built a case by feeding animals a victim's last meal, but more often than not poisoners walked free. As a result murder by poison flourished. It became so common in eliminating perceived difficulties, such as a wealthy parent who stayed alive too long, that the French nicknamed the metallic element arsenic *poudre de succession,* the inheritance powder.

Deborah Blum, *The Poisoner's Handbook,* 2010

Beware of the Jilted Nerd

In 2013, 19-year-old Nicholas Helman lived with his mother in Hatboro, Pennsylvania, a town of 8,000 in Montgomery County within the Philadelphia metropolitan area. One of the young man's neighbors in the Eleanor Courts apartment complex described Nicholas as the kid you went to school with for twelve years but don't remember.

Helman, a quiet unassuming Eagle Scout occasionally wore his uniform to work at the Target store in Warrington, Pennsylvania. He also spent a lot of time searching for geocaches--objects that are hidden and can be found through GPS coordinates posted on the Internet. Casual acquaintances thought that Helman was much younger than nineteen.

In the summer of 2013, Helman met a young woman his age at an Eagle Scout picnic. They began dating and he fell in love. When she left him for another man in November 2013, the devastated Helman began sending threatening emails to the new boyfriend. When the object of his wrath brushed off his threats, Helman decided to poison his competitor to death. This was not behavior befitting an Eagle Scout.

On March 7, 2014, Helman confided in a fellow Target employee that he had just placed an envelope in his rival's mailbox that contained a scratch-and-sniff birthday card laced with ricin, a deadly poison. (Ricin is a protein found in the caster oil plant. The pulp from just eight caster beans can kill an adult. As little as 500 micrograms of the poison, an amount that would fit on the head of a pin can be fatal.) Helman bragged to his confidant that anyone who came into contact with his ricin would be dead in a few days.

Helman identified his target as his ex-girlfriend's boyfriend, a guy who lived in Warminster, a Bucks County town 40 miles north of Philadelphia. The shocked employee wasted no time in calling the police.

Police officers, on the day Helman confided in his fellow worker, went to the Eleanor Courts apartment complex to question the suspect. Upon their arrival they arrested Helman as he tried to sneak off carrying a backpack and a piece of luggage.

Under police questioning, Helman admitted that he had placed an envelope containing a birthday card in his rival's mailbox. He said his intent was to scare his ex-girlfriend's boyfriend, not to hurt him. He was motivated by the desire to get the girl back. Helman claimed that the birthday card was harmless.

Police officers found, in Helman's backpack, a white bottle labeled "sodium hydroxide" that contained a crystal-like powder. The suspect also possessed a recipe in a notebook that listed ingredients such as caster beans, sodium hydroxide, mixing materials, and other substances.

Investigators telephoned the target's residence and spoke to his mother who said her daughter had just left the house to fetch the mail. The police caller instructed the mother to put the mail back into the box and wait for the police.

Officers booked Nicholas Helman into the Montgomery County Jail on the charge of harassment. Shortly after the hazardous materials team retrieved the plain white envelope without a stamp, address, or return address, Helman posted his $50,000 bond and walked out of jail.

After toxicological testing confirmed that the birthday card contained ricin, a Bucks County prosecutor charged Nicholas Helman with attempted first-degree murder. On March 19, 2014, FBI agents and local police officers, backed up by a SWAT team, surrounded the Helman apartment. Following a two-hour standoff, the suspect surrendered to the authorities. A judge denied Helman bail pending a psychiatric evaluation.

The next day, police officers found a stash of ricin tucked under a gas manhole cover in Hatboro not far from Helman's apartment.

The Husband From Hell

In 1992 Robert Girts and his third wife Diane lived in a house connected to a Parma Ohio funeral home that employed the 42-year-old mortician as director and embalmer. On the morning of September 2, 1992, Girts and a couple of his friends were driving back to Parma from nearby Cleveland where they had been helping Girts' brother move. That day, Diane Girts didn't show up for her job that started at noon. A fellow employee, worried because she was never late for work, phoned the funeral home. A funeral company employee checking on Diane noticed that her car was still in the driveway. He went to the front entrance of the dwelling and called to her through the screen door. When she didn't answer he entered the house and found Diane's nude body in the bathtub. She had been dead for several hours.

The death scene investigation revealed no evidence of foul play such as a burglary or signs of physical trauma. Moreover, detectives found no indication of suicide such as pills or a note. A forensic pathologist with the Cuyahoga County Coroner's Office performed the autopsy. Because the dead woman's post-mortem lividity featured a cherry color rather than purplish red, the forensic pathologist considered the possibility she had died of carbon monoxide poisoning. The pathologist, however, ruled out this cause of death when Diane's blood-carbon monoxide level tested normal. Following standard autopsy protocol, the forensic pathologist secured a sample of the subject's stomach contents--an undigested meal of pasta salad--for toxicological analysis. (The undigested meal suggested Diane had been dead for more than twelve hours.) As a result of inconclusive nature of the autopsy, the Cuyahoga Coroner ruled Diane Girts' death "undetermined."

On September 20, 1992, 18 days after the funeral home employee discovered Diane Girts' body in the bathtub, Robert Girts contacted a detective working on the case to inform him that he had discovered a handwritten note that indicated that his wife had killed herself. In that document she had supposedly written: "I hate Cleveland. I hate my job. I hate myself."

Robert Girts, the grieving husband, in his effort to control the direction of the investigation of his wife's sudden and unexplained death, informed detectives that she had been despondent over their recent move to Parma. Also, she had been having trouble with her weight and suffered depression over a series of miscarriages that suggested she wouldn't be able to give birth.

The toxicological analysis of the decedent's stomach contents revealed the presence of cyanide at twice the lethal dose. Based on this finding the coroner changed the manner of Diane Girts' death criminal homicide.

In January 1993, a chemist acquainted with Robert Girts told detectives that at his request in the spring of 1992, she had sent him two grams of potassium cyanide. Girts said he needed the poison to deal with a groundhog problem. Investigators believed the suspect had acquired the cyanide to deal with a wife problem. Detectives also knew that potassium cyanide is not used in the embalming process.

Investigators learned that the murder suspect, in February 2002, had resumed an affair with an interior designer who had broken off the relationship after learning he was married. To get this woman back, Girts had assured her that he and Diane would be divorced by July 1992. Two months after Diane turned up dead in her bathtub, Girts informed his girlfriend that his wife had died from an aneurysm. Detectives considered Girts' relationship with this woman, along with money, the motive for the murder. Upon Diane's death he had received $50,000 in life insurance proceeds.

Investigators digging into Girts' personal history in search of clues of past homicidal behavior discovered that in the late 1970s his first wife Terrie (nee Morris) had died at the age of 25. After the couple returned to Girts' hometown of Poland, Ohio after living in Hawaii, Terrie's feet swelled up and she became lethargic. In the hospital following a blood clot she slipped into a coma and died. The fact Terrie had spent a month in the hospital before she passed away might account for the fact there were no traces of poison in her body. Members of Terrie's family, who had tried to talk her out of marrying Robert in the first place, wanted her body autopsied out of suspicion she had poisoned. Robert wouldn't allow it.

On Terrie's death certificate the coroner listed the cause of death as a swollen heart. (This doesn't make sense on its face because a "swollen heart" is not a cause of death.) Investigators learned that Girts' second wife had divorced him. Prior to her death she had accused him of physical abuse.

In 1993, as part of the investigation of Diane Girts' death by poisoning, Terrie Girts' body was exhumed and autopsied. While the forensic pathologist concluded that she had not died of a swollen heart, he could not find evidence that she had been poisoned.

Charged with the murder Diane, Robert Girts went on trial in the summer of 1993. Except for a confession the defendant had allegedly made to an inmate in the Cuyahoga County Jail, the prosecution's case was circumstantial.

After the prosecution rested its case Girts took the stand and denied murdering his wife. On cross-examination the prosecutor asked the defendant if he had confessed to another inmate. The defense attorney objected to this line of questioning on the ground it was prejudicial. The judge overruled the objection. When the prosecutor asked this question again, Girts denied making the jailhouse confession. At that point the idea that the defendant had confessed to an inmate was planted in the minds of the jurors.

The Cuyahoga County jury found Robert Girts guilty of poisoning Diane to death. The judge sentenced him to life with the possibility of parole after twenty years. (This would make him eligible for parole in 2013.)

Girts appealed his murder conviction to the Eight District Court of Appeals in Cuyahoga County on the grounds that the trial judge should not have allowed the prosecutor, on cross-examination, to bring up the alleged jailhouse confession. On July 28, 1994, the state appellate court agreed. Citing prosecutorial misconduct, the justices overturned the murder conviction.

At his retrial in 1995, Robert Girts did not take the stand on his own behalf. The prosecutor, in his closing argument to the jury, cited the defendant's refusal to testify as evidence of his guilt. The second Cuyahoga County jury found Girts guilty of murder. This time Girts appealed his conviction on grounds that by referring to his decision not to take the stand in his own defense the prosecutor had violated his constitutional right against self-incrimination. On July 24, 1997 the state appeals court upheld the conviction.

In 2005, after serving 12 years behind bars at the Oakwood Correctional Facility in Lima, Ohio, Girts appealed his 1995 murder conviction to the Sixth Circuit Court of Appeals. Two years later, the federal appeals court, on grounds of prosecutorial misconduct, reversed Girts' conviction. The justices did not, however, order his immediate release from prison. But if they didn't try him by October 11, 2008 he would be set free on $100,000 bond. When the authorities in Ohio failed to bring Girts to trial for the third time within the 180-day deadline, the twice- convicted killer walked out of prison.

Robert Girts' returned to Poland, the bedroom community south of Youngstown. He moved in with a relative and for time reported twice a month to a probation officer at the Community Corrections Association. In the meantime, he filed a motion asking the appeals court to bar a third murder trial on grounds of double jeopardy. In March 2010, the federal appeals court denied Girts' motion. The decision paved the way for a third murder trial.

Since his release from prison in November 2008, Girts has taken a fourth wife, a woman named Ruth he met through the Internet. They lived in a trailer park in Brookfield, Ohio. On August 5, 2012, Ruth, a nurse who had just landed a job at the University of Pittsburgh Medical Center (UPMC) in nearby Farrell, Pennsylvania, called her supervisor to say she was quitting because her husband was stalking her. Ruth told the supervisor she was afraid for her life and was in hiding.

The UPMC nursing supervisor passed this information on to the Southwest Regional Police Department in Belle Vernon. An officer with that agency relayed the report to Dan Faustino, the Brookfield Chief of Police.

Brookfield officers drove out to the Girts' residence to check on Ruth. Robert met the officers at the house. He said his wife wasn't there. He said he had no idea where she was. Robert consented to a search of the house that confirmed his wife's absence. Later that day, a Brookfield officer got ahold of Ruth by phone. She told the officer that she had quit her nursing job in Farrell in order to hide from her husband. She said he had threatened to kill her. Ruth was so afraid of Robert she even refused to tell the officer where she was hiding. Ruth did inform the officer about her husband's two murder trials in Cuyahoga County. This led Chief Faustino to call the authorities in Cuyahoga County regarding the unfolding developments regarding Girts in Brookfield and Farrell.

On August 9, a judge granted a Cuyahoga County prosecutor's motion to convene an emergency bond revocation hearing. In light of Robert Girts' alleged threats against his current wife Ruth, the authorities wanted him back behind bars. After hearing testimony from officials familiar with Robert Girts' murder trials and appeals, and Ruth Girts' recent accusations against him, the judge did not revoke his $100,000 bond. Instead, the magistrate restricted Girts' travel to destinations in Mahoning County where he lived. He could also travel to Cuyahoga County to attend scheduled court appearances. The judge ordered Girts to stay away from his wife.

As the new phase of the Robert Girts murder saga unfolded, the 59-year-old's wife remained in hiding.

In January 2013, Cuyahoga County Judge Michael Jackson remanded Girts' bond and ordered him back to jail. Girts had been visiting Ruth at her new job. On each occasion he brought her coffee. After drinking the coffee Ruth would feel ill and vomit. Investigators believed Girts was poisoning Ruth with antifreeze. (He had searched the Internet under the word "antifreeze." Girts told detectives that his dog had stepped in the antifreeze and he was interested in the side effects. He also explained that he had been contemplating using antifreeze to kill himself. Ruth Girts did not seek medical treatment or submit to toxicological tests.

On January 31, 2014, in an effort to avoid a third trial for murdering his wife Diane in 1992, Girts pleaded guilty to the charge of involuntary manslaughter. In open court he described how he had put cyanide in a saltshaker to poison her. Girts also pleaded guilty to insurance fraud.

Following his guilty pleas, the authorities returned Girts to prison to serve a sentence of six to thirty years. The Ohio Parole Board will ultimately decide when to release him. Diane's relatives told Cuyahoga County Judge Michael Jackson that they intended to fight his release at every parole hearing.

The Judge Was Poisoned

In 2013, Judge Charles Hague lived with his wife of 45 years outside of Jefferson, Ohio in the northeastern part of the state. Since 1993 he had been an Ashtabula County common pleas juvenile/probate judge. Carla, his 70-year-old wife, had retired years ago as a nurse. The judge and Carla, parents of grown children, enjoyed a reputation in the community as outstanding citizens.

As is so often the case, outward signs of domestic tranquility are misleading. This unfortunate reality applied to Mr. and Mrs. Hague. The problem within that marriage exploded to the surface on September 15, 2013 when Carla telephoned one of her sons. She said the judge had become ill after consuming a glass of wine. Upon arrival at the house, the son took one look at his father and dialed 911.

Paramedics rushed the stricken judge to a local hospital from where medical personnel flew him to the Cleveland Clinic for emergency care. Following several days of treatment in Cleveland, the judge returned home to recuperate.

Judge Hague's relatives, on September 19, 3013, notified the Ashtabula County Sheriff's Office of foul play suspected in the judge's sudden illness four days earlier. More specifically, the relatives accused Mrs. Hague of spiking her husband's wine with antifreeze. (A toxicological analysis of the judge's blood confirmed the presence of ethylene glycol, a toxic ingredient in antifreeze.)

Sheriff's deputies arrested Carla Hague on December 2, 2013 on suspicion of attempted murder. Officers booked her into the Ashtabula County Jail. Eighteen days later, an Ashtabula County grand jury indicted the suspect of contaminating a substance for human consumption and attempted murder.

Carla Hague did not deny putting the antifreeze into her husband's wine. Her intent, she said, was not to kill the judge but to make him slightly ill. He suffered from pulmonary fibrosis, a serious respiratory condition. In

Carla's opinion, her husband had been adding to his health problem by drinking too much. She hoped that if the wine made him ill he would cut back on his use of alcohol.

At her arraignment, Carla pleaded not guilty to the charge of attempted murder. She posted her $100,000 surety bond on December 24, 2013.

On June 16, 2014, the local prosecutor, with Judge Hague's consent, allowed the defendant to plead guilty to felonious assault. In speaking to a reporter, the judge said, "I have no anger or animosity. I am beyond that. I'm gad to have this huge black spot behind us. I have moved on with my life. Carla can get on with hers." (Presumably they will be getting on with their lives without each other.)

Following the guilty plea the judge sentenced Carla Hague to two years in prison with eligibility for release in six months.

9 PROSTITUTION

Prostitutes And Serial Killers

The term "serial killing," coined by FBI profilers in the 1980s, pertains to two or more unrelated murders in distinctly separate incidents. These are killings with a "cooling-off" period in between. At any given time, according to FBI experts on the subject, there are between twenty and fifty serial killers going about their deadly business. I believe, based on national homicide statistics, that the number is closer to twenty. America produces 85 percent of the world's serial killers. While these murderers fall into several groups according to their motives, MO, and psychological profiles, they are all sociopaths who feel no guilt or remorse.

Serial killers who rape, torment and kill women--often runaways, prostitutes and others who live transient lives--are called lust killers. (In England they call them "recreational killers.") These men are primarily motivated by sex and sadism and have nothing but disdain for their victims. Before they actually kill anyone, most of these sociopaths fantasize about violent sex. At some point, their fantasies turn into reality. These predators prey on prostitutes because they are easy targets. A street walker will go missing, and no one will report it for days or weeks, if at all. Moreover, the police are not likely to give such cases much attention. As criminal homicides, these cases are difficult to solve because many of the bodies cannot be identified, and there is no substantial relationship between the victims and their killers.

What follows are the broad profiles of nine lust killers. Two of these men are black, and all of them murdered prostitutes. In no particular order, they are:

Garry Ridgway
Seattle, Washington
White male; born 1949; 90 victims (1982-2000)

Ridgway, known as the Green River Killer, is America's most prolific lust killer. This childhood bed-wetter with a low IQ grew into a religious fanatic fixated on prostitutes. A loner and an outdoorsman, Ridgway, divorced three times, had a son by his second wife. He targeted streetwalkers who worked in Seattle, and dumped their bodies on the banks of the Green River. He painted trucks for a living.

Arthur Shawcross
Rochester, New York
White male; born 1945; 12 victims (1988-1989)

In 1972, before Shawcross started killing prostitutes, he raped and murdered two children in Watertown, New York. After serving fourteen years in prison, he began targeting streetwalkers in Rochester, dumping their bodies in the Genesse River. Although he had a low IQ, he had served in the U.S. Army. He confessed to his murders before dying in 2008.

Bobby Joe Long
Tampa Bay, Florida
White male; born 1953; 10 victims (1984)

As a child growing up in Kenova, West Virginia, kids teased Long because he had an extra X chromosome that caused him to grow breasts. As a child he suffered several head injuries, and slept in his mother's bed until he was a teenager. Prior to killing women in the Tampa Bay area Long raped at least fifty women in Fort Lauderdale, Ocala and Miami where he was known in the press as the "Classified Ad Rapist." In 1974 he married his high school girlfriend with whom he fathered two children. They divorced in 1980. Three years later Long moved to Tampa Bay and in 1984 began abducting, raping and murdering women, most of whom were prostitutes. He took his victims to his apartment where he either strangled or bludgeoned them, or cut their throats. One of his victims escaped which led to his arrest and conviction. Long confessed to deriving sadistic pleasure from his crimes. He is currently on death row.

Maury Travis
St. Louis, Missouri
Black male; born 1965; 12-20 victims (2000-2002)

This hotel worker from Ferguson, Missouri outside of St. Louis, took prostitutes to his home where, in a basement torture chamber, he raped, tortured, and strangled his victims. He videotaped many of his atrocities. When investigators searched Travis' house, they found bondage equipment, a stun gun, and newspaper clippings featuring news of his murders. In 2002 he committed suicide in his St. Louis jail cell. In a letter to the *St. Louis Post-Dispatch*, Travis boasted that he had killed seventeen prostitutes.

Kendall Francois
Poughkeepsie, New York
Black male; born 1971; 8 victims (1996-1998)

This high school hall monitor took prostitutes to his home where he killed them by strangulation. His hatred of streetwalkers stemmed from the fact one of them had infected him with HIV. When the police searched his home, they found the decomposing bodies of several victims. He is serving a life sentence at the Attica Correctional Facility.

Robert Lee Yates
Spokane, Washington
White male; born 1952; 16 victims (1986-1988)

After working as a prison guard, Yates embarked on a medal-winning, nineteen-year career in the U.S. Army where he flew cargo planes and helicopters. All of his victims worked the streets in the skid row section of Spokane. He's currently on death row at Washington State Penitentiary.

Robert Hansen
Anchorage, Alaska
White male; born 1939; 21 victims (1980-1983)

This bipolar baker and police academy drill instructor came from a dysfunctional family, and was bullied at school. Before he began killing prostitutes, he burned down a school bus garage in Pocahontas, Iowa. Known as a quiet loner, Hansen fathered two children. He kidnapped his victims in Anchorage then released them into the Alaskan wilderness where he hunted them down like animals.

Doug Clark
Los Angeles, California
White male; born 1948; 8 victims (1980)

Along with his accomplice Carol M. Bundy, Clark became known as one of the "Sunset Strip Killers." The boiler operator at a Jergens Soap Factory fantasized about killing women during sex then, with the help of Bundy, graduated to the real thing. He shot his victims in the back of the head. At his trial he represented himself. He's now on death row. Carol Bundy, pursuant to a plea bargain, is doing life.

Dayton Leroy Rogers
Portland Oregon
White male; born 1953; 6 victims (1983-1987)

A mechanic who fixed small engines and was deeply in debt, Rogers took his victims into the woods where he raped and stabbed them to death. All of his victims were runaways hooked on dope. He's currently awaiting his fate on Oregon's death row.

The disturbing thing about all of these men is that they did not stand out in any way. They did not look like monsters, and in their daily lives did nothing that revealed who they really were. Notwithstanding their homicidal activities, they seemed ordinary. That's what made them so dangerous. And it made them hard to catch.

The Perils of Prostitution

Have you heard the one about the hooker, the trick with a bad ticker, and the bungled autopsy? You probably haven't because what happened to a prostitute named Natasha Vanwasshenova and her client Jonathan Hood is not that funny.

On November 23, 2010, Jonathan Hood, a resident of Rochester, Michigan, called a Dearborn escort service and requested a hooker and $80 worth of heroin. The 38-year-old, in the midst of a divorce, was under the influence of alcohol and heroin when 28-year-old Natasha Vanwasshenova arrived at Hood's suburban Detroit home with the requested drug.

After consuming more heroin and booze Mr. Hood and the prostitute soaked in his hot tub for 30 minutes after which he took a cold shower, then, while having sex with Vanwasshenova, died. She called 911, tried to revive him, and waited for the EMS personnel and the police.

The forensic pathologist with the Oakland County Medical Examiner's office who performed the autopsy ruled that Jonathan Hood had died of a heroin overdose. The forensic pathologist (who has not been publicly named) noted that Mr. Hood had an enlarged heart, and significant blockage in one of his arteries.

Since, according to this forensic pathologist, Vanwasshenova's heroin had killed Mr. Hood, a local prosecutor charged her with delivering a drug that caused the user's death. Arrested on this criminal homicide offense, and placed in the Oakland County Jail, Vanwasshenova, if found guilty, faced a maximum sentence of life in prison.

Sitting in her jail cell, Vanwasshenova must have wondered how having sex with a 38-year-old man had killed him, and why she was being held responsible for his death. Heroin, while not good for you, is not arsenic.

Had she known the authorities would charge her for causing this trick's demise, she might not have stuck around for the police.

Vanwasshenova's court appointed attorney, Charles Toby, when he read the autopsy report, wondered why the forensic pathologist hadn't taken Mr. Hood's enlarged heart and blocked artery into consideration in his cause of death ruling. With that in mind, attorney Toby asked Dr. Kirit Patel, the Chief Cardiologist at St. Joseph Mercy Hospital, to review the autopsy. Dr. Patel, after reading the police and autopsy reports, concluded that Jonathan Hood had died of "acute coronary thrombosis," not a heroin overdose. His weak heart had failed under the stress of the drug, booze, hot tub, cold shower, and sex.

In light of Dr. Kirit's post-mortem analysis, the local prosecutor reduced the charge against Vanwasshenova to delivering a controlled substance. Oakland County medical examiner, Dr. Ljubisa Dragovic, amended Mr. Hood's cause of death to heart attack.

In May 2012, after spending 14 months in the county jail, Vanwasshenova pleaded guilty to the drug delivery charge. She also apologized to Mr. Hood's relatives who were in the court room. Judge Leo Bowan sentenced her to two years probation, and ordered her released from custody.

Attorney Charles Toby, noting that his client had been in jail for 14 months on a minor drug crime, objected to the probated sentence. If Vanwasshenova returned to prostitution, she would be violating the terms of her probation, and if caught, could end up serving the rest of her drug delivery sentence behind bars. Perhaps her experience with Mr. Hood would point Vanwasshenova, the mother of four, in another direction, career-wise.

The Mother Pimp

In April 2012, a tipster called the Nebraska State Patrol to report a woman he had met on Craigslist. According to the informant, she had sent him sexually graphic photographs of her 14-year-old daughter. For a price, Michelle Randall offered to make the girl available for sex.

On April 26, an undercover state officer, posing as a potential John, arranged to meet the 35-year-old mother of three at a motel in Kearney, Nebraska. The suspect, accompanied by her 14-year-old daughter, offered to sell herself for $150, and/or the girl for $200. The officer flashed his badge and arrested the mother. A child protection agent took custody of the teen.

The arresting officer took Randall to the Buffalo County Jail where she was held on $250,000 bail under charges of soliciting the sexual assault of a child, and possession of child pornography.

Police and child protection personnel went to the pimp/prostitute's home near Minden, Nebraska where they found the suspect's other two daughters, ages 7 and 9, alone in the filthy house. The girls were placed into foster care.

The suspect, when questioned by the police, admitted allowing her 41-year-old boyfriend, over a period of 14 months, to have sex with her teenage daughter and her 7 year old. Randall also named some of the men who had paid to have sex with the girls.

Over the next few weeks, Nebraska police officers arrested 7 men, including the boyfriend, who had paid to have sex with the 14-year-old one or more times. Three of these men had sexually molested the 7-year-old sister. They were all charged with sexual assault.

A Columbus, Nebraska man, 37-year-old Donald Grafe, allegedly had sex with the 14-year-old at a Lincoln truck stop. The other arrestees include Logan Roepke, a 22-year-old man from McCook, Nebraska; 38-year-old Alexander Rahe from Omaha; 41-year-old Shad Chandler from Lincoln; and Brian McCarthy, 25, also from Lincoln. McCarthy, incarcerated in the Lancaster County Jail, had pornographic images of the 14-year-old on his cellphone.

In January 2013, in Buffalo County Court, the mom-pimp pleaded no contest to conspiracy to commit child sexual assault and two felony counts of child pornography possession.

The judge, noting that Randall had previous convictions for similar offenses, sentenced her to 80 years in prison. The men who had sex with the daughters were convicted and sent to prison as well.

It is disturbing to know that cases like this are not uncommon in the United States.

Winston Churchill on Prostitution

Sir Winston Churchill supposedly asked Lady Astor whether she would sleep with him for five million pounds. She said she supposed she would. Then he asked whether she would sleep with him for only five pounds. She answered, "What do you think I am?" His response was, "We've already established that; we're merely haggling over price."

Marcus Felson, *Crime and Everyday Life,* 1998

House-Call Hooker Robbed Her John

On May 1, 2013, a home-alone 14-year-old in Prospect Heights, Illinois, a suburb of Chicago, decided to avail himself of the services of a prostitute. Since he wasn't old enough to drive, the hooker would have to come to him. This is where the magic of the Internet enters the story. Through a website designed for sexual hook-ups, the adventurous youngster arranged to have 22-year-old Dareka Brooks, a prostitute from Milwaukee, come to his house.

The moment the hooker strolled into the suburban home, she took charge. She ordered the excited kid to go into his bedroom and take off his pants. Yeah, baby. As the hapless kid sat on his bed anticipating the real-life version of his wildest fantasies, the whore walked into the room and introduced him to the reality of her world. She sprayed him with a face-full of pepper juice, grabbed his iPad and piggy bank and got the hell out of there. This is *not* what the young devil had expected.

The stunned, ripped-off underage John could have avoided the wrath of his parents by lying about his lost iPad and piggy bank. Instead, he called the police with a description of the prostitute and her car. Good boy.

A detective "pinged" the victim's iPad after Brooks turned it on. This allowed the investigator to track the hooker to a motel in Elk Grove Village ten miles from Prospect Heights. Officers arrested Brooks at the motel where they recovered the kid's iPad and his piggy bank.

After being charged with armed robbery, a judge ordered Dareka Brooks held on $10,000 bond.

In June 2014 Brooks pleaded guilty to robbery. The judge sentenced her to five years in prison with a recommendation that she be sent to a correctional boot camp.

Honeymooning With a Hooker

Between May 8 and 11, 2013, Florida undercover officers with the Polk County Sheriff's Office ran a prostitution sting involving an online ad aimed a prospective Johns. The operation resulted in the arrests of 92 men. One of the suspects caught in the web was a 45-year-old youth minister. Another unlikely catch involved a young man who was on his honeymoon.

A 21-year-old Chicago area groom named Mohammed Ahmed was on his honeymoon in Orlando, Florida. After showing up at the place where he hoped to engage the prostitute, Ahmed was arrested by the cops running the sting. When Ahmed didn't return to his honeymoon suite at the Omni Orlando Resort at Championsgate, his bride called the police and reported him missing.

As it turned out, the newlywed was only missing from his bride. The authorities knew exactly where he was--sitting in the Polk County Jail facing charges of prostitution and possession of marijuana.

Because I believe that police officers should be spending their time and resources on more serious crimes I am not a fan of prostitution stings. But in Ahmed's case, the Polk County Sheriff's Office did his bride a huge favor. The fact her groom patronized a prostitute on their honeymoon might be an indication of what life will be like married to this man.

One Old Customer

According to New Castle, Pennsylvania police, two officers observed 35-year-old Brandy Lynn Bartley loitering on South Mill Street. They saw her get into a car driven by Harry Anthony Mooney, 83, about 9 PM on Wednesday, June 28, 2014. Officers arrested Bartley and searched her purse. They found a glass pipe commonly used to ingest crack cocaine.

A Lawrence County prosecutor charged Bartley with promoting prostitution and possession of drug paraphernalia. The 83-year-old suspect was charged with patronizing a prostitute….

New Castle News, June 20, 2014

The Teen Pimp

Montia Marie Parker lived in Maple Grove, a suburb of Minneapolis, Minnesota. The 18-year-old cheerleader was one of 1,800 students who attended Hopkins High School. In February 2013, Parker sent a text message to a 16-year-old member of the cheerleading squad asking if the girl was interested in performing sexual acts for money. The Hopkins High School sophomore, who received special education services due to "developmental cognitive delay," had been telling her friends that she needed money.

In response to the senior cheerleader's query, the 16-year-old, in a return text, said yes. She didn't want to engage in sexual intercourse for money, but she would perform oral sex for paying clients. Montia Parker asked the girl to send photographs of herself that were "not too nasty but kind of cute." When Parker received the photographs, she posted them on Backstage.com, a website that advertises juvenile prostitution.

Parker, on March 5, 2013, drove the high school sophomore to an apartment building in a nearby community to service a client willing to pay for oral sex. "You're up!" Parker said to her passenger as she pulled up to the address. The 16-year-old entered the building, and when she returned, handed Parker $60. The young pimp deposited the money into her bank account.

The next morning, Parker, identifying herself as her young sex worker's mother, called the school and reported that her "daughter" wasn't feeling well and would be staying at home that day. The young pimp drove her novice prostitute that morning to a John's house in Brooklyn Park. When the teenager met the John, he insisted in engaging in sexual intercourse. To the reluctant girl, Parker said, "You'll be fine. I didn't drive up here for nothing. Eventually you will need to have sex." The 16-year-old offered oral sex, but not sexual intercourse. The John refused, and the high school girls departed without a sale.

The sophomore's mother noticed changes in her daughter's behavior, and had also learned that she had skipped school on the pretext phone call. When the mom checked her daughter's cellphone, she discovered the text messages pertaining to prostitution. She called the police.

On May 22, 2013, police officers, on charges of sex trafficking and promoting prostitution, booked Montia Parker into the Hennepin County Jail. The next day the suspected pimp posted her $50,000 bond. If convicted as charged, Parker faced a maximum prison sentence of twenty years and a $50,000 fine.

In October 2013, Parker pleaded guilty to three prostitution-related counts. The judge sentenced her to three years in prison. She must also register as a sex offender.

While the sex trafficking in young girls by adult men is common criminal activity, a teenager pimping a fellow teen was not so common.

Prostitution in China

In China, prostitutes work out of "hair salons" with secret sex rooms in the back. They also ply their trade in upscale karaoke parlors. Except during periodic government "vice sweep" campaigns, corrupt police officers look the other way.

Rounded-up prostitutes are sent to "custody and education" detention centers where they are forced to work in one of 200 prison sweatshops. Without the benefit of trials, legal representation, or any form of due process, prostitutes caught in the net spend six months to two years in these forced labor jails.

Inmates at custody and education prisons manufacture products for export such as ornamental paper flowers, disposable chopsticks, toys, and dog diapers. Relatives who visit incarcerated prostitutes have to pay a fee for the opportunity. Abuse by prison personnel is commonplace within this correctional system.

When released from custody, prostitutes are told they owe the government for expenses related to food, medical exams, bedding, soap, and other personal items. The cost of a six-month stay in one of these hellholes amounts to the equivalent of $400. Most of the released prisoners go back to selling their bodies.

To make certain the prison factories are supplied with a steady flow of workers, cities and counties impose annual hooker arrest quotas. Each year in China the police arrest 18,000 to 28,000 prostitutes.

Feminists Debate Prostitution

Feminists across Western Europe are sounding the alarm. Prostitution, they claim, has become today's "white slavery," with women from Bulgaria and Romania, Africa and Asia, being forced, tricked or seduced into selling their bodies.

But in so doing, these activists are creating a schism in the [feminist] movement, between those who see prostitution as another form of male oppression and those who see it as a possible means of female empowerment.

Much of the debate is centered in Germany, where prostitution is legal. As a result, the German author Alice Schwarzer said, the country has become…"a paradise for johns from all over the Continent" that come in busloads to frequent the new "mega-brothels" in Cologne, Munich or Berlin

And, indeed, prostitution is big business in Germany. In bordellos along the borders with France and Poland, countries where prostitution is illegal, groups of visitors are often offered flat-rate packages. Though exact numbers are rare, experts estimate that there are as many as 400,000 prostitutes in Germany, serving more than a million clients and churning out a hefty revenue of 15 billion euros a year.

Mirian Lau, *The New York Times,* December 29, 2013

The Younger the Better

For prostitutes, the ages of 16 to 22 are the most sexually attractive ages, and precocious 14-year-olds can readily look 17 or 18. The value of prostitutes for attracting customers declines quickly into the late twenties.

Many prostitutes do not yet show the effects of drug abuse and a fast life by 21, but then the tendency to show their age accelerates...The younger ones attract more pickups, leaving the older ones to linger and to act more overtly to attract customers. Indeed, many younger prostitutes can do business simply by acting unpretentious....

Marcus Felson, *Crime and Everyday Life*, 1998

The Pimp From Hell

Sirgiorgio Clardy bounced from one foster home to another in Portland, Oregon because even as a kid no adult could handle him. In 2000, when he was thirteen, he attacked his foster dad with a baseball bat. Clardy also threatened and attacked teachers, school administrators, and classmates. He took brass knuckles to school and once tried to sexually assault a female student.

By 2013, the 26-year-old Clardy had been convicted of twenty felonies that included crimes such as forcing young women to work as prostitutes, assault, and robbery. When police officers arrested him, he'd threaten to rape their wives and children. When he wasn't incarcerated, Clardy made everyone who come into contact with him miserable, including the teenaged girls he forced into prostitution. This brutal pimp had no business living outside of prison walls.

In the summer of 2012, several 18-year-old prostitutes, against their will, were doing business for Clardy out of the Inn at the Convention Center, a motel on the edge of downtown Portland. During the course of that operation a john tried to leave the motel without paying one of Clardy's prostitutes. Clardy caught the john before he left the motel. The pimp knocked the freeloader down and used his feet to stomp the man's face. As the seriously injured john lay bleeding on the ground, Clardy took all the cash he possessed. It took plastic surgery to repair the damage to the prostitution patron's face.

Police officers arrested Clardy shortly after the assault. A Multnomah County prosecutor charged the violent pimp with compelling prostitution, first-degree robbery, and second-degree assault. The suspected pleaded not guilty to all charges.

In the months leading up to Clardy's trial he threatened and spit on several lawyers appointed to represent him. Eventually Judge Kelly Skye, realizing that no lawyer wanted to be near this man, declared that he would have to defend himself with the help of a legal advisor who would not be required to sit next to him in court. After awhile even the legal advisor asked the judge to be relieved from the unsavory assignment.

In July 2013, not long after Clardy's trial got underway in Portland's Multnomah County Circuit Court, the defendant spit on sheriff's deputies and threatened the judge. The next day, deputies rolled the defendant into court handcuffed to a wheelchair. To keep him from spitting on people, the deputies had covered Clardy's head in a mesh bag. Because Clardy refused to get dressed for trial, officers had wrapped him in a suicide smock.

A few days into the trial, notwithstanding the presence of nine deputy sheriffs, Judge Skye ordered the defendant into another courtroom where he'd watch the proceedings on a video monitor. The judge considered Clardy too disruptive to be physically present at his own trial.

The jurors concluded Clardy's two-week trial by finding him guilty of all charges. At the sentencing hearing a few days later, the prosecutor put Dr. Frank Colistro on the stand. The psychologist, in practice for thirty years, said, "I've evaluated serial murderers, serial rapists, and I'm going to tell you very few of those people reached the evaluation scores we're going to talk about here."

According to the forensic psychologist, Clardy was in the 100th percentile of the narcissistic psychopath scale. "People like Mr. Clardy" the doctor said, "are born bad. It's not something we can fix. That's why we have prisons."

The prosecutor had put Dr. Colistro on the stand to counter the defendant's claim that he heard voices and wanted to kill himself. Dr. Colistro testified that Clardy exemplified the textbook case of an anti-social psychopath, a man who thought he was smarter, more attractive, and better than anyone else. According to Dr. Colistro, Sirgiorgio Clardy was not mentally ill. This man was evil.

Judge Judy Skye, based upon Sirgiorgio Clardy's violent past, criminal record, courtroom behavior, and psychological evaluation, declared him a "dangerous offender". People so designated, if given the chance, would offend again. As someone beyond the reach of rehabilitation, Judge Skye sentenced Clardy to 100 years in prison with no chance of parole until he served 36 years. Clardy, upon hearing his sentence, swore at the judge and threatened the deputy sheriffs.

In January 2014, from his cell at the Eastern Oregon Correctional Institution, Clardy, through a handwritten, three-page complaint, filed a $100 million civil suit against, among others, Phil Knight, the chairman of the Nike Company. Clardy based his tort claim on the theory that Nike, on each shoe, does not provide a label that warns users that stomping a person's face while wearing this Nike product could cause serious injury to the stomped person. As a result of the defendant's omission, the plaintiff experienced "great mental suffering."

Clardy's lawsuit, the product of a sociopathic personality in the extreme, will obviously be dismissed as frivolous. When it is, Clardy will no doubt cuss at and spit on prison personnel.

Pimp Draws 17 to Life

Prosecutors say an Orange County, California man has been sentenced to 17 years to life in state prison for luring a teenager into prostitution. Chuncey Tarae Garcia received the sentence Friday, May 16, 2014 under a state law that increases penalties for human trafficking, especially the sex trafficking of children.

The 34-year-old was convicted in March 2014 of one count of human trafficking and one count of pimping a minor under 16, both felonies. Garcia was previously convicted of cocaine possession. Authorities say Garcia met the girl, a 14-year-old runaway identified as Jane Doe, last year through one of his prostitutes who recruited women for him.

Garcia was arrested during a routine traffic stop for a broken headlight. The officer became suspicious when he saw the girl in the car.

Associated Press, May 17, 2014

Super Bowl Prostitution

Big public events that attract tens of thousands of people also draw criminals such as thieves, drug dealers, and prostitutes. Many of the hookers are teenage women, runaways forced into the sex trade. For police administrators, big events are law enforcement and security headaches. If something goes wrong, there's hell to pay. For law enforcement, events like the Super Bowl are no-win propositions.

The Super Bowl presents an enormous challenge to law enforcement practitioners. While the first concern is terrorism, there is also the problem of crime. On February 2, 2014, the annual Super Bowl extravaganza will be held at MetLife Stadium in East Rutherford, New Jersey, the home of the NFL's New Jersey Giants. The proximity of this venue to New York City will make it an attractive base of operation for a small army of flesh traffickers.

Danielle Douglas, an anti-prostitution activist has said that the "Super Bowl is a huge arena for sex trafficking--men are coming to the event to have sex with women, men and/or children." For the past several years in New Jersey, police agencies have been waging a losing battle against pimps who keep young prostitutes on drugs and in conditions of involuntary servitude.

Early in 2013, the New Jersey legislature strengthened the state's human trafficking law. But in August of that year, a federal judge struck down the portion of the legislation that applied to criminalizing the placing of commercial sex ads online. According to the judge, that section of New Jersey's law conflicted with federal sex trafficking legislation. New Jersey's attorney general has appealed the federal ruling.

In anticipation of this year's big game, New Jersey Attorney General John Hoffman created a Super Bowl task force to deal with the expected wave of pimps and their sex slaves. Police officers assigned to Super Bowl detail are being trained to look for young women who seem frightened, or bear signs of physical abuse. Also receiving this training are hospitality workers and airport employees.

The state is publishing public information ads profiling exploited sex trade victims, and law enforcement hotlines have been put into operation. It's doubtful, however, than these measures will make much of a dent in the annual Super Bowl sex business.

Child Prostitution

Sixteen children as young as 13, and some of whom who had been reported missing by their families, were rescued from the sex trade in a law enforcement sting operation that targeted alleged pimps who brought the victims to New Jersey for Super Bowl weekend...More than 45 pimps and their associates were arrested in the operation conducted by law enforcement...Some admitted traveling to New Jersey from other states for the purpose of forcing women and children to have sex with Super Bowl tourists for money....The victims rescued during the sting operation range in ages 13 to 17 years old....

Associated Press, February 4, 2014

Free Sex For Vice Cops

You don't have to be a hardcore libertarian to question the wisdom of arresting and prosecuting adult prostitutes. Aside from cases involving the trafficking of underage sex slaves, this form of crime fighting is a waste of limited law enforcement manpower. Moreover, this type of vice control fosters police corruption and unprofessional behavior.

The criminalization of prostitution has affected law enforcement more than it has altered the oldest profession in the world. A recent study conducted by a professor at the University of Chicago and a professor from Columbia University revealed that a prostitute is taken into custody once every 450 tricks, and only one in ten of these arrests leads to more than a few days in jail. That doesn't mean, however, that police officers aren't bothering whores. One in every 30 tricks a prostitute performs is a freebie with a cop as payment for not being arrested. According to this study, a prostitute is much more likely to have sex with an on-duty police officer than to be arrested by one. The law enforcement freebie is simply a cost prostitutes pay to stay out of jail.

A former Massachusetts police officer pleaded guilty in 2013 to extorting sex from prostitutes he threatened to arrest. In August of that year, a passerby called 911 in Portland, Oregon when she saw a 50-year-old detective having sex with a prostitute in a vacant lot. The authorities threw the prostitute into jail but merely cited the detective for the minor offenses of patronizing a prostitute and indecent exposure. The cop was suspended without pay.

In West Sacramento, California, an officer was convicted of raping prostitutes in his police car. All over the country there have been cases of hookers raped by cops. A vast majority of these crimes go unreported. This is another price prostitutes pay for selling themselves for sex. While it's a rough business, there has never been a shortage of hookers. It's a matter of supply and demand, pure capitalism. Cops demand their cut that is often in the form of free sex.

In Hawaii, vice cops are allowed by law to have sex with prostitutes in order to make their cases. This incredibly stupid law was intended to solve the so-called "cop check" problem involving hookers who employ tactics to identify undercover cops to avoid arrest. Apparently in Honolulu vice cops are too stupid or lazy to pull off prostitution stings without going all the way. Vice cops in every other state have managed to get the job done without dropping their pants.

Recently a bill that would nullify the legal exemption that allows cops to commit what for civilians is a crime, passed the state's House of Representatives. The measure is being argued in the Senate.

Under Hawaii's vice law exemption, cops not only get free sex, they get it under the banner of crime fighting. It's amazing what these crime-fighting warriors are willing to sacrifice on our behalf.

The Hawaiian vice exemption encourages police behavior that in every other state is considered unprofessional and illegal. Moreover, it couldn't be good for marriage and other domestic relationships. Johnny, what does your dad do for a living? He arrests whores he has had sex with. Are they hiring down at the Honolulu PD?

The existence of taxpayer paid sex for Hawaiian vice cops is another reminder that you can never underestimate the stupidity of some legislators and police administrators.

The Prison Guard Pimp

On February 5, 2003, a judge sentenced 20-year-old Rasul Abernathy, a resident of Coatesville, a Philadelphia suburb in eastern Pennsylvania, to three to ten years for selling drugs. He began serving his time at the State Correctional Institution (SCI) in nearby Chester, Pennsylvania. Two months later, prison authorities transferred Abernathy to SCI-Greenburg, a Westmoreland County facility east of Pittsburgh in the southwestern part of the state.

On March 28, 2005, after serving slightly more than two years behind bars, Abernathy was granted parole. He returned to the Philadelphia area. After twenty months of freedom, Abernathy violated the conditions of his parole and landed back at SCI-Chester. Prison administrators, on February 6, 2007, transferred Abernathy back to the state prison in Greensburg.

On January 28, 2008, 29-year-old Postauntaramin Walker, a resident of North Versailles, a community outside of Pittsburgh, began working as a corrections officer at SCI-Greensburg. That's where she met inmate Rasul Abernathy. Upon his parole on September 24, 2008, Abernathy moved in with the prison guard.

Abernathy, in June 2012, encountered a 16-year-old girl who had run away from a western Pennsylvania juvenile facility. The girl accepted his invitation to live with him and Walker. Walker was still employed as a prison guard at SCI-Greensburg. She knew the authorities were looking for the girl.

A month after taking the runaway in, Abernathy and Walker turned the juvenile out as a teen prostitute. The pimps posted online ads featuring provocative photographs of the young sex worker. To ease the girls' anxiety over turning tricks, her ex-con and corrections officer handlers kept her supplied with marijuana, alcohol, and pain pills. Abernathy set the young prostitute's fees and took care of the business end of the vice operation. When the girl refused to cooperate, the pimps beat her.

In October 2012, the girl reached out to a counselor she knew from before and liked. She told the counselor about her life as an involuntary prostitute, but out of fear, did not identify her pimps. The counselor notified the authorities. A short time later, the police picked the girl up and placed her back into the juvenile facility.

Five months after re-entering the juvenile detention center, the girl escaped. She called Walker who welcomed her back into the sex trade. A few weeks after the young prostitute and her pimps were re-united in North Versailles, prison authorities transferred Walker across the state to SCI-Chester. Abernathy, Walker, and their young sex worker moved into an apartment in Coatesville outside of Philadelphia.

In March 2013, one of Abernathy's ex-con acquaintances raped the girl. Instead of punishing the rapist, Abernathy shrugged off the assault by calling it a "learning experience." The incident motivated the teen prostitute to run off and return to the Pittsburgh area. A few weeks later, she was back in the juvenile facility where she spilled the beans, this time identifying her pimps.

Back in the Philadelphia area, Abernathy and Walker were pimping out a 17-year-old male prostitute.

In November 2013, realizing that her career as a Pennsylvania corrections officer was about to end, Walker quit showing up for work at SCI-Chester.

In January 2014, a federal grand jury sitting in Philadelphia indicted Abernathy and Walker on charges of child sex trafficking and conspiring to engage in sex trafficking. The indictment pertained to the exploitation of the runaway girl. (The defendants' use of the Internet to promote their sex trade made the offense federal.)

FBI agents arrested Abernathy and the former state corrections officer in Philadelphia shortly after the indictment came down. Two months later, the same grand jury charged Abernathy, 32, and walker, 34, with forcing the 17-year-boy into the sex trade. The defendants also faced state charges of kidnapping, promoting prostitution, assault, and other offenses related to the corruption of minors.

The Paroled Prostitute Killers

In 1992, 23-year-old Steven Gordon, a resident of Orange County, California, was convicted of two counts of lewd and lascivious acts with girls under 14 and 10-years-old. Ten years later, in Riverside County, California, Gordon went to prison on a kidnapping conviction.

Twenty-one-year-old Franc Cano, another Orange County sexual predator, went to prison in 2008 for rape.

In April 2012, Gordon was on parole and wearing a federal GPS device. His friend Cano, also on parole, wore a state-issued ankle bracelet. That month, the two transients removed their tracking devices, and under the names Dexter McCoy and Joseph Madrid, boarded a Greyhound bus for Law Vegas.

On May 8, 2012, federal agents apprehended the two paroled sex offenders at the Circus Hotel and Casino in Las Vegas. Back in California, they both pleaded guilty to failure to register as sex offenders. Instead of sending these men back to prison where they belonged, the parolees were ordered to provide DNA samples. As further punishment, parole and probation authorities would monitor their computers. They were also required to check in once a month with the Anaheim Police Department. New GPS tracking devices were attached to each man and they were sent on their way.

On October 10, 2013, Kianna Jackson, a 20-year-old from Las Vegas, disappeared while she was in Santa Ana, California. In Santa Ana, she had been charged with prostitution and loitering to commit prostitution. Jackson wasn't the only sex worker that had gone missing in southern California during that period. Thirty-four-year-old Josephine Monique Vargas was last seen on October 24, 1913 after attending a family birthday party at a Santa Ana Red Roof Inn. Vargas had a history of drug abuse and prostitution.

Martha Anaya, a 28-year-old Santa Ana woman with a history of prostitution, was last seen on November 12, 2013. Before her disappearance, Anaya had asked her boyfriend to pick up her 5-year-old daughter so she could work her trade.

On March 14, 2014, the naked body of 21-year-old Jarrae Nykkole Estepp was found on a conveyor belt at an Anaheim trash-sorting plant. Estepp was known to work on a strip of beach in Anaheim known for prostitution. She had moved to southern California from Oklahoma.

On April 11, 2014, Anaheim police officers arrested Franc Cano, 27 and his traveling partner Steven Dean Gordon, 45, near the trash-sorting facility in Anaheim where Jarrae Estepp had been raped and murdered. (I presume the suspects are linked to this victim through DNA.)

On Monday, April 14, 2014, an Orange County prosecutor charged Cano and Gordon with four felony counts of special circumstances murder and four counts of rape. If convicted as charged, these men could be sentenced to life without parole. While they are also eligible for the death penalty, no California judge will impose that sentence.

Anaheim Police Lieutenant Bob Dunn, at a press conference on April 15, 2014, said the suspects may have raped and killed more women in southern California. The officer would not say if the bodies of the other three prostitutes had been found. According to Lieutenant Dunn, the suspects, when they raped and murdered the four victims, were wearing their GPS tracking devices.

The Crappiest Little Whorehouse in Texas

Fifteen women and three men were arrested on May 19, 2014 after a double prostitution sting in East Harris County, Texas.

Undercover officers went into the suspected locations, a bar and a cantina located just east of Houston, disguised as customers after several complaints. A makeshift bedroom was discovered in the restrooms. The group had a total of 21 charges of prostitution and other crimes.

dve.com, May 20, 2014

Condom Evidence

One of the key justifications for the criminalization of prostitution is public health, to curb the spread of sexually transmitted diseases such as AIDs. In New York City alone the government spends $1 million a year distributing free condoms with this very purpose in mind.

Every year in New York City, vice officers arrest 2,500 prostitutes. In a few cases, the fact the sex trade suspect possessed more condoms than what is considered customary has been used as evidence of prostitution.

Among sex workers, rumor has it that cops will arrest anyone in possession of more than three condoms. While there is not a three-condom rule, a lot of prostitutes no longer carry them in fear of being incriminated by this evidence. What can a prostitute say when the vice officer asks, "What are you doing with all of those condoms?"

The New York City Department of Health conducted a study in 2010 that revealed that a third of the city's hookers didn't carry condoms as a measure to avoid incriminating themselves.

Since more than 90 percent of prostitution arrests lead to plea bargained sentences, vice officers rarely need to make their cases using this type of evidence. In suburban New York's Nassau County, District Attorney Kathleen Rice has said that the evidentiary value of condoms does not outweigh the negative public health effect associated with the use of this prosecutorial technique. According to this prosecutor, "condom evidence is rarely of any value to a prosecution. If you need condom possession so badly in a case against a trafficker, you don't have a good case." Prosecutors in San Francisco and in Brooklyn, New York no longer use excessive condom possession as evidence in prostitution cases.

In 2013, the New York State Assembly passed a bill banning the introduction of condom possession into evidence at sex trafficking trials. A supporter of this first-of-its-kind legislation, Assemblyman Richard Gottfried, told a reporter with the *New York Times* that, "Sex workers are not a politically appealing constituency to most lawmakers." The New York State Senate has not taken up the bill.

Massage Parlor Raids

The message parlor has come to be regarded as a type of illegal brothel and is often located within neighborhood shopping districts. Massage parlors are usually relatively inconspicuous. There's not much publicity or advertisement, and the outer facade of the building is not very ostentatious or enticing to the casual shopper. Frequently, these message parlors advertise through small classified ads in local papers.

Police employ a method called "the duken" to close down massage parlors. The duken entails having a plainclothes police detective accost an unsuspecting customer about to enter the parlor. The officer will say something like, "We know who you are and what you are doing here, would you like your wife to find out about it?" Out of fear, the patron will introduce the officer to the employees of the massage parlor as a friend who wishes their services.

Once the detective gains entry, he plays the part of the customer coming in for the first time. The detective cannot carry a gun, identification cards, handcuffs or any object that would make the owner or employees of the massage parlor suspicious. Like the other patrons the officer then receives a massage.

Smart prostitution houses always tell their clients to go into a room, remove all their clothes, and wait for their girl. This is because most police departments will not allow their officers to remove their underwear when investigating houses of prostitution. And of course these prostitutes know this.

At no time may the detective suggest anything of a sexual nature to the masseuse. There must only be solicitation on the woman's part. The masseuse might attempt to sexually arouse the client while massaging him, but at this point there is no cause for arrest. As a enticement to get involved in sexual intercourse or oral sex many of these massage parlors will have televisions showing X-rated movies. Only after the masseuse suggests sexual intercourse or oral sex and states a monetary fee is she liable for arrest. At this time the undercover officer may make an arrest, even though no sexual intercourse or oral sex took place. Massage parlors usually employ only a few women as masseuses. Approximately two women do the massaging and soliciting. Their ages range from the mid-twenties to the mid-forties.

Mauro V. Corvasce and Joseph Paglino, *Modus Operandi*, 1995
A Hooker and Two Dead Johns

Alix Catherine Tichelman described herself on her Facebook page as a fetish ("bondage, dominance, sadism and masochism") model with more than 200 "client relationships." In plain words, the 26-year-old worked as a Silicon Valley prostitute. Her "clients" were wealthy Johns willing to shell out big fees for the rope, the whip, and who knows what else.

If you believed Tichelman's Facebook entries, the self-described high-end hooker graduated from high school in Deluth, Georgia before studying journalism at Georgia State University in Atlanta. (Maybe in college she heard that journalists were whores and decided to make real money in that profession.) Tichelman started her sex worker career at Larry Flynt's Hustler Club.

In early 2012, Tichelman began dating Dean Riopelle, the lead singer of a rock-and-roll band called "Impotent Sea Snakes." (Catchy.) Riopelle also owned the Masquerade Night Club in Atlanta, a popular music venue. Interestingly enough, Riopelle had earned a degree in construction engineering from the University of Florida. Eventually Tichelman moved into Riopelle's luxury home in Milton, Georgia.

On September 6, 2013, officers with the Milton Police Department responded to a domestic call that originated from the Riopelle house. Tichelman, the caller, accused her boyfriend of physical abuse. He returned the favor with assault accusations of his own. The officers departed without taking anyone into custody.

On September 19, 2013, Tichelman dialed 911 and to the dispatcher said, "I think my boyfriend overdosed on something. He, like, won't respond." Tichelman, in response to the emergency dispatcher's questions, said Riopelle's eyes were open but he was unconscious. She described his breathing as "on and off." The dispatcher overheard the caller say, "Hello Dean, are you awake?"

When the dispatcher asked Tichelman how she knew her boyfriend had overdosed on something, she said, "Because there's nothing else it could be." The dispatcher inquired if the overdose was intentional or accidental. "He was taking painkillers and drinking a lot," came the reply.

Dean Riopelle died a week later at a local hospital. The medical examiner's office, following the autopsy, identified the cause of death as excessive heroin and alcohol consumption. The medical examiner ruled the death an accident.

On November 23, 2013, about a month after Dean Riopelle's overdose fatality, a 51-year-old Google executive from Silicon Valley named Forrest Timothy Hayes enjoyed Tichelman's purchased company on his 50-foot yacht. (The vessel has also been described as a powerboat.) Later that day the authorities discovered Hayes' dead in one of the boat's bedrooms. (The boat was not at sea.)

In the course of the investigation into this sudden death, detectives with the Santa Cruz Police Department viewed the yacht's videotape footage that revealed just how the rich executive had died. Tichelman was seen injecting

Hayes with what investigators presumed to be a shot of heroin. Immediately after the needle went in, he clutched his chest and collapsed onto the floor. Tichelman responded to the obvious emergency by finishing her glass of wine then gathering up her belongings. As she casually strolled out of the bedroom, she stepped over his dead body. She did not call 911.

Santa Cruz detectives, on July 3, 2014, executed a search warrant at Tichelman's parents' home in Folsom, a upscale Silicon Valley community. Her father, Bart, was CEO of a tech firm that offered "energy efficient infrastructure" for data centers. At the Tichelman house, detectives carried away the suspect's laptop. On the computer, investigators found that Tichelman, just before Hayes' death, had made online inquires regarding how to defend oneself if accused of homicide in an overdose case.

On July 4, 2014, an undercover Santa Cruz officer, through the website SeekingArrangement.com, lured Alix Tichelman to a fancy hotel on the pretext of being a John willing to pay $1,000 for a session featuring fetish sex. The officer took the hooker into custody on suspicion of criminal homicide in the yacht owner's death.

At her arraignment on July 10, 2014, the judge informed the suspect she faced a charge of manslaughter along with several drug related crimes. She pleaded not guilty to these offenses. The judge set her bail at $1.5 million.

Homicide detectives, in the wake of Forrest Hayes' suspicious death, were looking into the Dean Riopelle overdose case. As a result of the Hayes case, SeekingArrangement.com was shut down. This upset Silicon Valley prostitutes who said they used the site to screen Johns with histories of violence. Affluent sex worker clients in the valley also used the site to arrange hooker dates. (I guess if you're a whore, doing business in an area populated by a lot of rich nerds is a good thing.)

10 CHURCH MURDER

Michigan's Killer Pastor

John Douglas White, the 55-year-old pastor of the Christ Community Fellowship Church located just west of Mount Pleasant, Michigan, lived by himself in a mobile home park in Broomfield Township near the town of Remus. This self-appointed man of the cloth possessed a background more in line with a person serving a life sentence in prison than a preacher of a tiny church in rural central Michigan. Pastor White, a perverted lust killer, had no business living outside prison walls where he could take advantage of women while masquerading as a man of God. He was a predatory sex killer in preacher's clothing.

In 1981, John White, then 24, choked and stabbed a 17-year-old girl in Battle Creek, Michigan. The victim survived, and White was allowed to plead no contest to assault with intent to do great bodily harm. (In my view, the no contest plea should be abolished.) The judge sentenced White to five years in prison. Corrections authorities let White out on parole after he had served two years behind bars.

John White and his wife, in 1994, were living in Comstock Township near Kalamazoo, Michigan. On July 11 of that year, 26-year-old Vicky Sue Wall was seen getting into White's pickup just before she disappeared. Shortly after Wall's relatives reported her missing, the 37-year-old violent sex offender checked himself into the Kalamazoo Regional Psychiatric Hospital. In September 1994, police found Vicky Sue Wall's badly decomposed body in the woods not far from her home. Arrested at the psychiatric facility, White admitted strangling the victim to death. The victim and White had an affair, and she had threatened to tell his wife. So he killed her. (I doubt the police, once they had the confession, conducted an investigation to determine if this was, in reality, the motive for Wall's murder.)

In the Vicky Sue Wall murder case, the authorities allowed White to strike a deal with the prosecutor. In return for his guilty plea to the ridiculous charge of involuntary manslaughter, the judge sentenced White to eight to fifteen years. At his May 1995 sentencing hearing, White told the judge that Vicky Sue Wall's death had been a "tragic accident." (How does one *accidentally* strangle someone to death?) John White walked out of prison in 2007 after serving twelve years of his sentence. White's wife divorced him.

In 2012, Pastor John White was engaged to a woman in his congregation whose 24-year-old daughter--Rebekah Gay--lived a few doors from him in the mobile home park. Because White was a preacher engaged to her mother, Rebekah allowed him to watch her 3-year-old son. She had no idea this preacher watched necrophilia pornography, and fantasized about having gruesome, perverted sex with her.

On October 31, 2012, at six in the morning, John White entered Rebekah Gay's trailer, struck her in the head with a hard rubber mallet then strangled her to death with a zip tie. After performing perverted sexual acts on Gay's body, White hauled her 5-foot-3, 118-pound corpse in his pickup to a ditch behind a stand of pine trees about a mile from the trailer park. It was there he dumped her body.

After hiding his victim's corpse, White returned to his trailer where he cleaned himself and his truck with paper towels. He walked to Gay's dwelling, got into her car, and drove it to a nearby bar and parked it there. He had also tossed Gay's cellphone into a dumpster, and threw away the rubber mallet. From the bar, White walked back to Gay's mobile home, dressed her son in his Halloween costume, then drove the boy to Mount Pleasant where, as prearranged, the boy's father picked him up for the day.

Crime scene investigators processed the victim's trailer for physical clues, and searched White's mobile home where they found the bloody towels and other incriminating evidence. When questioned by detectives with the Michigan State Police, John White confessed, then led the officers to Rebekah Gay's body.

On November 1, 2012, John White was arraigned in an Isabella County District Court on the charge of first-degree murder. The judge denied him bail.

The church official who had hired John White as pastor, said this to a reporter with *The Detroit News*: "He [White] was absolutely contrite. All kinds of people turn around and meet the Lord and they are a different person. He [White] was doing a lot of good in the community...He was doing a lot of good and Satan did not want him doing good, and Satan got to him."

So, according to one of Pastor White's congregants, White's cold-blooded lust murder of Rebekah Gay was the devil's doing. The devil didn't kill this woman, John White did.

In April 2013, White pleaded guilty to second-degree murder for killing Rebekah Gay. The judge sentenced him to 56 years and three months. On August 28, 2013, a prison guard at the Michigan Reformatory Correctional Institution in Ionia, found White dead in his cell. He hanged himself.

The Singing Minister of Death

In 1968, Arthur Burton "A.B." Schirmer, an ordained Methodist minister, married his first wife Jewel whom he met while they were 20-year-old students at Messiah College in southeast central Pennsylvania. In the late 1970s, as pastor of the Bainbridge and Marietta United Methodist Churches in southeastern Pennsylvania's Lancaster County, AB Schirmer and his wife Jewel sang duets at area churches and camp meetings. Later his son and two daughters joined the gospel group billed as the "Singing Schirmer Family."

In 1978, A.B. and his family moved to the town of Lebanon in southeast central Pennsylvania where he had been named pastor of the Bethany United Methodist Church (UMC). He and his wife Jewel lived in the church parsonage.

On April 24, 1999, the 50-year-old Bethany church pastor called 911 at 2:15 in the afternoon to report that when he returned to the parsonage after a jog, he found his wife Jewel lying unconscious at the foot of the basement stairs. Jewel Schirmer died the next day at the Penn State Milton S. Hershey Medical Center.

The forensic pathologist with the Lebanon County Coroner's Office who performed the autopsy noted that the deceased woman had, wrapped around one leg, an electrical cord from a shopping vac. She was also barefoot. The pastor's wife had suffered a fractured skull, and possessed numerous bruises on her upper body. The coroner's office reported that Jewel Schirmer had died from a traumatic brain injury, and ruled her manner of death as "undetermined." While her obituaries stated that she had died a "natural death," from falling down a flight of stairs (actually an accidental death), the coroner's office listed Jewel Schirmer's demise as undetermined because her injuries seemed too severe to have been caused by a fall down a flight of steps. Because his wife's death was not ruled a homicide, there was no police investigation into the incident, and no criminal charges filed against the singing minister.

In 2001, the year he became pastor of the United Methodist Church in Reeders, an eastern Pennsylvania town in Monroe County, A.B. Schirmer married his second wife, 49-year-old Betty Jean Shertzer, a music teacher.

On July 15, 2008, motorists driving along State Route 715, a wooded, two-lane highway not far from Reeders, saw a PT Cruiser sitting on the shoulder of the road next to a guardrail. Betty Schirmer was sitting in the front passenger's seat that was soaked in blood. She was bleeding from the head and unconscious. The passersby noticed severe bruising on the right side of her face. The vehicle showed only minor damage, and the pastor was uninjured. Although he possessed a cellphone, one of the motorists called 911.

The next day, at the Lehigh Valley Hospital, Betty Jean Schirmer died of "sustained multiple skull and facial fractures," and "brain injury." At the pastor's request, his second wife's body was cremated before it could be autopsied.

To the officer investigating the supposed traffic accident, the pastor said he had been driving his wife to the hospital after she complained of a pain in her jaw. While traveling between 45 and 55 MPH, he lost control of the car after over-steering to avoid a deer. The vehicle swerved back and forth across the road before slamming into the guardrail. Although Betty Schirmer's head injuries seemed out of proportion to the damage to the car, the authorities did not investigate the 56-year-old woman's death as a possible homicide. The fact the dead woman's husband was a Methodist minister probably had a lot to do with that decision. Had the authorities known about the circumstances surrounding the death of AB's first wife, Jewel, they might have looked closer into Betty Schirmer's suspicious demise.

On October 29, 2008, sudden, violent death raised its ugly head again in Pastor Schirmer's life. On that day, Joseph Musante, the husband of the pastor's personal assistant, was found dead in the church office behind the pastor's desk. Mr. Musante had been shot in the head in an apparent suicide. Investigators looking into the case were curious to know why this active member of the Reeders UMC congregation had taken his own life in the pastor's office. In pursuing that lead, investigators learned that Pastor Schirmer was having an affair with the dead man's wife, Cynthia.

A.B. Schirmer's proximity to the untimely violent deaths of two of his wives and the husband of his personal assistant and lover kick started a criminal investigation of his second wife Betty's July 2008 death. The fact the pastor was having an affair at the time of the so-called fatal traffic accident on State Route 715, added what had been missing until now: a motive for murder. Pursuant to the homicide investigation, the police conducted a search of Schirmer's church living quarters and found incriminating evidence: massive blood stains from Betty Schirmer, stains someone had tried to cleanup.

The discovery of blood stains in the Reeders Church parsonage provided homicide investigators with a plausible narrative of Betty Jean's death: the pastor had bludgeoned her in the parsonage, put her bleeding body into the PT Cruiser, staged the traffic accident on the remote highway, then sat in the car with his unconscious wife waiting for her to die. Before she passed away, passing motorists came along, and one of them called 911. The next day she died, and shortly after that, was cremated without an autopsy. With the death of the pastor's personal assistant's husband three months later, the path had been cleared for the pastor's third marriage to Cynthia.

After A.B. Schirmer became a prime murder suspect in this second wife's death, the pastor left the ministry. He joined a three-person evangelical singing group called "Beroean."

To bolster their case that this man of God had murdered his second wife, the police consulted an expert in traffic accident investigation. According to this expert, the damage to Schirmer's PT Cruiser suggested that when he hit the guardrail, he was only traveling 25 MPH, a speed that would not have resulted in Betty Schirmer's severe head trauma and brain damage.

In July 2010, the county coroner, a forensic pathologist named Dr. Samuel Land, ruled Betty Schirmer's manner of death a homicide. This opened the door to a criminal prosecution.

State police officers, on September 13, 2010 in Tannersville, Pennsylvania, took former pastor A. B. Schirmer into custody. The prosecutor charged him with the murder of his second wife Betty, and with the tampering of homicide evidence. At the time of his arrest, the gospel singer planned to marry for the third time. The ex-pastor would await his upcoming murder trial in the Monroe County Correctional Facility where he was incarcerated without bail.

On September 17, 2010, the Monroe County prosecutor convened a grand jury to look into the deaths of Schirmer's two wives. Dr. Wayne Ross, the forensic pathologist for Lancaster County, had studied photographs and other material pertaining to the 1999 death of Jewel Schirmer in the Lebanon UMC parsonage. Dr. Ross informed the grand jurors that the skull fracture Jewel had supposedly incurred from a fall down the basement steps would have required at least 750 pounds of pressure, a force way out of proportion to an accidental spill of this nature. Moreover, the forensic pathologist testified that the cuts to the victim's face were "highly suspicious, and could have been caused by an object striking her head. There were 14 separate impact injuries to her head and face," Dr. Ross said, "as well as numerous abrasions and contusions throughout her upper body and arms." According to Dr. Ross, one of the bruises was in the shape of a handprint.

Based on Dr. Ross' testimony, and other evidence presented at the Monroe County Grand Jury session, Dauphin County Chief Deputy

Coroner Lisa Potteiger changed Jewel Schirmer's manner of death from "undetermined" to "homicide."

In March 2013, a Monroe County Judge, after a jury found Schirmer guilty of first-degree murder, sentenced him to life in prison.

Texas Pastor Murdered by Man on PCP

At eleven o'clock on Monday morning, October 29, 2012, in Forest Hill, a suburban town outside of Fort Worth, Texas, Derrick Birdow crashed his Ford Crown Victoria into the Greater Sweethome Missionary Baptist Church, an 850-member congregation founded in 1995 by Reverend Danny Kirk. Kirk had been a football star at East Texas State University.

Shortly after the sedan smashed into the brick building, the 53-year-old pastor came out of the church to investigate the source of the commotion. He encountered 33-year-old Birdow who, after plowing into the structure, climbed out of his car apparently unhurt. With no warning, Birdow shoved Pastor Kirk against the car and began punching him in the head.

John Whitaker, a church maintenance employee, when he saw a man punching the pastor, ran outside to help him. While Whitaker was able to punch the attacker several times, his blows didn't faze Birdow who broke away from the altercation and fled into the church with the pastor and the janitor in pursuit.

The church secretary, aware that a crazy man had plowed his car into the building, had attacked the pastor, and was now inside the church, locked herself in her office and called 911. "My pastor is bleeding, he's been attacked," she said. "I'm not going out there. I need help real fast. Send policemen. I do need an ambulance."

The dispatcher asked, "Does your pastor know him?"

"I have no idea," answered the frightened secretary.

Inside the church, Derrick Birdow ran to the music room where he grabbed an electric guitar. As John Whitaker turned a corner in the hallway, Birdow used the instrument to blindside him with two blows to the head. Seriously injured, Whitaker went down. Birdow then began beating Pastor Kirk with the guitar, turning the scene into a bloodbath.

When officers with the Forest Hill Police Department burst into the church, they saw Birdow, covered in the minister's blood, beating him to death with the church musical instrument. One of the officers, through the use of a Taser gun, subdued the crazed attacker enough to slap on the handcuffs. As the police hauled the violent intruder to a patrol car, he continued to resist. After placing the suspect into the back of the cruiser and returning to the church, the officers realized they had not arrived in time to save Reverend Danny Kirk. Derrick Birdow had beaten the pastor to death.

A short time later, a police officer checking on Birdow in the back of the patrol car, found him unresponsive. Paramedics arrived at the scene, couldn't find a pulse, and rushed him to the John Peter Smith Hospital where he was pronounced dead.

In 2004, a Tarrant County judge sentenced Derrick Birdow to a five-year prison sentence for aggravated assault with a deadly weapon. Birdow had also been convicted in the county for the possession of controlled substances, DUI, and charges related to domestic violence. According to one of this man's relatives, Birdow had been having some "issues," and he hadn't "been himself." Birdow had also "been going through some stuff. He's not a happy dude." Derrick Birdow was not a member of Pastor Kirk's congregation, but his children may have attended the church. It is not known if Reverend Kirk and his killer were acquainted.

In February 2013, Tarrant County Medical Examiner Dr. Nizam Peerwani ruled that Derrick Birdow had died of PCP ingestion.

There should be no place more peaceful on a Monday morning in suburban Fort Worth than a Baptist church. But in America, when it comes to mayhem and murder, no place is off-limits. Nevertheless, the beating death of a Baptist minister at his own church by a man wielding an electric guitar, even by U.S. standards of drug-addled crime and mental illness, was more than unusual.

Murdered at the Organ

In 1982, after graduating from Lebanon Valley College in Annville, Pennsylvania, Darlene Sitler began teaching music to students in kindergarten to sixth grade. For thirty years she taught at the Northern Potter School District based in the tiny borough of Ulysses just south of the New York state border 140 miles northeast of Pittsburgh. Her husband, Gregory Eldred, taught music at the elementary school in Coudersport, the capital of Potter County 20 miles south of Ulysses. He was also a clarinet player with the Southern Tier Symphony. The couple attended the First United Presbyterian Church in Coudersport where Darlene played the organ and directed the choir. In April 2010, Darlene filed for divorce. The marital split became official four months later.

On Sunday, December 2, 2012, about twenty minutes into Pastor Evon Lloyd's service at the First United Presbyterian Church, Darlene's 52-year-old ex-husband, wearing a hooded beige jacket, entered the building through a side door. Eldred walked up the center aisle, and with a .40-caliber handgun, shot Darlene as she sat at the organ. The single shot caused her to fall into the organ pit. As the stunned congregation looked on Eldred walked calmly out of the church. One of the churchgoers called 911 as several witnesses to the shooting ran to the front of the church to attend to the wounded organist.

About three minutes after the shooting, Gregory Eldred walked back into the church. When Pastor Lloyd and others pleaded with him to put down his pistol, the music teacher threatened to shoot anyone who got in his way. "I want to finish this," he said. "I've got to see if she's dead." Eldred walked up to the organ pit and fired two bullets into his ex-wife. If she wasn't already dead, these two shots killed her.

Several members of the congregation swarmed the shooter, and in the course of subduing him, he fired off another shot that didn't hit anyone. A Pennsylvania State Trooper assigned to the Coudersport barracks arrived at the scene shortly thereafter.

After officers with the state police escorted Gregory Eldred out of the church, the entire congregation climbed aboard a school bus. The witnesses were driven to a place they were questioned by a team of police officers. Eldred, charged with first-degree murder, is being held without bond in the Potter County Jail.

Who knows how long it has been since anyone in this rural community has been murdered. And I'm sure, in the 180-year history of the Coudersport First United Presbyterian Church, nothing remotely like this has ever happened. The obvious question in this bizarre case is why did the music teacher kill his ex-wife, and why did he choose to commit the murder during a Sunday morning church service? It's possible the congregation, by subduing this man, prevented his suicide.

On July 10, 2013, Gregory Eldred pleaded guilty to first-degree murder in a common pleas court. The judge, pursuant to the plea agreement, sentenced him to life in prison.

The Killer Franciscan

Daniel Montgomery grew up in King of Prussia, Pennsylvania, a town outside of Philadelphia. After graduating from Catholic high school, he studied religion in the mid-west, and became a peace activist. In 1994, the 28-year-old joined the Franciscans, a Catholic religious order. An odd, socially awkward man with a volatile temper and a foul mouth, Montgomery didn't get along with his church colleagues and superiors.

In July 2002, after being bounced from one church to another, the misfit friar ended up in Cleveland at St. Stanislaus located in the city's Slavic Village neighborhood. Montgomery didn't fit in well at St. Stanislaus either. He offended fellow friars, parishioners, and the 68-year-old pastor of the church, William Gulas, affectionately known as "Father Willie." After three students accused Daniel Montgomery of touching them inappropriately, Father Gulas, in late November 2002, informed the troubled friar that he was being transferred to Our Lady of Lourdes Friary in Cedar Lake, Indiana. (Sounds like a case of passing the trash.)

At nine in the morning of December 2, 2002, when extinguishing a fire in Father Gulas' rectory office, firefighters stumbled upon his corpse. When questioned that morning by the police, Montgomery said that when the fire broke out, he had been asleep in his second-floor bedroom. A ringing telephone awoke him at which time he smelled smoke, then called 911. After trying to put out the fire, Montgomery fled the church without realizing that Father Gulas was in the burning first-floor office.

On the day after the St. Stanislaus fire, the Cuyahoga County Coroner announced that the blaze had not killed Pastor Gulas. Someone had shot the priest in the chest then torched his office.

On December 8, 2002, detectives brought Friar Montgomery in for further questioning. Following what evolved into a seven-hour interrogation, Montgomery confessed to murdering the St. Stanislaus pastor. The friar had been angry about being transferred to the church in Indiana. He had gone into the pastor's office that morning to ask Father Gulas to vacate the order. According to Montgomery, upon entering the pastor's office, he had said, "I can't [expletive] take it anymore." The angry friar then shot Father Gulas in the chest with a .38-caliber revolver he had purchased the day before from an employee of a neighborhood convenience store. (This person has never been identified.)

After killing the pastor, Montgomery dropped the revolver (which was never found) and walked down the hall where he acquired the red butane lighter he used to ignite papers on Father Gulas' desk. After setting the fire, Montgomery returned to his room and fell asleep. A call from a parishioner woke him up.

A Cuyahoga County grand jury, in January 2003, indicted Daniel Montgomery on the charge of aggravated murder. Nine months later the defendant pleaded guilty to a lesser homicide charge in order to avoid the death penalty. The judge sentenced him to 24 years to life. He began serving his time at the state prison in Marion, Ohio.

In the spring of 2011, a *Philadelphia Inquirer* reporter named John P. Martin decided to look into Montgomery's case. (Montgomery was now maintaining his innocence.) The journalist's investigation led to a four-part *Inquirer* series published in July 2011. Pursuant to his claims of innocence, Montgomery, through his new attorney, Barry Wilford, had filed a motion to withdraw his guilty plea in order that the case could go to trial. Attorney Wilford based his argument for reopening the murder case on three principal points: The prosecution had withheld exculpatory evidence;

interrogators ignored signs that Montgomery was confessing falsely; and his defense attorney, Henry Hilow, did not provide him with the best defense.

Problems in the prosecution's case against Montgomery included the fact the police never recovered the murder weapon. On the charred floor of Pastor Gulas' office, fire investigators found an open toolbox that once contained $1,600 in bingo proceeds. Father Gulas kept the padlocked box in his office safe. On the morning of the murder, a parishioner who supposedly had financial problems was seen coming out of the pastor's office. Assuming this is true, could this man have committed the murder? Another mystery in the case involved the fact that Pastor Gulas' cellphone ended up in the hands of a convicted drug dealer.

On the issue pertaining to the adequacy of Montgomery's defense, attorney Wilford argued that his client had not wanted to plead guilty. To back up this claim, Wilford cited parts of two letters Montgomery had sent to attorney Hilow months before his guilty plea. In a letter dated February 23, 2003 in which Montgomery asked to meet again with the psychiatrist who had examined him shortly after the murder, wrote: "I was in a state of schizophrenia that produced severe delusions in my thinking, causing me to make false statements on December 8, 2002 at the police interrogation. At that time I was suffering from delusions of grandeur that perhaps if I was no longer to be a Franciscan, then I was to be a martyr for a sinner, the killer and arsonist who committed the crime." On July 7, 2003, Montgomery had written: "I am firmly convinced that I must plead my innocence and follow God's law, which is above human law." (I have no idea what that means in the context of this case.)

At the July 2011 hearing to determine if the Gulas murder case should be reopened, and a trial convened, Cuyahoga County Assistant Prosecutor Salem Awadallah argued that there was nothing in Montgomery's motion to justify setting aside his guilty plea and going to trial. She pointed out that Montgomery had failed a polygraph test that had been arranged by attorney Wilford. The prosecutor noted that while the Cleveland police interrogation lasted seven hours, there was no evidence that suggested Montgomery's confession had been coerced.

Cuyahoga County Common Pleas Judge Joan Synenberg, on December 31, 2012, denied Daniel Montgomery's motion for a murder trial. She did not accompany her ruling with a written decision. Whenever an educated, adult defendant confesses and pleads guilty, without strong evidence of a false confession, or equally powerful evidence that someone else had committed the crime, the conviction will stand. In this case, Daniel Montgomery had failed to overcome the presumption of his guilt.

The Easter Morning Murder

Reverend David Howard had just finished his Easter service on Sunday, March 31, 2013 at the Hiawatha Church of God in Christ in the northeastern Ohio town of Ashtabula. As congregants began to file out of the church, Reshad Riddle entered the building carrying a handgun and yelling something about God and Allah. A couple of church members grabbed the minister and ushered him to safety inside an office in the back of the building. Other congregants hit the floor and dialed 911 on their cellphones.

The 25-year-old gunman walked up to Richard Riddle, his 52-year-old father, and shot him in the head. The victim died on the spot. Waving the gun in the air, Reshad Riddle screamed that the murder had been "the will of Allah. This is the will of God," he yelled.

Police officers stormed into the church and took the killer into custody before he shot anyone else.

In 2006, Reshad, then 18, was charged with felonious assault and kidnapping in connection with his attempt to cut his girlfriend's throat. A year later he was arrested for another felonious assault. Riddle was charged again in 2009 for possession of cocaine and tampering with evidence.

Ashtabula Chief of Police Robert Stell told an Associated Press reporter that, "There was no indication that the father and son had a bad relationship. Everyone thinks this was very surprising," he said. Really? Why wasn't this man in prison? Are they putting anyone away these days?

After a local prosecutor charged Riddle with aggravated murder, officers booked him into the Ashtabula County Jail. The judge set his bond at $1 million.

On December 20, 2013, a judge declared Reshad Riddle incompetent to stand trial. In this ruling, the judge relied on the testimony of two psychiatrists who had examined the defendant.

The Reservation Murder of a Nun

Twenty-one-year-old Reehahlio Carroll, a burglar and thief addicted to alcohol and drugs lived on the Navajo Indian Reservation in northwestern New Mexico. Just after midnight on November 1, 2009, he broke into a house trailer at the reservation's St. Berard Mission, an outpost inhabited by nuns attached to the Order of the Sisters of the Blessed Sacrament. The trailer Carroll forced his way into was the home of 64-year-old Sister Marguerite Bartz.

Carroll knew he was breaking into an occupied dwelling. (Under common law, breaking into an occupied home at night, by itself, was a capital crime.) Carroll entered Sister Marguerite's home to steal cash and anything he could sell to support his addictions. If the nun who lived there got in his way that would be her problem.

Sister Marguerite confronted the burglar when he entered her bedroom. Instead of backing out of the trailer, Carroll hit her in the head six times with his flashlight. As the nun lay bleeding and semi-conscious on the floor of the room, the home invader kicked and stomped her.

With Sister Marguerite dying in a pool of her own blood, Carroll rummaged through her trailer home for cash and valuables. Before leaving the scene and driving off in the nun's car, Carroll returned to the bedroom. To make sure he would be leaving a dead woman behind, Carroll finished the victim off by tying a shirt around her neck and mouth.

The following morning, when Sister Marguerite failed to show up for Mass, one of her mission colleagues discovered her corpse.

A couple of days after the cold-blooded killing, police officers arrested Reehallio Carroll. He was driving his victim's car.

Because crimes committed on Indian Reservations are federal offenses, the FBI took charge of the case. An assistant United States attorney out of Albuquerque charged Carroll with first-degree murder, a crime that under federal law carried a mandatory life sentence.

On April 5, 2013, U. S. District Court Judge William Johnson accepted Carroll's plea to second-degree murder. The judge sentenced Carroll to 40 years in prison.

Members of Sister Marguerite's family, as well as her fellow nuns at St. Berard approved of the guilty plea and reduced sentence. They spoke of "forgiveness, redemption, and rehabilitation." Rehabilitation? Good heavens. Mr. Carroll got off light because he murdered a nun. Had he killed a police officer, no one in the law enforcement community would be talking about forgiveness.

Score One for the Devil

There are people among us, ordinary-looking people pushing carts at Walmart, driving around in SUVs, watching their kids play soccer, sitting in movie theaters, and eating in restaurants, that for little or no reason, will take your life. As Charles Lindbergh once said after the murder of his 20-month-old son, life is like war. That's because there are too many people on this earth like Rene Patrick Bourassa, Jr.

On Sunday morning, June 6, 2010, Bourassa, a 34-year-old drifter with a shaved head, an ordinary face, and a tattoo featuring three skulls and a flaming dragon, was driving in eastern Arkansas on Highway 64. Slightly tall, thin, and clean-cut, Bourassa, if placed in a group of men his age, wouldn't stand out. Originally from Danielson, Connecticut, he had recently worked in a Dotham, Alabama barbecue restaurant, and had tended bar in Phoenix, Arizona and Wichita, Kansas.

At eight-thirty that Sunday morning, as Bourassa drove west toward the small town of Hamlin, Arkansas, 80-year-old Lillian Wilson was alone inside the Central Methodist Church. She had gone there to pick-up donation baskets that had been used to collect money for victims of a recent storm. As Bourassa approached the town, his car broke down. Leaving the vehicle along the highway, he walked to the church, and forced his way into the building.

About an hour after Bourassa broke into the Methodist Church, he pulled into a nearby Citgo station driving Lillian Wilson's car. A few miles down the highway from the gas station, he used Wilson's credit card to buy food at a Sonic convenience store.

As Patrick Bourassa drove west through Arkansas, the pastor of the Central Methodist Church discovered Lillian Wilson's body lying on the floor between two pews. She had been bludgeoned to death with a heavy brass cross.

A few days after the murder, police arrested Bourassa in Bremerton, Washington on Kitsap Peninsula west of Seattle. He still possessed Lillian Wilson's car, and admitted to the arresting officers that he had murdered the old woman in the Arkansas church.

On June 16, after waiving extradition, Bourassa, accompanied by his attorney, stood before a judge in Wynne, Arkansas. Advised that he had been charged with capital murder and several lesser charges, Bourassa pleaded not guilty. If convicted of the murder charge, he could be sentenced to life, or sent to death row. He would await his trial, with no bail, in the Cross County Jail.

On Monday, April 2, 2012, in Wynne, Arkansas, the jury selection phase of Bourassa's capital murder trial got underway. A week later, the prosecutor showed the jury a videotape of the defendant re-enacting how he had picked the brass cross off the communion table and used it to beat Lillian Wilson to death. In response to why he had killed an old woman he didn't know, Bourassa said it was because he became enraged when she told him that God loved him, and would forgive him.

Bourassa's attorneys did not dispute the fact their client had killed Lillian Wilson. It was their mission to convince the jury to find Bourassa guilty of a lesser homicide charge, and save him from execution. To get that result, the defense put two expert witnesses on the stand. A psychologist and a forensic psychiatrist testified that Bourassa was genetically predisposed to violence. These mental health practitioners told the jury that the defendant had suffered childhood abuse, and was bipolar. Moreover, he had a personality disorder. (No kidding.) Because these experts were not saying that Bourassa was not guilty by virtue of legal insanity, the relevance of this testimony was not clear. Surely they were not trying to make the jurors feel sorry for this man.

On Friday the thirteenth, 2012, after four hours of deliberation, the jury found Bourassa guilty of capital murder as well as the lesser charges. The defendant, at the reading of the verdict, showed no emotion. Having found Bourassa guilty, the jury had to sentence him to either life in prison or death. The next day, after deliberating two hours, the jury sentenced Bourassa to life without parole. The jurors had spared this killer's life because they didn't think Lillian Wilson, the woman he had murdered, would approve of the death sentence.

The Knife Attack in Albuquerque

On Sunday morning, April 28, 2013, all hell broke loose inside St. Jude Thaddeus Catholic Church in Albuquerque, New Mexico. The mass had just ended and the choir had begun its final hymn when a 24-year-old man who had been nervous acting and fidgety throughout the service vaulted over several pews toward the front of the church. Lawrence Capener, the crazed churchgoer, possessed a knife that he used to stab the choir director several times.

Gerald Madrid, the church flutist, came to Adam Alvarez's rescue by attempting to put Lawrence Capener into a bear hug. During the scuffle, Capener, before collapsing to the church floor under the weight of other churchgoers who mobbed him, stabbed the flutist five times in the back. Daren De Aquero, an off-duty Albuquerque police officer, put the subdued assailant into handcuffs.

Greg Aragon, an off-duty Albuquerque Fire Department Lieutenant, treated the choir director, the man who came to his aid, and a female member of the choir who had been slashed by Capener's knife. None of the victims incurred life-threatening injuries.

As Capener was led out of the church, an elderly parishioner spoke to him. She said, "God bless you, forgive yourself."

"You don't know about the Masons," the attacker replied.

Later that Sunday, a local prosecutor charged Lawrence Capener with three counts of aggravated battery. A magistrate set his bail at $250,000.

After detectives advised Capener of his *Miranda* rights, the subject informed his interrogators that he was "99 percent sure" that the choir director was a Mason involved in a conspiracy "that is far more reaching than I could or would believe." He apologized for stabbing the flutist and the woman in the choir.

While Capener did not belong to the 3,000-member church, his mother was an active parishioner. He had recently graduated from a community college, and had started a new job. According to people who know him, Capener struggled with mental illness.

In February 2014, Capener's attorney petitioned the court to lower his client's bail so he could live at home under the supervision of a GPS device. The judge, after hearing from Capener's victims, denied the request. The trial was scheduled for September 2014.

Murdered While Preaching

Lake Charles, Louisiana is located in the southwest part of the state. At 8:30 Friday evening, September 27, 2013, 53-year-old Woodrow Karey, armed with a shotgun, walked into the Tabernacle of Praise Worship Center in Lake Charles. Pastor Ronald J. Harris was standing in front of the church preaching to sixty revival service congregants when Karey blew him off his feet with a blast from his shotgun. As the preacher lay bleeding on the church floor, Karey stood over him and fired a second shot into his head, killing Reverend Harris instantly.

As congregants, including the pastor's wife, scrambled for cover, Woodrow Karey walked out of the church. Shortly thereafter the shooter called 911. Karey identified himself, and informed the dispatcher of what he had just done. He did not reveal *why* he had murdered the pastor. It is not known if the two men even knew each other. Karey said he wanted to turn himself in and informed the dispatcher where the police could find him.

In a matter of minutes after Woodrow Karey's 911 call deputies with the Calcasieu Parrish Sheriff's Office took him into custody without incident. Before being hauled off to jail, the shooter took the officers to a wooded area where he had hidden a .22-caliber pistol and a shotgun.

A parish prosecutor has changed Woodrow Karey with second-degree murder. He was held on $1 million bond at the Calacasieu Corrections Center. According to reports, Mr. Karey does not have a criminal record. The authorities did not reveal if he had a history of mental illness or some kind of grievance against the pastor or the church.

In December 2013, following Karey's indictment for the lesser offense of manslaughter, the judge reduced his bail to $500,000. In Louisiana, manslaughter carries a sentence of 10 to 40 years. The defendant's trial was scheduled for late 2014.

Human Torch Kills a Priest

Ocean City is a resort town on the southern tip of Fenwick Island off the coast of Maryland. In the summer the population swells to 300,000. In 2003, Reverend David Dingwell, his wife Brenda, and their three sons moved to Ocean City from the Canadian Province of British Columbia where he grew up. Father Dingwell came to Maryland to become the priest and rector of St. Paul's By-The-Sea Episcopal Church. His parishioners came to know him as Father David.

Just before ten in the morning of Tuesday, November 26, 2013, a man engulfed in flames stormed into St Paul's Shepherd's Crook Building where volunteers were in the pantry preparing to open that day's food distribution service. The man on fire, John Raymond Sterner, a 56-year-old resident of Ocean City who had been a regular beneficiary of the food service and the church's used clothing outlet, bear-hugged church volunteer Jessica Waters.

From the pantry Sterner ran into one of the ground floor church offices where the flaming man encountered parishioner Bruce Young who tried in vain to knock him to the floor where he could smother the fire. Sterner died in the ground floor office. His burning body started a fire in the church that produced a lot of smoke.

Ocean City firefighters doused the church fire before it destroyed much of the structure. In the second-floor rectory office they found the 51-year-old priest. Paramedics rushed Reverend Dingwell to Atlantic General Hospital where he died from smoke inhalation.

Jessica Waters, the pantry volunteer who had been embraced by the flaming Sterner, received treatment at John Hopkins Bayview Medical Center in Baltimore. Bruce Young, the parishioner who tried to help the human torch, received minor burns.

Twenty-five minutes before he ran into the church in flames, Sterner, at a Shell station a quarter mile from the church, was recorded on a surveillance camera pouring gasoline into a red container. It is presumed that just before running into the church building he doused himself with the accelerant and lit himself up.

The Chief Medical Examiner of Maryland performed the autopsies of Father Dingwell and John Raymond Sterner.

The man who started the fire that killed Reverend Dingwell had a history of crime dating back to June 1994. Over the years Sterner had been convicted of breaking and entering, malicious destruction of property, disturbing the peace, and numerous offenses related to alcohol intoxication. The police last arrested Sterner in July 2013 on the charge of second-degree assault. Police officers had taken Sterner to the Peninsula Regional Medical Center for psychiatric evaluation after two of his arrests. According to police reports, he showed signs of "emotional and mental crisis."

He was just the kind of person Reverend Dingwell and his parishioner volunteers helped every day.

The fact Sterner bear-hugged the pantry volunteer suggested this was a case of suicide by fire followed by the intent to kill others. Unlike most murder-suicide cases, this killer died before his murder victim.

Pastor Accused of Murdering His Wife

In 2013, Richard Shahan, the 53-year-old associate pastor of the First Baptist Church in Birmingham, Alabama, lived in Homewood, Alabama with his wife Karen. Reverend Shahan functioned as the church's children and family pastor and facilities director. Karen Shahan had a job at a nearby Hobby Lobby store. The couple lived in a rental house owned by the church.

After graduating in 1985 from the Southwestern Baptist Theological Seminary in Fort Worth, Texas, Shahan joined the staff at the First Baptist Church in Bryon, Texas where he was the associate pastor of education and family development. From 1989 to 1999 Reverend Shahan served at the Shades Mountain Baptist Church in Birmingham. In 2000 he became associate pastor in education and administration for the Hickory Grove Baptist Church in Charlotte, North Carolina where he worked seven years. From 2007 to 2009 Shahan was employed by the Kimble Knight Ministries in Brentwood, Tennessee. From Brentwood in 2009 he and his wife moved back to Birmingham where he joined the First Baptist Church in that city.

In 2003, while working in Charlotte, North Carolina, Shahan formed his own company, an Internet-based curriculum provider called One Vine, Inc. In 2010, while living in Birmingham, Pastor Shahan and his wife filed for personal bankruptcy. According to court records, the couple listed $443,500 in assets and $505,665 in debts. At the time they had a monthly income of $5,874 that did not include a $2,516 monthly housing allowance from the church.

In September 2012, Pastor Shahan took a leave of absence from the First Baptist Church in Birmingham in order to travel to Kazakhstan where he had acquired a visiting professor position at the Bible Institute in Almaty, Kazakhstan. He returned to Birmingham in May 2013.

On July 23, 2013, Karen Louise Shahan's co-workers at Hobby Lobby became concerned when the 52-year-old pastor's wife didn't show up for work. Calls to her home went unanswered. At 11:15 that Tuesday morning, police officers with the Homewood Police Department, pursuant to a welfare check, made a gruesome discovery. The officers found that someone had stabbed Karen Shahan to death in her bedroom. The victim's blood had been spilled throughout the dwelling. A crime scene investigator told reporters that this was the most brutal murder site he had ever witnessed.

Pastor Richard Shahan was not home the morning police discovered the body of his repeatedly stabbed wife. Detectives believed that the victim had been murdered Monday night or early the next day. There were no signs of forced entry, and nothing from the house had been stolen. The victim had not been sexually assaulted. Suspicion immediately fell upon the husband. The fact he was a pastor meant nothing to homicide detectives who know there is no such thing as an unlikely murder suspect.

Detectives, on August 7, 2013, questioned Pastor Shahan at the Homewood police station. When asked to account for his whereabouts that Monday night and Tuesday morning, the pastor said he had been out of town visiting one of the couple's two sons.

On August 8, 2013, the day after the station house interrogation, detectives took Shahan into custody "for investigative purposes." Under Alabama law, a suspect can only be held for investigation 48 hours. If the arrestee is not charged with a crime, he or she must be released.

Following the suspect's 48 hours behind bars, the authorities released him because the prosecutor didn't have enough evidence to level a homicide charge. Because he was a suspect in his wife's brutal murder, officials at the First Baptist Church placed pastor Shahan on paid administrative leave.

A Jefferson County prosecutor, shortly after Pastor Shahan announced on December 16, 2013 that he would be leaving the United States to do three years of mission work in Germany, charged him with first-degree murder. On New Years Day, 2014, police officers in Nashville, Tennessee arrested the suspect as he boarded a plane to Germany.

Investigators believed that Pastor Shahan murdered his wife so that he could start a new life overseas with his boyfriend.

On January 21, in Birmingham, family members posted Shahan's $100,000 bond. The next day a corrections official fitted him with an electronic monitoring device. As of August 2014, this case had not come to trial.

The Torture Murder of a Priest

Eric Freed, while living in Japan in 1979, was ordained a Catholic priest. Twenty years later Reverend Freed joined the greater Santa Rosa Diocese in northern California's Humboldt County. In 2003, Father Freed began teaching in the Religious Studies Department of Humboldt State University in Arcata, California. At the school, which is part of the 23-campus California State University system, Father Freed also directed the Newman

Center, a Catholic student organization. In August 2011 Reverend Freed became pastor of St. Bernard Church in the coastal city of Eureka located 275 miles north of San Francisco.

At nine in the morning, on New Year's Day 2014, Deacon Frank Weber went to the St. Bernard rectory after Father Freed failed to show up for morning mass. The deacon called 911 after discovering the priest dead from what appeared to be a head wound caused by a blunt object.

At the murder scene police officers found signs of forced entry as well as evidence of a struggle. Father Freed was last seen at 6:30 New Year's Eve following the evening service. The victim's gray 2010 Nissan Altima was nowhere to be found. Investigators had no immediate suspect.

Humboldt County Sheriff's Office deputies, early in the afternoon of Thursday, January 2, 2014, arrested a 43-year-old man from Redway, California named Garry Lee Bullock. The officers took him into custody for the murder of Father Freed near the southern Humboldt County town of Gaberville.

According to investigators there was no indication that the suspect and the victim knew each other, or had met before the church break-in. Detectives believed that Bullock had broken into the rectory looking for money. When he encountered the priest, the two men fought until the intruder struck Reverend Freed with a blunt instrument, a blow that killed him.

In tracing the suspect's activities in the days leading up to the murder, detectives working the Freed case learned that early Tuesday afternoon, December 31, 2013, Humboldt County deputies had arrested Bullock near Gaberville for public intoxication. After becoming agitated at the hospital where he was being evaluated, deputies handcuffed Bullock and booked him into the Humboldt County Jail.

Just after midnight, January 1, the authorities released Bullock. A few hours later a security guard found Bullock loitering near the St. Bernard Church rectory. The guard chased Bullock off church grounds. This could have been just before or after the suspect murdered the priest.

After he pleaded guilty to cocaine possession early in 2013, a judge placed Bullock on three years probation. The murder suspect has three daughters and once filed for bankruptcy. He has no history of violent crime.

On January 6, 2014, the Humboldt County Coroner announced that Reverend Freed had been beaten to death with a wooden stake and a metal gutter pipe. Bullock, held under $1.2 million bond, pleaded not guilty.

On January 21, 2014, Eureka Police detectives testified at the preliminary hearing to determine if the state had enough evidence to go forward with the case. When arrested for murder, officers found what looked like pieces of mushrooms in the pockets of Bullock's trousers. His hands were so swollen officers took him to the hospital for x-rays. The suspect's hands were also covered with abrasions from his knuckles to his wrists. Bullock also had scratches on his face, arms, and back.

According to the autopsy report, the victim had died either of blunt force trauma to the head and trachea or by suffocation caused by compression or having a broken vase shoved down his throat. The prosecuting attorney told the court that Bullock had tortured Father Reed "for his own sadistic purpose."

The judge ruled that the prosecution had presented sufficient evidence against Bullock for the case to go forward toward trial. As of July 2014, the case was pending.

Father Gerald Robinson

In 1980, 72-year-old Sister Margaret Ann Pahl worked at Mercy Hospital in Toledo, Ohio as the caretaker of the chapel. A strict taskmaster who didn't suffer fools, Sister Margaret worked closely with 42-year-old Father Gerald Robinson, one of the hospital's chaplains. Father Robinson was a popular priest in the heavily Catholic city of 300,000.

On April 5, 1980, on Holy Saturday, someone found Sister Margaret's bloody body on the chapel floor. She had been choked to near death, then stabbed 31 times in the chest, neck, and face. Some of the stab wounds in her chest formed the pattern of an upside down cross. The killer had also anointed her forehead with a smudge of her own blood. With her habit pulled up to her chest, and her undergarments pulled down around her ankles, the victim had been posed in a position of humiliation. While not raped, the killer had penetrated her with a cross.

Although detectives on the case immediately suspected Father Robinson of this ritualistic murder, he presided over Sister Margaret's funeral Mass four days after her homicide. The principal piece of crime scene evidence involved a bloodstain on the altar cloth consistent with the form of a sword-shaped letter opener in Father Robinson's apartment. The stain bore the vague print of the letter opener's dime-sized medallion bearing the image of the U.S. capitol. However, because the chief detective on the case was a Catholic, and didn't want to scandalize the church, Father Robinson was not arrested. The investigation floundered, and without a suspect, died on the vine.

In December 2003, a Lucas County cold-case investigative team reopened the 1980 murder. Father Robinson, over the past 23 years, had served in three Toledo Diocese parishes. The 65-year-old priest, in 2003, was administering to the sick and dying in several area Catholic homes and hospitals. The case came back to life after a woman wrote a letter to the police claiming that Father Robinson had sexually abused her as a child, molestation that involved Satanic ritualistic behavior that involved human sacrifice. (I don't know if this complainant passed a polygraph test, or made the accusation after some psychologist coaxed the memory out of her. After the Satanic hysteria in the 1980s McMartin preschool debacle, and the horrible injustice in the Memphis three case in the 1990s, this kind of allegation should draw serious skepticism.)

Following the exhumation of Sister Margaret's body, a forensic pathologist noted that a wound in the victim's jaw could have been made by the letter opener found in Father Robinson's apartment. A DNA analysis of the victim's fingernail scrapings, and underwear, excluded the priest. Nevertheless, in April 2006, the police went to Father Robinson's home and arrested him. From the Lucas County Jail where he was held without bail, the priest denied killing Sister Margaret.

While there was barely enough evidence to legally justify Father Robinson's arrest--no motive, no confession, no eyewitness, and no physical evidence directly linking him to the corpse--the priest went on trial for murder on April 24, 2006. The prosecutor showed the jury a videotape of the defendant's 2004 police interrogation. Father Robinson told his questioners that he had been stunned when one of the other hospital chaplains accused him of murdering Sister Margaret. When left alone for a few minutes in the interrogation room, the priest folded his hands and began to whisper the word "sister," then bowed his head in prayer. At one point he said, "Oh my Jesus." (I don't know exactly how the prosecution interpreted this as incriminating evidence.)

A prosecution forensic scientist testified that the letter opener "could not be ruled out" as the murder weapon. (The prosecutor, in his closing remarks, told the jury that the letter opener fit one of the victim's stab wounds "like a key in a lock." Instruments used in stabbings cannot be scientifically linked to their wounds this way. That statement alone should have been adequate ground for a reversal on appeal.) The forensic scientist also testified that the altar cloth bloodstains were "consistent with" the general shape of the letter opener. On cross-examination, this witness conceded that a pair of missing scissors could have left the bloodstain on the altar cloth.

On May 11, 2006, the jury, after 9 days of testimony, and 6 hours of deliberation, found Father Robinson guilty. The 70-year-old priest became the second priest in U.S. history to be convicted of criminal homicide. (The first was a priest named Hans Schmidt.) The judge sentenced Robinson to 15 years to life. Incarcerated at the Hocking Correctional Facility in southern Ohio, the priest will be first eligible for parole in 2016.

Two months after the murder trial, Ohio's 6th District Court of Appeals upheld the conviction. In December 2008, the Ohio Supreme Court declined to hear the case. About a year later, the U.S. Supreme Court refused to entertain the appeal as well.

While it seemed that Gerald Robinson had run out of legal remedies, his legal team, in 2010, petitioned the state appeals court for post-conviction relief on the grounds a 27-year-old confessed serial killer named Coral Eugene Watts murdered Sister Margaret. Watts, a black man, had stabbed 12 women to death in Texas, and at least one woman in Michigan. Police suspected him of killing another 80 victims. Watts had left many of the women with their blouses pulled up to their necks. He had not sexually molested any of his victims. They had all been posed in humiliating positions.

On April 11, 2011, the Ohio appeals court denied the Robinson petition. According to the appellate judges, Father Robinson's attorneys, at the time of his 2006 trial, knew of Watts as a possible suspect in Sister Margaret's murder, but chose not to pursue this as a defense strategy. Moreover, there were dissimilarities between the serial killer's *modus operandi* and Sister Margaret's homicide. For one thing, Coral Eugene Watts had typically stalked young women before he killed them outdoors.

A year later, the Robinson defense team again petitioned the state court of appeals to toss out the 2006 murder conviction. This time the priest's lawyers accused the prosecution of withholding key documents in the case. Regarding the issue of serial killer Watts, Robinson's trial attorneys didn't pursue that line of defense in 2006 because they erroneously thought he was serving time when Sister Margaret was murdered. As it turned out, on April 5, 1980, Watts was living in southern Michigan, just 40 miles from Toledo. As for *modus operandi*, the priest's attorneys found Watts' killings and the death of the nun "eerily similar." (Coral Eugene Watts died in 2007 of prostate cancer. He was 53 and serving time in a Michigan prison.)

On June 5, 2014, United States District Court Judge James Guin denied a request for the release of Father Robinson. The priest had suffered a heart attack a month earlier and, according to reports, didn't have long to live. The judge said he didn't have the jurisdictional authority to grant the motion. The next day, Friday morning, Father Robinson died while being cared for in the hospital unit at the Columbus, Ohio prison

The Attack in Phoenix

Father Joseph Terra and his assistant pastor, Reverend Kenneth Walker, resided in the rectory of the Mercy Mission Catholic Church in a seedy neighborhood in downtown Phoenix, Arizona. Father Walker, age 29 and from New York State had been ordained in May 2012.

Father Terra, at nine o'clock on the night of Wednesday, June 11, 2014, heard a noise coming from the church courtyard. Upon investigation, the 56-year-old priest came upon a man he did not know or recognize. The toothless, longhaired intruder, a man who looked like he lived on the streets, began attacking Father Terra with a blunt object made of iron. Under attack, the priest fled to the rectory where he grabbed a handgun kept in his bedroom. Because the longhaired assailant had bludgeoned the father's right hand, he was unable to fire the gun.

The intruder wrestled the gun from the priest and ordered him to get down on his hands and knees. After demanding money, the unkempt attacker shot Father Terra with the rectory gun.

Assistant pastor Walker heard the commotion and came to help his colleague. The intruder responded by shooting the reverend as well. With the pastors shot and bleeding in the church, the shooter ran out of the church, climbed into Father Walker's 2003 Mazda Tribute and drove off.

Pastor Walker, thirty minutes after Father Terra encountered the burglar in the church courtyard, called 911 to report that he and the unresponsive pastor had been shot by a white, longhaired man in his fifties.

As Father Walker waited for the police and ambulance crews, he administered last rites to his gravely wounded colleague.

Later that night Father Joseph Terra died while being treated at a nearby hospital. Doctors listed Father Walker in critical condition. He was, however, expected to survive the attack.

Shortly after the shootings, police officers came across Father Walker's Mazda parked four blocks from the church. A team of crime scene specialists processed the vehicle for physical evidence that could link the killer to the church murder.

Homicide detectives caught a break when a woman called and told them a homeless man recently out of prison had given her a black bag containing a camera. That camera belonged to one of the priests at the Mercy Mission Catholic Church.

At nine o'clock Sunday night, June 15, 2014, detectives arrested 54-year-old Gary Michael Moran for the murder of Father Terra and the attempted murder of Reverend Walker. Moran denied shooting the priests, then later confessed to the crimes. At his arraignment on Monday, June 16, 2014, Moran pleaded not guilty to the charges of murder, attempted murder, and aggravated assault. The judge ruled that Moran be held in the county jail on a $1 million cash-only bond.

So, who was this man who had snuck into a church and shot two priests? In 2005, Moran had entered a stranger's apartment, picked up a steak knife, and stabbed the male resident in the abdomen as he slept. Moran pleaded guilty to aggravated assault with a deadly weapon, and was sentenced to ten years in an Arizona state prison. On April 24, 2014, after serving eight years of that sentence, corrections authorities paroled this violent man.

On June 9, 2014, after meeting regularly with his parole officer, Moran failed to show up for a scheduled appointment. Besides the aggravated assault conviction, Moran had served time for car theft, burglary, and numerous drug related offenses. Since this life-long criminal's release from prison, he had been living on the streets of downtown Phoenix.

11 DRUGS

A Growing Problem

A governor broke with tradition [on January 8, 2014] and devoted his entire state of the state address to drug addiction. Peter Shumlin, the governor of Vermont, urged residents to open their eyes to the growing problem in their front yards, rather than leaving it only to law enforcement, medical personnel and addiction treatment providers. Shumlin argued the facts speak for themselves.

In Vermont, since 2000, there has been a 770 per cent increase in treatment for all opiates. He stated, "What started out as an OxyContin and prescription drug addiction problem in this state has now grown into a full-blown heroin crisis. And last year we had nearly double the number of deaths in Vermont from heroin overdose as the previous year."

In turns out Vermont is not the only state facing this crisis. According to the White House's Office of National Drug Control Policy, the number of deaths involving heroin surged 45 percent between 1999 and 2010.

Judy Woodruff, PBS News Hour, January 9, 2014

Drug-Addled Americans

According to a pair of Australian researchers, between 149 million and 271 million people worldwide took an illegal drug at least once in 2009. Other studies have shown that the heaviest drug users in the world are Americans. In 2009, 22 million Americans used illegal drugs. (This figure is low because it was based on self-reporting.) The narcotic of choice, marijuana was followed by meth, cocaine, ecstasy, and heroin. In addition, 9 million Americans abuse legal drugs and millions more take prescription pills.

Drugs and Crime

The great availability of illicit drugs contributes not only to more frequent crime it leads to more serious crime. The man who steals from stores and houses may have ideas about bank robberies flash through his mind, but without drugs he is too fearful to carry them out. Once he is on drugs, barriers to more daring ventures are overcome. The drugs do not *cause* a person to obtain a sawed-off shotgun and hold up a liquor store, or for that matter, commit any other crime. They simply make it more feasible for him to eliminate fears for the time being in order to act upon what he has previously considered. That is, drugs intensify and bring out tendencies already present within the individual user. They do not transform a responsible person into a criminal. The criminality comes first, the decision to use drugs later.

Dr. Stranton E. Samenow, *Inside the Criminal Mind*, 1984

Crazy Acting Naked Men: Four Cases

Within the past few weeks, police in Tempe Town, Lynx Lake, Phoenix, and Scottsdale, Arizona have arrested naked men high on synthetic drugs. They had shed their clothing because PCP, bath salts, and meth causes body temperatures to rise. The drugs also produce bizarre behavior that is often criminal. The recent cases in Arizona may be a harbinger of problems families and police officers will be facing due to the increasing popularity of these drugs.

Chris Brown

On June 20, 2012, at 11:30 AM in Tempe Town, a community 10 miles east of Phoenix, police received a call that a man was swimming in a municipal lake in violation of an ordinance prohibiting such activity. The trespasser, 38-year-old Chris Brown, was swimming in his birthday suit. When he refused to come out of the lake, rescuers climbed into a boat to fish him out of the water. On the shore, among Brown's clothing, police officers found drug paraphernalia.

The naked swimmer avoided apprehension for an hour, but eventually ended up in the rescue boat. The local prosecutor charged Chris Brown with indecent exposure, failure to identify, and possession of drug paraphernalia. Believed to have been high on some kind of synthetic drug, his case is pending.

In January 2013, the judge sentenced Brown to one year of probation.

Calvin Forrey

Yavapaia County sheriff's deputies, on June 25, 2012, responded to Calvin Forrey's home in Prescott, Arizona. A family member had called 911 to report that Forrey, naked and drug addled had become disorderly. The 27-year-old, who admitted to the responding officers that he had been using bath salts, was not arrested because he wasn't belligerent.

Four days later, a man at a Lynx Lake campground called the Yavapaia Sheriff's Office to report that a naked man "on drugs and out of his mind" had stolen his Jeep. When deputies arrived at the scene, they found Forrey, not far from where he had stolen the vehicle, screaming at the top of his lungs. The Prescott man had crashed the Jeep and was injured. Forrey's pit bull charged one of the officers who shot and killed the dog.

On Saturday morning, July 1, Calvin Forrey died in the Yavapai Regional Medical Center. Information regarding his cause of death has not been released. His blood is being analyzing to determine if he had been under the influence of bath salts or other synthetic drugs.

Unidentified Naked Man

In Phoenix, at 2:30 in the morning on July 4, 2012, a nude man driving a Budget rental truck plowed through the front lawn of a home and slammed into the house, ending up in one of the dwelling's bedrooms. Fortunately the room was at the time unoccupied. The naked man jumped out of the truck and fled the scene on foot. Later in the day police identified the driver and took him into custody.

John Brigham

On November 24, 2011, John Brigham, a 45-year-old from Gilbert, Arizona was staying at his Uncle Ed's house in Scottsdale. That day, a neighbor called 911 to report a man with nothing on but a bath towel around his waist was stacking furniture and other household items into a big pile in the front yard. The man was also dancing about this stack of stuff to loud music. This strange-acting man turned out to be John Brigham.

When police officers rolled up to Uncle Ed's house, they saw Brigham standing nude in the front doorway. The nephew admitted to the police he had been smoking marijuana and snorting meth, and referred to the mess he had made in his uncle's front yard as a sculpture constructed in anticipation of a visit from a witch.

An officer called Brigham's Uncle Ed who was in New York City at the time. The owner of the house confirmed that his nephew had permission to be in the home, but was not pleased that he had trashed the place. Although Uncle Ed agreed to press charges, he said he was worried about his nephew's mental state, and drug habit.

At the Scottsdale city lockup, Brigham, who had gotten dressed for the police, stripped again, and created a commotion by yelling and banging the bars to his cell. After getting him dressed, officers took Brigham to a nearby hospital for a mental evaluation. A few days later, the charges against him were dropped, and Brigham went home.

On June 29, while driving in Scottsdale, Brigham collided with another car, injuring the driver. Brigham got out of his damaged vehicle, took off his clothes, and started yelling and chanting. He then climbed onto the roof of another car and danced about in the nude.

Brigham's bizarre behavior took an ominous turn when he yanked a woman out of a Toyota Prius and drove off in her car traveling eastbound at a high rate of speed in the westbound lane. He hadn't gone far when he crashed the blue Prius into four cars. As Brigham tried to carjack a second vehicle, police officers took him into custody. One of the cars Brigham had smashed into contained a woman who was 8-months pregnant. Both of her legs had been broken. Brigham, in his reckless driving spree, had injured seven people.

The Maricopa County prosecutor charged Brigham with aggravated assault, robbery, and driving under the influence of drugs. He was held in the Maricopa County Jail on $100,000 cash-only bond. A toxicological test revealed he had been high on PCP. Brigham's preliminary hearing was set for July 13, 2012.

Following his plea-bargained carjacking conviction in December 2012, the judge sentenced Brigham to eight years in prison. He will serve five years on probation once he completed his prison term.

How to Spot a Junkie

Dope [heroin] can make you bad looking, especially if you're using a lot: you retain water, so your face grows puffy and aged, you develop blemishes your skin looks green. After quitting, you look worse for months before your former looks return.

Ann Marlowe, *How to Stop Time*, 1999

The Stoned Mother

On Friday, June 1, 2012, Catalina Clouser, a vacuous-faced 19-year-old with pink hair, a pot habit, and a 5-week-old baby, spent the evening at a Phoenix park near her home drinking and smoking marijuana with her boyfriend. Clouser had brought her baby to the park to enjoy the night, and inhale their second-hand smoke. Parenting in the age of drugs.

Later that night, Clouser and her boyfriend ran out of booze so he and Clouser, with the sleeping baby in the car seat, drove off to get more beer. Along the way, police pulled them over and charged him with driving under the influence. After the cops hauled the boyfriend off to jail, Clouser drove to her girlfriend's house on West Cholla Street.

At her friend's place, Clouser, distraught that the police had interrupted a fun night by busting her boyfriend, added to her high by smoking two bowls of marijuana. Around midnight, she staggered to her 2000 Ford Focus, laid the carrier containing the sleeping infant on the roof of the vehicle, slid behind the wheel, and drove off. As she motored mindlessly through the intersection of Cholla and 45th Avenue, the baby, wearing only a diaper, bounced off the car and landed in the street.

Arriving home, the stoned mother discovered that her baby wasn't in or on the car. Instead of calling 911, she phoned her friend and asked her to retrace the route she had taken from her house. Clouser said she would do the same from her place back to the friend's dwelling. In the meantime, passing motorists spotted the baby in the intersection and called 911. Miraculously, the child (probably half-stoned) had not been seriously injured.

Clouser and her girlfriend, when they converged at the intersection of Cholla and 45th Avenue, encountered police officers who were questioning the citizens who had called in the emergency. Identifying herself as the mother of the baby in the street, Clouser admitted she had driven off with the infant on her car roof. An officer at the scene arrested Clouser for aggravated DUI, and child abuse. Paramedics with the Phoenix Fire Department transported the baby, who appeared to be okay but hungry, to a nearby hospital. The next day, officials with the Arizona's child protective services took control of Clouser's baby.

Clouser bailed out of the Maricopa County Jail, and awaited her trial while under house arrest.

In April 2014, the judge sentenced Clouser to 16 years of supervised probation after she pleaded guilty to DUI and child abuse.

Heroin Chic

Popular folklore has it that people who do dope don't eat. That stereotype of the reed-thin drug addict is partially a matter of economics, and partially ideology. Yes, if you're a junkie living on the street, you're not likely to make eating your first priority. But for the rest of the heroin-using population, food consumption has more to do with metaphor. Some embrace the image of the junkie as vampire, a creature of the midnight, cut off from normal human needs, requiring only heroin. But just as many junkies maintain their weight....

The attenuated, fashionable body of "heroin chic" ads may be what you have in mind when you start doing dope but in reality long term use can make you bloated in odd places....

The frightening thin dope users I've known were either people with some kind of eating disorder that was articulated though heroin, or those who are unable to keep food down on dope.

Ann Marlowe, *How To Stop Time,* 1999

Designer Drugs

Since 2008, when the designer drug first came on the scene, hundreds of violent crimes, overdoses, and incidents of bizarre behavior have been linked to users of synthetic marijuana. Called Spice, K2, Yucatan, Skunk, and Moon Rocks, the drug consists of dried, shredded plant material sprayed with chemicals that when smoked produces an intense high. Marketed as a "safe" legal alternative to pot, the drug is sold openly in tobacco shops and gas stations.

Synthetic marijuana can cause bath salts-like euphoria, paranoia, and hallucinations. In addition to becoming agitated, aggressive, and violent, users have suffered seizures and heart attacks. Several states are considering making this group of mind-altering substances illegal. One of those states is Michigan, the site of a murder case that involved a high school student named Jonathan Hoffman.

After his divorced parents moved from West Bloomfield, Michigan to Scottsdale, Arizona, 17-year-old Jonathan Hoffman, in the fall of 2011, moved in with his grandparents so he could finish his senior year at Farmington Central High School. He had been accepted to East Michigan University where he planned on majoring in computer science. The boy's father, 56-year-old Michael Hoffman, a prominent divorce lawyer and co-founder of the law firm American Divorce Association for Men (ADAM), had recently retired. He and Jonathan's mother had been divorced 6 years and were living near each other in Scottsdale so they both could spend time with Jonathan's 15-year-old sister. While living at his grandparents' condo at Maple Place Villas in the Detroit suburb, Jonathan had been smoking the synthetic marijuana Spice. He had been arrested for possession of the drug, and was on probation. This had caused friction between him and his 74-year-old grandmother, a former schoolteacher named Sandra Layne.

Late in the afternoon of Friday, May 18, 2012, neighbors heard Jonathan and his grandmother yelling at each other from inside the condo. They were fighting over Jonathan's schoolwork and his drug abuse. Hearing several gunshots, several neighbors called 911. Jonathan himself phoned for help, screaming that he'd been shot several times, and that he was going to die. Three minutes into his 911 call, he exclaimed that he had been shot again.

Police officers rolled up to the scene at 5:25 PM and ordered Sandra Layne out of the dwelling. She walked out of the condo carrying a .40-caliber Glock semi-automatic pistol and announced that she had just "murdered" her grandson.

Emergency personnel rushed Jonathan to Botsford Hospital in Farmington Hills where he died less than an hour later. Police officers transported the married, 74-year-old mother of five to a holding cell in the West Bloomfield police station.

The Oakland County Medical Examiner determined that Jonathan Hoffman had been shot 10 times. (Later, a toxicological analysis showed that the victim had been high on Spice.)

An Oakland County prosecutor charged Sandra Layne with open murder, a general homicide charge which covers first and second degree murder. On May 21, following her arraignment at the West Bloomfield District Court, the judge ordered Layne to be held without bail in the Oakland County Jail. Her attorney, Mitch Ribitwer, told reporters that his client, married for 28 years, had never been in trouble before. "She's very distraught, very upset. It's a very difficult time."

In April 2013, Judge Denise Langford Morris, in exceeding sentencing guidelines, sentenced Layne to 20 to 40 years in prison.

The Blue Meth Scam

Kevin Abar, assistant special agent in charge of Homeland Security Investigations in New Mexico, says drug distributors are selling methamphetamine tinted blue in the Four Corners region. That mirrors AKMC's hit drama "Breaking Bad," which depicted an Albuquerque-based meth operation that cooked up the drug with a blue hue. Abar says tinting meth blue is a way for distributors to advertise and brand their product. But he says the blue meth being sold makes people sick. He says it has been cut with chemicals to make it blue and is not the "pure" product portrayed in "Breaking Bad."

Associated Press, January 14, 2014

Meth Contaminated Homes

Methamphetamine is an addictive, synthetic stimulant that causes the brain to release a surge of dopamine that, depending upon how it is ingested, and its potency, creates a high that lasts from a few minutes to 24 hours. Meth comes in two forms, powder and rock. The powder can be snorted, smoked, eaten, or dissolved into a drink. Rock, the crystalized form of the drug, is usually smoked or injected. One hit costs the meth user between $25 and $80. There are 1.4 million users of methamphetamine in the United States, and this number is rising.

Meth is addictive because it depletes the brain of dopamine. Once this happens, users are unable to experience pleasure without the chemicals. Addicts who try to quit become depressed, and in some cases, psychotic. The prolonged use of meth permanently destroys the brain, and can cause heart attacks and strokes.

Manufacturing or "cooking" meth is a multi-step operation that takes 48 hours to complete. The process produces toxic fumes, and there is always the potential for an explosion. There are a handful of large, commercial super labs, and thousands of small home laboratories. Super labs like the one featured on the AMC TV series "Breaking Bad" are staffed by trained chemists who purchase the key ingredients--ephedrine and pseudoephedrine--in bulk from chemical suppliers. A super lab can manufacture more than 100,000 doses per cook.

Amateur meth cooks who operate home labs use chemicals derived from over-the-counter cold, cough, and allergy medicines. These shade-tree chemists acquire ingredients such as ammonia and lye from everyday household items. For example, they can obtain red phosphorus by scraping it off matches. The operator of a home meth lab can only produce about 300 doses a cook, enough product for himself and a few sales.

The vast majority of meth factories raided by narcotics officers are amateur operations. In 2011, drug enforcement agents in the U.S. seized 10,287 residential meth labs. (One of the largest meth lab raids occurred in San Jose, California where, in March 2012, DEA agents seized 750 pounds of meth with a street value of $34 million.) Because of the highly toxic nature of meth production, these sites have to be professionally scrubbed.

The government spends about $200 million a year de-contaminating meth labs. But not all of the homes that were once meth labs are sanitized, and some of them go on the real estate market. People who move into these places become very sick. As a result, about half of the states have passed residential meth lab disclosure laws.

Unfortunately for John Bates, his wife Jessie, and their 7-year-old son, the state of Washington didn't have a meth disclosure law in 2007 when they purchased a house for $235,000 in Suquamish, a town near Seattle. Shortly after moving into the dwelling, their son Tyler developed breathing problems. Mr. Bates developed a variety of unexplained symptoms, and his wife kept getting horrible skin rashes. The family and their physicians didn't have a clue what was causing these ailments until a neighbor, 18 months after the onset of the illnesses, casually mentioned that the former occupant of the home had made his living cooking meth.

A state inspection of the Bates home revealed that toxic chemicals had soaked into the carpets, walls, studs, and flooring. Instead of shelling out $90,000 to replace the contaminated areas of the house, the Bates demolished the place and built a new home on the two-acre lot. The project cost them $184,000. Today the Bates family is healthy, and the state of Washington has a residential meth lab disclosure law.

Meth Cleanups

Tens of thousands of houses have been used as meth labs the last decade and a cottage industry is developing around cleaning them up. Many Americans are more aware of the production of the highly addictive drug thanks to AMC's hit show "Breaking Bad" which featured a high school chemistry teacher who turned into a meth cooker and dealer. In real life, cleanup contractors are the ones who deal with a property when a batch explodes or police raid an operation and shut it down.

However, there is little oversight of the growing industry in most states, opening the door for potential malfeasance...

To make a meth home safe, a certified contractor must remove and replace all contaminated materials, from walls to carpet to air conditioning vents. Next, a certified "industrial hygienist" tests the home to gauge whether it can be lived in or needs more cleaning.

Hygienists and contractors find homes in different states of repair. Homes with no fires or explosions are easier to clean, but there is often a pungent odor, contaminated cooktops, carpets and walls, leaky roofs and dirty furniture.

Adrian Sainz, Associated Press, December 27, 2013

The Hannibal Lector Syndrome

At five in the evening on Saturday, June 2, 2012, 21-year-old Brandon De Leon, accompanied by three other homeless men, walked into a Boston Market fast-food restaurant in North Miami Beach, Florida. High on marijuana, Xanax, and a bath salt called Cloud 9, De Leon had also consumed a bottle of rum and an alcohol and caffeine-laced drink called Four Loko.

The moment De Leon entered the restaurant he became belligerent. Cursing loudly, he challenged one of his homeless companions to a fight. As it happened, two uniformed police officers were eating there. As the officers approached the manifestly intoxicated and unruly man, he swore at them. De Leon was asking for trouble, and he got it.

Although De Leon resisted, the officers hustled him out of the place and onto the ground outside. Once handcuffed behind his back, and seated in the patrol car, De Leon began bashing his head against the glass divider between the back seat and the front interior of the police vehicle. As he slammed the glass with his head, De Leon yelled, "I'm going to eat you!"

At the police station, De Leon continued to behave like an animal intent on eating its prey by baring and gnashing his teeth. Several officers wrestled him to the floor, then carried the squirming, spitting, growling, and snapping maniac to a holding cell where De Leon tried to bite one of his captors in the hand as they put him in leg restraints. Once they had the prisoner physically under control, officers slipped a Hannibal Lecter-type "bite-mask" over his head.

Following drug testing procedures at Aventura Hospital, police officers transported the chained and masked De Leon to the Miami-Dade County Jail where he is being held on $7,500 bond.

Because of the recent rash of cases involving cannibalistic behavior, Brandon De Leon's Hannibal Lecter act became more than a local crime story. The intense interest in these type cases has brought a gruesome homicide, committed in 2009 by a San Antonio woman named Otty Sanchez, back into the news. Sanchez was found not guilty by reason of insanity for killing and eating parts of her 3-week-old baby. The schizophrenic said the devil made her do it.

In December 2010, Stephen Griffith, a Ph.D. student in England, murdered three women and ate the body parts of two of them. (He killed one of his victims with a crossbow.) In Russia, a chef, in August 2011, lured his victims to his apartment through a gay-dating website, then killed them with a butcher's knife. He made meatballs and sausages from their corpses.

More recent murders of this nature include Miami's Rudy Eugene who chewed the face off a homeless man, and Alexander Kinyua, the Morgan State University student who allegedly ate a portion of his victim's heart and brain. In Sweden, a professor, in a fit of jealous rage, cut off and ate his wife's lips. He has been charged with attempted murder, and is undergoing psychiatric evaluation.

Perhaps the most disturbing cases involving cannibalistic behavior have unfolded in Japan and Canada, countries we normally don't associate with violent crime. In May 2012, a man named Mao Sugiyama advertised a meal where five diners each paid 100,000 yen to eat, in a banquet setting, Sugiyama's surgically removed genitals. Sugiyama and the five diners who ate his flesh were charged with a crime. In Japan, consensual cannibalism is not illegal. (I'm not sure if it's a crime here.)

The Canadian case involved Luka Magnotta, the porn star snuff-video maker who ate parts of his dismembered victim, then mailed four of Jun Lin's body parts to two addresses in Ottawa, and two in Vancouver.

The use of designer drugs were linked to 31-year-old Rudy Eugene, the Miami causeway flesh-eater, and Brandon De Leon, the homeless man transported to the Miami-Dade County Jail in the Hannibal Lecter mask. In De Leon's case, he was under the influence, among other substances, of the bath salt Cloud 9 (also called Ivory Wave), a synthetic form of cocaine. Legal in the United States, Cloud 9 can be purchased online, in smoke shops, convenience stores, and at gas stations. (It is illegal in the United Kingdom and Australia.) Cloud 9 comes in 500mg packets containing instructions on how to add it to bath water for a soothing and relaxing soak. There is also a warning not to sniff or inject the product. (I once saw a warning on a curling iron that read: "Not for internal use.")

Cloud 9 users snort, smoke, and eat the bath salt. The drug produces a euphoric ecstasy-like sensation combined with an amphetamine-like high. Cloud 9 has been known to produce violent and bizarre hallucinations, extreme paranoid delusions, acute agitation, and thoughts of suicide. When the drug wears off, users suffer painful hangovers.

Does the use of Cloud 9 and other designer drugs turn people into Hannibal Lecter types? According to Deborah Schurman-Kauflin in a 2011 *Psychology Today* article, "Most cannibals are extreme loners. They do not have friends and they are bitter about it. Killing and eating a victim ensures that the offender is never alone."

Jack Levin, the co-director of the Center on Violence and Conflict at Northeastern University in Boston, in discussing America's most infamous cannibal, Jeffrey Dahmer, pointed out that Dahmer was a loner. Levin believed that Dahmer, who killed and ate parts of 17 young men, consumed his victims out of "affection." According to Levin, this was Dahmer's way of physically possessing the objects of his love.

While cannibalism was in the news in the United States and around the world, it is still an extremely rare form of deviant behavior.

Free Crack Pipes

Crack pipe distribution programs have been successful in Canada, said Laura Thomas, a member of the HIV Prevention Planning Council [HPPC), the group that recently suggested San Francisco consider a similar program. Why give out free crack pipes? Unlike used needles, which pierce the skin and can immediately infect someone who shares it, the sharing of crack pipes doesn't have that same likelihood of physical contamination of HIV.

Instead, officials said, the main focus of this program would be as an outreach effort. Crack users are a population identified as a major risk to have HIV and they often become disconnected from medical services and stop taking their medicine. "It may seem counter intuitive, but it's a great program," says Thomas. "Once you can bring people into your program, make them feel respected, taken care of, then they're more likely to come back and get on HIV meds and want to be engaged and taking care of their health."...

Daniel Greenfield, January 26, 2014

The Zombie Apocalypse

The Memorial weekend "causeway cannibal" case in Miami that involved the fatal police shooting of Rudy Eugene, the person who chewed off the face of a homeless man, ignited the morbid imagination of millions of people fascinated with zombies, cannibalism, and the specter of a "zombie apocalypse." The Rudy Eugene case also increased awareness of the bath salt trend, and how designer drugs made people dangerous. Other recent cases of cannibalistic behavior included the Texas woman who killed and ate part of her newborn baby, and the college student in Maryland who consumed part of a man's brain and heart.

Zombies, the stars of horror movies, TV series ("The Walking Dead"), novels, and comic books, along with vampires, their more romantic, blood-sucking cousins, have worked their way into American culture. The term "zombie apocalypse" pertains to human-like creatures that rise from the dead, as the world is ending, to prey upon the living to replenish their brains and blood. In the wake of the causeway cannibal case in Miami, people were wondering if the bath salt epidemic had created a class of zombie-like flesh eaters.

Mind altering bath salts are not those household products people put in bath water. While in some states the drug can still be purchased at convenience stores, gas stations, and head shops, these designer hallucinogenic powders are extremely toxic. Although the active ingredients in bath salts have been outlawed by congress, drug designers have been able to replace the banned chemicals with modified substances that are even worse.

Besides making the user intensely high, bath salts, like LSD, create bizarre hallucinations. And like PCP, Ecstasy, and crystal meth, they give users supernatural strength, and can turn them violent.

So, could the abuse of bath salts and similar synthetic designer drugs turn people into flesh-eating zombies? No. While taking these toxic chemicals can make a stupid person even less bright, a crazy person crazier, and an otherwise nonviolent person dangerous, they do not give users a taste for human flesh. Bath salts are responsible for bizarre and violent behavior, but they don't turn people into cannibals.

Death by Heroin

With deaths from heroin and opioid prescription pills soaring, New York Attorney General Eric T. Schneiderman on April 3, 2014 announced a push to have law enforcement officers across the state carry a drug that is effectively an antidote to overdose. The program, to be funded primarily from $5 million in criminal and civil seizures from drug dealers, would help provide a kit with the drug, naloxone, and the training to use it to every state and local officer in New York. [Drug dealers, I image are behind this program. Fatal overdosing costs them customers.]

The authorities have increasingly seen naloxone, also known under its brand name Narcan, as a potent weapon against a national surge in drug overdoses. Last month, the Justice Department encouraged emergency medical workers across the country to begin carrying the drug. The move to broaden access in New York is the latest tactic employed by state officials to combat abuse of pills and the rising specter of heroin use...In New York City, there was an 84 percent jump in heroin overdose deaths between 2010 and 2012...[While naloxone may save lives, it won't play a role in reducing drug abuse.]

The drug naloxone, which has been available for decades in emergency rooms, works on the opiate molecules that attach to the brain and, during an overdose, fatally slows a person's breathing. Naloxone effectively bumps them away, restoring breathing in minutes and giving medical workers time to get a hospital.

For years only paramedics carried the drug. In 2012, a pilot program in Suffolk County, New York trained emergency technicians and half the police officers to administer the drug...Last year, the New York Police Department trained some 180 officers to use the drug on Staten Island, which has the city's most acute problem with heroin and pill overdoses, saving three people in the first three months. The department is currently looking to expand the program across the borough and around the city.

The state's Good Samaritan law protects those who call the police during an overdose, even if they too were using illegal drugs. Those who administer naloxone are also protected from liability. The drug, which is not habit forming and gives no high to an overdosing user, is nontoxic....

David Goodman, *The New York Times,* April 3, 2014

Teacher to Cocaine Crazed Spree Killer

Anthony (Tony) Giancola, as a student at Boca Ciega High School in Gulfport, Florida just south of St. Petersburg in Pinellas County, showed a lot of promise. He played football, was class president, and had the lead role in the school play *South Pacific.* Although accepted for admission at West Point, he attended the U.S. Coast Guard Academy.

Giancola began his teaching career in 1991 at the Dorothy Thomas Exceptional Center, a K-12 school for at-risk children with special needs. By 2005 he was head of the school. In the summer of 2006, Pinellas School District administrators made Giancola principal at the Van Buren Middle School in Tampa. Although he made $90,000 a year, Giancola had a $100-a-day cocaine habit. In February 2007, the principal purchased cocaine, while in his school office, from an undercover narcotics officer. After the drug transaction, the officer arrested Giancola and searched his car where he found marijuana and two glass pipes containing traces of cocaine. The narcotics arrest ended Giancola's career, and led to a year in jail followed by three years of probation.

In 2009, Giancola's wife divorced him, and a year later, in St. Petersburg, police arrested him as he sat in his car at three in the morning. He was charged with violating his probation, prowling, and loitering. At this point in his life, Tony Giancola was a mere shadow of his former self, and living on the fringes of society.

On Friday, June 22, 2012, at 10:45 AM in Lealman, Florida, a Pinellas County town 20 miles west of Tampa, Giancola walked into a group home for the hearing impaired and stabbed 27-year-old Justin Vand who died at the scene. Next, he stabbed Mary Allis, 59, who would die later that day at a local hospital. Giancola, using the same knife attacked 25-year-old Whitney Gilbert, and Janice Rhoden, 44. These women survived their stab wounds.

After stabbing four people at the group home, Giancola drove to nearby Pinellas Park, and at the Kenvin's Motel, attacked the man and woman who ran the place with a hammer. The married 57-year-olds were taken to the hospital and treated for their injuries. Mr. Kenvin remains in critical condition.

At 11:30 on the morning of the Kenvin's Motel rampage, Giancola pulled his Ford sedan up to a house in Penellas Park and asked a group of people sitting on the front porch where he could meet a prostitute. When they told him to get lost, he plowed his car into the porch, injuring three women and a man. A witness at the scene took down the license number to his car.

As Giancola drove from the hit and run scene, he struck a 13-year-old boy riding a bicycle. Kole Price received minor injuries from the collision. When the boy realized the driver was trying to run him down, he found protection behind a telephone pole.

Giancola drove to a nearby Egg Plotter restaurant where he called his mother. Shortly after the call, she and his sister put the blood-covered Giancola into their car and drove him to the mother's house. When Giancola climbed into the car he said, "You'll be proud of me, I just killed 10 drug dealers."

When Giancola and the two women arrived at his mother's house, she called the sheriff's office. But before deputies arrived at the dwelling, he was gone. A short time later the police found Giancola hiding in a clump of brush next to a canal in St. Petersburg.

In the course of Giancola's crime spree, the former school principal had stabbed four people, killing two of them. He attacked the two motel operators with a hammer, injured four people on the porch, and ran over a boy on a bicycle. The Pinellas County prosecutor charged Tony Giancola with two counts of first-degree murder, two counts of attempted murder, and several counts of aggravated assault. If convicted, Giancola could be sent to prison for life.

Other than being high on cocaine, investigators didn't know why Giancola attacked these eleven people. There was nothing connecting the groups of victims to each other, or to Giancola. Police believed the murders and assaults were spontaneous and random.

In September 2013, the judge sentenced Giancola to six consecutive life sentences after the former teacher pleaded guilty to two murders, four counts of attempted murder and two counts of aggravated batter. By pleading guilty, Giancola avoided the death sentence.

A Meth Crazed Killer

Sisters Britny Haarup, 19, and Ashley Key 22, lived together in a house in Edgerton, Missouri, 35 miles north of Kansas City. Ashley Key, the mother of a 4-year-old girl, had been running with a bad crowd, and had sought her sister's help in turning her life around. On Friday afternoon, July 13, 2012, Britny Haarup's fiancée, Matt Meyers, stopped by the house and found the sisters missing, and Haarup's 6 month and18-month-old daughters alone in the same crib. Because Haarup would never leave the infants alone in the house, Meyers suspected foul play. She had left her cellphone and purse behind, and in the living room Meyers found Ashley's handbag and a pair of her shoes. And most troubling of all, a comforter on the couch contained bloodstains. (Police later learned that several guns had been taken from the house.)

On the afternoon of the disappearances, deputies with the Platte County Sheriff's Office spoke to witnesses who had seen a white, 2002 Dodge Ram pickup truck parked near the sister's house at 9:30 that morning. The next day, a deputy found a truck meeting that description several miles from the sister's house parked near the Platte-Clay County line. The vehicle, registered to a Clifford D. Miller, bore no evidence of a crime, inside or out.

On Sunday morning, July 15, 2012, Platte County detectives questioned Clifford D. Miller, "a person of interest," at his girlfriend's house in Parksville, a suburb of Kansas City. Miller, from Trimble, Missouri in southwest Clinton County, confessed to murdering Haarup and Key, and agreed to lead the police to the field where he had dumped their bodies. Following the confession, the officers took Miller into custody.

The sisters' bodies were recovered that Sunday, and transported to the Medical Examiner's Office in Jackson County for identification and autopsy.

When interrogated at his girlfriend's house, Miller said he had been smoking methamphetamine on Friday, July 13, 2012. With the intent of having sex with Britny Haarup, (they knew each other but had not engaged in sex) he drove his 2002 Dodge pickup to her house in Edgerton. When he walked into the dwelling through the unlocked front door, Ashley Key, asleep on the sofa, woke up and confronted him. Miller punched her several times, struck her in the head with a hard object from the coffee table then smothered her with the comforter on the couch.

Still thinking about having sex with Haarup, Miller walked into her bedroom. When Britny screamed, he hit her with a blunt object then smothered her with a pillow.

After murdering the sisters in their home, Clifford Miller hung around and smoked more meth. High on the drug, he wrapped his victims' bodies in bed sheets and carried them to his pickup truck. After depositing the murdered women in a field several miles from their house, he abandoned his vehicle and called his girlfriend in Parksville.

The Platte County prosecutor charged Clifford Miller with two counts of first-degree murder. If convicted he faced the possibility of the death sentence.

In April 2013, Clifford Miller pleaded guilty to two counts of first-degree murder. The judge sentenced him to life in prison with no chance of parole.

Celebrity Heroin Deaths

Philip Seymour Hoffman, Cory Monteith, and Janis Joplin all died of heroin overdoses. The narcotic also killed River Phoenix and John Belushi...Drug experts say that heroin use among entertainers may be surprising because it is not talked about the same way that cocaine or party drugs are discussed...The addiction experts noted that while cocaine has a reputation for being appealing to business people for its ability to give them energy and focus, heroin's appeal is that it allows users to escape reality, a temptation for some in high-stress or highly visible professions....

Coleen Curry, ABC News, February 4, 2014

The Addicted Attorney

Kenneth Markman, after graduating from UCLA and Loyola Law School, began practicing criminal defense law in 1991. Between 2000 and 2010, the state bar association suspended him twice for not paying his membership dues. It was during this period that the attorney went from representing drug addicts and dealers to becoming one.

On October 21, 2011, Markman was in the attorney's room on the 11th floor of the Criminal Justice Center in downtown Los Angeles. He had scheduled a meeting with his client, Jorge Zaragoza. Zaragoza, a drug-dealing gang member with a history of violent crime, had been convicted of attempted carjacking. In a few days a judge would be handing down Zaragoza's sentence.

Detectives with the Los Angeles Sheriff's Office suspected that Markman was smuggling narcotics to his clients who were incarcerated in the Los Angeles County Jail. As the attorney waited for his opportunity to speak with Zaragoza, a sheriff's deputy accompanied by a drug-sniffing dog, entered the room. The dog immediately "alerted" to the presence of drugs in Markman's possession.

From the inside pocket of the attorney's suit jacket, the deputy removed a package wrapped tightly with electrical tape. The bundle contained twenty-six balloons of heroin and methamphetamine. Markman's briefcase contained a quantity of marijuana and three mini-hypodermic syringes.

Charged with seven drug-related felony counts, the attorney was booked into the county Inmate Reception Center. The judge set his bail at $145,000. If convicted of trying to smuggle $30,000 worth of narcotics into the Los Angeles County Jail, Markman faced up to four years in prison.

The accused attorney posted his bond and was released from custody. On November 8, 2011, a security officer screening visitors to the Antelope Valley Court House noticed something suspicious as Markman's briefcase passed through the X-ray machine. The attorney grabbed his wallet out of the tray and tried to flee. A Los Angeles Sheriff's deputy caught up to him before he got out of the building. In his wallet the officer found two bundles of rock cocaine. The attorney's briefcase contained several pieces of drug paraphernalia.

After being booked again for trying to smuggle drugs to an incarcerated client, Markman made his $25,000 bail.

In February 2013, Kenneth Markman pleaded no contest to the October 2011 drug smuggling charges. Pursuant to a plea deal, the judge, a month later, sentenced the suspended attorney to a year in the Los Angeles County Jail. That sentence included three years of probation that involved one year of drug treatment.

The Heroin High

The specialness of your first heroin high is to invoke the deep satisfaction of your first cup of coffee in the morning. Your subsequent coffees may be pleasant enough, but they're all marred by not being the first. And heroin use is one of the indisputable cases where the good old days really were the good old days. The initial highs did feel better than the drug will ever make you feel again.

The chemistry of the drug is ruthless: it is designed to disappoint you. Yes, once in a while there's a night when you get exactly where you're trying to go. Magic. Then you chase that memory for a month. But precisely because you so want to get there it becomes harder and harder. Your mind starts playing tricks on you. Scrutinizing the high, it weakens. You wonder if you're quite as high as you should be...Ah for the good old days when heroin felt wonderful. If I had to offer up a one-sentence definition of addiction, I'd call it a form of mourning for the irrecoverable glories of the first time.

Ann Marlowe, *How To Stop Time,* 1999

The Drug Pushing Priest

In 1996, Father Kevin Wallin became pastor of the St. Peter's Catholic Church in Danbury, Connecticut. Six years later, the 50-year-old priest was transferred to the St. Augustine Parish in Bridgeport. Citing health and personal problems, Father Wallin asked for and was granted a sabbatical in July 2011. A year later, the Diocese of Bridgeport suspended Wallin from public ministry.

While performing his duties as a Catholic priest, Father Wallin was buying and selling crystal methamphetamine out of his apartment in Waterbury.

From September 20, 2012 to January 3, 2013, a state narcotics undercover agent purchased 23 grams of crystal meth from Wallin in six transactions. Because the priest was part of an interstate drug operation, the state turned the case over to the FBI.

On January 3, 2013, FBI agents who had been working with the state drug task force arrested Father Wallin at his Waterbury apartment where searchers recovered a quantity of meth, drug paraphernalia, and drug packaging materials.

Based on the state undercover buys, federal wiretaps, and informant drug purchases, Father Wallin was charged with the federal offense of conspiracy to distribute 500 grams of crystal meth. Four co-conspirators in California, between June and December 2012, had mailed the priest $300,000 worth of meth.

Dubbed by the local media as "Monsignor Meth," Father Wallin also owned an adult video and sex-toy shop in North Haven, Connecticut. (I guess that made him the "Porno Priest" as well.)

On April 2, 2013, the defrocked Wallin pleaded guilty before a federal judge in Hartford, Connecticut. Pursuant to the plea agreement, the judge, in June 2013 sentenced the 61-year-old drug dealer to 11 to 14 years in prison.

Small Crime, Big Sentence

In 1991, 22-year-old Timothy Tyler, an avid user of the hallucinogenic drug LSD, was a so-called "Deadhead" who traveled the country attending Grateful Dead concerts. That year, while en route to a rock concert in California, DEA agents arrested Tyler on the charge of conspiracy to possess LSD with the intent to distribute.

Tyler, from his home in Florida, had mailed five grams of the drug to an out-of-state friend. As it turned out, the friend had become a DEA snitch.

Tyler had been arrested twice before on LSD charges. On both of these occasions the judge had sentenced him to probation.

In 1986, five years before Tyler's third LSD arrest, Congress passed the Anti-Drug Abuse Act that contained a "three strikes and you're out" provision. Under the new federal sentencing guidelines, judges, without regard to a defendant's age, lack of violent crime record, mental state, or drug addiction, were required to impose a sentence of life without parole on a defendant's third drug conviction.

Under the 1986 Anti-Drug Act, prosecutors were supposed to use the law to bring down major drug traffickers. Instead, as could be predicted, prosecutors went after low-level drug offenders like Timothy Tyler. Federal prosecutors did this because it was easy, and made them look like real crime-fighters. (The three strikes and you're out sentencing provision is no longer in effect.)

The federal prosecutor in Florida offered Tyler a plea bargain. If he agreed to testify against his co-defendants, Tyler would go to prison for ten years. Since his father was one of the co-defendants in the case, Tyler turned down the deal. Unfortunately for him, his public defender attorney failed to inform him of the mandatory life without parole sentence for three-time losers. Tyler pleaded guilty, but refused to testify against the others. When he learned of the mandatory life sentence law, he tried to withdraw his guilty plea but it was too late.

In 1992, a federal district judge imprisoned Tyler to life without parole. His father was handed a lesser sentence and died in prison on April 2001. Tyler is currently serving his time at the federal prison in Waymart, Pennsylvania in the northeastern corner of the state.

On April 23, 2014, Deputy U.S. Attorney General James Cole announced proposed changes to the presidential clemency criteria. Pursuant to the new policy, clemency could be granted to persons who meet the following conditions: The clemency applicant must be a low-level, nonviolent offender without a significant criminal history. If convicted today for the same offense, the modern sentence would be shorter than the one imposed. To be eligible for clemency under the new policy, the applicant must also have served at least ten years of his sentence, and his prison record must reflect good conduct.

The clemency policy announcement gave Timothy Tyler some hope he might not spend the rest of his life behind bars for mailing five grams of LSD in 1991.

First Grader Brings Stash to School

Authorities say a man and a woman are facing charges after a first-grader brought 11 packs of heroin to a Philadelphia school. School officials say 20 students at Barry Elementary School in the city's Cobbs Creek section were taken to a hospital after a teacher saw a 6-year-old girl playing with one of the packets.

No injuries were reported, although police said one of the packets appeared to have been bitten and a girl was complaining of stomach pains. Police and prosecutors said Wednesday, June 11, 2014 that 28-year-old Christopher Troy-Jenkins White and 32-year-old Marie Hunter were charged with endangerment and narcotics possession....

elitebartend.com, June 11, 2014

The Pot Smoking Toddler

In late November 2013, someone called 911 to report that the parents of a two-year-old had helped, observed or encouraged their toddler to breathe smoke from a lighted bowl of marijuana. The alleged incident took placed in Mayfield, New York, an upstate town in Chautauqua County not far from Buffalo.

On December 5, 2013, deputies with the Chautauqua County Sheriff's Office arrested the parents and the grandfather of the weed-exposed child. George Kelsey, 18, Jessica Kelsey, 17, and 54-year-old Don Baker were booked into the Chautauqua County Jail on charges of second-degree reckless endangerment and endangering the welfare of a child. A magistrate set each of the suspect's bail at $20,000.

The two-year-old victim was placed into the care of a child protection agency pending the outcome of the case.

If the endangerment charges proved true, these stupid, drug-addled parents would lose permanent custody of their child. The case, as of July 2014, remained unresolved.

In a nation of potheads, kids under twelve are the only sober citizens left.

Buying Heroin at McDonald's

A McDonald's employee in Pittsburgh, Pennsylvania was arrested on January 29, 2014 after undercover police officers said they discovered her selling heroin in Happy Meal Boxes....Shantia Dennis, 26, was arrested after undercover law enforcement officials conducted a drug buy....

Customers looking for heroin were instructed to go through the drive-through and say, "I'd like to order a toy." The customer would then be told to proceed to the first window, where they would be handed a Happy Meal Box containing heroin. [I imagine the drug buyer would pay someone else for the heroin at another location.]

During the drug buy, the undercover officers recovered 10 stamp bags of heroin, as well as a small amount of marijuana....

Allie Malloy, CNN, January 30, 2014

A Pair of Drug-Ruined Lives

Nickie Ann Circelli and her husband Sal were divorced in 2010. Due to years of drug abuse, the 36-year-old lifelong resident of Suffern, New York, lost custody of her four children. That year, police in the town of 12,000 in the foothills of Ramapo Mountains, arrested Nickie and a man named Michael Chase in connection with the theft of $4,800 worth of power tools from trucks in a Home Depot parking lot. She pleaded guilty and spent a few months in jail.

Nickie Circelli, a former employee of a local insurance company, moved in with her mother when she got out of jail. But when her mother died in 2013, Nickie took up residence with her 70-year-old uncle, William Valenti. Mr. Valenti owned a house in Suffern.

Another local drug addict, 40-year-old Gary Crockett, had also moved in to "Uncle Bill's" house. For 19 years, Gary had worked at the Mahwah Warehouse and Delivery Company in Mahwah, New Jersey. But a year earlier he quit his job after having an argument with the co-owner. Crockett didn't like being criticized for "moving too slowly." At the time, Crockett was living downtown in a apartment above the Suffern Furniture Gallery.

Circelli and Crockett, while residing under Mr. Valenti's roof, had been passing forged checks to withdraw small sums of money from his bank account. Mr. Valenti gave the couple a deadline to pay back the $1,500 they had stolen. If they didn't return his money, he threatened to report them to the police.

On Monday morning, April 28, 2014, during an argument over the stolen money, Crockett murdered William Valenti. (The Rockland County Medical Examiner determined that the victim had died of suffocation. His body was discovered in his bed.)

Following the murder, the couple took dead man's Chevrolet Malibu and drove it to the Bronx, New York. They parked the vehicle and walked to the George Washington Bridge. Just before noon, about half way across the span, Circelli and Crockett jumped to their deaths.

At the Suffern murder scene, investigators found two suicide notes signed by Circelli under her maiden name, Hunt. In the note addressed to her family, Circelli wrote: "To the four most amazing kids who the world has ever seen and ever will. I beg you to remember the Nickie that I used to be, before I was introduced to heroin."

The second suicide note read: "I know that I'm taking the cowardly way out. I just don't want to hurt people anymore. Anything that goes into the paper, please make sure my last name is Hunt; I don't want to hurt my kids anymore than I already have."

Prescription Drug Abuse

Up until the late 1980s, prescriptions for narcotic painkillers were limited to cancer patients and people with other terminal illnesses. That changed when influential physicians, in medical journal articles, argued that it was inhumane to keep these narcotics from patients who simply needed relief from pain. As a result, the use of pain killing drugs quadrupled between 1999 and 2010. Currently, physicians write about 300 million painkiller prescriptions a year with hydrocodone the most popular followed by morphine, codeine, dilaudid, OxyContin, and Xanax.

In November 2012, reporters with the *Los Angeles Times* reviewed coroners' office records from four southern California counties (Los Angeles, Orange, Ventura, and San Diego) covering the period 2006 through 2011. The inquiry revealed that more people died from prescription drug overdoses than from heroin and cocaine overdoses. The journalists identified 3,733 overdose deaths from prescription drugs. In half of the cases, the deceased had a doctor's prescription for at least one of the drugs that contributed to the fatal overdose. The deaths frequently resulted from several drugs prescribed by more than one physician.

The *Los Angeles Times* study revealed that a small group of doctors accounted for a disproportionate number of fatal overdoses. Seventy-one physicians had written prescriptions that contributed to 298 overdose deaths. Each of these medical practitioners had prescribed drugs to three or more patients who died.

The ages of the 298 overdose victims ranged from 21 to 79. A majority of these patients had histories of mental illness or addiction, including previous overdoses or stints in drug rehabilitation centers. Many of these prescription drug users were middle-aged teachers, nurses, and police officers introduced to addictive painkillers through bad backs, sore knees, and other painful ailments.

The 71 physicians associated with three or more fatal overdose cases were pain specialists, general practitioners, and psychiatrists who worked alone without the peer scrutiny provided by hospitals, group practices, and HMOs. Four of the doctors had been convicted of drug-related crimes, and a fifth was awaiting trial.

One of the physicians in the group of doctors who had not been charged with a crime was a 49-year-old pain specialist from Huntington Beach, California named Dr. Van H. Vu. The Vietnam native had 17 of his patients die as a result of prescription painkiller overdoses. Dr. Vu earned his undergraduate and medical degrees from the University of Washington, and served a residency in anesthesiology at the University of California. He was board-certified in anesthesiology and in pain medicine.

Other physicians referred their patients to Dr. Vu. These doctors turned to him as a physician of last resort for people who suffered chronic pain. Many of these patients came to the pain specialist already hooked on prescription narcotics. While 17 of his patients overdosed fatally, Dr. Vu pointed out that he had successfully treated thousands of patients with these drugs. As quoted in the *Los Angeles Times*, Dr. Vu said: "I am doing the best I can in this very difficult field. I consider myself to be one of the best. But we have limits....I am a physician. I feel terrible when someone loses their life. I'm the one who should be prolonging life, so I'm saddened by that."

On March 14, 2014, members of the California Medical Board filed a 15-page complaint accusing Dr. Vu of negligently prescribing powerful narcotics to patients who overdosed on the medication. The medical authorities sought to suspend or revoke the doctor's medical license.

While it may be unfair to compare Dr. Vu to pill-pushing quacks like the feel-good doctors who supplied Elvis Presley and Michael Jackson with their drugs, physicians who function principally as legal drug dealers should be prosecuted for homicide when their patients fatally overdose. From an investigative point of view, however, it's not always easy distinguishing between physicians dedicated to the relief of suffering and their drug-pushing counterparts.

12 HOMICIDE DEFENSES

Justifiable Homicide

There is no crime called "homicide." It is simply an umbrella term that includes various types of *lawful homicide* [executions, valid police involved shootings, and self defense) as well as *unlawful homicide* (involuntary manslaughter, voluntary manslaughter, felony murder, second-degree murder, and first-degree murder]. The categories of lawful homicide are awfully narrow. One of them is *justifiable homicide,* which applies mainly to self-defense but can also apply to the defense of one's home from intruders. The latter is known as the *castle defense*...In these cases, the killing is intentional but "justified" by the circumstances.

When the act of killing is truly unintentional [as opposed to reckless] the law calls this *excusable homicide.* Despite the name, it is not enough to say "excuse me" to the victim in order to fit into this category. Rather, the defendant must show that the killing was accidental; for example, when a driver hits a pedestrian who ran into the street without warning. [If a drunken driver accidentally runs over someone that might constitute involuntary manslaughter.]

Adam Freedman, *The Party of the First Part,* 2007

Playing the Stupid Card

At one in the morning, after watching a movie at a friend's house, 20-year-old Sabina Rose O'Donnell borrowed a bicycle to ride to her north

Philadelphia apartment a few blocks away. She never made it home. Later that day, June 2, 2010, police discovered her body in a trash-littered lot behind her apartment building. At the scene, investigators found jewelry, a camera, and a paycheck made payable to the victim. With her bra wrapped tightly around her neck, the victim had been raped, beaten, and strangled to death. He killer had left his bloody undershirt near her body.

According to videotapes from neighborhood surveillance cameras, police were able to place 18-year-old Donte Johnson in the area at the time of the murder. After two Philadelphia officers arrested Johnson on June 10, 2010, he admitted biking around the neighborhood that night, but denied any knowledge of the murder. His interrogators explained to him how DNA analysis of his sperm could link him to the woman's body. Upon hearing this, Johnson said he and the victim had consensual sex two days before her death. When the detectives questioned that story, Johnson tried another way of neutralizing the DNA evidence: he said that after stumbling across her body, he had masturbated over the corpse. The interrogators explained that this didn't explain away the bloody undershirt. At this point, Johnson confessed to the rape and murder.

Assistant district attorney Richard Sax charged Donte Johnson with first-degree murder, rape, and robbery. Soon after Johnson's court-appointed defense attorneys entered the case, the suspect took back his confession, and turned down a negotiated guilty plea. The defense challenged the reliability of the DNA evidence linking Johnson to the body and the murder site, and made the argument that the prosecution couldn't use his recanted confession. Johnson was now claiming that at the time of Sabina Rose O'Donnell's rape and murder, he was at home with his family.

At a pre-trial hearing on April 30, 2012 to determine if the prosecution could introduce Johnson's confession, defense attorney Gary Server put a private forensic neuropsychologist on the stand. Dr. Gerald Cooke testified that Johnson, with a damaged brain and an IQ of 73, had the mental capacity of an 11-year-old. Because the suspect was almost retarded, his interrogators could have easily manipulated him into confessing to a crime he didn't commit.

In arguing for the exclusion of Johnson's confession, attorney Server said, "The detective speaks to Mr. Johnson and he thinks he's talking to an adult, when in reality he's speaking to a child." The defense attorney also noted that when questioned by the police, his client had been drunk and high on drugs.

The police officers that arrested Johnson took the stand and testified that the suspect, sober and coherent, knew exactly what was going on when they took him into custody. According to the police officers, Johnson did not act or speak like an 11-year-old child. The judge, after hearing both sides of the argument, ruled that the prosecutor could introduce Johnson's confession at his trial. The defense attorneys could make the false confession claim to the jury.

On May 1, after opening statements to the jury from both sides, the prosecutor presented the state's case. Surveillance cameras placed the defendant in the vicinity that night, Johnson had confessed to the rape and murder, and DNA linked him to the bloody shirt and the victim's body. From a prosecutor's point of view, as murder cases go, this was about as good as it gets.

By comparison, Johnson's defense--that DNA analysts make mistakes, the confession is false, and his family says he was at home with them that night--was weak.

To convince the jury that police interrogators had taken advantage of Johnson's feeble mind to wrangle a false confession out of him, the defense showed the videotaped testimony of the neuropsychologist, Dr. Gerald Cooke. According to Dr. Cooke--who earned $9,300 for his intelligence testing and testimony--Donte Johnson has trouble solving problems, reasoning, and thinking quickly. His mother gave birth to Donte when she was 16; early in his youth he had suffered some kind of brain damage; and since turning 14, he has been using drugs and binge drinking. According to the psychologist, this simpleton has never held a job, and has had sex with scores of women.

Donte Johnson's attorneys chose not to put their client on the stand. Perhaps they didn't want to risk a witness box confession like in one of those old Perry Mason TV episodes. Moreover, having tried to make the jurors feel sorry for the defendant, the attorneys wanted to keep him under wraps. Following the closing arguments, and the judge's instructions, the case went to the jury.

Jurors, after deliberating 4 hours, found Donte Johnson guilty of first degree-murder and rape. The judge sentenced him to life plus 40 to 80 years. In speaking to the judge after receiving his sentence, Johnson said, "How can you clearly say I did anything? If I did something I would take responsibility."

The Historic Dilemma

In the summer of 1884, four English sailors were stranded at sea in a small lifeboat in the South Atlantic, over a thousand miles from land. Their ship, the *Migonette*, had gone down in a storm, and they had escaped to the lifeboat, with only two cans of preserved turnips and no fresh water. Thomas Dudley was the captain, Edwin Stephens was the first mate, and Edmund Brooks was a sailor--"all men of excellent character," according to newspaper accounts.

The fourth member of the crew was the cabin boy, Richard Parker, age seventeen. He was an orphan, on his first voyage at sea. He had signed up against the advice of his friends, "in the hopefulness of youthful ambition," thinking the journey would make a man of him. Sadly, it was not to be.

From the lifeboat, the four stranded sailors watched the horizon, hoping a ship might pass and rescue them. For the first three days, they ate small rations of turnips. On the fourth day, they caught a turtle. They subsisted on the turtle and the remaining turnips for the next few days. And then for eight days they ate nothing.

By now Parker, the cabin boy was lying in the corner of the lifeboat. He had drunk seawater, against the advice of the others, and became ill. He appeared to be dying. On the nineteenth day of their ordeal, Dudley, the captain, suggested drawing lots to determine who would die so that the others might live. But Brooks refused, and no lots were drawn.

The next day came, and still no ship was in sight. Dudley told Brooks to avert his gaze and motioned to Stephens that Parker had to be killed. Dudley offered a prayer, told the boy his time had come, then killed him with a penknife, stabbing him in the jugular vein. Brooks emerged from his conscientious objection to share in the gruesome bounty. For four days, the three men fed on the body and blood of the cabin boy.

And then help came. Dudley describes their rescue in his diary, with staggering euphemism: "On the 24th day, as we were having our breakfast," a ship appeared at last. The three survivors were picked up. Upon their return to England, they were arrested and tried. Brooks turned state's witness. Dudley and Stephens went to trial. They freely confessed that they had killed and eaten Parker. They claimed they had done so out of necessity.

Michael J. Sandel, *Justice*, 2009

The Rich Kid's Defense

On the night of June 15, 2013, in Fort Worth, Texas, 16-year-old Ethan Couch and seven of his friends stole two cases of beer from a local Walmart store. A few hours later, Couch, behind the wheel of his wealthy family's F-350 pickup, sped down a poorly lit rural road. With his blood-alcohol level three times the legal limit and seven passengers in the cab--two in the back of the truck--he lost control of the vehicle.

Couch's truck plowed into vehicles parked along the side of the road. The two boys in the bed of the truck were flung out of the pickup and severely injured. Breanna Mitchell, whose SUV had broken down and was off the road, was killed. Brian Jennings, Shelby Boyles, and Hollie Boyles, people who had pulled off the road to help Breanna, also died in the crash.

Ethan Couch, on the advise of his attorneys, pleaded guilty to four counts of intoxication manslaughter. This meant the only issue left to be resolved in the case involved his punishment. Was he a troubled kid who needed psychological treatment, or a spoiled brat who required incarceration? If punishment was appropriate in this case, how severe? Did it matter that he was only sixteen? These were questions that would have to be resolved by juvenile court judge Jean Boyd.

At Ethan Couch's sentence hearing held in Fort Worth on December 10, 2013, Tarrant County Assistant District Attorney Richard Alpert proposed that the defendant be incarcerated for twenty years. In addressing Judge Boyd, Alpert said, "If the boy, who is from an affluent family, is cushioned by the family's wealth, there can be no doubt that he will be in another courthouse one day blaming the leniency he received here." The prosecutor pointed out that inmates in Texas who needed it received drug and alcohol treatment.

One of the defendant's attorneys, Scott Brown, argued that his client required rehabilitation more than he needed treatment. (Perhaps, but the families of the victim needed for him to be punished. Sentencing should be more than just about what's good for the defendant.)

Couch's attorney recommended a two-year treatment program at a $1,200-a-day rehabilitation center near Newport Beach, California followed by a period of probation. The $450,000-a-year program in southern California featured equine sports, yoga, and massages. According to attorney Brown, the boy's parents were willing to pick up the California rehabilitation tab.

Dr. Dick Miller, a clinical psychologist from Bedford, Texas testified at the sentencing hearing on the defendant's behalf. According to Dr. Miller, Ethan Couch suffered from what he called "affluenza," a syndrome caused by rich parents who didn't set limits and discipline their children. As a result of being spoiled rotten, Ethan didn't know how to behave appropriately.

Judge Boyd stunned the prosecutor and friends and families of the four victims when she sentenced the teenager to ten years of probation. The judge said she would find a treatment program for the boy in the state of Texas. If he violated the terms of his probation, he could be sent to a juvenile detention facility.

Eric Boyles lost his wife Hollie and his daughter Shelby in Couch's drunken crash. In speaking to a CNN correspondent, he said, "There are absolutely no consequences for what occurred that day...Money always seems to keep you out of trouble. Ultimately today, I feel that money did prevail.

In responding to Judge Boyd's decision, prosecutor Alpert told a reporter that "We are disappointed by the punishment assessed but we have no power under the law to change or overturn it."

In horrific homicides like this, if there is no retribution, the public will lose confidence in the criminal justice system. While rich people do not always get their way in criminal court, the public perception is that they do.

The Innocent Defendant

In many criminal trials the most important and difficult part of the defending attorney's job comes during the first half of the trial, when the prosecution is presenting its evidence. Discrediting the prosecution's case is at least as important as presenting the defense's own story.

The guilty defendant often has an advantage over the truly innocent defendant: he knows what actually happened. If he is clever, he can carefully tailor his defense to fit the recoverable facts. The secret advantage for the side of truth and justice is that so many criminals who think they're clever are mistaken. The innocent defendant, on the other hand, usually doesn't know what really happened and is at a loss to explain away the evidence connecting him to the crime.

Michael Kurland, *How to Try a Murder,* 1997

Provocation

In March 2013, Ralph Wald, a 69-year-old retired Army Lieutenant Colonel who fought in Vietnam, lived with his wife Johnna Flores in Brandon, Florida. The couple had been married since October 2012. She was 41.

On Sunday, March 10, 2013, just before midnight, Wald got out of bed for a drink of water. En route to the kitchen he saw Johnna on the living room floor having sex with a man he didn't recognize. Wald immediately returned to his bedroom where he picked up his .38-caliber revolver. Back in the living room a few moments later, he shot his wife's sex partner in the stomach and head. The man died on the spot.

After shooting 32-year-old Walter Lee Copley, who turned out to be one of Johnna's old flames from Riverview, Florida, Mr. Wald called the police. To the dispatcher he said that he had just shot a man he caught "fornicating" with his wife in their home. After the call, Mr. Wald laid down his gun and waited for the authorities to arrive at the death scene.

Deputies with the Hillsborough County Sheriff's Office took Mr. Wald into custody that night. The next day, Hillsborough County Assistant State

Attorney Chris Moody charged Ralph Wald with second-degree murder. A judge denied the murder suspect bail.

The Wald case went to trial in Tampa, Florida just eleven weeks after Mr. Copley's death. Prosecutor Moody, in his opening remarks, told the jury that the defendant, who suffered from erectile dysfunction, killed the victim in a jealous rage.

Defense attorney Joe Episcopo argued that his client thought Mr. Copley was an intruder raping his wife. Under Florida's stand your ground self-defense doctrine, the defendant has no duty to retreat from his own home.

On the second day of the three-day trial, Johnna Flores took the stand for the defense. She testified that when her husband shot Mr. Copley she was "black-out" drunk from too much cognac. As a result, she had virtually no memory of the shooting.

The defendant followed his wife to the stand. According to the witness, he and Johnna had planned to see a therapist regarding their sexual problem. "In fact," he said, "she would joke a lot with me that we were a perfect couple. She didn't want to do it, and I couldn't do it." The witness said he hoped to salvage his marriage. "I love my wife," he said.

Prosecutor Moody, in his closing argument to the jury, said this about Mr. Copley: "It's a personal insult to conduct that kind of activity in a man's home, his castle. It cuts to the quick. It's brazen. That kind of deep and personal insult when you find another man having sex in your living room and you can't have sex yourself. This would make you want to lash out--and the defendant did."

Defense attorney Episcopo, in addressing the jurors, said, "This was a military man trained to know what to do with the enemy. You take your gun and you kill the enemy."

On May 30, 2013, the jury, after just two hours of deliberation, found the defendant not guilty. Ralph Wald embraced his two lawyers as his wife Johnna cried tears of joy.

Members of Walter Copley's family who were in the courtroom when the verdict was read were not happy with the outcome of the case.

Murder Trials are Imperfect

In most murder trials the only person who knows the true story of the crime is the defendant, and then only if he or she is guilty. Circumstantial evidence is suspect, eyewitnesses are unreliable, forensic evidence is only as good as the laboratory that developed it. On the other hand, circumstantial evidence, if properly interpreted, can tell the story of the crime;

eyewitnesses can be good observers; and a professionally run forensics laboratory can develop evidence that is trustworthy.

But these conditions may not be assumed. States' attorneys have been known to be overly zealous in pressing their cases; defense attorneys have been know to be less dedicated, or less competent than desired; and many people have spent years, even decades, in prison before a new circumstance showed that they were wrongly convicted. The introduction of DNA analysis has freed hundreds of people who were shown to have been wrongfully convicted--many on eyewitness testimony. [Also on jailhouse informants and junk science.]

There is another side to this judicial coin: people who have committed murder and have been tried and found not guilty due to inadequate evidence, incompetent prosecution, a brilliant defense, or a jury not disposed to convict. [The above factors explain the O.J. Simpson acquittal.] This is, perhaps, a shame in the individual case, but it does society little harm in the long run, since no one would commit murder simply in the hope that his or her prosecution would be inept. Murder has the lowest recidivist rate of any major crime. It is much more likely that a mugger or a convenience-store robber will kill someone than it is for a murderer found not guilty to kill again. Society would be more seriously harmed if the popular perception were that citizens were regularly convicted of crimes they did not commit.

Michael Kurland, *How to Try a Murder,* 2002

It Was An Accident

In 2009, 17-year-old Jason Beckman lived with his 52-year-old father, Jay Beckman, in South Miami, Florida. The South Miami High School student's mother had died of cancer in 1998 when he was six. Mr. Beckman, since 2006, had been a South Miami City Commissioner.

In the afternoon of April 13, 2009, Jason Beckman called 911 to report an accidental shooting that had killed his father. Miami-Dade police officers found Jay Beckman in his bathroom shower stall with his face blow away from a close-range shotgun blast.

When questioned at the police station, Jason Beckman said he had taken his father's Browning Citori 12-gauge, double barrel shotgun out of the closet and assembled it. He carried the gun into his father's bathroom to show him that he knew how to assemble and load the weapon. In the bathroom he slipped and fell causing the shotgun to discharge. The boy claimed that his father's death had been a tragic accident. At this point, although Jason's story didn't make a whole lot of sense, detectives had no reason to suspect an intentional killing.

A local prosecutor, on the theory the fatal shooting had been an accident, charged Jason Beckman with manslaughter by firearm, a lesser homicide offense involving negligent behavior rather than specific criminal intent.

As the investigation into the violent death progressed, detectives began to question whether the shooting had been an accident. Among Jason's belongings investigators found a list of people he said he wanted to kill. Jay Beckman's name was at the top of the hit list. A Beckman neighbor told officers that Jason, for years, had made no secret of the fact he planned to kill his father some day. Jason's friends came forward and confirmed the boy's hatred of his father and his stated plans to murder him.

Jason, when questioned by detectives a second time, stuck to his original account of the shooting. He did, however, say that his father had threatened to kill him.

In light of the new, incriminating evidence, the prosecutor upgraded the charge against Jason Beckman to first-degree murder. Investigators now believed the killing had been intentional and pre-meditated.

The Beckman trial got underway on November 4, 2013. Prosecutor Jessica Dobbins, in her opening statement to the jury, said, "We are here today because the defendant regularly talked about his hatred for his father and his desire to kill him." Defense attorney Tara Kawass told the jurors that Jason was not an aggressive person. "No one was scared of him," she said.

On November 8, two of the defendant's classmates took the stand for the prosecution. According to both witnesses Jason kept a list of people who had crossed him. Moreover, the defendant had told several people, "countless times," that he hated his father and intended to kill him.

Jailhouse snitch Michael Nistal took the stand for the prosecution. In 2008 the burglar had been involved in a high-speed police chase that ended with his brother being shot to death by the police. In 2009, while incarcerated at the Turner Guilford Knight Correction Center in West Miami, one of Nistal's fellow prisoners--Jason Beckman--told him why he had murdered his father.

According to the jailhouse informant, just before the shooting, Jason asked his father what he thought of an actress named Megan Fox. Nistal testified that, "Jason's father told him he [Jason] wouldn't know what to do with that. So he [the defendant] went and got a shotgun and blew his father's head off." After the shooting, according to Nistal, Jason poked his father's body to see if he was still alive.

Nistal testified that Beckman had told him that he planned to beat the murder rap by claiming the shooting was an accident or by asserting self-defense or insanity. According to the witness, Jason knew right from wrong and was not mentally ill when he committed the murder.

Tara Kawass, Beckman's attorney, did her best to convince the jury that testimony from jailhouse snitches was notoriously unreliable evidence. She said that Nistal, who was serving a seven-year stretch in prison, exchanged his bogus testimony for a lighter sentence. Attorney Kawass did not put her client on the stand to testify on his own behalf.

On November 8, 2013 the jury, at eight o'clock that night, announced its verdict. The jurors found Jason Beckman guilty as charged. In Florida, first-degree murder carried a sentence that ranged between 25 years and life.

The defendant, when he heard the verdict, shook his head. "I don't understand," he said. "I really don't."

In June 2014, the judge sentenced Jason Beckman to 25 years to life.

Post-Traumatic Stress Disorder

The post-traumatic stress disorder (PTSD) is a fairly recent entry in psychiatric terminology; in fact, it was only officially recognized with the publication of the third edition of the *Diagnostic and Statistical Manual of Disorders* in 1980, known as *DSM-III*. In World Wars I and II there had been what was known to laymen as "shell shock" and to mental health professions as "combat neurosis," a battlefield condition in which men become too traumatized to function properly. A fairly large proportion of discharges from the army were due to this condition, and the problem remains a serious one for all those who participate in combat, with its attendant horrors and stresses.

During the 1950s when *DSM-I* was published, there was a condition referred to as "transient situational disorder," which was sometimes used to encompass battlefield stress. It was the initials TSD that were lifted from this previous neurosis and made to fit a condition that seemed to have sprung up in American survivors of the war in Vietnam, and which became known as PTSD--or, in layman's terms, "the Vietnam syndrome."

I had discovered, over the years, that while there were people who really did suffer from post-traumatic stress disorder--had difficulty in living normal lives after returning from the brink of death experienced either in war or as a result of some other traumatic event--many other claims of PTSD were just a lot of poppycock, a form of malingering. The diagnosis of PTSD had become fashionable in certain psychiatric circles, mainly those that dealt with people in and out of veterans' hospitals. Other psychiatrists, just as well qualified, who also dealt with war veterans, had not seen many genuine cases. Also, the United States had been involved in several traumatic wars earlier in this century, and while there had been a few diagnosed cases of what was then called *battlefield shock*, most of the people who did experience these sort of shocks recovered and went on to lead normal lives. Could the experience of fighting in Vietnam have been worse than the experience of fighting in Korea? Could it have been worse than fighting in Europe or fighting in the Pacific Islands during World War II? Were American servicemen of the 1960s and 1970s so much more emotionally fragile that those who served in earlier conflicts?

Robert K. Ressler, *I Have Lived in the Monster*, 1997

The Frame Up

In 2001, Dino Guglielmelli, the owner of Creations Garden, a $48 million natural cream and nutritional supplement business, met Monica Olsen, a Romanian-born model twenty years younger than him. The 39-year-old tycoon had been married twice before. Both of those marriages had been brief.

Not long after the two met, Monica moved into Gugglielmelli's six-bedroom, 7,000-square foot mansion on three acres north of Los Angeles. The couple married in April 2003, and by 2008, had two daughters. They also possessed a Maserati, a Porsche, and a BMW.

The Food and Drug Administration, in 2009, tightened the federal regulations regarding the manufacture and marketing of nutritional supplements. This, along with the economic recession, took its toll on Gugglielmelli's business. By 2011, the company, along with his marriage, had collapsed.

Dino Gugglielmelli, in October 2012, in filing for divorce, described Monica as a bad mother that "never made dinner for the children." According to court documents, Guglielmelli complained that nannies had raised the children, and domestic employees cleaned the house.

In January 2013, after Mr. Gugglielmelli accused Monica of attacking him with a kitchen knife, she lost custody of the children and moved out of the mansion. Shortly after her departure, Gugglielmelli acquired a young girlfriend. Although he was facing bankruptcy, he lavished this woman with $200,000 in gifts. He used other people's money to impress his young squeeze.

In the spring of 2013, the justice system exonerated Monica in the domestic knife assault case. A family court judge, in August of that year, was about to award her $300,000 in back alimony payments. The federal government, the economy, and his pending divorce put an end to Gugglielmelli's lavish style of living. He did not like what the future held for him.

On October 1, 2013, Gugglielmelli met 47-year-old Richard Euhrmann in a Los Angeles restaurant. Euhrmann, a short time before this meeting, had gone to the Los Angeles County Sheriff's Office with information that Gugglielmelli had asked him to murder his estranged wife, Monica. For that reason, Euhrmann showed up at the restaurant wired for sound.

During the meeting, Gugglielmelli allegedly offered his friend $80,000 to pull off the hit. "I'll be happy when it's over," he reportedly said. As the two men walked out of the restaurant, deputies took Gugglielmelli into custody.

A Los Angeles County prosecutor charged the former millionaire with attempted murder and solicitation of murder. After being booked into the county's Men's Central Jail, the judge set Gugglielmelli's bond at $10 million.

At a pre-trial hearing in late 2013, Gugglielmelli's attorney, Anthony Brooklier, described Richard Euhrmann, the man Guglielmelli had allegedly asked to kill Monica, as an opportunist and liar who had set up his client. (If this were true, I don't know what Euhrmann had gained from setting up his friend.)

With her estranged husband behind bars for plotting to kill her, Monica moved back into the Gugglielmelli mansion.

In May 2014, county jail officials moved the high-profile inmate into solitary confinement at the notorious Twin Towers correctional facility. The 9,500-prison complex was named one of the ten worst jails in the world. (I'm sure it's not a nice place, but this is hard to believe. I base this opinion on the fact I've watched a lot of "Locked Up Abroad" TV episodes.)

After receiving word that several of Guglielmelli's fellow inmates had approached him with offers to kill Richard Euhrmann, the principal witness against Gugglielmelli, corrections officials had decided to isolate him from the jail population. Gugglielmelli was also denied the privilege of seeing visitors. Richard Euhrmann, fearing for his life, went into hiding.

Monica, the alleged target of the murder-for-hire plot, said she also worried about being killed by a hit man. Traumatized by the case, she has put the mansion up for sale. She asked $3.5 million for the house. Monica was also trying to breathe new life back into her beauty cream and baby skin care business.

On June 13, 2014 in San Fernando Superior Court, Gugglielmelli pleaded guilty to one count of attempted murder. The judge sentenced him to nine years in prison.

Drug-Addled

In 2013, 30-year-old Marcel Hill and Camia Gamet, 38, shared an apartment in Jackson, Michigan a town of 34,000 in the south central part of the state.

308

Raised in foster homes, Gamet claimed to have been raped by a foster dad. People who knew Gamet were aware of her violent streak and abuse of drugs, a combination that made her unpredictable and dangerous.

Marcel Hill, a high school graduate and fast food worker, was by contrast friendly and child-like. According to members of his family, he suffered "cognitive limitations," that made it difficult for him to handle simple everyday tasks like paying his bills. Unlike Gamet, he didn't have a violent bone in his body. This odd couple relationship would cost Mr. Hill his life.

A year or so earlier, Camia Gamet, in a fit of rage, stabbed Marcel Hill with a knife, then stitched up his wound herself. Neither one of them reported the assault to the authorities. On another occasion, she sent Marcel to the hospital with a punctured lung. That assault did not lead to her arrest. But in March 2013, a Jackson County prosecutor charged Gamet with domestic violence and felonious assault after she pounded Marcel on the head with a hammer. Because he was afraid to press the matter, and refused to cooperate with law enforcement personnel, the prosecutor had no choice but to close the case.

In the early morning hours of Saturday, May 18, 2013, a neighbor called 911 to report domestic violence at the odd couple's dwelling. Responding police officers found a blood-covered Gamet staggering around and slurring her words outside the apartment. Inside, officers found smashed furniture, a broken floor lamp, a bloody filet knife, and a damaged frying pan covered in blood.

Amid all of the destruction and gore, officers discovered Marcel Hill. He had been repeatedly bludgeoned with hard objects--presumably the broken lamp and the frying pan--stabbed eleven times, and cut wide open in the torso with the knife.

Police officers arrested Gamet that night. On Wednesday, May 20, 2013, a Jackson County prosecutor charged Camia with open criminal homicide. (This meant a jury or a judge could determine the appropriate degree of murder in the event of a conviction.)

The Gamet murder trial got underway in late February 2014. In her opening statement to the jury, Chief Assistant Prosecutor Kati Rezmierski portrayed the defendant as a violent person and a proven liar. According to the prosecutor, Gamet had deliberately and knowingly beaten, stabbed and slashed the victim to death.

Defense attorney Anthony Raduazo told the jury that his client had awaken from a drug-induced stupor that night to the sound of shattering glass. Believing that an intruder was attacking her, she grabbed the lamp and the knife and used these objects to defend herself. Attorney Raduazo said the defendant had acted out of a "fear-driven rage," noting that in the encounter she had herself received cuts and bruises.

After six days of prosecution testimony, the defense attorney put Gamet on the stand to testify on her own behalf. In telling her story of self-defense, Gamet did not come off as a very credible or sympathetic witness.

In his closing remarks to the jury, attorney Raduazo said, "She is a woman and she is asleep and she is full of drugs and she is full of liquor. Did she react in a thoughtful manner? Or did she jump up and try to defend herself?" Raduazo pointed out that Gamet had not tried to dispose of Hill's body or clean up the death scene. "If this was preplanned and premeditated," he said, "it was a heck of a bad plan."

Prosecutor Rezmierski, when it came her turn to address the jurors for the last time, said, "The victim did not die quickly. He knew his death was coming. The victim tried to protect himself and flee, but he was no match for the defendant. He never was a match." As to Gamet's supposed injuries, the prosecutor said, "She has barely a scratch, and he's eviscerated."

On March 5, 2014, following a short period of deliberation, the jury returned a verdict of first-degree murder.

At Camia Gamet's sentencing hearing on April 16, 2014, County Circuit Court Judge John McBain saw the convicted murderer roll her eyes and snicker during a court presentation by one of Marcel Hill's aunts. The sight infuriated the judge who, in speaking directly to Gamet said, "You gutted him like a fish in the apartment! You were relentless! You stabbed, you stabbed, you stabbed, you stabbed, you stabbed until he was dead! I agree with the family, I hope you die in prison! You know, if this was a death penalty state, you'd be getting the chair!"

Judge McBain sentenced Camia Gamet to life in prison without the possibility of parole. Afterward, defense attorney Raduazo told reporters he would appeal his client's verdict and the sentence. No doubt Judge McBain's outburst will constitute an issue in the appeal.

The Insanity Defense

Evil or Criminally Insane

On July 21, 2011, 32-year-old Anders Behring Breivik set off a bomb in Oslo, Norway that killed eight. Breivik, later that day, opened fire at a summer camp on Utoya Island, killing sixty-nine people of which most were children. Breivik's bombing and shooting spree also injured 151 in the city and on the island. The mass murderer surrendered without incident to a SWAT team that showed incredible restraint.

After confessing to the bombing and shooting spree, Breivik told his interrogators that he was a commander of a resistance movement aiming to overthrow European governments and replace them with "patriotic" regimes that will deport Muslim immigrants.

A pair of psychiatrists, on thirteen visits, spent 36 hours talking with Breivik. The doctors concluded that because Breivik was a paranoid schizophrenic, he was not a proper candidate for conviction and imprisonment as a criminal. A forensic panel representing the district court will make the final ruling on Breivik's mental condition and whether he should be brought to justice as a mass murderer.

As it stands, because Breivik "lost touch with reality," the criminal justice system in Norway will treat the murders not as crimes, but as symptoms of this killer's mental illness. These victims, in other words, were killed by paranoid schizophrenia, not an evil, cold-blooded murderer.

Norwegian critics of the decision not to try Breivik as a criminal defendant have called attention to the extensive planning and gruesome efficiency characterizing Breivik's slaughter of his helpless victims. In the opinion of the Swedish forensic psychiatrist Anders Forsman, Breivik carried out his murderous mission in a rational way. He was, in Forsman's words, an "efficient killing machine."

Norway has a rather lenient legal insanity defense doctrine that merely requires that a defendant be in a state of psychosis during the commission of the crime. It is therefore not surprising that Norway has a tradition of not criminally punishing defendants who are adjudicated mentally ill.

Had Anders Breivik embarked on his murderous rampage in the United States, he'd have almost no chance of successfully raising the insanity defense. This is because in America, most states operate under the M'Naghten Rule. Under this doctrine of legal insanity, a criminal defendant is *not* insane unless: "At the time of the commission of the act, the defendant was laboring under such a defect of reason, from disease of the mind, as not to know the nature and quality of the act he was doing, or if he did know it, that he did not know what he was doing was wrong." Popularly referred to as the "right/wrong test," a defense attorney has to prove by a preponderance of the evidence, that his client did not realize the act in question was wrong. Regardless of how mentally ill defendants are, almost all of them knew that what they were doing was wrong. In other words, in most states, merely because a criminal defendant has been diagnosed a paranoid schizophrenic is not enough. For this reason, very few defendants succeed in being found not guilty by reason of insanity. In the United States, the law requires a degree of mental impairment that in reality doesn't exist.

Juries do not find serial killers such as Ted Bundy legally insane. The Unabomber Ted Kaczynski, diagnosed as a paranoid schizophrenic, was convicted of murder in 1996 and sent to prison. It is doubtful that Jared Loughner, the mental case that wounded Congresswoman Gabrielle

Giffords and killed six others, will end up in a facility for the criminally insane instead of prison.

Juries don't completely trust the social scientific findings of psychiatrists who testify for the defense. And jurors don't want to replace the concept of good and evil with sane and insane. Serial killers and mass murderers, to jurors, while obviously mentally ill, are still evil and dangerous people. In America, evil people who murder are going to be punished criminally. That doesn't mean, however, that they don't receive medical attention in prison. But it does mean, whether "rehabilitated" or not, they are never getting out.

John Hinckley, Jr. the disturbed man that shot President Ronald Reagan in 1981 was found not guilty by reason of insanity. That is because he was tried in federal court that applies a different standard of legal insanity. Hinckley's attorneys recently asked the court to continue Hinckley's extended visits outside the mental facility. They have also requested that he be released from the facility so he can live with or be near his mother in Williamsburg, Virginia. If the court grants Hinckley his release, the decision will displease a majority of Americans. And it probably won't go over too well in Williamsburg.

The Crazy Cop Killer

During the winter of 1974, 16-year-old Alan A. Randall committed more than a dozen burglaries in and around Summit, Wisconsin, a town of 4,000 in Waukesha, County. In January 1975, Randall broke into the Summit Police Department. When officers Wayne Olson and Robert Atkins pulled up to police headquarters in their patrol car, Randall, instead of either giving himself up or making a run for it, opened fire on the officers, killing them both. The burglar-turned cop killer drove from the scene in the dead officers' bullet-ridden police vehicle. That night, he committed another burglary then went home to bed.

Tried as an adult two years later, the jury found Alan Randall guilty of two counts of first-degree murder. (He had also been charged with murdering his neighbor, a man named Ronald Hoeft. Due to procedural problems with the prosecution in that case, that charge was dropped.) Because Randall's attorney had raised the defense of legal insanity, the trial went into a second phase centered on the issue of his mental state at the time of the murders. The jury, having heard testimony from psychiatrists who had diagnosed Randall of having a personality disorder, found him not guilty by reason of insanity.

Today, a defendant with a so-called personality disorder would not be adjudged legally insane because people with this disorder are not psychotic, or in any way delusional. They are fully aware of what they have done, and that the act of murder is wrong. In other words, these defendants are bad people rather than insane people. Ted Bundy had a personality disorder, John Hinckley was nuts.

Having been declared legally insane, Alan Randall, rather than being sent to prison for a specific period of time, was packed off to a mental institution for an indefinite period. He would be eligible for release when psychiatrists said he was cured of his mental illness. Since Randall was not insane, he was, at least in theory, eligible for release the day they admitted him into the Central State Hospital in northeast Wisconsin.

In 1980, doctors took Randall off his anti-psychotic medication. A model patient--the best mental patients are the ones who aren't insane-- Randall was transferred to the Mendota Mental Institution in Madison where he was allowed to work full time at an art gallery.

In 1989, Randall's attorney began petitioning the court for his release on grounds he had been cured of the mental illness behind the murders he had committed fourteen years earlier. By now, Randall's psychiatrists had dropped the personality disorder diagnosis. In 1990 and 1991, judges denied Randall's quest for freedom. In 1992, the shrinks quit spending time with this mental patient altogether. Randall didn't need psychiatrists who had plenty of real nuts to deal with at the institution.

Randall lost another bid for freedom in 1995. Finally, in April 2013, after 36 years in a mental institution, a six-member jury recommended that the 54-year-old cop killer be released back into society. Since Randall had not been sent to the mental institution to be punished, the issue wasn't whether he had been punished enough. Because he wasn't crazy, he didn't belong in a mental institution. The patient was not let out of the facility immediately because it would take several months to find him a suitable home in some county other than Waukesha.

While Randall's release order did not create public outrage, some of the murder victims' relatives were disappointed. A widow of one of the murdered officers told reporters that in her opinion Mr. Randall, who had never publicly apologized for the murders, was not contrite. Waukesha District Attorney Brad Schimel said there was no basis upon which the state could appeal the jury's recommendation to free this killer of two cops.

Alan Randall's attorney, Craig Powell, assured reporters that his client posed no threat to the community. "He's a much different person now than when he was a kid." Had Alan Randall been sentenced to prison in 1977 instead of being committed to a mental institution, he would have been eligible for parole as early as 1992. That, of course, doesn't mean that he would have been released so soon after the murders.

In September 2013, Alan Randall, the cop killer who lived 36 years in an insane asylum, became a free man. I'm not sure what's worse: losing your mind in prison, or remaining sane in a nuthouse.

The M'Naghten Rule

On Friday, January 20, 1843, in a shot heard around the world, Scottish woodcutter and conspiracy theorist Daniel M'Naghten fired at and killed Edward Drummond, private secretary of Sir Robert Peel. M'Naghten was under the impression that he was shooting at Sir Robert, then Prime Minister of Great Britain. He was further under the delusion that Sir Robert Peel, the founder of the first London Police force was part of a cabal, along with the Pope and the Society of Jesus, that plotted to abridge the rights of British subjects and that had deliberately set out to spy on and persecute him.

That M'Naghten was insane there was no doubt; nine medical experts testified for the defense, and none for the prosecution. That insanity was accepted as a defense came as a surprise, and that M'Naghten was acquitted "by reason of insanity" came as a shock. [In many states the insanity defense doctrine is called The M'Naghten Rule.]

Michael Kurland, *How To Try a Murder*, 1997

How Crazy Do You Have To Be?

Psychiatrists diagnosed David Tarloff with schizophrenia in 1991 when the 23-year-old was in college. Over the next seventeen years, the Queens, New York resident, on twelve occasions, ended up in a hospital mental ward. There was no question that the man was mentally ill.

Tarloff lived with his mother in an apartment until 2004 when she moved into a nursing home. By 2008, the 40-year-old schizophrenic had convinced himself that nursing home personnel were abusing his mother. That's when he concocted a plan to rob Dr. Kent Shinbach, the psychiatrist who had initially treated him in 1991. With the money he hoped to acquire by using the doctor's ATM code, Tarloff planned to pull his mother out of the nursing home and take her away to Hawaii.

In February 2008, after making several phone inquiries, Tarloff learned that Dr. Shinbach had offices on Manhattan's Upper East Side. In preparation for the robbery, Tarloff purchased a rubber meat mallet and a cleaver that he packed into a suitcase filled with adult diapers and clothing for his mother.

On February 8, 2008, Tarloff showed up at Dr. Shinbach's office armed with the meat cleaver and the mallet. But instead of encountering his robbery target, he was confronted by Dr. Kathryn Faughey, the 56-year-old psychotherapist who shared office space with Dr. Shinbach.

In the Manhattan doctor's office, Tarloff smashed Faughey's skull with the mallet, then hacked her to death with the meat cleaver. He also attacked Dr. Shinbach when the psychiatrist tried to rescue his colleague. Tarloff fled the bloody scene on foot and was taken into custody shortly thereafter. Dr. Shinbach survived his wounds.

The Manhattan District Attorneys Office charged Tarloff with first-degree murder. The defendant's attorney acknowledged what his client had done, but pleaded him not guilty by reason of insanity. If a jury found that at the moment Tarloff killed Dr. Faughey, he was so mentally ill he couldn't appreciate the nature and quality of his act, they could return a verdict of not guilty. Instead of serving a fixed prison term, Tarloff would be placed into an institution for the criminally insane. The doctors who treated him would determine the length of his sentence. If at some point the psychiatrists considered him sane enough for society, he could be discharged from the mental institution. (It is for this reason that most jurors are uncomfortable with the insanity defense, particularly in cases of extreme violence.)

Under American law, criminal defendants are presumed innocent and sane. That means the prosecution has to prove guilt beyond a reasonable doubt. The defense, in insanity cases, has the burden of proving, by a preponderance of the evidence (a less rigorous standard of proof) that the defendant was out of touch with reality when he committed the homicide. Since even seriously psychotic murder defendants are aware they are killing their victims, not guilty by reason of insanity verdicts are rare. This is particularly true in rural communities where jurors prefer to send mentally ill murderers to prison.

David Tarloff's murder trial got underway in March 2013. A month later, following the testimony of a set of dueling psychiatrists, the case went to the jury. After ten days of deliberation, the jury foreman informed the judge that the panel had not been able to reach a unanimous verdict of guilt. The trial judge had no choice but to declare a mistrial.

The Manhattan prosecutor in charge of the case announced his intention to try David Tarloff again. Cases like this tend to be won or lost in the jury selection process. Given the history of the insanity defense, the odds of a guilty verdict favor the prosecution. The prosecutor, the second time around, will probably beef-up his roster of psychiatric witnesses. As of July 2014, the Tarloff case had not come to trial.

The Forensic Psychiatrist

When John Hinckley was found "not guilty by reason of insanity" after having shot President Ronald Reagan and two of his aides [in 1981] in full view of the national press corps, public furor brought the controversy concerning the use of psychiatric testimony in criminal trials to a boil.

Critics [of psychiatrists in the courtroom], most of whom demand that psychiatrists be banished from all criminal trials, possess either a minimal or distorted understanding of just what a forensic psychiatrist does...[The critics] have forgotten that well before a psychiatrist ever entered an American courtroom, our legal system was already greatly concerned not only with *what* a man did wrong, but *why* he did it--what was going on in his head at the moment of his offense.

It is a cornerstone of our system of justice that if a man perceives himself as innocent at the time of his offense, if he had not *intended* a wrongful outcome, then he is less culpable than someone whose crime was *deliberate* and committed with malice aforethought. Because of the preeminence of the principle that there are *degrees* of criminal liability, criminal trials necessarily go beyond the black-and-white issue of whether or not the accused pulled the trigger, and into the murky labyrinth of his intentions and motivations--his state of mind.

Dr. Martin Blinder, *Lovers, Killers, Husbands and Wives*, 1997

Playing the System

In the 1957 musical *West Side Story*, Stephen Sondheim parodied what then was the current thinking about juvenile delinquency in the song, "Gee, Officer Krupke." Delinquents were punks because their fathers were drunks. They were misunderstood rather than no good. They were suffering from a "social disease," and society "had played them a terrible trick." They needed an analyst, not a judge, because it was "just their neurosis" acting up. In short, their criminal behavior was regarded as symptomatic of a deep-seated psychological or sociological problem. Little has changed since then in terms of deeply ingrained beliefs about the causes of crime....

When a person commits a particularly sordid crime, his sanity may be questioned. Three men pick up two girls who are thumbing a lift. A joyride turns into a nightmare when the teenagers are driven to a desolate mountainous area where they are bound and repeatedly raped. Two of their tormentors dig a hole and tell them to say their prayers. However, the men decide to prolong the torture and take the girls to an apartment where they brutalize them again. Eventually, the court considers the rapists to be "mentally disordered sex offenders" and sends them to a psychiatric hospital, where they spend less time than one-third of the time they would have spent in prison.

Criminals learn to fool the psychiatrists and the courts in order to serve "easy time" in a hospital with the prospect of getting out more quickly than they would from a prison. From other criminals and from their attorneys, even unsophisticated street criminals learn the ploy of insanity. The game is for the criminal to convince others that he is sick, so that he can beat the charge. After he is admitted to the hospital, he plays the psychiatric game of mouthing insights and behaving properly so that he can convince the staff that he is recovering and deserves to be released.

Stanton E. Samenow, *Criminal Justice*, 1994

What Drove This Woman to Kill?

Police in Livermore, California, a suburban community 45 miles east of San Francisco, received calls, at ten-thirty on the morning of Saturday, April 26, 2014, regarding a disturbed woman in the 4,400-acre Del Valle Regional Park. The woman, according to the callers, was screaming as she repeatedly rammed her Honda Civil into a rock wall at the end of Arroyo Road in the remote Camp Arroyo section of the sprawling park.

Officers with the Livermore Police Department, accompanied by California Highway Patrol (CHP) officers, responded to the badly damaged Honda that sat in a ditch off Arroyo Road. The female driver had left the scene. Her whereabouts at the time were unknown. Officers noticed an empty car seat in the back of the damaged vehicle.

Two hours after the police calls, off-duty Livermore Chief of Police Mike Harris, his wife and their two daughters, had returned to their car after a hike in the Camp Arroyo section of the park. Earlier that morning Harris and his family had driven past the wrecked Honda. He didn't stop because there were several officers already at the scene. Harris and his family were about to get into their car that was parked about 200 yards from the Honda.

Shortly after the chief's daughters climbed into the family vehicle, a young woman wearing a sweatshirt and jeans caked in blood approached the Harris family. In her arms she carried a blond-haired, 7-month-old boy dressed in Cookie Monster diapers and a blue striped pullover. The child was also covered in blood. The distraught woman handed the boy to the chief. "Take him! Take him!" she yelled before climbing into the car with the chief's daughters.

The police chief assumed that the woman and her son had been injured in the nearby wrecked Honda. He alerted officers and paramedic personnel who were down the road investigating the accident. A member of the emergency crew, shortly after starting CPR on the boy, realized that he was dead. The child had been stabbed to death.

Police officers escorted the woman, 23-year-old Ashley Newton, to the Santa Rita Jail where she was booked on suspicion of murder. Originally from North Carolina, Newton resided in San Jose. Before that she had lived in the bay area town of Fremont, California.

On Sunday, April 27, 2014, detectives questioned Newton at the Santa Rita Jail. She said she had stabbed her son with a pocketknife. (The bloody weapon had been recovered from the park.) Sounding paranoid and detached from reality, Newton was unable to articulate a motive for killing her son.

That day, detectives in San Jose interviewed the dead child's father. He said he had last spoken to Newton the day before she stabbed their son to death. She had been suffering from depression. A police spokesperson announced that toxicology tests would determine if drugs or alcohol had played a role in the killing.

On Monday, April 28, an Orange County prosecutor charged Newton with first-degree murder. The judge denied her bail and ordered psychiatric tests. This case was pending as of July 2014.

Rejecting the Insanity Defense

Parker Schenecker, an Army intelligence officer, met Julie Powers, an Army linguist (Russian) in 1987 when they were deployed in Germany. Shortly after they were married in Louisiana in 1991, a psychologist began treating her for depression. Three years later, she gave birth to Calyx, and in 1997, their son Beau.

Not long after having Beau, Julie began taking anti-depression medication on a daily basis. In 2001, psychiatrists diagnosed her as suffering from bipolar disorder and severe depression. According to these physicians, she had a personality disorder as well. (There is no effective way to treat the latter.) During her nine months of treatment at Walter Reed Army Medical Center in Maryland outside of Washington, D.C., she labored under the false belief that a brain tumor was causing her mental illness. Julie held this belief after brain scans proved negative. During this time, Parker Schenecker hired a nanny to take care of the children.

In 2009, while being treated in south Florida for mental illness, Julie expressed a desire to take her psychiatrist's comb and use his DNA to get pregnant.

On November 6, 2010, while residing in an upscale neighborhood in Tampa, Florida, 15-year-old Calyx told a school counselor that her mother had slapped her in the face when they returned from her cross-country practice. The counselor reported the matter to the authorities, and that day, a Tampa police officer, accompanied by a child protection social worker paid Julie a home visit. Julie admitted hitting Calyx with her open hand during an argument four days earlier. The police officer decided not to make an arrest in the case.

On January 15, 2011, Colonel Schenecker, while assigned as an intelligence officer with U.S. Central Command in Qatar, wrote a long email to the psychiatrist in Florida treating Julie. The colonel expressed concern about Julie's bellicose relationship with Calyx. It seemed the two of them never stopped fighting.

Colonel Schenecker wrote: "Julie can no longer control Calyx and Calyx has been disrespectful and verbally abusive toward Julie." Colonel Schenecker also noted that his wife had taken to the bottle. "Drinking starts to affect the kids--they start mentioning it to me." Julie had also, according to the colonel, been driving erratically which had resulted in a traffic accident.

Julie Schenecker wrote an email addressed to her family on January 27, 2011. The message read: "It's really difficult and I'm so sick mentally. I minimally take care of the kids, sad to say. Beau has also developed Calyx's attitude--makes me cry every evening. Seeing what they've become, I will end this soon. I am at my wits end."

The day following Julie's email to her family, her mother Nancy called the police to report that she had not been able to reach her daughter. Due to Julie's mental state, Nancy was concerned that something was wrong. In response to the mother's request for a welfare visit, officers were dispatched to the Schenecker house. There, in the garage, they found Beau in Julie's SUV. The boy had been shot twice in the head.

In Calyx's room, officers discovered the 16-year-old lying on her bed with a fatal bullet wound to the back of her head. Both children had been shot with the .38-caliber revolver found at the scene. The bodies had been covered with blankets. The officers also recovered a journal at the scene in which Julie described her plan to kill her children and herself.

Police officers found, on the back porch, Julie Schenecker. Wearing a blood-soaked bathrobe, she was asleep and under the influence of prescription pills. She awoke and told the officers why she had shot her children to death. She said she had done this because they had "talked back and were mouthy."

Officers took Julie into custody at the death scene. At the police station, they continued to question her. Julie said she had shot Beau in the car after they had returned home from his soccer practice. She said she killed Calyx in her room as she did homework on her computer. Julie showed no emotion or remorse as she described killing her children.

Julie Schenecker informed her interrogators that five days before shooting her children to death, she had driven 27 miles to a small Florida town where she purchased the revolver at a store called Lock N Load.

(When buying the weapon, she told the counterman that there had been a rash of burglaries in her neighborhood.)

After questioning her at the police station, detectives took Julie to a nearby hospital for observation. She told a doctor that she had a "pre-existing" medical condition. Following her discharge from the medical center on January 29, 2011, officers booked the murder suspect into Hillsborough County's Falkenburg Road Jail on two counts of first-degree murder. The judge denied her bond.

The homicide suspect's attorneys, at her February 16, 2011 arraignment, pleaded her not guilty. The lawyers announced they planned to launch an insanity defense on her behalf. Under Florida law, legal insanity is statutorily defined as a mental disease or defect present at the time of the crime that rendered the defendant incapable of appreciating the nature and quality of the criminal act. In other words, the mental illness had destroyed the defendant's ability to distinguish between right and wrong. In Florida, as well as most other states, the so-called "M'Naghten right-wrong test," due to the fact that even seriously mentally ill people are aware of what they are doing when they kill someone, is a difficult defense to prove. Proving that the defendant's actions were driven by the mental illness and nothing else is usually an uphill task. (A defendant must prove legal insanity by a preponderance of the evidence. That means the prosecution does not have the burden of proving the defendant was sane, that is presumed along with innocence.)

Colonel Schenecker divorced Julie in May 2011. Following a dispute over the distribution of family assets, he sued her in civil court for the wrongful death of their children. Julie's civil attorneys in the case countered that the plaintiff was equally responsible for the children's deaths. In support of this argument, they cited the emails the colonel had sent to her psychiatrist less than two weeks before the killings. In these emails he expressed his concern for the wellbeing of the children.

The Julie Schenecker double murder trial got underway on April 28, 2014 in Tampa, Florida. Following jury selection and the opening statements from each side, the prosecutor put police officers, detectives, crime scene people, and a forensic pathologist on the stand. On May 5, 2014, crime scene specialist Matthew Evans testified that he had recovered numerous bottles of prescription pills at the murder house that included Lithium and Oxycodone.

The prosecutor asked Matthew Evans to read from portions of the journal taken from the house. From this document, Evans read the following to the jury: "The best job I ever had was having/bringing up my babies. This is why I had to bring them with me. It's possible they've inherited my DNA and would live their lives depressed or bipolar! I believe I saved them from the pain. I wouldn't wish this on nobody--ever."

According to the defendant's journal, she had worried that if she committed suicide, her children would have to live with the stigma associated with their mother's act of self-destruction. "If you're wondering why I decided to take out the kids it was to protect them from embarrassment the rest of their lives."

A detective followed the crime scene investigator to the stand. The detective played an audiotape of the defendant's police station interview. Slurring her words, Schenecker explained in detail how she had shot her children to death and why. She also listed all of the prescription medicine she had been taking.

The following day, now retired Army Colonel Parker Schenecker, took the stand for the prosecution. The 53-year-old described to the jury the domestic turmoil of living with a mentally disturbed wife. During his testimony, he never referred to her by name, referring to Julie as the "defendant."

On May 9, 2014, after the prosecution rested its case, The Schenecker defense took center stage. Michelle Frisco, a 43-year-old house cleaner who worked for the defendant, said that Julie had been upset because Beau had become as disrespectful as his older sister. The defendant also told the witness that she drank heavily when her husband was deployed out of the country.

Dr. Demian Obregon, a University of Southern Florida psychologist, testified that he had treated the defendant for various mental disorders. The medicine she took produced side effects such as "lip-smacking," and "leg-jerking." According to this witness, Julie, in August 2010, had starting expressing suicidal thoughts. In December of that year, she had revealed deep feelings of being both helpless and hopeless.

Throughout the trial, Julie Schenecker sat passively with her attorneys at the defense table. But that changed suddenly in the middle of Dr. Obergron's testimony. When the psychologist told the jury he had warned her against mixing alcohol with her bipolar medicine, she yelled "Liar! You told me two drinks a day, two Oxys a day!"

The trial judge responded to the outburst by ordering the jurors out of the courtroom. The judge then issued a strong warning to the defendant. If she engaged in this type of behavior again, there would be serious consequences. Such outbursts would not be tolerated.

On Monday, May 12, 2014, Dr. Eldra Solomon, another psychologist, took the stand for the defense. Hired by Julie's attorneys to examine and evaluate their client's mental state on the days leading up to the killings, Dr. Solomon testified that Julie, on the day she decided to buy the gun, "had her first clear thought in weeks." And that thought involved killing her children so they could all go to heaven together. "People who are not in a psychotic state," Dr. Solomon said, "do not kill their children."

Dr. Michael Malher, a medical doctor and psychiatrist, had also been hired by the defense as an expert insanity defense witness. In his expert opinion, Julie Schenecker, at the time of the killings, was insane pursuant to the criteria of the M'Naghten right-wrong test.

In cross-examining the defense insanity witnesses, the prosecutor, in an effort to undermine their credibility, implied that they were nothing more than insanity defense hired guns.

On May 13, the defense wound-up its case with another expert who found that the defendant, at the time of the killings, was in a psychotic state. The defense also called Colonel Schenecker to the stand. The witness described his ex-wife as a 50-year-old with the judgment of a 10-year-old, and painted a picture of what it was like for him and his family to live with a person who was seriously mentally ill. Following the colonel's testimony, the defense rested its case.

The prosecutor, on May 14, 2014, in the rebuttal phase of the trial, pressed the argument that the double murder had been motivated by anger. The three rebuttal witnesses on this day were psychiatrists who testified that the defendant had operated under a clear, calculated plan to kill her children. These prosecution experts explained to the jury why the defendant, under Florida's right-wrong test, was not legally insane. When shooting her children, she had known exactly what she was doing. The defendant was not acting pursuant to any delusions, or instructions from voices in her head. She had been driven by anger, not mental illness.

On Thursday morning, May 15, 2014, following the closing arguments and the judge's instructions to the jury, the jurors walked out of the courtroom to deliberate the defendant's fate. Just two hours later, at three o'clock, the jury returned to the courtroom with its verdict: guilty of two counts of first-degree murder. This jury obviously did not buy the Schenecker insanity defense.

In addressing the judge in advance of the sentence, Julie Schenecker tearfully apologized for killing her children. She said, "They are alive and enjoying everything and anything heaven has to offer. Jesus is protecting them and keeping them safe until we get there." Immediately after this irony-laced statement, the judge handed Schenecker the mandated sentence of two life terms without the possibility of parole.

Self Defense

What Does the Physical Evidence Say?

We went to a scene where the husband shot his wife. His story was she came at him with a knife and tried to stab him. So he was saying he killed her in self-defense. But there were a couple of things that just didn't make sense.

There *was* a knife in her hand. But it was in the wrong direction to be used as a stabbing-type instrument. It was apparent that he had placed the knife in her hand after he shot her and probably, in his panic, faced it the wrong way.

There was blood on the palm of her hand where she had touched the entrance wound when she was shot. The normal reaction is to grab where it hurts, and she *did*. And she had blood on her hand, but there was no blood on the knife.

Connie Fletcher, *Crime Scene*, 2006

Killing Intruders

On November 21, 2012, the day before Thanksgiving, a resident in a neighborhood in Little Falls Township south of Little Falls, Minnesota, phoned the Morrison County Sheriff's Office to report a suspicious car parked at the foot of his driveway. To the officers who rolled up to the red Mitsubishi Eclipse, the lone occupant of the vehicle, 17-year-old Nicholas Brady, said that he and his 18-year-old cousin, Haile Kifer, had been riding around when they ran out of gas. He was a junior at Pillager High School in Little Falls, and Haile was a year ahead of him. She had left the vehicle to find a gas station. One of the deputies gave Brady, a nice-looking kid interested in wrestling and the martial art of taekwondo, a ride home. His cousin Haile, a high school gymnast, diver, cross country runner, and softball player, had nothing in her background that would arouse a police officer's suspicion.

Byron Smith, a 64-year-old retiree, lived in a modest, township home located a few miles north of Little Falls. In recent months, Mr. Smith had been plagued by a series of home burglaries committed by teenagers looking for drugs, money, and guns. In October 2012, burglars had broken into his house and stolen weapons and other items. The fact Byron Smith had been a physical security expert who specialized in preventing criminal intrusion into government buildings, had added to his frustration and anger over being a repeat burglary victim.

In 2007, Byron Smith, after serving overseas in places like Bangkok, Thailand, Beijing, China, and Cairo, Egypt, retired from the U.S. State Department. He had been one of a handful of highly trained security engineers responsible for making our embassies and consulates difficult for terrorists and spies to physically penetrate. An expert on anti-intrusion building design, locks, access control, alarms, video surveillance, protective lighting, and physical barriers, Smith had overseen the construction and renovation of these government facilities.

Byron Smith's job not only required technical knowledge and experience it came with top security clearance. This meant he had been thoroughly investigated for mental illnesses, personality disorders, and possible substance abuse. Moreover, he had to live a straight-arrow lifestyle to avoid the potential of blackmail. Mr. Smith was also familiar with handguns and assault rifles. It is not difficult to understand why this man had a particular dislike, even hatred, for criminal intruders.

On Thanksgiving night, November 22, 2012, a day after the Morrison County Deputies checked out the suspicious Mitsubishi south of Little Falls, Byron Smith, while sitting in his basement, heard the sound of breaking window glass. The sound of footsteps on the first floor told him that he had at least two burglars in his dwelling. The government retiree grabbed his Ruger Mini-14 assault rifle and waited.

Mr. Smith readied his rifle when he saw the feet of one of the burglars on his basement stairs. When the intruder's torso came into view, Mr. Smith fired twice, striking and killing Nicholas Brady. Mr. Smith dragged the 17-year-old's corpse into the basement and laid it out next to his workbench.

Not long after he had killed the high school student, another set of feet appeared on the stairway. As Haile Kifer descended into Smith's basement far enough for the homeowner to see up to her waist, he fired the Ruger. The girl collapsed and her body tumbled down the steps. She was still alive, and gasping for air. Byron Smith interpreted the sounds the wounded girl made as she struggled for air as laughter. He tried to shoot her again, but his rifle jammed. Mr. Smith dragged Haile deeper into his basement and laid her body next to her cousin Nicholas. After securing a handgun, Mr. Smith placed its muzzle under the girl's chin. He pulled the trigger, killing her.

Instead of calling the police and reporting that he had shot and killed two intruders in his house, Byron Smith decided to spend the night with the dead bodies lying in his basement. The next morning, Smith called a neighbor and asked if he could recommend a good attorney. The neighbor replied that he didn't know any lawyers. At this point Smith informed the neighbor that he had killed a couple of burglars the previous night. He asked the neighbor to call the authorities.

While homicide investigators were processing the death scene, deputies searched Haile Kifer's red Mitsubishi parked a few blocks from Mr. Smith's house. The officers identified the vehicle as the suspicious car they had checked on the day before. At that time they had questioned Nicholas Brady, the boy who lay dead in Smith's basement. Inside the car, searchers found six bottles of medicine that had been prescribed to a Little Falls Township man named Richard Johnson. They also recovered a jar of pennies and some foreign coins.

A Morrison County prosecutor, based upon Byron Smith's account of the shootings, charged him with two counts of second-degree murder. While under Minnesota law the occupant of a dwelling can legally use deadly force against an intruder, the homicide defense doesn't apply if the burglar was killed *after* the threat had been neutralized. Byron Smith, when describing to the police what happened to Haile Kifer, said, "If you're trying to shoot somebody and they laugh at you, you go again." Mr. Smith characterized his follow-up shooting of the girl as a "good clean finishing shot under her chin up into the cranium." Neither of the teen intruders had been armed.

On Sunday, November 25, 2012, three days after the fatal shootings, 68-year-old Richard Johnson, upon returning to his Little Falls Township home after vacationing in Spain, found his dwelling ransacked by intruders. The burglars had used a crowbar to smash a sliding glass door. The home invaders had stolen bottles of prescription medicine Mr. Johnson took to treat diabetes and high cholesterol. The burglars had also taken a collection of foreign coins and some pennies. The police had recovered these items three days earlier from Haile Kifer's red Mitsubishi. Investigators figured that Brady and Kifer had burglarized Mr. Johnson's home on the day before Thanksgiving about the time one of Johnson's neighbors reported the suspicious car.

Byron Smith was held in the Morrison County Jail on $2 million bond.

It seemed that Nicholas Brady and Haile Kifer had been breaking into older people's homes looking for drugs, money, and guns. House burglary is a dangerous business, and it had gotten these youngsters killed. They were smart kids and should have known better. As for the man who shot them, his life, at least as he knew it, is over. But Byron Smith should have known that the way he killed the 18-year-old girl, burglar or not, was murder. You can shoot home invaders, but the law won't let you execute them.

In April 2014, a jury, after deliberating just three hours, found the defendant guilty as charged. The judge sentenced him to life in prison.

A Decision Not to Prosecute

In 2010, in Kalispell, Montana, a town of 20,000 in the northwest corner of the state, 38-year-old Dan Fredenberg, a divorced father of two, met and started dating a 20-year-old cocktail waitress named Heather King. After Heather became pregnant with twins, she and Dan got married. The marriage didn't work out. He drank too much, they had financial problems, and he was a bit of a lady's man. The couple fought, and talked frequently of divorce.

In June 2012, Heather informed her husband that she was having a friendly but nonsexual relationship with Brice Harper, a 24-year-old resident of Kalispell. Dan Fredenberg did not take the news very well and was understandably jealous. (He probably didn't believe the nonsexual part.) That month the two men were involved in a nonphysical confrontation at Fat Boy's Bar & Grille in Kalispell.

On September 22, 2012, Brice Harper called Heather Fredenberg with a request. He was moving out of town the next day and wondered if she could come to his duplex and help him clean house. Heather put her twin sons into her car and made the five-minute trip to Harper's dwelling. That day, while at Harper's place, Heather and her husband exchanged angry text messages. When they spoke on the phone, Dan asked his wife if she was with Harper. She didn't answer his question so he swore at her and hung up.

At eight-thirty that night, Heather, about to leave Harper's house, put the twins into her car. Before going home, she asked Harper to ride around the block with her. Perhaps he could determine what was making the clunking noise coming from under the hood of her car. Harper climbed into the vehicle. They hadn't traveled very far when Heather realized her husband was following them. When she pulled back into Harper's driveway to drop him off, Heather suggested that he go directly into his house and lock the doors. Harper replied that he was not afraid of her husband. He also told her he owned a gun. Anticipating trouble, Heather backed out of the driveway, but did not pull away from Harper's house.

Dan Fredenberg, who was not armed, climbed out of his car, walked up Harper's driveway and into his garage through the open door. Harper came out of his house and into his garage carrying a handgun. From a distance of a few feet, he shot Fredenberg three times.

As Dan Fredenberg bled on the floor of Brice Harper's garage, Heather, screaming at the top of her lungs, ran to him. "Call 911," he said. Pronounced dead a short time later at the Kalispell Regional Medical Center, these had been his last words.

Ed Corrigan, the Flathead County attorney, had to determine if under Montana's so-called "castle doctrine" (because a man's home is his "castle," he does not have to retreat from using deadly force against an intruder), Brice Harper had committed murder. Did this killer have the legal right to stand his ground against an unarmed intruder in his garage?

In most of the twenty states that justify the killing of a home invader by the dwelling's legal occupant, the use of deadly force is an affirmative defense to criminal homicide. This means that the use of lethal force under these circumstances is presumed unjustified, placing the burden of proving this defense on the accused. (The defendant must prove his case by a preponderance of the evidence, a less rigorous evidentiary standard than proof beyond a reasonable doubt needed to rebut the presumption of innocence.)

In Montana, the state legislature, in 2009, modified this self-defense doctrine by shifting the burden of proof to the prosecution. In other words, the state has to prove that the homicide defendant's actions were outside the castle doctrine. On October 9, 2012, the county attorney, in a 4-page letter to the Kalispell Police Department (the dead man's father was a retired police officer), announced his decision not to prosecute Brice Harper for criminal homicide. Prosecutor Ed Corrigan wrote that under Montana's revised statute, "you [referring to the defendant] didn't have to claim that you were afraid for your life. You just have to claim that he [the victim] was in the house illegally. [An attached garage is considered part of a dwelling.] If you think someone's going to punch you in the nose or engage in a fistfight, that's sufficient grounds to engage in lethal force."

It is not good jurisprudence to write a law that makes the use of deadly force, under certain circumstances, legal. There is a danger that this type of law will actually encourage violence. The better approach is to allow the use of deadly force, under clearly defined circumstances, as a homicide defense, a defense the accused has the burden of proving.

In another state, Brice Harper would probably have been prosecuted for voluntary manslaughter on the grounds he had used excessive force against an unarmed man. In his defense, he could have argued that he felt that his life was in danger, and because the confrontation took place in his house, he didn't have to retreat. In my view, Harper may have had a difficult time convincing a jury that his life was in danger. Moreover, jurors may not have liked the fact Harper had been fooling around with the dead man's wife.

A Florida Stand Your Ground Case

Marissa Alexander, when she married Rico Gray in June 2010, was six months pregnant with their child. She had two children from a previous marriage, and Gray had five with five other women. One of his sons, and two of Marissa's children, lived with them in their rented Jacksonville, Florida home. She was 30 and he was 35.

Rico Gray had physically abused his former partners, and was beating up Marissa. In July 2010, he had thrown his pregnant wife across the room then given her a black eye with a head butt. Marissa and her children moved out of the house and into her mother's place. She also filed for an order of protection against her husband.

At the domestic violence injunction hearing, Rico Gray reportedly said this to the judge: "I got five baby mamas and I put my hand on every last one of them except one. The way I was with women they had to walk on eggshells around me. You know, they never knew what I was thinking...or what I might do...hit them, push them." The judge granted the order of protection.

Marissa had the baby on July 23, 2010, and on August 1, returned to the rented house to gather up more of her clothes. While there, she showed Gray a cellphone photograph of their baby. After she entered the bathroom, Gray, looked through her cellphone and came across text messages she had sent to her former husband that suggested she planned to leave him permanently and get back with the ex-spouse. Enraged, Gray stormed into the bathroom and allegedly said, "If I can't have you, no one can." He put his hands on her throat, threw her against the door, and threatened to kill her.

Breaking free, Marissa ran into the attached garage, and from her car, grabbed her handgun. (It was licensed.) She returned to the house (She claimed she couldn't exit the dwelling through the garage because the automatic door opener didn't work.) and encountered Gray standing in the kitchen next to his two sons. Fearing for her life, she (according to her account) fired a warning shot into the air. (Ballistics analysis, however, suggested that the bullet hit a wall and ricocheted up into the ceiling.)

Rico Gray called 911, and in reporting the shooting to the dispatcher, sounded more angry than frightened. A short time later a SWAT team surrounded the house. Marissa was arrested and charged with three counts of aggravated assault. (Three counts because she had allegedly endangered three people.) Under Florida's so-called 10-20-life law, any person convicted of aggravated assault involving the discharge of a gun is subject to a mandatory 20-year sentence.

A few days after her arrest, Marissa was released on bail under orders from the judge to stay clear of her husband. But four months later, Marissa, in violation of the judge's order, went back to the house and punched Gray in the face. (She would later plead no contest to domestic battery.)

With the approach of Marissa's aggravated assault by handgun trial, prosecutor Angela Corey, explained to the defendant that if convicted she would be sentenced to 20 years. The prosecutor offered her a deal: if she pleaded guilty to a lesser charge, the judge would sentence her to three years in prison. Marissa rejected the plea bargain offer.

In defending Marissa Alexander, her attorney planned to rely on Florida's "stand your ground" law that was in the news as a result of the George Zimmerman/Trayvon Martin murder case. (Angela Corey, the state's attorney in Marissa's case was the leading special prosecutor in the February 2012 Sanford, Florida shooting.) Under the "stand your ground" self-defense doctrine, a person who is threatened with death or serious bodily injury in a place where he has a right to be, has no duty under the law to retreat, and can meet force with force.

In a pre-trial hearing on the stand your ground issue, Judge James Daniel ruled that the law didn't apply to Marissa Alexander because she had no reason to fear for her life in that confrontation with her husband. The defendant could therefore not rely on self-defense, and the stand your ground doctrine. On March 16, 2012, a jury found Alexander guilty of the three aggravated assault counts, and the judge, bound by Florida's 10-20-life law, sentenced her to 20 years in prison.

Critics of mandatory sentencing laws, along with anti-domestic violence advocates, have expressed outrage over the outcome of the Marissa Alexander case. Other than winning an appeal, Marissa Alexander's only other legal remedy involves a grant of clemency by Florida Governor Rick Scott. For that to happen, a member of the state clemency board will have to initiate the action. Marissa can only make application herself after she has served half of her sentence.

In the George Zimmerman/Trayvon Martin murder trial, on July 13, 2013, the jury found defendant Zimmerman not guilty of second-degree murder. He was also acquitted of the lesser homicide offense of manslaughter. In this case, the jury of six women found that because Zimmerman reasonably feared for his life during a fight with Trayvon Martin, the neighborhood watch leader was legally justified in standing his ground, and eventually using deadly force against the 17-year-old. The jury must have accepted the defense theory that at the time of his death, the 17-year-old was on top of the defendant, banging his head against the sidewalk. Following the February 2012 shooting, Zimmerman told police officers that he had been afraid the attacker would get control of his handgun.

While the justice system failed Marissa Alexander, it worked for George Zimmerman. However, it will take a politician to help Alexander.

Self Defense or Cold-Blooded Murder?

Police officers in the northwest New Mexico town of Farmington, on the morning of June 10, 2011, discovered the body of Dr. Jim Nordstrom. The victim was buried in a woodpile behind his upscale house. The previous night, someone had bludgeoned the 55-year-old physician to death. One of the victim's fingers had been nearly severed in what the forensic pathologist identified as a defensive wound. The killer had stolen the doctor's pickup truck as well as his credit cards.

Not long after finding the doctor's body behind his Foothills neighborhood home, police officers arrested 17-year-old John Mayes. Rob Mayes, Farmington's city manager, had adopted John, a boy who had grown up in Ukraine where he had been abused.

Detectives, over a two-day period, conducted five interrogation sessions during which time John Mayes confessed to killing the doctor. The interrogations were recorded and preceded by *Miranda* warnings. Mayes also signed forms in which he waived his constitutional right to remain silent. The young murder suspect did not, however, have an attorney present during the police interrogations.

John Mayes told his questioners that on June 9, 2011 he had run away from home. When he came upon the house in the Foothills neighborhood, he snuck inside and hid in a bedroom. (I believe he entered the dwelling through an unlocked window.) At the time of the intrusion, Dr. Nordstrom was in his living room watching television. About an hour after Mayes entered the house, the doctor walked into the bedroom. That's when Mayes struck him in the head eight times with the handle of a pool cue.

With the doctor dead in his own home, Mayes stole his credit cards and his pickup truck. After taking a four-hour nap in the stolen vehicle, Mayes ate a meal at a Burger King. When he finished his hamburger he used the victim's credit cards to go on a $3,000 shopping spree.

Later that night, Mayes returned to the murder scene to clean up the blood and to bury the body in the victim's backyard. After tiring of digging a grave, Mayes dragged the corpse to the woodpile.

San Juan County Chief Deputy District Attorney Brent Capshaw charged John Mayes with first-degree murder and the lesser offenses of aggravated burglary, tampering with evidence, vehicle theft, and fraudulent use of credit cards. After being booked into the San Juan County Jail, the magistrate denied the suspect bond.

John Mayes, represented by attorney Stephen Taylor, pleaded not guilty at a preliminary heard held in August 2011. Attorney Taylor advised the court he was challenging the constitutionality of his client's initial five statements to the police on the grounds he had not *knowingly* waived his *Miranda* rights. (The judge later ruled that the confessions had been constitutionally acquired and could therefore be introduced into evidence at Mayes' trial.)

Speaking from the stand at his preliminary hearing, John Mayes offered a version of the events of June 9, 2011 that were far less incriminating than the substance of his statements to the police. Rather than sneaking into the doctor's home that night, he came upon Dr. Nordstrom outside of his Foothills neighborhood house just when the doctor was washing his pickup truck. Mayes told the doctor he had run away from home and asked if he could spend the night at his place. Dr. Nordstrom said that he could.

That night, Mayes and the doctor watched a James Bond film on television. After the movie, the doctor gave Mayes a tour of the house after which they played a couple games of pool. Dr. Nordstrom asked Mayes if he would like to "try something new." When the physician made a sexual advance, Mayes beat him to death with a pool cue.

Mayes admitted that after killing Dr. Nordstrom he stole his truck and used his credit cards before returning to the house to hide the body.

Pursuant to a change of venue, the John Mayes murder trial got underway on November 13, 2013 in a McKinley County court in Gallup, New Mexico. Neither side disputed the fact Mayes had killed the doctor in his home. What the jury had to determine was whether or not the defendant had committed the act in self-defense.

After the prosecution rested its case, a presentation based heavily on the five statements Mayes had made to the police following his arrest, the defense brought psychologist Gary White and forensic psychologist Maxann Schwartz to the stand. Both witnesses testified that Mayes' behavior that night had been influenced by a personality disorder that affects people who as children had been neglected or abused. The psychologists said the defendant suffered from "reactive attachment disorder," or RAD. People with his disorder often seek attention from strangers but become aggressive when these individuals try to be nice to them.

On November 20, 2013, a psychologist from Boise State University named Dr. Charles Honts took the stand for the defense to testify that he had given Mayes a polygraph test early in 2013. Prosecutor Brent Capshaw objected to this witness on grounds he was not a qualified polygraph examiner. (In 2005 a U. S. magistrate judge in Atlanta had prohibited Dr. Honts from giving polygraph testimony in a murder trial. The judge said, "The court attributes little weight to Dr. Honts' opinions.)

After Judge William Birdsall overruled the prosecutor's objections to this witness, Dr. Honts took the stand and said he had asked Mayes four polygraph questions: Did Nordstrom invite you into his home? Did you play pool with Nordstrom? Did he slap you on the butt? Did you hide in the bedroom waiting to hit Nordstrom? The witness testified that the defendant answered yes to the first three questions and no to the fourth. According to Dr. Honts, his polygraph examination revealed that Mayes was truthful in his responses.

On rebuttal, Peter Pierangeli, a polygraph examiner from Albuquerque took the stand for the prosecution and testified that Dr. Honts did not ask the defendant appropriate questions. His polygraph results were therefore unreliable. According to Pierangeli, if Dr. Honts wanted to get to the truth, he would have asked Mayes if Dr. Nordstrom had sexually assaulted him.

John Mayes did not take the witness stand on his own behalf.

The defense attorney, in his closing remarks to the jury, pointed out that the police, by not seizing Dr. Nordstrom's computer and a prescription bottle found in his bedroom, had botched the investigation. The defense attorney told the jurors that Dr. Honts' polygraph test, by itself, created reasonable doubt that his client was guilty of murder.

On Monday, November 25, 2013, after deliberating ten hours over a period of two days, the jury found John Mayes guilty of second-degree murder. The jurors found the defendant guilty of the lesser charges as well. The conviction carried a maximum sentence of 31 years in prison. The jurors must have accepted enough of the defendant's story to believe Dr. Nordstrom had *not* been the victim of a cold-blooded murder. The jury had also rejected the notion of self-defense in the case.

Had John Mayes been convicted of first-degree murder, his sentence would have been life without parole. The judge sentenced Mayes to thirty years in prison.

13 LIGHT SENTENCES

Murder

Holland's Boy Hit Man

Joyce Winsie Hau, a 14-year-old member of the Chinese-Dutch community in Arnhem, Holland, fell out with her best friend, a 15-year-old girl referred to by the Dutch authorities as Polly W. Joyce angered Polly and Polly's boyfriend, 15-year-old Wesley C., when she gossiped about their sexual escapades on Facebook and other social media. This anger set in motion a plot, hatched by Polly and Wesley, to have Joyce Hau murdered.

Polly and Wesley (names more in tune with a children's book than a murder for hire case), offered Jinhau K., an acquaintance of Joyce's, 16 pounds (roughly $50), to commit the homicide. The pair of teen masterminds, over a period of several weeks in late 2011, met frequently with the boy hit man to plan the murder. During these meetings, Polly and her boyfriend provided Jinhau with the homicide target's address, and other information including when Joyce would most likely be home. After the murder, the masterminds promised to take their hit man out for drinks. (I don't know how these kids got around, the minimum driving age in Holland, or how easy it is for youngsters in that country to get their hands on alcohol.)

On January 14, 2012, Jinhau K. showed up at the Hau residence, and when invited into the house by Mr. Chun Nam Hau, the knife-wielding boy stabbed the father and his daughter. The attack took place in the hallway just inside the dwelling's front entrance. Mr. Hau survived the attack, but Joyce Hau did not. Joyce's younger brother who was not harmed witnessed the murder and attempted murder.

Shortly after the home assault and murder, the police arrested Jinhau K. In his confession, the boy named the two teen murder-for-hire masterminds. Soon after that, the police arrested Polly W. and Wesley C.

In August 2012, Jinhau K. went on trial as a juvenile before a district court judge in Arnhem. Following testimony from Chun Nam Hau and Joyce Hau's younger brother, the judge heard from the defendant who testified that he had committed the assault and murder out of fear that if he had refused to carry out the plot, Polly W. and Wesley C. would have killed him.

The judge, in ruling that the defendant had plenty of opportunity to pull out of the murder conspiracy, said, "In their reports the psychologist and psychiatrist state that the pressure the defendant says he felt, was never so high that he was unable to resist it. There were several moments where the defendant could have called in the help of others, or could have come to his senses." (What senses? This kid must be some kind of idiot.)

On September 3, 2012, the Arnhem judge sentenced Jinhau K. to one year in a juvenile detention center, the maximum penalty under Dutch law for a murderer between the ages 12 to 16. (I don't know why the judge didn't add another year for the attempted murder of Mr. Hau.) Upon completing his one-year sentence, Jinhau K. will undergo 3 years of psychiatric treatment at another facility. When the teen hit man turns 18, he will be completely free from court supervision.

Members of Holland's Chinese-Dutch community were shocked and outraged by such a light sentence for the cold-blooded murder of a girl, and the attempted murder of her father. As for the two teenage murder-for-hire masterminds, the charges against them were dropped. If the hit man only qualifies for one year of juvenile detention, what's the point of bothering with the degenerate kids who set these bloody crimes into motion?

In Holland, the media called Joyce Hau's killing the "Facebook Murder Case." I would call it the case of the Dutch teens that got away with murder. It's not snappy, but it's closer to the truth.

No Justice For Arlene

On October 28, 1978, Arlene Roberts' neighbors at the Lakeshore Manor Mobile Home Park in Renton, Washington near Seattle checked in on the 80-year-old after she hadn't been seen for several days. They were shocked by what they saw upon entering her ransacked trailer. Someone had brutally murdered this woman.

King County Sheriff's deputies found the victim half-naked and gagged with her hands and feet bound by one of her nylon stockings. The killer had strangled Roberts to death with a ligature fashioned from the victim's hair net.

Although a crime scene investigator gathered physical evidence from the scene, including several latent fingerprints that did not belong to the victim, no suspects were developed, and the investigation slowed to a crawl then died on the vine.

Early in 2011, 33 years after this sadistic murder, King County cold case investigators re-opened the Roberts homicide case. When detectives entered three of the crime scene latent prints into the Automatic Fingerprint Identification System (AFIS) computer--including a print that had been developed off a bank statement, and a print off a traveler's check--the computer search produced three "hits" or matches. All of the submitted fingerprints belonged to Ronald Wayne MacDonald, a then 17-year-old burglar who lived seven blocks from the murder scene.

A background investigation of the murder suspect revealed that shortly after Arlene Roberts' murder, MacDonald moved to Florida where he was arrested several times for burglary for which he served numerous stretches in prison. In the 1990's, while living around the Reno, Nevada area, police had arrested him on burglary charges in 1992 and 2001.

In June 2011, King County investigators traveled to Reno to interrogate the Roberts case murder suspect. When the detectives confronted MacDonald with the crime scene fingerprint evidence, he confessed to strangling the elderly woman to death in 1978. Two months later, the authorities in Nevada took MacDonald into custody on the charge of first-degree murder. In September 2011 he was back in King County, Washington awaiting his trial under a $2 million bond.

At the opening of the MacDonald murder trial in June 2012, the defendant and the prosecutor entered into a so-called Alford plea agreement. (An Alford plea allows a defendant to agree to a sentencing deal without admitting guilt.) Pursuant to this plea, MacDonald pleaded guilty to second-degree manslaughter, a lesser homicide offense that carried a maximum sentence of five years.

On August 8, 2012, the judge sentenced the 51-year-old murderer to 16 months, with credit given for time served. That meant that Ronald Wayne MacDonald, following his sentencing hearing, walked out of the courtroom. For 34 years he had gotten away with committing a brutal murder, served a year in jail, and now was free again.

Letting a vicious killer off the hook begs the question: *Why?* The King County prosecutor's rationale for giving away the criminal justice store was as stupid as the Alford plea. According to the prosecutor, the medical examiner that performed Arlene Roberts' autopsy, and the crime scene technician who had processed the latent fingerprint evidence, were dead. So what? Arlene Roberts obviously hadn't killed herself, or died naturally.

Calling this crime a second-degree manslaughter was insane. And how did the death of the crime scene fingerprint technician affect anything? He must have written a report regarding his discoveries, and taken photographs. Fingerprints speak for themselves.

According to the Roberts case prosecutor, the cold case investigators, when they interrogated MacDonald in June 2011, didn't audio record or video tape his confession. Other than revealing their incompetence, so what? MacDonald must have signed a statement, and even if he hadn't, the detectives could take the stand and testify from their notes.

This King County prosecutor had a murder confession, plus the defendant's crime scene fingerprints. He should have made, on behalf of Arlene Roberts and her family, a better deal.

The Professor Gets Off Light

In 1972, Rafael Robb graduated from Hebrew University in Jerusalem, Israel with a bachelor's degree in economics. A few years later, he immigrated to the United States where, in 1991, he earned a Ph.D. in economics from UCLA. In 1984, now a U.S. citizen, Dr. Robb joined the teaching staff at the University of Pennsylvania. He married Ellen Gregory, a woman seven years younger than him, in 1990. Four years later, the couple had a daughter, Olivia.

As Rafael Robb's marriage fell apart, Professor Robb's career at the University of Pennsylvania flourished. In 2004, after having published dozens of important papers on game theory, a mathematical discipline used to analyze political, economic, and military strategies, the professor was granted tenure. He also became a Fellow of the Economics Society, one of the highest honors in the discipline.

In the afternoon of December 22, 2006, Professor Robb, using the non-emergency phone number rather than 911, reported that he had just discovered, upon returning home from work, that an intruder had beaten his wife to death in the kitchen of their Upper Merion, Pennsylvania home. Because Ellen Robb had been beaten beyond recognition, the responding police officers thought she had been murdered by a close-range shotgun blast to the face.

From Ellen Robb's relatives and friends, homicide detectives learned that the victim, after years of marital abuse, had recently hired a divorce attorney who planned to demand $4,000 a month in spousal support. Ellen, after living with the professor for the sake of their 12-year-old daughter, had finally decided to move out of the house.

Montgomery County District Attorney Bruce L. Castor, Jr., on January 9, 2007, charged Rafael Robb with first-degree murder. Homicide detectives considered Robb's attempt to cover his tracks by staging a home invasion quite amateurish. They believed Robb had murdered his wife to avoid the financial consequences of the upcoming divorce. Robb's attorney announced that he would produce, at the upcoming trial, security-camera footage what would prove that his client hadn't been home when his wife was murdered. Homicide investigators found numerous holes in Robb's so-called alibi.

On November 27, 2007, on the day Rafael Robb's trial was scheduled to begin, the defendant, pursuant to a plea bargain arrangement, took the opportunity to plead guilty to voluntary manslaughter, a lesser homicide offense. Standing before Common Pleas Court Judge Paul W. Tressler, the defendant said that he and Ellen, on the morning of her death, had argued over a trip she planned to take with their daughter, Olivia. "The discussion," Robb said, "was very tense. We were both anxious." (Anxious?) According to the defendant's version of the killing, when Ellen pushed him, he "just lost it." By losing it, Robb meant that he walked into the living room, grabbed an exercise bar used to do chin-ups, and used the blunt object to beat his wife's head into pulp. "I just kept flailing it," he said.

Judge Tressler, after he called the Robb homicide "the worst physical bludgeoning" he had ever seen, sentenced Rafael Robb to a five-to-ten-year prison term. The light sentence for such a brutal killing committed by an abusive husband who had tried to stage a fake burglary, shocked the victim's family and supporters.

In March 2012, after serving less than five years of his lenient sentence at a minimum security prison near Mercer, Pennsylvania 70 miles north of Pittsburgh, Rafael Robb filed a request to serve the remainder of his sentence in a Philadelphia halfway house. The Montgomery County prosecutor strenuously opposed Robb's attempt to get into a halfway facility.

Notwithstanding objections from the prosecutor and members of Ellen Robb's family still upset about the light sentence, the Pennsylvania Board of Probation and Parole, in October 2012, shocked everyone by granting Rafael Robb early parole.

On January 29, 2013, the Pennsylvania Parole Board, after meeting with Ellen Robb's family, reversed its decision to grant the ex-professor's release. His next parole review was scheduled for September 14, 2014.

Rafael Robb should have been found guilty of first-degree murder and sentenced to life without parole. Just because this brutal killer was a prominent scholar should not justify the authorities letting him get away with murdering his estranged wife in order to save the cost of a divorce. The prosecutor, in negotiating Robb's guilty plea, gave away the store.

Lenient Sentence for the Accomplice

In 2000, Peggy Sue Thomas, as Ms. Washington, participated in the U.S. Continental Beauty Pageant in Las Vegas. The 34-year-old beautician didn't win or make the top ten. Three years later, Thomas was working in a Freeland Washington beauty salon owned by Brenna Douglas who confided in her that her 32-year-old husband Russell Douglas was abusive. When Thomas relayed this information to her boyfriend James Huden, he decided to kill Russell Douglas out of revenge. (Huden had been abused as a child, and he was supposedly taking out his anger on Douglas. He and the intended victim had never met.)

On December 26, 2003, Thomas asked Russell Douglas to meet her in a remote area on Whidbey Island 30 miles north of Seattle. Thomas lured Douglas to this spot on the pretext she had a gift for his wife Brenna. As Russell Douglas waited in his Chevrolet Geo Tracker for Peggy Sue, he came face-to-face with James Huden who shot the sunglasses-wearing victim between the eyes with a .380-caliber pistol.

Homicide detectives initially suspected that Russell Douglas had been shot to death in a murder for hire plot cooked-up by his wife, the beneficiary of his $500,000 life insurance policy. Investigators caught a break in the case in August 2004 when a friend of James Huden's who had known him in Port Charlotte, Florida, called the Island County Sheriff's Office with a hot tip. The tipster, Bill Hill, said he had played in Huden's band called Buck Naked and the Xhibitionists. According to Hill, Huden had murdered Russell Douglas because Douglas had been abusing his wife. Huden's girlfriend, Peggy Sue Thomas had set the victim up by luring him to the remote spot on Whidbey Island.

Douglas case investigators received a second break in the case that summer. A man named Keith Ogden came forward with information regarding the murder weapon used in the execution-style killing. Ogden said he had showed Huden how to disassemble, clean, and fire the .380-caliber Bersa. He had also advised Huden on how to use a pillow or a plastic soda bottle to muffle the muzzle sound.

James Huden, aware that the authorities were closing in on him, fled to Veracruz, Mexico in the fall of 2004. In Mexico, under the name Maestro Jim, Huden made a living as a guitar player in his band, Buck Naked and the Xhibitionists.

In 2006, Peggy Sue Thomas, while working in Las Vegas as a limo driver, met Mark Allen, the millionaire owner of the 2009 Kentucky Derby winner, Mind That Bird. After marrying Allen, Thomas took up residence at his horse ranch in New Mexico. After the divorce a few years later, Thomas, the beneficiary of a large settlement, moved back to Whidbey Island, Washington.

The Mexican police, in June 2011, arrested James Huden on a federal unlawful flight warrant issued in the United States. U.S. Marshals returned the fugitive to Washington where he was scheduled to stand trial for the eight-year-old murder of Russell Douglas.

Huden, after turning down a plea bargain deal where he'd identify Peggy Sue Thomas as his murder accomplice, went on trial in July 2012. The defendant's wife Jean took the stand for the prosecution and testified that Huden and Thomas had confessed to her regarding their roles in the Douglas murder. Two other men testified that Huden had confessed to them as well. Because James Huden did not take the stand on his own behalf, he did not implicate Peggy Sue in the murder.

Following eight days of testimony, the jury found the defendant guilty of first-degree murder with aggravating circumstances (using a firearm). A month later, the judge sentenced 59-year-old James Edward Huden to 80 years in prison. (According to the Douglas case prosecutor, one of Thomas' latent fingerprints had been lifted from the murder weapon.)

The Huden-Thomas-Douglas murder saga came to an end on January 27, 2013 when Peggy Sue, now 47, pleaded guilty to the lesser charge of rendering criminal assistance. The guilty plea came one week before she was scheduled to go on trial for murder.

At Thomas' sentencing hearing a month after the guilty plea, Jim Douglas, the victim's father, said this to the judge: "It seems a travesty of justice that she [Thomas] would be sentenced to less than four years in prison for the cold and premeditated act that could not have happened without her involvement." The judge, ignoring the plea for more serious punishment, sentenced Thomas to four years in prison.

Peggy Sue Thomas was as much responsible for Russell Douglas' murder as the man who pulled the trigger. James Huden got 80 years. She got off light.

Shame on Ruby

In 1957, 21-year-old Ruby Klokow, a resident of Sheboygan, a Michigan Lake town of 50,000 in southern Wisconsin, physically abused and murdered her 6-month-old daughter, Jeaneen. Following the baby's suspicious death, Klokow told the police the child had fallen off the sofa. Although the autopsy revealed two brain hemorrhages, a partially collapsed lung, and three scalp bruises, injuries inconsistent with a fall from a couch, the Sheboygan County Corner ruled the baby's death accidental. As a result of this bogus manner of death ruling, the police did not conduct a homicide investigation. This stunning example of criminal justice incompetence (or indifference) is particularly tragic because the dead child had a two-year-old brother, and Klokow would give birth again.

In 1964, Ruby Klokow's infant son Scott died mysteriously in his crib. Given the suspicious death of her daughter Jeaneen seven years earlier, it's hard to understand why the authorities in Sheboygan didn't investigate the passing of this child. (Had there been an autopsy, there would have been signs of past injuries caused by abuse.) Instead of putting this homicidal mother away for life, local criminal justice personnel made it possible for this woman to continue practicing her sadistic style of parenting.

Finally, in 2008, Klokow's 53-year-old son James, who was two-years-old when his mother murdered his sister Jeaneen, came forward with his own story of parental abuse. According to James Klokow, his mother repeatedly beat him as far back as he could remember. At school he would lie to his teachers regarding how he had collected all of the bruises on his body, including choke marks on his neck. His mother frequently made him stand in a corner all day long during which time she threw knives and scissors at him. She also blinded him in one eye. When he turned thirteen, James, suffering from post-traumatic stress disorder, ran away from home. After that, he was abused by a series of foster parents until the age of eighteen.

After James Klokow came forward with his story of child abuse, Judy Post, Ruby Klokow's younger sister, told the authorities that Ruby had physically abused her when they were children. Post also reported having seen Ruby throw her infant daughter Jeaneen to the ground.

In February 2011, a Sheboygan County prosecutor charged the 74-year-old Klokow with second-degree murder in the 1957 death of Jeaneen. A forensic pathologist took the stand at a preliminary hearing and testified that the infant's autopsy revealed injuries too severe to have been caused by a fall off a sofa. Klokow's attorney, after getting her released on bail, delayed matters by claiming that his client was not mentally competent to stand trial.

On February 25, 2013, the day Ruby Klokow was scheduled to go on trial for the murder of her daughter, she entered a plea of no contest to the second-degree murder charge.

Sheboygan County Judge Angela Sutkiewicz, pursuant to a plea-bargain agreement worked out between the defendant's attorney and the prosecutor, sentenced Klokow to 45 days in jail and ten years probation.

To reporters following the no contest plea, Klokow's attorney, Kirk Obear, said trying his client for murder after all of these years would be "unfair" because so many witnesses have died. The defense attorney went on to say that Klokow was "dealing with a lot of heartache."

District Attorney Joe DeCecco in explaining to the media why he signed-off on the plea deal mentioned Klokow's age and poor health. The prosecutor also said that because the statute of limitations did not allow him to charge Klokow with the lesser murder that, under the circumstances, may have been difficult.

It's not that the prosecution in this case didn't have evidence. In addition to the defendant's confession, the district attorney had her sister's testimony, and a compelling witness in her son, James Klokow. This prosecutor, in the name of justice, should have pushed forward with the trial. What did he have to lose? What's the point of 45 days in jail, and ten years of probation?

Judge Goes Soft On Baby Killer

On November 1, 2011, police officers in Cortez, Colorado, a town of 8,000 in the southwest corner of the state, responded to a call involving an infant who was not breathing. At the residence shared by Dylan Kuhn and his girlfriend April Coleman, police discovered the corpse of their 6-month-old daughter, Sailor Serenity Kuhn.

Officers found the baby lying half off the bed with a blanket wrapped around her neck. One didn't have to be a trained, experienced homicide detective to know this was the scene of a crime rather than a natural or accidental death.

According to the 19-year-old father of the dead baby, she had been crying in her bed when he returned home from a Halloween party. He calmed her down and went to bed himself. The next morning, Kuhn found the baby with the blanket wrapped around her neck. Kuhn said that a few days before her death, the infant had fallen off the couch and bumped her head.

Following the autopsy, the Montezuma County Medical Examiner announced that the child's fatal injuries, a subdural hematoma and hemorrhaging in her optic nerve sheath, revealed that someone had slammed the child violently against a soft but unyielding surface such as a mattress. The medical examiner ruled the baby's manner of death a homicide. The head trauma was too severe to have been caused by a fall off a sofa.When police interrogators confronted Kuhn with the forensic pathologist's findings, he admitted slamming the baby down hard on the mattress. He also confessed to placing the blanket around his daughter's neck to throw off investigators. He said he didn't mean to hurt his daughter. As to why he had lied to the police, Kuhn said he was scared, and worried what his girlfriend would think of him if he told the truth. The Montezuma County district attorney charged Dylan Kuhn with child abuse causing death, and the offense of manslaughter.

Several months after Kuhn's arrest, District Attorney Russell Wasley, perhaps because of procedural mistakes made by the police and his office, approached Kuhn with a plea-bargain offer. If the defendant came clean, the prosecutor would drop the child abuse causing death charge. If the defendant pleaded guilty to manslaughter, the worst sentence he could get would be four years in prison.

In accepting the deal, Kuhn admitted that he had "aggressively" put the baby to bed that night. She had been crying, he became frustrated, told her to "shut-up" then slammed her body against the mattress. "I put her to bed too hard," he said. After his confession, Kuhn asked to consult with a defense attorney. The defendant said he was too young to understand how much trouble he might be in. (Kuhn was 19, old enough to vote and serve in the military. Under Colorado law, he is considered an adult. He had assaulted and killed his 6-month-old daughter. He wasn't retarded, or insane. He knew he had committed a terrible crime. That's why he lied to the police.)

On October 2, 2012, Dylan Kuhn entered his guilty plea to the charge of manslaughter before District Court Judge Douglas Walker. Before imposing his sentence, Judge Walker heard from Kuhn's girlfriend (and mother of the dead baby) and his mother. According to April Coleman, Kuhn had always been good to his daughter. The defendant's mother, Vicki Espinoza, told the court that she was worried about what might happen to her son if he had to serve time in prison. "I don't know why it [the case] went this far," she said. "It was an accident."

Judge Walker agreed with the defendant's mother that prison might not be a good thing for her son. The judge also noted that the defendant was young, and had no history of violent crime prior to killing his daughter. In addressing Kuhn, the judge said, "I am giving you an opportunity. Make the best of this opportunity, if nothing else, to honor your daughter's memory."

The judge's "opportunity" was this: He sentenced Dylan Kuhn to 90 days in jail, and four years of probation. Lest critics characterized this sentence as insanely lenient, Judge Walker ordered Kuhn to take parenting classes. The judge also ordered Kuhn to undergo mental and substance abuse evaluation. And finally, Kuhn, during his four-year probationary period, was prohibited from being alone with any child under the age of ten.

Murder Mastermind Gets Off Light

Lee D. Smith lived with his wife Lana and their daughter in Basehor, Kansas, a suburban community of 5,000 across the line from Kansas City, Missouri. The 37-year-old and his wife had been arguing about money that led to his decision to hire someone to kill her.

On May 8, 2012, Smith offed the job to a man who seemed interested.

Smith drove the potential hit man to his wife's place of work and showed him where she parked her car. Smith also outlined her daily routine, and described what she looked like to the man he hoped would kill her. Smith even offered this man advice on how to accomplish the job. He suggested catching his murder target's attention by calling out her name then shooting her when she turned in response. The man solicited for the hit accepted the assignment, and was given $400 in upfront money. Smith promised the rest--$1,800--when his wife was dead.

The next day, instead of carrying out the murder of Lana Smith, the would-be hit man went to the police. Working as an undercover operative, the phony hit man called the murder-for-hire mastermind and reported that he was holding his wife and his daughter hostage. Did Mr. Smith want them both murdered? Smith instructed the informant to release his daughter. But kill his wife, he said.

The undercover hit man, an hour later, called Smith. He informed the murder-for-hire mastermind that his wife was dead. They agreed to meet later that afternoon at a grocery store where Smith would pay the hit man the balance due on the murder contract. Before he had a chance to meet the hit man, Smith received a call from a police officer that asked him to come to the station to pick up his daughter. When Smith showed up for the girl, officers took him into custody.

The local police turned the Smith case over to the FBI, and on May 28, 2012, an Assistant United States Attorney in Kansas City charged Lee Smith with soliciting his wife's murder. In October, Smith pleaded guilty to the federal charge.

A federal judge in Kansas City, on February 28, 2013, sentenced the murder-for-hire mastermind to eight years in prison. Eight years. Had Smith picked a triggerman that had been willing to complete the job, his wife would be dead. How is this any different than Smith putting a gun to his wife's head, a firearm he thought was loaded, and pulling the trigger?

The Rock Star Who Wanted His Wife Dead

In 2000, 19-year-old guitarist Tim Lambesis, a graduate of a San Diego area Christian high school, formed a heavy mental band called "As I Lay Dying" (the title of a William Faulkner novel). The group's sixth album came out in the fall of 2012 prior to a tour of Asia. The band was scheduled to kick-off a U.S. tour from Oklahoma City on May 30, 2013. Many of the band's songs included Christian themes of forgiveness and struggle.

In 2011, Lambesis and his wife Meggan separated. According to divorce papers, she accused him of becoming emotionally distant from her and the three children they adopted from Ethiopia. She complained that he had become obsessed with bodybuilding and touring. Meggan also accused her estranged husband of having a "string of women."

In April 2013, the 32-year-old rock star, on two occasions, confided to a man who worked out at his gym that he wanted to have his wife killed. Lambesis told this man his wife made it difficult for him to visit his children. The man in the gym Lambesis reached out to reported Lambesis' homicidal wishes to the San Diego County Sheriff's Office. Shortly thereafter, Lambesis met with an undercover police officer posing as a hit man named "Red".

In the recorded murder-for-hire meeting, the heavy metal rocker handed Red an envelope containing $1,000 in cash, a photograph of his wife, the security gate code to the Encinitas, California estate, and a list of dates in which Lambesis would have an alibi. According to court documents, the murder-for-hire mastermind also gave the undercover sheriff's department officer instructions on how to kill Meggan Lambesis.

At two in the afternoon of Tuesday, May 7, 2013, San Diego sheriff's deputies arrested Lambesis as he shopped at a mall in Oceanside. The officers booked him into the Vista Jail on the charge of solicitation of murder.

The day after his arrest, at his arraignment, Lambesis pleaded not guilty to the murder solicitation charge. The judge set his bail at $3 million. Forty-eight days later Lambesis posted his bond. The judge required him to wear a GPS device.

The murder-for-hire suspect's attorney told reporters that a man in the gym had set up his client. If convicted as charged Lambesis faced up to nine years in prison. His fans and people who know the entertainer expressed shock over the murder-for-hire accusation.

On September 16, 2013, the Superior Court Judge, after hearing preliminary hearing testimony from the undercover officer and other prosecution witnesses, bound the murder-for-hire case over for trial.

In February 2014, Lambesis pleaded guilty in a Vista, California courtroom of soliciting an undercover officer to murder his wife. At his sentencing hearing on May 16, 2014, the former rock star's attorney said his client suffered brain damage as a result of using steroids. The deputy district attorney dismissed the claim. She called it a flimsy, illogical excuse for what in reality was a calculated plan to have a person murdered.

The judge sentenced Lambesis to six years in prison.

How Many Murder Victims?

On April 11, 2011, police officers in Reno, Nevada arrested 77-year-old Joseph Naso on four first-degree murder charges filed against him in Marin

County California. The former commercial photographer stood accused of raping and murdering four Bay Area prostitutes between 1977 and 1994. The victims, Roxene Roggasch, Carmen Colen, Pamela Parsons, and Tracy Tafoya ranged in age from 18 to 38, and each had first and last names that began with the same letter.

Forensic scientists had connected Naso to two of the victims through DNA. A search of his house produced several nude photographs of women who appeared unconscious or dead. Police officers also found a so-called "rape diary" containing narrative accounts of women and girls who had been picked up and raped. The murder suspect's house was also littered with female mannequin parts and women's lingerie. In Naso's safety deposit box, searchers found a passport bearing the name Sara Dylan. (A skull, found years earlier in Nevada, matched Dylan's mother's DNA.) Naso's safety deposit box also contained $152,400 in cash.

The Joseph Naso serial murder trial got underway in San Rafael California in June 2013. The prosecutor, in her opening statement to the jury, said the state would prove that Naso had drugged, raped, and photographed the four victims. He strangled them to death then dumped their nude bodies in remote areas in northern California.

Naso, who represented himself at the trial, told the jury that he was not the monster the prosecution was trying to make him out to be. The defendant said the nude women he had photographed had been willing models. "I don't kill people, and there's no evidence of that in my writings and photography."

Following two months of evidence that featured the defendant's rape diary, the nude photographs, and the DNA evidence linking Naso to two of the murder victims, the case went to the jury. During the trial, Naso, as his own attorney, was a courtroom fool and tried the patience of the judge. On August 19, 2013, after deliberating seven hours over a period of two days, the jury found the defendant guilty of the four counts of first-degree murder. The verdict also included a finding of special circumstances that made Naso eligible for the death penalty.

While the jury recommended the death penalty in the Naso case, there was no chance the state would put him to death. In 2006 a federal judge had put California's executions on hold until the state modified its execution protocols. Naso joined the 725 inmates who lived on California's death row. While some politicians and judges threw roadblocks in the path of the state's death penalty procedure, juries in California continued to impose the death sentence. (In July 2014, the California Supreme Court ruled the death penalty unconstitutional.)

Homicide investigators believed that Naso raped and murdered three 11-year-old girls between 1971 and 1973 in Rochester, New York. Naso had been living in the city when these murders occurred. These victims had first and last names that began with the same letter. One of the girls, Carmen Colon, had the same name of one of the women Naso killed in California. Detectives also believed that Joseph Naso murdered at least ten other women. Naso, following the verdict, insisted that he had not raped or killed anyone.

Unfit for Civilized Society

Donald Williams, Jr., born and raised in a crime-ridden Philadelphia neighborhood to parents who physically abused him and spent their welfare money on crack, murdered a man in 1994. The 20-year-old with a low I.Q. and no idea how to make his way in civilized society, had assaulted his former girlfriend, then killed her boyfriend. Convicted of third-degree murder in 1996, the judge sentenced Williams to ten years in prison. (In Pennsylvania, third-degree murder convictions are almost always the result of plea deals.)

Early in 2009, Williams began dating a woman from Reading, Pennsylvania named Maria Serrano. In May of that year, after letting him move in with her, Serrano kicked the 35-year-old out of her house. The infuriated ex-con took up residence in a halfway house in Reading.

On June 25, 2009, Williams returned to Serrano's home. That night he raped her. But he didn't leave it at that. While she took a shower, he stabbed her with a screwdriver. Williams then threw the 49-year-old woman down her basement steps, doused her with gasoline, lit her up and left her for dead.

Serrano dialed 911 and screamed, "Oh my God, I am bleeding! Hurry up! There is a fire. I am burning all over the place! There is a fire in the house! Hurry up!" Paramedics rushed the badly burned woman to the Lehigh Valley Burn Center near Allentown, Pennsylvania. On August 8, 2009, she died of her injuries.

A Berks County prosecutor charged Williams, who was already in custody on the rape, arson, and aggravated assault charges, with first-degree murder. The prosecutor said he would seek the death penalty in this case.

The Williams trial got underway on September 12, 2013 before Berks County Judge Scott D. Keller and a jury of seven women and five men. When Assistant District Attorney Dennis J. Skayhan rested his case, there was no doubt who had tortured and murdered Maria Serrano. Before she died, the victim had identified Williams as her attacker. A state forensic expert had connected the defendant to the rape though his DNA.

Public defender Paul Yessler put Williams on the stand. The defendant did not deny that he had raped, stabbed, and set fire to the woman he had thrown down a flight of stairs. In a bold and obvious lie that did not go over well with the jurors, Williams claimed to have "flipped-out" that night after catching Serrano having sex with his younger brother.

Prosecutor Skayhan, as part of his closing argument, played the victim's 911 tape. Public defender Yessler, in his closing statement, emphasized the defendant's 83 I.Q., his ghetto upbringing, and his childhood abuse. In referring to Williams, Yessler said, "This guy did not have a chance from the get-go."

Six days after the opening of the trial, the jury, after deliberating six hours, found Williams guilty of rape, arson, and first-degree murder. The defendant showed no emotion at the reading of the verdict.

Because the prosecution sought the death penalty in this case, the judge scheduled a two-day sentence hearing. In arguing for the death sentence, prosecutor Skayhan focused on how the tortured victim had died a slow, agonizing death. Public defender Yessler, in pushing for life, highlighted the defendant's low I.Q. and inability to control his impulses.

The jury, after deliberating two hours on the sentencing issue, informed Judge Keller that a consensus could not be reached. The judge had no choice but to sentence Donald Williams to life in prison without parole.

In speaking directly to the convicted murderer, Judge Keller made no secret of where he stood on the question of punishment in this case. "You deserved the death penalty," he said without trying to disguise his disgust at the jury's performance. "It was torture in any man or woman's world. You inflicted a considerable amount of pain and suffering on a victim which is unnecessary, heinous, atrocious, and cruel."

While few would disagree with the judge's analysis of this murderer, William's low I.Q. would probably have kept him out of the death chamber anyway. Appellate judges do not like the idea of executing stupid people.

A Suspicious Drowning

After a party on the night of June 18, 1993, 35-year-old Jon Lang's wife Debbie died in the couple's swimming pool. The drowning took place in Patterson Township not far from the western Pennsylvania town of Industry. The Beaver County coroner ruled the death accidental.

Nineteen years after Debbie Lang's drowning, a coroner's jury sitting in Beaver, Pennsylvania ruled that Debbie Lang's death had been caused by a criminal act. In November 2012, a Beaver County prosecutor charged Jon Lang, now 54, with the murder of his wife.

Whenever a suspect is charged with murder decades after the questioned death, the newly discovered evidence is usually a crime scene fingerprint identification or DNA evidence that links the defendant to the victim or the site of the murder. It's forensic science that usually saves the day in cold-case murder investigations.

In the Lang case, however, the evidence supporting the long delayed murder charge lacked the incriminating value of physical evidence. The incriminating evidence was in the form of the most unreliable evidence of all--eyewitness testimony.

The new testimony in the Lang murder consisted of an event the witness had seen nineteen years ago when he was 16-years-old. Jamie Darlington told a panel of Beaver County coroner's jurors that on June 18, 1993, he was a guest at the Long residence. That night, when Darlington looked out a second-story window, he saw Jon Lang push his wife into the swimming pool. According to the witness, Mr. Long kept his struggling wife submerged by holding her down with a long-handled pool skimmer.

According to the 25-year-old's coroner's jury testimony, Mr. Lang became aware that he had been seen murdering his wife. When Lang entered the house after the drowning, he threatened the boy. "You didn't hear anything," he said. "And you didn't see nothing." Darlington said he didn't report the homicide out of fear for his own life.

William Difenderfer, Jon Lang's attorney, called Jamie Darlington's testimony "preposterous." The attorney asserted that Darlington was telling this story now because he was himself in trouble with the law. (In this regard, Darlington was not unlike a jailhouse snitch, the absolute bottom of the evidentiary totem pole.)

In speaking to a local television reporter after the coroner's jury verdict, Gloria Caler, a Lang neighbor in 1993, said, "I just never believed it was an accident because the lady couldn't swim and the pool was green and it was like, who would want to go swimming in a pool like that? At the time I never thought it was an accident, but nothing came about it."

On December 9, 2013, the first day of Jon Lang's murder trial, the defendant pleaded no contest to voluntary manslaughter, a lesser homicide offense. While the no-contest plea was not an acknowledgement of criminal culpability, it could nevertheless be interpreted as an admission of guilt. Why else would Jon Lang allow himself to be convicted on such flimsy evidence?

The Beaver County Judge sentenced Jon Lang to three to six years in prison, a light sentence if he murdered his wife in cold blood.

The Shunned Amish Mastermind

In 2009, Eli Weaver, his wife Barbara, and their five children resided in central Ohio's Amish heartland. He owned a gun shop near his Wayne County farm near Apple Creek. Over the past several years, leaders of the Amish community had thrown him out of the church for running around with English women he had met online. Eli would ask for forgiveness, be accepted back into the fold then get into trouble again with the same un-Amish behavior.

The 23-year-old Amish man, in 2003, met an English woman named Barbara Raber. The 33-year-old from Millersburg, Ohio made extra money driving Amish people from place to place. The relationship between Eli and his driver eventually became sexual.

Beginning in the fall of 2008, Weaver and Raber began discussing how to murder his wife. In 2009, they exchanged a series of text messages in which they discussed various plans on how to pull off the crime.

At seven on the morning of June 2, 2009, one of the Weaver children ran to a neighbor's house with shocking news. Someone, during the night, had shot and killed his mother in her bed. Eli, at that moment, was fishing on Lake Erie. The neighbor and the boy entered the Weaver house where Barbara Weaver lay in her blood-soaked bed with a gaping gunshot wound in her chest.

At 11:30 that morning, Wayne County Coroner Dr. Amy Joliff pronounced Barbara Weaver dead at the scene. Dr. Lisa Kohler, the Summit County Chief Medical Examiner, performed the autopsy. According to the forensic pathologist, the victim had been killed by a single shotgun blast to the right side of her chest. Several shotgun pellets were removed from the corpse. Dr. Kohler estimated the time of death as sometime between midnight and three o'clock that morning.

John Gardner, a firearms expert with the Ohio Bureau of Criminal Investigation identified the death scene pellets as number six shot. This ammunition could have been fired from shotguns of four different gauges. Gardner believed the murder weapon was a .410-gauge shotgun.

Detectives with the Wayne County Sheriff's Office seized two .410 shotguns from Eli Weaver's gun shop. Officers also recovered a box of .410 shells with one round missing. Investigators in the murder house found an amount of cash sitting on a table suggesting that robbery had not been the motive in this killing.

Questioned by detectives upon his return from the Lake Erie fishing trip, Eli denied any involvement in his wife's murder.

On June 10, 2009, detectives arrested Eli Weaver after he confessed to helping Barbara Weaver murder his wife. She had pulled the trigger while he was fishing.

That day, pursuant to a search of Raber's house in Millersburg, officers found a notebook in which she had written out a list of various poisons. At the police station following her arrest, she denied knowledge of the murder. She explained the incriminating text messages to and from Eli as nothing more than joking around.

The day after Raber's arrest, upon further questioning, she admitted going to the Weaver house around four in the morning armed with a .410-gauge shotgun. Eli had left the basement door unlocked for her. She said her intent was merely to frighten Barbara Weaver, but when she entered the bedroom, the gun discharged accidentally. Raber's interrogators didn't buy the accidental shooting story, but asked her to sign a written statement to that effect. She refused and asked to see a lawyer. The interrogation, at that point, came to an end.

On August 17, 2009, Eli Weaver agreed to plead guilty to conspiracy to commit murder. As part of the plea deal, he promised to testify for the prosecution at Barbara Raber's murder trial.

The Raber murder trial got underway on September 16, 2009 in Wooster, Ohio with Judge Robert J. Brown presiding. Wayne County prosecutor Edna J. Boyle, following testimony from the county coroner, the medical examiner, and several police officers, put Dena Unangst on the stand. Unangst had been the defendant's cellmate at the Wayne County Jail. According to this witness, Raber admitted to her that she had purchased a .410 shotgun after Eli Weaver, on numerous occasions, begged her to murder his wife. Raber also asked Unangst if she knew how long a fingerprint could last on a gun. (Under ideal conditions, 50 years or more.)

Larry Miller, the owner of the gun store took the stand and testified that the defendant had purchased a .410 on November 15, 2008.

On September 30, 2009, prosecutor Boyle put the shunned Amish man on the stand. Elie Weaver, now 29, testified that when he mentioned getting rid of his wife, a woman he didn't love, Raber "ran away with the idea." At one point, during one of their homicide planning conversations, she gave him a bottle of what she called "poison pills." Eli said he rejected poisoning as a way of killing his wife.

On the day before the murder, Eli informed Raber that at three the next morning he would be leaving the house on a fishing trip. He'd leave the basement door open for her. Shortly after he left the house that morning, Raber sent him a text in which she asked how she was supposed to see in the dark. "It's too scary," she wrote. Eli advised her to take a flashlight.

At 3:25 AM Raber texted that, "I'm scared, where are you?" Texting that he was in Wooster, Eli cautioned Raber not to leave anything behind at the murder scene.

According to the prosecutor's star witness, on June 9, the day before Eli and his trigger woman were arrested, they had a conversation in his barn. She described the night she killed Barbara Weaver and said she was "sorry for everything." Before parting company, Raber asked Eli how to clean a gun so it looked like it hadn't been recently fired.

Assistant public defender John J. Leonard tried to convince the jury that Eli Weaver, not his client, had murdered the victim. The defense attorney explained Raber's incriminating statement to detectives as the produce of fear and confusion. Leonard rested his defense without putting Barbara Raber on the stand.

On October 1, 2009, the jury found the defendant guilty as charged. Judge Brown sentenced the 39-year-old woman to 23 years in prison. The judge sentenced Eli Weaver to 15 years to life.

Weaver's light sentence illustrates, from the point of view of a guilty murder mastermind, the value of pleading guilty and testifying against an accomplice. Raber's sentence, given the cold-bloodedness of the killing and the innocence of the victim, was also lenient.

Rape

A Fake Crime and Ridiculous Sentence

In 2008, Linsey and Gary Attridge were married in the central Scotland town of Grangemouth. The 26-year-old bride had grown up in Grangemouth where her mother worked as a seamstress and her father was a window cleaner. Linsey and her new husband, a financial advisor, honeymooned in Malta.

Less than two years after the wedding, Linsey was unhappy with her marriage. In August 2010, after meeting kickboxing instructor Nick Smith online, Linsey and her daughter moved into the 32-year-old's house in the northern city of Aberdeen. By the summer of 2011, that relationship had fallen apart after Linsey confessed to having sex with one of Nick Smith's friends while he slept. Although they were no longer a couple, Nick allowed Linsey and her daughter, to whom he had become a surrogate father, to continue living in his house.

In August 2011, while browsing through Facebook pages, Linsey came across a photograph of 26-year-old Philip McDonald, a cook at a downtown Aberdeen cafe. He was pictured with his 14-year-old brother James. Philip lived outside of the city in a modest flat with his partner Kelly Fraser and their daughter. To Linsey, Philip and James McDonald were total strangers.

A few days after stumbling across the Facebook photograph, Linsey Attridge, in a scheme to rekindle her relationship with Nick Smith, decided to falsely report that that Philip and James McDonald had broken into her house and brutally raped her. Before alerting the authorities, she staged the crime by overturning furniture, punching herself in the face, and ripping her clothing.

Police officers who responded to the false rape report found a woman who looked and acted as though she had been beaten and sexually assaulted. She submitted herself to various physical examinations including tests for sexually transmitted diseases. In an act of extreme self-centered cruelty, Linsey Attridge identified Philip and James McDonald as her rapists. (Since they were total strangers, I don't know how Linsey explained knowing who her attackers were.)

Two days after receiving the false crime report, police officers arrested the younger brother at his mother's house. James McDonald was a student at a residential school for teenagers with behavioral problems. Less than an hour after taking James into custody, police officers walked into the cafe where Philip worked as a cook.

On the worst day of Philip McDonald's life, the detectives who showed up at the cafe told Philip that he and his brother were the prime suspects in a brutal rape case. The officers asked the shocked and frightened young man to accompany them to the police station for questioning. In the police vehicle en route to police headquarters, the officers identified the victim and described the home invasion and crime. Philip broke down and cried. (The officers probably took that as a sign of guilt.)

At the police station, detectives photographed, fingerprinted, and swabbed the rape suspect for DNA. During the five-hour interrogation, when a detective revealed exactly when the crime had taken place, Philip was relieved. While the two men were raping Linsey Attridge, Philip was at home putting his daughter to bed. Several members of his family were in the house with him that night. His relatives would vouch for his whereabouts at the time of the rape. He had an alibi.

The detectives questioning Philip were not interested in his so-called alibi. Everyone had an alibi. Big deal. Philip didn't realize that police investigators, once they have a suspect in their cross-hairs, are extremely reluctant, even in the face of exonerating evidence, to change targets.

Over the next two months Philip McDonald's life was a living hell. He couldn't be out in public without being harassed, and had to enroll his daughter in another school. By October 2011, Linsey Attridge's story began to unravel. When pressed by skeptical detectives, she admitted that she had made the entire story up. She had done it in an effort to attract attention and sympathy from her estranged boyfriend, Nick Smith. In so doing, she had put Philip and his brother through hell, wasted police resources, and made the detectives look like monkeys. Cops hate people who lie to them about as much as they hate rapists.

Shortly after Linsey Attridge's false report confession, a pair of detectives walked into the cafe to inform Philip that he was in the clear. That was it. Out of the blue he was accused of rape, and out of the blue he was told that his ordeal had ended. The cops left the restaurant without offering even an insincere apology.

A local prosecutor charged Linsey Attridge with the crime of filing a false report. In June 2013, the defendant pleaded guilty to the charge in an

Aberdeen courtroom. The judge shocked everyone by sentencing Attridge to 200 hours of community service and two years probation. Nick Smith, her former boyfriend, was in the courtroom that day. He told reporters outside the court house that he thought the judge's sentence was "ridiculous." He was right.

Blaming the Victim

Police in Billings Montana in 2008 arrested 49-year-old Stacey Dean Rambold, a teacher at the local high school. Rambold stood accused of having a sexual relationship with Cherice Morales, a 14-year-old student. A Yellowstone County prosecutor charged Rambold with three counts of sexual intercourse without consent. (By law, a person under the age of 16 cannot consent to sex with an adult. In some states the crime is called statutory rape.)

In 2004 administrators at Billings Senior High School had warned Rambold against touching or being alone with female students.

Cherice Moralises, just before her 17th birthday in 2010, committed suicide. At the time of this troubled girl's death, the criminal case against her former teacher was pending. The girl's mother, Auliea Halon, sued the school district for wrongful death. The case was quickly settled for $91,000.

The Yellowstone County prosecutor, as a result of Morales' suicide, offered Stacey Rambold a deal. If he confessed to one count of sexual intercourse without consent, and promised to enter a sex offender treatment program, the charges would be dropped. Rambold accepted the offer.

In August 2012, Rambold began skipping meetings with his counselors, and didn't tell them about unsupervised visits he was having with girls. In November, the head of the sex treatment facility kicked him out of the program. When Deputy Chief Yellowstone County prosecutor Rod Souza learned that Rambold had violated the terms of their agreement, he reinstated the original charges against the former teacher.

Rambold's attorney, Jay Lansing, told reporters that the girls Rambold had visited without supervision were members of his family. Moreover, his client had enrolled in another sex treatment program.

On August 26, 2013, the Rambold case came before 66-year-old District Court Judge G. Todd Baugh. Before being elected to the bench in 1985, Baugh had served as a federal magistrate. Prior to that, he practiced law in Billings. The judge was running, unopposed, for his fifth term on the bench.

In September 2011, Judge Baugh had sentenced a 26-year-old defendant to 50 years in prison for the rape on an 11-year-old girl. A year later he sent a man to prison for 25 years for possessing child pornography. Judge Baugh did not have a reputation for going easy on sex offenders.

At the Rambold hearing, Judge Baugh dismissed the new charges against the defendant. The judge said that Rambold's being kicked out of the sex program did not justify the 2008 sexual intercourse without consent charges. The remaining issue before the judge involved Rambold's sentence based upon his 2010 admission of guilt on the single count of sexual intercourse without consent.

Yellowstone County Chief Deputy prosecutor Rod Souza proposed a 20-year sentence with 10 years suspended. Defense attorney Jay Lansing suggested that because Rambold had lost his job, his license to teach, his house and his wife, he had been punished enough. Attorney Lansing asked Judge Baugh to suspend all but 30 days of a 15-year sentence. The attorney pointed out that Mr. Rambold had continued his sex rehabilitation program with another treatment facility.

Judge Baugh said that he had reviewed the videotaped police interviews of Cherice Morales. From this he had concluded that even though the victim was 35 years younger than her teacher, she was "as much in control of the situation" as the defendant. Judge Baugh said that the 14-year-old was "older than her chronological age." The judge considered this a major mitigating factor in the case.

Judge Baugh suspended all but 30 days of Rambold's 15-year sentence. After spending a month in jail, the former teacher would be on probation for 15 years. He would also have to register as a sex offender.

Upon hearing this sentence, the dead girl's mother, Auilea Hanlon, stormed out of the courtroom. When she spoke to reports after the hearing, Hanlon said, " I guess somehow it makes a rape more acceptable if you can blame the victim, even if she was only fourteen."

In a matter of hours following the sentence, local citizens were signing an online petition that called for Judge Baugh to resign. Marion Bradley, the director of the Montana National Organization for Women told reporters, "Rape is rape. She was 14-years-old, and she was not an age where she could give consent, and he groomed her like any pedophile. Unless we show our outrage, none of our children are safe."

On the day following his controversial and extremely unpopular sentencing of the former high school teacher, Judge Baugh, in speaking to reporters, stood by his ruling. "Obviously," he said, "a 14-year-old can't consent. I think that people have in mind that this was some violent, forcible, horrible rape. It was horrible enough as it is, just given her age, but it wasn't this forcible beat-up rape. I think what people are seeing is a sentence for rape of 30 days. Obviously on the face of it, if you look at it that way, it's crazy. No wonder people are upset. I'd be upset, too, if that happened."

The next day, Judge Baugh did concede that he deserved to be criticized for his "chronological age" comment. He apologized for that but it was too late for apologies.

Yellowstone County Attorney Scott Twito, in responding to Judge Baugh's sentence, said, "I have no legal authority whatsoever to appeal a sentence handed down by a judge."

As of August 29, 2013, the day hundreds of anti-Baugh demonstrators gathered in Billings to protest the sentence, the online petition calling for the judges' resignation had collected 26,350 signatures.

Soft On Rapists: Two Judges

On December 27, 2012, 44-year-old soccer coach Timothy Lyman hosted a party for his players at his Oakdale, California house. The coach provided his young partygoers with vodka and rum. One of his guests, a 16-year-old girl, after having consensual sex with a boy her age in one of Lyman's bedrooms, passed out from the effects of alcohol. She awoke to find her coach performing oral sex on her.

On November 12, 2013, after Timothy Lyman pleaded no contest to rape, Stanislaus County Judge Marie Silveira sentenced the coach to three years probation. Lyman was also ordered to sign up as a sex offender. The prosecutor and members of the victim's family were shocked and outraged by the judge's light sentence.

In speaking to reporters after Lyman's sentencing, the victim's father said, "Whoever would do this to a 16-year-old girl is just sick. This has devastated my family. There have been lots of sleepless nights for my daughter and sleepless nights for myself. I'm just sick."

In 2007, 19-year-old Austin Smith Clem had, on two occasions, forcible sex with 14-year-old Courtney Andrews. The rapes took place in Athens, Alabama. Clem swore the girl to secrecy. Moreover, if she told anyone, he threatened to harm her and her parents.

Four years later, at age 23, Clem forcibly raped Andrews who was then eighteen. This time she asked a friend to report the assault to her parents.

In September 2013, the Limestone County jury, after deliberating just two hours, found Austin Smith Clem guilty of two counts of second-degree rape and one count of first-degree rape. On November 13, 2013, Judge James Woodroof sentenced the convicted rapist to a non-custody correctional program designed to make offenders "likely to maintain a productive and law abiding life as a result of accountability, guidance, and direction to services needed."

Clem, after completing the two-year program for "nonviolent, low-level offenders," would be placed on probation for three years. He would also have to pay a $2,381 fine and register as a sex offender.

In response to Judge Woodroof's sentence, Courtney Andrews told reporters that she was "livid" and afraid for her family. The rape victim's father said this: "We thought justice was finally being served, and although the system was very slow, it was not totally broken. We were forced to hear a judge hand down a light sentence."

House Detention

In 2008, Mandy Wise kicked her husband, David Wise, out of their home in Indianapolis, Indiana then filed for divorce. After eleven years of marriage, she had discovered, on his cell phone, video recordings of him having sex with her. She was unconscious. The tapes revealed to Mandy that she had been surreptitiously drugged and raped by her husband.

When confronted with the tapes, David responded with the following email: "I was taking advantage of you in your sleep and you kept coming to me and telling me it was not okay. I needed to stop." He did not admit to drugging her, and they never, according to Mandy, discussed the matter prior to her discovery of the videotapes.

In January 2010, not long after the finalization of the divorce, Mandy, now going by her maiden name Boardman, complained to the police that her ex-husband had been harassing her with repeated phone calls and text messages. She also claimed that David Wise had threatened to kill the man she was then engaged to. A judge granted her a protection order, but Wise was not charged with any crime.

In 2011, two years after the divorce, Mandy reported the rapes to the police. As evidence, she submitted a DVD copy of the sex tapes. When asked to explain the delay in reporting the rapes and submitting the evidence, Mandy said she didn't want their two children to grow up without a father.

A Marion County prosecutor charged David Wise with one count of rape, and five felony counts of criminal deviate conduct. If convicted as charged, he faced a maximum sentence of forty years in prison. After spending 24 days in the county detention center, David Wise made bail and was released to await his trial.

The David Wise rape trial began in April 2014 in Indianapolis. Mandy Boardman's testimony for the prosecution comprised the principal evidence in the three-day proceeding. She took the stand and told the jury that on numerous occasions she awoke with the feeling that her body had been "messed with." One time she woke up with a pill still dissolving in her mouth. She had also discovered, in the bedroom, eyedroppers that were not hers.

Following two days of testimony, the case went to the jury. After a brief deliberation, the jurors returned a verdict of guilty on all counts. The judge set Friday, May 16, 2014 as the sentencing date. On that day, the prosecutor asked the judge to sentence Wise to twenty years in prison. The convicted man's attorney argued for two years of house detention.

Marion County Superior Court Judge Kurt Eisgruber, on May 16, sentenced the 52-year-old rapist to twenty years with twelve years suspended. David Wise would serve the remaining eight years wearing a GPS monitoring device in his home. Following the house detention, he would serve two years of probation.

Following the sentencing hearing, Wise's attorney, Elizabeth Milliken, told reporters that she planned to appeal her client's conviction.

On Monday, May 19, 2014, Mandy Boardman, in speaking to a reporter with the *Indianapolis Star*, said, "I was very pleased with the conviction. The sentencing was a punch in the gut by the justice system. During the reading of the sentence the judge looked at me before he gave the final decision. I was told that I needed to forgive my attacker and move on. I received zero justice on Friday." (If this victim needed to forgive anyone, it was the judge.)

Boardman, to a reporter with the *Los Angeles Times,* added: "I never thought he [Wise] would be at home, being able to have the same rights and privileges that I do."

Crimes Committed on Parole

Repeat Offenders

Most crimes are committed by repeat offenders often arrested but rarely imprisoned…Among that small percentage of hardened, repeat offenders who are apprehended, convicted, and imprisoned, few will spend very long under lock and key. And within a short time after release on parole, most resume their criminal careers. Proof of this lies in many studies showing that paroled inmates have high rates of "recidivism" (or relapse into crime). Depending on how recidivism is measured, fully a third to half of all paroled inmates are returned to prison within a year or two--and this despite the very low chance of being arrested for any of their subsequent crimes. As every criminal knows, the "criminal justice system" is a sham.

Robert James Bidinotto, *Criminal Justice?* 1994

Cop Killers

In October 2009, a Philadelphia judge sentenced Rafael Jones, a 21-year-old thug, to four years in prison for a variety of crimes involving firearms. As a juvenile, Jones had a record of drug dealing, auto theft, and gun possession. He lived in a North Philadelphia neighborhood with his grandmother, Ada Banks. After serving two years behind bars, Jones walked out of prison on parole. He returned to his high-crime neighborhood where, early in 2012, he was shot and wounded by another North Philadelphia street criminal.

Early in July 2012, police arrested Jones on a parole violation related to the illegal possession of a gun. While incarcerated in the Curran-Fromhold Correctional Facility, Jones's state parole officer asked his grandmother, Ada Banks, if Jones could live with her, under house arrest, after his release. She said no. Banks didn't want Jones back in his old neighborhood where he had gotten into so much trouble. She suggested the prison authorities send Jones to his aunt's house in a better part of the city. The parole officer, rather than make the arrangements with the aunt, instructed Jones' grandmother to send the parolee to his aunt's house when got out of jail and showed up at her place. You know, the old honor system.

On July 25, at Jones' parole hearing, Common Pleas Judge Susan I. Schuman set August 8, 2012 as Jones' release date. The judge emailed prison officials to instruct Jones to report directly to his grandmother's house where someone from the state board of probation and parole would outfit him with an electronic monitoring ankle bracelet. (The judge wasn't aware that the grandmother was supposed to send Jones on to his aunt's house.) Signals from Jones' house arrest device would be monitored in Harrisburg, Pennsylvania. If Jones left the dwelling for an unauthorized reason, the parole office in Philadelphia would either receive an email or telephone alert from Harrisburg. Jones, although under house arrest, could leave the premises to look for a job, to complete his GED, or to do community service work.

On August 8, the day Jones got out of jail, the state parole officer didn't escort Jones from the prison directly to his aunt's house where he was supposed to be outfitted with the house arrest electronic equipment. Instead, the parolee walked out of prison unsupervised. The fact he didn't report to his grandmother's house, or check in to his aunt's place, should not have shocked anyone. As one would expect, he returned to the streets in North Philadelphia where he wasted no time getting his hands on the tool of his only trade, a handgun.

At six in the morning of August 18, just ten days after leaving prison, Rafael Jones and 19-year-old Chancies McFarland, an associate with a long juvenile record of crime and violence who was currently out on bail in connection with a drug case, were prowling the North Philadelphia neighborhood in search of someone to rob. The two robbers in search of a victim came upon Moses Walker, Jr., a 40-year-old Philadelphia police officer. After completing his night shift at the 22nd district police station in North Philadelphia, the 19-year veteran of the force had changed into his street clothes and was walking toward the bus station.

When confronted by Jones and McFarland who had been stalking him for robbery, Walker reached for his sidearm. Before the off-duty officer could protect himself, the two muggers shot him in the chest, stomach, and arm. Officer Moses Walker died on the street where he was shot.

Following officer Moses' murder, the city of Philadelphia and the police union posted a reward of $100,000 for information leading to the identification of the cop-killers. Several people came forward with information that led to Jones' arrest on August 24, 2012. Charged with murder and robbery, he was placed in custody without bail. On Sunday, August 26, McFarland was arrested in Alabama.

What is the point of parole if violent criminals released from prison early are not closely supervised. Did anyone really expect Rafael Jones to *voluntarily* show up at his grandmother's house, go on to his aunt's place, then call the parole authorities so they could come and install the electronic house arrest bracelet?

If Rafael Jones had murdered another street thug, this case would have been just another Philadelphia shooting incident. But Jones and his accomplice murdered a police officer. This made all the difference in the world.

Setting a Violent Man Free

In 2007, after being convicted of assault with intent to do great bodily harm, an Isabella County judge in central Michigan sentenced Erie Lee Ramsey to five to fifteen years behind bars. The 25-year-old felon from Mount Pleasant, a town 120 miles northwest of Detroit, had previous felony convictions for destruction of police property, resisting arrest, and assault with a dangerous weapon. Ramsey had proven himself to be a violent, lawless person unfit for life outside of prison.

In the summer of 2012, a Michigan parole board set this violent man free after he had served his minimum sentence of five years. During his relatively short prison stretch, Ramsey had been cited for inmate misconduct six times. Putting this prisoner back into society turned out to be a stupid, disastrous decision by so-called experts in the corrections field.

At nine-thirty on the night of January 16, 2013, Eric Ramsey drove his pickup onto the campus of Central Michigan University. He arrived on campus with the intent of abducting, raping, and murdering the first vulnerable woman who crossed his path. Outside the Student Activity Center, Ramsey approached a senior from Grand Rapids as she walked toward her car. He stuck a BB handgun into the victim's face, opened the door to her 2003 Ford Escape, and ordered her into the vehicle. Ramsey climbed in behind the wheel, and drove the abductee to his house in Mount Pleasant where he bound her with tape and raped her.

Later that night, Ramsey forced the terrified college student back into her car. He also placed two cans of gasoline in the vehicle, and drove north out of Mount Pleasant. When they reached nearby Lincoln Township, Ramsey informed his victim that he was going to kill her. (I presume he intended to use the gasoline to torch the Ford Escape with her in it.) Moments after Ramsey announced his plan to murder his captive, she opened her back passenger seat door and rolled out of the moving vehicle.

The young woman, not seriously injured from her vehicular escape, jumped to her feet and ran to the closest house where she pounded on the door and screamed for help. A 14-year-old boy, at home with his 11-year-old sister and a younger brother who was two, let the frantic woman into their dwelling. As the victim used the teenager's cellphone to call 911, he armed himself with a hunting knife.

Eric Ramsey climbed out of the Ford Escape, grabbed the two cans of gasoline, and walked up to the house occupied by the victim and the boy who had taken her in. Using the gasoline as an accelerant, Ramsey set fire to the place, climbed back into the victim's car, and drove off. Shortly after Ramsey torched the house, the occupants' parent arrived home, and using an extinguisher, doused the small blaze.

Just after midnight, a Michigan State Police officer spotted Ramsey and the Ford Escape in Gaylord, an Otsego County town north of Mount Pleasant. Ramsey intentionally drove his victim's car into the state patrol vehicle, veered off onto a field, jumped out of the damaged vehicle, and ran. In Gaylord, Ramsey stole a Ford F-350 sanitation truck, rammed another state police car, and continued north into Crawford County. Near the town of Fredric about 70 miles north of Mount Pleasant, Ramsey plowed the city garbage truck into a police car driven by a Crawford County sheriff's deputy. Just before climbing out of the sanitation vehicle, Ramsey posted the following message on his Facebook page: "Well folks, I'm about to be shot." (In the era of social media, even fleeing felons find time to post real-time messages.)

Ramsey had correctly predicted his fate. The Crawford County Deputy whose car Ramsey had disabled shot him dead.

Eric Lee Ramsey was not some drug-addled mental case who flipped-out and embarked on a criminal rampage. He had carried out a planned kidnapping and rape of a total stranger. Had this young woman not escaped, he would have murdered her and set her body on fire. If this wasn't bad enough, the 30-year-old felon had set fire to a house occupied by four people, and tried to kill three police officers.

Members of the parole board who let this dangerous man out of prison ten years early are responsible for the college student's abduction and rape. It's a miracle she is alive, and that holds true for the three police officers Ramsey crashed into.

Letting Out a Murderous Pedophile

Sidney Jerome DeAvila, a Stockton, California pedophile with a long history of sex crime, was sentenced to a prison psychiatric hospital after a child molestation conviction in 2011. The 38-year-old criminally insane sexual predator should have remained in custody for the remainder of his miserable life. Although allowing this man back into society guaranteed more victims, state parole officials released him from the prison mental facility in May 2012. Correction officials did not let DeAvila out because he was no longer dangerous. They freed him because some judge determined that the state psychiatric hospital was too crowded.

DeAvila was just one of thousands of violent criminals the state of California has paroled early because there is no room for them in its prisons and jails. Because getting into prison and jail has become so difficult in the state, parole violators like DeAvila have no incentive not to break parole. DeAvila was supposed to wear a GPS tracking device around his ankle that triggers an alarm if it's tampered with. Removing the device constitutes a parole violation. Because removing tracking devices doesn't lead to jail time, parolees have no incentive to wear them. As a result, DeAvila's parole officer had no idea where he was or what he was up to.

The Stockton police, on February 13, 2013, arrested DeAvila for the tenth time since his release from the state psychiatric facility. Every one of his arrests involved violations of the terms of his parole, and included public drunkenness, possession of drugs, and the removal of his GPS tracking device. On each these occasions, officers would book him into the San Joaquin County Jail.

In the past, before the court ordered the thinning out of the state's prison and jail population, parole violators would be held in county jails until their state parole revocation hearings. If found in violation they'd be sent back to prison to serve up to another year behind bars.

In DeAvila's case, he'd only spend a few nights in the San Joaquin lockup before being released back into society. Following his tenth parole violation arrest on February 13, 2013, he remained in the overcrowded San Joaquin Jail one week before walking free.

On February 26, just six days after DeAvila's last jail release, neighbors discovered the corpse of Rachael Russell, the parole violator's grandmother. Her body had been dumped in a wheelbarrow found in her backyard. Later that day, Stockton police officers arrested the high-risk parolee for the murder of his grandmother.

Going Easy on a Child Pornography Buff

In 2007, 67-year-old Richard Bistline lived with his ailing wife in Mount Vernon, a central Ohio town of 17,000 not far from Columbus, the state capital. In October of that year, FBI agents came to his home, arrested him for possessing child pornography, and seized his home computer. A search of Bistline's computer revealed 305 images and 56 videos of eight to ten-year-old girls being raped by adult men. Bistline had downloaded this material from an online program called "Limewire" which provided access to child pornography without a fee.

Three years after his arrest, Bistline pleaded guilty in a Columbus U. S. District Court to one count of possessing child pornography. The Sentencing Guidelines for this federal offense, as established by Congress, consisted of a sentence of between 63 and 78 months in prison.

Assistant United States Attorney Deborah A. Solove, in preparation for Bistline's sentencing hearing before federal judge James L. Graham, submitted a detailed memorandum outlining the government's argument for a sentence that fell within the established guidelines.

Judge Graham, a 1986 Reagan appointee who was Bistline's age, opened the sentence hearing with statements that telegraphed his decision to be lenient with the child porn possessor. Noting that mere possession of this kind of material did not constitute a very serious offense, Judge Graham declared the federal Sentencing Guidelines for the crime "seriously flawed." The judge also stated that in determining who should go to prison and who shouldn't, the age and health of the convicted person are important considerations. Judge Graham said that he was worried that Mr. Bistline, who over the past decade had suffered two strokes, would not receive adequate health care in prison. Moreover, if he sent this man away, who would care for his sick wife?

Judge Graham shocked the federal prosecutor when he handed down his sentence of one night in the federal courthouse lockup. That was it. *No* prison time for a man caught in possession of images and videos of young girls being raped by adult men.

After prosecutor Solove objected to the sentence as being extremely lenient, and outside the bounds of the guidelines, Judge Graham convened a second sentencing hearing two months later. At that hearing, the judge simply added ten years of supervised release to his original sentence. Still, no prison time for Mr. Bistline.

Assistant Unites States Attorney Deborah Solove appealed Judge Graham's sentence to the 6th Circuit Court of Appeals in Cincinnati on the grounds the district court judge had improperly rejected the federal Sentencing Guidelines in this case.

In January 2012, the panel of three appellate judges handed down its decision. The federal appeals court justices held that a district court judge, without a "compelling" reason, must not ignore sentencing guidelines created by the U. S. Congress. The justices ruled that in the Bistline case, Judge Graham's personal belief that the guidelines were too harsh for the possession of child porn did not constitute a "compelling" reason for ignoring them.

In justifying this legal decision, the appellate court laid out the following rationale: "Knowing possession of child pornography...is not a crime of inadvertence, of pop-up [computer] screens and viruses that can incriminate an innocent person. Possession of child pornography instead becomes a crime when a defendant knowingly acquires the images--in this case, affirmatively, deliberately, and repeatedly, hundreds of times over, in a period exceeding a year."

The 6th Circuit justices noted that Mr. Bistline never expressed genuine remorse for his actions. In fact, the defendant said he didn't understand why the possession of child pornography was even a crime. (Bistline was also angry with FBI agents for seizing his illegally downloaded music along with the child pornography.)

The 6th Circuit Court of Appeals justices ruled that Judge Graham's sentence "... did not remotely meet the criteria that Congress laid out. We vacate Bistline's sentence and remand his case for prompt imposition of one that does."

In January 2013, at Bistline's third sentencing hearing, federal prosecutor Solove urged Judge Graham to sentence the defendant to five years in prison. Intent on keeping this man out of prison, Judge Graham sentenced him to three years of home confinement. This sentence was a far cry from the recommended sentence of 63 to 78 months behind bars. If Judge Graham thought the federal sentencing guideline for the possession of child pornography was too harsh, he should run for Congress. Otherwise he should follow the law.

Rich Pedophile Gets Break

In 2005, 38-year-old Robert H. Richards IV resided with his wife Tracy and their two children, a 3-year-old girl and a boy aged 19 months. The heir to a pair of family fortunes lived in a 5,800-square-foot mansion in Greenville,

Delaware. Richards, a member of the du Pont family, the people who built a worldwide chemical empire, and the son of a prominent Delaware attorney, also owned a luxury home in the exclusive North Shores neighborhood near Rehoboth Beach.

In October 2007, Richards' daughter, now almost six, told her grandmother, Donna Burg, that her father had sexually assaulted her several times in 2005. According to the girl, her father had penetrated her with his finger at night in her bedroom. He told his daughter to keep what he had done to her a secret. The grandmother passed this information on to the victim's mother, Tracy Richards. The mother took her daughter to a pediatrician who confirmed that she had been sexually assaulted.

In December 2007, a grand jury sitting in New Castle County indicted Robert Richards on two counts of second-degree rape. If convicted of these felonies, Richards faced a mandatory prison sentence. Following his arrest, Richards retained the services of a high-powered Delaware defense attorney named Eugene J. Maurer, Jr.

Having denied his daughter's accusations, Richards agreed to take a polygraph test. When advised by the lie detection examiner that he had failed the test, Richards confessed to sexually assaulting his daughter. He said he was mentally ill and in need of psychiatric treatment.

In June 2008, attorney Maurer and New Castle County prosecutor Renee Hrivnak agreed on a plea arrangement. According to the deal, Richards would plead guilty to one count of fourth-degree rape. This was not an offense that called for an automatic stretch in prison.

Superior Court Judge Jan Jurden, in January 2009, sentenced Richards to Level 2 probation. Under the terms of his sentence, Richards would visit a case officer once a month. He also paid a $4,395 fine to the Delaware Violent Crimes Compensation Board.

Judge Jurden, in justifying the probated sentence, wrote that prison life would be especially difficult for Mr. Richards, and that he would not fare well behind bars. In her mind, prison was for drug dealers, robbers, and murderers, not for child rapists in need of psychiatric treatment.

In March 2014, Robert Richards' ex-wife Tracy filed a lawsuit against him on behalf of their children. The plaintiff is seeking compensatory and punitive damages for assault, negligence, and the intentional infliction of emotional stress on his daughter and her younger brother.

According to the affidavit in support of the lawsuit, Richards, in anticipation of a second polygraph test in April 2010, expressed concern about something he had done to his son in December 2005. Richards was worried that he had sexually assaulted the then 19-month-old boy. Richards promised that whatever he had done to that child, it would not happen again.

Richard's incriminating remarks sparked by the lie detector test in 2010 following his probated sentence for sexually assaulting his daughter, were not make public until Tracy Richards filed her lawsuit. The new information inflamed a public already angry over what seemed to be Richards' preferential treatment by the prosecutor and Judge Jurden.

Notwithstanding public outrage over this case, it was not likely that prosecutors in Delaware would charge Richards for crimes allegedly involving his son in 2005. Criminal defendants with money have a better chance of staying out of prison than people who can't afford influential lawyers. Apparently this even applied to pedophiles.

Justice Delayed is Not Justice

In Harrisburg, Pennsylvania on June 12, 1959, 23-year-old Joseph Lewis Miller blasted John and Donna Lumpkins with a 12-gauge shotgun. Mr. Lumpkins died of his injuries on July 4 of that year. Donna Lumpkins, his wife, survived her wounds.

On January 22, 1960, Joseph Miller pleaded guilty to the John Lumpkins murder and the attempted murder of the victim's wife. The judge sentenced Miller to life in prison. Throughout the late 1960s, Miller made several requests to have his life sentence commuted. On February 9, 1971, Miller got his wish when Governor Raymond P. Shaffer granted his motion. After serving 11 years and 6 months behind bars, Miller began his life as an ex-con on lifetime parole. Governor Shaffer's decision in this case would end up costing another man his life.

On January 15, 1981, Miller, at age 45, shot Thomas Walker to death in the parking lot outside a Harrisburg bar. After being charged with murder and several firearms violations a month later, Miller was nowhere to be found. He became a fugitive from justice.

In 2010, in the northeastern Texas town of Mineola, Miller, a deacon in the New Life Family Baptist Church, married a 58-year-old member of the congregation named Gennell. He was 74-years-old and living under the name Eugene Eubanks. Miller, a wanted killer, had established himself as a pillar of the community. But he was a man with a secret.

In the early morning hours of April 21, 2014, a team of U.S. Marshals showed up in Mineola with a warrant for the longtime fugitive's arrest. The marshals took Joseph Miller, aka Eugene Eubanks, into custody and booked him into the Wood County Jail where he would await his extradition back to Pennsylvania. According to Miller's wife Gennell Eubanks, Eugene suffered from early stage Alzheimer's disease and arthritis. He also had been having problems with his heart.

After the marshals hauled her 78-year-old husband off to jail, Gennell Eubanks told a reporter from Pennsylvania that she had not known her husband's real name. Regarding the shooting death of Thomas Walker in 1981, she said, "Eugene said it was an accident. He was trying to protect his brother, because a man was trying to kill him. I believe my husband. He wasn't trying to kill that man; it just happened. He isn't going to lie to me," she said, "because he is a deacon. He was trying to do what's right." As Miller was being taken out of his house in handcuffs, he said this to his 62-year-old wife: "Take care of yourself, and trust in the Lord. He will see you through."

Miller had not told Gennell Eubanks about his 1959 murder of John Lumpkins and the shooting of the victim's wife. Gennell had no idea her husband of four years had spent more than eleven years in a Pennsylvania prison. This deacon knew how to keep a secret.

14 EXECUTIONS

A Satiric Take on Hanging

I am not greatly concerned with the condemned man, but rather with the system, for it is the system that can be improved. The death of an individual is a trifle when we think of war and the general slaughter and butchery that is synonymous...What is the death of even the most important individual? And cannot death itself, even death by execution, be made, and frequently is made, into an admirable thing? Christianity itself might not have taken its great hold upon the imagination of the world if Christ had not been executed. Out of evil good can come; and the end justifies the means.

Charles Duff, *A Handbook on Hanging*, 1961

Three Executions

In 1966, 19-year-old Robert Waterhouse, during a home burglary on Long Island, New York, murdered a 77-year-old woman. He pleaded guilty to second-degree murder, and was sentenced to life in prison. But in the state of New York, a life sentence doesn't always mean a life behind bars. In 1975, after serving just eight years, Waterhouse was granted parole, and walked out of prison.

Four years later, after leaving a St. Petersburg bar with 29-year-old Deborah Kammerer, Waterhouse beat and raped her on the beach, then dragged her body into Tampa Bay where she drowned. In 1980, based on the victim's blood, hair, and other trace evidence found in Waterhouse's car, a jury convicted him of murder. A judge imposed the death sentence.

(Waterhouse admitted having sex with the victim that night, but denied killing her.)

Scheduled to die in 1985, Waterhouse appealed his sentence. Three years later, the Florida Supreme Court invalidated his death sentence because jurors at his sentence hearing had not been presented evidence that may have mitigated his guilt. At a second sentence hearing before another jury in 1990, jurors recommended the death penalty by a 12 to 0 vote. Waterhouse returned to death row.

On St. Valentine's day, 2013, after living on death row for 31 years, the 65-year-old double murderer died by lethal injection at the Florida State Prison in Raiford. Waterhouse was the 72nd inmate to be put to death in Florida since 1972.

In 1983, Mark Wiles, a 22-year-old farmhand, was sent to prison for stealing cash and property from his employers, the owners of the Klima family horse farm in Rootstown, Ohio. Although Wiles had been stealing from the family for some time, Mrs. Klima wrote a letter to the parole board in support of his bid for early release. In October 1984, Wiles left prison on parole.

Mark Wiles, a serial thief and sociopath, returned to the northern Ohio farm on August 7, 1985 to burglarize the Klima house that he believed was at the time unoccupied. In the dwelling, while helping himself to his former employer's property, Wiles encountered 15-year-old Mark Klima. To eliminate a witness who would have sent him back to prison, Wiles stabbed the boy 24 times, leaving the kitchen knife stuck in his back.

A panel of three judges, in 1986, found Wiles guilty of capital murder. Notwithstanding testimony on the defendant's behalf that 12 days before the murder Wiles had suffered a head injury that affected his impulse control, the judges sentenced him to death.

Following numerous appeals, hearings, and delays, the 49-year-old inmate died by lethal injection on April 18, 2012 at the Southern Ohio Facility in Lucasville. Wiles became the 47th prisoner to be executed since Ohio re-instated the death penalty in 1999.

On September 24, 2006, 22-year-old Shannon Johnson shot and killed Cameron Hamlin as Hamlin sat in his car in downtown Wilmington, Delaware with Johnson's ex-girlfriend. The woman managed to flee the scene without injury. Two months later, Johnson tracked her down, but when he tried to shoot her, his gun jammed. Once again, his intended victim escaped death.

In 2008, a jury found Johnson guilty of capital murder, and recommended the death penalty. The defendant's lawyer argued that because his client was mentally retarded, he was not eligible for execution. (Victims murdered by people with low IQs are just as dead as people murdered by geniuses.) The Delaware Supreme Court rejected the argument, and upheld the sentence. At that point, Johnson waived his right to further appeals.

Shannon Johnson, on April 20, 2012, died of lethal injection at James T. Vaughn Correction Center in Smyrna, Delaware. Before dying a few minutes before 3 AM (the execution deadline), the condemned man uttered a few words in Arabic. He was the second inmate in Delaware to be executed in twelve months.

Born To Be Executed

When he was 3-years-old, Steven L. Nelson set fire to his mother's bed. His father abused the boy, and by the time he was ten, Steven was being medicated for attention deficit disorder. But the child's emotional and personality problems were deeper than that. The drugs only made him more hyperactive, and impossible to control.

As a teen, Steven continued to be a disciplinary problem in school, and got into trouble with the law. He seemed to enjoy disturbing the peace, causing trouble, and inflicting pain on others. He ended up in juvenile detention centers in Oklahoma and Texas. One didn't have to be an expert in deviant behavior to predict bad things for this young man as well as the people unfortunate enough to cross his path. Had he been accidentally run over by a bus, it would have been a gift to society.

On March 3, 2011 in North Arlington, Texas, the 25-year-old sadistic sociopath, in the course of robbing a Baptist church, murdered the pastor, 28-year-old Clint Dobson. He beat, bound, then with a plastic bag, suffocated his victim. Nelson also viciously assaulted Judy Elliott, the church secretary. Left for dead, she survived the attack.

A week after the murder of Pastor Dobson, and the attempted murder of his secretary, the police arrested Nelson. Although this cold-blooded killer was off the street, he was still an extremely dangerous man. While incarcerated in the Tarrant County Jail in Fort Worth, Texas, Nelson, while in the recreation area of the lockup, attacked another inmate. Nelson beat 30-year-old Jonathan Holden with a broom handle then strangled the mentally retarded man to death with a blanket. After murdering Holden, Nelson showed-off to inmates who had witnessed the homicide by doing the Chuck Berry hop, using the broomstick as his guitar.

Knowing that he was going to be convicted for murdering Pastor Dobson, Nelson, with nothing to lose, killed another man just for the thrill of it.

On October 8, 2012, after the five-day trial, a jury in Fort Worth found Steven Nelson guilty of capital murder in the brutal, sadistic killing of Pastor Dobson. Following the verdict, the penalty phase of the murder trial got underway before the same jurors. The jury would have to decide whether to sentence this man to life in prison without parole, or condemn him to die by lethal injection.

After a week of testimony from prosecution witnesses, Nelson's defense attorneys put experts on the stand in a futile attempt to make their client slightly more sympathetic than the vicious, recreational murderer that he was.

Dr. Antoinette McGarrahan, a psychiatrist with the University of Texas Southwestern Medical Center, labeled Nelson a violent psychopath, and said he will pose a danger to people exposed to him in prison. The witness also debunked Nelson's claim that he had multiple personalities. On October 16, the jury, after deliberating Nelson's fate for 90 minutes, issued their sentence verdict: death by lethal injection.

Nelson, true to form, was not done creating havoc. After sheriff deputies placed him in a courthouse holding pen he flooded the cell, and the courtroom, with black, fire-retardant infused water from the sprinkler head he had broken. Courthouse personnel scrambled to save boxes of evidence from being ruined by the foul-smelling liquid. As the courthouse people rushed to save the evidence, they could hear Nelson howling like a wolf in his cell. Firefighters who responded to the scene shut off the water to the sprinkler system.

The Death Penalty Debate

To some extent, the debate about capital punishment has been going on almost since the founding of the Republic. At that time, each state, following the English tradition, imposed death for a long list of felonies. But the same humanism that posited the equal value of all men and animated democracy necessarily led to many questions about a punishment that vested such fierce power over citizens in the state and assumed individuals were irredeemable. Thomas Jefferson was among the earliest advocates of restricting executions, and in 1794, Pennsylvania limited capital punishment to first-degree murder. In 1846, Michigan became the first American state to outlaw capital punishment for killers.

For most Americans, the death penalty debate goes no further than asking whether they "believe" in capital punishment. There is good reason for this, of course, because the threshold issues define us so profoundly as individuals and as a society that it is almost impossible to move past them. What are the goals of punishment? What do we think about the perfectibility of human beings and the perdurability of evil? What value do we place on life--of the murderer and the victim? What kind of power do we want in the hands of government, and what do we hope the state can accomplish when it wields it?

Scott Turow, *Ultimate Punishment*, 2003

Too Fat To Execute

America's weight problem has changed the way we live and die, and has affected how we punish, or can't punish, some of our worst criminals. While the U.S. Supreme Court has not prohibited the execution of certain types of murderers, it has mandated that the state must kill condemned prisoners in a "dignified and humane manner." I would argue that how a prisoner is dispatched is less a matter of dignity and humanity than aesthetics. For this reason, death sentence prisoners no longer end up swinging from the end of a rope, being gunned down by a firing squad, or giving off smoke while twitching in an electric chair. These methods, while effective, look unprofessional, and barbaric. In states where certain criminals are still executed, the government has to use methods that do not offend our tender sensitivities. The execution business has to be politically correct. This is why juries have been reluctant to recommend the death sentence for women, people younger than 21, and folks with low I.Q.s. Of the 3,222 people currently on death row, only 61 are women. Wives convicted of murdering their husbands spend, on average, 6 years in prison. Men who murder their wives are, on average, sent away for 17 years. (In terms of race, 42 percent of the death row population is black, 12 percent Latino, and 44 percent white.)

Today, death row inmates are killed by lethal injection. This method of execution fits in nicely with our pharmaceutical culture. We take drugs to get well, to sleep, and to get high, so why not use drugs to execute certain murderers in the 32 states where the death penalty is still legal. But now there is a growing concern about executing people with drugs. Over the past twenty years, several death row prisoners have tried to escape their fates by claiming they are too obese to be humanely injected. In Ohio this has been a recurring correctional issue.

In May 2007, an executioner in Ohio ran into difficulty when he tried to kill, by injection, 38-year-old Christopher Newton. Six years earlier, while serving time for burglary, Newton murdered his cellmate. Now it was his time to go. Because of his weight it took the executioner two hours and ten attempts to find a receptive vein for the lethal dose of pentobarbital. During the prolonged execution, Newton was actually allowed to go to the bathroom. It would be his last bathroom break, however.

Nineteen-year-old Richard Cooey, in 1986, threw chunks of concrete off a bridge over Interstate 77 near Akron, Ohio. The act caused the deaths of two University of Akron students. As Cooey's execution date drew near, the 5-foot-7, 267-pound inmate alleged that prison food and lack of exercise had made him too fat to painlessly execute. (In the old days, after a year on bread and water, many inmates hanged themselves, or self-executed. Just kidding.) According to the 41-year-old Ohio prisoner, the executioner's difficulty in finding a friendly vein would cause him stress and discomfort. On October 14, 2008, the Ohio executioner, probably under a little stress himself, had no problem introducing the pentobarbital into Mr. Cooey's system.

In 1983, Ronald Post murdered Helen Vantz, a hotel desk clerk in Elyria, Ohio. A jury found him guilty and a judge sentenced him to death. There wasn't any question regarding his guilt. Post didn't exercise and he ate too much. He ballooned up to 400 pounds. In an effort to get control of his weight, Post asked the government to pay for gastric bypass surgery.

In 1997, claiming that prison health care providers were having difficulty finding his veins for medication, Ronald Post argued that to execute him this way would amount to a violation of his Eighth Amendment right against cruel and unusual punishment.

After the federal appellate judge refused to take Ronald Post off death row, prison authorities in Ohio scheduled his execution by lethal injection for January 16, 2013. Assuming the execution is carried out, Post will have lived almost twenty years on death row. In November 2012, Mr. Post, now claiming to weigh 480 pounds, filed another appeal in which he argued that he had grown so fat his veins were even less accessible. The prison didn't own a gurney sturdy enough to roll him into the death chamber. According to Post's attorney, executing his client under these circumstances would comprise "a substantial risk that any attempt to execute him will result in serious physical and psychological pain to him...." The lawyer added that Mr. Post's execution would consist of "a torturous and lingering death."

State authorities opposing Ronald Post's attempt to see the other side of January 16, 2013, argued that in fact, the death row inmate only weighted 396 pounds. In this case it really didn't matter how much this man weighed. The federal appeals court in Cincinnati has already ruled against Mr. Post on the weight issue. For this reason, come spring, he will probably not be among the living. Moreover, the state of Ohio, given all of its resources, will find a heavy-duty gurney, and an executioner who can locate hard-to-find veins. As for dignified and humane, who knows? I'm not sure any execution can meet that test.

If our procedurally oriented criminal justice system were efficient and reliable enough to dispatch first-degree murderers within two years of their convictions, death row inmates wouldn't have time to get so fat. After ten or twenty years on death row, many of these inmates also find religion, and become different people. The person being executed is not the same person who committed the crime. (The Karla Faye Tucker case in Texas is a good example of this. While on death row, Karla found Jesus. To the dismay of protesting evangelicals, Texas went ahead and executed her anyway. I don't think the state has dispatched a female since.)

There are those death row inmates who, while smart enough to have committed first-degree murder, when the time comes around to execute them, are not intelligent enough to kill. It seems cruel and unusual to execute slow-witted killers. So, if a death row inmate isn't fat, or hasn't found Jesus, he can pretend to be stupid.

On December 17, 2012, Governor John Kasich granted Ronald Post clemency on the grounds he had poor legal representation at his trial.

The Science of Electrocution

Divorced from the emotional and ethical aspects of the matter, electrocution can be pictured as a purely physical process. The body--seen as a conductor of electricity--is a leathery bag containing a solution of electrolytes. Though electricity does not move in a perfectly straight line as is passes from entrance to exit, the greatest density of current is along the line connecting the two points of contact. But because the human body is a complex object for the current to pass though--unlike a uniform substance such as copper wire or salt water--the actual resistance of the body may vary greatly during the time the electricity is moving through it. The effects of the shock are often impossible to predict.

To make electrocution as efficient and expedient a process as possible, certain techniques of preparation have been developed. Like a patient being readied for surgery, the prisoner to be executed goes though an exacting process before the actual procedure occurs. Very important is the maximizing of contact. The prisoner's scalp is shaved down to stubble; a safety razor is used then to clear a spot at the center of the head. This is the place where the soaked sponge of the death cap will make contact. Similarly, an area approximately six inches above the ankle is shaved, to make the optimum connection with the ground pad....

Everything possible is done to ensure that the mechanism works as desired. The connection at head and leg soaked with conductive Electro-Creme or paste-like brine solution--is the most efficient way of transferring electrical current into the body. Voltages and amperages are finely calibrated. The system itself is checked and rechecked, tested and inspected. Hundreds of previous executions give the prison personnel a good idea of what to expect. A controlled environment, witnesses, accurate analytic tools, the frequent presence of doctors and nurses lend the execution the air of a scientific experiment. But the body is always a variable.

Th. Metzger, *Blood & Volts*, 1996

Say Goodbye to A Baby Killer

On the night of September 29, 1988, in the northern Ohio town of Mansfield, 31-year-old Steve Smith walked into his live-in girlfriend's bedroom carrying her six-month-old daughter. Smith was nude and had been drinking. The lifeless infant in his arms bore bruises and cuts.

Kesha Frye took her daughter to a neighbor's house where she called 911. At the hospital, doctors tried for an hour to revive Autumn Frye before pronouncing the baby dead. An autopsy revealed that the infant had been raped.

A year after his arrest, Steve Smith went on trial for aggravated murder. On the advice of his attorneys, the defendant did not take the stand on his own behalf. The jury found him guilty as charged, and the judge sentenced him to death.

On April 2, 2013, after living twelve years on death row, Smith appeared before the Ohio Parole Board that was considering his petition to reduce his sentence to life. Smith admitted raping the infant, but said he hadn't intended to kill her. The parole board and Governor John Kasich denied Smith's motion for a life sentence.

At ten-thirty in the morning of May 1, 2013, the Ohio executioner at the state prison in Lucasville injected a lethal dose of pentobarbital into the body of the 46-year-old prisoner. Steve Smith's 20-year-old daughter and a handful of others watched him go. If the baby-killer made a statement before the pentobarbital got into his system, his last words have not escaped the prison.

Guillotine Chic

Almost from its first victim on April 25, 1792, the guillotine became a fetishistic object for the French during their revolution. Men had it tattooed on their bodies; women wore dangling guillotine earrings and brooches; the design was incorporated into plates, cups, snuffboxes; children played with toy versions, decapitating mice; elegant ladies lopped off the heads of dolls and out squirted a red perfume, in which they soaked their handkerchiefs.

Richard Zacks, *An Underground Education*, 1997

The Era of the Electric Chair

Quite often, the centerpiece of a police or crime museum is an electric chair. To some, "Old Sparky" is a symbol of a bygone era when convicted murderers got what was coming to them swiftly and electronically. Others believe the electric chair represents government brutality and cruel and unusual punishment. Still others are drawn to these old "hot seats" by morbid curiosity. Currently, only four states--Alabama, Florida, South Carolina, and Virginia--have operational electric chairs. In these states a death row inmate can choose between lethal injection and electrocution. Over the past years, prisoners faced with this dark dilemma, have chosen the needle over the voltage. Since 1890, about 4,000 inmates have been electrocuted in the United States. It would be wishful thinking to believe that all of them were guilty of the crimes charged.

In the 1920s and 30s, Robert G. Elliott, an electrician (of course) from Long Island, the official executioner for six states, electrocuted 387 inmates. For this he charged the state $150 a pop. When he threw the switch (or turned the wheel) on two or more at one setting (so to speak), he discounted his fee. Some of Elliot's most infamous clients included Bruno Richard Hauptmann (1936), the killer of the Lindbergh baby; Ruth Snyder and Judd Grey (1928), the murderers of Ruth's husband Albert; and Nicola Sacco and Bartolomeo Vanzetti (1927), the Italian anarchists convicted of killing a Boston area bank guard. Elliott, somewhat of a celebrity, and obviously proud of his singular contribution to the American system of criminal justice, wrote a memoir called "Agent of Death" that came out in 1940 less than a year after his own demise. His book, long out of print and written by a co-author, has become a collector's item.

In 1981, Allen Lee "Tiny" Davis murdered a pregnant woman and her two children during a home invasion robbery in Jacksonville, Florida. A year later a jury found him guilty of first-degree murder. The judge sentenced him to death. In 1998, as Davis' execution date approached, the 54-year-old death row inmate's attorney argued that his 355 pound client was too heavy for the state's broken-down 76-year-old electric chair. Since it was built in 1923, the Florida State Prison's electric chair had dispatched 200 prisoners, and was worn out. Witnesses to the chair's performance in 1997 saw, when the juice was applied, a flame from the condemned man's head shoot a foot into the air. So, in 1998, following this unpleasant tableau, the prison, with Allen "Tiny" Davis in mind, oversaw the construction of a new, heavy-duty electric chair, one that could accommodate a 355 pound guest. On July 8, 1999, the executioner ran 2,300 volts through the metal cap on Davis's head for two minutes. It wasn't pretty, there was some blood and a lot of groaning, but the new chair did its job.

If a crime buff is interested in the electric chair that sent Ruth Snyder and Judd Grey to hell in 1927, he or she can see a replica of it at the Sing Sing Prison Museum in Ossining, New York. Snyder was the first women executed in the United States since 1899. After her, more would follow. The real chair is in prison storage. The hot seat Robert Elliott activated to electrocute Bruno Richard Hauptmann sits in the New Jersey Police Museum and Learning Center in West Trenton. In that state they call it "Old Smokey."

At the American Police Hall of Fame and Museum in Titusville, Florida, visitors can be photographed sitting in a replica electric chair. An Old Sparky is on display in Moundsville, West Virginia as part of a tourist attraction that used to be part of the West Virginia State Penitentiary. Before 1950, death sentence inmates in West Virginia were hanged--85 of them since 1866. The state has abolished the death penalty.

In Springer, New Mexico, at the Santa Fe Trail Museum, a female mannequin sits in the state's first and only electric chair. (I'm not a museum curator, but this seems like an odd choice.) The electric chair at the Texas Prison System in Huntsville, built by an inmate, fried 361 prisoners from 1924 to 1964.

The centerpiece of a recent exhibit at the Ohio Historical Center in Columbus featured an electric chair that put 312 men and one woman to death between 1887 and 1963. The exhibit, in a state that has kept the death penalty, has created some controversy.

Lethal Injection for a Woman in Texas

In 1997, 36-year-old Kimberly LaGayle McCarthy, a nursing home occupational therapist living in Lancaster, Texas fifteen miles south of Dallas, was hooked on crack cocaine. Married to Aaron Michaels, the founder of the New Black Panther Party, McCarthy possessed a criminal record that included forgery, prostitution, and theft of services. She and Michaels had one child, a son.

On July 21, 1997, McCarthy telephoned her neighbor, Dorothy Booth, to inform her she was coming to Booth's house to borrow a cup of sugar. In reality, the purpose of the visit was to murder and rob the 71-year-old former El Centro College psychology professor. In Booth's home, McCarthy stabbed the victim five times with a 10-inch butcher's knife before repeatedly clubbing the dying woman with a heavy candelabrum.

In stealing the victim's diamond wedding ring, McCarthy used the big knife to cut off Booth's finger. In possession of the murder victim's credit cards and ring, McCarthy drove from the murder scene to a pawnshop in

Booth's Mercedes-Benz. The next day, police officers booked McCarthy into the Dallas County Jail on the charge of murder.

The McCarthy case went to trial a year after the brutal, cold-blooded murder. The defendant's attorney tried to convince the jury the victim had been murdered by a pair of unnamed drug dealers. The prosecution, however, linked the defendant to the murder knife through DNA analysis. Following a short deliberation, the jury found McCarthy guilty as charged.

At the sentencing hearing, the Dallas County District Attorney, through DNA evidence, connected McCarthy to two similar murders committed in December 1988. Maggie Harding, 81-years-old, had been stabbed with a knife then clubbed with a meat-tenderizing mallet. Jettie Lucas, 85, had been stabbed then beaten with a claw hammer. Both victims had been robbed. (Although indicted in both of these cases, McCarthy did not go to trial for these murders.)

On November 24, 1998, the judge who had presided over McCarthy's murder trial sentenced her to die by lethal injection. McCarthy would spend the next fifteen years living on death row at the Texas state prison in Huntsville, Texas.

As is common practice in death penalty cases, McCarthy's legal team filed a series of appeals. In 2002, a federal appellate court granted McCarthy a new trial. The Dallas County District Attorney, relying on the DNA evidence connecting the defendant to the Booth murder scene, re-tried McCarthy a few months after the appeals court decision. The second jury required little time in finding her guilty. The judge that presided over the second trial sentenced her to death.

In July 2002, four years after Dorothy Booth's murder, McCarthy's attorneys, having exhausted all other appellate remedies, asked the United States Supreme Court to hear their client's appeal. The high court declined to entertain the condemned woman's case. The prison authorities in Texas set McCarthy's execution for January 29, 2013.

On January 29, 2013, a few hours before McCarthy's appointment with Huntsville's executioner, the governor granted the 52-year-old prisoner a temporary stay of execution. A month before the new execution date, April 3, 2013, the lethal injection was re-scheduled for June 26, 2013.

At 6:27 in the evening of June 26, twenty minutes after the executioner administered the lethal dose, a doctor pronounced Kimberly McCarthy dead. The murder victim's daughter, granddaughter, and godson witnessed the execution. The executed woman's attorney, University of Texas Law Professor Maurie Levin, told reporters that her client's case had been plagued by "shameful errors" of racial bias during the jury selection phase of McCarthy's trials. Levin also claimed that McCarthy's had been denied effective legal representation.

Kimberly McCarthy was the first woman executed in the United States since 2010. Thirteen women, since 1976, have been put to death. During this period, executioners across the country have dispatched 1,300 men. Nationwide, there are currently 63 women on death row.

Does The Death Penalty Deter?

When we look closely into it, there are two categories of people who commit murder: (1) Those who are sane (know the nature and quality or consequences of their act) but *hope to escape the penalty*; (2) Those who are insane, and these either do not know or do not care what they do. Homicides are either the one or the other, so it is difficult to appreciate the deterring effect of the death penalty upon their minds. I am not a psychologist or metaphysician, or even a theologian, so I cannot resolve this difficult problem except by saying that, if a man knows what will happen as a result of an act of his, and hopes so strongly to escape the consequences that he actually commits the act, a contemplation of the possible penalty does not seem to hinder him.

Charles Duff, *A Handbook on Hanging,* 2001

A History of Death House Pharmacology

By 2010, 35 states still impose the death penalty in cases involving inmates who have committed the most heinous murders. Not all of these states, however, actually carry out the executions. In the states that do, the mode of execution is lethal injection. Chemicals have replaced the electric chair. Inmates are no longer electrocuted they are poisoned to death.

Death house executioners, in dispatching the condemned, administer a lethal cocktail comprised of three drugs. The first drug to go in--sodium thiopental--renders the recipient unconscious. The second chemical paralyzes the inmate while the third stops his heart. The key ingredient in the cocktail, the vodka in the screwdriver as it were, is the sodium thiopental, a drug used by all of the states where death row prisoners are actually executed.

Late in 2010, the only company that manufactured sodium thiopental--mainly used as an anesthesia, and to induce medical comas--announced a shortage of the drug. A spokesperson for the Hospira company blamed the scarcity on a problem with the manufacturer's raw material suppliers. Cut off from the drug, executions in California, Arkansas, Tennessee, and Maryland were delayed.

In December 2010, the executioner in Oklahoma who sent 58-year-old John David Duty to his grave for killing a cellmate, substituted sodium thiopental with a sedative used to treat severe epilepsy. A Danish company called Lundbeck manufactured the drug pentobarbital, sold under the brand name Nembutal. The pharmaceutical was also used to put down animals.

In August 2011, an executioner in Virginia used pentobarbital as part of the lethal mix to kill a 30-year-old inmate named Jerry Jackson. Jackson had been convicted in 2002 for breaking into 88-year-old Ruth Phillips' house where he raped and murdered the woman. Phillips woke up to find him burglarizing the place. When she confronted the intruder, he sexually assaulted, then killed her. Following the Jackson execution, the Lundbeck Company, objecting to one of its products being used to kill inmates, restricted the drug's distribution in an effort to keep it out of America's execution chambers.

In 2011, 23 death row prisoners in the United States were either buried or cremated with pentobarbital in their blood. In Ohio that year, for the first time in the nation, an executioner dispatched a prisoner by using pentobarbital only. Death penalty opponents, claiming that the one-drug method caused inmates to die more slowly, objected to the procedure.

In March 2012, with the cost of pentobarbital going through the roof, the state of Texas spent $1,200 on the deadly cocktail used to kill 52-year-old Keith Thurmond. The condemned man had been convicted in 2002 of murdering his estranged wife and her lover during an argument over child custody.

Texas prison administrators, in July 2012, adopted Ohio's one-drug policy in an effort to save taxpayers' money. The executioner injected pentobarbital into 33-year-old Yokamon Hearn fourteen years after he had murdered a Dallas stockbroker. A death chamber physician pronounced the prisoner dead 25 minutes following his lethal injection.

In 2012, the states of Arizona, Washington, Idaho, and Georgia also began executing inmates with pentobarbital only.

Correction officials in Texas, in July 2013, announced that they were running out of pentobarbital. Because the European Commission, in December 2011, had ordered companies in the European Union to stop exporting the drug to the United States for execution, states had no way of replenishing their supply of the drug.

A Serial Killer Executed in Tennessee

In 1988 a judge in Texas sent a drifter named Paul Dennis Reid to prison for twenty years. Seven years later a parole board set the 27-year-old serial armed robber free. Reid left the state in 1995 for Nashville, Tennessee in hopes of becoming a country western star. Instead of performing at the Grand Ole Opry, Reid ended up washing dishes at a number of Shoney's restaurants in and around Nashville.

On February 16, 1997, the day after the manager of a Shoney's fired him, Reid walked into Captain D's restaurant in Nashville and shot, execution style, two employees. The armed robber and cold-blooded killer, on March 23, 1995, murdered three McDonald's workers in Hermitage, Tennessee. A month later, he killed two Baskin-Robbins employees in nearby Clarksville.

Police officers arrested Reid in June 1997 in Cheatham County, Tennessee. He was taken into custody while trying to kidnap one of his former Shoney's restaurant bosses.

Convicted of seven first-degree murders in 1999, Paul Dennis Reid landed on death row at the Riverbend Maximum prison in Nashville. He claimed that the "military government" had him under constant surveillance and was the force behind his murder convictions. Reid said his trials had been "scripted" by the government.

Immediately after the serial killer's convictions, his team of lawyers began appealing his seven death sentences on the grounds he was too mentally ill to execute. By 2002, several execution dates had come and gone. It was around this time that Reid informed his attorneys to stop appealing his case. Arguing that the death row prisoner was not mentally competent, and therefore couldn't determine his own fate, his attorneys ignored his request.

In 2003, to a newspaper reporter with Clarksville's *Leaf-Chronicle*, Reid said he had "sincere, profound empathy" for his victims' families. (I'm sure that made them feel better.) "I would say to them that if I have violated you or offended you in any manner, I plead for your forgiveness."

A pair of Tennessee courts in 2008 ruled that Reid was mentally sound enough to be executed. Four years later, the state Supreme Court declared that Reid's attorneys could not continue to appeal against the condemned man's wishes. By now Reid had been on death row fourteen years.

At six o'clock on the evening of Friday, November 1, 2013, after being treated two weeks at a Nashville hospital for an undisclosed illness, Paul Dennis Reid died. He was fifty-five years old.

Doyle Brown, the father of one of Reid's victims at the McDonald's in Hermitage, said this to an Associated Press reporter who asked him how he felt about the death of the man who had murdered his daughter: "I'm glad he's dead. I wish it happened through the criminal justice system several years ago rather than him just getting sick and dying."

Members of Reid's family, people who had fought for years to keep him from being executed, mourned his death. They didn't view their relative as an evil, cold-blooded serial killer but as a victim of severe mental illness.

Since sane people can fake mental illness, and crazy people can, on occasion act perfectly normal, Reid's true nature will remain a mystery. Regardless of whether or not he was evil, Paul Dennis Reid was unfit to live outside a one-man prison cell.

Say Goodbye to Three Killers

In 1968, 42-year-old Edward Harold Schad strangled a male sex partner to death in Utah. Ten years later on August 9, 1978, the paroled killer carjacked Lorimer Grove's Cadillac in Bisbee, Arizona. Police discovered Grove's body along a highway near Prescott, Arizona with a sash-like cord knotted around his neck.

After he murdered Mr. Grove, Schad drove around the country in the stolen Cadillac cashing forged checks drawn on the dead man's bank account. Schad also made purchases with the victim's credit cards. A year later a jury found Schad guilty of first-degree murder. A judge sentenced him to death.

At ten in the morning of Wednesday, October 9, 2013, at the Arizona State Prison at Florence, the oldest man on the state's death row received his lethal dose of pentobarbital. When the warden asked the 71-year-old if he had any last words, Schad said, "Well, after 34 years [on death row], I'm free to fly away home. Thank you, Warden. Those are my last words."

In Arizona, 121 death row inmates await their executions. Two of the condemned prisoners are women. Since supplies of pentobarbital are limited, I wonder if the state has enough of this lethal drug to carry out its execution mandate.

On September 2, 1986, 26-year-old Ronald Clinton Lott broke into 83-year-old Anna Laura Fowler's home in Oklahoma City. The intruder beat, raped, and strangled the old woman to death. On January 11, 1987, Lott broke into the home across the street from his first victim's dwelling. In that house he tortured, raped, and murdered 93-year-old Zelma Cutler.

A jury in Oklahoma City found Ronald Lott guilty of two counts of first-degree murder. The judge sentenced him to death.

At 6:06 in the evening of Tuesday, December 10, 2013, the executioner at the Oklahoma State Penitentiary in McAlester administered Lott's lethal injection. The 53-year-old had no last words. Lott was the fifth Oklahoma prisoner to be put to death in 2013.

In August 1994, 22-year-old Allen Nicklasson met a convicted killer named Dennis Skillicorn at a drug rehabilitation center in Kansas City, Missouri. On August 22, 1994, Nicklasson, Skillicorn, and a third man, Tim De Graffenreid, decided to drive across the state to St. Louis where they planned to buy drugs. En route, Nicklasson's 1883 Chevrolet Caprice broke down on Interstate 70 near Kingdom City, Missouri. The next day, after a local mechanic worked on the car, the trio of violent losers got back on the road despite the mechanic's warning that the repairs had been temporary. Not long after resuming the trip, the Chevy broke down again.

On August 23, Richard Drummond spotted the three stranded motorists standing alone I-70 next to the disabled Chevy. The 47-year-old AT & T supervisor pulled off the highway to help. When Mr. Drummond got out of his Dodge Intrepid, Nicklasson put a gun to his head and took him hostage.

Nicklasson ordered Drummond to drive the Dodge to a secluded place where Nicklasson shot Drummond execution style in the back of the head. (The victim's body was found eight days later.) Years later, in recalling the moment he killed Drummond, Nicklasson said, "I felt euphoria. I finally got back for all the beatings I took as a child."

Two days after he murdered Richard Drummond, Nicklasson, with his two degenerate friends in the dead man's car, drove to Arizona where, in the desert, the Dodge broke down. The three men walked in the desert until they came upon a house occupied by Joseph and Charlene Babcock. Once inside the dwelling, Nicklasson shot Charlene to death and forced her husband to drive the killers back to the broken down Dodge. It was there Nicklasson murdered Mr. Babcock and stole his car.

The three fugitives were caught shortly after the murders by police officers in Arizona. After being found guilty in that state of murdering Mr. and Mrs. Babcock, a judge sentenced Nicklasson to life in prison. Tim De Graffenreid, in return for his guilty plea and cooperation with the authorities, received life sentences in Arizona and later in Missouri.

In Missouri, following his conviction for the cold-blooded murder of Richard Drummond, a judge sent Nicklasson to death row. Another Missouri judge sentenced Dennis Skillicorn to death. In 2009 they executed Skillicorn for his role in the Drummond murder.

Allen Nicklasson's time finally came at 10:52 in the morning of December 11, 2013. The executioner at the Missouri State Prison in Bonne Terre injected the 41-year-old killer with enough pentobarbital to stop his heart. This murderer of three innocent, helpless people had no last words.

An Execution in Missouri

By 1991, 33-year-old Herbert Smulls had spent several years behind bars for armed robbery and other crimes. On July 27, 1991, Smulls and a 15-year-old accomplice named Normon Brown walked into the F & M Crown Jewelers store in Chesterfield, Missouri with the intent of robbing the establishment. Smulls told the owners of the St. Louis County jewelry store,

Stephen and Florence Honickman, that he wanted to buy a diamond ring for his fiancée.

Instead of purchasing a ring, Smulls pulled out a handgun and shot the owners. He killed 51-year-old Stephen Honickman on the spot. When Smulls and Brown fled the scene, they left behind Florence Honickman who was still alive but lying in a poor of her own blood. Smulls had shot her in the arm and side. She survived the shooting by playing dead.

Fifteen minutes after the robbery-murder, a police officer pulled Smulls off the road on a traffic stop. Inside the car officers found handguns and the stolen jewelry.

Upon Florence Honickman's recovery, she identified Smulls and Brown as the armed robbers and Smulls at the man who had shot her and her husband.

In 1993, a judge sentenced Normon Brown to life in prison without parole. The judge handed Smulls the death sentence. The murderer was sent to Missouri's death row.

In 1989, executioners in Missouri began dispatching death row inmates by injecting them with a lethal, three-drug cocktail. The first drug midazalam helped calm the inmate. Hydromorphine, a strong narcotic, reduced pain. Sodium thiopental, the killer drug, stopped the heart.

Recently, the overseas companies that manufacture and distribute the above drugs stopped exporting them to the U.S. if they are to be used to execute prisoners. As a result, Missouri and other states have switched to a single execution drug, pentobarbital. If Smulls' execution, scheduled for 12:01 AM, January 29, 2014, went ahead as planned, he'd be getting a shot of pentobarbital.

A few days before the 56-year-old's execution date, Cheryl Pilante, one of the lawyers fervently fighting to save his life, asked the U.S. Supreme Court for a temporary stay of execution. Just two and a half hours before Smulls' date with death, the Supreme Court granted the stay. Justice Samuel Alito signed the order temporarily delaying the punishment.

Smulls' execution had been put on hold because corrections officials with the state of Missouri refused to disclose the identify of the compounding pharmacy that mixed the pentobarbital. Attorney Pilate argued that Missouri's execution secret made it impossible to know whether the drug would cause Mr. Smulls any pain.

In expressing grave concern for her client, attorney Pilate said, "I frankly cannot begin to tell you how distressing this situation is, that the state is going to execute a prisoner in his mid-50s who made one series of colossal *mistakes* that were in many ways out of character, because he is not a violent person."

What? He's not a violent person? His cold-blooded murder was *out of character*? If defense attorneys are paid to embarrass themselves on behalf of their clients, Pilate deserves a bonus.

St. Louis County prosecutor Bob McCulloch characterized the drug purchase issue a smokescreen designed to save the life of a vicious killer. He also accused Pilate of trying to divert attention from her client's horrific crime.

On January 29, the Supreme Court lifted the temporary stay of execution. Later that morning, the state executioner in Bonne Terre, Missouri administered the lethal drug. Herbert Smulls was pronounced dead at 10:20 AM. Only his attorneys and a few others were sad to see him go.

Most U.S. citizens do not oppose the death penalty as a matter of principle. Regarding inmates like Herbert Smulls, few citizens are concerned they may feel some pain at the end. We all have to occasionally endure pain and anxiety in our daily lives. And because of people like Herbert Smulls, victims of crime are certainly no strangers to suffering.

So what is behind this obsessive quest to insure that cold-blooded killers are dispatched without discomfort? Who really cares that Mr. Smulls was anxious about dying, and worried about pain? Who isn't?

Executing Dimwits

Throw a ball in any prison and it will bounce off a lot of stupid men. If these vicious rapists, thugs, and murderers were smart, they wouldn't be behind bars. Thank heavens so many criminals *are* dimwits. Moreover, it's not stupidity that makes a person violent. Most stupid people obey the law and wouldn't hurt a fly. So, just because a cold-blooded, sadistic killer has an IQ so low he can't get into community college is no reason to cut him a break when it comes time for the death penalty. Take Freddie Lee Hall.

In February 1978, 33-year-old Freddie Lee Hall was out on parole in connection with a recent conviction for assault with intent to rape. Given his long history of violent crime, it's hard to believe he wasn't in prison. Hall and one of his criminal associates, on February 21, 1978, were in Leesburg, Florida looking for a car to steal for use in an armed robbery.

That afternoon, Hall and his accomplice spotted 21-year-old Karol Hurst coming out of the Pantry Pride Grocery Store. She was seven months pregnant. As Hurst walked toward her car the men accosted her and forced the terrified victim into Hall's vehicle.

Hall drove off with the abducted woman in his car. The accomplice followed in the victim's vehicle. Hall drove Hurst to a wooded area where the two thugs raped and beat her savagely. After that they shot her to death execution style. To hide the body, Hall dragged the pregnant corpse deeper into the woods.

That night, in the murdered woman's car, Hall and his friend drove to the convenience store in Hernando County they planned to hold-up. As they sat in the parking lot waiting for the right moment to strike, a suspicious clerk inside the store called the sheriff's station. The sheriff's office happened to be across the street from where Hall and his accomplice were casing out the robbery.

Deputy Lonnie Coburn pulled into the parking lot and confronted the suspicious men. After getting the drop on the deputy, Hall shot the officer to death with his own service revolver.

A jury found Freddie Lee Hall guilty of two counts of first-degree murder on June 23, 1978. Jurors, by an eight to four vote, recommended the death penalty. The judge, four days later, sentenced Hall to death row.

At Hall's sentencing hearing, his lawyers had argued that their client was too stupid to execute. Public school officials in the 1960s had labeled him as "mentally retarded." Ten years before his death sentence, Hall had scored as low as 60 and as high as 80 on IQ tests. According to the American Psychiatric Association's *Manual of Mental Disorders,* an IQ of 70, plus or minus five points represents the upper range of intellectual disability.

Over the years, Hall's anti-capital punishment attorneys arranged to have him examined by a battery of psychiatrists and other medical practitioners who declared the death row inmate mentally disabled.

In 2002 the United States Supreme Court barred states from executing "mentally disabled" prisoners. The high court left the determination of who is so afflicted to the states. In Florida, as measured by an IQ test, the threshold for concluding that an inmate is mentally disabled is a score below 70. (In Florida, people with IQs as high as 75 are classified as mentally disabled for purposes of state welfare.)

On March 3, 2014, Hall's attorneys appeared before the U.S. Supreme Court on behalf of Freddie Lee Hall. The death house lawyers, in challenging Florida's mental threshold for execution, argued that IQ tests alone were insufficient in establishing mental disability.

Justice Antonin Scalia pointed out the brutality of Hall's crime, and noted that it had taken several steps for Hall to abduct then kill the pregnant woman. The killing of the police officer was certainly premeditated. Didn't the crime itself reflect sufficient mental capacity?

The decision in *Hall v. Florida* will come down in June 2014.

If a criminal is smart enough to read, get a driver's license, plan a robbery, and make an effort not to get caught, he's smart enough to execute.

The One-Drug Send Off

Anti-capital punishment activists and death house lawyers have been making a fuss over the fact that several states have recently executed their condemned prisoners with a single toxic drug, pentobarbital. In the past, executioners used a three-drug cocktail. Because the other two drugs are manufactured in country's that oppose the death penalty, these chemicals are no long available for this purpose in the U.S. Since the rope, the electric chair, the firing squad and the gas chamber are no longer execution options, states that still believe in capital punishment have no choice but to make do with pentobarbital. This has enraged anti-capital punishment advocates who consider the one-drug send-off cruel and unusual punishment. But this is nothing new. Capital punishment opponents object to the death penalty, period. They would complain if rapists and killers were tickled to death.

In Missouri, when judges and the governor were confronted with the choice of executing a prisoner with pentobarbital or commuting his sentence to life, they chose the deadly dose. This was not good news for Jeffrey Ferguson, a 59-year-old kidnapper, rapist, and murderer who had been living on Missouri's death row for nineteen years.

At eleven o'clock on the night of February 10, 1989, in St. Charles, Missouri, a suburb of St. Louis, 34-year-old Jeffrey Ferguson and his friend Kenneth Ousley pulled into a Shell gas station not far from Interstate 70. Across the street at the Mobile station, a 17-year-old employee named Kelli Hall was out front checking the fuel level in one of the station's underground gas tanks. The teenager caught Ferguson's eye.

Ferguson, with Ousley in his Chevrolet Blazer, pulled into the Mobile station. Ferguson got out of his SUV, approached the girl, and ordered her at gunpoint into the vehicle. The two men, with the girl in the backseat, drove off with the intention of raping and killing her.

In a remote area a few miles from St. Charles, Ferguson and Ousley tortured, raped, then murdered Kelli Hall by shooting her in the head with a .32-caliber handgun. They dumped her body in a farmer's field in Maryland Heights, Missouri.

Two weeks after the senseless, random lust killing, the owner of the St. Louis County farm stumbled across the victim's corpse near a shed. The teenager was naked except for a pair of socks.

In1993, Kenneth Ousley pleaded guilty to second-degree murder. The judge sentenced him to life with the possibility of parole. Two years later, Ferguson went on trial for kidnapping, rape, and first-degree murder. Taking the stand on his own behalf, the sociopath claimed that he could not have participated in the rape and murder because at the time he was passed out drunk in his truck. This story contradicted the defendant's confession to detectives shortly after his arrest.

The jury found Ferguson guilty as charged and recommended the death penalty. The judge sentenced him to death in December 1995. (At the time most Americans were wrapped up in the O.J. Simpson double murder case.)

After he had been in prison for some time, Ferguson expressed deep remorse for raping and murdering the 17-year-old girl. He also became religious, counseled inmates, and helped start a prison hospice program. All the while his team of attorneys appealed his case to the 8th Circuit Court of Appeals and ultimately to the U.S. Supreme Court. They lost all of their appeals.

Shortly after midnight on March 26, 2014, following a burst of last-minute pleas for a stay of execution, the executioner at the state prison in Bonne Terre, Missouri injected Ferguson with the lethal dose of pentobarbital. While several death penalty sob sisters pointed out in horror that Ferguson did not die quickly, the drug eventually did its job.

St. Louis County prosecutor Bob McCulloch, in speaking to reporters following the execution, said that Ferguson's good deeds in prison did not make up for what he had done to that innocent teenager. The prosecutor called Ferguson's crime "unspeakable," a word Ferguson's supporters would use to describe his death.

Dispatching a Rape Murderer

Dennis McGuire, 53, whose arguments that the new lethal injection protocol could cause terror and agony [like that of his victim] were rejected by a federal judge, was pronounced dead at 10:53 AM on January 14, 2014. Ohio adopted the new protocol--a combination of the sedative midozolam and the painkiller hydropmorphone--after the manufacturer of the old drug, pentobarbital, stopped selling it for lethal injections.

McGuire was convicted of raping, sodomizing and slashing the throat of an acquaintance Joy Stewart, who was eight months pregnant at the time of her murder in 1989....

McGuire was...given a last meal of roast beef, toasted bagel with cream cheese and onion, butter pecan ice cream, fried chicken, potato salad, fried potatoes with onion a Coca-Cola.

[Because it took the executioner 25 minutes to kill McGuire, his family has filed as unusual punishment lawsuit against the state of Ohio. At least Mr. McGuire was sent off with a full stomach.]

Tracy Connor, NBC News, January 16, 2014

All's Well That Ends Well

On June 3, 1999, in Perry, Oklahoma, 23-year-old Clayton Lockett, a violent criminal, accompanied by a pair of crime associates, invaded a home and severely beat the occupant. While Lockett assaulted 23-year-old Bobby Lee Bornt over a debt, a girl just out of high school knocked on Bornt's front door. Lockett appeared in the doorway and pulled the girl into the house.

After hitting the stunned visitor in the face with a shotgun, Lockett put the gun to her head and ordered her to invite her 18-year-old friend, Stephanie Neiman, into the duplex. Neiman had graduated from Perry High School less than a month earlier. She had been a good student, and played in the band.

The nightmare for these girls began with Lockett and his accomplices raping Nieman's friend and beating her with the shotgun. After the rape and beatings, Lockett bound the girls with duct tape and drove them and Bornt, in Neiman's pickup truck, to a remote area a few miles away. En route, he informed his captives that he planned to kill all three of them and bury their bodies in the woods. The terrified girls begged for their lives.

At the designated spot, Lockett made the rape victim dig a grave. When the hole was big enough, Lockett told Neiman to get into the grave. He pointed his shotgun at her and pulled the trigger. The weapon jammed. Lockett walked away, cleared the gun, and returned to the site where he shot and wounded Neiman. He forced the other girl to bury Stephanie Neiman alive. The 18-year-old was murdered because she had refused to promise Lockett that she wouldn't report the rape and kidnapping to the police.

Lockett and his degenerate friends drove the rape victim and Bornt back to the duplex. Lockett threatened to kill his traumatized victims if they went to the police.

As it turned out, one of the accomplices notified the authorities in the hopes of saving his neck. A local prosecutor charged Clayton Lockett with first-degree murder, rape, robbery, kidnapping, assault and battery, and burglary. Upon his arrest, the cold-blooded rapist and sadistic killer confessed to shooting the girl and having her buried alive.

In 2000, a jury found Lockett guilty as charged, and sentenced him to death. He ended up on death row at the Oklahoma State Penitentiary in McAlester.

After fourteen years of legal appeals, and a last minute stay, Governor Mary Fallin ordered Lockett's execution to take place on April 29, 2014. That evening, an hour before his scheduled death, Lockett fought with prison officers and had to be Taser stunned before being strapped onto the gurney. The executioner, after struggling to find a vein, administered the three-drug cocktail--midazalam to render Lockett unconscious, vecuronium to stop his breathing, and potassium chloride--to stop his heart.

Seven minutes after the drugs were put into Lockett's body, he was still conscious. Ten minutes later, after being declared dead, the condemned man moved his head and tried to climb off the gurney. He was also heard muttering the word, "man." At this point, a corrections official lowered the blind to spare witnesses the sight of a slower than planned execution.

Forty-three minutes after the executioner injected Lockett with the three drugs, he died of a heart attack. The potassium chloride had done its job, albeit a bit slowly.

As could be expected, death house lawyers, anti-capital punishment activists, and hand-wringing media types agonized over Lockett's imperfect execution. These death row sob sisters characterized his death as torture, an ordeal, and a nightmare, and called for the abolishment of the death penalty.

Where were these outrage mongers when Lockett shot Stephanie Neiman and buried her alive? In this case, who in their right mind would shed a tear for such a cruel, cold-blooded killer? So what if Mr. Lockett didn't pass gently and quickly into the night? A lot of people die slow, agonizing deaths, citizens who never committed rape or murder. Clayton Lockett is gone, and the world is a better place without him.

Since 1976, not counting Clayton Lockett, 1,203 inmates have been executed by lethal injection in the United States. Over the years, state corrections officials have done their best to find more humane ways to put condemned criminals to death. In the 19th and 20th centuries, death row inmates were hanged, electrocuted, suffocated in gas chambers, and shot. Hanging is still an option in New Hampshire and Washington. In Arizona, Missouri, and Wyoming, the gas chamber remains a death penalty choice.

Many correction experts believe the firing squad is the quickest and least painful way to execute a convict. In 1977, the firing squad was used to execute Gary Gilmore who asked to be so dispatched.

Saving a Killer

In 1991, 19-year-old Robert Campbell and another violent criminal abducted a 20-year-old bank clerk as she filled her car with gas at a Houston service station. The victim, Angela Rendon, had just purchased a bridal gown for her upcoming wedding.

The two criminal degenerates drove Campbell to a field where they robbed, raped, and beat her. After the vicious assaults, Campbell ordered the terrified victim to run for her life. As she fled her captors, he calmly shot her in the back.

A year after this senseless, cold-blooded murder, a jury found Campbell guilty of capital murder. The judge sentenced him to death. In this depressing case, there has never been a question of Campbell's murderous intent or guilt.

After living twenty-two years as a Texas death row inmate, Robert Campbell was finally scheduled to die by lethal injection on Tuesday night, May 13, 2014. University of Texas law professor Laurie Levin, one of Campbell's death house attorneys working feverishly to save his life, filed a last-minute motion for a stay of execution with the 5th Circuit Court of Appeals. Levin based the federal petition on the fact the Texas Department of Corrections had not revealed the manufacturing source of the pentobarbital purchased for the execution. (If it hadn't been for this issue, there would have been something else for Levin to base an appeal on.)

According to this eleventh-hour plea, prisoners have a right to know whether or not the pentobarbital has been manufactured under "pristine conditions" that would assure that the drug was safe. (What in the hell is a *safe* execution drug? Pentobarbital is not supposed to be *safe*--it's used to *kill* cold-blooded murders. We're not talking about medicine here.)

According to Professor Levin, if Campbell's execution was not blocked, the results could be "disastrous." (Again, from the executioner's point of view, the results are supposed to be *disastrous.*)

On another save-the-killer front, death house lawyers claimed that Campbell, with an I.Q. of 69, was too stupid to execute pursuant to a 2002 U.S. Supreme Court decision that prohibited states from executing criminal dimwits.

Robert Campbell's energetic and devoted legal team also asked Texas Governor Rick Perry to grant an executive stay of execution on Campbell's behalf.

On May 13, 2014, the day he was scheduled to die by lethal injection, the federal court of appeals stayed Campbell's execution. Had the executioner dispatched Campbell, he would have been the first condemned man to be put to death since the executioner in Oklahoma ran into trouble disposing of Clayton Lockett. Had Campbell been executed as scheduled according to the wishes of the jury, he would have been the eighth death row inmate killed this year by the state of Texas.

Bring Back Firing Squads

A lawmaker in Wyoming says the state ought to take action now to avoid a constitutional crisis if lethal injection for convicts is ever outlawed and pass a bill to allow for the return of firing squads.... Senator Bruce Burns said that Wyoming state law only allows for a gas chamber to be used in place of a lethal injection...but that causes a dilemma in his mind. "The state of Wyoming doesn't have a gas chamber...so the procedure and expense to build one would be impractical. I consider the gas chamber to be cruel and unusual, so I want the firing squad because they also have it in Utah."

Cheryl K. Chumley, *The Washington Times,* January 14, 2014

The Modern History of the Death Penalty

While the death penalty is still lawful in 31 states, only Alabama, Arizona, Florida, Georgia, Mississippi, Missouri, Ohio, Oklahoma, Virginia, and Texas actually execute their death row inmates. Contrary to popular belief, the U.S. Supreme Court has never ruled that the death penalty itself amounts to cruel and unusual punishment in violation of the Constitution's Eighth Amendment.

Since the mid-1980s, the states that carry out the death penalty have used lethal injection as the principal method of execution. Considered a more humane way to kill condemned prisoners than its predecessors the electric chair and the gas chamber, the use of drugs instead of electricity and lethal gas is more a matter of appearance--aesthetics if you will--than concern for the condemned.

Since 1976, 1,204 inmates have been executed by lethal injection. Four states--Alabama, Florida, South Carolina, and Virginia--still allow death row prisoners to choose between deadly drugs and the electric chair.

The Electric Chair

On August 6, 1890, William Kemmler, a convicted murderer serving time at New York's Auburn Prison, earned the distinction of becoming the first person in America to die in the electric chair. The state of Ohio followed New York by replacing hanging with electrocution in 1897. Massachusetts adopted the chair in 1900, New Jersey in 1906, and Virginia in 1908. By the 1930s most of the death penalty states used the electric chair as the primary method of execution. The other states killed their death row inmates by gas, by firing squad, or by rope. The state of Kansas continued to hang its prisoners into the early 1960s.

The state of Nebraska was one of the last jurisdictions to employ the electric chair as its sole method of killing murderers. In February 2008, the practice ended when the Nebraska Supreme Court ruled that electrocution was in itself cruel and unusual punishment in violation of the state's constitution.

The Gas Chamber

Death in a gas chamber usually took six to eighteen minutes. The execution ritual began with the condemned inmate being led into the death chamber and strapped into a chair by his arms, waist, ankles, and chest. A mask was placed over the prisoner's face, and the chamber sealed. The executioner poured sulfuric acid down a tube into a metal container on the floor, a canister that contained cyanide pellets. The mixture of the chemicals produced a cloud of lethal gas.

An open curtain allowed witnesses to observe the inmate inside the chamber. At the designated moment, the executioner hit an electric switch that combined the chemicals that produced the killing agent.

The gas chamber was an expensive form of execution. Moreover, one could argue that because the condemned man contributed to his own death by breathing in the gas, it was the most cruel. Dr. Allen McLean Hamilton, a toxicologist, first proposed the gassing of death row inmates to the state of Nevada in 1921. That year, state legislators abolished the electric chair in favor of the gas chamber. On February 8, 1924, a Chinese immigrant named Gee Jon became the first person in America to be executed by gas. He died in the chamber inside the Nevada State Penitentiary in Carson City.

Eventually adopted by eleven states as the official method of execution, lethal gas killed 594 prisoners in the U.S. from 1924 to 1999.

The Caryl Chessman Case

Caryl Chessman was an armed robber and serial rapist who spent most of his adult life behind bars. In 1948, a Los Angeles jury found him guilty of 17 counts of robbery, kidnapping, and rape. Among his crimes he had dragged--kidnapped--a 17-year-old girl named Mary Alice Meza out of her car and forced her to give him oral sex. He committed a similar offense against another victim, Regina Johnson. Under California law at the time, a kidnapping that involved bodily injury was a capital offense. Under this law, the judge sentenced Chessman to die in the gas chamber.

Following his highly publicized trial, Chessman continued to argue his innocence through essays and books. His two memoirs, written behind bars, became bestsellers. During his twelve years on San Quentin's death row, Chessman filed dozens of appeals, and managed to avoid eight execution dates. Following his failed last-minute attempt to avoid death with a writ of *habeas corpus* filed with the California Supreme Court, Chessman died of asphyxiation on May 2, 1960 in San Quentin's gas chamber. He is the only person to die in the gas chamber for a crime other than murder.

Lethal Injection

By the 21st century, state executioners were injecting death row inmates with a three-drug cocktail that included pentobarbital. When the European manufacturers of this deadly drug stopped exporting it and other killing agents to the United States, executioners found themselves in a fix. Some began using a single drug--usually pentobarbital if they had it--while others concocted new, experimental cocktails made of drugs available in the United States.

Anti-capital punishment activists have used the lethal drug supply problem to further their push to have the death penalty abolished altogether. But for these crusaders, if it's not the inhumanity of using untested drugs, it's something else. These death house lawyers and political activists object to executing prisoners who, when they murdered, were under eighteen; inmates who are fat with hard-to-find veins; killers with low I.Q.s; and in the case of a Missouri murderer named Russell Bucklew, a death row inmate who isn't *healthy* enough to be humanely executed.

Back to Bullets

In 2014, politicians in Utah, Wyoming, and Missouri proposed bringing back the firing squad. In Utah, legislators abolished death by firing squad in 2004, citing the excessive media attention surrounding this form of execution. Still, murderers sentenced before 2004 have the option to die by shooting. In 2010, Ronnie Lee Gardner, a man who fatally shot a Salt Lake City attorney in 1985 in Gardner's attempt to flee the court house selected the firing squad over lethal injection. Five police officers used .30-caliber Winchester rifles to carry out Gardner's execution. Unlike Clayton Lockett in Oklahoma, Mr. Gardner died instantly. Nevertheless, those who oppose capital punishment, fret that the executioners might miss their target, causing a slow and painful death. There is, however, a simple solution to this problem: give each executioner *two* bullets.

The Return of the Electric Chair

On May 22, 2014, Tennessee Governor Bill Hallam signed a bill allowing the state to electrocute death row inmates in the event the state is unable to acquire the proper drugs for the execution. Lawmakers had overwhelmingly passed the bill the previous month. And most people in the state support the new law. According to a recent Vanderbilt University poll, 56 percent of registered voters in the state welcome the return of the chair.

Corrections officials in Tennessee have been dealing with the lethal drug shortage. Electricity, on the other hand, doesn't come from Europe, and is in good supply.

In Tennessee, Daryl Holton, in 2009, became the last man in the state to die in the electric chair. In 1997, the Gulf War veteran murdered his three sons and a stepdaughter with a high-powered rifle in their Shelbyville, Tennessee garage. Death by electrocution had been his choice of execution.

The Thrill is Gone

During the late Middle Age (1000-1500), executions took place in the marketplace or in the village square, but by then they had become more formal, dignified, even ceremonial undertakings. Procedures were more elaborate; rage was blunted by formalities. For the grievous offenders of this time--a category including heretics--executions were elaborate highly planned exhibitions orchestrated by high officials. Rage was absent altogether in these pageants, but other strong emotions reigned. Most notably, there was excitement and awe, especially before the might and majesty of the Inquisition.

Executions marked by a restrained ceremony were the norm during the early modern period (1500-1800). Crowds of spectators might have lapsed into unseemly behavior, but such behavior was sharply at odds with the formal execution script. These executions featured ritual and etiquette, as in the late Middle Age, but little pomp or circumstance. Milder feelings, such as those of devotion were given an outlet in ceremony; excitement or awe was deemed inappropriately expressive. Officials and spectators were instead expected to show a quiet reverence, tinged by sadness.

In the modern period (from 1800 on), ceremony gradually gave way to bureaucratic procedure played out behind prison walls, in isolation from the community. Feelings are absent, or at least suppressed, in bureaucratically administered executions. With bureaucratic procedure, there is a functional routine dominated by hierarchy and task. Officials perform mechanically before a small, silent gathering of authorized witnesses who behave with marked restraint. Executions have come to be seen as "dirty work." Hence, there is no communal involvement of any sort. The proceedings are antiseptically arranged; few of us get our hands soiled.

Robert Johnson, *Death Work, Second Edition*, 1998

California's Death Penalty Unconstitutional

Since 1979, 900 inmates in California have been sentenced to death. But only thirteen have been executed. One of those unexecuted death row prisoners, Ernest Dewayne Jones, murdered and raped his girlfriend's mother in 1993. In 2011, Jones filed a petition with the federal court for the abolishment of the death penalty in the state. The lawyers filing the motion petitioned the judge to replace executions with life without parole sentences.

In 2006, another federal judge in California placed the state's death penalty on hold until corrections officials overhauled their lethal injections procedures and protocol. The California Department of Corrections and Rehabilitation, in an effort to comply with this judge's mandate, built a new execution chamber on the grounds of San Quentin in northern California.

On July 16, 2014, U.S. District Court Judge Cormac J. Carney declared California's death penalty unconstitutional. The judge wrote that "arbitrary factors" such as the manner in which corrections bureaucrats determined who would be executed and who wouldn't, made the process unfair and unpredictable. Moreover, the state's lethal injection procedures, according to the judge, created a risk an inmate might suffer pain during the execution.

In concluding that California's execution law and procedures violated the U.S. Constitution's Eighth Amendment right against cruel and unusual punishment, Judge Carney wrote: "As for the random few for whom execution does become a reality, they have languished so long on death row that their executions serve no retributive or deterrent purpose." [No retributive purpose? Tell that the families of the people these cold-blooded killers had murdered without regard for the pain and suffering of their victims.]

Since most of California's death row inmates die of old age before their dates with the executioner, the federal judge's ruling will have little practical affect on the state's criminal justice system.

The improvement of the state's execution facility in response to the 2006 federal ruling turned out to be another example of California tax money poured down the drain.

15 MISCELLANEOUS CRIME

Perjury

More than 90 percent of the criminal cases in American are not tried before a jury. Bargained guilty pleas have essentially replaced the cumbersome and costly trial process. Still, tens of millions of Americans receive jury duty summonses every year. (Our criminal justice system would collapse if just 20 percent of defendants demanded a jury trial. The entire system is set up for guilty pleas based on negotiated sentencing deals. Legislators make maximum sentences for even minor crimes extremely high to give prosecutors more bargaining power.)

In high-profile criminal trials, the outcome of the case is pretty much determined by which side does the best job of jury selection. O. J. Simpson got off because his attorneys won the jury selection battle. To a certain degree, these trials are over before the first witness takes the stand. Wealthy defendants often hire juror picking consultants who help design a defense-friendly jury. These psychological profilers match jurors to defendants by analyzing such factors as body language, hairstyles, clothing, gender, marital status, age, race, education, and occupation. In high-profile cases, the jury selection process can go on for months.

Juries, in general, do not represent a cross-section of American society. Entire categories of people never see the jury box. For various reasons, juries rarely include professors, cops, physicians, nurses, small business owners, small company employees, college students, young mothers, and lawyers. Most juries are made up of retirees, government workers, employees of large corporations, and people who are unemployed. As a law graduate, criminal justice professor, small business owner, and former FBI agent, I couldn't buy my way onto a jury. I've never made it from the big room full of prospective jurors to the courtroom where lawyers from each side choose the final twelve.

There are all kinds of reasons and ways for a prospective juror to get out of jury duty. People can be excused for poor health, a criminal record, an upcoming wedding, family demands, mental illness, various economic hardships, and the stated inability to render an unbiased decision. In Michigan, lawmakers recently approved a bill that exempts breast-feeding mothers from jury duty. While prospective jurors are not above telling lies to get out of sitting on a jury, prosecutions for this form of lying under oath are extremely rare. That makes the following case so unusual.

In June 2011, Susan Cole, a 57-year-old beautician and Mary Kay cosmetics saleswoman, received a summons for jury duty. She arrived at the courthouse in Denver with her hair in curlers, and dressed according to her idea of how mentally ill people present themselves. She wore too much lipstick, reindeer socks (I have no idea what they are), and mismatched sneakers. She had put on a tee shirt that read: "Ask Me About My Bestseller." (In 2007 Cole, under the pen name Char Cole, had self-published a relationship, self-help book/memoir called "Seven Institutions With El-Way Secrets." My advice to this author: next time you publish a book, select a title that makes sense.)

When Judge Anne Mansfield asked Cole if she had a history of mental illness, the prospective juror said, "Yeah, I have some mental issues...I broke out of domestic violence in the military [after her divorce she joined the Army] and have a lot of repercussions. I get very confused in the morning when I try to get ready." (Like forgetting to take out her curlers.) The prospective juror said that as a result of the domestic violence, she suffered from Post Traumatic Stress Disorder (PTSD). Cole also told the judge she was homeless, and living on the street. Judge Mansfield asked if anyone objected to the dismissal of this woman. No one did, and Cole went home.

On October 17, 2011, on Denver's "Dave Logan Show," a radio call-in program, callers were telling stories about how they had avoided jury duty. Susan Cole joined in the fun by calling the show and telling how she had recently gotten out of jury duty by impersonating a mentally ill person. Obviously aware that she was admitting to a crime Cole called in under her pen name, Char.

In justifying her jury avoiding ploy, Cole told the radio audience that she was simply too busy for jury duty. Rather than being ashamed of having lied under oath to avoid a basic civic responsibility, Cole seemed quite proud of herself: "I put black eyebrows on. I put red lipstick on. I left my hair in my curlers, and I put on a tee-shirt that said, 'Ask Me About My Bestseller.' [When did mentally ill homeless women start putting up their hair?] For about two weeks after, when my roommate and I would think about it, or I would tell my clients about it, we would cry we would laugh so hard."

One of the "Dave Logan Show" listeners, Anne Mansfield, the judge Susan Cole had lied to, didn't find her story so funny. The judge knew exactly who this caller was, and notified the prosecutor's office. The prosecutor initiated a criminal investigation.

Detectives looking into the case found no mention of spousal abuse, or PTSD, in Cole's divorce records. Moreover, her military file contained no documentation supporting such a diagnosis. On March 22, 2012, police arrested Cole on charges of first-degree perjury, and attempt to influence a public servant (the judge).

Before being hauled off to jail, Cole told detectives that the military had lost her medical records. And the only person who had diagnosed her with PTSD, a Jefferson County court counselor, has since died. Cole said that in her book, she writes of being imprisoned five days in a military mental institution. She also claimed that on the night before her jury duty appearance, she had been traumatized by news that her cousin had been killed in a motorcycle accident. As it turned out, her cousin hadn't been involved in the crash. Assuming this is not a load of crap, how does this explain why she had prepared for jury duty by dressing up like a mentally ill person? Why would a "traumatized" person go to such lengths?

On November 13, 2012, after pleading guilty to second-degree burglary, the judge sentenced Cole to two years in prison.

Bank Robbery

Shortly after the Pilgrims planted their feet on Plymouth Rock, there was a problem with thieves. Crime crept like a plague from the boats of the Pilgrims, bringing to the new land all of the old conditions--both good and bad--that had defined Europe throughout the centuries. Robbing banks, however, had never been an established practice in the Old World. Instead, it can be chalked up as one of the great innovations in civilization brought to fruition in the new frontier nation--the United States.

L. R. Kirchner, *Robbing Banks*, 2003

Archaeological Looting

The lobbying efforts of the Society for American Archaeology, an international organization dedicated to the research, interpretation, and protection of the archaeological heritage of the Americas, led to the passage of the Archaeological Resource Protection Act (ARPA), federal legislation signed into law in October 1979 by President Jimmy Carter. Under Title 16 of the United States Code, Sections 470, ARPA preserves archaeological resources on federal and Indian lands with the aim to prevent the loss of irreplaceable artifacts that are part of the nation's cultural heritage.

At its core, ARPA makes it a federal crime to excavate, remove, damage, alter, and/or deface (without a government permit) archaeological resources from protected areas. It is also a federal offense, under this law, to traffic interstate in artifacts acquired in violation of the act or in breach of local or state law. Under ARPA, an "archaeological resource" is an item of past human existence or archaeological interest more than a hundred years old.

First-time ARPA offenders, in cases where the value of the artifacts and the cost of restoration and repair of the damaged archaeological site is less than $500, can be fined no more than $10,000 or imprisoned for more than a year. However, if the value or restoration costs exceed $500, the offender can be fined up to $20,000 and imprisoned for two years on each count. Repeat ARPA offenders can be fined $100,000 and sent to prison for five years on each count. Under ARPA, federal authorities can pursue violators civilly or in criminal court, imposing fines and confiscating vehicles and equipment used in the commission of the prohibited activity.

Earl K. Shumway

Earl K. Shumway, the central figure in the country's first major ARPA case, came from a family of archaeological looters. Earl grew up in Moab, Utah, a Mormon town seventy miles north of the four corners village of Blanding, where, in June 2009, FBI and Bureau of Land Management (BLM) agents raided the homes of eleven ARPA defendants. DeLoy Shumway, Earl's father, spent years plundering Anasazi ruins for pottery and other artifacts in the Puebloan region of the Colorado Plateau in southeastern Utah. In the early 1980s, Earl's distant cousin, Casey Shumway, had the distinction of being the nation's first ARPA defendant convicted of the offense.

From 700 to 1300, the Peublo (also referred to as the Anasazi) people grew beans and corn and built masonry structures--so-called cliff dwellings--into canyon alcoves that still show rock petroglyphs depicting animals, human figures, and prehistoric tools. Just before the turn of the fourteenth century, social upheaval and prolonged drought caused these people to migrate south. They never returned, but left in Utah's San Juan County alone, a place the size of Connecticut, 28,000 known archaeological sites.

In 1850, Mormon settlers to southwestern Utah found, scattered virtually everywhere, prehistoric tools, flint projectile points, and shards of Anasazi pottery. The collecting of prehistoric pottery began in the late 1800s after Richard Wetherill and his brother, Colorado ranchers, discovered Anasazi ruins in Mesa Verdi. In the canyon cliff dwellings they found decorated pottery, jewelry, tools, sandals, and woven blankets. The brothers also discovered thousands of gravesites containing human skeletons wrapped in blankets.

The Wetherill discoveries launched a lucrative trade in Native American artifacts fueled by competition between the Smithsonian and other U. S. museums, and a growing interest among the general pubic in Indian relic collecting.

Up until 1930, archaeologists and curators at the University of Utah paid artifact hunters two dollars for every piece of pottery (called "pots" by collectors) they brought to the school. Earl Shumway's grandfather, in the 1920s, sold 370 pieces of Anasazi pottery to the university. In those days he could acquire up to seventeen pots in a single day, and in a productive month, dig up two hundred, many of which ended up in a local museum.

Craig Childs, in his book *Finders Keepers*, chronicles the early relationship between the region's pot hunters and the university: "In the 1920s an archaeologist named Andrew Kerr from the University of Utah in Salt Lake appeared after he heard that an entire quarter of the state was filthy with archaeology right near the surface, graves practically springing from the ground. Kerr hired local residents to dig; his head diggers were members of the Shumway family who had already done a good deal of private excavation. The Shumways did most of the work while Kerr sat back. They showed him how to locate the best caches of artifacts, how to dig without breaking pots. Meanwhile, Kerr encouraged them and paid them to become even better at it. Showing little regard for scientific method, he wanted only the most visually stunning artifacts which he shipped back to the university museum."

According to William Hurst, an archaeologist and lifelong resident of Blanding, Utah, Anasazi projectile points, tools, and pottery, during the 1950s and 1960s, were everywhere and easy to find. Most of the local collectors were surface hunters who picked up pieces from cultivated fields. In those days, collecting arrowheads in and around Blanding was like picking up seashells from a beach.

A Blanding resident and artifact collector, speaking about what it was like in the 1950s and 1960s, said this to a journalist writing about the plundering of Anasazi sites: "This was our way of life. You could find artifacts just everywhere. You can go in any direction from Blanding and they'll be mounds and dwellings and arrowheads and artifacts." In the same article, Toni Turk, the then mayor of Blanding, also described how it was for collectors in those days: "The pottery was so commonplace that kids would use them for target practice, they would throw rocks at them. There was nothing particularly special about them. Some people started seeing in them some art value for themselves and they'd start collecting."

Blanding mayor Turk also spoke of archaeological looters like Earl Shumway and his father. "Some people went in with heavy machinery. It took a lot of labor off the effort to dig up graves. They dug down to get the treasures. These are people who stepped across the lines of propriety. They got into looting graves and grave goods."

According to Wayne Dance, the Assistant United States Attorney (AUSA) for the Utah District from 1990 to 2007, the prosecutor who targeted Earl Shumway and ended up prosecuting more ARPA subjects than any AUSA in the country, the bulk of Anasazi looting took place within a hundred mile, north-south corridor stretching from Moab to the town of Bluff on the edge of the Navajo Reservation near the Arizona state line.

In 1985, a federal grand jury sitting in Salt Lake City, indicted Earl K. Shumway, then twenty-five, on four felony counts in violation of the Archaeological Resources Protection Act. The fierce and flamboyant looter with the wild shock of red hair and matching mustache, had openly bragged about how much money he made selling Anasazi pottery, baskets, human remains, and other artifacts from hundreds of archaeological sites which he left littered with empty Mountain Dew cans.

Because Shumway also boasted of carrying a .44 magnum revolver he'd use on anyone who'd confront him while digging for artifacts, federal agents despised and feared him. The AUSA charged Shumway with the removal and sale of thirty-four prehistoric baskets excavated from Horse Rock Ruin on federal land near Allen Canyon, Manti-La Sal National Forest in southeastern Utah. Shumway and his crew had been digging on this site since 1981. Tried and convicted in 1986, Shumway, to avoid serving time in prison, identified, for the FBI, a long list of artifact collectors living in Blanding. In turning snitch, he avoided prison and settled scores with collectors he didn't like. His information also led to a series of ARPA SWAT raids that year. All of those cases were eventually dropped.

After informing on collectors, Earl Shumway returned to looting archaeological sites on federal land. In November 1994, a former Shumway business partner told the FBI that Shumway had been plundering artifacts at Horse Rock Ruin. The snitch said that Shumway had cheated him out of his share of the loot. Shortly after his arrest, Shumway pleaded guilty to three ARPA counts and a federal firearms charge. In return for his guilty plea, the judge sentenced the serial looter to probation.

In June 1995, just seven months after Shumway's guilty plea, AUSA Wayne Dance, having successfully prosecuted forty ARPA defendants, convinced members of a federal grand jury in Utah to indict Shumway on a pair of four-year-old ARPA cases.

In 1991, Shumway had met helicopter pilot Michael Miller at a pool hall in Moab. After regaling Miller with stories of his archaeological adventures and the big money he made selling Anasazi pottery, baskets, and human remains, Miller contacted a helicopter pilot named John Ruhl and asked him to fly the pair around in search of potential sites. Shumway's father had taught Earl how to use aircraft in search for ruins. With diggers on the ground and a lookout in the sky, looters could easily avoid detection. Shumway, with Ruhl's knowledge, rented a helicopter by telling Ruhl's employer he was a film scout.

Ruhl flew Miller and Shumway to Dop-Ki Cave in Utah's Canyonlands National Park, a 350,000-acre tract where they dug up the skeleton of an infant wrapped in a blanket inside a burial basket. Shumway took the blanket and all of the bones except the skull. A few days later, Ruhl flew Shumway and Miller to Horse Rock Ruin where they spent the night. The next morning, Shumway dug up a pair of ancient sandals and a sleeping mat.

At Shumway's November 1995 trial, AUSA Dance, through DNA analysis, connected the defendant to a cigarette butt found at the Dop-Ki Cave site. The jurors, based upon the first use of DNA evidence in an ARPA case, found Shumway guilty.

Convicted of seven felony counts, Judge David K. Winder, appalled at Shumway's callous handling of the infant's remains, exceeded ARPA's punishment guidelines by sentencing the looter to six and a half years in prison. The judge also fined him $3,500. Shumway appealed his sentence to the Tenth Circuit Court of Appeals that reduced it to five years, three months.

While being transported to prison, a group of Native American prisoners gave Shumway a severe beating. In 2003, three years after getting out of prison, Earl K. Shumway died of cancer. He was forty-six-years-old.

Making Funny Money

The most difficult, intricate crime involves counterfeiting money. Let me rephrase that. The most difficult, intricate crime is *successful* counterfeiting. Unsuccessful counterfeiters are everywhere, particularly in prison, having failed to live up to their expectations.

Chuck Sheppard, *America's Lest Successful Criminals*, 1993

The Counterfeit Ring

In the old days, counterfeiters made funny money the hard way: they laboriously, and with great skill and craftsmanship, engraved metal, facsimile plates. The quality of their fake twenties and hundred-dollar bills depended upon the engraving detail, the color of the ink, and the softness, strength, and feel of the paper used to approximate the government's secret blend. In those days only a handful of forgers possessed the skill and equipment needed to counterfeit money. This made them easy to identify, and to catch. But with ink in their blood, these men, the minute they got out of prison, returned to their illicit trades. The most skillful counterfeiters were driven by the challenge to produce fake money indistinguishable from the real thing.

In the late Twentieth Century, with advances in computer, photocopy, and graphic arts technology, counterfeiters could produce half-decent fake bills by simply copying real money. At that time, American paper currency was the easiest money in the world to counterfeit. In an effort to render bills more difficult to replicate, the U. S. Treasury Department redesigned the larger denominations. (At one time the government printed $500 and $1,000-dollar bills. The largest denomination today is $100.)

The U.S. government's anti-counterfeiting measures included adding holograms, embedded inks whose colors change depending on the angle of light, more color, and larger presidential portraits. The first bills to be redesigned were the tens, twenties, and fifties. The government didn't issue the new 100s until February 2011. The 5-dollar bill has not been changed.

The redesigned currency has driven the amateurs out of the funny money business, but it hasn't discouraged counterfeiters like Heath J. Kellogg. In 2011, the 36-year-old counterfeiter owned and operated a graphic and web design shop in Marietta, Georgia. In February of that year, Kellogg, who has a history of forged check convictions, allegedly began producing fake $50-dollar bills. (Fifties are rarely counterfeited.)

According to court documents, Kellogg approximated the security threads in government bills by using pens with colored ink that showed up under ultraviolet lamps. He printed out the facsimile fronts and backs separately, then glued the sheets together.

In May 2011, a bank in Atlanta sent the Secret Service seven fake 50-dollar bills. Three months later, agents arrested a man in Conyers, Georgia who was passing $50-dollar bills that matched the seven fakes that passed through the bank in Atlanta.

The counterfeit bill passer had purchased his fake bills with a face value of $2,000 for $900 in genuine money. The arrestee identified Mr. Kellogg as the manufacturer of the fake fifties, and agreed to cooperate with the Secret Service.

Agents arrested a second member of the counterfeit distribution ring who also became an undercover Secret Service operative. On November 15, 2012, following the execution of two search warrants and two controlled undercover buys of counterfeit currency from the suspect, agents arrested Heath Kellogg.

The Assistant United States attorney in the Northern District of Georgia charged Kellogg with conspiracy to manufacture and distribute counterfeit U.S. currency. Five other men were charged in connection with the passing of Mr. Kellogg's contraband product. The federal prosecutor believed that Kellogg and his accomplices injected $1.1 million worth of fake $50-dollar bills into the local economy.

In November 2013, a jury found Mr. Kellogg guilty as charged. On March 24, 2014, the federal judge sentenced him to 12 years in prison.

Two days after the counterfeiter's sentencing, the judge sent accomplice Stacy P. Smith to prison for three years. Following his prison stretch, Smith faced three years of supervised release. The judge sentenced four other members of the Kellogg counterfeiting ring in March 2014. Those sentences ranged from 18-months behind bars to five years probation.

The Great Impostor

While most people aren't con artists, charlatans, and swindlers, many are, in various degrees, cheats and pretenders. Men without military experience impersonate war heroes, politicians pretend to lead, bureaucrats impersonate competent employees, and job applicants falsely claim qualifications and work histories. It's not uncommon for young men to break the law by impersonating cops and FBI agents. Because most law enforcement impostors are inept, they are quickly caught.

In 1937, 16-year-old Ferdinand Waldo Demara, Jr. ran away from his home in Lawrence, Massachusetts. He took up residence with Cistercian monks in Rhode Island then in 1941, joined the U. S. Army. A year later, Demara went AWOL. Under the name Anthony Ignolia, he lived in another monastery before signing up with the Navy. Demara next faked his suicide, adopted the name Robert Lincoln French, and began playing the role of a religiously oriented psychologist. This led to a teaching position in a college psychology department.

Bored with teaching, Demara worked as an orderly in a Los Angeles sanitarium then moved to Washington State where he taught at St. Martin's College. The FBI interrupted his impersonation career by arresting him for desertion. That resulted in an 18-month stretch in a federal prison.

Following his release from the federal penitentiary, Demara joined the Brothers of Christian Instruction order in Maine. There, Demara became friends with a young physician that led to the impostor becoming a trauma surgeon aboard a Royal Canadian Navy destroyer during the Korean War. Demara actually operated on 16 South Korean soldiers wounded in combat.

He managed this by speed-reading surgical textbooks. All of his patients survived. Later exposed as a phony physician, the Canadian Navy did not press charges.

In 1951, as Brother John Payne of the Christian Brothers of Instruction, Demara founded a college called La Mennais College of Alfred Maine. He left the state shortly thereafter. (In 1959, the college moved to Canton, Ohio, and in 1960, changed its name to Walsh College.)

In the early 1960s, Demara worked as a prison administrator in Huntsville, Texas, and as a counselor at the Union Rescue Mission in Los Angeles. In 1967, at age 46, he received a Graduate Certificate in Bible from Multnomah Bible College in Portland, Oregon. In the late 1970s, Demara became a chaplain at a hospital in Anaheim, California. He became ill in 1980, and on June 7, 1982, died at the age of 62.

Demara had become famous in the late 1950s after he sold his story to *Life Magazine*. In 1961, Tony Curtis played him in a popular movie called "The Great Impostor." Demara credited his impostor success to his high IQ, his photographic memory, and his understanding of institutional politics.

Police Officer Impersonators: Four Cases

Years ago when starting out in St. Louis as an FBI agent I worked on a squad that, among other things, handled impersonation cases. Because I felt that *I* was impersonating a FBI agent, and getting paid for it, I didn't like these assignments. While it is a federal crime to impersonate a federal law enforcement officer, federal prosecutors will not press a case unless the perpetrator misrepresented to acquire something of value. In the cases I worked the impersonators were trying to impress someone, often a woman, or simply trying to make their lives seem more exciting. (The beauty of impersonating a FBI agent over actually being one is that the impersonator doesn't have the paperwork associated with the job.) I questioned several of these people and found them harmless and in some cases pathetic.

Naftali Berrill, the director of a private consulting firm called New York Forensics believes that police impersonators come in two flavors, and that both types pose a danger to themselves and to others. One group consists of criminal predators who employ the ruse to gain entry into a house or a car with the intent of robbery, rape or murder. (Serial killer Ted Bundy lured some of his victims into his Volkswagen by impersonating a police detective.) Many of these predator impersonators are violent sociopaths.

According to Berrill the second group of impersonators are men who are mentally or emotionally disturbed. Many of these people deal with feelings of inadequacy by using the indicia of law enforcement to exert power over others. Many of them are also depressed and lonely. Some are suicidal while a few might be capable of much worse. Police impersonators, as the cases below reveal, come from all walks of life. And not all of them were losers in their real lives.

Raised in Argentina, Alfredo Borodowski earned his degree in law in 1996 at the University of Buenos Aires. After immigrating to the U.S. he became an ordained rabbi. In 2013, Borodowski lived in the Westchester County community of Larchmont, New York where he presided as rabbi of the Sulam Yaakov Congregation.

In 2013, in the Westchester towns of White Plains, Yonkers, Greenburgh, and Mamaroneck, Rabbi Borodowski began impersonating a police officer by flashing a fake badge at motorists who annoyed him by either driving too slowly or erratically. In one case a 26-year-old driver told police officers that a man (Borodowski) chased him down, and as a police officer, scolded him for swerving in front of him.

Borodowski yelled at a 24-year-old woman for driving too slowly in a school zone. In White Plains, the rabbi tailgated a man then ordered him off the road by flashing a badge. The motorist's offense: Driving too slowly. The rabbi cop impersonator, on the Sprain Brook Parkway, chased a 30-year-old woman three miles then banged on her widow as she waited at a traffic light. According to this motorist, "He pulled out a badge and told me that he's going to have me arrested. First he said it was for slow driving. Then he said, 'no, I'm going to lock you up for erratic driving.' When the light turned green he jumped into his car and peeled off."

When real police officers took Rabbi Borodowski into custody, he denied impersonating a police officer. "What happened," he said, "was that the girl was driving too slow, and I hate it when people do this because it causes traffic backups. She must have been going 15 miles per hour so I told her, 'police! I am calling the police.'"

In February 2014, Rabbi Borodowski, the self-appointed crusader against slow driving, pleaded guilty in exchange for a fine instead of time in jail. The police impersonator also promised to seek psychiatric counseling.

On August 9, 2013, a police officer in Old Lyme, Connecticut, in response to a call from a citizen who spotted a man walking along a beach road with a handgun holstered at his side, came upon a blue 2004 Ford Crown Victoria that looked like a police car. The officer took note of the two-way radio and police-style emergency lights. The Ford's license plate revealed that the vehicle was registered to Bruce W. Browne, a resident of Wolcott, Connecticut. The officer learned that the owner of the police-style car was the estranged, half-brother of Scott Brown, the former U.S. Senator from Massachusetts. (Senator Brown does not spell his last name with the silent e.)

Earlier that day, Mr. Browne had approached three boaters as a law enforcement officer. (Browne had served a stint with the U.S. Coast Guard Reserves.)

Inside Bruce Browne's Ford Crown Victoria police officers discovered a cache of police related equipment that included three loaded 9 mm pistols, a black nylon duty belt with two sets of handcuffs, an expandable baton, and twelve loaded pistol magazines. Mr. Browne also possessed a bulletproof vest with "POLICE" embroidered on the front and back. A silver TSA (Transportation Security Administration) badge was attached to the police vest.

A local Connecticut prosecutor charged Bruce Browne with impersonating a police officer, breach of peace, interfering with a police officer, and possession of a dangerous weapon in a vehicle. The suspect posted his $50,000 bail.

In February 2014, the 49-year-old Browne pleaded guilty to impersonating a police officer and falsifying a military discharge certificate. Two months later, in Bridgeport, Connecticut, the judge sentenced Browne to a prison term of one year and a day. (Without the extra day, the crime would have been a misdemeanor offense served in a local jail. By adding the day, the case became a felony that involved a stretch in prison.)

In September 2013, an officer with the Indianapolis, Indiana Police Department spotted, along a funeral procession route for a police officer killed in the line of duty, 38-year-old Ninh Nguyen. Nguyen, wore a police uniform that included a duty belt with a holstered gun, two sets of handcuffs, and a Taser. The Indianapolis officer, from past experience with Nguyen, knew he was a police impersonator. The officers saw the fake cop taking photographs of the funeral procession from his black 2012 Dodge Charger. Nguyen had equipped the vehicle with a siren, flashing lights, and a two-way radio.

Following Nguyen's arrest, a Marion County prosecutor charged him with impersonating a public servant, a felony that carries a sentence in Indiana of six months to three years in prison. The prosecutor also charged Nguyen with theft of city property. The suspect pleaded not guilty to all charges, posted his bond and was released from jail.

In the trunk on Nguyen's phony police car, officers found an AR-15 semi-automatic rifle and police equipment that had been stolen from the Indianapolis Police Department. A search of his house produced a 37-millimeter grenade launcher, more assault rifles, shotguns, more handguns, and several thousand rounds of ammunition.

This was not the first time Mr. Nguyen had been in trouble with the law for this type of behavior. In 2004, while driving a white Ford Crown Victoria with strobe lights, Nguyen pulled over a motorist for speeding. The cop impersonator wore a security officer's uniform. Two years later the authorities charged Nguyen with the unlawful use of a police radio, a misdemeanor offense. A local prosecutor dismissed that offense. In 2012 police were investigating Nguyen in connection with a peeping Tom accusation. That case did not lead to an arrest.

As of August 2014, Mr. Nguyen awaits his trial on the police impersonation and theft charges.

On Monday evening, June 2, 2014, in St. Augustine, Florida, a St. Johns County detective behind the wheel of an unmarked police car on the International Golf Parkway, passed a 1999 Ford Crown Victoria. Matthew Michael Lee McMahon, the driver of the car, turned on his red and blue emergency lights, pulled up alongside the police officer, and with a stern look on his face, gave him the slow-down hand gesture. The real officer pulled out of traffic and came to a stop on the shoulder of the highway. When McMahon didn't take the bait the St. Johns County officer pursued McMahon and pulled him over.

That night McMahon found himself sitting in the county jail. The next morning a local prosecutor charged him with the improper display of blue lights. The accused impersonator paid his $5,500 bond and walked out of the St. Johns County Detention Facility. As of August 2014 his case had not come to trial.

Note to police impersonators: It's never a good idea to enforce the law on a cop. If you do, the cop will return the favor.

Hit and Run

America's Silent Crime Wave

Those who accidentally injure or kill pedestrians and others with their vehicles then leave the scene of the accident, come from all walks of life. Most of them are ordinary people who do not live lives of crime. They flee the site of the mishap for different reasons. Hit-and-run drivers don't stop because they are intoxicated, driving on suspended driver's licenses, don't have insurance, are accompanied by someone they shouldn't be with, or are being sought by the authorities. Hit-and-run victims also represent a cross-section of American society.

Hit-and-run cases are difficult to solve because so many of them occur at night with no witnesses. Even if investigators link a particular car or truck to the victim through hair follicle, textile, or DNA evidence, the prosecutor still has to place the defendant in that vehicle. Judges in hit-and-run cases resulting in injury or death are often reluctant to send convicted defendants to prison. These are not intentional crimes, and those convicted are usually not hardened criminals. Families of hit-and-run victims believe these defendants get off light.

Nationwide there are about 6 million traffic accidents a year. At least ten percent of these crashes involve hit-and-run drivers. Of the 600,000 or so hit-and-run cases every year, about a third result in injury or death. Los Angeles, according to a recent journalistic study by *L. A. Weekly*, is in the midst of a hit-and-run epidemic. Every year, more than 4,000 people in the city of 3.8 million are hurt or killed by hit-and-run drivers. Almost half of the city's traffic accidents are hit-and-run cases. The staggering rate of this crime has overwhelmed the Los Angeles police.

Because the hit-and-run accident has become such a commonplace event, these cases do not attract a lot of coverage in the media. Exceptions involve drivers who are professional athletes, TV actors, politicians, or anyone remotely famous. A hit-and-run case made national news in 1999 when 43-year-old Bryon Smith ran over the horror novelist, Stephen King. King was jogging on a remote road near North Lovell, Maine when Smith plowed into him. The writer nearly lost a leg, and Smith lost his driver's license. A year after the judge gave Smith a suspended sentence, the hit-and-run driver committed suicide.

On January 14, 2013, a "hit-and-run" Google search covering a period of 24 hours, revealed more than thirty cases across America, a fraction of the actual number. In Los Angeles County, a hit and run driver killed 31-year-old twin sisters Tanisha and Tamaya Davis as they brawled in the middle of the street at three in the morning. The driver has not been identified.

In the early morning hours of January 14, sheriff's deputies found a hit-and-run victim lying dead on the road in North Charleston, North Carolina. In Framingham, Oregon, a 58-year-old man was seriously injured at 7:30 in the evening when a motorist ran over him as he crossed the street. The police are looking for a blue Toyota sedan. A hit-and-run driver on the south side of Indianapolis killed a female pedestrian at elven-thirty in the morning. In Houston, Texas, at ten-thirty at night, a 64-year-old man was killed when he tried to cross a busy road that had no crosswalk. He was hit by a gray Toyota pickup. A man in Brooklyn, New York was injured by a motorist while riding a bicycle at four in the morning. A driver on a road in Poulsbo, Washington hit two female pedestrians from behind. The injured women ended up in a roadside ditch. The case has not been solved.

A Bad Driving Record

On Saturday, January 13, 2013, a hit-and-run driver struck 28-year-old Catherine Calalang and her 20-year-old cousin Laurene Jiminez as they walked along a road in Camden County, New Jersey. Calalang had five teeth knocked out, and suffered facial injuries. Jiminez suffered serious head injuries. The next day, Voorhees Township police received an anonymous tip that led them to Magnolia, New Jersey where they found a damaged Ford Fusion parked on the street. The vehicle, registered to 44-year-old Michele Toussaint of Berlin, New Jersey, contained physical evidence linking it to the hit-and-run.

Michele Toussaint, since 1991, had 52 driver's license arrests and 16 moving traffic violations. (Toussaint's husband had been killed in a traffic accident.) She was charged with leaving the scene of an accident, endangering an injured victim, and causing injury while driving on a suspended license. Toussaint was taken into custody on January 13 and placed into the Camden County Correctional Facility under $62,500 bail. Toussaint told the arresting officers that she was about to turn herself in.

As of July 2014 Toussaint had not been tried or sentenced.

No Prison Time

In October 2011, 80-year-old Helen Fettes, while driving on a road in Olmsted, Ohio in the Cleveland area, killed 13-year-old Charlie Kho. After running the boy over, Fettes drove away. In November 2012, after pleading no contest to aggravated vehicular homicide, the judge sentenced Fettes to five years of house arrest. The judge also suspended Fettes' driving privileges for life, and ordered her to pay $125,000 in restitution.

The Brooklyn Hit-and-Run Murders

Nachman and Raizy Glauber were members of the ultra-Orthodox Satmar Hasidic Jewish community in the Williamsville section of Brooklyn, New York. He was studying to become a rabbi, and she worked at a hardware distribution store. The 21-year-olds were married a year ago after having been paired by a matchmaker. Raizy was seven months pregnant with their first child.

On Saturday, March 2, 2013, Raizy became worried because she could no longer feel the baby. The couple didn't own a car, so Nachman called a car service to drive them to Long Island College Hospital. Around midnight, Pedro Nunez Delacruz arrived at the Glauber apartment in his livery car. The couple climbed into the back seat of his black 2008 Toyota Camry. Raizy was seated behind the driver.

A few minutes after being picked up by Delacruz, the livery car, while moving through a Brooklyn intersection, was struck by a 2010 gray BMW traveling 60 miles per hour. Ejected from the livery cab, Raizy's body came to rest beneath a parked tractor-trailer. Nachman was left pinned inside the crushed Toyota. (The Toyota's engine ended up in the back seat where Raizy Glauber had been sitting.)

Following the collision, the driver of the BMW, 44-year-old Julio Acevedo, climbed out of the sedan and sat on the curb to collect himself. A few minutes later, he returned to the mangled BMW and helped a female passenger out of the car. Acevedo and his companion walked away from the crash, disappearing into the gathering crowd.

Raizy Glauber, who spoke to paramedics, died in the ambulance as it sped to Bellevue Hospital in Manhattan. Pronounced dead on arrival, doctors delivered her baby by cesarean. The premature baby was born alive.

Doctors pronounced Nachman Glauber dead on arrival at Manhattan's Beth Israel Hospital.

The next day, a spokesperson for the New York Medical Examiner's Office announced that the Glauber had been killed by blunt-force trauma. At 5:30 on the morning of the crash, the baby died from the same cause.

The livery car driver, 32-year-old Pedro Delacruz, was released from Bellevue Hospital on Monday, March 4 after being treated for minor injuries. In the meantime, New York City detectives had learned that the BMW was registered to a resident of the Bronx named Takia Walker. The 29-year-old told detectives that Acevedo had borrowed the vehicle from a mutual friend. She said she had never met him.

Julio Acevedo had a long history of crime and incarceration. He had spent eight years in prison after being convicted of manslaughter in connection with the death of a Brooklyn hood named Kelvin Martin. Martin was the original "50 Cent," the inspiration for the rapper of the same name.

Once out of prison, Acevedo continued to run afoul of the law. Police, on various occasions, arrested him for such crimes as robbery, reckless endangerment, and possession of a weapon. On February 17, 2013, officers pulled Acevedo over in Brooklyn for driving erratically in a 1997 BMW bearing Pennsylvania plates. With an alcohol blood content level of .13, the officers charged the ex-con with driving under the influence. Acevedo told the arresting officers that he had consumed a couple of beers at a baby shower. The next day, following his arraignment, the judge released Acevedo with a court appearance scheduled for April 10, 2013.

Acevedo's last known address is in a Brooklyn public housing project where his mother resides. One of his friends told reporters that the hit-and-run suspect wants to turn himself in because "he has remorse." A reward of $15,000 has been offered for information leading to his arrest.

Isaac Abraham, a spokesman for the Orthodox Jewish community, called for the maximum punishment for Acevedo. "We in the community are demanding that the prosecutor charge the driver of the BMW that caused the death of this couple and infant with triple homicide. This coward left the scene of the accident, not even bothering to check on the people in the car."

On Tuesday, March 5, Acevedo, while hiding from the police, spoke to a reporter with the *Daily News of New York*. According to the fugitive, just before the accident, he had been speeding away from a gunman who was trying to kill him. Acevedo said he had met with a lawyer who was arranging his surrender to the authorities.

Acevedo, on Wednesday evening, March 6, turned himself in to police officers in Bethlehem, Pennsylvania. He approached the officers as they sat in their cars in front of a convenience store. The next day, Acevedo, charged with negligent homicide, three counts of assault, leaving the scene of an accident, and reckless driving, was arraigned in a Brooklyn court. Judge Stephen Antignani suspended his driver's license and denied him bail. The suspect's wife and young daughter were in the courtroom with him.

In July 2013, the New York City Department of Transportation installed a traffic light at the Brooklyn intersection where the Glauber had been killed.

The Acevedo case, as of July 2014 had not gone to trial. Gayle Dampf, an assistant district attorney in the vehicle crimes bureau, will represent the state. In New York, the vehicular homicide law requires that the defendant, at the time of the crash, was committing at least two traffic infractions. In the Acevedo case, because the suspect was not arrested for some time after the accident, the prosecution will have a difficult time proving his intoxication. Speeding alone will not be enough.

The Amy Senser Case

Amy Senser and her husband Joe lived in Edina, Minnesota, an upscale Minneapolis suburb. Joe Senser, a NFL tight end with the Minnesota Vikings in the early 1980s, co-owned four Minneapolis-St. Paul area sports bars. A knee injury had ended his 4-year career with the Vikings. The businessman and sports commentator was a well-liked local celebrity. His attractive, 45-year-old wife Amy was also well known and popular. But on the night of August 23, 2011, Amy and Joe Senser's successful lives would take a sudden and tragic turn.

On the night that changed everything for the Senser family, Amy and her daughters were attending a Katy Perry concert at the Xcell Energy Center in St. Paul. Ninety minutes into the show, Amy developed a headache and decided to drive home. She called Joe who agreed to pick up the girls after the concert.

According to Amy's version of what happened, while driving Joe's Mercedes-Benz SUV on I-94's Riverside exit off-ramp, a poorly lit section of the highway under construction, she felt a jolt and thought she'd hit a pothole or had bumped a construction barrel. In fact, the right front of her vehicle had hit and killed a man from Laos named Anousone Phantauong. The 38-year-old chef at a Thai restaurant was pouring gasoline into his car that had rolled to a stop on the shoulder of the exit ramp.

After the collision, Amy got lost, and called her husband. At one point, in her confusion, she came full circle and got off the interstate using the same Riverside exit. This time the area was lit up with the flashing lights of emergency vehicles. She did not associate this activity with the earlier jolt she had felt from either a pothole, or a construction barrel.

The next morning, according to Amy Senser's account, Joe called her outside and asked how the Mercedes' right headlight and fog light had gotten knocked out. By then, they both had seen TV reports of Phantauong's death, and the search for the hit and run driver. Realizing what had happened the previous night, the Sensers called their lawyer, and later that day, surrendered the damaged Mercedes to the police.

Because of who the Sensers were the case became a real-life version of the Tom Wolfe novel, *Bonfire of the Vanities*. It was also a media sensation.

In speaking to the police, Amy admitted that just before the Katy Perry concert, she had gone to a nearby restaurant where she had consumed less than a full glass of wine. She insisted, however, that she had not been intoxicated when her car hit and killed Mr. Phantauong. Investigators believed she had been drunk, and because of that, had not stopped after plowing into the victim. Detectives were convinced she wanted to sober up before reporting the fatal accident.

In November 2011, the Hennepin County prosecutor, Deborah Russell, charged Any Senser with three vehicular related felonies: driving in a grossly negligent manner; leaving the scene of an accident; and failure to promptly report an accident. If convicted of all three charges, the defendant could face up to 30 years in prison. Because she hadn't confessed, and no witness to the accident had come forward, the case against Amy Senser was entirely circumstantial. To find her guilty, the jury would have to infer her state of mind that night. If they believed her testimony, they would have to acquit her.

To find the defendant guilty of reckless driving, the jury would also have to infer she had been intoxicated at the time of the accident. The fact she had clipped Mr. Phantauong, a man who had placed himself in harm's way by standing just off a poorly lit exit ramp, was not, by itself, enough to establish gross negligence on her part. If the jurors did not find that she was drunk, they would probably not find that the accident was a result of reckless driving.

The highly anticipated, media intense Amy Senser trial commenced on April 23, 2012. In an effort to prove that the defendant had been driving drunk that night, prosecutor Russell put a motorist on the stand. Shortly after the accident, the witness saw, on I-94, a Mercedes SUV being driven in an erratic manner. The witness passed this vehicle when it slowed to 40 MPH, and when she looked into her rearview mirror, noticed that the car's right front lights were out.

Defense attorney Eric Nelson put on only one witness, Amy Senser. The defendant denied she had been intoxicated when her car hit what she thought was a pothole or a construction barrel. As for her erratic driving on I-94, she had dropped her cellphone between the seat and the center console, and was trying to fish it out.

On May 2, 2012, the jury of 7 men and 5 women, after a grueling deliberation period of 19 hours, found Amy Senser guilty of two of the three felonies. Jurors acquitted the defendant of the gross negligent charge. Amy, who faced up to 20 years on prison, showed no emotion as the verdicts were read.

At a post-trial press conference, attorney Eric Nelson said he would appeal his client's conviction on the grounds she had met the requirements of the state accident notification law. One of the jurors who spoke to reporters said, "It was just a very challenging case for us to come to a consensus."

On July 10, 2012, the judge sentenced Amy Senser to three years, five months in prison.

Hit and Run Victim Solves His Own Case

When a hit and run driver in Smyrna, Georgia struck Jacob Rogers, a 39-year-old riding his bicycle to work, police told the victim it would be difficult to find the suspect. That's when he decided to conduct his own investigation. He had stopped that morning on July 17, 2014 at an entrance to an apartment complex. What happened next caught him by surprise. "I didn't see anything so I proceeded, and that's when I got hit," he said.

A female driver of a silver colored Volkswagen pulled out of the apartment complex and ran into Rogers. "So I'm still on my bike," he said, "and she forced her way through me." The Volkswagen pushed him aside and took off.

Rogers said that although he wasn't hurt seriously, he suffered pain in the foot that was on the bike pedal struck by vehicle. Part of the pedal broke off, and Rogers couldn't find the piece at the hit and run site.

The next day, Rogers went back to the apartment complex to look for a silver Volkswagen. "The first car that I saw was a silver Volkswagen," he said. I took a picture of the rear license plate and checked the front for damage." In front grill he found the missing piece from his left bike pedal lodged in the vehicle.

A police officer resident of the apartment complex ran the license plate. Shortly thereafter Smyrna police officers arrested the car's owner. They took 20-year-old Pablynne Silva into custody. A local prosecutor charged her with misdemeanor hit and run, an offense punishable by a fine of $1,000 and up to a year in jail.

Pablynne told officers she had driven off after hitting the man on the bike out of fear of getting into trouble with the law.

Kidnapping

Imprisoned in New Jersey

One could describe law enforcement as peeking under rocks in search of criminals and evidence of their crimes. Every so often the police turn over a rock and are surprised by what they find. On August 9, 2012, members of the New Jersey State Police Street Gang Unit, while searching an apartment in Paterson for drugs, discovered something they hadn't anticipated--a woman who may have lived ten years locked inside a bedroom. The apartment belonged to a 42-year-old suspected drug dealer and member of the Latin Kings street gang named Michael Mendez.

Most of Mendez's public housing neighbors had not been aware that the woman, 44-year-old Nancy Rodriguez Duran, had been living in the former roofer's apartment. (Mendez, because of lung problems and bipolar disorder, has been on disability for several years.) Over the past decade, only a few of his fellow apartment dwellers had seen Duran outside of the three-story brick complex. Even then the sightings were rare. Mendez had resided on the apartment's third floor for more than twelve years.

Inside Duran's small, padlocked (from the outside) bedroom, officers found a pail used as a chamber pot, a bed, a television, and a telephone. Searchers also discovered, in Mendez's possession, 4,200 prescription pills, 190 grams of marijuana, and $23,000 in cash. The pills alone had a street value of $100,000.

New Jersey State Police Officers took Michael Mendez into custody at the Paterson apartment and hauled him to the Passaic County Jail. Charged with possession of controlled substances with the intent to distribute, kidnapping, false imprisonment, and criminal restraint, Mendez was held on $1 million bail. The authorities transported Nancy Rodriguez Duran to a nearby hospital for medical evaluation. While Mendez has two previous convictions for aggravated assault, he has only served three months behind bars.

On August 14, before Mendez's preliminary hearing in Paterson, Nancy Rodriguez Duran, in speaking to reporters, denied having been held in Mendez's apartment bedroom against her will. "He padlocked the door with my consent," she said. "I like being inside, I don't like to go out. It's not that he was keeping mc there...Why would he keep me in a room for ten years? How could I be so healthy? I should be dead by now."

The Mendez case was handled by the New Jersey State Attorney General's office. The central legal question in this case was whether or not an adult can consent to being locked in a room for the better part of ten years. (People being held captive aren't given access to a telephone.)

Perhaps Duran had been abducted against her will, then over the years, developed the so-called Stockholm Syndrome, a psychological state in which the prisoner develops empathy for her captor. Was this woman the victim of what psychologists call traumatic bonding? (If this case has been resolved, there is no record of it online.)

The Bunker Hostage Case

Two years ago, shortly after moving into his rural house in Midland City, Alabama, a town of 2,300 not far from Dothan in the southeast corner of the state, 65-year-old Jimmy Lee Dykes began building his underground storm shelter. The retired truck driver and Navy veteran worked on the project every day between two and three in the morning for eighteen months. He stocked his underground sanctuary with food, wired it for electricity, and moved in a TV set and other amenities.

People who lived near Mr. Dykes considered him a neighbor from hell. Paranoid, combative, and violent, Dykes, pursuant to a variety of neighborhood disputes and feuds, had threatened to shoot people. He had been seen patrolling his property at night with a flashlight and a shotgun. Back in December, Dykes fired two shots at a pickup truck occupied by two people who resided in the area. As a result of that incident, Dykes had a court appearance in nearby Ozark, Alabama where he faced a charge of menacing.

On Tuesday, January 29, 2013, the day before his court appearance, Jimmy Lee Dykes became more than just an armed eccentric who hated people. At 3:40 in the afternoon, Dykes boarded a school bus near his house carrying twenty-two elementary school children. He pulled out a handgun and ordered the little passengers out of the vehicle. He then grabbed a 6-year-old boy who was so frightened he fainted. When the bus driver, 66-year-old Charles Poland, Jr. tried to save the child, Dykes shot him four times. (Mr. Poland later died from his wounds.)

From the hijacked bus, Dykes took the boy to his underground bunker that became the site of an ongoing hostage standoff. A short time later local, county and state police officers surrounded Dykes' underground fort. A SWAT team and paramedic units were also on hand. FBI hostage negotiators had also responded to the scene.

The abducted boy's parents were doubly concerned because the child required medication that had to be taken daily. At one point, officers who were talking to Dykes through a PVC pipe dropped the boy's medication into the bunker through the pipe. According to reports, Dykes has assured the hostage negotiators that the child has not been injured.

On Thursday, some 36 hours into the standoff, a hostage negotiator said, "Give up. You need to exit the shelter, put down any weapons you might have and approach the police. This isn't going to end itself. You need to come out and talk to us. We are not going away."

On Monday, February 4, 2013 at three in the afternoon, FBI agents stormed the bunker, killed the hostage taker and rescued the boy. The hostage negotiators, while they were unable to talk Dykes out of the storm shelter, kept the boy alive long enough for Dykes to be worn down then killed.

A Kidnapping Hoax

High school basketball standout Sierra "CeCe" Sims, in August 2008, arrived at Alabama's Auburn University with a full athletic scholarship. As a high school player in Brentwood, Tennessee, CeCe had led her team to three regional titles. The five-foot-seven inch point guard, a former Teen pageant contestant, also played the guitar. (Her father, Tommy Sims co-wrote the Grammy-winning Eric Clapton hit, "Change the World.")

The 18-year-old college freshman, a member of the Auburn Tiger's women's basketball team, a powerhouse in the Southeastern Conference, had to deal with being away from home, academic life on the university level, and living up to expectations on the basketball court.

Shortly after arriving at the university, CeCe began drinking heavily every night. In late September she called her mother Kathie and said she wanted to come home. Kathie told her distraught daughter to talk to coach Nell Fortner. Taking her mother's advice, CeCe called the coach. When CeCe hung up the phone after their chat, the coach felt that everything would be fine for the freshman prospect.

The next morning, when CeCe failed to show up for the six o'clock practice, Fortner became concerned. When the coach made inquiries regarding CeCe's whereabouts, her roommate said at 2:30 that morning she had stormed out of the dormitory and rode off into the night on her bicycle. None of her acquaintances had seen her since.

Not long after campus searchers couldn't find CeCe, university officials asked the authorities to issue an Amber Alert. Eighteen hours later, a parole officer looking for the missing student almost hit CeCe with his patrol car. When the officer approached the girl, she said, "I'm CeCe Sims."

Questioned at the local police department, CeCe told detectives she had been kidnapped by a man and a woman. The couple had pulled up alongside her in a pickup truck. After being dragged into the vehicle, the abductors forced her to drink alcohol and take pills. As a result of being drugged, she couldn't recall in detail what had happened to her.

Under close questioning by detectives, CeCe's story didn't hold up. In an effort to get the student to reveal where she had been since leaving the dorm at 2:30 the previous morning, officers threatened her with the possibility of being charged with a crime. Notwithstanding that threat, she stuck to her highly implausible story.

The police did not open a kidnapping investigation, and CeCe was not charged with false reporting. She dropped out of school and returned home to Brentwood, Tennessee.

In 2014, CeCe Sims posted a video on the Internet acknowledging that she had indeed made up the kidnapping story in September of 2008. When she left the dormitory that night she had ridden her bike to a nearby Walmart where she hid for almost eighteen hours.

According to CeCe Sims, the pressure at Auburn had been too much for her. "I didn't want to disappoint my parents," she said, "so I thought, what better way to say I was kidnapped? That way I wouldn't have to quit and be known as a quitter."

When the story broke regarding CeCe and the kidnapping hoax, former Auburn coach Nell Fortner described to an ABC reporter the pressure student/athletes are under at schools like Auburn. "Your schedule might take you to the Bahamas or to Hawaii. They are going to get a great education but pay heavily for that because working out is tough. They are up at five in the morning, and they don't get to bed until eleven at night."

Snatching a Baby

On February 2, 2014, 18-year-old Brianna Marshall gave birth to a six-pound, 20-inch boy she and her boyfriend Bruce Powell named Kayden. The couple resided in Beloit, a town of 7,700 50 miles south of Madison, Wisconsin near the Illinois border.

At four-thirty in the morning of Thursday, February 6, 2014, Brianna called 911 and reported that Kayden was missing. Brianna told responding officers with the Beloit Police Department that when she checked the baby's crib, located in the room where she and Bruce slept, the infant was gone. Police officers found no evidence of a break-in and there was no ransom note.

According to the parents, they last saw Kayden at one-thirty that morning when their houseguest, Brianna's half-sister Kristen Rose Smith, left Beloit en route to her home in Denver, Colorado.

A police officer reached Smith by calling her cellphone. At five-thirty that morning, Smith pulled into the Kum and Go gas station off Interstate 80 in West Branch, Iowa. From the gas station and convenience store, 180 miles from Beloit, Smith flagged down a local police officer.

After searching Smith's car and finding baby clothing but no infant, officers with the West Branch Police Department took the half-sister into custody on an outstanding warrant issued from Texas. She was wanted in that state on charges of tampering with government records and fraud. Officers booked Kristen Smith into the Cedar County Jail.

Back in Beloit, 40 officers representing the FBI, Rock County Sheriff's Office, and the Beloit Police Department, were working on the missing persons case.

The missing baby's mother, in speaking to a local CNN reporter on Friday, February 6, said: "I held that baby one time and that was the last time I seen that baby and held him." Brianna Marshall said that she, her husband, and the infant were about to move to Denver, Colorado. That explained the baby clothing in the half-sister's car.

At a press conference held on the afternoon of Friday, February 7, 2014, Beloit chief of police Steven Kopp announced that Baby Kayden Powell had been found alive and well that morning. The infant had been swaddled in blankets inside a tote bag in an exterior storage crate at the Kum and Go gas station in West Branch. The baby had survived for 29 hours in subzero temperatures.

After being taken into custody in Iowa, Kristen Smith agreed to take a polygraph test. When she denied abducting the baby, she failed the exam. Following the infant's recovery she admitted she had taken the baby, and that she had pretended to be pregnant. Before flagging the police car at the gas station, she hid the baby for later retrieval. Police officers disrupted that plan by taking her into custody on the Texas warrants.

Remarkably, the baby showed no signs of frostbite or hypothermia. A physician at the University of Wisconsin Health Center explained that infants possess a thin layer of fat they can metabolize into heat.

On June 25, 2014, a federal grand jury indicted Smith of one count of kidnapping a baby. If convicted she faced a minimum sentence of 25 years in prison.

Sex Slave Trucker

A Utah truck driver kept sex slaves in his semitrailer for months at a time while he traveled the country, filing down their teeth, forcing them to alter their appearance and beating them until they nearly passed out...Timothy Jay Vafeades, 54, made an initial appearance on March 12, 2014 in U.S. District Court in Fargo, North Dakota, and will be transferred to Utah for further proceedings.

The charges against Vafeades include kidnapping, transportation for illegal sexual activity, and possession of child pornography, and could bring a life sentence if he is convicted...An arrest warrant filed on March 11, 2014 in Salt Lake City claims Vafeades kidnapped a 19-year-old female relative who had come from Florida in May 2013 to work with him on the truck, the "Twilight Express." After a week, the teen told Vafeades she wanted to go home, but she later informed authorities that he strangled her until she blacked out and used threats and violence to keep her with him for the next six months while they traveled to Washington state, Nevada, Texas, Tennessee and other places.

Despite her pleas, Vafeades forced the teenager to have sex with him more than 100 times during their time together. He chipped down the girl's teeth and made her wear a fake set of teeth. He wore his own false teeth that featured vampire fangs....

Vafeades was arrested at a Clay County Minnesota weight station on November 26, 2013 after officers noticed bruises on the teenager and turned up a 1999 restraining order barring Vafeades from contacting the girl. After his arrest, a second woman went to authorities to report she had been held captive in Vafeades' truck....

Michelle Rindels, Associated Press, March 13, 2014

Unintentional Homicide

Murder Versus Manslaughter

The acid test of murder is intention and what the law calls guilty mind. Guilty intention is described as malice aforethought and this distinguishes it from manslaughter. The classic definition of murder based on malice aforethought goes back to English Common Law and takes account of the age and mental status of the offender. Lord Chief Justice Edward Coke (1552-1634) set this out when he referred to "a man of sound memory and at the age of discretion." In practical terms, this meant an individual who was not insane and aged at least ten years.

Robin Odell, *The Mammoth Book of Bizarre Crimes,* 2010

Jessica Herrera's Nightmare

As drivers, we all occasionally speed, cross the centerline, roll through stop signs, and get distracted. There is no such thing as perfection behind the wheel. No one wants to cause an accident, particularly one that results in injury or death. Whenever a driver's carelessness causes or contributes to a traffic accident that results in the death of another driver or passenger, a prosecutor has to decide if this act of negligence rises to the level of criminal homicide. Ordinary negligence that falls short of recklessness--the total disregard for the safety of others--should be treated as a civil wrong rather than a criminal act. Vehicular homicide should only apply to motorists who are driving extremely fast, are drunk, high on drugs, or fleeing from the police. The criminalization of all fatal traffic accidents is not a good idea.

On June 11, 2011, in Santa Barbara County, California, Christopher Martinez slowed down on Highway 246 east of the town of Lompoc to turn into a driveway that led back to a winery. The 28-year-old was showing up for his first day of work. As he slowed to negotiate the turn, Jessica Herrera, driving the car behind him, rear-ended his vehicle. The collision pushed Martinez's car into the opposite lane where it was struck broadside by a pickup truck carrying two people.

Paramedics rushed Christopher Martinez to the Marian Regional Medical Center in Santa Maria with severe head trauma and a collapsed lung. He died the next day.

A Santa Barbara County prosecutor charged the 22-year-old Herrera with misdemeanor vehicular manslaughter, a crime that carried a maximum sentence of one year in jail and a $1,000 fine. In May 2012, five Herrera trial jurors refused to find the defendant guilty. That caused the judge to declare a mistrial.

Prosecutor Mark Smith decided to retry Herrera for vehicular homicide. On February 8, 2013, the second trial got underway in the Santa Barbara County Court in Lompoc. In his opening remarks to the jury, prosecutor Smith accused the defendant of driving too fast for conditions (65 mph in a 55 mph zone) and being inattentive.

Herrera's attorney, Dillon Forsyth, argued that the crash that took Christopher Martinez's life was a tragic accident. To the jury he said, "There is no evidence a crime occurred. This is a circumstantial case. There is really no credible evidence that what occurred was anything but an accident. The fact is we simply don't know what happened." The defense attorney also pointed out that there were no signs that a driveway was coming up, and that brake lights and turn signals on Martinez's car might not have been working.

On February 13, 2013, after more than a day of deliberation, the jury reported to the judge that it was deadlocked eleven to one in favor of conviction. Another hung jury, another mistrial.

I'm surprised that so many jurors in these two trials actually voted for Herrera's conviction. Even assuming Jessica Herrera had been driving ten miles over the speed limit at the time of the accident, I don't believe she was *criminally* responsible for Christopher Martinez's death. I hope the Santa Barbara County District Attorney's Office drops this case. A third trial would amount to prosecutorial harassment.

The Body in the Freezer

In July 2010, a family member found 80-year-old Maria de Jesus Arroyo unconscious in her Boyle Heights home in Los Angeles. At the White Memorial Medical Centre, an emergency room doctor declared Arroyo dead from a heart attack.

A few days later, Arroyo's body was taken out of the hospital freezer and transported to a funeral home where it would be on display. When the mortician zipped open the body bag, he found the corpse uncharacteristically face down in the postmortem container. Moreover, the frozen woman's nose had been broken, and her face was covered in cuts and bruises. Family members who had seen Mrs. Arroyo just before the ambulance rushed her to the hospital hadn't noticed any injuries. They assumed that hospital personnel had in some way mishandled the body.

Mrs. Arroyo's husband and eight of their children filed a lawsuit against the White Memorial Medical Centre alleging abuse of corpse. In December 2011, at a hearing pertaining to the suit, Dr. William Manion, a forensic pathologist hired by the family, testified that Mrs. Arroyo had not died of a heart attack.

It was Dr. Manion's opinion that Mrs. Arroyo had died from asphyxiation and hypothermia. In other words, hospital personnel had put a body bag containing a live person into the hospital freezer. Mrs. Arroyo had regained consciousness inside the bag and struggled to get out. In so doing, she broke her nose and cut and bruised her face. If this were true, this woman had undergone a terrifying death. Instead of saving her life, hospital personnel had killed her in a most horrible way.

In May 2012, the Arroyo family attorney, Scott Schutzman, upgraded the lawsuit against the hospital to medical malpractice. (If Mrs. Arroyo had in fact died in the hospital morgue freezer, some of the people responsible for her ending up there could also face charges of negligent homicide.) According to Dr. Manion, this had not been a natural death.

In 2013, a Los Angeles Superior Court judge threw out the Arroyo lawsuit because the one-year statute of limitations for malpractice suits had run out before the case had been filed. The Arroyo family appealed that decision.

In March 2014, justices sitting on the California 2nd District Court of Appeal overturned the lower court ruling. The one-year statute of limitations did not start running in this case until the plaintiffs learned that Mrs. Arroyo might have gone into the hospital freezer alive. According to the appellate judges, the family had no reason to suspect Mrs. Arroyo had died *after* being placed into the body bag. The Arroyo lawsuit, therefore, could move forward.

Who Shot Blake?

Blake Randell Wardell resided in Honea Path, South Carolina, a town in the northeast part of the state. In the early morning hours of Wednesday, May 14, 2014, the 26-year-old Wardell, a man his age named Timothy Fisher, Taylor Ann Kelly, and eight or nine others, were hanging out at a house in Honea Path. (The reporting on this case has been so weak there is no information regarding who owned or lived in this house.)

At 2:45 that morning, someone in the group (presumably) called 911 to report a shooting. Deputies with the Anderson County Sheriff's office, upon arrival at the house, found Wardell unresponsive and bleeding from the chest as he lay in a pool of blood on the garage floor. Paramedics arrived but were unable to revive Wardell who they pronounced dead at the scene.

According to those questioned at the death site, Wardell had found, in the house, an old bulletproof Kevlar flak jacket. He put on the vest and asked someone to test it out by shooting him.

Taylor Ann Kelly, a recent graduate of Belton-Honea Path High School, took responsibility for the shooting death. She told the police that she had fired the small-caliber bullet that passed through the lining on the edge of the bulletproof vest into Wardell's heart. (This didn't make any sense. I presume detectives questioned the others at the scene who confirmed that Kelly was the one who had fired the fatal bullet.)

Officers took the 18-year-girl into custody and booked her into the Anderson County Detention Center on the charge of involuntary manslaughter.

In South Carolina, as in most states, the homicide offense of involuntary manslaughter involves, as criminal intent, the reckless disregard for human life. The fact the victim in this case had supposedly consented to being recklessly shot, would not comprise a legal defense to this charge. According to the law, there are certain things people cannot legally consent to. Being shot is one of them. In South Carolina, involuntary manslaughter carried a maximum penalty of five years in prison. The judge set the 18-year-old suspect's bail at $10,000.

On May 16, 2014, an Anderson County prosecutor reduced the charge against Taylor Kelly to accessory after the fact of a felony. According to investigators, she had lied to police officers about shooting the victim. She had apparently confessed to protect the real shooter in the case--25-year-old Timothy Fisher.

The Anderson County prosecutor charged Fisher with involuntary manslaughter. Officers booked him into the county detention center. The authorities have not revealed exactly why the girl had lied for this man. Did she do it voluntarily? Are Kelly and Fisher in some kind of relationship? Does Fisher have a criminal record? What was his relationship to Blake Wardell? The police did say that neither alcohol nor drugs played a role in the shooting.

This case called for a careful and professionally conducted investigation to uncover possible motives for murder. The criminal investigation should include a thorough forensic ballistics analysis that would determine if the fatal bullet had actually passed through a bulletproof vest. And finally, all witnesses to the shooting should be asked to take polygraph tests.

Drunk Mother Smothers Baby

A Maryland woman who killed her 2-month-old daughter by passing out drunk on top of her while breast-feeding was going to jail. Twenty-two-year-old Yadina Morales of Hagerstown was sentenced on June 3, 2014 to fifteen months after entering an Alford plea to involuntary manslaughter. (An Alford plea is not an admission of guilt but an acknowledgment that the state had enough evidence to convict.)

Prosecutors agreed to drop some charges, including child abuse and reckless endangerment, as a part of the plea deal. Morales was arrested in November 2013 after the girl's father came home and found her passed out on top of the unresponsive infant. Morales registered a blood-alcohol level of 0.256, more than three times the level needed for a drunken driving conviction. The judge said her actions were grossly negligent.

David Disheau, Associated Press, June 3, 2014

Rough Sex or Murder

On June 5, 2014, a highway cutting of high grass along a road in Geneva, Wisconsin, a town in Walworth County 50 miles southwest of Milwaukee, exposed a pair of large suitcases. The overpowering odor of rotting flesh caused the highway employee to notify the police.

Each of the suitcases contained a badly decomposed body of a woman. Through dental records the authorities identified the women as 37-year-old Laura Simonson and 21-year-old Jenny Gamez. The forensic pathologist, due to the condition of the bodies, could not establish their causes of death. Neither woman, however, had been shot.

One of Laura Simonson's relatives reported the mother of seven from Farmington, Wisconsin missing on November 22, 2013. While her cause of death was unknown, before she died someone had tied a rope around her neck. That person also stuffed a ball attached to a collar into her mouth. The gag collar looked like a device commonly used by sadomasochists in bondage/slave sexual activity. According to family members, Simonson had struggled with mental illness.

No one had been looking for the younger woman, Jenny Gamez. According to her foster parents, Gamez had left their home in Cottage Grove, Oregon to start a new life. In 2008, as a fifteen-year-old, she had given birth to a son. The baby's father, in 2010, gained full custody of the child. In keeping with the sadomasochistic theme of the case, someone had tied Gamez's hands behind her back.

On June 27, 2014, police officers arrested 52-year-old Steven M. Zelich at his home in West Allis, Wisconsin. Zelich had been seen with each woman on separate occasions in Wisconsin and Minnesota. A Wisconsin prosecutor charged Zelich with two counts of hiding a corpse.

In 1989, the then 27-year-old Zelich started working in West Allis as a police officer. Three years later, following an off-duty altercation with a prostitute, the chief of police forced him to resign. Since 2007 Zelich had been an employee of a contract security guard company.

Zelich's sexual tastes, in light of evidence of bondage associated with the bodies in the suitcases, led detectives to suspect he was the last person to see these women alive. On a bondage and sadomasochism website, Zelich solicited sexual partners with the following message: "Seeking no limit enslavement, imprisonment, captivity, animalization [no clue] ideally in a farm/caged situation."

Following his arrest, Zelich told detectives he met the 21-year-old Gamez through the sex website. In November of 2013, he spent several nights with her in a Kenosha County Hotel where they had sadomasochistic sex that included bondage. Upon her accidental death in the course of this activity, he stuffed her body into a suitcase and took the corpse home.

After connecting with the 37-year-old Simonson through the sadomasochistic Internet site, they engaged in bondage sex at the Microtel Inn & Suites in Rochester, Minnesota. This took place on November 21, 2013. Simonson had checked into the motel under her own name but never checked out. After she died while having sex with him, Zelich placed her body into a suitcase that ended up in his house with the other corpse.

In late May or early June 2014, Zelich dumped the suitcases along the road in Geneva, Wisconsin. According to Zelich's attorney the women, as willing participants in rough sex, died accidentally. By dumping the suitcases along the road, Zelich wanted the bodies to be discovered. The attorney did not believe that homicide charges in this case would be appropriate.

This was a tough case. Why didn't Zelich immediately report the deaths to the authorities? Moreover, the fact that *two* woman died while having sex with him suggested foul play. Have other women died under similar circumstance? Perhaps a polygraph examiner could shed some light on the matter.

Vehicular Homicide: Three Cases

Nobody likes a hypocrite. We are particularly offended (and intrigued) when people we generally admire such as physicians, professors, clergymen, law enforcement officers, generals, teachers, certain celebrities, and counselors commit crimes or behave badly. However, because of low expectations, we are less shocked when politicians, bureaucrats, lawyers, and Wall Street types break the law or act like jerks. In terms of what we expect from people, there are different standards of behavior. For example, in murder for hire cases, the upper-middle class mastermind is almost always considered more immoral, and criminally culpable, than the lower-class hit man. This is true even when the contract killer has murdered a complete stranger simply for the money.

Years ago, when the head mistress of an elite New England girl's school shot and killed her lover in a fit of jealousy, this otherwise ordinary criminal homicide became a celebrated case. Ministers have gone to prison to having their wives killed, and FBI agents have been convicted of first-degree murder. On a smaller criminological scale, the public is shocked when female public school teachers are caught having affairs with their male students. I remember a case involving a high-profile gun control advocate who shot an intruder with an unregistered firearm. These cases attract media attention because they feature hypocrisy.

In October 2012, Colin McGrattan, an anger management counselor in Stockton, California, murdered his ex-wife, her sister, and the victim's aunt before killing himself. McGrattan had recently lost a legal dispute with his former spouse. Unable to control his anger, he killed three people and himself. On matters of anger management, this man obviously didn't take his own advice.

Even though we have low expectations for politicians and bureaucrats, cases occasionally pop up that are egregious enough to, if not shock us, grab our attention. In 2007, Sheila Burgess, a Massachusetts political fund-raiser for democrat candidates, collected her reward when Governor Deval Patrick appointed her to the position of State Highway Safety Director. Since this was a political appointment, it's not surprising that Burgess didn't have experience in the fields of public safety, transportation, or public administration.

On August 24, 2012, Burgess, while driving her state-issued vehicle on a sunny, Sunday afternoon near Milton, Massachusetts, drove off the road, wrecked the car, and injured herself in the head. Although she told the police she had swerved off the highway to avoid an oncoming vehicle, she may have been texting.

The Highway Safety Director's traffic accident prompted a newspaper inquiry into Burgess' driving history. On November 18, 2012, the day after the paper revealed that Sheila Burgess had a record of 34 traffic violations, the governor removed her from office. (Because she was a government employee, dismissal was out of the question.) Instead of firing this woman, the governor assigned Burgess to a "different role" within the same department. As director of the agency, Burgess' annual salary had been $87,000. (I presume Burgess had accepted a pay cut.)

In the fall of 2010, 50-year-old Sherri Lynn Wilkins began counseling substance abusers at the Twin Town Treatment Center in Torrance, California. In charge of the evening group sessions, she counseled up to 50 drug and alcohol abusers at a time. It was her job to help these people either get sober, or stay off drugs. While Wilkins had earned a degree in drug counseling from Loyola Marymount University, it was her background as an alcoholic and heroin addict that in the bizarre world of substance abuse counseling that qualified her for the position. While giving her street credibility, the fact she "had been there" also meant she might relapse, an event that, in my opinion, would not be in the best interests of the people she was being paid to help. (I've often wondered if it might be a better idea to employ counselors who have managed to get through life without getting hooked on drugs or booze. Maybe this would give them a different kind of credibility.)

Sherri Lynn Watkin's background, before she began her counseling career, is as follows: In 1992, a Los Angeles County judge sentenced her to 16 months in jail for petty theft. Two years later, another judge set her away for nine years for burglary. All of her crimes were related to her substance addiction. In May 2010, the Los Angeles police arrested Wilkins for hit and run in Torrance. Because she had not been driving under the influence, the case against her was dropped. But in July 2010, the authorities in Los Angeles charged Wilkins with leaving the scene of an accident, and driving under the influence of a controlled substance. For some reason this case was also dismissed.

At eleven-thirty on the night of November 24, 2012, Sherri Wilkins, while speeding west on Torrance Boulevard, slammed into 31-year-old Phillip Moreno who was crossing the street near his home. The impact knocked Moreno out of his shoes and threw him up on the hood of Wilkins' car. Wilkins continued driving with the dying man lying on her hood, his body lodged into her windshield.

At a traffic light two miles from where Moreno had been struck and thrown up onto the car, several motorists swarmed Wilkins' vehicle and grabbed her ignition key. An ambulance rushed Mr. Moreno to a local hospital where, a few hours later, he died. Los Angeles police officers took the substance abuse counselor into custody. Watkins' blood-alcohol content registered twice the legal limit for driving.

On November 27, a Los Angeles County prosecutor charged Sherri Wilkins with vehicular manslaughter and driving under the influence. She was booked into the Los Angeles County Jail under $2.25 million bond.

In April 2014, a jury in Torrance found Sherri Wilkins guilty of second-degree murder as well as several lesser offenses including hit and run. Two months later, Superior Court Judge Henry Hall sentenced the 54-year-old to 55 years to life in prison. The judge said, "Ms. Wilkins demonstrated an extraordinary callousness in fleeing the scene and trying to shake Mr. Moreno's body off her car. Ms. Wilkins is not what we normally see. She's not a classic violent criminal. But you have to evaluate her history. (According to her own testimony, Wilkins' drug addiction started after she was involved in a traffic accident at the age of fifteen. Her back had been broken, and she suffered shattered bones in her ankles and legs. She began medicating herself with heroin because it was "cheaper than going to the doctor.") In justifying the stiff sentence, Judge Hall added, "She had an insatiable desire to become intoxicated."

Wilkins' attorney, Deputy Public Defender Nan Whitfield, said she would appeal the sentence. To reporters outside the courthouse, Whitfield said, "Nobody likes a drunk driver. Because she was a drug and alcohol counselor, she's held to a higher standard."

16 MURDER

The Group Therapy Confession

In 1984, 17-year-old Shane Absalon lived in a west Fort Worth, Texas apartment building with his parents. Ginger Hayden, a year older than him, lived in the same complex with her mother. She and Absalon had attended the same high school in Fort Worth. On September 4, 1984, after recently starting class at the University of Texas at Arlington (situated halfway between Fort Worth and Dallas), Ginger, her boyfriend Jeff Green, and Shane Absalon, were gathered in her apartment drinking beer and watching television.

At 6:15 the next morning, Ginger's mother, Sharon Hayden Harvey, was awaken by the ringing of Ginger's alarm clock. When Sharon entered the bedroom to see why Ginger hadn't turned off her alarm, she discovered her daughter lying on the floor next to her bed in a pool of blood. The hysterical mother dialed the operator and screamed, "My baby's dead!"

According to the Tarrant County forensic pathologist who performed the autopsy, Ginger Hayden had been stabbed 57 times with a kitchen knife, and had bled to death. Wounds on the victim's arms and hands suggested she had put up a fight.

Detectives with the Fort Worth Police Department questioned Shane Absalon on September 12, 1984. Absalon said that Ginger and her boyfriend were in the apartment when he left the place at 11:30 that night. When asked if he was willing to take a polygraph test, Absalon said that he would. But the next day, stating that he was acting on the advice of his attorney, the suspect declined to submit to the lie detector test.

For whatever reason, the investigation of Ginger Hayden's brutal murder ground to a halt and died on the vine. In the meantime, Shane Absalon, during the two years following the homicide, turned into a drunk

431

and drug abuser with a history of arrests for crimes such as burglary, arson, and assault. In July 1986, he pleaded guilty in Tarrant County to smashing a vehicle with a club while intoxicated. The judge sentenced him to a one-year period of probation. Pursuant to his sentence, Absalon was ordered to enter a drug and alcohol treatment program in Richardson, Texas called Straight Inc. (This outfit was later closed down following charges of patient abuse.)

In 2001, 18 years after Ginger Hayden's murder, cold-case investigators in Fort Worth re-opened the investigation that focused on Shane Absalon as the prime suspect. Detectives believed that he had murdered Hayden after she refused to have sex with him. Among other evidence of his guilt, a neighbor had seen the suspect, after he said he had left the apartment that night, climb over a fence and knock on the victim's sliding patio door. But the police needed more, and it wasn't until 2009 that they had enough evidence to support his arrest. After acquiring DNA samples from Absalon, forensic experts were able to link him to the murder scene.

On August 20, 2010, Absalon was taken into custody at his home in Sierra Vista, Arizona where he lived with his wife and young child. At the time he was working as a welder. A month later, a grand jury sitting in Fort Worth indicted Absalon for capital murder. If convicted, he would be automatically sentenced to life in prison. Because he had been a juvenile at the time of the murder, the defendant was not eligible for the death penalty. Moreover, under the applicable 1984 law, the 43-year-old would be eligible for parole after serving 20 years of his sentence.

Word of Shane Absalon's arrest reached at least three former patients who were treated with him in 1986 for alcohol and drug abuse at Straight Inc. These people had attended group therapy sessions with Absalon. The news of his arrest for Ginger Hayden's murder prompted the former patients to tell the Fort Worth police that during a group therapy session two years after the murder, Shane Absalon had confessed to killing a girl he knew. (It's a mystery to me why these former drug-alcohol patients hadn't informed on Absalon immediately after his confession.)

Shane Absalon's trial got underway on September 17, 2012. Following the testimony of a DNA analyst who linked the defendant to the murder scene, the prosecutor put three of the former Straight Inc. patients on the stand to state their recollections of the defendant's group therapy confession. (Absalon's attorney, Gary Udashen, had objected to the introduction of this evidence, but had been overruled by the judge.)

The first Straight Inc. witness, Sean Garrett, informed the jurors that "He [the defendant] told me he was angry. He told me he wanted more of a relationship with her [the victim], that he wanted to be more than just friends. Her response was no, and he was real embarrassed. He stabbed her until he was tired, and thought she was dead. His intentions were to kill her." According to this witness, after stabbing Hayden to death, Absalon cleaned up in the bathroom, threw his jacket and shoes in a nearby trash bin, and went back to his apartment.

Former patient Stefany Knight took the stand and said, "Shane stood up to admit to wrongdoing when he was high on heroin. He said he killed a girl...stabbed her with a knife." Michele Valencia, the third Straight, Inc. witness, testified that Absalon's confession had made her physically ill.

Defense attorney Gary Udashen, in cross-examining Michele Valencia, got her to admit that members of the rehabilitation center's poorly trained staff had pressured patients into confessing to crimes and former bad behavior. In this witness' opinion, some patients made false confessions just to please staff members running the group therapy sessions. "There was some brainwashing going on...I learned to conform. I had to get out," she said.

Gary Udashen, in addressing the crime scene DNA evidence in his closing remarks to the jury, referred to unidentified semen on the victim's bed quilt, and unidentified blood and tissue under Hayden's fingernails. The fact the defendant's DNA was in the apartment was not surprising because he had been there many times. Suggesting that Ginger Hayden had been murdered by a serial killer who had been loose in the Fort Worth area at the time of her death, the defense attorney said, "The person who killed Ginger Hayden is still out there, and the police need to find that person. That person is not Shane Absalon."

On September 21, 2012, the jury, following a short deliberation, found the defendant guilty of capital murder. Absalon looked stunned after the foreman of the jury read the verdict. The convicted man's wife ran out of the courtroom in tears. Absalon will not be eligible for parole until after he turned 65.

Social Work Can Be Dangerous

Stephanie Ross, after graduating in 2009 from the University of South Florida with a bachelor's degree in psychology, landed a job as a counselor at a central Florida high school. In September 2012, the 25-year-old began working for a firm that according to its corporate literature, provided a "...comprehensive approach to managing the health needs most costly and complex members." Ross' employer, Integra Health Management Company, arranged health care for clients diagnosed with chronic illnesses. Ross had been hired as a service person responsible for visiting the homes of disabled people.

One of Ross' mentally deranged clients, 53-year-old Lucious Smith, lived in a one-story, cement-block apartment complex in Dade City a town thirty miles north of Tampa. Smith, an anti-social person who was seriously mentally disturbed, paranoid, and violent, embodied the kind of man nobody wants as a neighbor, co-worker, relative, customer, or mental health patient. Residents of the neighborhood perceived Smith as more than just a bellicose pain-in-the-neck, they considered him physically dangerous. Because association with this man brought trouble, he was a person to avoid.

Since 1981, Lucious Smith had served four separate stints in Florida's prison system for committing various crimes of violence. In 2005, after doing seven years for aggravated battery with a deadly weapon, Smith moved into the small apartment in Dade City. (Since he didn't have a job, he must have been on the public dole). Over the next six years, police were called to investigate 60 criminal complaints against Smith that included assault, trespassing, public intoxication, and disorderly conduct. Smith constantly fought and threatened his neighbors, and as a result of his bad behavior, had been banned from the local convenience store.

As part of her job, Stephanie Ross visited Lucious Smith in his apartment. After three house visitations, Ross placed a notation in Smith's file that he made her "very uncomfortable."

On the morning of December 10, 2012, Stephanie Ross was in Dade City delivering insurance paperwork to Mr. Smith. Shortly after entering Smith's apartment, neighbors and other witnesses saw Lucious Smith chasing a young woman down the street. Stephanie was yelling, "Help me! Help me!" As she ran, Smith stabbed her in the back with a butcher's knife. Smith caught his fleeing victim by her ponytail and threw her to the ground. He climbed on top of his bleeding victim and plunged the knife several more times into her body.

As people ran to Stephanie Ross' aid, Smith got up and casually strolled back to his apartment. A motorist pulled up to the bloody scene and drove Ross to a nearby hospital where she died a few hours later.

Not long after the fatal knife attack, police officers found Smith waiting for them outside his apartment. They arrested him without incident and hauled him to the Pasco County Jail where he was held without bond. A local prosecutor has charged Smith with first-degree murder. Shortly thereafter a grand jury indicted him on that charge.

In February 2013, two psychologists hired by Smith's defense attorney testified at a preliminary hearing that Mr. Smith was still mentally ill and therefore not competent to stand trial. A psychiatrist hired by the state disagreed. As a result, the judge ruled the defendant mentally competent. However, in May 2013, after further examinations of Mr. Smith, the state mental health expert changed his mind. This led the judge to change his mind and rule the defendant incompetent for trial. Judge Pat Siracusa ordered that Mr. Smith be treated at a state mental hospital until doctors determine he was competent to stand trial.

Why Teens Kill

There are many reasons why teens kill...If I were to narrow it down to the top three reasons, the order would be as follows:
   1. Abusive families and bullying
   2. Violent entertainment and pornography
   3. Anger, depression, and suicide

Phil Chalmers, *Inside the Mind of a Teen Killer*, 2009

Duke Lacrosse Accuser Accused

In 2006, 27-year-old Crystal Mangum claimed that three Duke University lacrosse players gang-raped her at a team party. The students had hired her as a stripper. The case grabbed national headlines because the accused were privileged young white men and the victim was working-class black.

When it became obvious that Mangum had fabricated her story of rape, North Carolina's attorney general declared the three Duke students innocent. The case ruined the career of Mike Nifong, the politically ambitious Durham County prosecutor who had championed Mangum's false allegations. The state bar association disbarred Nifong for his bad faith, overzealous prosecution of the innocent college students. The Duke Lacrosse case represents what can happen when politics and race override the pursuit of justice.

Another Durham County prosecutor, in February 2010, charged Crystal Mangum with attempted murder in connection with a row she had with her live-in boyfriend. According to the victim, she trashed his car then set fire to a pile of his clothes. At the time of the fire, children were in the apartment.

Just before the trial, the prosecutor replaced the attempted murder charge with felony-arson and contributing to the abuse of minors. In December 2010 a jury found Mangum guilty of the child abuse charge after failing to reach a consensus on the felony-arson count. The judge sentenced Mangum to the amount of time she had served in jail awaiting trial.

A 911 operator in Durham, North Carolina, on April 3, 2011, received an emergency call from the nephew of a 46-year-old man named Reginald Daye. Mr. Daye, another Mangum boyfriend, shared an apartment with her.

According to this 911 caller, Mr. Daye needed emergency medical assistance. Crystal Mangum had stabbed him with a kitchen knife.

Paramedics rushed Reginald Daye to Duke University Hospital where he underwent emergency surgery to repair the knife wound. Police officers arrested Mangum that day at a nearby apartment. Charged with assault with a deadly weapon with the intent to kill, the police booked Mangum into the Durham County Jail. The magistrate set her bond at $300,000.

Ten days after his surgery Reginald Daye died from the knife attack. The prosecutor immediately upgraded the charge against Mangum to first-degree murder.

In February 2013, Mangum gained temporary freedom after someone posted her bond. Acting as her own attorney, she claimed she had killed Reginald Daye in self-defense.

By the time the Mangum murder case went to trial on November 11, 2013, the accused had acquired the services of two defense attorneys. Assistant District Attorney Charlene Franks, in her opening remarks before the jury, said that the defendant, armed with a kitchen knife, had chased the victim down. Ten days later he died from his wounds.

According to the defense version of the case, Mangum, to protect herself against an enraged and jealous boyfriend, locked herself in the bathroom. When Daye kicked down the door and started beating her, she used the kitchen knife to "poke him in the side." According to the defense, Daye had died not from the stabbing but from complications arising from his surgery.

On November 22, 2013, the jury, after a six-hour deliberation, rejected Mangum's version of the events leading up to Reginald Daye's violent death. The panel found the defendant guilty of second-degree murder. The judge sentenced Mangum to a minimum 14 years in prison. At maximum, she could spend 18 years behind bars.

If Crystal Mangum is released after serving her minimum sentence, she will walk out of prison at age 48. If she conducts herself behind bars like she has lived her life on the outside, she's in for a difficult 14 years.

Physical Evidence

Clues are tangible signs that prove--or seem to prove--that no crime can be committed by thoughts only, and that we live in a world regulated by mechanical laws. The dead man was not killed by a ghostly hand but by a murderer of flesh and blood.

Theodore Reik, *The Unknown Murderer*, 1945

A Pair of Murders Over Nothing

Just because murder is a serious criminal offense does not mean that murderers always have equally serious motives to kill. In the world of criminal homicide, the motive does not always match the crime. Authors of detective novels give their fictitious murderers good reasons to kill such as sweet revenge, big money, passionate sex, jealous love, and burning hatred. In crime fiction the killer and the killed usually know each other well. In novels, murderers are, if not nice people, fascinating folks with interesting reasons to commit the ultimate crime.

In real life, people who commit criminal homicide are often wildly insane, drug-addled, or just plain stupid. Nonfiction killers are frequently uninteresting people who kill for trivial, idiotic reasons. Quite often, in real life, the murder victim is as insane, drug-addled or stupid as the person who killed him. In the more tragic cases, these mindless murderers take the lives of decent people who simply had the misfortune of crossing their lethal paths. If there is anything interesting in these under-motivated murder cases, it is the fact they are *real*. The advantage of writing about nonfiction crime is that these cases do not have to make a whole lot of sense. They just have to be true. Crime fiction, on the other hand, has to be believable and make sense.

At 7:40 in the evening of November 20, 2012, Michael D. Dunn and his girlfriend pulled into a service station in Jacksonville, Florida. That day, the couple had attended the wedding of Mr. Dunn's son. The 45-year-old software developer and his girlfriend were en route to Dunn's home 160 miles away in Satellite Beach, Florida. Dunn parked his vehicle and waited behind the wheel as his girlfriend entered the gas station's convenience store.

Mr. Dunn had pulled into the service station alongside a SUV occupied by three teenagers who were listening to music Dunn considered much too loud. He asked the boys to lower the sound level. The kids didn't take kindly to his request that led to an exchange of angry words. Suddenly, Michael Dunn picked up a handgun and fired eight shots into the car. Two of the bullets struck 17-year-old Jordan Davis who was sitting in the back seat. The high school junior, who was about to start his first job at McDonald's, died in the SUV.

The shooter's girlfriend ran out of the convenience store, and as she climbed into Dunn's vehicle, asked, "What's going on?"

"I just fired at those kids," Dunn replied as the couple drove away.

The next day, police officers arrested Michael Dunn at his home in Satellite Beach. (A witness had written down his license number.) Dunn told his police questioners that he had fired his pistol in self-defense after one of the kids in the SUV pointed a shotgun at him. Dunn's self-defense justification suffered a blow when investigators failed to find any weapons in the SUV. (There were no drugs in the car, and none of the boys had ever been in trouble with the law.)

A grand jury sitting in Jacksonville indicted Michael Dunn of first-degree murder, and three counts of attempted murder. If convicted of killing Jordan Davis, he faced life in prison without parole.

In February 2014, a Duval County jury, after deliberating 32 hours over a four-day period, found Dunn guilty of three counts of second-degree murder. The jury also found the defendant guilty of shooting or throwing a deadly missile. The jurors, however, could not agree on the first-degree murder counts. The judge sentenced Dunn to twenty years in prison.

In 2006, James Pak sold his Korean Yankee Landscape Company, a Biddeford, Maine business he had owned since 1964. In 2012, Mr. Pak lived with his wife in a cape cod-style home in the town of Bedford located 15 miles south of Portland. He rented out an apartment attached to his house to 44-year-old Susan Johnson who lived there with her son who was six and his 19-year-old brother, Derrick Thompson. Derrick worked as an auto detailer at a nearby car dealership. His girlfriend Alivia Welch worked as a waitress at a local coffee shop. She was eighteen.

Around six o'clock in the evening of Saturday, December 29, 2012, Bedford police officers responded to a call to defuse a dispute between Mr. Pak and his tenants. The 74-year-old landlord was upset because Derrick Thompson and his mother had parked their cars in his driveway. (The town had banned overnight parking on the street to clear the way for snow removal crews.) After speaking with Mr. Pak and his renters, the officers left the scene without taking anyone into custody.

At seven that night, shortly after the police thought they had resolved the dispute, and calmed the landlord down, they were called back to the Pak house on reports of shots being fired in the rented apartment. Upon their arrival, the officers discovered that Mr. Pak had shot Derrick Thompson and his girlfriend, Alivia Welch, killing them both. He had also shot and wounded Derrick's mother, Susan Johnson.

Following a three-hour police standoff at his home, James Pak surrendered to the authorities. Among other crimes, he was charged with two counts of first-degree murder.

In June 2014 James Pak changed his plea to not guilty by reason of insanity.

Drug dealers and members of street gangs regularly murder each other over minor slights, petty arguments, and even disrespectful looks. For these habitual criminals it's their chosen way of life. Unless some innocent bystander goes down in the crossfire, the general public couldn't care less about these deaths. One violent crook is dead, and his killer is off to prison for life.

Michael Dunn and James Pak were murderers who weren't career criminals or even drains on society. Because they were not stupid men, their homicidal behavior made no sense. These men ruined their lives over nothing. And their victims did nothing to deserve their sudden and violent deaths. That is what makes these spontaneous homicides so tragic, and hard to understand. (On January 5, 2013, a man in Kings Park, Long Island named Clarence Newcomb, beat his 82-year-old grandmother to death. The 25-year-old and the victim had been arguing over what TV show to watch.)

Lust as A Motive to Murder

The Marquis de Sade knew whereof he spoke. As the first of the seven deadly sins, lust commands a special place in the lexicon of transgression. It's a trigger-happy emotion that can turn from inarticulate ardor to homicidal mania on a dime. Lust is the sin that drives ordinary people to extraordinary measures, one corpse--or more--at a time.

A Miscellany of Murder, The Monday Murder Club, 2011

Killer Boobs

In April 2010, Claire Smedley from Blackpool, England told a British newspaper reporter that she had nearly killed her boyfriend with her size 40LL breasts. (While I know bullet calibers, I have no idea what 40LLs look like other than they are big.) With her boyfriend Steven's face buried in her super-bust, Claire misinterpreted his flailing for oxygen as sexual excitement. After barely escaping breast asphyxiation, Steven ended the relationship. He's now dating a flat-chested woman named Paula. (Just kidding.)

In Germany, a lawyer named Tim Schmidt claimed that his girlfriend, a woman armed with a pair of 38DDs attempted to suffocate him by breast. Mr. Schmidt described his near-death experience to a German newspaper reporter: "I asked her why she wanted to smother me to death with her breasts. She told me: 'Pleasure--I wanted your death to be as pleasurable as possible.' " (Really? I can't image, as I'm fighting for my last breath, thinking, *these are nice.*)

Ambulance personnel and Snohomish County sheriff's deputies, shortly after midnight on Saturday, January 12, 2013, responded to a 911 domestic disturbance call from a mobile home in the Airport Inn Trailer Park outside Everett, Washington. Residents Donna Lange and her boyfriend (who has not been named) had been drinking alcohol and smoking pot all night with a man and two other women. The 51-year-old Lange and her boyfriend had gotten into a fight. The fight escalated and moved to the back of the trailer house. At some point, Lange allegedly threw the 5-foot, 7-inch, 175-pound man to the floor. The 5-foot, 6-inch, 195-pound Lange then climbed on top of the downed drunk and passed out. The victim lay trapped under her body with his face buried in her breasts.

When the police and the medics stormed into the trailer, they found the boyfriend still lying on the floor. He was not breathing. In his hands were clumps of Lange's hair. CPR didn't help, and upon arrival at the Swedish Hospital in Edmonds, medical personnel pronounced the 50-year-old boyfriend dead. Cause of death: suffocation.

Questioned at the hospital, Donna Lange told police officers that she had no knowledge how her boyfriend had died. A few days later, a Snohomish County prosecutor charged Donna Lange with second-degree manslaughter. (A lesser homicide charge involving an accidental death caused by reckless behavior, or during the commission of a crime that is not a felony.) If convicted, Lange could be sentenced to a maximum five years in prison.

As of August 2014 the Lange case had not been resolved.

The Sea Hag Case

In and around the town of Conch Key, an unincorporated community in the Florida Keys, 62-year-old Carolyn Dukeshire was known as "The Sea Hag." (When I saw Dukeshire's mug shot I thought Hulk Hogan had been arrested.)

On the night of July 29, 2012, Martin Mazur and his friends, after an evening of drinking at the Brass Monkey Bar, were sitting outside of his dwelling finishing off a few beers. His neighbor, Carolyn Dukeshire, approached the group and asked Mazur if he had a cold Busch Light for her. "I have absolutely nothing for you," he replied.

Mazur's last words had barely left his mouth when Dukeshire pulled out a handgun and shot him five times. The victim was hit in the stomach, back, and wrist. He died a few hours later at a nearby hospital.

One of the witnesses to the murder called 911. Deputies from the Monroe County Sheriff's Office arrested Dukeshire at the scene of the shooting. Charged with first-degree murder, the judge denied her bail. (Prior to the murder, Dukeshire had not been arrested for any serious crimes.)

On January 31, 2013, the defendant, after submitting a statement to the judge that she felt bad about murdering Martin Mazur over a can of beer, was allowed to plead guilty to second-degree murder. The judge sentenced

The Sea Hag to thirty years in prison. It's doubtful that she will live long enough to see her next beer.

Infanticide

Infanticide has been committed throughout human history for a multiplicity of reasons--personal, political, superstitious, and strategic. Whether or not a culture supports the perpetrators of infanticide, it is, like other forms of violence, highly mutable [subject to change]. In many cultures, offspring weren't considered to be fully human until they reached a certain age, one or two, sometimes three years old. Perhaps the most common cause of violence against infants arose from the need to space children in the absence of birth control. The Japanese word for infanticide means, "weeding," as in the thinning of rice saplings. Today, in some of the poorest communities in the world, infanticide as birth control takes a passive-aggressive form: babies are given birth to then simply not fed.

Cultures have also engaged in crude forms of eugenics, turning against twins, against girls, against deformities--as some societies continue to do, now, through selective abortion. Infants have been killed, as well, during famine, or in the midst of war, or as an offering in ritual sacrifice.

Patricia Pearson, *When She Was Bad,* 1998

Three Dead Babies

In 2004, 24-year-old Katie Stockton and her 4-year-old son lived with her parents in a rural home near Rockton, Illinois in the northern part of the state. After becoming pregnant in March of that year, Stockton continued using cocaine, and kept her pregnancy secret. On December 17, 2004, under clandestine circumstances, Stockton gave birth to a living baby.

Because she didn't want anyone to know about the baby's existence, Stockton stuffed the breathing infant, the placenta, and her bloody garments into an orange shopping sack that she placed into a white, plastic trash bag. Knowing the consequences of her act, the new mother dumped the trash bag and the baby alongside a road 100 feet from her parent's house.

Days later, the baby was found dead from either exposure or suffocation. A forensic toxicologist determined that the infant--referred to as Baby Crystal--had been infected with hepatitis. The baby also had traces of cocaine in her system.

Detectives questioned Katie Stockton about the murdered infant. She denied having given birth to the dumped baby. She also refused to provide the authorities with a sample of her DNA. Without enough evidence to support a court order that required Stockton to supply the DNA evidence, the case fizzled-out.

Four years later, Baby Crystal's murder was under investigation by a team of cold-case homicide detectives who considered Stockton the prime suspect. An officer who had the suspect under surveillance recovered a cigarette butt she had discarded. The DNA on the cigarette butt matched the bloody clothing found inside the trash bag with the dead baby.

Detectives, in August 2009, arrested Stockton on the charge of first-degree murder. Notwithstanding the DNA results, she denied being Baby Crystal's mother. Shortly after the arrest, investigators located Stockton's blue Saturn. The vehicle had been parked for years in an impound lot. Police officers searched the car, and in the trunk, found the skeletal remains of two other infants. The babies had been stuffed into a pair of bags hidden beneath the spare tire.

Stockton was not charged with the murders of the two infants in the car because forensic pathologists couldn't establish if the baby's had been born alive. Later DNA analysis revealed that the infants in Stockton's vehicle were Baby Crystal's sisters. The three dead babies had three different fathers.

In February 2013, Stockton, facing life in prison (Illinois abolished its death penalty), pleaded guilty to first-degree murder in hopes the judge would show her mercy. At her April 5 sentencing hearing before Winnebago County Judge John Truitt, public defender David Doll asked that Stockton be given a prison term of 25 years. The defense attorney described his client as a good person who struggled with drug addiction.

The defendant, in speaking directly to Judge Truitt, said, "I was in a very dark place for many years. I apologize to those I hurt and ask forgiveness. I'm truly sorry for the pain and hurt they have endured."

Judge Truitt, apparently unmoved by the murder defendant's apology, sentenced the 32-year-old woman to 50 years behind bars.

Remarkable Cases

Of the cases presented here (*A Companion to Murder*), some have been chosen because the people involved in them are strange and remarkable, passionate, revengeful, avaricious, stupid, ambitious, resourceful, pitiable, tragic, even comic, beyond the ordinary. Others have been chosen because the interplay of motive behind the crime has some special interest; others for the sake of some brilliant stroke of detection. Other cases are to be valued for their particular atmosphere or mood; others because they illustrate some tenet of the law as it applies to the crime of murder; others, again, because they display the forensic skill of a great advocate.

Spenser Shew, *A Companion to Murder*, 1961

A Murder Suicide Without the Suicide

Sixty-four-year-old Eugene Maraventano, his wife Janet, and their 27-year-old son Bryan lived in Goodyear, Arizona, a suburb of Phoenix. On April 6, 2013, Maraventano called 911 to report he had killed his wife and son. To the dispatcher her said, "I can't kill myself. I stabbed them to death. My wife had cancer."

When police officers rolled up to the two-story stucco house, they encountered Mr. Maraventano walking out of the dwelling wearing clothing soaked in blood. (He had murdered his 63-year-old wife and their son four days earlier, but had just attempted suicide. The blood was his.)

Inside the Maraventano house, police discovered Janet dead in the master bedroom. The carpet, bed, and bedroom door were stained with the victim's blood. A bloody 14-inch kitchen knife lay on the nightstand next to the bed.

In another bedroom, officers discovered Bryan Maraventano dead on the floor not far from the doorway. He had been stabbed as well.

Later on the day of the 911 call, a police interrogator asked Mr. Maraventano the obvious question: Why did he kill his wife and son? The subject explained that he suspected he had infected his wife with a sexually transmitted disease he picked up from patronizing prostitutes when he worked in New York City. After her cancer diagnosis, he was worried she would test positive for HIV. He had killed his wife to spare incurring her wrath and disapproval.

As to why he had murdered his son, Mr. Maraventano said that the kid had no life. He didn't have a job or a girlfriend, and just sat around the house all day playing video games. He figured Bryan had some kind of mental disability, and wouldn't be able to make it on his own.

After the cold-blooded murder, Maraventano tried to kill himself by cutting his wrists and putting a plastic bag over his head. When he couldn't commit suicide using these techniques, he placed a knife handle against a wall and pushed himself into it. That didn't work either, so he gave up trying.

Following treatment for his self-inflicted wounds at a local hospital, Eugene Maraventano, charged with two counts of first- degree murder, was placed in the county jail under $2 million bond.

Maraventano's December 2013 trial was postponed. The case remained unresolved as of August 2014.

Serial Killer Hysteria

Psychiatry is not to blame for the emergence of the late-twentieth-century fictional monster known as the serial killer, but the psychiatric concept of criminal violence as an unconsciously motivated explosion of rage bolsters the credibility of what is in fact a bureaucratic invention....

Ultraviolent criminals sometimes commit a series of murders...Such serial homicides are committed most commonly by violent drug dealers, professional murderers and armed robbers in the course of doing business...The notion of an irrational, predatory "serial killer" emerged in the early 1980s amid widespread hysteria about the danger to children from pornographers, satanic cults, lethal day-care centers and kidnappers...The 1983 [Senate] hearings on child kidnapping and serial homicide by the Juvenile Justice Sub Committee, chaired by Senator Arlen Spector, [was] the public forum from which emerged the popular notion of a multitude of predatory serial killers scourging the land....

Specter's subcommittee estimated that there had been as many as 3,600 "random and senseless [serial] murders" in 1981; by the time that number had whispered its way around the circle of public discussion, it was inflated to estimates of 4,000 or 5,000 serial-killer victims per year (out of about 23,000 total U. S. homicides)...The actual number of [serial killer] victims is closer to two hundred a year. [That may have been true in the 80s and 90s, but the number of yearly victims is now much lower than 200.]

Richard Rhodes, *Why They Kill*, 1999

The Murder of an Adopted Son

Andrew Burd was born in Corpus Christi, Texas on July 28, 2002. The 16-year-old girl who gave birth to him had used, during her pregnancy, meth, crack cocaine, LSD, and marijuana. The expectant mother had also consumed alcohol, took Xanax, and smoked cigarettes. The baby's 17-year-old father worked for a traveling carnival.

Andrew was a year old when his mother took him to an emergency room with a broken arm. A doctor suspected child abuse and called Child Protective Services (CPS). Nothing came of the CPS investigation, and the baby was returned to his mother. Eventually, after repeated evidence of child abuse, CPS agents, on the grounds that Andrew was in "immediate danger," took him from his young parents. The agency placed the two and a half-year-old toddler into foster care where he was shuffled from one home to another.

In 2006, Corpus Christi residents Larry and Hannah Overton heard about Andrew Burd through their evangelical, nondenominational church, Calvary Chapel of the Coastlands. The couple resided in a modest ranch-style house with their four young children. Twenty-nine-year-old Hannah was six months pregnant at the time. Although the family struggled financially from what Larry Overton earned as a landscape lighting installer, the couple expressed interest in adopting Andrew.

In 1984, when Hannah Overton was seven-years-old, her father, Bennie Saenz, an evangelical preacher, was arrested and charged with murder. Convicted of bludgeoning a 16-year-old girl to death, then dumping her body along the shore of Padre Island, the Corpus Christi preacher went to prison for 23 years. (I presume he was released in 2007.)

Before her marriage to Larry, Hannah had worked as a volunteer in an orphanage in Reynosa, Mexico across the border from Corpus Christi. As a married couple, Larry and Hannah had performed missionary work for their church. By all accounts they were decent people, loving parents who had never been in trouble with the authorities. Moreover, Larry and Hannah did not have histories of mental illness.

In the spring of 2006, Andrew Burd joined the Overton family on a six-month probationary basis. On October 2, 2006, not long after the official adoption, the four-year-old became suddenly ill. He began vomiting and struggled with his breathing. Hannah, instead of immediately calling 911, telephoned Larry at work. He rushed home. When Andrew became unresponsive, the Overtons rushed him to a nearby urgent care clinic. When nurses at the clinic failed to revive Andrew with CPR, paramedics transported the boy to Corpus Christi's Driscoll Hospital.

Medical personnel at the urgent care clinic, suspicious of child abuse, notified the police shortly after Andrew was admitted to the hospital. Within hours of Andrew's hospitalization, police with the Corpus Christi Police Department searched the Overton residence.

In the evening of October 3, 2006, Andrew Burd died. Dr. Ray Fernandez, the Nueces County Medical Examiner, performed the autopsy. The forensic pathologist, finding some bleeding of the brain, external scratches and bruises, and twice the level of sodium in the dead child's blood, ruled the manner of death homicide. Dr. Fernandez identified the boy's cause of death as "acute sodium toxicity with blunt force trauma as a contributing factor." (Dr. Fernandez did not acknowledge that the brain hemorrhaging could have been caused by the sodium content in Andrew's blood.)

Child Protection Services agents took the other Overton children out of their home and placed them with relatives. (Eventually the children would be placed under the care of Hannah Overton's mother.) A few days after Andrew's death, Corpus Christi detective Michael Hess, an investigator who specialized in child abuse cases, interrogated Hannah Overton at the police station. She had agreed to be questioned without the presence of counsel.

Detective Hess made it clear that he believed that Hannah, feeling overburdened with so many young children had murdered her adopted son. "I don't see," he said, "what caused the trauma to the brain. I don't see what caused the salt content. Did you at any time strike him?" (At this point, Hannah Overton should have asked for an attorney.)

The five-hour grilling at the police station ended without a confession. In his report, Detective Hess wrote: "It should be noted that during the entire conversation (conversation?), Hannah Overton showed no emotion." Notwithstanding Hannah Overton's insistence that she had done nothing to harm her adopted son, Nueces County Assistant District Attorney Sandra Eastwood, a child protection crusader, charged the mother of five (she had since had her baby) with capital murder. Under Texas law, if convicted as charged, Hannah Overton would go to prison for life without the chance of parole.

The televised Hannah Overton murder trial got underway in Corpus Christi in August 2007. Prosecutor Eastwood, in her opening remarks to the jury, said, "We don't know precisely how she [the defendant] got [the salt] down Andrew, but we know that he [the child] was very, very, obedient."

Dr. Ray Fernandez, the Nueces County Medical Examiner testified that he had seen "burn-like scarring" on Andrew's arm that had likely been caused by "contact with a hot surface." (Judge Jose Longoria did not allow Dr. Fernandez to state that blunt force trauma had contributed to Andrew's death. The judge, due to insufficient scientific evidence to back up this part of the pathologist's testimony, ruled it inadmissible.)

Dr. Alexander Rotta, a pediatric critical care specialist from Indianapolis, Indiana testified, "The body had so many bruises and scratches it would be difficult to describe them all." Dr. Rotta told the jurors that the sodium content in Andrew's blood amounted to six teaspoons of salt. In the doctor's expert opinion, Andrew Burd's death had *not* been accidental.

After Detective Michael Hess played a video of the defendant's interrogation, one of the nurses who had performed CPR on Andrew at the urgent care clinic testified that the defendant, during the emergency, had not behaved like a panic-stricken parent. In fact, she often had a smile on her face. Two other urgent care clinic employees took the stand and gave similar testimony. One of these witnesses said that she had heard the defendant tell someone at the clinic that the boy had stopped breathing after he had been "punished." (While children are "punished" all the time, jurors probably interpreted this comment as evidence of child abuse.)

At the close of the state's case, defense attorneys David Jones and Chris Pinedo brought Harvard educated forensic pathologist Dr. Judy Melinek to the stand. Dr. Melinek identified the sores on Andrew's body as being consistent with mosquito bites that had been excessively scratched. The witness, on the issue of how all of that sodium had entered Andrew's system, said that in all probability the child suffered from a rare eating disorder called pica. Children with this malady have an uncontrollable desire to consume inappropriate substances such as salt.

Hannah Overton took the stand on her own behalf and did not come off as a convincing or even sympathetic witness. (Her attorneys, given the accusations in the case, had no choice but to put her on the stand.) At this stage of the trial, given the testimony of the medical examiner, the pediatrician from Indiana, and the urgent care clinic personnel, the jurors had probably made up their minds.

The three-week trial came to an end when the jury, after deliberating eleven hours, found Hannah Overton guilty of capital murder. (She would eventually be sent to the maximum-security women's prison outside of Waco, Texas.) Overton's attorneys, shortly after the verdict, polled the jury. The defense attorneys were stunned to learn that *all* of the jurors had found the defendant guilty for intentionally not getting Andrew immediate medical help. None of the jurors had been convinced beyond a reasonable doubt that the defendant had poisoned her child with salt.

Two days after the guilty verdict, Dr. Edgar Cortes, the emergency room physician on duty at Driscoll Hospital the day Andrew arrived, and the pediatrician who had resuscitated the patient before he was sent to the intensive care unit, wrote a letter to the Overton defense team. Dr. Cortes informed the lawyers that while he had been scheduled to testify for the prosecution, prosecutor Sandra Eastwood never called him to the stand. The doctor wasn't called because in his opinion, Andrew Burd's death had been accidental. Dr. Cortes, had he taken the stand, would have testified that Andrew had been a hyperactive child who suffered from an autism spectrum disorder. (Dr. Cortes had studied Andrew's medical records.) This would account for the boy's inappropriate eating habits, obsessive scratching and picking, and head banging.

In the months following the guilty verdict, three prominent appellate attorneys--Cynthia Orr, John Raley, and Gerry Goldstein--took an interest in the Overton case. The attorneys filed an appeal alleging newly discovered exonerating evidence, ineffective legal representation at trial, and the withholding of exculpatory evidence from the defense by prosecutor Sandra Eastwood.

In 2009, the Texas Circuit Court of Criminal Appeals upheld the Overton capital murder conviction. The justices found no proof that the state had known of Dr. Edgar Cortes' cause and manner of death opinion. The appellate judges also rejected the newly discovered evidence and ineffective counsel claims.

In the spring of 2010, the Overton appellate team petitioned for the right to have access to the prosecution's file on the case. Prior to the trial, prosecutor Eastwood, when asked by defense attorneys for access to documents related to Andrew's stomach contents, claimed that such a report didn't exist. The appellate attorneys, when they were given the opportunity to examine the prosecution's file, found the gastric contents report. Not only did they find the report, according to this document, Andrew's stomach contents did *not* reveal elevated amounts of salt when he arrived at the urgent care clinic.

Hannah Overton's appellate team also discovered that prosecutor Eastwood had scheduled, for testimony, Dr. Michael Moritz, the clinical director of pediatric nephrology at the Children's Hospital of Pittsburgh. Dr. Moritz specialized in children's kidney diseases, and in 2007, had published a paper on accidental child salt poisoning cases. Dr. Moritz had found that a vast majority of these cases involved boys between the age of one and six. Moreover, they had all had been in foster care, or were from abusive homes. All of these boys suffered from the eating disorder, pica.

Dr. Moritz told the appellate team that he had waited days in the Corpus Christi courthouse for his turn to take the stand. When the doctor told prosecutor Eastwood that he had to return to Pittsburgh, she arranged for a video deposition that because of time was not completed. Had he taken the stand, Dr. Moritz would have testified that in his expert opinion, Andrew's death had been accidental.

Appellate attorney Cynthia Orr, about the time of the Dr. Moritz revelation, received a letter from Anna Jimenez, the former Nueces County prosecutor who had worked on the Overton case with Sandra Eastwood. Regarding whether Eastwood had withheld exculpatory evidence from the defense, Jimenez wrote: "I fear she [Eastwood] may have purposely withheld evidence that may have been favorable to Hannah Overton's defense."

In April 2011, Cynthia Orr petitioned the Texas Court of Criminal Appeals for an evidentiary hearing on the Overton case. Ten months later, in February 2012, appellate judge Cathy Cochran ordered the Corpus Christi trial court judge to hold such a proceeding to entertain the appellate team's assertion that Hanna Overton, an innocent person, had been wrongfully convicted of murder.

The evidentiary hearing began on April 24, 2012. Chris Pinedo, one of Overton's trial attorneys, took the stand. Pinedo testified that he had asked prosecutor Sandra Eastwood for a sample of Andrew's gastric contents that had been acquired by Driscoll Hospital personnel. Attorney Pinedo wanted to have an independent scientist analyze this evidence for sodium content. The defense attorney was told that such evidence did not exist. Because he had acquired photographs of the stomach contents that had been taken at the Nueces County Medical Examiner's Office, attorney Pinedo knew that he had been lied to.

Forensic pathologist Dr. Judy Melinek testified that because Neuces County medical examiner, Dr. Ray Fernandez, had failed to adequately analyze Andrew's hypothalamus and pituitary glands, his cause and manner of death conclusions were questionable.

Dr. Edgar Cortes, the emergency medicine pediatrician who had attended to Andrew at Driscoll Hospital before the boy's death, took the stand and described how he had waited at the courthouse to testify as a prosecution witness. "I told Assistant District Attorney Sandra Eastwood, 'I hope you're going to come forward with some other [homicide] charge than capital murder because I don't think this was capital murder.' " When asked by attorney Orr why prosecutor Eastwood hadn't put him on the stand, Dr. Cortes said, "I felt like the prosecution had its own theory about what happened." (That was fine as long as the prosecution's theory was backed up by proof beyond a reasonable doubt.)

Dr. Michael Moritz, the clinical director of pediatric nephrology at Children's Hospital of Pittsburgh, one of the nation's leading experts on salt poisoning, took the stand on day two of the Overton evidentiary hearing. Dr. Moritz said he believed that if Andrew Burd had ingested a lethal dose of salt, he had fed it to himself. The doctor testified that intentional, force-fed salt poisoning was extremely rare.

Day three of the Overton hearing featured the testimony of former prosecutor Sandra Eastwood. In 2010, Eastwood had been fired from the Nueces County District Attorney's office after she had informed the district attorney that she had been romantically involved with a sex offender. During the Overton trial in 2007, Eastwood, an alcoholic, had been functioning under the influence of alcohol and prescription diet pills. Her responses to Cynthia Orr's questions were vague, confusing, and often contradictory. The witness said that her drinking and pill taking had destroyed her memory of the Overton case. As a witness, Eastwood come off more pathetic than evil.

Eastwood's former assistant in the Overton case, Anna Jimenez, followed her to the stand. According to Jimenez, Eastwood had made the following comment to her: "I will do anything to win this case." Jimenez testified that in her opinion, Sandra Eastwood's behavior during the Overton murder trial was "so far out." The witness testified further that she believed that Hannah Overton should have been charged with a lesser homicide offense. Regarding Eastwood's claim that the boy's gastric contents evidence did not exist, Jimenez said, "She is not truthful."

On the sixth and final day of the Overton evidentiary proceeding, David Jones, one of Overton's trial attorneys, broke down on the stand. "I failed miserably," he said. "There's probably not a day since this verdict that I don't regret spending more time on this case. I should have done more."

On June 1, 2012, a month after the conclusion of the Overton hearing, District Court Judge Jose Longoria issued his recommendation to the Texas Court of Criminal Appeals. In a 14-page opinion, Judge Longoria explained why he saw *no* new evidence that would have altered the outcome of Overton's murder trial. "The court," he wrote, "concludes that all of the supposedly newly discovered evidence actually was clearly known and discussed at the time of the trial."

Hannah Overton's appellate team, as well as a large group of people who believed she was an innocent mother who had been railroaded into prison by an overzealous prosecutor, were stunned by Judge Longoria's opinion. The imprisoned woman's fate rests with the Texas Court of Criminal Appeals. In making their decision on whether or not to grant Overton a new trial, the appeals court justices are not bound by District Court Judge Longoria's recommendation.

In April 2014, the Court of Criminal Appeals sitting in Austin, Texas heard oral arguments presented by Overton's attorneys on the issue of whether she should be granted a new trial. As of July 2014, the appellate court has not handed down its decision.

Murder Trial Drama

For sheer human interest, the ability to catch public attention and cleave to it from start to finish, nothing else in real life equals a good murder trial. A prominent victim, or, even better, a prominent defendant; a bit of mystery surrounding the facts of the case; two teams of high-powered attorneys facing each other across the courtroom; a cluster of witnesses, each contributing a few tantalizing facts to a tale of human fallibility; a battery of expert witnesses to explain the unexplainable; a man's or woman's life or freedom hanging in the balance--these are the makings of high drama. As Shakespeare taught us, good drama is an intimate mixture of both tragedy and farce.

Michael Kurland, *How to Try a Murder,* 2002

Rotting Corpses in Detroit

Beginning in the 1950s, the middle class in Detroit, Michigan began moving to the suburbs. The exodus accelerated in 1967 following the race riots, and it hasn't stopped. Between 2000 and 2010, 750,000 residents have moved out of the city. Detroit now has a population of 700,000 living in a place built for 2 million.

The massive migration from crime, taxes, lousy schools, and falling real estate values has left vast sections of the city virtually abandoned. Because of its dwindling tax base, the city can't afford to demolish more than 30,000 vacant houses. (Youngstown, Ohio has a similar problem.) These urban wastelands consist of empty dwellings, crumbling buildings, crack houses, abandoned vehicles, and vacant lots. And there is garbage everywhere.

In rural, small town, and suburban America, when someone commits murder and needs to dispose of the body, they deposit the corpse in the woods, in a rural field, or toss it into a river, pond, or lake. Not in Detroit. Murderers in that city took their dead victims to these dying neighborhoods where weeks later they were found decomposing in empty buildings, abandoned vehicles, trash-littered alleyways, and overgrown lots.

In 2012, more than a dozen homicide victims were dumped in these decaying areas of Detroit. The place became a dumping ground for killers. Because the police didn't patrol these districts, the corpses laid around for days and weeks stinking up the city.

The Art of Dismemberment

To profane a dead body by cutting it to pieces has always seemed, at least to our Western eyes, an act of bestial brutality. It is one thing to do murder. It is quite another to destroy the murder victim's identity, and this is the effect of dismemberment....

Taking apart a fresh human body is no mean task. You will work up a sweat doing it. I have seen every tool imaginable used for this grisly purpose, from the ancient stone choppers used by early man millions of years ago...to the Rambo knives, hacksaws and chain saws of today. It is a bloody, messy, dangerous business. Saws and knives can slip and wound you while you are using them. Bone itself can be quite sharp.

Many dismemberments are done in bathtubs--more things come out of bathtubs than bathtub gin...Most of my [dismemberment] cases seem to involve motorcycle gang members or people involved in the drug trade.

Dr. William R. Maples, *Dead Men Do Tell Tales*, 1994

Kill the Lawyer

In Greenwood, Mississippi, attorney Lee Abraham got wind of a murder-for-hire plot against him by two husbands of women he had represented several years before in a pair of divorce cases. The attorney had reason to believe that a local physician, 70-year-old Dr. Arnold Smith, and a 54-year-old brick mason named William Paul Muller, were the masterminds behind the plan to kill him. Apparently these men still hated the lawyer who had won settlements for their wives. Instead of moving on with their lives, they wanted revenge.

On Saturday night, April 28, 2012, two agents with the Mississippi Attorney General's Office investigating the case were in Abraham's office talking to him about the alleged murder plot. That night, 23-year-old Keaira Byrd and his 25-year-old accomplice Derrick Lacy burst into the law office. (According to some reports, the agents knew the hit men were coming and were waiting for them.) Byrd, armed with an assault rifle, and wearing a ski mask, fired the first shot. The agents returned fire, killing Byrd on the spot. Derrick Lacy was shot in the lower back. One of the attorney general agents received a minor wound. Attorney Abraham, the target of the hit, escaped injury.

Derrick Lacy, as he was airlifted to the University of Mississippi Medical Center in Jackson, told an investigator that he had overheard Dr. Smith offer Keaira Byrd money to kill the lawyer.

The day after the shootings, a Leflore County prosecutor charged the oncologist and the brick mason with conspiracy to commit murder. The arraignment magistrate denied Dr. Smith bail. William Paul Muller paid his $250,000 bond and was released. On his Facebook page, Mr. Muller proclaimed his innocence.

Following Dr. Smith's arrest, his attorney arranged to have him evaluated by a mental health expert who concluded that the physician was not mentally competent to stand trial. In January 2013, in response to the prosecution's request, Circuit Court Judge Breland Hilburn ordered Dr. Smith to undergo a psychiatric evaluation at the Mississippi State Hospital at Whitfield.

Because of institutional overcrowding, a hospital bed for Dr. Smith didn't become available until June 4, 3013. (Mississippi must have a serious problem with mental illness.) As of August 2014 the Smith case remained on hold.

No Smoking Gun

In November 2006, 29-year-old Jason Young and his 26-year-old wife Michelle lived in a suburban home outside of Raleigh, North Carolina. They had a 2-year-old daughter named Cassidy. Michelle was five months pregnant with their second child. It was not a happy marriage. He had several girlfriends, and as a salesman for a medical software company, he spent a lot of time on the road. Michelle told friends and relatives that she hated her life.

On the morning of November 3, 2006 Jason was out of town. The previous night he had checked into a Hampton Inn in Huntsville, Virginia 169 miles from Raleigh. At nine that morning, he left a voicemail for Michelle's younger sister, Meredith Fisher. Jason asked Meredith to stop by his house and retrieve some papers for him. (I presume he told Meredith he had called home and didn't get an answer.)

Later that morning, Meredith Fisher entered the Young house on Jason's behalf. When she climbed the stairs to the second floor she was shocked by the sight of bloody footprints. In the master bedroom she discovered her sister lying facedown in a pool of blood. The victim, wearing a white sweatshirt and black sweatpants, had been bludgeoned to death beyond recognition. Meredith found Cassidy hiding under the covers of her parents' bed. She had not been harmed, but her socks were saturated in her mother's blood. Meredith Fisher called 911.

According to the forensic pathologist who performed the autopsy, the assailant had struck Michelle Young at least thirty times in the head. The attacker had tried to kill the victim by manual strangulation before beating her to death. The extent of the head wounds suggested an attack by an enraged, out-of-control killer who hated the victim.

The authorities, from the beginning, suspected that Jason Young had snuck back to North Carolina from Virginia, murdered his wife then returned to the Hampton Inn. The killer had not forced his way into the house, nothing had been taken, and the little girl's life had been spared. At the time of the murder, Jason was having an affair with one of his wife's friends. The couple had been fighting, and Jason had made no secret of the fact he wanted out of the marriage.

From a prosecutor's point of view, there were serious holes in the Jason Young case. The suspect had an alibi 169 miles from the murder scene, and there was no physical evidence linking him to the carnage. Moreover, no one had seen him at the house on the night of the murder. Even worse, investigators had not identified the murder weapon. As a result of these prosecutorial weaknesses, the Wake County District Attorney's Office did not charge Jason with the murder of his wife.Michelle Young's parents were convinced that Jason had murdered their daughter. When it became apparent that the authorities were not taking action, they filed a wrongful death suit against him. In March 2009, two years and four months after the homicide, the civil court jury, applying a standard of proof that is less demanding than a criminal trial's proof beyond a reasonable doubt, found the defendant responsible for Michelle's brutal killing. The jurors awarded the plaintiffs $15.5 million in damages.

Eight months after the civil court verdict, a Wake County prosecutor, based on a three-year homicide investigation conducted by the City-County Bureau of Investigation, charged Jason Young with first-degree murder. Police officers, on the afternoon of December 15, 2009, arrested Young after pulling over his car in Brevard, a town in southwest North Carolina. The local magistrate denied him bail.

The Jason Young murder case went to trial in Raleigh in June 2011. The prosecutor, following his opening statement in which he alleged that the defendant had drugged his daughter that night with adult-strength Tylenol and a prescription sedative, put on an entirely circumstantial case that relied heavily on motive.

The defense attorney hammered home the fact the prosecution could not place the defendant at the scene of the murder. The state did not have a confession, an eyewitness, or even the murder weapon. Jason took the stand on his own behalf and told the jurors that when his wife was murdered, he was sleeping in a hotel 169 miles away. He said he had loved his wife and their unborn child.

On Monday morning, June 27, 2011, the foreman of the jury of seven men and five women told the judge that the jurors were "immovably hung" on the verdict. "We currently sit," he said, "at a six to six ration and do not appear to be able to make any further movement. Where do we go from here?"

The trial judge instructed the jurors to return to the jury room and try to reach a verdict. But later in the day, after deliberating a total of twelve hours, the foreman announced that they were deadlocked in an eight to four vote in favor of acquittal. The judge declared a mistrial.

The Wake County District Attorney, determined to bring Jason Young to justice, announced that he would try him again. Jason, who had been incarcerated in the Wake County Jail since his arrest in December 2009, went on trial for the second time on February 10, 2012.

The prosecutor, in his opening statement, alleged that the defendant had checked into the Hillsville Hampton Inn just before eleven on the night of November 2, 2006. An hour later he left the building through an emergency exit he had propped open with a rock to avoid using his computer card key to re-enter the hotel. According to the prosecutor, the defendant arrived at his Birchleaf Drive home at around three in the morning. Shortly after his arrival, he drugged his daughter and murdered his wife. After cleaning up and disposing of his bloody shirt, shoes, and trousers, and ditching or cleaning off the murder weapon, he returned to the hotel, arriving there around seven in the morning.

Following the testimony of the victim's sister, Meredith Fisher, and the testimony of several other prosecution witnesses, a Hampton Inn hotel clerk took the stand. According to this witness, he had found the emergency door on the first-floor stairwell propped open with a rock, He also noticed that in the same stairwell, someone had unplugged the security camera and turned its lens toward the ceiling.

One of the City-County Bureau of Investigation crime scene officers testified that it appeared that someone had moved the victim's body to get into the defendant's closet. The detective said that despite all of the blood on the upstairs floor, the killer had sanitized certain items such as the sink drain. The investigator said he did find traces of blood on the knob to the door leading from the house to the garage. This witness had been present when, on the day after the murder, the suspect's body was checked for signs of trauma related to the killing. No injuries were found.

A second detective testified that the dark shirt the defendant was seen wearing on hotel surveillance video footage was not in the suitcase he had used on that trip. The implication was that the defendant had disposed of the bloody garment.

Included among the prosecution witnesses who took the stand over the next two weeks were two daycare employees who said they had seen Cassidy Young acting out her mother's beating. The girl was using a doll to demonstrate the attack. A therapist took the stand and testified that a week before her death, the victim had come to her seeking counseling to cope with her unhappy marriage. In the therapist's opinion Michelle Young's husband had been verbally abused her.

Jason Young's mother and father took the stand for the defense. On November 3, 2006 Jason had driven from the Hampton Inn in Virginia to his parents' home in Brevard, North Carolina. His mother testified that when they broke the news to him that Michelle had been murdered "you saw the color just drain from his face."

On February 29, 2012 the defense rested its case without calling Jason to the stand. (The defense attorney was probably worried that the prosecutor, having studied Jason's direct testimony from the first trial, would rip him apart on cross-examination.)

The prosecutor, in his closing argument to the jury, said, "This woman wasn't just murdered, she suffered a beating the likes of which we seldom see. This woman was punished. The assailant struck her over thirty times with a weapon of some sort, and she was undoubtedly unconscious after the second or third blow."

The defense attorney pointed out the weaknesses in the prosecution's case, talked about reasonable doubt, and reminded the jury that being a bad husband did not make his client a murderer.

On March 5, 2012, after the jury of eight women and four men had deliberated eight hours, the judge, before a packed courtroom, read the verdict: guilty of first-degree murder. The 38-year-old defendant, after the judge announced the verdict, showed no emotion. Facing a mandatory life sentence without the chance of parole, Jason Young was escorted out of the room in handcuffs.

Following the trial, several of the jurors spoke to reporters. Two members of the jury said that the lack of physical evidence in the case pointed more to the defendant's guilt than his innocence. For example, what happened to the shirt and shoes he was seen wearing on the hotel surveillance footage? A third juror found it incriminating that Cassidy had not been murdered, and possibly cleaned-up after the attack.

The prosecutor in the Jason Young murder trial, the second time around, turned a weakness--a lack of physical evidence—into something positive. In the era of the "CSI" television shows, advanced DNA technology, and high forensic expectations on the part of juries, this was an unusual case.

Murdering a Great Grandmother

In the summer of 2012, Antonio D. Barbeau, a 13-year-old escapee from a juvenile detention center, was living in Sheboygan Falls, Wisconsin with the family of his 13-year-old friend, Nathan P. Paape. On September 17, 2012, Paape's mother drove the eighth graders to the Sheboygan Falls home of Barbeau's great-grandmother. Paape's mother didn't realize that Barbeau carried a concealed hatchet, and that her son possessed a hammer. She didn't know that the boys intended to murder and rob the 78-year-old woman, Barbara Olson.

The boys entered Olson's house through an unlocked door to her attached garage. The target of the murder/robbery, when she realized why the boys had come to her home, threatened to call Barbeau's mother. At that point Barbeau knocked his great-grandmother off her feet by hitting her in the back of the head with the blunt end of his hatchet. As she lay on the floor trying to protect her head with her hands, Barbeau hit her again, and again. Nathan Paape joined in with his hammer. To finish off the dying woman, Barbeau struck her twice in the back of the head with the blade part of the bloodied hatchet.

The young murderers rummaged through the dead woman's house looking for cash and valuables. They gathered up the victim's purse, some loose change, and a few pieces of her jewelry. Barbeau slipped the blood-soaked watch off his great-grandmother's wrist.

The boys had planned to load the old woman's body into her car and drive it to a spot where they'd abandoned the vehicle and the corpse. When they couldn't stuff the body into the car, they left it in the garage beneath a blanket.

The cold-blooded killers tossed the bloody murder instruments into the trunk, and drove off in the victim's car. They parked the Olson vehicle in a lot to a Sheboygan Falls bowling alley. Leaving the keys in the ignition with the stolen jewelry placed on the front seat in plain view, they walked away, hoping that someone would steal the car and eventually take the fall for murdering the woman lying dead in her garage.

A few blocks from the abandoned vehicle, Barbeau and Paape sat down for a meal at a pizza parlor. After eating their pizzas, the boys walked to Paape's house. Along the way, they tossed Barbara Olson's handbag into a storm drain. At Paape's home, they changed into fresh clothes and hid their bloody garments and the gold watch Barbeau had taken off the corpse.

Later on the day of this senseless murder, Mrs. Olson's daughter discovered her body. Police officers quickly figured out who had murdered the victim. Investigators recovered her purse from the street drain, the murder weapons from the stolen car, and the killers' bloody clothing and the victim's gold watch from Nathan Paape's house.

In a matter of days, Antonio Barbeau confessed, and in so doing, implicated his friend. On September 21, 2012, four days after the murder, a Sheboygan County prosecutor changed each suspect with first-degree intentional homicide. The magistrate set each of the defendants' bail at $1 million.

Nathan Paape went on trial for first-degree intentional homicide in June 2013. Under Wisconsin law, Paape, because of his age, couldn't be sentenced to life without the possibility of parole. But if convicted as charged, the judge could sentence him to a maximum of forty years in prison before he was eligible for release.

One of the first prosecution witnesses, Dr. Doug Kelley with the Fond du Lac County Medical Examiner's Office, testified that Barbara Olson had been struck in the head with the blunt instrument at least twenty-five times. The star prosecution witness, Antonia Barbeau, testified that he and the defendant had hatched the murder/robbery scheme together. Barbeau told the jurors that he and Paape took turns hitting the woman in her own home.

Defense attorneys put their client on the stand to testify on his own behalf. According to the defendant, the crime had been Barbeau's idea. After they entered the victim's house, Paape said he hit the old woman twice with his hammer. He only did it because he was afraid that if he didn't, Barbeau would attack him. The defendant claimed that when his mother drove them to Olson's dwelling, he didn't think that Barbeau would actually carryout the plan to kill the woman.

Following the one-week trial, the jury, after a quick deliberation, found Nathan Paape guilty as charged. A few days after the verdict, Antonio Barbeau withdrew his not guilty by mental disease plea. He agreed to plead no contest to first-degree intentional homicide.

On August 12, 2013, Barbeau appeared before Circuit Court Judge Timothy Van Akkeren who presided at his sentence hearing. His attorney presented a psychiatrist who testified that Barbeau had "cognitive issues" stemming from being hit by a car when he was 10-years-old. Judge Van Akkeren, obviously unimpressed with the psychiatrist's testimony, sentenced Barbeau to life. The 14-year-old would not be eligible for parole until November 24, 2048 when he turned fifty.

The next day Judge Van Akkeren, before sentencing Nathan Paape, said, "Mr. Paape is a follower in this case. I do find there is less culpability." The judge sentenced Paape to life in prison with eligibility for parole on December 2, 2043, Paape's 45th birthday.

Recreational Murder: Three Cases

No society has been free of criminal homicide. People have always murdered for sex, money, and revenge. While deviant and unlawful, this form of homicidal behavior is at least *human*. However, murdering a total stranger for the thrill and power of taking a life reflects a form of moral depravity that borders on *inhuman*. In the United States recently, in three separate cases, black teenage boys murdered three white people they didn't know. These boys had no reason whatsoever to kill the victims. If such senseless, random black on white killings mark the beginning of a criminal trend, America is in trouble. No one will be safe and race relations will deteriorate.

On Friday, August 16, 2013, Christopher Lane, an Australian who attended Oklahoma's East Central University, was in the town of Duncan visiting his girlfriend. That afternoon, while jogging along Country Club Road, Lane caught the attention of three black teenagers as he ran passed the place where they were hanging out. One of the boys said, "There's our target."

The trio piled into a black vehicle with 17-year-old Michael Dewayne Jones behind the wheel. James Francis Edwards, Jr., 15, climbed into the front passenger seat. Chancy Luna, a 16-year-old, sat in the back of the car armed with a .22-caliber handgun. As the vehicle pulled up behind the college baseball player, Luna shot him in the back. As the car sped off, Lane staggered then collapsed on the side of the road.

Witnesses who heard the gunshot saw a black vehicle drive away as Lane staggered and collapsed. Several people ran to Lane's aid. As a woman called 911, another bystander performed CPR on the fallen student. Christopher Lane died on the side of the road.

A few hours after the shooting, detectives, while reviewing surveillance camera footage, noticed a black vehicle pull in behind a hotel shortly after the murder. Eleven minutes later the car drove off. Three hours after the murder, a police officer spotted the car in front of a house on Country Club Road. This led to the arrests of Jones, Edwards, and Luna.

According to reports, Edward and Luna, when questioned by detectives, denied any knowledge of the murder. Michael Jones, the 17-year-old driver, confessed. "We were bored," he said, "and didn't have anything to do so we decided to kill somebody."

Prosecutor Jason Hicks charged Edwards and Luna with first-degree murder. Michael Jones has been charged as an accessory to the murder. On August 20, 2013, a judge denied Edwards and Luna bail. Jones is being held on $1 million bond. At the arraignment, prosecutor Hicks said, "I'm appalled. This is not supposed to happen in this community."

Earlier in the year, James Edwards tweeted that "90 % of white people are nasty. #HATE THEM." A few days after the George Zimmerman acquittal, the 15-year-old tweeted, "Ayeee I knocced out 5 woods" (a derogatory word for white people).

On Thursday morning, March 21, 2013, in the small southeastern Georgia coastal town of Brunswick, Sherry West pushed her 13-month-old son in a stroller not far from her house in the Old Town historic district. Two young black males approached the 41-year-old mother and her child at quarter after nine that morning. The older kid, described by Sherry West as between 13 and 15-years-old, pulled a handgun and demanded money. The robber's companion, as described by the victim, looked to be between 10 and 12-years old. The older boy, who was wearing a red shirt, when told by the mother that she didn't have any money, said, "Well, I'm going to kill your baby."

The terrified mother tried to use her body to protect her son. "Please don't kill my baby," she pleaded.

The young robber, after pushing the mother aside, shot the sleeping child in the face. Before fleeing on foot, the gunman shot Sherry West in the leg. A second bullet grazed her head. As the boys ran off, the wounded mother called 911, and tried in vain to save her baby by administering CPR.

The next day, police arrested 17-year-old DeMarquis Elkins on charges of aggravated assault, robbery, and murder. The prosecutor charged his 15-year-old friend, Dominique Lang, with felony-murder.

Following a change of venue, DeMarquis Elkins was tried for murder in Cobb County north of Atlanta. Dominique Lang was the state's star witness. In September 2013 the jury found Elkins guilty of first-degree murder. The judge sentenced him to life in prison without parole.

On Wednesday evening, August 21, 2013, 88-year-old World War II veteran Delbert Belton was waiting for a friend in the parking lot outside of the Eagles Lodge in Spokane, Washington. Two black teenagers approached the elderly man and began hitting him in the head with heavy flashlights. The young men, both dressed entirely in black, fled the scene with the old man dying on the lot. Mr. Belton, who had been shot on the beaches of Okinawa in 1945, died later that night. His friends had called him "Shorty."

The next day police officers arrested a juvenile who turned himself in. On August 26, the police arrested 16-year-old Kenan D. Adams-Kinard. As of August 2014, this case had not come to trial.

Murder by Stranger

Before I coined the term *serial killer* in the mid-1970s, such murders were referred to as *stranger murders* to differentiate them from murders in which the victim is killed by those he or she knew, usually family members.

One reason that Jack the Ripper frightened those who heard or read about him when he was active [in 1888 London] was the notion that he killed strangers--leading to the idea that ordinary people out for a walk at night would now have to be afraid of any stranger who crossed their path. At that time, such murders were entirely uncommon in Great Britain and everywhere else. The great individual killers (as opposed to military ones) in history had been of the Bluebeard sort, those who killed their wives, one by one, or massacred their families. For most people the emotional components of intra-familial violence seemed understandable; most people, at some time or another, had considered raising an angry hand toward a spouse or a child, and could comprehend how, in a fit of rage, such an emotion could escalate into murder. But the emotional components of stranger murder seemed incomprehensible.

Robert K. Ressler, *I Have Lived in the Monster,* 1997

Stranger Than Fiction

It might be thought that murder presented as fictional entertainment on cinema and television screens is frequently implausible. Yet in its bizarre, extraordinary and frequently farcical consequences the real thing is often better. Truth really is stranger than fiction. The details of murder frequently fall into that category where the conclusion is, "You couldn't make that up."...

Murder seems to attract weird behavior beyond the basic elements of one person killing another. Tremaryne Durham, for instance, a murder suspect in custody in the United States, became fed up with the monotonous institutional food he was served in prison and arranged a plea bargain deal whereby he would admit guilt in return for a chicken dinner.

Robin Odell, *The Mammoth Book of Bizarre Crimes*, 2010

The Man Who Cooked His Wife

In 2002, Frederick Joseph Hengl and his wife Anna Faris moved into a two-bedroom bungalow on North Ditmar Street a block from City Hall in Oceanside, California. Ten years later, residents of the neighborhood considered the 68-year-old Hengl, and his 73-year-old spouse, more than a little odd. Bearded, bespectacled, and bone-thin, Hengl regularly appeared in public dressed in women's clothing and wearing make-up. Ann Faris often walked the streets armed with a butcher's knife. Neighbors wondered why she always wore the same outfit, a blue sweater and denim-like pants. The fact people could smell her suggested she didn't bother much with personal hygiene. Occasionally Faris would stand in her front yard and take off her clothes.

On November 11, 2012, the odd couple's neighbors began detecting a foul odor coming from the Hengl house. They also heard sounds of a power saw coming from inside the dwelling. The stench grew unbearable after Hengl, to draw the odor out of the house, installed a window fan. A neighbor called the police.

On November 16 at eleven o'clock in the morning, Oceanside police officers pulled up to the Hengl bungalow. An officer knocked on the front door but no one answered. Assuming that the place was at the moment unoccupied, officers climbed into the dwelling through a window at the rear of the house. As the police officer entered the foul-smelling bungalow, Frederick Hengl slipped out the front door and walked away.

Inside, amid the stench of rotting flesh, the police discovered three pans of meat cooking on the kitchen stove. In the freezer compartment of the refrigerator, they came upon a plastic bag containing a human head. (Later identified as Anna Faris.) A meat grinder that had been recently used sat nearby. In the bathroom, the police found a power saw, a boning knife, and other cutting instruments. It didn't take Sherlock Holmes to figure out what had taken place under this roof. Scattered throughout the first floor, officers found pieces of freshly cut bone.

Shortly after the gruesome discovery in the bungalow on North Ditmar Street, police officers found and arrested Frederick Hengl. From his house he had walked to a local bar. Perhaps he was enjoying what he knew would be his last alcoholic beverage.

According to a forensic pathologist with the San Diego County Medical Examiner's Office, Anna Faris had died on or about November 1. Crime scene investigators reported that they found "no evidence of cannibalism." (Then why was Hengl cooking the meat?)

A San Diego County prosecutor charged Frederick Hengl with murder, willful cruelty to an elder, and committing an unlawful act with human remains. If convicted of murder, he could be sentenced to 25 years to life. On November 21, the day before Thanksgiving, Hengl pleaded not guilty to all charges before a superior court judge who set his bail at $5 million. Hengl's attorney advised the court that his client had a bad heart, and required medical treatment.

On September 27, 2013, while in the San Diego County Jail's infirmary, Frederick Hengl died of prostate cancer. From the day of his arrest, Hengl denied killing his wife who reportedly suffered from Alzheimer's disease.

To make a case of criminal homicide against Mr. Hengl, the state would have had to prove she did not die a natural death. Under the circumstances, this would have been difficult. With Hengl's passing, no one will ever know the exact circumstances of Anna Faris' death, or why her husband had butchered and cooked her body. While they were a strange couple, they were not necessarily a killer and a murder victim.

The Murderer Who Was Murdered

William Keitel and his wife Michele were married in 1989. The couple resided a few miles north of Pittsburgh in Ohio Township, Pennsylvania. In October 1996, following a tumultuous marriage and two children--William, 5 and Abbee, 3--William and Michele separated. Shortly after the split, Michele, 35, became engaged to Charles Dunkle, a 34-year-old from nearby Moon Township.

In the evening of New Year's Day 1998, 45-year-old William Keitel sat in his Mercedes in the parking lot of the Stop 'N Go convenience store on Mount Nebo Road. He and his father, William Keitel senior, were waiting for Michele to arrive with the children pursuant to an a prearranged exchange. As on numerous occasions in the past, Michele had either forgotten about the exchange or was late.

At nine-thirty that night, after William called the police, Michele, accompanied by the children, her father, and her fiancée, pulled into the convenience store lot.

As William pulled out of the Stop 'N Go parking lot with his children in the car, Michele saw that he was armed with a handgun. (William had been issued a permit to carry the .38-caliber revolver.) Screaming that he had a gun, Michele ran after the Mercedes as it eased back onto Mount Nebo Road.

William, realizing that his estranged wife was chasing his car, pulled into a neighboring beer distributorship parking area and climbed out of his vehicle with the gun in his hand. As Michele, her father--Mr. Charles Walker--and Charles Dunkle rushed him, William shot Dunkle in the chest at close range. With Michele on her knees next to Dunkle's body, William placed the barrel of the .38 to her forehead and pulled the trigger. When Mr. Walker tried to disarm William, the father-in-law was shot in the stomach.

Michele Keitel and Charles Dunkle died on the beer distributorship's parking lot. Charles Walker survived his bullet wound. The Keitel children witnessed the mayhem a few feet away from their father's car.

Charged with first-degree murder of Michele Keitel, third-degree murder of Charles Dunkle, and the aggravated assault of Charles Walker, William Keitel went on trial in Pittsburgh in October 1998. His attorney, William Diffenderfer, presented a case of self-defense that included putting his client on the stand to testify on his own behalf. Allegheny County prosecutor Edward Borowski, in the murder of Michele Keitel, sought the death penalty.

The jury, following the one-month trial, found William Keitel guilty as charged. The jurors, however, rejected the death sentence by an eight to four vote. In January 1999, Common Pleas Judge Jeffery A. Manning sentenced Keitel to life in prison without parole. Three months later, prison administrators assigned him to the State Correctional Institution at Houtzdale located in Clearfield County, Pennsylvania.

In 2010, William Keitel's 18-year-son, a high school senior, died when his car collided with a telephone pole.

At one in the afternoon of August 2, 2013, after returning to his cell following a work assignment, William Keitel's 43-year-old cellmate beat him severely. The 59-year-old convicted murderer was rushed by helicopter to a hospital in Altoona, Pennsylvania where, nine days later, he died from the beating.

The federal appeal of William Keitel's conviction and sentence, pending before the 3rd Circuit Court of Appeals in Philadelphia, died with him.

Perjured Testimony

During the early morning hours of November 1, 2001, a person or persons attacked sports editor Kent Heitholt as he approached his car in the parking lot next to the *Columbia Daily Tribune* office in Columbia, Missouri. Around the time of the assault two young white men were seen in the vicinity. The attackers had beaten Mr. Heitholt with their fists then strangled him with his own belt. His watch had been stolen but his wallet was still in his car.

In the months following the Heitholt murder, detectives with the Columbia Police Department ran down thousands of leads but came up empty handed. As time passed and the case remained unsolved, local criminal justice leaders felt building pressure to solve this brutal murder of a prominent citizen.

In an act of investigative desperation the authorities, in November 2003, published a composite police sketch of the two men seen near the newspaper office that night. (Police sketches are not only useless to crime investigators. They drawings make things worse by generating false leads and false hopes of a case solution.)

In March 2004 an anonymous caller to the crime stopper's hotline in Columbia reported that a 19-year-old local man named Chuck Erickson had been telling people that he might have been involved in the Heitholt murder.

Chuck Erickson, in March 2004, had just come off a probated sentence related to a drug conviction. When Mr. Heitholt was beaten and strangled to death, the drug addict would have been seventeen. Detectives assigned to the case were thrilled to have such a promising lead.

At police headquarters, detectives put Erickson through an intense and prolonged interrogation that was only partially recorded. Erickson told his questioners that because one of the men depicted in the police sketches looked like him, he started wondering if maybe in a drug and alcohol blackout he had been involved in Mr. Heitholt's violent death. Perhaps he and his friend since childhood, Ryan Ferguson, had committed the murder. They had been drinking that night in a bar not far from the crime scene. Maybe they had robbed the newspaperman in order to keep drinking.

Had the detectives grilling Erickson not been so desperate to solve the Heitholt case, they might have recognized several indications that Erickson and his friend were not good murder suspects. The robbery motive didn't hold water because Mr. Heitholt had been murdered one hour after the bars had closed that night. Moreover, Erickson had to be told that the victim had been strangled with his own belt, and shown exactly where in the parking lot Heitholt had been attacked.

When detectives brought Ryan Ferguson in for questioning, he insisted that he had nothing to do with Mr. Heitholt's murder. He maintained that position throughout the interrogation. Not only did Ferguson strongly deny any involvement in the homicide, investigators didn't have a single piece of physical evidence linking him to the crime scene.

Notwithstanding having nothing but the word of a former drug addict who had no memory of what he had done that night, detectives continued to press their case against both suspects.

In the months that followed, Chuck Erickson, in return for the promise of a relatively light sentence, agreed to testify against his friend. This meant that Erickson's memory, colored by heavy coaching, would have to significantly improve. And it did.

In October 2005, in Columbia, Missouri, Ryan Ferguson went on trial for the Heitholt murder. Prosecutor Kevin Crane put Chuck Erickson on the stand. The witness testified that he and the defendant had attacked the victim that night in the newspaper office parking lot. Prosecutor Crane also produced a witness, a janitor named Jerry Trump, who said he had seen Erickson and the defendant that night not far from the murder scene. For some reason Mr. Trump had waited several years before coming forward with his information.

Two men--a drug addict with a remarkably improved memory, and a witness who came forward at the last minute--comprised the sum total of the prosecution's case. In the name of justice, the trial judge should have directed a not guilty verdict based on the fact the government had not carried its burden of proof. But instead, the case went to the jury and the jurors found Ryan Ferguson guilty as charged. The judge sentenced him to forty years in prison.

In 2010, Missouri's Western District appellate court heard arguments regarding the Ferguson conviction. While the justices questioned the star prosecution witness' credibility, they declined to rule on the case. Instead, the appeals court judges recommended that the case be reviewed before a different lower court judge.

The lower court hearing on the Ferguson conviction took place in April 2012. At this proceeding Chuck Erickson admitted under oath that he had lied at Ferguson's murder trial to save his own skin. Jerry Trump, the prosecution's miracle witness, took the stand and confessed that he had committed perjury as well.

The lower court review judge, after hearing from Erickson and Trump, ruled that Erickson's testimony at Ferguson's 2005 murder trial was indeed credible. In other words, he was telling the truth then but lying now. Although the janitor's testimony was not reliable, the judge said it was an inconsequential factor in Ferguson's conviction.

On January 13, 2013, the Ferguson legal team appealed the review judge's ruling. In September justices with the Western District Appeals Court considered the revised testimony of Chick Erickston and Jerry

Trump. On November 5, 2013, the Missouri appeals court vacated Ryan Ferguson's murder conviction. After spending almost ten years behind bars, Mr. Ferguson was a free man.

A Deadly Love Triangle

In 2010, Anthony Taglianetti and his wife Mary resided with their four children in Woodbridge, Virginia. Anthony, a former Marine, practiced law. Later that year they separated. Mary and the children moved out of the house in Virginia and relocated in Saratoga Springs, New York.

Shortly after taking up residence in Saratoga Springs, Mary signed up with the online dating site Match.com where she met Keith Reed Jr. She did not tell the 51-year-old superintendent of the Clymer, New York school district that she was married. After Mr. Reed and the 40-year-old woman exchanged a few emails, they met for dinner. After that they became romantically involved. Keith Reed still did not know that he was dating a married woman.

Keith Reed, the father of three college age daughters, lived alone in the farming community of 1,500 70 miles southwest of Buffalo, New York. The school superintendent had been divorced for several years.

In 2011, Mary Taglianetti, after reconciling with her husband, moved back to Woodbridge, Virginia. But in 2012, while still living with him and their children, she began exchanging sexually explicit emails and telephone calls with Keith Reed who still wasn't aware that she was married. The online relationship came to an end when Anthony Taglianetti discovered one of the lurid email messages Mary had forgotten to erase from her computer.

A furious Anthony Taglianetti sent several angry emails to Keith Reed who insisted he had no idea the woman he had been swapping erotic emails with was married. Mr. Reed made it clear he wanted nothing more to do with Mr. Taglianetti or his dishonest wife.

On September 23, 2012, Edward Bailey, the principal of Clymer Central High School, reported Keith Reed missing after the superintendent didn't show up for a conference in Saratoga Springs. Mr. Bailey went to Reed's house where he found his dog locked in the garage. Mr. Reed was not in the dwelling.

Deputies with the Chautauqua County Sheriff's Office questioned the missing man's neighbors who reported hearing gunshots coming from the vicinity of Reed's house around 9:30 PM two days before. On September 24, 2014, a deputy sheriff found Mr. Reed's body amid a row of thick shrubs about 150 feet from his house. He had been shot three times.

Detectives working the case caught their first break when Mary Taglianetti, on September 26, 2012, told them she suspected that her angry and jealous husband murdered Keith Reed.

Investigators learned that on September 21, 2012, Anthony Taglianetti drove 350 miles to Clymer, New York where they believed he shot and killed Keith Reed. According to these detectives, Taglianetti, after murdering the victim, drove straight back to Woodbridge, Virginia. The next day he took one of his children to a local museum.

A Chautauqua County prosecutor charged Anthony Taglianetti with second-degree murder. On September 31, 2012, U.S. Marshals and local police officers pulled the murder suspect over as he drove along a rural road in the Shenandoah Valley National Forest in Virginia. Inside Taglianetti's vehicle officers found a .367-Magnum revolver wrapped in one of his wife's offending emails.

Through DNA analysis, a forensic scientist identified Keith Reed's blood on the suspect's handgun. Ballistics tests revealed that this .357-Magnum had fired the death scene bullets.

The Taglianetti murder trial got underway on October 31, 2013 in Chautauqua County, New York. District Attorney David W. Foley, in his opening statement to the jury, emphasized the physical evidence pointing to the defendant's guilt.

Public defender Nathaniel L. Barone, in his opening remarks, said, "This is not a story of an affair gone wrong or a crazed husband seeking justice. It's not as simple as Mr. Taglianetti driving up and killing Keith Reed because of an email. That's not what happened--the defendant is innocent. Mr. Taglianetti did not murder Keith Reed Jr."

The defense attorney, after declaring his client innocent, attacked Mary Taglianetti, one of the prosecution's star witnesses. He characterized her as a "master manipulator" and urged jurors to weigh her testimony carefully. "Mary Taglianetti is a liar," he said.

On November 9, 2013, following the testimony of 46 witnesses over a nine-day period, the jury of five women and seven men, after three hours of deliberation, found the 45-year-old defendant guilty as charged. On February 24, 2014, the Chautauqua County judge sentenced Anthony Taglianetti to 25 years to life in prison.

Homicide by Gun

The high-profile tragedies that glue us to the TV screen are a very small part of the overall homicide problem, and they're not representative of it. If you take Sandy Hook and the Oak Creek Sikh temple shooting and Aurora and Virginia Tech and Columbine, 95 people were killed in those shootings.

And each of those deaths is horrific. But we lose on average 88 per day to firearm violence.

Bill Dedman, NBC News, December 12, 2013

No-Body Murder Cases

Many missing persons cases involving young woman turn into homicide investigations when the victims are found dead. However, there are thousands of cases in which the missing women are not found but presumed dead. Many women that disappeared without a trace were murdered by killers who did a good job of disposing of the their bodies. It's no secret that if the police don't have a corpse they probably won't be able to arrest anyone for murder. Notwithstanding disappearances that are highly suspicious it generally comes down to this unpleasant reality: if there's no body there's no homicide case.

There are, however, exceptions to this rule. Prosecutors have pressed charges in homicide cases that do not feature a body. In these so-called no-body cases, prosecutors work without an autopsy report, have no time of death based upon postmortem biological changes, or physical evidence establishing the victims' exact causes of death. Moreover, there are no death scene photographs in no-body cases.

Based on his research of no-body cases, Thomas A. Di Biase believes that in the United States, from 1843 to 2013, 380 homicide cases have gone to trial without the victims' remains. According to Di Biase, a former federal prosecutor, the conviction rate pertaining to these prosecutions is 89 percent.

In a homicide case, the *corpus delecti* of the crime--the body or main element of the offense-- consists of proof that an unlawful death has occurred. The best evidence of an unlawful death is the corpse itself.

So, without a body, can a prosecutor, by law, acquire a homicide conviction? That legal question was settled in a 1960 California appellate case titled, *U.S. v. Scott.* The state appeals court justices decided that a homicide defendant in a case without a body can lawfully be found guilty if the prosecution presents circumstantial evidence of an unlawful death that excludes other reasonable hypotheses regarding the missing person's fate. The prosecutor must also present sufficient evidence that the defendant was the person who unlawfully killed the missing person.

Because juries understandably are uncomfortable with no-body homicide cases, prosecutors need strong circumstantial evidence that the missing person is dead and that the defendant is responsible for that death. In establishing the necessary proof, it helps if detectives have located a probable killing site. Such a place might be a bed soaked in a large quantity of blood. The crime scene might also feature other types of physical evidence that suggests the occurrence of lethal violence. This evidence of course must be linked to the missing person, ideally through DNA analysis.

It would also be ideal if the prosecutor can place the defendant at the scene of the violence through fingerprints, hair follicles, semen, blood, shoe impressions, handwriting, or fiber evidence.

The no-body case prosecutor will be helped if the defendant possessed a strong motive to kill the victim such as jealousy, lust, money, or revenge. If the defendant offers an alibi, the prosecution must be able to break that alibi. The presence of physical evidence linking the defendant to the crime scene would have that effect.

Other circumstantial evidence against a homicide defendant in a no-body case might include conflicting statements by the defendant to the police, or a history of violence between the defendant and the missing person. Secretly recorded death threats by the defendant against the victim would also be relevant.

If the no-body prosecutor doesn't have physical evidence from a probable crime scene to work with, a conviction won't be possible unless the defendant confessed to the police, a friend, or to a jailhouse snitch. The confession of an accomplice that implicates the defendant is good.

Attorneys representing defendants in no-body cases usually portray the murder evidence as circumstantial, and therefore weak. Defense lawyers often remind jurors that they cannot convict the defendant if they have any reasonable doubt regarding his or her guilt.

While the conviction rate of no-body cases brought to trial is high, only a small percentage of no-body suspects are charged with criminal homicide. Without a body, there was simply too much reasonable doubt to overcome.

The Sex Killer

In 2011, after graduating from high school in Westborough, Massachusetts, Elizabeth Marriott attended Manchester Community College in New Hampshire. Following her freshman year in Manchester she transferred to the University of New Hampshire in Durham. The 19-year-old marine biology major commuted to the university's main campus from her aunt and uncle's home in Chester. To help pay for her schooling she worked at the Target store in the neighboring community of Greenland.

Elizabeth, who went by "Lizzi," walked out of class at nine at night on October 9, 2012 with the intent of visiting friends at an apartment in Dover a town of 30,000 in the southeast corner of the state not far from the university. Her friends notified the authorities when Lizzi didn't show up in Dover and couldn't be located elsewhere.

Three days after Marriott's disappearance, detectives questioned 29-year-old Seth Mazzaglia who was a resident of Dover. The 2006 graduate of the University of New Hampshire had earned a bachelor's degree in theater. Over the past ten years, Mazzaglia, more of a character actor than a leading man type, had performed in plays and musicals around southeast New Hampshire. According to his Facebook page he had a black belt in karate, instructed others in the martial arts, and liked to juggle. Mazzaglia also professed to have a special interest in stagecraft fighting.

Mazzaglia told detectives that he met Lizzi Marriott in the summer of 2011 when they worked at the Greenland, New Hampshire Target store. He said he now worked in the video game section of the Best Buy store in Newington, New Hampshire.

Mazzaglia informed his questioners that he and his 19-year-old girlfriend, Kathryn McDonough, a high school dropout, had invited Marriott to join them in his apartment on October 9 for three-way, bondage sex. Mazzaglia said that Marriott did not show up that evening.

When questioned again later in the day Mazzaglia changed his story. He said he had gone out for a run and upon his return to the apartment found Marriott dead with a ligature mark around her neck. He explained that earlier that evening McDonough and another man had engaged in bondage sex with Marriott. Later in the interrogation session Mazzaglia reluctantly admitted that he was the man in the threesome that night.

Mazzaglia said that he, McDonough, and Marriott played strip poker. That led to sexual intercourse involving a rope-restraint used to limit Marriott's ability to breathe. During that voluntary activity, Marriott suffered a seizure and died. The death, according to Mazzaglia, was an accidental event in the course of consensual but rough sex.

Instead of reporting the death to the authorities Mazzaglia tied a grocery bag over the dead woman's head. At eleven o'clock that night, McDonough's friend, Roberta Gerkin and her housemate, came to the apartment at McDonough's request. Gerkin, according to a statement she gave the police, said she saw a white female lying on the floor with a grocery bag covering her head.

Gerkin told detectives that she used a box cutter to removed the sack. When she did so it exposed the victim's bluish tinted face. Meanwhile, according to Gerkin, Mazzaglia and his girlfriend engaged in a discussion of how they would dispose of the body.

During his session with detectives Mazzaglia said he used Marriott's Mazda to haul her body to Pierce Island in Portsmouth, New Hampshire where he and McDonough dumped the corpse into the Piscataqua River. When Marriott's torso remained above the water she pushed it under. The pair then drove Marriott's car to the University of New Hampshire where they left it in a student parking lot. The couple discarded Marriott's clothing in trash bins on campus.

Police officers and volunteers searched for Marriott's body in the Piscataqua River around the 27-acre island. They found no trace of her remains. Notwithstanding the absence of a body, a Strafford County prosecutor charged Mazzaglia with first-degree murder. Police officers arrested him on October 13, 2012. The judge denied the murder suspect bail.

On December 24, 2012 detectives arrested Kathryn McDonough on the charges of conspiracy and hindering prosecution. She posted her $35,000 bond and walked out of jail on the condition she stayed with her parents in Portsmouth, New Hampshire. In 2013 McDonough pleaded guilty to the charges. The judge, aware that she had agreed to help the prosecution against Mazzaglia, sentenced her to 18 months to three years in prison. Given her role in Lizzi Marriott's death, this depraved young woman had gotten off light. Because the prosecutor in the no-body case needed McDonough's testimony to establish the murder, and the defendant's role in it, McDonough escaped a stiffer sentence.

The Seth Mazzaglia no-body murder case got underway in Dover, New Hampshire on Monday, June 2, 2014. Two days later, Kathryn McDonough, the prosecution's star witness, took the stand under government immunity from the charge of first-degree murder. The witness said that on October 9, 2012 she lured Marriott to Mazzaglia's apartment with the promise of watching a movie or playing a video game. In reality she wanted to please Mazzaglia with a new sex partner.

Following a game of strip poker, Mazzaglia said he wanted Marriott and McDonough to kiss. Marriott refused. Mazzaglia next suggested that Marriott watch as he and McDonough had sex. Marriott said she wasn't interested. Unaccustomed to not getting his way, Mazzaglia strangled Marriott with a soft cotton rope used in bondage sex. After witnessing the murder McDonough went into the bathroom. When she returned, she saw her boyfriend having sex with the corpse.

McDonough testified that she and Mazzaglia stuffed the victim's body into a large suitcase and drove to the Piscataqua River where they knew the currents were strong. The couple tossed the body over a railing but the five-foot-five, 130-pound body landed on the rocks short of the water line. McDonough climbed down and dragged the corpse into the river.

On cross-examination, Mazzaglia's attorney, Joachim Barth, proposed that McDonough had killed Lizzi Marriott when the victim refused to have sex with the defendant. Barth reminded the witness that when she first spoke with the police she had taken responsibility for Marriott's death. The defense attorney suggested that the witness had changed her story in return for government immunity and a light sentence.

Defense attorney Barth also grilled the witness about her claim to have alternative personalities--different characters she used as a "coping mechanism." McDonough said she was not controlled by the voices she heard in her head. During the cross-examination McDonough revealed that Mazzaglia believed that he had been a dragon in a past life. Being around him she said strengthened her own beliefs in the supernatural.

On June 27, 2014, following 19 days of testimony that did not include the defendant taking the stand on his own behalf, the jury found Mazzaglia guilty of first-degree murder by strangulation. The jury also found him guilty of first-degree murder while committing a felonious assault. The panel of seven women and five men also found the defendant guilty of conspiracy to tamper with evidence as well as the destruction of physical evidence.

Pursuant to New Hampshire law Mazzaglia will spend the rest of his life in prison. Lizzi Marriott's remains have not been recovered.

A Child Killer

By November 2011, Imani Benton, a 26-year-old resident of Lakehurst, New Jersey, terminated her relationship with Arthur Morgan III, the father of their two-year-old daughter, Tierra. The couple had fought constantly, and on several occasions, had taken each other to court. He continued to deny the breakup even after she returned the engagement ring and the other jewelry he had given her. The two of them had also traded accusations of child abuse. As a result of Benton's domestic complaints, state child protection agents had conducted four separate investigations that ended up clearing Morgan of these accusations. As a result, he continued to have access to his daughter.

On November 15, Morgan's boss at Creative Building Supplies Company in Lakewood, New Jersey, fired him.

On November 21, 2011, just eight hours after he had called Imani Benton a bad mother and a whore, Morgan made arrangements with her to take Tierra to see a movie about dancing penguins. Four hours after the father said he would return the toddler to her mother, she called the police to report Tierra missing.

Police officers from thirteen New Jersey law enforcement agencies looked for the missing girl. Her father had also disappeared. The search came to an end when Tierra's body was found in Shark River Park twenty miles north of her Lakehurst home.

Homicide investigators believed that Arthur Morgan had dropped the girl's car seat, with her strapped in it, fifteen feet into a creek below an overpass. A car jack weighted down the car seat. The drowned girl, still wearing her Pink Hello Kitty hat, had landed in three feet of water. (According to the father who did not deny throwing his daughter off the bridge, he heard her scream from the creek as he got back into his car.)

After leaving his daughter to drown in the creek beneath the overpass, Arthur Morgan drove to a friend's house where he had a few drinks. The next day, he boarded a train for San Diego, California.

At four in the afternoon of November 29, 2011, agents with the U.S. Marshals Service arrested Morgan at a house in San Diego. (He was arrested on a federal unlawful flight to avoid prosecution warrant. These UFAP warrants are dismissed after the fugitive is returned to the local jurisdiction.)

Back in New Jersey a few days after his apprehension, Morgan faced the charge of first-degree murder. Over the objection of his court-appointed lawyer, the arraignment judge set Morgan's bond at $10 million. Peter J. Warshaw Jr., the Monmouth County prosecutor in charge of the case, said he would seek the maximum penalty of life without parole. (New Jersey has abolished the death penalty.)

The Arthur Morgan child murder trial got underway in a Freehold, New Jersey superior court on March 12, 2014. In his opening remarks to the jury, prosecutor Warshaw accused the defendant of killing his daughter simply because he was angry that Benton had ended their relationship. According to the prosecutor, Morgan killed Tierra to get back at his former girlfriend. Mr. Warshaw called the killing a "knowing and purposeful murder" motivated by pride and revenge.

The public defender told the jurors that her client was merely guilty of reckless manslaughter, a lesser degree of criminal homicide that carries a maximum sentence of five years in prison. Given the undisputed facts of this case, that would be a hard sell.

The murdered girl's mother, Imani Benton, took the stand as the prosecution's star witness. To the jury, Benton read a letter the defendant had sent her from the San Diego jail shortly after his arrest. In that letter, Morgan, in justifying the murder, accused members of Benton's family of abusing Tierra. He referred to their behavior as "heinous and depraved." Morgan also blamed the girl's mother for her death: "You should have come with us to the movie. It would have been so different, I'm sure. That was the plan, to go as a family."

Regarding the defendant's self-serving letter, Imani Benton testified that, "If I would have gone to the movie, we wouldn't have gone to the movie. We all would be dead."

One of the defendant's co-workers at the Lakewood lumber yard testified that Morgan had been paid every Tuesday, and by Friday, he was broke. According to Tulio Bazan, the defendant spent a lot of money on clothes. "He showed me the Gucci sunglasses, a Gucci wallet, and the Gucci shoes." Morgan told the witness that the wallet itself cost him $400.

In mid-April 2014, the jury in Freehold, New Jersey, following a short period of deliberation, found Arthur Morgan guilty as charged.

Six weeks after the guilty verdict, at his May 28 sentence hearing, the convicted murderer apologized to Imani Benton for the breakdown of their relationship. (He didn't apologize for killing their daughter.) "I want to say I'm sorry for the deterioration of what I thought was a beautiful friendship between the two of us that blossomed into a daughter. For anybody that was truly affected by this, I hope we can all heal from the situation, knowing that Tierra is in a better place." (In other words, he is the victim in this story.)

As one might expect from a narcissistic sociopath with a god-complex, the convicted murderer whined about the media coverage of the trial. He said he didn't like newspaper photographs that depicted him as either angry or inappropriately jolly. He informed the court that had he known that reporters would make negative comments about is designer court room attire, he would have dressed more modestly.

The whining sociopath also rambled on about how badly his murder victim had been treated by members of Benton's family. He contrasted that behavior to how, before he murdered his daughter out of wounded pride, he had been such an excellent father.

Judge Anthony Mellaci, Jr., before handing down Morgan's sentence, lamented that New Jersey no longer imposed the death penalty. "You'd be candidate number one for its imposition," he said. "Your actions were horrific, unthinkable and appalling. This child was alive when she was placed in the water in pitch darkness. She had to suffer the unthinkable action of having water rush in and fill her lungs while strapped into that car seat. This child suffered before she died."

Judge Mellaci sentenced the remorseless sociopath to life in prison without the possibility of parole.

The Hickory Street Four

On the night of January 9, 2013, 24-year-old Joshua Miner and his girlfriend, Alisa Massaro, 18, were drinking and doing drugs at a house in Joliet, Illinois, a town of 150,000 forty miles southwest of Chicago. They were partying in Massaro's Hickory Street home where she resided with her father, Phillip. Bethany McKee, an 18-year-old who lived in Shorewood, Illinois was at the booze and drug party as well. Adam Landerman, a 19-year-old whose father worked as a sergeant with the Joliet Police

Department, rounded out the group. Mr. Massaro, the father of the host, was in the house that night.

Joshua Miner, the oldest partygoer, possessed a serious criminal record. When he was sixteen he pleaded guilty to filming a child pornography video. In 2010, a jury convicted him of residential burglary. Instead of prison, the judge enrolled the heavy drug user into a boot camp program. (In addition to numerous accusations of violence toward women, Miner faced more current, pending, child pornography charges.) Joshua Miner was not the kind of person one would want associating with one's children. He was not a man you would welcome into your home, or for that matter, into your neighborhood. As the oldest and most criminally experienced member of the party group, Miner assumed the role of leader.

Later that evening, Joshua Miner invited two more people to the Hickory Street house. These young men, Eric Glover and Terrence Rankin, were acquainted with the party attendees. The 22-year-old men no idea what lay in store for them.

On Friday, January 11, 2013, Bethany McKee's father, a resident of Shorewood, Illinois, reported to the police that his daughter had just called him with a disturbing request. She and her friends needed help in disposing of the bodies of two men murdered a day or so earlier in the house on Hickory Street.

When the Joliet police stormed into the Massaro home they found two of the original partygoers, Minder and Landerman, still boozing it up, snorting cocaine, and playing video games. Eric Glover and Terrence Rankin were in the house as well, but they were dead. Both men had been strangled, and someone and had tied plastic bags around their heads.

Bethany McKee had left the house before the police stormed into the dwelling. Police officers picked her up a short time later in Kankakee, Illinois. Alisa Massaro's father, the owner of the dwelling, was at the murder scene when police joined the party.

Not long after being taken into custody, the four partygoers opened-up to detectives about the double murder. Joshua Miner informed his interrogators that he had lured Glover and Rankin to the party by giving them the impression they would be having sex with Massaro and McKee. Once in the house, Miner and Landerman strangled the victims to death. (I don't know if by ligature or by hand.) The victims were killed for their cash and drugs.

Miner said he planned to dismember the bodies and dump the remains in a river or lake or put the body parts into trash bags and curb them in another town on garbage day. Landerman, in furtherance of the garbage disposal plan, had purchased rubber gloves, bleach, a saw, and a blowtorch. Police arrested the men before they had the chance to dismember the victims for disposal.

Joshua Miner, in spilling his guts to detectives, painted Alisa Massaro as a woman as depraved and sexually deviant as himself. According to the 24-year-old child pornographer, Alisa had fantasized about having sex with a dead man. (I'm not sure how that would work.) After Miner and the police officer's son strangled the victims, they lined-up their bodies side-by-side and covered them with a blanket. Miner and Massaro then engaged in sex on top of the corpses.

Bethany McKee, the 18-year-old who had asked her father for help in disposing of the bodies, told detectives that Joshua Miner had planned to save the victims' teeth as trophies. After helping Miner murder Glover and Rankin, Adam Landerman, according to McKee, danced around the room and speculated about how much money the dead men carried in their pockets. Miner and Landerman then drove off in Eric Glover's car to score cocaine from Miner's drug supplier.

On Monday, January 14, 2013, a Will County prosecutor charged the four suspects with two counts each of first-degree murder. The judge set bail for each defendant at $10 million. Fortunately for these defendants, Illinois does not have the death penalty. In the local media, the accused killers were referred to as the "Hickory Street Four." The sensational nature of the case led to a court battle over how much information the authorities were allowed to share with reporters. Not long after the arrests, a judge issued a gag order in the case.

In May 2014, Alisa Massaro, the daughter of the man who owned the Hickory Street house, pleaded guilty to two counts of robbery and two counts of concealing a homicide. Will County Judge Gerald Kinney sentenced her to ten years in prison. Given time served and other factors, Massaro could be out of prison in less than four years. As part of the plea deal, Massaro agreed to testify against the other three defendants at their upcoming murder trials.

17 CAMPUS CRIME

The Clery Act

Over the years, colleges and universities have overcharged students and underreported crime. While useless courses and academic programs are bad enough, sweeping serious campus crime under the rug is even worse. The reportage and publication of campus crime, for any institution of higher learning, is bad for business. No parent wants to send a kid to a college to get raped, robbed, or murdered. These things happen in real life, not in the Disneyesque college experience. These beautiful and expensive institutions, if not sites of great learning, should at least be places where students are relatively safe from violent crime. Over the years, particularly in the big schools, crimes committed by male athletes have not only been suppressed, they've been covered-up.

The underreporting of serious crime by college and university administrators led to the passage, in 1990, of the Jeanne Clery Disclosure of Campus Security Policy and Campus Crime Statistics Act. Under this federal statute, named after a 19-year-old Lehigh University freshman who was raped and murdered in her dormitory in 1986, requires, among other things, that schools keep and disclose information about crime on and near their campuses. Covered offenses include criminal homicide, sexual offenses, robbery, aggravated assault, burglary, arson, motor vehicle theft, and alcohol and drug crimes. Violation of the Clery Act can result in fines up to $27,500 per violation, and exclusion from the federal student aid program.

In December 2006, Laura Dickinson, a freshman at Eastern Michigan University, was found in her dorm room naked from the waist down with a pillow over her head. The chief of the university police department reported "no reason to suspect foul play," and told the student's parents she had died of natural causes. Two months passed before this death was investigated as a murder. In the meantime, the killer roamed the campus in search of other victims. The president of Eastern Michigan lost his job, and the U.S. Department of Education fined the school $357,500. The university also ended up paying the victim's family $2.5 million.

In 2006 and 2010, freshmen women at Dominican College in Orangeburg, New York and at Notre Dame, committed suicide after their complaints of sexual assaults against football players were covered-up. After state and federal investigations, both schools agreed to change their crime reporting policies. (Change their policies from what?) The U.S. Department of Education, under the Clery Act, fined Dominican $20,000 for crime underreporting.

In Texas, the U.S. Department of Education, in 2009, fined Tarleton State University (part of the Texas A&M University system) $137,000 for not accurately reporting its crime statistics. According to the student newspaper, administrators at Tarleton State "underreported the number of forcible sex offenses, drug-law violations, and burglaries between 2003 and 2005." During that period, 10 sex offenses on campus were not reported to the police. The school only reported 29 of more than 60 burglaries.

In recent years, the Department of Education accused administrators at Marquette University of mishandling sexual assault accusations against four athletes. Arizona State, in a case involving the rape of a student by a football player with a history of sexual aggression, was criticized for sweeping this campus crime under the rug.

At Penn State, in 2002, when an assistant football coach reported to coach Joe Paterno that he saw Jerry Sandusky raping a 10-year-old boy in the locker room showers, coach Paterno, instead of reporting the accusation to the police, passed the information on to a university administrator.

In May 2012, Department of Education auditors were on the campus of Roxbury Community College in Boston looking into allegations that at least three sexual assault cases were not reported to the police. Since 2008, the college had only reported six on-campus crimes: one robbery and 5 aggravated assaults that were characterized as "fist-fights." These crime statistics were low for an urban campus.

Campus SWAT

As a result of the fear mongering that followed public school and college campus spree shootings, the aging security guard on many campuses has been replaced by the SWAT equipped and trained commando. The militarization of campus security has not, however, made our colleges and universities safer. It could be argued that militarized campus policing has had the opposite effect.

The Adu-Brempong Case

On March 2, 2010, in Gainsville, Florida, members of the University of Florida's Critical Incident Response Team (CIRT) responded to a 911 call that a 35-year-old doctoral student from Ghana was screaming inside his on-campus apartment. Kofi Adu-Brempong was having psychotic delusions brought on by his fear that his student visa would be denied.

Adu-Brempong, a man disabled by childhood polio, refused to come to his door and speak to the police. This led to an eleven-hour standoff that ended with the CIRT officers breaking into the apartment. After failing to subdue Adu-Brempong with a Taser gun and a beanbag device, a CIRT officer shot the deranged man in the head with his Bushmaster M-4 rifle. According to the police, the subject had attacked them with a knife and a pipe.

Adu-Brempong survived his head wound and was charged with one count of aggravated assault with a deadly weapon without intent to kill, and five counts of resisting an officer with violence. A judge, ruling that the police did not have sufficient evidence to support these charges, dismissed the case against Adu-Brempong.

On August 11, 2011, the University of Florida Police Department announced that its internal investigation had found the Adu-Brempong shooting unjustified. The head of the CIRT unit, a 17-year veteran of the force, was fired. According to the internal review of the shooting, the CIRT officers should not have been deployed in this case.

As a result of the shooting, a group of educators and filmmakers produced a documentary about the case called "In His Own Home." The film revealed that the CIRT officer who shot Adu-Brempong remained on the force until they fired him for roughing up a white student driving a Mercedes.

The Professor Who Liked Meth

In high school, I had a French teacher who came unglued in front of the class. She had acted strange for weeks, but nobody reported her. School officials eventually hauled the disturbed teacher out of the classroom, and we never saw her again. I found this quite tragic because she had been an easy-grader. Her replacement was a monster that flunked half the class.

During my college years I encountered a couple of oddball professors, but witnessed nothing that compared to what Michigan State University students experienced on October 1, 2012 when math professor John McCarthy went off the deep end.

Professor McCarthy, described by his students as an eccentric who smoked meth, taught in MSU's Engineering Building. Just before one o'clock on the day his students will never forget, he started shouting in class. The professor pressed his hands and his face against a window, and stated to scream at the top of his lungs. (I was a college professor for thirty years, and while I occasionally lost my temper, I never had the urge to scream into window glass.) The out of control professor walked out of the classroom and continued to make a lot of noise as he paced up and down the hallway. At this point someone called 911.

Professor McCarthy returned to the classroom, and with his terrified students looking on, took off his clothes, except for his socks. (Not a good look under any circumstance.) He then ran naked about the room screaming, "There is no God," and ranting about computers, Steve Jobs, and that everything in life was just an act. At this point, students were fleeing the classroom for their lives.

Fifteen minutes after the 911 alert, a period that seemed to the students like an eternity, police officers entered the classroom, placed the naked man into handcuffs, and hauled him off to a local hospital for observation.

Professor John McCarthy was not charged with a crime.

Having a Riot at School

An annual celebration at Iowa State University got out of hand when a rowdy crowd began overturning cars and knocking down light poles. Police said the crowd began amassing late on the night of April 8, 2014 in the Campustown area in Ames. The students pelted officers with rocks and beer cans.

The rioters overturned at least two cars and knocked down two light poles. One of the poles struck and seriously hurt a student. The injured person was airlifted to a hospital in Des Moines.

University president Steven Leath said his university cabinet would gather to evaluate options for the remainder of the week's activities for the annual Veishea celebration, one of the oldest campus traditions, showcasing a variety of educational and entertainment events.

University administrators should start a new tradition--no more "celebrations." That won't happen because if it did, the students would riot. In the end, following a lot of academic hot air, life would go on as usual in college fantasyland. In academia, it's the students who rule. (The most powerful individual on any big campus is the football coach of a winning team.)

Death Over Disgrace

Dr. James Aune, the holder of a Ph.D. in Rhetoric from Northwestern University, joined the faculty at Texas A & M in 1996. He published a book about Rhetoric theory and the First Amendment in 2003, and eight years later, was named head of the university's Department of Communication. He lived with his wife in College Station, Texas. The short, pudgy academic with the full beard, long, unruly hair and glasses, cut the figure of the stereotypic college professor.

In December 2012, a 37-year-old man from Metairie, Louisiana named Daniel T. Duplaisir, under the email address pretty-gurl985@yahoo.com, sent sexually explicit photographs of one of his underage female relatives to Dr. Aune and several other men. The 59-year-old professor took the bait, and with the girl, who called herself Karen McCall, set up a website on MocoSpace.com. Over the next five or six weeks, the professor and the girl communicated online. These exchanges included the transmission of sexually explicit photos of each other.

On January 7, 2013, Duplaisir, holding himself out as Karen McCall's outraged father, sent Professor Aune a message demanding $5,000 in hush money. The extortionist wrote: "If I do not hear from you I swear to God Almighty that the police, your place of employment, students, ALL OVER THE INTERNET--ALL OF THEM will be able to see your conversations, texts, pictures you sent. And if by some miracle you get away with this, I will use every chance I get to make sure every place or person associated with you knows and sees what you have done. Last chance. You better make the right move." Duplaisir demanded the money by January 8, 2013.

Shortly after he received the extortion demand, the professor transferred $1,000 to Duplaisir. In an email to the girl, he wrote: "I answered and said I would do whatever he wanted...I sent him $1,000 and then promised more in January. I am scared shitless about this, and can't figure out how to come up with more money."

At ten-thirty in the morning of January 8, 2013, 90 minutes before Duplaisir's extortion payoff deadline, Professor Aune sent him the following email: "Killing myself now, and you will be prosecuted for blackmail." One minute after sending the message, the 59-year-old professor jumped to his death from the sixth floor of a campus garage.

On March 26, 2013, FBI agents arrested Daniel Duplaisir in Metairie, Louisiana, an unincorporated community within metropolitan New Orleans. The suspect was charged with the federal crimes of using a phone and the Internet to extort money. At his arraignment in a federal courtroom in Houston, Duplaisir pleaded not guilty to all charges. He was held without bail.

In 2011, the authorities in Louisiana had charged Duplaisir with aggravated incest and oral sexual battery for allegedly abusing the girl Professor Aune thought was Karen McCall.

In the immediate aftermath of the professor's death, his family, friends and colleagues were baffled by the suicide. (Had the extortion plot not been uncovered, I'm sure there would have been suspicions that Dr. Aune had been murdered.) What's truly hard to understand in this case is why a man of Professor Aune's intelligence and stature would establish a sexual, online relationship with a young girl. As a professor of communications, didn't he realize that his exchanges with this Internet personality were quasi-public?

On November 18, 2013, federal judge Lynn N. Hughes, after a jury found Duplaisir guilty, sentenced him to one year in prison.

Professor Aune must have gone through hell between the period of Duplaisir's extortion demand and his suicide. It's tragic that a person like Daniel Duplaisir had exploited and destroyed a man who was, by all accounts, an outstanding professor.

The Stiletto Heel Murder Case

Dr. Alf Stefan Anderson, a native of Sweden, joined the staff of the University of Houston in December 2009 as a full-time research professor specializing in women's reproductive health. In 2013, he resided on the 18th floor of a luxury high-rise condo in the city's museum district. The 59-year-old professor had an on-again, off-again relationship with Ana Trujillo (pronounced troo-HEE-yoh), a 44-year-old Mexican native.

Dr. Anderson and Trujillo got into an argument on the night of June 8, 2013 while having drinks at a nightclub in Houston. In the taxi on the way back to his condo, she was still angry and yelling at him. The fight had started when another man at the bar offered to buy her a drink.

At four o'clock that morning Trujillo called 911 from Dr. Anderson's high-rise dwelling. Responding police officers and paramedic personnel were met at the door by Trujillo whose clothing and hands were covered in blood. The professor was lying on his back in the hallway with twenty to twenty-five puncture wounds in his face, arms and neck. He was unresponsive.

Next to Dr. Anderson's punctured head lay a bloody blue suede woman's shoe with six-inch stiletto heels. This was the weapon that had caused the wounds and presumably killed the professor.

Trujillo told the officers she had stabbed her boyfriend with the size-nine pump after he'd grabbed her and wrestled her to the ground. Unable to breathe, she had attacked him with the shoe in self-defense.

Police officers took Trujillo into custody at the scene. Later that day, a Harris County prosecutor charged her with capital murder. Following a short period behind bars, the murder suspect posted her $100,000 bail and was released.

The Trujillo trial opened in late March 2014. In his opening remarks, the prosecutor told the jury that the defendant, in a fit of rage, had attacked the victim, causing him to fall backward and injure himself. As he lay helpless on the condo floor, she sat on him and from that position gave it to him with the stiletto shoe. At one point she tried to stop him from breathing by applying pressure to his neck.

The prosecutor portrayed the professor as a mild-mannered nice guy and the defendant as a hothead.

The defense attorney argued that his client had acted in self- defense against an alcohol-fueled assault. Dr. Lee Ann Grossberg, a private forensic pathologist, took the stand for the defense. The witness had reviewed death scene photographs, the autopsy report, police documents, and medical records pertaining to the case. According to the expert witness, "I did not see any one injury that would have been fatal to Dr. Anderson. Natural causes may have contributed to his death."

The defense pathologist testified that if the responding officers and medical crew had performed CPR on Dr. Anderson, or at least used an electronic monitor to measure his heart activity, they may have saved his life.

Without a confession, surveillance footage of the altercation, or an eyewitness account, the stiletto murder represents the classic circumstantial case. The jurors, based on the interpretation of the death scene--particularly the number and nature of the puncture wounds, the unusual murder weapon as well as other circumstances of the case--would have to infer the defendant's guilt. In other words, if murder in this case seemed more reasonable that self-defense, Trujillo would go to prison.

On April 8, 2014, the jury found the defendant guilty as charged. Ana Trujillo showed little emotion as the verdict was read. She faced up to life behind bars.

The punishment phase of the Trujillo trial began the day following the guilty verdict. A police officer testified that Trujillo had been arrested twice for drunken driving. A former security guard took the stand and described how Trujillo had once attacked him. Another witness told jurors that Trujillo had broken into his apartment.

Ana Trujillo took the stand at her sentencing hearing and said, "I never meant to hurt him. It was never my intent. I loved him. I wanted to get away." Following her testimony, the defense attorney asked the judge to send her to prison for two years.

On April 11, 2014, the trial judge sentenced the 45-year-old Trujillo to life.

A Knockout Game Assault

A Massachusetts college sophomore was under arrest for a string of vicious, totally random, "knockout game"-style attacks against three fellow students. Dillon Destefano walked up to three people he didn't know and sucker-punched them in the face...Police said the incidents occurred in the early morning hours of Sunday, February 2, 2014 at or near Endicott College, a small private school in a small New England town about 25 miles north of Boston. The victims were walking home.

Destefano, 19, was a resident of New Jersey. As a freshman he was on the roster of the men's hockey team. Two of Destefano's alleged victims suffered major injuries. The sophomore pleaded not guilty to the aggravated assault and battery charges.

Destefano, who has been diagnosed with Crohn's disease, had a previous brush with fame about a decade ago when he met hockey great Wayne Gretzky for a portion of a televised Make-a-Wish Foundation Special on ESPN....Destefano was nine-years-old at the time....

Eric Owens, The Daily Caller, February 8, 2014

A Professor's Dark Past

In 1967, when he was fifteen, James Gordon Wolcott lived in the central Texas town of Georgetown where Southwestern University is located. His father Dr. Gordon Wolcott headed up the university's Biology Department. His mother Elizabeth, an outgoing woman, was active in the religious community. James and his 17-year-old sister Libby attended Georgetown High School.

At ten on the night of August 4, 1967, James and Libby returned home after attending a rock concert with friends in nearby Austin. Just after midnight, James sniffed model airplane glue to give himself a "boost." Armed with a .22 rifle, he walked into the living room and killed his father by shooting him twice in the chest. In Libby's room, James killed his sister by shooting her in the chest and in the face. The teenager found his mother in her bedroom where he shot her twice in the head and once in the chest.

With his father and sister dead, and his mother in her room dying, James hid the rifle in the attic crawlspace above his bedroom closet. After the disposal of the weapon, James ran out of the house and flagged down a car occupied by three college students. After telling these students that someone had killed his family, they returned with him to the house. Inside the dwelling, the students found Mrs. Wolcott hanging onto her life in her bedroom. One of the young men called for an ambulance and the police. (This was pre-911.)

On the front porch of the Wolcott house, James kept yelling, "How could this happen!" He, of course, knew exactly how it happened. When it occurred to the college kids that the killer could still be in the dwelling, they fled the scene.

Later that morning, Elizabeth Wolcott died at the hospital. A minister who happened to be a Wolcott neighbor took James to his parsonage. A few hours later, when a Texas Ranger asked James if he had killed his family, the youngster said, "Yes, sir." At that point James had the presence of mind to describe in detail what he had done. At the killing site, he showed police officers where he hid the rifle.

When asked the obvious question of *why*, James said he *hated* his family. He later told psychiatrists that his mother chewed her food so loudly he had to leave the room. His sister had an annoying Texas accent, and his father made him cut his hippie hair and wouldn't allow him to wear anti-Vietnam war buttons or attend peace rallies.

Several psychiatrists interviewed James at the Williamson County Jail. From the young mass killer they learned that he had been sniffing glue for several months. James also told the shrinks that he had contemplated suicide. He said that his parents and sister had tried to drive him insane. He killed them before they had a chance to murder him.

Although James and members of his family did not have histories of mental illness, the psychiatrists concluded that the boy, although he had an IQ of 134, suffered from paranoid schizophrenia. (There may have been doctors who disagreed with this conclusion.) Notwithstanding the diagnosis of schizophrenia, the psychiatrists declared the defendant mentally competent to stand trial as an adult.

The murder defendant's attorney Will Kelly McClain set up a defense based on legal insanity. In October 1967, following a short trial, the all-male jury found James Wolcott not guilty by reason of insanity. The jurors believed that James had been so mentally impaired he had no idea that killing his family was wrong. (Since the Wolcott verdict, only a handful of Texas murder defendants have been declared not guilty by reason of insanity. This rarely happens because there is no such thing as a mental illness so severe that it completely destroys a killer's appreciation of what he is doing. In the history of Texas jurisprudence, the James Wolcott case is an anomaly.)

In February 1968, the trial judge sent James Wolcott to the Rusk State Hospital in Nacodoches, Texas. He was to be incarcerated there until he regained his sanity. That sentence placed his fate in the hands of psychiatrists.

In 1974, seven years after the mass killing in the Texas college town, Rusk State Hospital psychiatrists declared the 21-year-old killer sane. The young man had made a remarkable recovery for someone who had been so mentally ill that he didn't realize that shooting his family to death was wrong.

As the only surviving child of his deceased parents, James Wolcott inherited their estate, and started receiving a monthly stipend from his father's university pension fund.

Upon his departure from Rusk State Hospital, James took up residence in Austin, Texas where he enrolled at Stephen F. Austin University. Just two years later, he had a Bachelor's Degree in psychology.

At some point in the late 1970s, James Wolcott changed his name to James David St. James. In 1980, Mr. St. James, having acquired his Master's Degree, began his doctoral work in psychology at the University of Illinois. In 1988, Dr. St. James began teaching psychology at Millikin University, a Presbyterian liberal arts institution in Decatur, Illinois. No one at the school knew that the psychology professor had shot three members of his family to death twenty years earlier. Had he included this relevant background information on his job application, it is doubtful the university would have hired him. Having been declared criminally insane, even in the field of academic psychology, is not a job-hunting selling point.

In July 2013, a Texas journalist named Ann Marie Gardner published an article that revealed Dr. St. James' homicidal past. When the story broke, the academic, who did not have a family of his own, headed the Behavioral Sciences Department at Millikin University. While the secretive professor's colleagues and students were probably shocked, no one at the school voiced disapproval. In fact, at least in academic circles, Dr. St. James emerged from his exposure as a hero, a poster-boy for the power and glory of the behavioral sciences. (Had he been working for a plumbing company, he would have been fired.) If the professor's colleagues and students were stunned by the creepy irony of Dr. St. James' story, no one said so. (University campuses are not places where people can speak freely.)

There are probably members of the Wolcott family who are still psychologically scarred by James Wolcott's killing spree. There was no indication, however, that what took place that night in 1967 had any lingering affect on the killer himself. And there was no evidence that Dr. St. James was still schizophrenic. This is interesting because the disease is *incurable*. All of the homicidal schizophrenics I have written about struggled with the malady their entire lives. One of these men couldn't take it anymore and committed suicide.

One possible explanation for James Wolcott's rapid and apparent total recovery from this devastating disease is that he wasn't insane in the first place. Following his arrest, James told his interrogators that he had been thinking about killing his family for a week. Was it possible that Wolcott, a brilliant sociopath, had pulled one over on the psychiatrists, the criminal justice system, and academia?

A Culture of Rape

In February 2012, Occidental College professors Caroline Heldman and Danielle Dirks publicly accused President Jonathan Veitch and his administration of discouraging campus rape victims from reporting the assaults to the police. The professors and students who supported their cause asserted that Veitch and his people not only suppressed crime reporting on the Los Angeles campus, they handed down weak sanctions against the students responsible for rapes and other sexual offenses. The activist professors and those who backed them also accused college administrators of retaliating against professors and students who publicly criticized the school's handling of sex crimes. According to the complainants, this malfeasance had been going on since 2009.

As part of their effort to reform Occidental's campus sex crime policy, Professors Heldman and Dirks helped concerned students file federal complaints against the school that accused the administration of civil rights violations as well as violations of the Clery Act.

Because colleges and university administrations across the country have a long history of under-reporting campus crime, congress passed the Clery Act. Under this law, colleges and universities that receive federal money are required to maintain and fully disclose campus and near-campus crime statistics. Institutions that do not comply with the Clery Act can be fined up to $35,000 per violation.

College and university administrators hate the Clery Act and do whatever they can to get around it. Since crime is bad for business, it's still grossly under-reported on most campuses. Given the high cost of higher education and the fierce competition for students, a campus that is not perceived as an oasis of safety and luxury will lose out in the market place. Colleges and universities no longer sell education, they sell lifestyle.

Following the filing of the federal complaints, President Veitch agreed to tighten the school's policy regarding the handling of campus rape. But in the summer of 2013, a student who said she had been raped on campus in February of that year complained on television that the college had not honored its agreement to report these crimes and take aggressive action against perpetrators.

Infuriated by this public accusation, President Veitch accused the complaining student and Professor Dirks of maliciously embarrassing him and the college on the evening news. The president's thin-skinned response drew public criticism. As a result, he was forced to apologize for taking out his anger on the wrong people. (College and University presidents, the kings and queens of academia, have huge egos and suffer from degrees of self-love that is borderline pathological. They therefore have no tolerance for people who criticize them.)

On September 19, 2013, the *Los Angeles Times* reported that Occidental College had reached a confidential monetary settlement with at least ten students who had been raped on campus. In all of these cases, the college had either squelched or downplayed the crimes.

On the day following the *Times* article, President Veitch, in an attempt to garner faculty support for his reappointment as president (his 5-year contract was up for renewal), gave a 20-minute, emotional speech at an all-faculty meeting. Now that the scandal was supposedly behind them, the president called for intra-campus civility. (In academia, "civility" is a code word for speech suppression. There is more free speech in Russia than on many American college campuses.)

In his faculty address, rather than focus on how his administration had let down crime victims and misled the public, President Veitch talked about himself. He said he had been "shell-shocked" by the accusations, and that the "controversy" had taken a toll "on my health and my soul." (Outside of academia, who talks like that?) While the president admitted that mistakes had been made, he assured faculty members that Occidental College had some of the strongest sexual assault policies in the country. (That might be true, but no thanks to him.)

President Veitch, when his 5-year contract runs out, should be shown the door. And he should be sent packing without one of those typically over-generous severance packages. No golden parachute for this man. If he is one-tenth as great as I'm sure he thinks he is, getting a new job should be no problem.

Dorm Room Ricin

A Georgetown University student who made deadly ricin in his dorm room was arrested in Washington, D.C. on March 21, 2014 for illegal possession of a biological toxin...The student, Daniel Harry Milzman, made the white powder with materials he bought at local stores, including The Home Depot and American Plant Company...He found the recipe for making ricin by doing a search on his iPhone....

Wearing goggles and a dust mask for protection, Milzman used Epsom salts and castor beans, among other materials, to make the ricin in his dorm room about a month ago...He stored what he had made in plastic bags sealed with hockey tape.

On Tuesday evening, March 18, 2014, Milzman showed some of his ricin to his residential advisor who promptly contacted the university's counseling services who in turn called the police....Milzman described his efforts during an interview with FBI agents later that day....The FBI Laboratory tested the contents of the bags and confirmed they contained the ricin toxin...

Reuters, March 22, 2014

Useless Courses Rip Off Parents

Recent polls indicate that most Americans believe that acquiring a higher education isn't worth the time or the money. Having a college degree once meant something, and provided the graduate with at least the opportunity to get a decent job. Modern employers are not so impressed. The job market is flooded with degree holders who are unfit for the higher paying positions. That people with bachelor degrees are smarter and more informed than people who haven't graduated from a four-year college is no longer a safe assumption.

On average, students in public supported colleges and universities spend $20,000 a year. (This includes room and board.) Private schools cost twice as much. This means that a college education costs between $80,000 and $160,000. How many parents with more than one child can afford this? Not many. The average college graduate enters the job market owing, for his or her education alone, $24,000. They also have to pay off credit card debt, and car loans. No wonder they are so disappointed when they can't land the high-paying jobs. With the cost of higher education so high, and so many graduates unemployed or under-employed, it's no longer a given that a college education, as a business proposition, is a wise investment.

Studies have shown that college and university services are less geared for student needs than for the needs of administrators and professors. Too many college courses reflect the interests of the people who teach them rather than the interests of the students who take them. Many courses are products of the professors' pet interests, or are designed, not for the teaching of useful and demanding subjects, but to draw students.

One way to fill up a classroom is to create a course about sex. This is one subject college graduates are well versed in. If the professor is a historian, he can offer a course called The History of Sex. There's also the

Sociology of Sex; The Philosophy of Sex; The Physiology of Sex; the Psychology of Sex; and The Politics of Sex. Some actual course titles include: Sex in Ancient Rome; The Adultery Novel; Those Sexy Victorians; The Phallus; Sex, Rugs, Salt, and Coal (I have no idea what that one is about); Purity and Porn is America; Cyberporn and Society; FemSex; God, Sex, Chocolate: Desire and the Spiritual Path; and Dirty Pictures.

There are entire academic departments devoted to gay studies. Swarthmore students are offered a course called Interrogating Gender: Centuries of Dramatic Cross-Dressing. At the University of South Carolina one can take a course entitled GaGa for Gaga: Sex, Gender, and Identify. Not to be outdone, the University of California, Los Angeles, offers a course called Queer Musicology.

Look through any college catalogue and you'll find courses on UFO's, ghosts, vampires, zombies, and witchcraft. College kids can enroll in courses devoted to the study of people such as David Beckham, Lady Gaga, Oprah Winfrey, Tupac, and dozens of other sports and entertainment "icons." College students today take courses called The Art of Walking; Tree Climbing; Whitewater Skills; Golf; Knitting for Noobs; Finding Dates Worth Keeping; Getting Dressed; How to Watch Television; and my favorite--Underwater Basket Weaving. (In the old days, if you were weaving baskets, you were in a mental institution. Now, you are in college.)

Several universities, including Georgetown, offer courses featuring the old TV series "Star Trek." Students at the University of Texas can sign up for a course called Invented Languages: Klingon and Beyond. Language students at the University of Wisconsin can take Elvish (a language spoken in the *Lord of the Rings* trilogy.) Many of these Klingon and Elvish speaking students can barely handle English.

Physics students at Frostburg University can study the magic featured in Harry Potter books. Inquiring minds at Occidental College can earn credits by taking a course called, The Unbearable Whiteness of Barbie. Students at the University of Iowa can avail themselves of a course called Elvis As Anthology. The University of California Irvine offers a course called The Science of Superheroes.

At Alfred University, some professor teaches a course called Nip, Tuck, Perm, Pierce, and Tattoo: Adventures with Embodied Culture. According to the course description: "Students are encouraged to think about teeth whitening, tanning, shaving, and hair-dying." Since kids think about this stuff anyway, perhaps this professor could encourage students to think about things that are at least *academic*. But wait--there's more: class projects include a visit to a tattoo-and-piercing studio. (Maybe owned by the professor's spouse.) University of California Berkeley students can avail themselves of Joy of Garbage.

At the University of Minnesota, if you're a numbskull who's worried about satisfying the physical science requirement, there is a course for you. It's called Geology and Cinema (Professors use the word "cinema" instead of "movie" because "cinema" sounds so academic.) where students sit in class and watch movies that feature geological subject matter as in "Tremors," and "Journey to the Center of the Earth." (If I were this professor, I'd include a field trip to Disneyworld.) At Pitzer College there's a course called Learning from YouTube. According to the catalogue, "YouTube is a phenomenon that should be studied." (Anything referred to as a "phenomenon" must be important.)

For Ohio State students who don't know how to watch a football game, there's a course called Sport For The Spectator. (Again, notice the word "Spectator." How many people who attend sporting events think of themselves as "spectators?") Hopefully this professor gives several lectures that deal with the technique, and meaning, of face-painting, or "facial art." Temple University has a course called UFOs in American Society.

For pre-law students at the University of California at Berkeley, there's Arguing with Judge Judy: Popular "Logic" on TV Judge Shows. This course is of particular value to students who would rather play a judge on television than assume the role in real life. For students who want to be TV lawyers, I recommend the Perry Mason series. There is probably a college course around called: The Jurisprudence of Perry Mason.

Appalachian State University offers a history course called, "What if Harry Potter is Real?" Students who take this course will explore questions such as "who decides what history is, and who decides how it is used or misused. How can fantasy reshape how we look at history?"

Students lucky enough to attend the University of Wisconsin at Madison can avail themselves of Theatrical Fencing. This offering from the Department of Kinesiology provides the student with this pearl of wisdom: "Good theatrical fencing is distinct from the art of sword craft, and is worthy of study." Indeed. What value is an academic program without at least one course on theatrical sword craft? And finally, at New York University, students can earn four college credits by taking a course called Disc Jockey: History, Culture, and Technique. (The technique element suggests a big lab fee.) Many college graduates don't know what came first, World War I or World War II, but they all know the history of the D J. At the University of Pennsylvania one can take a course called The Feminist Critique of Christianity.

It's no wonder that if you throw a stick in your local shopping mall it'll hit nine retail employees with college degrees. And all of them are in debt and quite a few can speak Klingon.

In his 2013 book, *The New School,* University of Tennessee law professor Glenn H. Reynolds makes the case that college graduates can't find good jobs and pay off their huge debts because colleges and universities overcharge and underperform. One way to quickly improve the quality of higher education would be to eliminate stupid courses like the ones above.

Hooked on Meth

Samuel Ryan See grew up in California's Central Valley where he attended California State University in his hometown of Bakersfield. After acquiring his Bachelors of Arts Degree, See earned a Ph.D. from the University of California, Los Angeles.

In May 2013, the 34-year-old assistant professor of English and American Studies at Yale University married Sunder Ganglani, a former student at the Yale School of Drama. The two men took up residence in a house in New Haven, Connecticut.

Professor See's academic focus, as described on his Facebook page, included "British and American Modernist Literature and Sexuality Studies." In addition to writing about sexual orientation in modern literature, Dr. See moonlighted, under the alias Ryan Cochran, as a male escort. In one of Ryan Cochran's Internet profiles, See described himself as loving sex and being with men. "I can get into all kinds of sexual and social situations--just name your pleasure. I'm down to earth, humble, personally generous, and horny a lot of the time." Professor See was, in other words, a male prostitute.

Dr. See, on leave from Yale University during the fall semester 2013, was not getting along with his 32-year-old husband. On September 18, 2013, officers with the New Haven Police Department, after responding to a domestic call at See's residence, arrested See and Sunder Ganglani for breaching the peace and third-degree assault.

After a judge issued orders of protection requiring that the two men stay away from each other, Ganglani moved to New York City.

At five in the evening of Saturday, November 23, 2013, Ganglani, in violation of his protection order, showed up at the New Haven house to retrieve some of his possessions. Two hours later the estranged couple were engaged in a heated argument. The fight became so intense a third man in the house called the police.

When the responding officers couldn't calm down the combatants they placed both men under arrest for violating their protection orders. This infuriated See who couldn't believe he was being arrested in his own home. The situation escalated when See fought against being handcuffed. In the scuffle with officers, Professor See fell and sustained a cut above his right eye.

While being escorted in handcuffs to the police vehicle, See, in addressing the arresting officer, said, "I will kill you. I will destroy you."

Following his treatment at the Yale-New Haven Hospital, police officers booked Professor See into the police department jail on the additional charges of interfering with police and second-degree threatening. He was placed into a cell at nine-fifteen that night.

At six o'clock the next morning, when a guard checked on Professor See, he found the prisoner unresponsive. The officer called for paramedic help then tried to revive Dr. See with CPR. Fifteen minutes later, emergency service responders pronounced the inmate dead.

The forensic pathologist who performed Dr. See's autopsy ruled out trauma as the cause of death. This meant that another inmate had not killed the professor.

In January 2014, Chief State Medical Examiner Dr. James Gill announced that professor See had died of a heart attack brought on by methamphetamine and amphetamine intoxication. The manner of death went into the books as accidental.

Death by Hazing

Since 2008 there have been 16 hazing deaths at U.S. colleges and universities. Victims of these unintentional, senseless killings were members of fraternities, school bands, or sports teams that had long histories of putting new members through right-of-passage rituals. These young people died because they desperately wanted to belong. Despite the efforts of university administrators and others to break this tradition, hazing will continue and students will die as a result.

Chen Hsien Deng, a 19-year-old freshman finance major at Baruch College in Manhattan, New York, joined the Pi Delta Psi fraternity. According to its published profile, this fraternal organization is an Asian-American group with a mission to "spread Asian-American cultural awareness." Founded in 1994, the organization has chapters in twenty states and the District or Columbia.

On Friday, December 6, 2013, thirty members of Pi Delta Psi left New York City en route to the Poconos Mountain region in northeastern Pennsylvania. Chen Deng was one of four fraternity pledges participating in the weekend getaway. The group had rented a house in Tunkhannock Township in Monroe County.

On Sunday, December 8, 2013, at eight-fifteen in the morning, three of Deng's fraternity brothers drove him to the Geisinger Wyoming Valley Hospital emergency room in Danville, Pennsylvania. Doctors found the freshman unresponsive and immediately placed him on life support. Twenty-four hours later, Chen Deng died.

Two days later, a spokesperson for the Luzerne County Coroner's Office announced that Chen Deng had died from "closed head injuries due to blunt force trauma."

Investigators with the Poconos Mountain Regional Police Department found marijuana and hallucinogenic mushrooms in the rented house in Tunkhannock.

At the hospital, detectives spoke to Sheldon Wong, the fraternity's "pledge educator." Wong said that Deng had injured his head when he fell backward in the snow while wrestling another fraternity brother. Charles Lai, another member of the fraternity told a different story. According to Lai, Deng had died during a hazing ritual called "The Gauntlet." In this initiation game, a blindfolded pledge is repeatedly tackled as he runs a gauntlet of fraternity brothers while carrying a backpack full of sand. After Deng was knocked unconscious in the snow outside the rented house, fraternity brothers carried him into the dwelling.

Before driving Deng to the hospital, fraternity members removed and replaced his wet clothing. Next, someone made an Internet search regarding the unconscious pledge's symptoms. The Internet inquiry also included determining the location of the nearest hospital. An hour after Deng collapsed in the snow, the three Pi Delta Psi fraternity brothers drove him to the emergency room in Danville.

At the hospital, one of the fraternity brothers called the rented house in Tunkhannock and instructed someone there to dispose of all fraternity memorabilia as well as anything else that would reveal what had happened to the dead pledge.

On February 14, 2014 the coroner ruled that the student had died of "closed head injuries due to blunt force head trauma." The corner labeled the death homicide. As of August 2014, no criminal charges have been filed against members of the fraternity.

A Nice Place for Pot

Four University of Utah students were found in a well-concealed igloo after a security guard heard voices and detected the smell of marijuana coming from the area. The igloo was an impressive five feet high, with solid ten-inch thick walls, and even had a crudely hinged cardboard door. It was built in a wooded area on campus grounds.

One student was cited with possession of drug paraphernalia, and all were referred for possible disciplinary action. It was unclear if the students themselves had constructed the igloo, or simply taken advantage of its presence. The igloo was taken down by campus security with a sledgehammer. [Had the igloo been raided by a SWAT team, officers would have punched a hole in the roof and dropped in a stun grenade.]...

John Baiata, NBC News, February 27, 2014

Campus Phone Sex

Over the past ten years, Resa Cooper-Morning, a cultural diversity coordinator in the Ethnic Studies Department at the University of Colorado at Denver, has been living a double life. Employed by the university since 1992, Resa, in 2003, began supplementing her $68,000-a-year salary by charging phone sex callers $1.49 a minute for her pornographic talk.

Cooper-Morning advertised her services through her website, msresa.com. The site also offered soft-core videos of the university administrator with titles such as "Stripping Before the Camera," and "Erotica in Pink." The site included a link to her phone sex service that promised to "rock every part of your body." Internet viewers could also purchase memberships to Cooper-Morning's virtual world.

Internet visitors desiring sexy phone talk were encouraged to call Resa between seven in the morning and "late at night", Monday through Friday. This made her available to sex callers Monday through Friday, 7 AM to 3PM, her university working hours. This meant the 54-year-old was talking dirty for money on university's time. (I guess you could argue that a lot of employees talk dirty on company time. The only difference here is that Cooper-Morning allegedly did it for money.)

Big wigs at the University of Colorado were informed of Cooper-Morning's clandestine business by a producer with the local CBS-TV affiliate working on a segment about Cooper-Morning's erotic website. The show was scheduled to air on December 12, 3003. Shortly after the notification, the diversity coordinator was placed on paid administrative leave.

Blair Cooper, Resa's daughter-in-law, appeared in the CBS-produced segment that aired as scheduled. According to Cooper, "she [Resa] was taking calls at work. I've been in her office and she's said, 'oh, let me be right back, I have a phone call.' She takes them very discreetly, shuts her door and takes phone calls on Colorado University of Denver's pay."

Following an internal investigation, a university administrator announced, in January 2014, that Cooper-Morning had not broken any laws. As a result she kept her $68,000 a year job. It's obvious that in academia the bar for professional behavior is extremely low.

How Many Kids in Class Are Enrolled in the School?

In October 2013, a student the University of North Carolina at Chapel Hill wanted to fly to India to attend a wedding. If she took the trip she'd miss two days of class, absences she couldn't afford. To solve her problem, the young woman decided to find a classroom stand-in.

In the Raleigh section of Craigslist the wedding-bound girl posted a photograph of herself and an offer of $100 to any female who met her general description willing to attend the classes on her behalf. According to the posting, the job required "sitting in the classroom and raising one's hand during attendance."

Getting away with this class-skipping ploy is one advantage of taking classes attended by hundreds of students. This little academic episode begged the questions: why do professors even bother keeping attendance records. Why should a professor care if kids are skipping class? It's students' money that's wasted. One wonders how many college students make extra money filling empty seats for classroom slackers. It's a lot easier than babysitting.

In Pittsburgh, Pennsylvania, an enterprising person pushed the college stand-in game to its limits. This man wanted someone, under his name, to acquire a four-year degree from Harvard University. This man claimed to have a 4.0 high school grade average and high SAT scores.

The Pittsburgh Craigslist posting read: "I am looking for someone to attend Harvard University pretending to be me for four years, starting August 2014. I will pay for your tuition, books, housing, transportation and living expenses and pay $40,000 a year with a $10,000 bonus after graduation. All you have to do is attend all classes, pass all tests, and finish all assigned work while pretending you are me."

According to the terms of this education scam, all persons applying for the assignment were required to sign nondisclosure agreements.

Because for most people a Harvard degree is not worth the cost, I think this is a better deal for the stand-in than the pretender. Since no one ever flunks out of Harvard, the stand-in can slack off by hiring seat-fillers whenever he wants to skip class.

The Harvard Bomb Hoaxer

At 8:40 in the morning of Monday, December 16, 2013, officials at Harvard University in Cambridge, Massachusetts received a bomb threat via email. The sender of the email wrote that "shrapnel bombs" were hidden in Emerson, Thayer, and Sever Halls as well as in the Science Center. As more than 100 police, federal agents, and emergency personnel rushed to the university, Harvard security officers began evacuating the four buildings. The bomb threat came on the first day of final exam week.

Four hours after the threat, after bomb searchers failed to find any suspicious devices, faculty, students, and others were allowed back into the buildings. The feared terrorist attack turned out to be a hoax.

Shortly after the bomb threat disruption that had little effect on students, university sob sisters sprang into action. In an all-student email from the Faculty of Arts and Sciences, students were advised that if they felt unable to take an exam for *any reason* "including anxiety, loss of study time, lack of access to material and belongings left in one of the affected buildings, or travel schedule" they could skip the final and take a grade based on coursework to date. (At Harvard, professors not only make it easy for academic slackers, they provide them with a menu of excuses. No wonder kids want to get into this school.)

Because the Faculty of Arts and Sciences email came under intense ridicule, the professors sent a follow up memo that required bomb threat affected students to acquire documentation from the school's mental health service. (Universities today have mental health services. When I was in college, if you went nuts your parents pulled you out of school. That's why you tried not to go crazy, or lost your mind after graduation.)

Later on the day of the bomb hoax, investigators traced the email threat back to a 20-year-old Harvard sophomore named Eldo Kim. The naturalized citizen from South Korea graduated from high school in Mukilteo, Washington. He played the viola and had interned with a newspaper in Seoul. On the staff of the *Harvard Independent,* Kim's academic focus involved psychology and sociology.

On the day of the disruption, FBI agents arrested Eldo Kim on federal charges related to the bomb threats. If convicted as charged, he faced up to five years in prison. He could also be fined $250,000. Freed on $100,000 bond, the authorities released Kim to the custody of his sister who resided in Massachusetts.

According to Ian Gold, the federal public defender appointed to represent the bomb hoax suspect, Kim had emailed the bomb threat to avoid taking a final exam in his government class. Attorney Gold told reporters that his client had been having difficulty coping with his studies and the upcoming anniversary of his father's death. "It's finals time at Harvard," attorney Gold said. "In one way, we're looking at the equivalent of pulling a fire alarm…It's important to keep in mind we're dealing with a 20-year-old man who was under a great deal of pressure."

Harvard law professor Alan Dershowitz, in addressing the media, took issue with the "great deal of academic pressure" defense. Dershowitz pointed out that due to run-away grade inflation, it's very difficult to flunk out of Harvard. The median grade awarded to Harvard students is A-minus.

"I doubt that anyone who got into Harvard would fail a government exam," said Dershowitz. "People come to Harvard with major problems. It's not that Harvard causes them." (Students at Ivy League schools intimidate their professors. For that reason Harvard professors function more like camp counselors than demanding teachers.)

Eldo Kim may or may not have entered Harvard with some sort of mental or emotional problem. However, if he didn't have a problem before, he had one now.

As of August 2014, Kim had not been indicted by a federal grand jury. Since he confessed to the bomb calls, the delay is puzzling.

Kidnapping Hoax

A Penn State student [main campus, State College] who told police she had been kidnapped from a campus sidewalk faced charges of making a false report. Police said on March 31, 2014 that Samantha Sernekos, 20, of Landing, New Jersey, admitted to authorities that the January 25 incident had not happened.

Police Chief Tyrone Parham said authorities examined surveillance video and other evidence during a two-month investigation and concluded no crime had occurred. Campus police ramped up their night patrols after the student reported she had been pulled into a vehicle, driven off campus and escaped as her abductors were trying to assault her....

Associated Press, March 31, 2014

A Fund Raiser's Suicide

In 1975, a 22-year-old student from Taiwan (an island 200 miles off the coast of mainland China) named Cecilia Chang, enrolled in the Asian Studies Master's Degree program at St. John's University in Queens, New York. After Chang acquired the degree in 1977, the university hired her as an Asian Studies professor. Three years later, university administrators promoted Chang to the position of Dean of the Institute For Asian Studies. Having exhibited the ability to raise money for the program from the Taiwanese and other Asian governments, Chang's job as dean involved fund-raising. She spent the next decade traveling the world, living high on donor contributions to the school and her university expense account.

In October 1986, Cecilia Chang's husband, Ruey Fung, filed for divorce and sought custody of the couples' toddler son. Four years later, in the midst of a contentious domestic struggle over money and child custody,

Ruey Fung was shot outside a warehouse in the Bushwick section of Brooklyn.

Ruey Fung died from his wounds eleven days after the shooting. But before he passed away, homicide detectives were able to question him at the hospital. Unable to speak, Mr. Fung wrote: "I know the man who shot me, but I do not know his name. Cecilia Chang was the person who paid the guy to shoot me." Ruey Fung claimed that his wife wanted him dead so she wouldn't have to split their estate that included a hosiery business. With his death, she would also gain custody of the boy.

Because NYC homicide detectives were unable to identity the man who shot and killed Mr. Fung, the investigation died on the vine. Notwithstanding her husband's deathbed murder accusation and police suspicion that Chang had engaged the services of a hit man, her fund-raising career at St. John's University continued to flourish.

In 2001, Cecilia Chang began spending an inordinate amount of time in Connecticut at the Foxwoods Casino where she lost tens of thousands of dollars playing high-stakes baccarat. Her wagering strategy of doubling her bet each time she lost compounded her casino losses.

A grand jury sitting in Queens, New York, in 2010, indicted Chang on 205 counts of fraud and embezzlement. She stood accused of stealing huge amounts of money from St. John's University. In addition to embezzling $1 million from the institution, Chang was accused of using her $350,000 a year expense account, and donor money, to finance skiing and surfing trips for her son, fund his law school tuition, and even pay for his dog's veterinary bills.

Dean Chang also faced charges of theft, fraud, and corruption in federal court. In 2011, after being charged federally, the judge placed her under house arrest. In the fall of 2012, the federal case against Chang went to trial in Brooklyn, New York. When the Assistant United States Attorney rested the government's case, it was clear to people following the trial that the defendant was guilty.

On November 5, 2012, convinced she could convince the jury that she was innocent of all charges, Chang took the stand on her own behalf. It quickly became obvious that the jurors not only didn't like her, they didn't believe her testimony. At one point during her testimony, jurors actually laughed loudly at something she said. At this point in the trial, Cecilia Chang realized that in all probability she would be spending the next twenty years in federal prison.

On Tuesday, the day after her devastatingly bad afternoon on the stand, Chang, in her $1.7 million home in the Jamaica section of Queens, committed suicide. The 59-year-old was found hanging from a ladder that folded down from her attic. Chang had also slit her wrists. She left behind several suicide notes, written in Mandarin, in which, in true sociopathic fashion, she blamed St. John's University for her problems and her suicide.

Cecilia Chang had gotten accustomed to having all the money she needed to lavishly entertain herself, her son, and all of her friends in high places. She felt entitled to use university and donor money to live extravagantly, and to cover her gambling loses. In my view, the university bears some responsibility for Chang's financial excesses. No university employee should be allowed a $350,000 a year expense account.

Campus Sex Crime

A new federal report says sex crimes reported at American colleges and universities went up in the last decade even as overall campus crime decreased. The report, released on June 10, 2014 from the U.S. Education Department, says 3,330 forcible sex offenses on college campuses were reported in 2011, a 51 percent increase from the 2,200 reported in 2001. The number of crimes in every other category, such as burglary, declined during the same period....

Associated Press, June 10, 2014

Naming Names

It wasn't a secret that on the campus of Columbia University in New York City, rape had been a campus problem for years. On April 25, 2014, twenty-three Columbia students filed a Clery Act complaint with the U.S. Department of Education. Through this document, the university stood accused of discouraging campus rape allegations to the authorities. These complainants also accused university administrators of protecting students suspected of rape by refusing to kick them out of school.

On May 7, 2014, a group of activists wrote the names of four accused rapists on the stalls in a Hamilton Hall women's restroom. Under the headings "Sexual Assault Violators" and "Rapists on Campus," the published names were written in four different sets of handwriting with each writer using a different color marker. The last person on the lists was labeled a "serial rapist."

The Hamilton Hall bathroom rape lists had been posted less than 24 hours when university officials got wind of the "graffiti" and removed it. This not only prompted the activists to spread their message to other women's restrooms, it resulted in the publication of rape list flyers that were posted around the campus. For university administrators, the lists presented a public relations nightmare.

On May 16, 2014, after Columbia student Emma Sulkowicz filed a rape complaint against one of the students on the rape lists with the New York City Police Department, the school paper, the *Spectator*, published this male undergraduate's name.

A few days after the rapist's name appeared in the *Spectator*, Emma Sulkowicz, one of the Clery Act complainants, held a press conference. In describing her experience at the New York City Police Department, Sulkowicz said, "the officer basically treated me as if I was the criminal. After you've been physically violated the last thing you want is to have a policemen who is high on his own power telling you that everything you've just experienced is invalid."

Regarding the Columbia rape lists, campus opinion seemed divided between students who considered the lists the work of out-of-control vigilantes, and others who praised these students for standing up for victims' rights.

18 BAD COPS

Pittsburgh's Depression Era Cops

In the 1930s a young man didn't get on the Pittsburgh Police force by passing a test. He got the job because he had pull--a priest he knew, a relative in uniform, or the sponsorship of a ward chairman. Most recruits had ended their schooling early, in some cases so early they couldn't read or write. Some came from neighborhoods where joining the police force was considered an act of treason. Had it not been for the Great Depression, many of these men would have found work in the mills, driving a truck, or in the building trades. But when the bottom fell out of the employment market, police department jobs looked good. This was a time when people who couldn't find work either lived off their relatives, stole, begged, or starved.

In those days, the city didn't supply its officers with the tools of the trade. A rookie had to purchase his own uniform, badge, billy club, gun, and callbox key. If he planned on firing his revolver, he'd have to buy his own ammunition, and if he wanted to hit what he shot at, he'd have to arrange for his own firearms training.

One night on Pittsburgh's South Side, a rookie responding to a grocery store hold-up saw the robber running out of the place with a gun in his hand. The young cop, in fumbling with his second-hand revolver, accidentally shot the hold-up man in the shoulder. The wounded robber stopped in his tracks, dropped his gun, and surrendered. But before the rookie could collect his thoughts, a pair of seasoned patrolmen come on the scene and took credit for the arrest. By stealing the pinch, the veterans got promoted to the detective bureau. The rookie got nothing but a little wiser. This was police training, 1930's style.

Every cop in Pittsburgh began his career as a substitute officer. Subs were expected to attend roll call at the beginning of each shift--three times a day--until someone was needed to replace a regular officer who hadn't shown up for duty. A sub might report for work three times a day for weeks before getting an assignment. If a sub didn't get work he didn't get paid, and when he was assigned temporary shift duty, he was paid what the man who had called off earned. Cops who joined the force in the 1930s worked from three to six years as subs before they got on the job full time.

A few Pittsburgh cops had German backgrounds, and some were Italian, but most were Irish because Irish politicians controlled the city. But this western Pennsylvania mill town wasn't all Irish. The city had a thriving Chinatown as well as Polish, Russian, German, and Italian neighborhoods. Most of the city's black population lived in the Hill District, a neighborhood east of the downtown business district. One of the best-known and respected foot patrolmen of the era was a black officer who walked the beat on the South Side, and on the Hill, a pair of black cops in plainclothes worked vice. But black cops were never promoted, and only white officers were allowed inside a patrol car.

During the depression, sprawling shantytowns sprung up around the city. There was a large encampment in the woods near Tropical Avenue in the Banksville section of town. The residents of this makeshift ghetto fed and clothed themselves off a nearby garbage dump. On the fringes of downtown, homeless people the police called "cavemen" camped in caves they had dug out of the hillsides. Occasionally a caveman or two would drink too much moonshine and stagger into the business district where the police would scoop them up and haul them off to jail in a paddy wagon.

A pair of devastating floods hit Pittsburgh in 1936 and 1937, and downtown, police in rowboats had to rescue customers and employees from the second story of Kaufman's Department Store. In 1936, a Pittsburgh patrolman lost his life when he slipped into the swollen Ohio River between two barges.

In the thirties, Pittsburgh police officers directed traffic, operated the city run ambulance service, rode paddy wagons, or walked a beat. There were a handful of detectives, vice cops, and a few patrol car and motorcycle officers. Sergeants and lieutenants and their clerical personnel worked inside a dozen station houses throughout the city. Station number 1 was located downtown, number 2 on the Hill, 3 in Lawrenceville, 4 in Oakland, 5 in East Liberty, 7 on the South Side, and so on.

In those days, cops didn't carry two-way radios. They kept in touch by telephoning the station every hour or so from call boxes situated along their beats. Patrol cars were equipped with one-way radios that meant that radio messages could be received in the car but not transmitted. To acknowledge a transmission from the radio dispatcher, one of the patrol car officers had to telephone the station from a call box.

Since law enforcement is an around-the-clock operation, the workday is divided into three, eight-hour shifts, or "turns" as Pittsburgh cops called them. In the old days, every station house had a sergeant on duty during each turn. These sergeants exercised absolute authority over the cops on the beat, and they seldom left the station except to check on a patrolman suspected of sleeping or drinking on the job. Offending patrol officers were assigned so-called "penalty beats" for thirty days. These beats were located in the remote sections of the city and involved long walks between call boxes.

Officers on patrol shook doors, reported in on callboxes, and handled disturbances such as barroom fights, and domestic flare-ups. Downtown, cops wearing white gloves directed traffic while officers on paddy wagon duty hauled drunks, crazy people, tramps, and prostitutes to jail. The ambulance crew picked up the sick, the old, and the injured, and carried corpses, often ripe, down endless flights of hillside stairways. Beat cops, besides maintaining order, rendered a variety of unofficial social services. A distraught wife could speak to a patrolman about her drunken husband, and the officer might walk into the bar and yank the domestic slacker onto the street for a lecture and a warning.

In the 1930s, Pittsburgh police officers were paid in cash. In many police households there was a difference between what the officer earned and the amount he turned over to his wife. In other words, a lot of cops skimmed a little off the top for themselves. One police officer's wife, after her husband suffered a heart attack, went to the station to pick up his pay. When she counted it out, she thought he had been given him a raise. A cop they called "Bullet" because he was quick to use his gun, hid a fifty-dollar bill in the barrel of his revolver. When confronted by a rabid dog, he shot his gun, and his stash.

The prohibition era featured a wave of violent crime in New York and Chicago. In Pittsburgh three bootleggers from Stowe Township, the Volpe brothers, were gunned-down on the Hill in a St. Valentine's Day style massacre. The Volves were murdered on the corner of Chatam and Wylie Streets by rival bootleggers from New York City.

Pittsburgh in the 1930s had it share of whorehouses, called "sporting houses," and a few of them were palatial. The most spectacular sporting house was located on the North Side where Three Rivers Stadium once sat. The police called this cluster of cathouses the "blackberry patch." The madams paid local politicians and ranking police officers for protection. One whorehouse proprietor even built a special men's room for cops on the beat. Detectives used prostitutes as confidential informants, and every so often a vice cop would arrange an illegal, whorehouse abortion for the daughter of a judge or prominent politician.

Gamblers rolled dice in pool halls, bars, after-hour clubs, and casinos. Ordinary citizens played the daily number for a nickel or a dime--a racket said to have originated in Pittsburgh by Gus Greenlee, Bill Synder, and a guy named Woggie Harris. The gambling bosses paid for police protection, but every so often the cops would raid a joint to remind the racketeers what they were paying for.

Policing in the 1930s was nothing like it is today. Cops were all male, mostly Irish, undereducated, and undertrained. There were no hiring standards, and corruption was institutionalized. Because there was almost no public accountability, police brutality was simply part of the job. While the official pay was extremely low, cops made up the difference through petty graft. If a police officer could handle offenders and kept his political fences mended, he had a job for life. For most people, the depression era was a terrible time, but for cops, it was, in many ways, the best of times.

Zero Tolerance Policing

It seems that more and more police officers are authoritarian types who see everything as either black or white. When it comes to enforcing the law there is no gray. If a cop sees a person breaking the letter of a minor law, or is engaged in behavior he simply doesn't like, that person could be on his way to jail in handcuffs. Policing in this country is becoming more heavy-handed, more zero-tolerant. The police are not only over-enforcing the law (the so-called broken window theory), they are manufacturing crime out of noncriminal behavior. This could be called the criminalization of America.

One form of zero-tolerant, heavy-handed policing involved the criminalization of school kid misbehavior such as arresting grade school children for schoolyard fights (assault); carving their initials in their desks (vandalism); truancy; drawing pictures depicting violence; general classroom misbehavior (disorderly conduct), possessing an aspirin tablet; and carrying something as dangerous as a pocket knife. Any kid caught playing with matches could be labeled a potential pathological fire setter and sent off for psychological help.

Otherwise law-abiding adults have to deal with speed traps; sobriety checkpoints; jaywalking tickets; rolling through stop sign busts; and thousands of regulatory infractions such as holding a yard sale without a permit. If you park your car in the wrong place, or let the meter expire, in addition to paying a fine, you may have to ransom your vehicle out of an impound lot.

If, in the war against real criminals, police need the cooperation of law obeying citizens, zero-tolerance policing is not a good way to get it. Too many officers seem unable or unwilling to distinguish between a burglar and someone trespassing across someone's yard to find his dog. Because militarized law enforcement is replacing community based policing, cops have become isolated from the public they are paid to serve. They do not see themselves as public servants but as crime-fighting warriors. Officers with this mindset see everyone as a potential enemy combatant. In this way of thinking, it's not good guys versus criminals, but cops versus everyone else.

What a Way to Go

William Martinez, an Atlanta police officer who lived in Lawrenceville, Georgia with his wife Sugeidy and their 7 and 9-year-old sons, wasn't feeling well. While only 31, Martinez had a history of high blood pressure, and had been told by doctors he was at risk for clogged arteries. After experiencing shortness of breath and chest pains that radiated into his arms, Martinez, on March 5, 2009, made an appointment with Dr. Sreenivasulu Gangasani at the Cardiovascular Group in Lawrenceville. The physician examined Martinez, and scheduled a stress test for March 13.

At three in the morning of March 12, 2009, the day before his stress test, Martinez and a male friend were in an Atlanta airport motel having a threesome with a woman. When, in the throes of this activity, Martinez rolled off the bed and became unresponsive, one of his sex partners called 911.

EMT responders failed to revive Martinez at the motel. A short time later he was pronounced dead at a nearby hospital. The officer had died of atheroschlerotic coronary artery disease (hardening of the arteries).

A few months after Mr. Martinez died from sexual exertion at the Atlanta motel, his widow sued Dr. Gangasani and the Cardiovascular Group for malpractice. According to the plaintiff, the heart doctor had failed to warn Martinez that strenuous physical activity might kill him.

The defendant's attorney, Gary Lovell, Jr., argued that Mr. Martinez, a man who knew he had a bad heart, and had a history of ignoring doctors' orders, was solely responsible for his own death. Instead of administering his own stress test in the motel room, Mr. Martinez should have waited for the treadmill version at the cardiovascular facility. While walking on a treadmill at the medical center might not be as exciting as 3-way sex, it's less stressful, and a lot safer. If Mr. Martinez was smart enough to be an Atlanta police officer, he should have known this. (With his bad ticker, I'm surprised he was in law enforcement. He must have had a desk job.)

The Martinez malpractice case went to trial on May 21, 2012. Eight days later, the Gwinnett County jury awarded the widow $3 million. The damages would have been $5 million had the jury not found Mr. Martinez 40 percent liable for his own demise. Apportioning personal responsibility in this case involves an interesting calculation that begs the question: how can you do that? Dr. Gangasani didn't cause Mr. Martinez's heart condition, nor did he give the patient permission to have a middle-of-the-night sex orgy. Dr. Gangasani is a heart specialist, not a life coach. Had officer Martinez twisted his spine that night, would some hapless chiropractor have ended up in court?

Cops Versus Cameras

In Illinois you can be arrested for videotaping an on-duty police officer. Citizen's using their cellphones to record police abuse have been arrested, handcuffed and hauled off to jail. Under Illinois law one cannot audiotape a phone conversation without the consent of the other party. The police use this law to justify arresting people who have videotaped them in public.

In 2007, Simon Glik videotaped a Boston police officer using excessive force. The police arrested Glik for this activity. The video-taper fought the case and won. He then sued the Boston Police Department for violating is First Amendment right to record police activity. He won that case as well.

In California, it's legal to videotape a police officer if the video taker is in a public place and has a right to be there. Police in the state fought against this law and lost.

In Philadelphia the police have arrested many videotaping citizens. The arresting officers have confiscated and destroyed the offending cellphones. Public outrage over this over-enforcement led the police commissioner, in October 2011, to issue a departmental order declaring it legal for citizens in the city to videotape police officers doing their jobs. Rank and file police officers were not pleased with this decision.

Speed Traps

One of the worst speed traps in America was on U.S. Route 19 as it passes north and south through Summersville, West Virginia. At this popular interstate shortcut to and from Florida, the speed limit dropped from 65 to 50 MPH at a place where traffic cops laid in wait with radar guns. Police in Summersville were writing between 10,000 and 18,000 speeding tickets a year, generating millions in revenue for the town of 3,250.

Local businessman Charles McCue objected to the speed trap on the grounds it scared away business. He banned police officers from using his shopping center parking lot as a place to clock passing motorists. When that didn't solve the problem, he put up a giant billboard along Route 19 warning drivers of the upcoming speed trap. Although the police were not amused, Charles McCue became a hero to thousands of motorists who managed to get through this town without paying a fine.

In central Florida, police officers routinely pulled over and fined motorists who flashed their headlights to warn oncoming drivers of an upcoming speed trap. In justifying these tickets, the cops cited a Florida statute that prohibits the flashing of lights except as a means of indicating a turn or to indicate when a vehicle is stopped on the road. Motorists stopped for trying to save their fellow citizens the cost of speeding tickets were fined around a hundred dollars. They were charged with "Improper Flashing of High-Beams." Traffic cops considered this motorist-to-motorist form of communication "obnoxious and disrespectful" and equated it to obstruction of justice. These officers saw no difference between warning someone of a drug bust and telling a fellow motorist to slow down to avoid a speeding ticket.

One of the fined "high-beam" flashers filed a class-action lawsuit against the state of Florida on behalf of 2,400 people who had been ticketed for this activity between 2005 and 2010. A few days after the filing of the suit, the head of the Florida Highway Patrol ordered officers to stop ticketing the light flashers until the case is resolved in the courts.

Help Not Wanted

On September 8, 2011, Alan Ehrlich encountered a traffic-light outage at a major intersection in South Pasadena, California. To bring some order to the traffic chaos, Ehrlich took matters into his own hands. He put on a bright orange shirt and began directing traffic. Within ten minutes he had traffic flowing smoothly again. When a police officer arrived at the scene, instead of thanking Ehrlich and taking over the job, he wrote him a ticket and drove off. Once again traffic became snarled at this intersection. Officers do not appreciate citizens who think they can do police work.

Expired Plates: Big Deal

In Washington, D. C., the police are authorized to arrest drivers if their license plates are more than thirty days out of date. These offenders, under D. C. law, can be fined up to $1,000 and jailed up to thirty days.

In October 2011, a naval officer was pulled over in D. C. for having an expired Florida plate. The Navy man carried a Maryland driver's license, but lived in D. C. (He kept his legal residence in Florida for voting and income tax purposes.) Because he was in the military, the officer didn't change his driver's license every time he moved from one state to another. (Military personnel are exempt from having to acquire a new driver's license every time they move.) The naval officer tried to explain all of this to the police officer. He promised to go home and immediately renew his Florida tags online.

The D. C. cop ordered the officer out of his car. When a second policeman arrived at the scene, they handcuffed the motorist and hauled him off to jail where they fingerprinted him and took his mug shot. The police released the officer three hours later. While he was incarcerated, his wife, who had sent him out for some fast food, had no idea what had happened to him. The judge who dismissed the case told the Navy man that in two years he could request to have his arrest record sealed.

Accused but Still On Duty

Let's say two women, in separate cases, accused a police officer of sexual misconduct. Should that cop, while these allegations were being investigated, remain on duty, or be placed on administrative leave? According to Ocean City (Maryland) Police Chief Bernadette Di Pino, a member of the executive committee of the International Association of Chiefs of Police (IACP), there were no national guidelines or policies dealing with this question. In Maryland, an uncharged officer could be taken off the street if the allegations seemed credible. In most jurisdictions, however, accused police officers stayed on the job until they were charged with a crime.

Adam Skweres, after graduating from Pittsburgh Allderdice High School, joined the U.S. Army Reserves and served a tour of duty in Iraq. In 2005, after taking a few college courses, the 29-year-old applied for a job with the Pittsburgh Police Department. As part of the hiring process, city psychologist Dr. Irvin P. R. Guyett, in determining if Skweres was psychologically fit for police duty, reviewed the results of the candidate's background investigation. Based on polygraph test results, what neighbors and others said about the applicant, his financial history, and the psychologist's interview of the candidate, Dr. Guyett concluded that Skweres was "not psychologically fit for police work." (Dr. Guyett has been evaluating police candidates for 20 years.)

Unwilling to take no for an answer, Skweres appealed Dr. Guyett's findings, and the rejection of his application, to the civil service commission. In 2006, the city appointed another psychologist, Dr. Alexander Levy, to re-evaluate the candidate. Dr. Levy, after presumably looking at the same data available to Dr. Guyett, found Skweres "psychologically suited for police work." Based on this second expert opinion, the city allowed Skweres to join the next available police academy class. Upon graduation from the police academy, the new officer was assigned to the Zone 3 station on Pittsburgh's south side.

In June 2008, a woman filed a sexual misconduct complaint against Officer Skweres. After this woman had testified as a victim in one of his cases, Skweres, as he escorted her out of the courtroom, asked to speak to her privately. Skweres said he knew that this woman and her husband were dealing with the county office of Children, Youth and Families (CYF). If she agreed to give him oral sex, Skweres would write the CYF a positive letter on their behalf. If she refused, he would write the agency a negative letter. He allegedly said that he just needed 30 minutes of her time. The woman refused, and filed a complaint with the Pittsburgh Police Department.

Two weeks later, Officer Skweres told a woman who had been in a minor traffic accident that he was writing her up, but the ticket would disappear if she gave him oral sex. According to this woman's complaint, Skweres looked at his sidearm and told her that if she told anyone about his proposal, he'd make sure she never spoke to anyone again.

Although presented with two credible citizen complaints of coercion and sexual misconduct against one of its officers, supervisors at the Pittsburgh Police Department, because they didn't have sufficient cause, did not remove Officer Skweres from active duty. Pursuant to regulations enforced by the local Fraternal Order of the Police, this officer, until charged with a crime, would stay on the job.

In December 2011, Officer Skweres entered a home in the Belthoover section of the city where the girlfriend of a man he had recently arrested lived. After asking her how much she loved the arrestee, Skweres allegedly offered to help the boyfriend if she stripped and performed oral sex on him. In making the proposal, which was more of a demand, he unclipped his holster to intimidate her. This woman filed a complaint with the Pittsburgh Police Department. Officer Skweres remained on duty.

Officer Skweres, on February 11, 2012, showed up at the home of a girlfriend of another man he had arrested. Indicating that he knew he was being watched and didn't want to be recorded, Skweres communicated with the woman by writing messages on a notepad. He instructed her not to talk, and told her to lift her skirt to show she wasn't wearing a wire. (He was not being watched.) When Skweres did speak, he did so in the kitchen where he had water running in the sink to cover his voice.

After offering to help this woman's incarcerated boyfriend, Skweres allegedly forced the victim to give him oral sex. He cleaned himself off with a towel, put it into his pocket, and left the house. This victim reported the crime to the FBI.

Five days later, at 5:15 P.M., officers with the Pittsburgh Police Department arrested Officer Skweres at his home. Charged with official oppression, indecent assault, rape, and criminal coercion, Skweres was placed into the Allegheny County Jail where, for his protection, he was isolated from the other inmates. A judge set his bond at $300,000. The department suspended Skweres without pay.

On February 21, 2012, detectives searching Officer Adam Skweres's house and SUV found marijuana and crack cocaine. His lawyer told reporters that his client would be pleading not guilty to the sexual misconduct and criminal coercion charges.

In defending the police department's decision not to remove Officer Skweres from active duty after the 2008 complaints, Mayor Luke Ravenstahl told a reporter with the *Pittsburgh Post-Gazette* that it wasn't until the fourth alleged victim filed her complaint with the FBI that the department had the "hard evidence" they needed to make the arrest, and take this officer off the street. The head of the police union told the same reporter that officers can't be taken off duty simply because a civilian makes a complaint. "If we remove someone every time an accusation was thrown at an officer, we wouldn't have any officers on the street who are hardworking and aggressive." (Really? Are there that many citizen complaints?)

In March 2013, officer Skweres pleaded guilty to sexual assault and intimidation. The judge sentenced him to three years in prison.

Samuel Walker, a professor emeritus at the University of Nebraska, a nationally known author and scholar on the subject of policing, said the following to a reporter with the *Pittsburgh Tribune-Review*: "Common sense would say if you have suspicions about this person's conduct, you take him off the street, period. If there were two complaints back in 2008, that raises the significance of it even further. There should have been something done."

Protect People From Cops, Not Cops From People

Lawmakers in Kansas were considering a bill that would make it much harder for citizens to report instances of police abuse, while simultaneously putting internal affairs investigations at even greater risk of succumbing to police corruption. House Bill No. 2698 required citizens to swear an affidavit before submitting a complaint against an officer. If any part of the complaint turned out to be erroneous, the citizen would be prosecuted for filing a false complaint.

It got worse. The bill also established that police officers accused of abuse could not be questioned until after they read and reviewed all aspects of the complaint. Ironically, this was exactly the opposite of how police interrogate citizens. Suspects are never given the opportunity to review the entire case against them before being questioned.

The bill would also mandate that all investigations are final. If one police agency found a cop to be innocent, no other agency would be allowed to review the case--even if the latter agency was a higher authority such as the state police.

Robby Soave, The Daily Caller, March 18, 2014

Policing the Police

Police departments cannot police themselves anymore than federal politicians can resist using insider information to make killings in the stock market. Politicians get rich and police officers get away with corruption and misbehavior. Departmental internal affairs units put in place to unearth and investigate police corruption, wrongdoing and misconduct, are, for the most part, window-dressing.

In New York City, recent cases of police corruption were not uncovered by the department's Internal Affairs Bureau but exposed by outside agencies such as the FBI and the Queens District Attorney's Office. The Mayor's Commission to Combat Police Corruption, a tiny group responsible for monitoring the Internal Affairs Bureau, has no subpoena power and must rely on the department's good will. The watchdog group is therefore toothless.

Recently, outside agencies uncovered, within the NYPD, cases of evidence planting (drugs), gun smuggling, and a false arrest to cover the crime of a cop's cousin. In the recent NYPD ticket-fixing scandal, a scheme uncovered by the Internal Affairs Bureau, internal affairs investigators initially did not want to pursue the case, directing detectives to focus more narrowly on the drug case (involving an officer) that uncovered the racket. Also, one of the IA officers on the case has been indicted for leaking information to the subjects of the inquiry.

Law enforcement agencies that investigate their own police involved shooting cases almost always justify the use of deadly force. Every year, in numerous cases, after officers have been cleared in-house, outside agencies draw contrary conclusions. Because cops do not trust outsiders, have secrets, and by nature are paranoid, they resist outside independent monitoring.

They Still Fix Tickets?

Following a long-running internal affairs and grand jury investigation in The Bronx New York, sixteen New York City police officers were indicted on October 20 for ticket fixing and various counts of corruption. Two of the defendants were officials in the Patrolman's Benevolent Association, the city's largest police union. Also facing charges were two sergeants and a lieutenant. The lieutenant, who had worked on the case when assigned to internal affairs, was indicted for leaking wiretap information to the ticket-fixing defendants. Police Commissioner Raymond W. Kelly reminded the media that the scandal represented a tiny fraction of the 35,000-member department.

According to the District Attorney's Office, more than 800 traffic summonses were fixed during the three-year investigation. When the investigative dust settled, more than 400 police officers faced criminal charges or disciplinary action. The investigation began in December 2008 with an anonymous tip that an officer had been protecting a drug dealer. In the suspect's wiretapped conversations, internal affairs investigators learned about the ticket-fixing racket.

It's surprising that, given computers and modern technology, it's still possible for a cop to fix a traffic ticket. Mayor Bloomberg, when asked about rumors of the scandal, said it was almost impossible in New York City to fix a ticket. Apparently the mayor was wrong.

The Hoboken SWAT Scandal

It all started in November 2007 when dozens of photographs surfaced in the New Jersey media showing members of the Hoboken Police Department's SWAT team partying with Hooter waitresses in Tuscaloosa, Alabama. Some of the shots were mildly racy, and others featured the Hooter girls handling various SWAT weapons, and clowning around with the officers. The photographs had been taken in the fall of 2006 when the officers, during one of several trips to Kenner, Louisiana, on Hurricane Katrina humanitarian missions, stopped over in Tuscaloosa. Exactly how hurricane victims in Louisiana needed a New Jersey SWAT team was never explained.

One of the more disturbing photographs featured the commander of the SWAT squad, Lieutenant Angelo Andriani, wearing a napkin with eyeholes cut out meant to look like a Ku Klux Klan hood. A month before the photographs were published, five Hispanic Hoboken police officers filed a lawsuit against Andriani accusing him of creating a racist and hostile work environment. In November 2007, public safety director Bill Bergin permanently disbanded the SWAT team.

The *Jersey Journal*, in February 2008, acquired videotape showing Lieutenant Andriani's gun being passed around at a party in New Orleans hosted by a Louisiana developer and his wife. When the weapon came back around to Andriani, he slipped the magazine out of the gun and distributed the bullets to partygoers. Chief of Police Carmen La Bruno can be seen laughing as the Lieutenant's gun is being passed around.

The New York Times, in March 2008, ran a story based on an internal police report leaked to the media. According to Hoboken Police Department's internal affairs investigators, SWAT team members had each been contributing $20 a month to an equipment and gear fund controlled by Lieutenant Andriani, and that Andriani had diverted and misused the money. The report also included allegations that Andriani had forced off-duty police officers to work at his home in Verona, New Jersey. Regarding the Hoboken paramilitary unit, the author of the internal affairs report had written that the "SWAT team had provided virtually no meaningful service to the city." A few days after the article appeared, the public safety director placed Lieutenant Andriani on paid administrative leave. Nine other members of the former SWAT squad, while kept on regular duty, received a variety of "behavior unbecoming" citations.

Hoboken police chief Carmen La Bruno, after 37 years on the job, retired on July 1, 2008 with a $525,000 cash payout, and a $148,000 pension for life. (This did not include benefits.) A year later, the public safety director placed Andriani on an $11,000 per month, two-year suspension, essentially a paid vacation mandated by his employment contract. The lieutenant, insisting that he had done nothing wrong, accused his accusers of being politically motivated.

In January 2010, Angelo Andriani was back in the news after reportedly creating a disturbance at Tampa International Airport by allegedly flashing his badge and berating airline employees for allowing a flight crew to move ahead of him in a screening line.

In May 2011, the city of Hoboken settled the lawsuit against Andriani by the five Hispanic police officers. The $2 million in damages would be split evenly among the defendants.

Before the $2 million dollar settlement, and after Andriani's two-year suspension, he was fired. He challenged the termination, and in October 2010, an administrative law judge ruled that Andriani should have been suspended without pay for three months instead of fired. In March 2012, the civil service commission amended the ruling to a six-month suspension.

Sexy in Tucson

In August 2012, internal affairs investigators with the Tucson Arizona Police Department learned that between May and August 2011, Lieutenant Diana Lopez, via her personal cellphone, had sent sexually explicit videos of herself to a subordinate officer on the force. The subordinate showed the videos to several other Tucson Police Officers who kept the whole thing quiet for about a year.

The Tucson Chief of Police, in February 2013, on grounds that Lieutenant Lopez had violated departmental regulations and standards of conduct, demoted her to patrol sergeant. Assistant Chief Kathleen Robinson, in her departmental report, wrote: "Lopez used extremely poor judgment in sending these images undermining her credibility as a commander. Her actions have negatively affected not only her reputation, but the reputation and mission of the Tucson Police Department."

Officer Lopez's attorney, Michael Piccarreta, announced that his client was considering filing a civil lawsuit against the city and the department for wrongful demotion. Lopez would also, according to the attorney, appeal her demotion to the state Civil Service Commission.

Attorney Piccarreta, in speaking to a local reporter about the case said, "The case raises constitutional issues when there is lawful off-duty behavior, and a wrongdoer [the subordinate officer] violates your trust and privacy rights without your permission or consent by making it public."

In the summer of 2013, the state Civil Service Commission upheld Lopez's demotion.

In May 2014, Superior Court Judge Charles Harrington reversed the department's demotion of Lopez. The judge rationalized his decision on the fact the police department did not have an explicit policy warning officers against making and showing sexually explicit materials. (In order to foresee and list all the stupid things a police officer might do, the department's manual of professional conduct would have to be massive.)

In addressing attorney Piccarreta's points, I'm not sure how the police department violated officer Lopez's constitutional rights by demoting her for sending sex videos to a lower ranking member of the force. On the violation of privacy issue, cellphone images carry no expectancy of privacy. In fact, one can expect that sexually oriented videos sent by cellphone will eventually go public.

While attorney Piccarreta's strongest argument might have been the off-duty activity aspect, police officers, in reality, are never off-duty. If you punch an off-duty cop you will be arrested on the spot.

Judge Harrington, in interfering with the internal administrative workings of a police department, lowered the bar regarding what is considered professional police conduct. The fact this officer wasn't fired for embarrassing the profession reveals how unprofessional law enforcement has become. Public employees have become immune from being fired. Citizens have lost control of a government that serves itself rather than the public.

The Lost Prisoner

One could say that 2012 was not a good year for federal law enforcement. The ATF has been embarrassed by the Fast and Furious debacle; an ICE agent shot his supervisor, then was shot and killed by another agent; an ICE officer was convicted of embezzling a huge sum of government money; TSA screeners were accused of taking bribes from drug smugglers; and Secret Service agents were caught partying with prostitutes in Columbia. Just when one would think it couldn't get worse, the Drug Enforcement Agency (DEA) pulled one of the most bone-headed blunders in the history of the federal government's war on drugs.

On Saturday, April 21, 23-year-old University of California at San Diego engineering student Daniel Chong was smoking pot in a house in University City with eight of his friends. That day, DEA agents raided the place as a suspected Ecstasy pill distribution center. The agents recovered 18,000 Ecstasy pills, several guns, ammunition, and other drugs, and took Chong and the other eight suspects into custody.

After the 9 arrestees were fingerprinted, photographed, and questioned at the DEA office in Kearny Mesa, agents released one suspect, took seven to a detention facility, and placed the handcuffed Daniel Chong into a holding cell in the DEA office complex. Although being swept up in a federal drug raid was bad enough, Daniel Chong's ordeal had just begun.

Because Chong was placed into a windowless 5 by 10 foot room with no sink or toilet, he didn't expect to be there very long. But as the hours dragged on, and no one came to release him, or take him elsewhere, Chong began to worry. To call attention to his isolation, he screamed for help and frantically kicked at the door. Hungry, in need of a bathroom, scared, and in a state of panic, Chong began to lose control of his body, and his emotions.

A day or so into his confinement, Chong found a plastic bag containing white powder a previous detainee had hidden inside a folded blanket. Chong ingested the powdery stuff that turned out to be methamphetamine. (You can be cavity-searched at the airport, but apparently not in a DEA office.) The abandoned office prisoner drank his own urine, and by his third day in captivity, began hallucinating. In an effort to kill himself Chong used his teeth to break out the glass in his eyewear, then swallowed the shards. As DEA personnel went about their business just yards from him, Chong, locked into his private hell, completely lost his mind.

On Saturday, April 25, someone in the DEA office discovered Mr. Chong. They had simply forgotten about him. (I'm not sure why the people Chong had been arrested with didn't alert someone, or make inquires with the DEA. It's really hard to believe that someone can go missing inside a law enforcement facility.) When the bureaucrat discovered the incoherent, waste-covered, raving mad drug detainee, he weighed 15 pounds less than when they had placed him into the room. Had he been there much longer, the DEA people would have discovered a corpse.

Rushed to Sharp Memorial Hospital, Chong, suffering from a failing kidney, a perforated lung, severe dehydration, and numerous other ailments, was placed into an intensive care unit. He left the hospital four days later.

On May 2, Chong's attorney announced his plan to file a $20 million lawsuit against the DEA. On August 1, 2013, the DEA settled the Chong case out of court for $4.1 million.

Camera Shy Cops

A Massachusetts man who recorded video footage of a profane cop was arrested and jailed, even though state law explicitly permits the recording of public officials. The video evidence was taken into police custody and mysteriously destroyed....

George Thompson, a 51-year-old citizen of Fall River, Massachusetts, was sitting on his front porch when he noticed Officer Thomas Barboza sitting in a patrol car and having a heated, profane cell phone conversation. Thompson began recording the officer's call using his own cell phone. When Barboza noticed, he approached Thompson.

Thompson freely admitted that he was filming Barboza--something that state law explicitly permits. But Barboza arrested him anyway....

Police Chief Daniel Racine launched an investigation to determine who deleted the footage, and said the guilty party will face justice. "If a Fall River police officer erased that video, he's fired and I would suspect the district attorney would take out charges," Racine said in a statement.

Thompson had complained about Barboza before. The officer regularly parked on the street and conducted profane phone conversations within earshot of other people--something Thompson didn't like. "Why don't you cool it with the language there?" said Thompson. "

"Why don't you shut the [expletive] up and mind your own [expletive] business?" the cop replied.

Robby Soave, The Daily Caller, March 11, 2014

Extortion

The Baltimore Police Department, with 3,100 sworn officers, is the nation's eighth largest city police force. Like all big city police departments, Baltimore has its history of scandals, embarrassments, and graft.

In Baltimore, and other cities, the towing and repair of vehicles involved in traffic accidents is a big business. To regulate this enterprise, the city of Baltimore authorizes a number of so-called medallion tow trucks. Police officers at accident sites are not allowed to call in unauthorized towing vehicles. So in Baltimore, if you are in the towing and auto repair business, and don't have the approval of the city, if you are not a medallion company, you're frozen out of a lucrative source of income.

In 2009, an employee of a medallion firm who was also vice president of the association representing medallion tow operators filed a complaint with the Baltimore Police Department. According to the complainant, certain Baltimore police officers were calling unauthorized tow trucks to the scenes of accidents. Hernan Mejia and his brother Edwin operated these trucks. The brothers owned the Majestic Body Shop. In return for this unauthorized business, the brothers were paying kickbacks to traffic site cops who summoned their trucks. (Once the damaged vehicles were brought to the shop, employees allegedly banged them up some more to rip off insurance companies. Who knows how common a practice this is around the country.) Authorities with the Baltimore Police Department turned the Majestic Body Shop complaint over to the FBI.

After a series of phone taps, FBI agents identified 17 city officers who had received Majestic Body Shop bribes totaling $1 million. In 2011, the kickback suspects were lured to the Baltimore police academy where they were confronted by police brass and FBI agents. Stripped of their guns and badges, the suspects were arrested, and hauled off to jail. By May 2012, 14 Baltimore officers had pleaded guilty to federal charges of extortion. Ten cops have been convicted and sentenced to prison. The owners of the Majestic Body Shop have also pleaded guilty to the federal racketeering offenses.

In the 1960s and 70s, America's big city police departments were thoroughly corrupt. Graft was the rule, not the exception. Cops on the take justified this behavior by telling each other they risked their lives every day for low pay and lousy benefits. Today, big city police officers are well paid, and enjoy benefits envied by most private sector employees. And with lower violent crime rates, and more militarized policing, the job is a lot safer.

Police corruption, then and now, is simply a matter of dishonesty and greed. Some cops simply can't resist the opportunity to pocket easy money. If we paid these crooks more, and let them retire at 40 instead of 55, they would still be corrupt. The good news in the Majestic Body Shop case was that the Baltimore Police Department, instead of covering up this graft, called in the FBI.

Take the Settlement

At 1:45 in the morning of September 26, 2007, a couple returning to their home in Millcreek, a suburban community adjacent to Erie, Pennsylvania, encountered a pair of burglars. When one of the intruders pointed a gun at the homeowners, the husband tried to disarm him. In the scuffle, the burglar fired a shot into the ceiling then ran out of the house with his partner. The burglars sped from the scene in a white minivan.

Shortly after the incident in Millcreek, a pair of Erie police officers looking for the fleeing burglars, happened upon Maria Jordan parked in front of her house in a white minivan. Maria was about to pick up her husband, the night shift manager at a local Taco Bell.

The Erie police officers ordered Maria out of the van at gunpoint, told her to hit the ground, then handcuffed the prone woman behind her back. Once they placed Maria into the patrol car (calling her an "idiot," and a "retard"), the officers entered the Jordon house where, at gunpoint, they hauled Maria's 10-year-old stepson out of bed, and arrested her father. After handcuffing the boy and Jose Arenas, the officers searched the dwelling. They found nothing incriminating in the house, removed the handcuffs from the people they had arrested then took leave of the citizens they had traumatized. (Other than being annoyed they had wasted time on these people I doubt these officers gave these arrests and intrusions a second thought.)

In 2009, Maria, her father, and her stepson sued the Erie Police Department in federal court for violating their civil rights. According to the complaint, the false arrests and police manhandling had caused the family "worry, humiliation, and anxiety." In defense of their actions, the officers said they should not be sued for doing their jobs. (Since when is making false arrests part of the job?) The city offered to settle the case out of court for $10,000. The plaintiffs turned down the offer, and the suit moved forward.

On May 11, 2012, following a 4-day trial in the Erie federal court house, the jury found that the two Erie police officers had in fact violated the plaintiffs' civil rights. While finding that the defendants had acted improperly, these jurors didn't believe the false arrests and house search harmed the family in any way. As a result, in what could be interpreted as an insult, the jury awarded Maria Jordan $2, and her stepson and father $1 each.

If the plaintiffs were angered and insulted by the token damages, they didn't let on. In fact, Maria's husband told a local reporter the family was pleased by the verdict because they had sought justice, not money.

On May 26, 2012, the assistant city solicitor, unwilling to leave well enough alone, filed a motion asking the federal judge to order the plaintiffs to pay some of the city's legal costs created by the lawsuit. According to the Erie solicitor, Pennsylvania law "obligated a prevailing plaintiff to pay the defendant's post-offer costs after rejecting an offer more favorable than the judgment." The city wanted the judge to order the Jordons--the wronged parties in the suit--to pay $5,085 of the city's legal expenses.

In March 2013, the judge dismissed the solicitor's case.

The Rise and Decline of a Police Chief

It's not surprising that a crime-ridden city in long decline has a troubled and shrinking police department and a disgraced chief. Between 2000 and 2010, 750,000 middle-class residents of Detroit moved out of the city to the suburbs. Today, there are 700,000 people living in a city that in the 1950s had a population of 2 million.

Because of massive budget cuts, the Detroit Police Department had gotten smaller while the crime problem grew. Police response times, even to major crime scenes, had significantly slowed. In 2012, a man who had committed a murder called the Detroit Police Department and asked to be picked-up. When no one showed, the killer walked to a precinct station where he turned himself in. In Detroit, it was actually hard to get arrested.

When Ralph Godbee joined the Detroit Police Department in 1986, the city had not entered its final stage of decline and decomposition. The 19-year-old high school graduate, after just a few years on patrol, was assigned to the elite Executive Protection Unit. (That's how it works in a lot of police departments. You have to have someone upstairs who likes you.) In 1995, when Godbee was just 26, the chief named him commander of the unit.

Seven years after taking over the Executive Protection Unit, Chief Jerry Oliver appointed Godbee commander of the 1st Precinct. In 2005, Godbee made Assistant Chief of Police, but three years later the chief demoted him. Godbee retired and started a private security agency. Just a year into Godbee's retirement, Chief Warren Evans brought him back into law enforcement by making him the Assistant Chief of Police.

In July 2010, Detroit Mayor Dave Bing promoted Ralph Godbee to interim chief of police after Chief Warren Evans stepped down as a result of a sexual affair with a subordinate police officer. The following month, Godbee, after having taken up with the same female officer, Lieutenant

Monique Patterson, filed for divorce. Notwithstanding Godbee's relationship with officer Patterson, Mayor Bing promoted him to the permanent position of chief of police.

The beginning of the end of Chief Godbee's law enforcement career came on October 2, 2012 when Mayor Dave Bing suspended him for thirty days. The assistant chief, Chester Logan, took over his duties. Like his predecessor, Warren Evans, Godbee's problem involved an affair with a subordinate departmental employee. In Godbee's case, the woman was an internal affairs officer named Angelica Robinson.

Angelica Robinson's attorney said this to a reporter with the *Detroit Free Press*: "She was trying to cut it off (I hope he didn't mean this literally) and he [Godbee] didn't like that. And apparently she was very depressed, and the concern was whether or not she was going to take her own life. Godbee got wind of that. I guess he tried to intervene." Other Detroit media outlets reported that Angelic Robinson became upset after discovering that Godbee attended the International Association of Chiefs of Police conference in San Diego with another woman.

Ralph Godbee, on October 4, 2012, announced his intention to step down as Detroit's chief of police. Retired Detroit police officer David Malhalab, a longtime Godbee critic, in speaking to a reporter with *The Detroit News*, said: "Godbee was a stink bomb waiting to go off. I've said from day one that because of his past actions, he shouldn't have been the face of the DPD. But Mayor Bing went ahead and appointed him anyway. Now he's reaping the consequences of his bad choices."

In police work, the higher up you go, the less power you have. The cop on the street, armed with the discretionary power of arrest, exercises the real muscle. Street officers also come under the protection of civil service and police unions. A street cop can abuse his authority and behave in a manner unbecoming a police officer and still keep his job. The chief, on the other hand, is wedged between the rank-and-file officers and the major. He is vulnerable to politics and bad publicity. Chief Godbee knew this, but risked his career and good name anyway. He may or may not have turned out to be an effective police administrator, but we will never know because of his reckless choices.

Ralph Godbee's career, like the sad city of Detroit, started in glory and ended in ignominy.

Police Pensions Are Sacred

Round Lake Beach is a northern Illinois town of 26,000 on the Wisconsin state line. In 2009, Round Lake Beach police officer Leroy Kuffel, a 29-year veteran of the force, got into serious trouble. In February and March of that year, the 52-year-old cop had sex with his son's ex-girlfriend. She was sixteen. Following his arrest, Kuffel admitted giving the teen gifts, and taking her out to dinner, but he denied have sexual relations with the minor.

In January 2010, following a three-day trial in a Lake County court, the jury found Kuffel guilty of aggravated criminal sexual abuse. (Had the girl been a few months younger, he could have been charged with statutory rape.) The state prosecutor recommended that Kuffel be sentenced up to seven years in prison. The defendant's attorney pushed for a probated sentence. In speaking to the court, Kuffel apologized for what he called "bad decisions."

Sentencing-wise, Judge Daniel Shanes took the middle ground. He sentenced Kuffel to sixty days in the county jail followed by thirty months of nighttime incarceration at a halfway house where the inmate would be allowed to work during the day. The judge also ordered the ex-police officer to seek sex offender treatment. (Since Kuffel considered his relationship with the minor nothing more than a "bad decision," I'm not sure what good that would do.) At the conclusion of the thirty-month work-release program, Kuffel would be under probation for three years.

On September 20, 2009, while working during the day and spending nights in custody, Kuffel began receiving his $48,000 a year police pension. Following a legal challenge by Round Lake Beach municipal authorities, the town's mayor, in January 2013, announced that Illinois state law required that Kuffel, notwithstanding his sex offense conviction, be paid his police pension.

Under Illinois law, no pension benefits will be paid to a retired police officer convicted of any felony relating to, arising from, or in connection with his law enforcement job. Since Officer Kuffel had been off-duty when he had sex with the minor, the above law did not apply to him. (One could argue that Kuffel's victim might have been intimidated or impressed by the fact he was a cop.) Had Kuffel, while off-duty, murdered his wife, under Illinois law, he'd still be eligible for his pension benefits.

By 2013, Kuffel's increased monthly pension benefits were based on an annual payout of $53,709. When the ex-cop turns 65, he'll rake in $70,079 a year. If Kuffel lives to the year 2026, he will have received, in total pension benefits (not including health care), more than $1 million. Not bad for a registered sex offender.

Manipulation of Crime Data

Crime statistics have always been unreliable indicators of crime rates because a substantial percentage of felonies are not reported to the police. This is particularly true in cases of spousal abuse, child molestation, and rape. Even criminal homicides are underreported. And of the crimes that do get reported to the authorities, not all of them become part of the official record. Crime statistics do, however, reveal trends, and for that reason they are important.

Politicians and police administrators hate high crime rates because they are afraid the public will blame increases in crime on them. Because mayors and police chiefs take credit for low crime rates, they are held responsible when the numbers go the other direction. This is a problem that politicians and police administrators have brought upon themselves. If politicians were honest (an odd thought), they would inform the public that the police have little control over the rate of crime in their jurisdictions. That's because law enforcement is not about preventing crime as much as reacting to it after the fact. The level of crime in a particular city has little bearing on the quality of that municipality's law enforcement services. While there are many ways to judge a police department, the local crime rate is not one of them.

Because politicians and police administrators have misled the public into believing they are protecting us from criminals, they try to control crime statistics the only way they can, by manipulating the reporting process. This kind of bureaucratic skullduggery has been going on forever.

In New York City during police commissioner Raymond Kelly's tenure, he has taken credit for the city's declining crime rates. But in 2011, New York's crime statistics revealed a slight increase over 2010, and so far in 2012, this trend has continued. So it's not surprising that when researchers with *The New York Times* reviewed 100 police reports submitted over the past four months, they found that the police were falsely downgrading felony offenses to misdemeanor crimes (that are not counted) to manipulate crime stats and mislead the public.

In an article published on September 16, 2012, *The New York Times* published examples of several cases that feature obvious felonies reported by the police as misdemeanors. (A friend of mine who worked 20 years as a patrolman in New York City, has said the first thing you learn as a NYC cop is that *nothing* is on the level.) What follows are examples of how the NYC police control crime statistics by mischaracterizing felonies as misdemeanors.

In 2010 a 17-year-old gunman fired several shots into a group of young men on the street in the Bronx. Nearby two teenage girls were hit by the shooter's stray bullets. Because their injuries were minor, police officers, in their reports, didn't mention that two girls had been shot in the shooting spree.

In Brooklyn, the police characterized an attempted rape as "forcible touching," a misdemeanor. When a prosecutor in the Brooklyn district attorney's office learned of the facts of this case, he charged the subject with attempted rape, a felony. After a man in a domestic violence case choked his wife to the point of unconsciousness, the police wrote up the crime as a misdemeanor offense even though the attack clearly fell within the legal guidelines of a felonious assault.

Numerous New York City police officers admitted to the reporters reviewing these cases that they are encouraged, whenever possible, to downgrade felonies to misdemeanors in order to keep the city's crime rates low, and the politicians happy. Sometimes police supervisors will actually show up at a crime scene to make sure officers are following this program of crime statistics manipulation. Sergeants and lieutenants have been known to modify police reports to achieve this result.

Crime rates fluctuate but what never changes is the fact that in law enforcement, nothing is on the level. My ex-cop friend was right.

The Federal Agent Tried for Murder

On November 4, 2011, 27-year-old Christopher Deedy, a U. S. State Department Special Agent from Arlington, Virginia, was in Hawaii as a member of the State Department's Diplomatic Security unit. Deedy and the other federal agents were in Honolulu to protect Hilary Clinton and President Obama at the upcoming Asian Pacific Economic Conference scheduled for November 7 through November 13.

On the night of November 4, Deedy and a couple of his friends were barhopping in the city. At 2:30 the following morning, the off-duty agent, dressed in shorts, flip-flops, and a dress shirt that covered the 9 mm Glock on his hip, were having coffee at a McDonalds. Kollin K. Elderts, a 23-year-old Hawaiian man who had been arrested in 2008 for disorderly conduct, and in 2010 for driving under the influence, was giving a white McDonalds customer he didn't know a hard time. Elderts called this man, Michael Perrine, a "haole," a Hawaiian word used by the locals as a racial slur against Caucasians of European decent. Perrine, who had been minding his own business, said he didn't understand why Elderts was singling him out for this verbal abuse. "I'm a local, too," he said. "I live here."

Agent Deedy walked over to Elderts' table and asked him why he was picking on Mr. Perrine. Mr. Elderts did not appreciate the interference. Angry words escalated into a physical confrontation. What happened next depended upon who was telling the story. The only facts not in dispute were these: Agent Deedy and the Hawaiian man fought. At some point in the confrontation the agent pulled his gun and fired three shots. One of the bullets hit and killed Mr. Elderts.

The Honolulu coroner retrieved a single bullet from Elderts' body. Detectives dug two slugs out of a McDonald's wall. The autopsy report revealed that Elderts had consumed marijuana and cocaine that night. He also had a blood-alcohol level of 0.12, a percentage well above the state's legal limit for driving.

Not long after Mr. Elderts' death, a state grand jury in Honolulu indicted agent Deedy for second-degree murder. Assistant deputy prosecutor Janice Futa did not include, as a backup charge, the lesser offense of manslaughter. That meant it was second-degree murder or nothing. Deedy posted his $250,000 bail and returned to Virginia to await his trial.

The Elderts shooting death exacerbated racial tensions in Hawaii. The local media compared the killing of an unarmed man of color by a white man with the Treyvon Martin case that was unfolding at the time in Florida. According to narrative created by reporters and correspondents in the print and television media, a wannabe cop had killed Martin. A federal law enforcement officer shot Elders to death. For Christopher Deedy, the timing was not helpful.

The Deedy murder trial got underway in a Honolulu courtroom in mid-July 2013. Circuit Court Judge Karen Ahn oversaw the selection of seven men and five women for the jury. Six of the jurors were of Hawaiian decent. The other members of the jury were Caucasian. Prosecutor Futa, with the defendant's wife and parents looking on, delivered her opening statement to the jurors. In the prosecution's version of the facts, Deedy's first shot missed Mr. Elderts. The second shot, fired before the two men fell to the floor and fought, killed the victim. The defendant's third shot missed.

In describing her theory of the case, Prosecutor Futa said, "The defendant...draws from his right hip area the gun. Kollin [Elderts] turns around and sees him and the defendant is within three feet of Kollin Elderts and fires his gun. He misses Kollin. Now having been shot at by the defendant, Elderts lunges toward him reaching for the gun. They grapple in front of the [McDonalds] counter and [another] shot rang out. After the shots, Kollin falls on top of the defendant onto the floor. The third bullet was fired. After the third bullet was fired, the gun jams."

In her opening statement, the prosecutor portrayed Deedy as an inexperienced agent (George Zimmerman was a wannabe cop) who had consumed alcohol against State Department policy while carrying a firearm. Deedy had "stuck his nose" in the situation at McDonalds "that was not his business." Futa informed the jurors that the McDonald surveillance videotape of the incident was "frustratingly fuzzy."

The defense version of the shooting differed from the prosecution's theory. According to the defense, it was the third shot, fired when the two men were fighting on the floor that killed Mr. Elderts.

Defense attorney Brook Hart, in addressing the jury, said, "The evidence will show that the defendant used a number of measured steps to try to sway Mr. Edlerts...from his violent assault. Referring to Elderts' racial slur, Hart said, "These are now fighting words. This is a threat of violence. This is what Deedy is trained to respond to, although he wasn't here to respond to the laws of harassment or bullying. He's a federal agent and his job is to serve the community." (His job was to protect Clinton and Obama.)

According to the defense attorney, when the defendant showed Elderts his State Department badge and credentials, Elderts said, "What, you gonna shoot me? You got a gun? Shoot me. I'm gonna gut you."

Attorney Hart informed the jurors that the State Department authorizes its agents to carry weapons when they are off-duty. She said that her client, on the night of the shooting, was not intoxicated.

As in the Treyvon Martin case where George Zimmerman's head injuries proved valuable to the defense, Attorney Hart pointed out that Agent Deedy's nose had been broken and his face badly pummeled. In summing up, the defense attorney said, "Special Agent Deedy was compelled to discharge his gun resulting in the death of Elderts. Agent Deedy acted responsibly and in self-defense."

On August 6, 2013, following 18 days of prosecution testimony, attorney Hart put the defendant on the stand. Agent Deedy testified that on the night in question, Mr. Elderts had drawn his attention with his "hysterical laughing" and taunting of Mr. Perrine. When Elderts ignored the McDonalds cashier's request to leave Mr. Perrine alone, Deedy walked over to Elderts' table and asked him what was going on. Sounding a bit self-important, the witness said, "From my trained perspective I believed it was appropriate for me to intervene, to further assess the situation because this was not a mutual interaction going on."

When Agent Deedy interceded on Mr. Perrine's behalf, Elderts called *him* a "haole." According to the witness, "I needed to portray a stronger command presence." This is when he identified himself as a federal law enforcement officer. (The surveillance footage shows Deedy displaying his badge and credentials.) Not impressed, Mr. Elderts continued to taunt the agent. When Elderts slid out from behind his table, the agent knew there would be trouble. In describing this moment to the jury, Deedy said, "I think I was in actual shock. This was very quick, there was a lot going through my head. My brain was going in a thousand directions."

Attorney Hart asked her witness, "Why didn't you just leave the restaurant?"

Deedy answered that because he was a trained law enforcement office, he couldn't responsibly back down. "I injected myself into the situation because I sensed the propensity for violence. For me at this point to run would be irresponsible."

Agent Deedy described to the jury how he had tried to disable Elderts with a kick to his left shin. He missed and hit the meaty part of his opponent's thigh. At that moment the agent knew he was in for a fight. When his attacker tried to grab his gun, the defendant said he had no choice but to utilize deadly force in defense of his life.

The defense rested after three days of the defendant's testimony. The case went to the jury on August 15, 2013. On Monday, August 19, the jury foreman advised Judge Ahn that the panel could not reach a unanimous verdict. Judge Ahn declared a mistrial. The defendant was free to accompany his wife and his parents back to Virginia.

Following the verdict, prosecutor Futa told reporters that she was "very disappointed." She said she didn't regret not giving the jury the manslaughter option. Defense attorney Hart, in speaking to the press, said that her client "pleaded not guilty and is not guilty. The jury," she said, "did not find him guilty."

Because the jury did not acquit agent Deedy, he was not home free. Not only that, Kollin Elderts' family sued him for wrongful death.

Deedy's retrial was scheduled for August 2014.

The Sucker Punch

On Sunday, September 30, 2012, Philadelphia police were out in force to provide security for the city's annual Puerto Rican Day Parade. A group of officers, just off the parade route, were putting a man into handcuffs when someone nearby threw water or something like silly string on them. Lieutenant Jonathan Josey, in reaction to this harmless act, grabbed 39-year-old Aida Guzmani whose back was to him. Josey turned her around, punched her in the face, and then hit her in the back of the head. The mother of three collapsed to the ground with blood running out of her nose and mouth. Other officers slapped handcuffs on the stunned Guzmani, lifted her to her feet, and hauled the bloodied woman off. She was charged with disorderly conduct.

A witness to officer Josey's assault recorded the event on her cellphone, then posted he 94-second video on YouTube where, over the next couple of weeks, it was seen by millions of viewers. It's hard to imagine anyone who has watched the video concluding the officer Josey's actions were justified. The Philadelphia Highway Patrol Lieutenant's attack on Guzmani seemed unprovoked, and entirely uncalled for.

The day after officer Josey decked Aida Guzmani, he was placed on "restricted status," meaning assigned to a desk until internal affairs officers completed their investigation. But as more and more online viewers witnessed this egregious overreaction, the Philadelphia's police commissioner and the mayor came under increasing pressure to act more aggressively against this officer. A week or so after the incident, the police commissioner suspended Lieutenant Josey "with the intent to dismiss." The department also dropped the disorderly conduct charges against the woman he slugged.

In response to growing public outrage of Lieutenant Josey's gratuitous brutality, Philadelphia Mayor Michael Nutter, in publicly apologizing for this officer's indefensible behavior, used the words "appalled," "sickened," and "ashamed." This apology did not sit well with members of the Philadelphia Police Department. (Cops never apologize, and don't look kindly on people who do it for them.)

So, who is this female-punching, 19-year veteran of the Philadelphia Police Department? In 2006, Josey, pursuant to some puerile contest sponsored by the *Philadelphia Daily News*, nominated himself as the city's sexiest man. In support of his quest for the title, the cop submitted a photograph of himself in a pair of red shorts, a shot that featured his pierced nipple. According to Josey's sexiest man resume, the officer described his most outstanding character traits as charm, and a "magnetic personality." (Really.) This charming and magnetic law enforcement hunk wanted to make it known that he was in search of a "sexy, sexy, sexy" woman.

In 2007, the city settled a lawsuit against officer Josey brought by a man who claimed the officer had inappropriately kicked, punched, and threw him against a wall. In March 2010, Josey shot and killed a man who was robbing a 7-Eleven store. The department cleared him of this shooting, and no criminal charges were filed. During his career, Officer Josey has been the subject of 13 complaints for both verbal and physical abuse. (Who knows, in the Philadelphia Police Department, this may be a *good* record.)

Shortly after the police commissioner announced Lieutenant Josey's dismissal, John McNesby, the president of the local chapter of the Fraternal Order of Police (FOP), announced that the organization would be holding a fund-raiser for their fellow union member. The proceeds would go for Josey's living expenses.

FOP President McNesby, said this to a reporter: "It was inappropriate for the city to apologize to this woman [he couldn't bring himself to utter her name] and drop the charges until the [internal affairs] investigation was completed." (Perhaps the FOP could have held-off the fund-raiser until the facts were in.)

Police officers have become increasingly thin-skinned and militant. They don't like outside interference and criticism by people they think have no idea what it's like to enforce the law. Police officers also hate civilian cellphone cameras. Had the Josey-Guzmani incident not been caught on video, one of Philadelphia's most sexy men would still be on the force.

Bad Cops are Hard to Fire

Police officers accused of serious misconduct including physical abuse are able to keep their jobs and benefits--sometimes only temporarily, but always longer than they should have--thanks to legislation written and lobbied for by well-funded police unions. That legislation is called the "Law Enforcement Bill of Rights," and its sole purpose is to shield cops from the laws they are paid to enforce...

When a citizen files a complaint against an officer, departmental leadership reviews the complaint and decides whether to investigate. If the department decides to pursue the complaint, it must inform the officer and his union. That's where the special treatment begins, but it doesn't end there.

Unlike a member of the pubic, the officer gets a "cooling off" period before he has to respond to any questions. Unlike a member of the public, the officer under investigation is privy to the names of his complainants and their testimony against him before he is ever interrogated. Unlike a member of the public, the officer under investigation is to be interrogated "at a reasonable hour," with a union member present. Unlike a member of the pubic, officers can only be questioned by one person during his interrogation. Unlike a member of the public, the officer can be interrogated for only "reasonable periods," which "shall be timed to allow for such personal necessities and rest periods as are reasonably necessary." Unlike a member of the pubic, the officer under investigation cannot be "threatened with disciplinary action" at any point during his interrogation. If he is threatened with punishment, whatever he says following the threat cannot be used against him.

What happens after the interrogation again varies from state to state. But under nearly every law enforcement bill of rights, the following additional privileges are granted to officers: Their departments cannot publicly acknowledge that the officer is under investigation; if the officer is cleared of wrongdoing or the charges are dropped, the department may not publicly acknowledge that the investigation ever took place, or reveal the nature of the complaint. The officer cannot be questioned or investigated by "non-government agents," which *means no civilian review boards*. If the officer is suspended as a result of the investigation, he must continue to receive full pay and benefits until his case is resolved. In most states, the charging department must subsidize the accused officer's legal defense....

Mike Riggs, reason.com, October 19, 2002

The Cannibal Cop Case

Gilberto Valle, a 6-year New York City police officer assigned to the 26th Precinct in Harlem, lived with his wife and child in the Forest Hills section of Queens. On an online dating site called OKCupid, the 28-year-old police officer described himself as a "very calm individual" with "an endless supply of hilarious short stories from work that can't be made up. I'll try anything," he wrote, "and I'm not picky at all." According to his online profile, Valle attended Archbishop Molloy High School in Queens, and the University of Maryland, College Park.

Based upon an investigation conducted by the FBI over several months, officer Valle was not calm, or funny. And what he was allegedly willing to try was more than a little disturbing.

According to court documents related to the federal investigation, Gilberto Valle, and several unnamed co-conspirators, had used the Internet to acquire potential female victims to kidnap, rape, torture, murder, cook, and eat. In his search for targets, Valle had used federal and state law enforcement crime-victim databases. The suspect corresponded with his like-minded co-conspirators through online dating forums. In addition to his use of the Internet to identify and lure women, Valle conducted physical surveillances of their homes and workplaces. He used this data to draw up and revise detailed kidnap/murder "operation plans."

In February 2012, Valle, in an online communication with a co-conspirator who had expressed a desire to rape a woman, offered to kidnap a victim for this man for a fee of $5,000. Pursuant to his offer, Valle wrote: "It is going to be hard to contain myself when I knock her out, but I am aspiring to be a professional kidnapper, and that's business." Later in the conversation, Valle wrote: "She will be alive. I think I would rather not get involve in the rape. You paid for her. She is all yours, and I don't want to be tempted the next time I abduct a girl."

On July 2, 2012, Valle and a co-conspirator conducted a disturbing online conversation in which Valle wrote: "I was thinking of tying her body onto some kind of apparatus. Cook her over a low heat, keep her alive as long as possible."

"How big is your oven," asked the co-conspirator.

"Big enough to fit one of these girls if I folded their legs...the abduction will have to be flawless...I know all of them."

In another Internet exchange regarding a specific woman, Valle wrote: "I can just show up at her home unannounced, it will not alert her, and I can knock her out, wait until dark and kidnap her right out of her home."

Valle's co-conspirator offered Valle some kidnap advice: "You really would be better to grab a stranger. The first thing the police force will do is check out [the victim's] friends [as suspects]."

"Her family is out of state."

"I have anesthetic gasses," replied the helpful co-conspirator.

"I can make chloroform here," Valle replied.

In another July 2012 conversation, one of Gilberto Valle's co-sickies asked, "How was your meal?"

"I am meeting her on Sunday," came the reply.

FBI agents, on Wednesday, October 24, 2012, arrested Gilberto Valle at his home on charges of conspiracy to commit kidnapping, and intentionally and knowingly accessing a computer without authorization. (The bureau moved in because Valle had recently had lunch with a woman the FBI feared he would abduct.) From Valle's home in Queens, agents seized a computer that contained personal data--names, addresses, physical descriptions, and photographs--of 100 women. Valle's computer also held hundreds of incriminating emails and instant message chats between the suspect and his co-conspirators.

In March 2013, a jury in Manhattan found the defendant guilty as charged. In July 2014, however, a federal judge, except for the count of illegally using the federal databank to target victims, overturned Valle's conviction. Instead of facing up to life in prison, Valle walked out of the jail having already served enough time to satisfy the punishment for the lesser offense.

This judge did not believe Valle's writings and behavior rose above the mere expression of his bizarre fantasies. In America people are punished for criminal actions, not thoughts. Because fantasies of murder often preclude the real thing, this was a close and controversial decision.

A Dishonest Detective

In December 1989, 25-year-old Debra Milke lived in Phoenix, Arizona with her 4-year-old son Christopher and her boyfriend, James Styers. A few days before Christmas, Milke asked Styers to drive Christopher to the mall so he could visit Santa Claus. Instead of taking the boy to the shopping mall, Styers and a friend drove him to a secluded ravine outside of town where Styers shot the boy three times in the head. Detectives and prosecutors believed that Debra Milke had arranged the murder of her son for a $50,000 insurance payout.

Styers confessed to the homicide. At his trial, neither he nor his friend implicated Milke in a murder-for-hire plot. No other witnesses came forward with incriminating evidence against the mother.

Evidence that Debra Milke had plotted the murder came from a Phoenix detective named Armando Saldate. According to the detective, Milke told him that her role in the conspiracy to murder her son had been "a bad judgment call." Milke's interrogation had not been recorded, and Saldate was the only officer involved in her questioning. Milke proclaimed her innocence from the beginning, and denied making any kind of confession to Detective Saldate or anyone else. A local prosecutor, relying on the detective's credibility, charged Milke with murder, conspiracy to commit murder, child abuse, and kidnapping.

Detective Saldate, at Milke's October 1990 murder trial, testified that the mother had confessed to him regarding her role in her son's homicide. The defendant took the stand, professed her innocence, and called the detective a liar. As is often the case, jurors believed the police officer over the defendant. The jury returned a guilty verdict. A few months later the judge sentenced Debra Milke to death.

As it turned out, Detective Armando Saldate was in fact a notorious liar. Prior to his interrogation of Milke he had been caught committing perjury in four criminal trials. His credibility was so comprised judges refused to accept into evidence confessions this detective had acquired.

On March 14, 2013, Chief Federal Judge Alex Kozinski of the 9th Circuit Court of Appeals overturned Milke's conviction and vacated her sentence. The 49-year-old had been on Arizona's death row for 22 years. Based on Detective Saldate's history of perjury and other incidents of police misconduct, Judge Kozinski ruled that Milke's confession should have been excluded from her trial. Without this dishonest detective's tainted testimony the prosecution had no case. In rationalizing his decision, Judge Kozinski wrote: "No civilized system of justice should have to depend on such flimsy evidence, quite possibly tainted by dishonest or overzealousness, to decide whether to take someone's life or liberty."

On September 6, 2013, Judge Rosa Mroz of the Maricopa County Superior Court set the 49-year-old prisoner free on $250,000 bond. County prosecutors planned to bring Milke back to trial by the end of September. On the strength of the disgraced detective's testimony, the prosecution will be seeking the death penalty.

In January 2014 Judge Mroz denied a motion to dismiss the murder charges against Milke. As of August 2014, the case has not come up for trial.

Hiring Unfit Officers

The Los Angeles County Sheriff's Department hired dozens of officers even though background investigators found they had committed serious misconduct on or off duty...The department made the hires in 2010 after taking over patrols of parks and government buildings from a little-known LA County police force. Officers from that agency were given first shot at new jobs with the Sheriff's Department. Investigators gave them lie detector tests and delved into their employment records and personal lives...

Ultimately, about 280 county officers were given jobs, including applicants who had accidentally fired their weapons, had sex at work, and solicited prostitutes...

For nearly 100 hires, background investigators discovered evidence of dishonesty, such as making untrue statements or falsifying police records. At least 15 were caught cheating on the department's own polygraph exams.

Twenty-nine of those given jobs had previously been fired or presumed to resign from other law enforcement agencies over concerns about misconduct or workplace performance problems. Nearly 200 had been rejected from other agencies because of past misdeeds, failed entrance exams or other issues. [So much for hiring the best and the brightest in law enforcement. The fact that governmental agencies conduct job candidate background investigations means nothing if they hire unfit people anyway.]

Robert Faturechi and Ben Poston, *The Los Angeles Times*, December 1, 2013

To Protect and Speed

Nobody likes being pulled over for speeding. It just ruins your day. And I hate it when the cop asks, "Do you know how fast your were going?" If you answer "no," you sound like an idiot. If you answer "yes," you're essentially confessing. Anyway, it really doesn't matter if you knew you were speeding or not because it's an offense that doesn't require criminal intent.

The police want us to believe their jobs are extremely dangerous and difficult, you know, war is hell and all of that. But let's face it, besides the good salaries and outstanding benefits (early retirement and generous pensions), there are a lot of advantages to being a cop. Perhaps the greatest joy in law enforcement is that cops don't ticket each other for speeding. They have a license to speed--off-duty, and in their personal vehicles. If I were still teaching, and a criminal justice student asked me why he or she should become a cop, I'd say, "Free speeding!"

In the state of Florida, police officers, as a group, are the most egregious speeders. A three-month investigation by *Sun Sentinel* journalists found that 800 cops from a dozen law enforcement agencies were driving 90 to 130 mph to and from work in their take-home patrol cars. Since 99 percent of these officers were not stopped for speeding, how did the newspaper come up with this information? They figured out how fast cops were driving by analyzing state highway toll records. They simply measured the time it took officers to travel from one toll plaza to the next. Moreover, according to the *Sun Sentinel* investigation, speeding Florida officers, since 2004, have caused 320 vehicular accidents resulting in 19 deaths. Only one of these officers went to jail, and that was for 60 days.

In the fall of 2011, while commuting from his home in Coconut Creek to his job as an officer with the Miami Police Department, a Florida State police officer clocked Fausto Lopez going 120 mph. The stopped 36-year-old cop offered a familiar explanation for speeding: he was late for work.

According to an analysis of toll records by journalists with the *Sun Sentinel,* officer Lopez was the king of law enforcement speeders. During the year before his October 11, 2011 traffic stop, Lopez averaged 90 mph over a period of 237 days of driving. But Lopez's Coral Springs attorney has assured the public that his client is a good driver. "Certainly," said the lawyer, "he at no time has put any member of the public in any type of danger." Fair enough, but can you see yourself defending a speeding ticket by telling the officer that you are a good driver? Good luck with that. To a police officer, or a judge, driving 90 mph makes you a *bad* driver. But we are mere civilians, and civilians get speeding tickets handed out by people who are worse drivers than we are.

Cops Are Hard To Convict

A jury acquitted two former Fullerton, California police officers on trial in the beating death on July 5, 2011 of Kelly Thomas, a mentally ill and homeless man. "I'm just horrified. They got away with murdering my son," Cathy Thomas, the victim's mother, told reporters…The victim's father, Ron Thomas, said that everyone now needs to be afraid. "This is carte blanche to police officers to do whatever they want."…Surveillance camera footage showed Thomas being beaten, clubbed and stunned with a Taser by police. The video sparked a nationwide outcry.

Chuck Conder, CNN, January 13, 2014

Skeletons in the Closet

John Marra's modest entry into law enforcement took place on July 11, 2005 when the 29-year-old became a part-time reserve police officer in Uniontown, Ohio, a Stark County village of 2,800 in the northeastern part of the state. A little over two years after being on the job, Marra entered into an intimate relationship with a 16-year-old girl. He sent her inappropriate text messages, and while on duty, kissed and fondled her at her place of employment, a Subway restaurant.

In May 2008, the 32-year-old police officer pleaded no contest to dereliction of duty, a second-degree misdemeanor. The Stark County judge sentenced Marra to two years probation and 100 hours of community service. The judge also ordered Marra not to have further contact with the girl or members of her family. As part of the plea deal, Marra agreed to resign from the Uniontown Police Department.

In 2010, shortly after his period of probation expired, Marra joined the police department in Brady Lake, Ohio, a small Portage County town in the Akron metropolitan area. In December 2013, following the retirement of the chief of police, the major named Marra acting head of the agency. On March 17, 2014, the village council approved Marra's appointment as the chief of the Brady Lake Police Department.

Marra's promotion, given his history with the Uniontown Police Department raised eyebrows. In April 2014, members of the local print and television news media asked Mayor Hal Lehman if someone, in anticipation of Marra's appointment, had conducted a background investigation. The mayor replied that such an inquiry had been made and said, "We are done with the issue." Another reporter asked the mayor if he would provide the media with a copy of the investigative report. Mayor Lehman said he did not have a copy of that document.

Mayor Lehman, when asked specifically about the new police chief's dereliction of duty conviction five years earlier, had nothing to say other than the matter was settled.

Chief Marra, aware that his 2008 conviction might prove troublesome to the advancement of his law enforcement career, petitioned the court to seal the records of the case. If granted his request, this information would be no longer available to the public.

The Portage County prosecutor's officer opposed the Marra petition. Recognizing that offenses less serious than a first-degree misdemeanor can be removed from public scrutiny, the prosecutor trying to preserve Marra's conviction history argued that this particular case was an exception because of Marra's intimate involvement with a 16-year-old girl. Had Marra not agreed to plead in the case, he would have been convicted of a more serious offense. Moreover, as a public official, the chief of police should be held to a higher standard of conduct than an ordinary citizen. Chief Marra had violated that standard.

On May 1, 2014, following a brief hearing on Marra's petition, Portage County Judge John Poulos approved the sealing of all documents pertaining to the 2008 dereliction of duty conviction in Uniontown, Ohio. Judge Poulos based his decision on the fact the petitioner had been convicted of a second-degree misdemeanor that, under Ohio law, allowed the sealing of these crime records. The judge obviously didn't buy the argument that public officials should be held to a higher standard than the rest of us.

We give our law enforcement officers enormous power over our lives. In return, they owe us honesty, trustworthiness, good character, and sound judgment. Officer John Marra, with regard to the girl, exhibited an alarming lack of good judgment as well as a troubling and perhaps pathological flaw in his character.

The citizens of Brady Lake who pay the chief's salary, and are subject to his power and authority, have a right to know such things as the degree to which Marra had coerced or stalked the girl. It may also be important to know how this case came to light, and how the officer initially reacted to the accusations.

Because public officials should be subjected to a much higher standard, the citizens of this community might want to take a second look at the judge, and the mayor of Brady Lake.

Planted Evidence

California cops planted drugs in a woman's house to frame her after finding nothing in their illegal search of her home...Allison Ross filed a federal lawsuit against the Santa Clara sheriff's department, a crime lab, and twelve officers she claimed participated in a conspiracy to plant drugs in her house and frame her for a crime she did not commit.

Ross was initially charged with being under the influence of methamphetamine, but the case against her was thrown out after the district attorney determined that the police made false statements about Ross's arrest...

Most shocking of all, Ross's lawsuit alleged that police vehicle video footage actually recorded the police discussing their plan to plant drugs inside her house. The incident transpired on New Year's Eve of 2009. Deputies arrested Ross's husband for unspecified reasons while he was at a neighbor's house. They then came to Ross's home, detained her and searched the premises. Ross...said she heard one officer tell another that they had not acquired a warrant. Officers then ransacked the house, but found nothing criminal.

The police video footage caught the officers admitting as much. "The house is clean, there is no meth in the house," said one officer...The officer then discussed taking white powder from the police vehicle and planting it in the house...Police reported that they found two bags of white powder inside the dwelling, although that was proven to be false. Ross also believed the crime lab tampered with evidence....

Robby Soave, The Daily Caller, April 24, 2014

19 BOMBING

The Historic Mass Murder in the Sky

In 1955, Jack Gilbert Graham insured his mother's life for $37,000 and then planted a bomb [in her luggage] on United Airlines Flight 629 that she boarded at Denver, Colorado. The device exploded just ten minutes after takeoff, killing all 44 passengers and crew. Graham, who had nurtured a hatred of his mother ever since she placed him in an orphanage for the first eight years of his life, readily confessed and was sent to the Colorado Penitentiary gas chamber in January 1957.

Brian Lane, *Chronicle of 20th Century Murder*, 1993

Bombs on Planes

In 2013, a TSA undercover inspector with a fake bomb in his pants got through two checkpoints at the Newark-Liberty International Airport in New Jersey. He was actually cleared to board a plane.

Had the bomb been real, it would have been powerful enough to blow a large hole in the aircraft that could have knocked the plane out of the sky.

In a *New York Post* expose, a former TSA officer revealed that many TSA employees don't have high school degrees, and were employed by the TSA because they weren't qualified for decent jobs in the private sector. Some, according to the *Post* article, have criminal records. Many TSA employees hope to use the job as a stepping-stone to a better federal position.

According to the whistleblower, undercover TSA inspectors carrying fake bombs and other weapons regularly got through security while security agents were patting down old ladies and harassing children in wheelchairs.

Bomb Maker Killed by Own Device

Kevin Harris lived by himself in a modest, one-story house in a quiet residential neighborhood in the southern California city of Costa Mesa. The 52-year-old, by covering his home in aluminum foil, attaching copies of his anti-government newsletters to a front yard tree, and videotaping his neighbors, revealed that he was strange, and probably mentally ill. He also established himself as an anti-social loner with his Internet writings that included the statement: "I am the only one who can get into my house. I think it may be dangerous for you to come to my house alone."

In America, we have more than our share of oddballs. Most of these people, usually men, are harmless eccentrics. Some of them, however, are psychotic, paranoid, and dangerous. Ted Kaczynski, the so-called "Unabomber", fell into this category. Unfortunately, there's no sure-fire way to distinguish the Ted Kaczynski types from the common garden-variety conspiracy kooks. When the distinction becomes clear, it's usually too late.

Mr. Harris, in a 17,000-word Internet-published manifesto called, "The Picker: A True Story of Assassination, Terrorism, and High Treason," describes the nefarious and clandestine activities of government agents. The author of this rambling manifesto had obviously convinced himself that secret government operatives are using a weapon called a "picker," a device that deposits germs on a victim's skin on contact. Government agents armed with these secret devices are infecting dissenters with illnesses like cancer and AIDS. According to Harris, government agents also use the deadly tool to cause various enemies of the state to die in freak accidents.

The Costa Mesa conspiracy theorizer, in his manifesto, said: "I have had personal experience with both domestic and foreign operatives using pickers within the U. S. at the request of the U. S. Government. The rationale stated here should give you a reasonable indication that pickers are used in this country, but it is not absolute proof. The diseases of the ex-spouses, which I will describe, provide a proof so strong that some of these attacks will have to stop...."

"Many years ago I met a woman who had just divorced a government agent. She had also just had a radical mastectomy. She was afraid of her ex-husband, afraid for her life. That a woman should have to live (and die) in fear of this 'public servant' struck me as very wrong. Since then I have met a couple of other women who have broken off marriages with government agents. In each case the woman was diagnosed with cancer within a year of breaking up....

"These women didn't get cancer because divorce and mortal fear are stressful. Emotional stress as a factor in carcinogenesis can account for a few percentage points at most. That is too small an influence to be reliably detectable. This is a cancer rate that is thousands of percent too high. Among other things, several attempts on my own life have confirmed to me that these cancers are intentional assaults...."

At six-fifteen in the evening of Sunday, April 14, 2013, several of Kevin Harris' neighbors called 911 to report he was sprawled out on his front lawn. After the ambulance rolled up to the aluminum-wrapped house, Mr. Harris refused treatment. The paramedics drove off, and Mr. Harris disappeared inside his strange looking dwelling.

Ninety minutes following the medical emergency, neighbors called 911 again to report a powerful explosion at the Harris house. Police arrived to find the front entrance to Harris' house shattered from an explosion. The resident of the dwelling lay dead in the doorway. Near his corpse Costa Mesa police officers saw an unexploded pipe bomb.

Dozens of homes in the neighborhood were evacuated as FBI agents, the Orange County Bomb Squad, and a Huntington Beach hazardous materials team searched the Harris dwelling for additional bombs and explosive substances. They found three more pipe bombs on the premises.

Because Kevin Harris was alone in the house when one of his pipe bombs detonated, the authorities have no way of knowing if he had killed himself intentionally, or had accidentally triggered one of his explosive devices. Perhaps he had mistakenly set-off his own booby-trap.

One of Mr. Harris' brothers told a reporter that Kevin was the youngest of five boys. Although all of his siblings were highly educated professionals, Kevin was the smartest one in the family. (His manifesto suggested that Kevin had been well educated as well, possibly in the hard sciences.)

The day after the Costa Mesa house explosion, terrorists detonated two bombs at the Boston Marathon.

U.S. Terrorists on Welfare

Americans who grew up in the 1950s were programed to respect and obey the law, work hard, and raise their children without state interference. They also paid their taxes. Today, I image that most people of this generation remain true to these values. I've been fortunate to live in this country my entire life. I earned a wage for forty years, paid my taxes, have never been to jail, and helped raise a family. I don't like paying taxes which I believe are too high, but I pay them anyway because that's part of the social contract that binds us as a nation. It's also against the law to cheat the government.

Citizens of my generation were taught to play by the rules. You don't drive unless you have a valid driver's license, an updated inspection sticker, and car insurance. I still consider shoplifting and bad check passing as well as illegal drug possession crimes of moral turpitude. Growing up, I don't think I had met anyone who had been in jail. In the past, cops were treated with respect even if they didn't deserve it.

Today, when I go to the doctor's office, if I don't have my social security data and my insurance papers, the doctor won't see me. There are no excuses. When I go to vote, I expect to be asked to produce a driver's license or some other form of identification. That requirement doesn't offend me because it makes sense. You are only allowed to vote once, and you have to be a U. S. citizen.

Years ago, the U. S. government lent me money to go to college. I paid it back. Not repaying the loan didn't cross my mind. In those days, people who didn't pay their bills were considered deadbeats. The vast majority of citizens who were on welfare back then were on the dole temporarily because they were ashamed and embarrassed by having to rely on the government. Welfare was not a way of life. People didn't feel entitled to a free lunch.

In the wake of the Boston Marathon Bombings, the terrorists' mother was on television criticizing the United States government for framing and not protecting her two sons. She and her husband had lived in this country ten years. They left the country but their boys stayed here. While the family lived in Massachusetts they were on state welfare. The boys had free rides in college, and while they were plotting to kill Americans, were living off welfare checks.

Since the bombings, a Massachusetts state legislator was on TV revealing how easy it was in that state to get on welfare. All a resident had to do was ask for the money. Social security numbers were not required. In other words, bureaucrats in Massachusetts had no idea who they are giving taxpayer money to. As it turned out, they were giving it to a pair of terrorists who set off two bombs at the Boston Marathon. This gave new meaning to the phrase state-sponsored terrorism.

America's First Murder by Bomb

The earliest case that I have found of the use of a bomb to commit murder was in 1854, when William Arrison sent one to the head of an asylum where he had been confined.

Thomas M. McDade, *The Annals of Murder*, 1961

The Phony War on Terrorism

On Monday, April 29, 2013, a 16-year-old girl in a high school chemistry class in the central Florida town of Bartow mixed a couple of household products in an eight-ounce plastic bottle. When Kiera Wilmot, a student with good grades and no history of trouble making, shook the mix, a mild explosion blew off the bottle cap. (She probably had placed cough drops or Tylenol pills into a bottle of soda.) The result of the experiment startled the student more than anyone.

No one was hurt, the tiny explosion caused no property damage, and the student had not intended anything malicious. (In my day, when mischievous kids got too old to put tacks on teachers' desk chairs, a few of them dropped cherry bombs into school toilets. Getting caught blowing up a public commode usually resulted in a paddling and a brief expulsion. Unless the student was a known juvenile delinquent, the matter was handled in-house. Police and prosecutors did not get involved.)

The administrators at Bartow High School, following Wilmot's harmless chemistry experiment, called in the authorities. Notwithstanding the student's background, lack of criminal intent, and the absence of physical harm or property damage, a local prosecutor charged the student with possession and discharge of a *weapon* on school property and discharging a *destructive device*. Having been charged with these felonies, school administrators had no choice but to expel the suspected bomber. If convicted of these crimes, Wilmot will have to finish her high school years in an expulsion program.

Kathleen Nolan, author of *Police in the Hallways*, told an education reporter that the Wilmot case "...is an example of the absurdity of zero tolerance and the over-use of police intervention in schools...This young woman, all because of misguided curiosity, now faces expulsion and felony charges which could negatively impact her future opportunities and alter the course of her life."

When looking for the source of such insanity, you usually don't have to look beyond the U. S. Congress. In 1994, Congress passed a law that forced states that received federal education funds to enact legislation that required mandatory one-year expulsions for students who brought firearms to school. As one can be expect, school officials and criminal justice practitioners took this law and went to hell with the joke.

The beauty of a zero-tolerance enforcement policy is that it exempts bureaucrats from having to think. It also protects them from making decisions and taking responsibility for those decisions. It's a policy for people without the guts to lead.

Although Kiera Wilmot didn't bring a firearm or a bomb to school, Bartow High administrators notified law enforcement authorities. Once the knucklehead prosecutor decided to treat the student as a terrorist, the school had to kick her out. With Wilmot expelled from school, the mindless school administrators and the crusading prosecutor can tell themselves that Bartow High is now a safer place.

When comparing the Wilmot story to the tale of government incompetence, inaction, and political correctness that led to the Boston Marathon Bombings, it's hard not to conclude that the people in charge of protecting our country possess weird priorities and have no sense of proportion.

At Home Kids Have no Right to Privacy

In Tempe, Arizona, a cleaning lady, in May 2013, discovered what looked like an improvised explosive device (IED) in an 18-year-old boy's bedroom. She took the suspicious-looking object to the local fire station where it was x-rayed and determined to be a live bomb capable of detonation. Members of a bomb squad disabled the device. While not a big IED, the bomb was powerful enough to destroy property and even kill people.

The cleaning lady, when questioned by detectives, showed them photographs she had taken of other items in Joshua Prater's room that included bomb-making materials. Police officers, after searching Prater's room, took him into custody. He was charged with possession of an explosive device. Bomb making is dangerous business. This kid was lucky he didn't blow up his room and himself.

According to media reports, the bomb-marker's parents told detectives that friends of their son's taught him how to make IEDs. (The old bad-influence defense.) While it is hard to imagine parents who would allow their child to build bombs in his room, it was not clear if these parents knew what their son was up to before the cleaning lady took action.

This story makes you wonder if today's parents know what their children are doing. It also raises the touchy issue of whether or not parents should regularly search their kids' rooms. Invading their child's privacy may make many parents feel guilty. This form of parental control will also create a lot of outrage and angst. Nobody likes to be compared to Hitler.

Recent studies have shown that kids today have extremely high opinions of themselves. (I blame this on Mr. Rogers.) They also feel entitled to things they are unwilling to work for. Parents should remind themselves that children are notorious liars and profoundly ignorant of how things work in life. Kids think they know everything because they know so little.

In a parent's home, a child has no legal right to privacy. In the domestic environment parents are the cops, prosecutors and judges. They have a right to know, and the duty to find out, if their kids have drugs, pornography, guns, or bombs in their rooms. And the only way to be absolutely certain that they do not possess these things involves periodic searches. Children should not be allowed to lock their doors. If they do have locks, parents should have the keys. Kids need to know that privacy is for adults. When they live in their own homes and clean their own rooms mom and dad can be locked out.

Dry Ice Bomb at Disneyland

At four in the afternoon of May 28, 2013, parents who had brought their children to Mickey's Toontown section of Anaheim, California's Disneyland, were startled by a small but loud explosion that tore the lid off a trash can near a kiddy ride called Roger Rabbit's Car Toon Spin. While no one suffered injuries from the blast, officials of the famous theme park evacuated the Toontown area.

At the site of the low-order explosion, detectives found fragments of a plastic water bottle that led them to conclude that a so-called dry ice bomb had been the source of the explosion. A maker of such a device adds chunks of dry ice to a quarter-full bottle of water. Once sealed, the water warms the dry ice that produces carbon dioxide that builds inside the container and eventually ruptures the bottle. These simply made little bombs, if moved, can blow off the handler's fingers. As booby-traps, dry ice bombs function as little anti-personnel devices.

Because dry ice was used at Disneyland to keep refreshments like ice cream and sodas cold, detectives figured there was a good chance the bomber worked for the theme park. As it turned out they were right.

On Wednesday, May 29, 2013, officers with the Anaheim Police Department arrested a 22-year-old man from Long Beach named Christian Barnes. Barnes, a so-called "outdoor vending cast member" peddled soda drinks and bottled water from a mobile cart. Charged with possession of a destructive device in a public place, the Disneyland employee was booked into the Orange County Jail. A magistrate set his bond at $1 million.

It's hard to imagine a rational motive for a crime like this. Some kid dropping a piece of garbage into that trash container could have lost his hand. The fact that Barnes worked at the theme park suggested he didn't have a criminal record.

On Thursday, May 30, Barnes pleaded not guilty to the felony charge that carried a maximum sentence of six years in prison. The judge reduced his bail to $500.000.

According to prosecutors, Barnes placed dry ice into two bottles and locked one inside his vending cart. When a co-worker took over the cart one of the bottles exploded. Barnes then took the second device and placed it into the trashcan.

In November 2013, Barnes pleaded guilty to one misdemeanor count of possession of a destructive device. The judge sentenced him to 36 days in jail, three years of probation, and 100 hours of community service. The judge also ordered the former Disneyland employee to stay away from the park.

Big theme parks have been relatively safe places from crime. Recently, at Disney's Animal Kingdom in Orlando, Florida, a grandmother, after getting off the Dinosaur ride, found a .380-caliber pistol on her seat. She handed the gun over to a park attendant. A few minutes later, a man returned to the site and claimed the weapon. It had fallen out of his pocket during the bumpy ride. Security personnel escorted him out of the park.

The Disney Animal Kingdom incident exposes the reality that millions of people walk through hundreds of turnstiles into parks all over the country without being searched or exposed to metal detectors. There is no way to keep guns and dry ice bombs out of these places. If going to a theme park becomes as inconvenient and intrusive as getting on an airplane, Mickey and his friends will find themselves alone among the Roger Rabbit rides and phony dinosaurs.

Bomb Threats are Not Funny

Earl Dennison Woods, Jr., the 58-year-old half-brother of Tiger Woods, the world famous professional golfer, worked for the Department of Economic Security, a state agency headquartered in Phoenix, Arizona that provides social services for needy children, the elderly, and the disabled.

In an April 2012 interview with a TV correspondent with ESPN, Earl Woods said that Tiger hadn't spoken to any of his half-siblings since their father, Earl Woods, Sr. died in 2006. According to the ESPN report, Earl said, "I'd like to slap Tiger, wake him up. I'd like to say, 'Don't come knocking on the door when you need a bone-marrow transplant.' " Earl Woods said he was upset with Tiger for not helping his half-brother Kevin who suffered from multiple sclerosis and was confined to a wheelchair. "Maybe when you see the world like he does you don't see what other people are going through. But seriously, you've got problems with you knee? That's nothing compared to what Kevin is going through. Nothing."

As reported in *Golf Digest*, Tiger Wood was close to Earl Jr.'s daughter Cheyenne who turned pro last year on the European Ladies' Golf Tour.

At eight-thirty in the morning of Friday, December 13, 2013, someone called the front desk at the Department of Economic Security headquarters and reported that a bomb had been planted in the building that would blow the place up. As one hundred DES employees filed out of the structure, police officers and firefighters searched the premises for a bomb. Before the emergency responders completed their sweep, Earl Woods informed a supervisor that he was the one who had called in the bomb threat. He said he did it as a joke, a prank.

After repeating his admission to detectives, the officers placed Mr. Woods under arrest. Shortly thereafter the apologetic bomb hoaxer was booked into the Maricopa County Jail on the misdemeanor charge of using an "electronic device (a telephone) to terrify, intimidate, threaten or harass others."

According to Earl Woods, he was surprised that people took his joke so seriously. Really? On the theory that Mr. Woods is not a stupid man who must have foreseen the consequences of his "joke," one has to suspect that behind his bomb threat lies a motive that is pathological or associated someway with drugs or alcohol. Otherwise, this crime makes no sense whatsoever.

As of August 2014, the Woods case remained unresolved.

The Car Bomb

Edgar J. Steele, in 2010, resided with his wife Cyndi on a horse ranch near the town of Sagle in northern Idaho. Ten years earlier the lawyer, who billed himself as the "attorney for the damned," represented Aryan Nations founder and leader Richard Butler in a civil suit the white supremacist lost.

In January 2010, the 65-year-old Steele solicited a man (who was not identified in the media) to kill his 50-year-old wife and her mother by staging a fatal car accident. According to the murder-for-hire plan, Steele would pay the hit man $25,000. If his wife's life insurance paid off, Steele would kick in an additional $100,000 for the double-hit.

On June 9, 2010, the man Steele had solicited for murder got cold feet and called the FBI. The next time the would-be hit man and the mastermind met, the snitch secretly recorded Steele soliciting the murders of his wife and his mother-in-law.

Two days after the FBI learned of the murder-for-hire plot, agents arrested Steele at his home. While the attorney sat in the Kootenai County Jail, FBI agents questioned his wife.

According to Cyndi, between 2000 and 2010, her husband had sent 14,000 emails to hundreds of Ukrainian women. In 2000 she caught him soliciting relationships with Ukrainian women on Match.com. To lay a trap, Cyndi posted a phony profile of her own on Match.com under a fake name. Steele replied to her posting. Not long after Cyndi filed for divorce, she and her husband reconciled.

A few days following Steele's arrest Cyndi decided to get an oil change before driving to Oregon to visit her mother. When an employee of the oil change service looked under her SUV he discovered a pipe bomb. ATF agents responded to the scene and disarmed the device.

Shortly after the car bomb discovery, FBI agents arrested Larry Fairfax, a former Steele handyman. Fairfax confessed to planting the car bomb on May 20, 2010. According to Fairfax, Edgar Steele had given him $10,000 in silver coins as a down payment for the murder of Cyndi and her mother. As part of the murder-for-hire plan, Fairfax was supposed plant a pipe bomb under Steele's car, a device the lawyer could detonate to make himself look like an intended victim.

On June 15, 2010 a grand jury sitting in Coeur d' Arlene indicted Edgar Steele on two counts of using interstate commerce facilities in the commission of murder-for-hire. The grand jury also indicted him with tampering with a federal witness. (From his jail cell, Steele had called his wife to tell her that the voice on the audio taped containing conversations with the first hit man was not his voice.)

The government provided Steele, who claimed he was broke, with a federal public defender. However, by February 2011, Steele's supporters had raised $120,000 for his defense. That allowed the accused to hire Robert T. McAllister, a prominent trial attorney from Denver.

In 2011 Larry Fairfax pleaded guilty to federal charges related to the car bomb. In return for his promise to testify against Steele at his upcoming trial, the judge sentenced Fairfax to 27 months in prison. (The first hit man was never charged with a crime.)

The Edgar Steele murder-for-hire trial got underway on April 30, 2011 in Coeur d' Arlene, Idaho before federal judge B. Lynn Winmill. Assistant United States Attorney Traci Jo Whelan, to establish the defendant's motive in the case, introduced several love letters Steele had written from his jail cell to a Ukrainian woman named Tatyana Loginova.

The prosecutor also introduced the audiotaped murder-for-hire conversations between Steele and the first man solicited by the defendant. Larry Fairfax, the former handyman, took the stand and explained why he had planted the pipe bomb under Cyndi Steele's SUV.

Defense attorney Robert McAllister portrayed the government's case against his client as a conspiracy based on fabricated audio- tapes, perjured testimony, and FBI wrongdoing. According to McAllister, the federal government objected to Steele's political beliefs and wanted to silence him.

Cyndi Steele, one of the defendant's alleged murder-for-hire targets, took the stand to testify on her husband's behalf. (This is not the only murder-for-hire case where a targeted wife stood by her man.)

On May 5, 2011 the jury of eleven women and one man found Edgar Steele guilty on all counts. Seven months after this verdict Judge Winmill sentenced the murder-for-hire mastermind to fifty years in prison. Steele would serve his time at the federal corrections facility at Victorville, California.

Steele, with the help of a new lawyer, appealed his conviction to the 9th Circuit Court of Appeals in Denver. According to the appellant, Judge Winmill had improperly instructed the jury. Steele also claimed that he had been denied adequate counsel. This assertion was based on the fact that one month after the guilty verdict, attorney McAllister was disbarred for stealing money in an unrelated case. As a result, he had been so distracted by his own legal problems that he hadn't performed well for Steele.

In October 2013 the three-judge panel sitting on the 9th Circuit Court of Appeals affirmed Steel's murder-for-hire conviction. The decision, however, did not deter Steele's ardent supporters who believed the FBI framed him because of his anti-government politics. They continue to fight for his freedom.

A Deadly Package Bomb

Bewildered residents in rural Tennessee were grappling with fear and confusion as they tried to understand why someone would send a bomb to a neighbor. Retired lawyer John Setzer, 74, died Monday February 10, 2014 after "an unknown package exploded," the Tennessee Bureau of Investigation reported. Neighbors said the Lebanon, Tennessee blast was so powerful it blew out windows and damaged several rooms of the Setzer's house…On the Setzers' quiet, rural street, neighbors were terrified about whether a bomb might arrive in their mailboxes. [On February 13, 2014, a local prosecutor charged the victims' son-in-law, 49-year-old Richard Parker, with two counts of premeditated murder.]

Holly Yan and Dave Alsup, CNN February 12, 2014

The Tucson Car Bomb Murder Case

In 1986, Gary Lee Triano, a well-known real estate developer in Tucson, Arizona, made the mistake of his life when he married 28-year-old Pamela Phillips. Triano had made millions investing in bingo halls and slot-machine parlors in Arizona and California. He made his fortune before Congress authorized Native Americans to open full-blown gambling casinos.

In 1992, when Triano was broke, his wife of six years divorced him. The couple had two children together. Shortly after the breakup Phillips took out a $2 million insurance policy on her ex-husband's life. She moved to

Aspen, Colorado where she began working as a real estate agent. It was there she met and began dating a 44-year-old man named Ronald Young.

In 1994, Gary Triano filed for bankruptcy. He was $25 million in debt. He told his girlfriend in July 1996 that someone had been following him.

At 5:30 PM on Friday, November 1, 1996, after playing a round of golf at the Westin La Paloma Country Club with his friend Luis Ruben, Triano climbed behind the wheel of his 1989 Lincoln Town Car. Eight minutes after pulling out of the country club parking lot, the vehicle exploded and burst into flames. The blast killed Triano instantly.

Investigators determined that someone had wired a large black powder pipe bomb to Triano's car. Detectives had no idea who had murdered Triano. They questioned his ex-wife but didn't consider Phillips a suspect in the bombing. Without promising leads, the case quickly went cold.

In November 2005, nine years after the car bombing murder of the ex-millionaire, Tucson detectives caught a break in the form of an anonymous tip. According to the tipster, Pamela Phillips had paid Ronald Young $400,000 to murder her ex-husband. He had been compensated out of the $2 million life insurance payout.

FBI agents in Florida uncovered information connecting Young and Phillips in the Triano murder plot. The evidence included incriminating emails between the hit man and the mastermind, detailed records of their business transactions, meetings, and even recorded telephone calls in which the two discussed the murder plot.

Ronald Young, charged with first-degree murder and conspiracy to commit murder, went into hiding and became a fugitive.

In September 2006, FBI agents raided Phillips' house in Aspen, Colorado. On her computer agents found evidence of her involvement in her ex-husband's murder. However, before she was taken into custody, the murder-for-hire suspect fled the country and took up residence in Austria.

Gary Triano's two children, in November 2007, sued Pamela Phillips and Ronald Young for the wrongful death of their father. (The plaintiffs were awarded $10 million in damages two years later.)

On October 2008, FBI agents, after Ronald Young was featured on the TV show "America's Most Wanted," arrested him in California. The suspected hit man was now 66-years-old. Upon his extradition to Arizona the authorities booked him into the Pima County Jail. The judge set his bond at $5 million. Young pleaded not guilty to the charges of conspiracy to commit murder and first-degree murder.

A jury, in March 2010, found Ronald Young guilty as charged. The judge sentenced him to life in prison without chance of parole.

In December 2010, the authorities in Austria agreed to extradite Phillips to the U.S. on condition she would not, if found guilty, be sentenced to death. Prosecutors in Arizona agreed to this condition and the fugitive was sent home to face trial.

The Pamela Phillips murder-for-hire trial got underway in February 2014 in Tucson, Arizona. Prosecutor Nicol Green portrayed the defendant as a cold-blooded gold digger who hired a former boyfriend to kill Mr. Triano for the life insurance money.

Defense attorney Paul Eckerstrom painted his client as a victim of overzealous law enforcement. As a successful real estate agent in her own right, the lawyer claimed she didn't need Triano's insurance money. Regarding the $400,000 she had paid Ronald Young, Eckerstrom characterized the transaction as payment for Young's help in various business ventures.

In speculating who may have bombed Triano's Lincoln Town Car, attorney Eckerstrom said, "Gary Triano lived on the edge, the financial edge...He borrowed a lot of money from all sorts of people, many people who might be connected to organized crime."

On April 8, 2014, the jury found Pamela Phillips guilty of conspiracy to commit murder. The judge sentenced Phillips to life in prison.

20 STALKING

Anti-Stalking Laws

Most anti-stalking laws around the country discuss threats or threatening behavior. Most anti-stalking laws require, at minimum, that the victim *feel* threatened by the stalker's actions. In these states, the stalker may explicitly threaten the victim, but the law does not require that such a threat take place. As long as the stalker's other actions create a threatening climate for the victim, the law can be applied.

In other states, however, repeated harassment or following must be accompanied by an *explicit threat*. Most states that require a threat also require that it be "credible." In many states that require a credible threat, the defendant must have the "intent and/or apparent ability" to carry out the threat. Someone who clearly could not carry out the threat would not fit this requirement.

Melita Schaum and Karen Parrish, *Stalked*, 1995

The Politician From Hell

If you think all, or even most, politicians are above average spouses and parents, think again. Although they pretend to be better than the rest of us, some of these hypocrites and thieves turn out to be dangerous criminals. Take Steve Nunn, a state legislator from Kentucky who was a lousy husband, a raging hypocrite, *and* a dangerous criminal. His story should remind us that the people we vote into office, regardless of how good they look on the surface might be rotten to the core.

Steven Nunn was 15 when his father, Louie B. Nunn, became Kentucky's 52nd governor in 1967. A Republican, Nunn was re-elected to a second term, but in 1973, lost his bid for a seat in the U. S. Senate. Six years later, he ran for governor again, but lost. His career in elected politics was over.

In 1974, Steve, hoping to follow in his father's footsteps, enrolled in law school, but dropped out. He got married, and over the next five years, had three children. In 1990, at age 38, Nunn ran for the Kentucky state house of representatives, and won.

Steve's father, a hard-driven narcissist and BS artist who enjoyed subjecting his kid to ridicule, refused to be impressed with his son's election to state office. Like his father, Steve was a lousy husband who regularly cheated on his wife. In 1994 she divorced him. (In state politics, being a rotten husband is not a liability because most people have no idea who represents them locally.) Two years later, Steve's mother Beula, after 42 years of marriage to Louie B., sought a restraining order against the abusive ex-governor. Steve confronted his father over this, and the two men came to blows. After that, they stopped speaking to each other. Beula divorced Louie B. shortly thereafter.

Steve Nunn, in his third term as a state legislator, married Tracey Damron, a former flight attendant and daughter of a wealthy Kentucky coal magnate. A social butterfly who sparkled at fundraisers and social balls, Tracey became the perfect politician's wife. Two years later, in 1998, Steve co-sponsored a bill that imposed the death sentence on convicted killers who murdered women who had taken out restraining orders against them. The bill became Kentucky law.

In 2002, following reconciliation with Louie B., Tracy and Steve moved into the ex-governor's Pin Oak Farms mansion near Versailles, Kentucky. But a year later, the 51-year-old's political career took a bad turn. In a bid for the governorship, Steve lost badly in the Republican primary. And on January 29, 2004, his father, at age 81, died of a heart attack. Although Steve didn't have a healthy relationship with his father, the old man's death devastated him. The wheels of Steve's political career came off in 2006 when he lost his legislative seat to an unknown challenger.

Following the death of his father, Steve starting drinking heavily, patronizing prostitutes, and behaving irrationally. He also became, like his father, an abusive husband. Tracey divorced him in 2006. The following year, the 55-year-old political has-been met 20-year-old Amanda Ross, the daughter of a recently deceased public financier. After two months of dating, Steve moved into her Lexington, Kentucky apartment. In 2008, they became engaged.

Through his engagement to Amanda Ross, Steve landed the cabinet-level job of heading up a state agency that oversaw a variety of welfare programs including those dealing with spousal abuse. (Ex drug users get jobs as drug counselors why not hire ex-wife abusers to oversee spousal abuse?) Amanda Ross held a high-level state position as well.

Although Steve was back on his feet career-wise, he was still emotionally unstable, and drinking too much. His paranoia led him to suspect that Amanda was cheating on him. On February 17, 2009, in the midst of an argument in Ross' apartment, Steve, true to form, hit her. The next day, she petitioned the court for an emergency protection order, which a judge quickly granted. Under the restraining order, Nunn could have no contact with Ross for a period of a year. Within 48 hours of the judge's ruling, Nunn had no choice but to resign his cushy, high-paid government job.

Convinced that Ross had intentionally sabotaged his career, Nunn became obsessed with revenge. To embarrass and humiliate his former girlfriend, he showed his friends nude photographs he had taken of her. He then began to stalk her.

On September 11, 2009, as Amanda Ross left her apartment on her way to work, Nunn shot her to death. While no one witnessed the murder, homicide investigators had an obvious suspect--Steve Nunn. Later that day, police found him hiding in a cemetery. He had scratched his wrists in a phony suicide attempt.

Charged with first-degree murder, Nunn, to avoid the death penalty mandated by his own legislation, pleaded guilty in exchange for a sentence of life without parole.

Psychological Damage to Victims

Even after stalking victims feel assured that the stalking has ended, many find themselves having trouble learning to trust again--both others and themselves. A phase of overcompensating can take place, in which survivors of stalking tend to mistrust their own judgment in meeting people, or feel intensely suspicious of others, resulting in potential difficulties forming new relationships, whether personal or professional, intimate or casual. Existing relationships may also be affected; survivors may find themselves reacting with far greater caution and vigilance around others than is normal for them.

Melita Schaum and Karen Parrish, *Stalked*, 1995

No Protection From Scottye Miller

Scottye Leon Miller, a violent, sociopathic stalker of ex-girlfriends and other women unfortunate enough to have crossed his path, lived in Burien, Washington, a King County town of 33,000 located south of Seattle. Between 2002 and 2010, Miller had stalked, harassed, threatened, and assaulted several women. His arrest record featured 15 domestic violence related convictions, and six court protection order violations. It was just a matter of time before he killed one of his victims.

In 2008, the violent ex-con started dating Tricia Patricelli, a 30-year-old mother of two daughters who lived in the nearby city of Auburn. In January of the following year, Miller forced his way into Patricelli's apartment and assaulted her in front of her children. A local prosecutor charged the 30-year-old subject with burglary and third-degree assault. The defendant pleaded guilty and received a short sentence in the King County Jail. (Burglary is a felony. The judge should have sentenced Miller, given his criminal record, to twenty years.)

Miller served less than a year in jail on the Patricelli burglary/assault conviction. In January 2012, Tricia Patricelli called 911 and reported that he had threatened to kill her, and was chasing her in the parking lot of the apartment complex. "Please hurry, he is going to kill me!" she screamed. The police arrived and took Miller into custody. To the responding officers, Patricelli said, "You don't know who you are dealing with. He is going to kill me."

Scottye Miller, convicted of fourth-degree assault and harassment, was sentenced to another short stretch in the King County Jail. The fact he was behind bars, however, did not stop this man from continuing to terrorize his victim. While serving his time, Miller wrote Patricelli letters in which he promised to kill her when he got out of jail. Apparently in King County, victims of stalking and assault do not get relief even when their offenders are in custody. For a victim of this type of crime, this reality must be frightening as hell.

Scottye Miller, on October 12, 2012, walked out of jail a free man. This meant serious trouble for Tricia Patricelli, the object of the serial stalker's obsession and pathological wrath. The criminal justice system, at this point, had no solution for Patricelli's life-threatening predicament. It didn't take a psychic detective to predict bad things for this vulnerable woman.

At eight-thirty in the morning of October 30, 2012, just two weeks after Miller's release from the King County Jail, neighbors heard the screams of a woman coming from Tricia Patricelli's apartment. Moments after the woman went silent, witnesses saw a man meeting Miller's physical description walk out of the building. Someone called 911.

Responders to Patricelli's apartment found that Miller had stabbed her to death in the bathroom. He had stabbed his ex-girlfriend in the face, neck, torso, and back--22 times in all. Police arrested him shortly thereafter at a nearby bus stop. Miller denied any knowledge of the stabbing, but admitted that he had sent the dead woman text messages in which he had threatened to kill her. Miller told the arresting officers that he had been dating the victim for four years, and had lived with her, on and off, during half of that time.

Shortly after Patricelli's murder, investigators found three bloody knives, a pair of bloodstained gloves, and the victim's cellphone at the foot of a fence near the apartment complex. One of the knives was 8 inches long. During a second interrogation, Scottye Miller confessed to the killing. He said that in the midst of a fight in Patricelli's apartment, he just "snapped." After "snapping," Miller slipped on a pair of gloves, and using the three knives he had brought with him to Patricelli's place, started stabbing her. The bloody assault ended up in Patricelli's bathroom where she died.

On November 15, a King County judge arraigned Miller on the charge of first-degree murder. The homicidal stalker is back in jail under $1 million bond.

In December 2013, a jury found Miller guilty of first-degree murder. Two weeks after the verdict the judge sentenced him to 50 years in prison.

The Scottye Miller is a reminder of a frightening truth about our criminal justice system. The police cannot arrest dangerous people for what they might do in the future. Law enforcement authorities only spring into action *after* the harm is done. In this case it was too late to protect this victim's life. Our system of criminal justice is designed more for the protection of the criminal than it is for the safety of the victim. Women being stalked, threatened with death, and assaulted by pathological criminals like Scottye Miller cannot look to the police or the courts for protection. They either have to flee and hide, buy themselves a gun and do the job themselves, or hire a contract killer. None of these options are good, but neither is being hounded, assaulted, then murdered by some low-life sociopath.

Stalking Victims

Who are the victims of stalkers? A statistically small--but prominently visible--number are celebrities: Hollywood actors and actresses and highly visible athletes. Performing on television, in concerts, or in sports arenas, these figures are familiar to countless people worldwide....

While the stalking of celebrities often draws the most media attention, however, the vast majority of stalking takes place between ordinary people who have known each other intimately....

A broad arena of remaining cases exists in which victims are either casual acquaintances or random targets. These cases include the stalking of co-workers and most often tragically, the stalking of children.

Melita Schaum and Karen Parrish, *Stalked*, 1995

Two Stalkers, Two Sentences

In January 2010, Jessica (not the victim's real name) broke up with Dieter Heinz Werner, her 68-year-old boyfriend. Shortly after that, someone slashed her tires in the parking lot of a Houston, Texas movie complex. A month later, Jessica found a GPS tracking device attached to the undercarriage of her car. She suspected Werner, who had been bothering her with text messages and phone calls, of slashing her tires, and using the GPS device to keep track of her whereabouts.

That spring, the ex-boyfriend continued his harassment by sending Jessica hundreds of text messages. On April 3, 2010, he sent her a text that read: "Should have answered the phone and not ignored me again. Pissed me off. Now I show you." That day, after following her to a grocery store, Werner texted: "Pissed me off when I saw you at Krogers and you turned your head. I would never treat you like that."

On April 15, a witness at the same movie complex parking lot saw an elderly white man slashing someone's car tires with a pocketknife. The witness jotted the license number to the vandal's Mercedes convertible. The vehicle was registered to Dieter Heinz Werner. A couple of weeks later, a Harris County prosecutor charged Werner with stalking, a third degree felony. Werner was held without bond for a few days until a judge issued a protection order against the accused stalker. After being served with the restraining order, Werner paid his $75,000 bond and was released.

In late 2011, Dieter Werner was found guilty of the stalking offense. A few months later, the judge sentenced him to ten years in prison, the maximum penalty for a third degree felony. But in 2012, before Werner was transferred out of the Harris County Jail into the state prison system, he was paroled. After serving about a year behind bars, the convicted stalker walked free.

According to Texas corrections authorities, Werner had benefited from a so-called "parole in absentia." (Texas parole boards in the 1980s had issued these get-out-of prison passes when the state prison system couldn't handle all of the convicted felons.)

Victims' rights activists, as well as Werner's stalking victim, were outraged. The parole authorities had not even bothered to notify Jessica of her stalker's parole hearing. In Texas and other places, it's a fact that parole boards often do not inform victims when their criminals are released on parole.

In 2011, in the northern Georgia town of Ringgold, 25-year-old Jason Earl Dean and the 18-year-old girl he had become obsessed with, worked at the local Taco Bell. After Joan (not her real name) told Dean she did not want to go out with him, he continued asking her out for a date. This had gone on for a month. The harassment became so intense she changed shifts at work to get away from him. Undeterred, Dean continued to bother her.

On the night of August 8, 2011, Dean waited outside Taco Bell until Joan's shift ended. As she walked to her car, he came up to her with a pair of handcuffs that he slapped around her wrist, binding them arm-to-arm. She screamed for help that brought other employees out of the Taco Bell. Her fellow employees talked Dean into turning Joan free. The police rolled up to the scene shortly thereafter, but Dean had left. A few days later, police officers arrested him on a college campus in nearby Dalton, Georgia. A local prosecutor charged him with stalking and felonious restraint.

In January 2013, Jason Earl Dean entered a so-called "blind guilty plea" before Judge Ralph Van Pelt. (A blind plea means that no sentencing agreement has been reached between the prosecutor and the defense attorney. The defendant is essentially throwing himself on the mercy of the court.) Judge Van Pelt, showing no mercy for this stalker, sentenced him to four years in prison followed by six years of probation.

Entitled Reciprocity Syndrome

If the celebrity stalker thinks he's being rejected, he can feel humiliated and develop anger and hatred toward the star he loves. He thinks, "I have spent hundreds of hours writing and communicating and sending e-mails and presents to this celebrity; this celebrity figure owes me time, he owes me attention--how dare he ignore me." Narcissism is the aggressive underbelly of this idealized fantasy.

Reid Meloy, *Details*, April 2013

From Stalking to Murder

Early in 2010, Robert McLaughlin, a 62-year-old retired U.S. Postal employee from Painesville, Ohio, a Lake County town in the northeastern part of the state, asked Stacey Sutera out for a date. The 37-year-old teacher who lived in Canfield, a suburban town located on the western edge of the Youngstown metropolitan area, informed McLaughlin that she had no interested in him romantically. The two had known each other fifteen years. McLaughlin gave no indication that he had been hurt and angered by the rejection. Sutera said she hoped the two could remain, if not friends, at least friendly acquaintances.

Stacey Sutera's rejection of a much older man who had no reason to expect that he had any chance of developing a relationship with this young, attractive woman, changed her life in a way she could not have predicted, or imagined. The rejection turned this otherwise unremarkable, cowardly man into a stealthy and insidious monster.

Stacey Sutera's prolonged nightmare began on March 26, 2010 when someone used a key to scratch-up her car in the parking lot of a grocery store. Three months later, the superintendent of the Columbiana School District started receiving emails about a sexually oriented website that falsely featured Sutera. The anonymous writer of the emails began sending messages to Sutera in which he threatened to ruin her reputation. These emails were signed, "Your Enemy For Life." During this period, Sutera, who had remained in touch with McLauglin, spoke to him about her problem. He responded with sympathy and concern.

On July 29, 2010, Sutera filed a report with the Canfield Police Department that detailed the Internet harassment. Sutera had no idea who hated her enough to wage such a malicious campaign against her. Following the police report, Sutera's tormentor scratched a derogatory slur on her car, and began harassing her with a series of prank telephone calls.

In September 2010, Sutera received a fake, used condom in the mail, a gag item sold online to people out for revenge. The following month, Sutera's teaching colleagues received, through the mail, business cards bearing the teacher's name and address. The cards advertised Sutera's willingness to perform sexual acts for a fee. At this point it was obvious that Sutera's stalker had dedicated his life to ruining hers.

Stacey Sutera's ongoing nightmare intensified on December 1, 2010 when her stalker poisoned her dog to death. A week later, Canfield detectives learned that Robert McLaughlin had purchased the fake condom online, and had created the sexually explicit websites designed to embarrass and scandalize Sutera. When police officers informed Sutera who had been stalking her, she was stunned. What had she ever done to this man to incur his wrath? Why did he think she deserved to be treated like this?

On December 8, 2010, detectives with the Canfield Police Department searched McLaughlin's home in Painesville. The officers discovered information linking the suspect to the malicious website, a mailing list of Sutera's colleagues, the phony sex act business cards, photographs of her, and miscellaneous pornographic material. The next day detectives arrested McLaughlin on charges of pandering obscenity and menacing by stalking.

Sutera, on the day of McLaughlin's arrest, filed for a civil protection order before Judge Eugene J. Fehr of the Mahoning County Common Pleas Court. The judge granted the order that barred McLaughlin from possessing a firearm, and prohibited him from any further contact with Sutera. The order would remain in effect until July 2015. In her affidavit in support of the protection order, Sutera had written: "McLaughlin's actions are clearly designed to cause me mental illness and fear of physical harm. I live in constant fear. My dog has been killed. My daughter and I are in danger."

Robert McLaughlin, on December 17, 2010, after eight months of stalking Stacey Sutera, pleaded guilty in a Mahoning County Court to menacing by stalking. The judge sentenced him to six months in jail. Six months for ruining a woman's life. The judge had given Sutera just six months of temporary protection from a malicious nutcase.

Sutera, on January 8, 2011, filed a civil suit against McLaughlin claiming infliction of emotional stress, libel, and invasion of privacy. The plaintiff sought $1.5 million in damages.

A Mahoning County grand jury, in the spring of 2011, indicted McLaughlin on the felony charges of pandering obscenity, and three counts of possessing criminal tools (his computer). That fall the defendant pleaded guilty to these charges, and on November 29, 2011, Judge Maureen A. Sweeney shocked Sutera, her family, and friends by sentencing this aggressively vicious stalker to five years of probation. McLaughlin was also sentenced to 500 hours of community service and fined $2,500. The judge ordered him to enroll in an anger-management program. He would also have to register in the county as a tier I sex offender.

From Sutera's point of view, McLaughlin's sentence amounted to a slap in the wrist. The fact he would not serve time behind bars guaranteed that he would continue his program of personal destruction. Sutera suffered from multiple sclerosis and ulcers, and had nothing to look forward to but a future of worry and fear. Robert McLaughlin, a lowlife loser who couldn't handle being rejected by someone out of his league, had ruined the life of a once productive mother and teacher. Anger-management? Community service? Probation?

On February 8, 2012, a neighbor found Stacey Sutera lying dead outside her Carriage Hill apartment. She had been shot at close range. That day, a Mahoning County judge issued a warrant for Robert McLaughlin's arrest on the charge of capital murder. After harassing Stacey Sutera for almost two years, this degenerate, who should have been in prison, waited for the 40-year-old to come out of her dwelling. On the last day of her life, this degenerate stalker put a bullet in her head.

The next day, at his mother's gravesite, the 64-year-old McLaughlin used the same gun to kill himself. Who knows why this loser felt the need to take his life near his dead mother? Who cares? In McLaughlin's Painesville storage unit, investigators found a suicide note in which he had written out his plans to murder Sutera, and then kill himself. It's tragic that he hadn't killed himself a couple of years earlier after Sutera had rejected him. In his case, suicide would have been more effective than talking to some anger management counselor.

As of August 2014, the McLaughlin murder case had not come to trial.

Stacey Sutera had been powerless to protect herself from a man she knew would eventually kill her. She had reached out to the police and the courts for help and got nothing because the local criminal justice system was more concerned about protecting Robert McLaughlin's rights than Sutera's safety. Did the sentencing judge actually believe that an anger-management counselor could fix Robert McLaughlin? For criminal justice practitioners, the beauty of the system is that nobody is ever held accountable for anything. One wonders how many other women in Mahoning County, and elsewhere are being stalked by men who will eventually murder them.

Bailing Out Stalkers

Most first-time stalking offenses are charged as misdemeanors, and it is not infrequent that perpetrators are released after the arraignment "on their own recognizance"--also known as "personal bond"--without financial bail, that is, the posting of cash or a secured (monetary) bond. In the cases where financial bond is set, often the amounts seem extraordinarily high, yet perpetrators seem able to come up with the money and obtain release. An option in many jurisdictions is that the arrestee is allowed to post just 10 percent of the bond set by the magistrate.

Melita Schaum and Karen Parrish, *Stalked*, 1995

English Police Drop the Ball

On October 21, 2013, 33-year-old Helen Pearson, a resident of Exeter, England, while walking in the rain from her flat to a physical fitness class at a nearby gym, was stabbed in the back by an attacker armed with a large pair of scissors. The man dragged Pearson through the entrance gate of St. Bartholomew Cemetery where he pinned her to the ground, punched her, and stabbed her in the face and lower jaw.

When Sandra Robertson, a passing motorist, heard Pearson's screams, she jumped out of her vehicle and ran into the cemetery, known by the locals as the Catacombs, and pushed the assailant off the victim. This gave Pearson the chance to run out of the cemetery and take refuge at the Fitness First Gym. The attacker fled the scene as well.

Questioned at the gym by a police officer, the hysterical Pearson cried, "It was my stalker!" An ambulance crew rushed the victim to a nearby hospital. Her wounds, while serious, were not life threatening.

Helen Pearson's ordeal began in 2008 when her neighbor, an unemployed mechanic named Joseph Willis, asked if she would accompany him to a local pub to hear a band. She declined his invitation. Her rejection incurred Willis' wrath and turned him into an unrelenting stalker. During the next five years Willis devoted himself to making Pearson's life a living hell.

Early on, Willis made his intentions clear. He wrote Pearson a letter that read: "I want to see how you would cope if you were attacked. Would you fight back? Scream? Let the game begin." Willis' "game" included regularly pawing through her trash, visiting her Facebook page, disrupting her eating disorder support group (she suffered from obsessive compulsion disorder), harassing hang-up phone calls, depositing a dead cat on her doorstep, slashing her tires, and vandalizing her flat and her parents' home in Crediton. Willis also continued to send her poison letters in which he called her a "lying evil girl," and warned her to "watch her back."

On April 7, 2014, Willis' attempted murder trial got underway at the Crown Court in Exeter. Crown prosecutor Richard Crabb, in his opening statement to the jury, said, " The defendant was obsessed with Helen Pearson and consumed with hostility for reasons that may never become apparent. [Motive in cases like this is irrelevant.] Willis was consumed by hatred. He had done his best to make her life a misery and made clear threats against her in two letters."

Helen Pearson took the stand and described to the jury how the 49-year-old defendant had forced her and her family to live in fear. Her father installed security grilles on her windows, and set up a security camera at his house in Crediton. She changed cellphones every month or so, and lived in constant fear of being physically attacked. Pearson also kept a diary in which she had documented more than 100 incidents of harassment and vandalism.

In describing the October 21, 2013 attempted murder, Pearson said, "He came from behind. I did not hear him because it was raining heavily and I had my umbrella up. The first thing I knew was when I was stabbed in the back. I turned and saw it was Joe. I saw his eyes and he looked absolutely furious. The first blow pushed me to the ground, and he kicked me and was dragging me along. It was obvious he was planning to get me into the Catacombs. That was where I was going to end. I tried to get free. I felt another kick and stab from behind. I thought this is going on until I am completely dead."

Continuing with her account of the vicious attack, Pearson said, "I got my phone and was able to dial two nines but not the third. He got the phone away from me. He was deranged and so evil. He knew full well what he was doing and he was determined I was going to be dead. He was trying to drag me farther and farther from the cemetery entrance gates. I thought this is where he is going to get rid of the body. I thought I would be found and my mum and dad would not know what happened. [I would imagine that Mr. Pearson would have known exactly what had happened to his daughter, and who was responsible.]

"I had six stab wounds in total in my back. I remember seeing the scissors and turning my head and seeing them come down…I was struggling and screaming and pleading. I remember saying, 'Please, Joe. No!' He never spoke to me throughout the whole thing."

The victim-witness told the jury about her father's home security camera and her window bars. Because the police were useless and apparently uninterested in protecting this woman, the family hired a private detective in an effort to catch the stalker in the act. During Pearson's prolonged nightmare, she filed 125 complaints with the Devon and Cornwall Police Departments.

On April 15, 2014, the jury found Joseph Willis guilty of attempted murder. Outside the Exeter court house following the verdict, Helen Pearson, in speaking to a reporter with the BBC, said, "Every night you go to bed and you don't know what is going to happen and you constantly live in fear. You see that there's no way the stalking is ever gong to end." Pearson, feeling hopeless and vulnerable, said she had thought many times about ending her misery by killing herself.

Helen Pearson's father, Bernard Pearson, said this to the BBC: "Nobody with the police could see that the level of violence was rising, rising and rising." Mr. Pearson spoke of the family's intention of filing a formal complaint against the law enforcement agencies that failed to protect his daughter against the obsessed degenerate who had obviously intended at some point to murder her.

The Exeter Crown Court judge, in appreciation of Sandra Robertson's heroic life saving intervention on Helen Pearson's behalf, granted her a 500-pound reward.

In May 2014, Bernard Pearson filed a 48-page complaint against the Devon and Cornwall Police Departments. To a BBC reporter he said, "They failed us terribly. The attacks were getting worse and worse and the police failed to realize this and act."

The judge sentenced Willis to twenty years in prison.

The Versace Case

Andrew Cunanan stalked Gianni Versace [renowned fashion designer] before he killed him, often walking the same routes, sometimes following him.

The morning of the shooting [July 15, 1997], Versace left his house to walk to the News Cafe on Ocean Drive [Miami Beach] where he had his favorite gourmet coffee and picked up several newspapers and magazines. When he arrived back at his home on 11th Street, Cunanan walked up behind him and fired two shots into the back of Versace's head, killing him instantly.

The assassin then fled, and the case wasn't closed until Cunanan's dead body was found eight days later on a houseboat owned by a friend of Cunanan's who was in Germany at the time....

One FBI theory is that Versace once turned town Cunanan for a modeling job. Cunanan was a bar-hopper, drug-user (possibly including steroids and rage-inducing testosterone), and he often sold himself to older, wealthy men. It is now known that Cunanan and Versace were never involved sexually, but it is known that the two men had met at least once.

Stephen J. Spignesi, *In the Crosshairs*, 2003

21 ATTEMPTED MURDER

Defining Attempted Murder

In order for a defendant to be found guilty of attempted murder, that person must have deliberately attempted to kill someone. A person commits an attempt when, with intent to commit a specific offense, he does any act that constitutes a substantial step toward the commission of the crime. If a shooter tries to kill someone but fails because he didn't realize the weapon was unloaded, that is not a defense. In other words, impossibility is not a defense to attempted murder.

Armed and Mentally Ill

On May 15, 2005, 21-year-old Alice Boland from Beaufort, South Carolina was waiting in line at U.S. Customs at the Pierre Trudeau/Dorval International Airport in Montreal, Canada. After waiting longer than she considered appropriate, Boland lost her temper and became loud and unruly. When customs officials and others tried to calm the irrational young woman, she began screaming threats. "Give me a gun!" Boland screamed, "I am going to kill you. I am going to kill President Bush with a gun. Just give me a gun. I am going to find a gun and kill you all." Boland's public outburst revealed an unbalanced mental state and an obsession with guns and murder, a dangerous combination.

Officers with the Montreal Police Department took the American into custody. The next day, after a psychiatric evaluation and Boland's written promise to return to Canada to appear at a later court date, the authorities released her to the custody of her father who had flown to Montreal to accompany her back to South Carolina. (I'm sure the Canadian authorities were glad to get this crazy American out of their country.)

Ten days after Boland's mental meltdown in Montreal, a deputy with the Beaufort County Sheriff's Office accompanied by a Secret Service Agent, paid her a visit at home. (I'm guessing that between the time of the incident and the officers' visit, Boland had been receiving psychiatric treatment at some mental facility.) The deputy and the Secret Service agent, shortly into the interview, realized that Boland was still fuming over having to wait in line at the Montreal airport. The Secret Service agent asked Boland if she still harbored anger toward President George W. Bush. "Yes, hell yes," she replied. "I would shoot him. I would shoot him and the entire U.S. Congress. If I had a gun, I would shoot you, too." This was not what the deputy and the secret service agent had expected to hear.

The Beaufort County deputy placed Boland into handcuffs. The officers also searched the Boland house for guns, seizing an air rifle. The officers hauled Boland to the Beufort County jail on charges of making terroristic threats. To that offense, Boland pleaded not guilty by reason of insanity. After paying her bail, Boland's parents committed their daughter to a psychiatric facility. Psychiatrists at the institution found that Alice Boland was mentally ill. In 2009, the criminal charges her were dropped.

On February 1, 2013, Alice Boland was in Walterboro, South Carolina, a town of 6,000, 50 miles northwest of the coastal city of Charleston. Although federal law prohibits the sale of guns to mentally ill people, the 28-year-old former mental patient was in Colleton County to buy a firearm. She must have lied on the federal background check form because Bolton walked out of the store that day carrying a new Taurus PT-22 pistol.

On Monday, February 4, Alice Boland showed-up in downtown Charleston outside Ashley Hall, the state's only all-girl preparatory school. It was just before noon, a time when parents were waiting in the carpool line to pick-up their children. After pacing just outside the school's iron-rod fence, Boland pointed her .22-caliber handgun at a school administrator and pulled the trigger. The gun didn't discharge. Boland next aimed the pistol at an English teacher, but the gun still didn't work. (She didn't realize the pistol was in the locked position.)

Arrested by Charleston police officers, Boland, charged with two counts of attempted murder and other offenses, was incarcerated at the Al Cannon Detention Center in North Charleston. The judge set her bail at $900,000.

In March 2013 the judge ordered Boland to undergo psychiatric tests to determine if she was competent to stand trial. As of August 2014, the case remains unresolved.

It appears that notwithstanding federal gun control legislation, a mentally ill person can walk into a gun store and buy a firearm. Boland has not only spent time in a mental ward, she had made repeated threats to assassinate the president of the United States. If this is how gun control laws are enforced, what's the point of new gun legislation? Enacting more laws won't reduce the rate of gun violence in the United States. Gun-control politicians, while not the smartest people around, know this but have to pander to their anti-gun constituents.

The Incompetent Hit Man

Michael Kuhnhausen, in the fall of 2006, had tried to talk his wife Susan out of divorcing him, but she wouldn't change her mind. She was determined to end the marriage. The 58-year-old former custodial supervisor for a chain of adult video stores in Portland, Oregon, depended on his wife for support that included the insurance benefits she received from her job as an emergency room nurse. If Susan, seven years his junior, divorced him, he would end up homeless and broke. Michael had suggested marriage counseling, but Susan said that she was finished with him. Michael felt that his estranged wife had pushed him into a corner. He had convinced himself that he had only one option: to pay someone to kill her before the divorce became final. But first he had to find a hit man. Where do you find an assassin?

In 2005, when Michael worked for the adult video chain, he had hired 59-year-old Edward Dalton Haffey as a part time janitor. Haffey, a heavy cocaine user, had just finished a twenty-year stretch in an Oregon state prison for conspiracy to commit murder. Haffey had also been convicted of robbery, burglary, and numerous other crimes involving drugs. Kuhnhausen had every reason to believe that this lifelong violent criminal was an excellent candidate for his murder assignment. He offered the ex-con a $50,000 piece of Susan's life insurance payout. Dazzled by the prospect of so much easy money, Haffey jumped at the chance to kill his former boss' wife.

On September 6, 2006, Haffey, using the house key Michael had given him, entered Susan Kuhnhausen's Portland home. He deactivated the intrusion alarm, removed a claw hammer from his backpack, and waited for his prey. On the kitchen table was a note from Michael informing the murder target that he was spending the day at the beach. The stage had been set for the cold-blooded, home invasion killing.

As six in the evening, Susan Kuhnhausen, having completed her shift at the Providence Portland Medical Center, pulled into the driveway alongside the dwelling. She let herself into the house, and was wondering who had turned off the alarm when she received a glancing blow to the back of her head. She turned and came face-to-face with a man with stringy hair and a long beard. He stood about five-foot-nine and weighed 170 pounds.

Although two inches shorter than her attacker, Susan outweighed the intruder by eighty pounds. Before Haffey could strike her again, she wrestled him to the floor and managed to get the hit man into a chokehold. Susan squeezed as hard as she could, and within a matter of minutes, Haffey stopped breathing and went limp.

With a dead hit man lying on her kitchen floor, the slightly injured but badly shaken victim walked to a neighbor's house and called 911.

The responding police officers sized-up the situation quickly. Mrs. Kuhnhausen had interrupted a house burglar, the two had struggled, and he had died; an obvious case of justifiable homicide. As far as the authorities were concerned, this tough woman had eliminated a violent criminal from the community. She was, in the eyes of the police and residents of her neighborhood, a crime-fighting hero. Chalk up one for the homeowner.

A detective found, in Haffey's backpack, a day-planner with the September 6 notation: "Call Mike." When the investigator came across Michael Kuhnhausen's cell phone number in the dead man's planner, a different picture began to emerge. That Haffey had known Mr. Kuhnhausen wasn't suspicious because Michael had been his boss. But it didn't explain Haffey's possession of the house key, and the fact he had known the alarm code. Once detectives learned of the pending divorce and how it would affect Mr. Kuhnhausen, he became the suspect in a murder-for-hire case. As crimes like this go, this one had come out badly for the hit man.

Edward Haffey's autopsy helped explain why the victim had overpowered him. According to the medical examiner, at the time of this death, Haffey's body contained a near lethal dose of cocaine. He had been too drug-addled to successfully pull off the hit. As it turned out, Haffey had been an unworthy candidate to carry out Michael's murder-for-hire assignment.

Barry Somers, a former prison acquaintance of Haffey's, saw the Kuhnhausen story on the local television news and called the police. In August 2006, Haffey had bragged that a man was paying him $50,000 to kill his wife. Haffey had wanted to know if Somers, for $5,000, would lend him a hand. Somers told Haffey he wouldn't help kill a person for a mere $5,000. A human life was worth more than that.

Three days before the murder-for-hire date, Haffey told his cocaine dealer that he would be coming into some big money after he killed a woman for her husband. He said the husband was paying him $25,000 upfront and the rest when he completed the job. The drug dealer, when he heard about the case in the news media, also called the police.

According to another police witness named Harold Jones, a few days before Mrs. Kuhnhausen choked Edward Haffey to death, Jones had driven the would-be hit man to an Applebee's Restaurant where Haffey met with

Mr. Kuhnhausen. On the way to the restaurant, Haffey told Jones that he was meeting with a man who was willing to pay him $50,000 to kill his wife.

On September 14, 2006, eight days following the botched hit, police officers arrested Michael Kuhnhausen on charges of attempted murder and conspiracy to commit murder. The magistrate set his bail at $500,000. Kuhnhausen's lawyer, in speaking to reporters, insisted that his client was innocent. According to the defense attorney, Haffey, acting on his own, had entered the house though a window in order to steal drug money.

In August 2007, Michael Kuhnhausen pleaded guilty to the attempted murder and conspiracy charges. A month later, just before the judge sentenced him to ten years in prison, Kuhnhausen said, "I hurt a lot of people over the past year and I'm sorry. That's all I can say, I'm sorry." (The failed murder-for-hire mastermind was probably sorry that his hit man turned out to be a drug-addled idiot.)

A Bungled Murder-For-Hire Scheme

Paul Driggers knew that if he filed for divorce, his wife Janice (not her real name) would fight for custody of their children. Driggers knew that Janice, because of his background of crime that included a ten year stretch in prison, would win that battle. To solve his problem, the 53-year-old Idaho man came up with a plan to file for divorce without his wife knowing about it. The idea behind his plan involved winning the divorce suit through his uninformed wife's default.

In February 2005, after creating a false mail drop address for himself and his wife in Post Falls, Idaho, Driggers traveled to Bannock County in the southern part of the state where he filed for divorce. Janice, oblivious to what he was up to, failed to respond to the court papers sent to the phony address. Through this scene, Paul Driggers divorced his wife without her knowledge. Janice was also unaware that the judge had awarded Driggers full custody of their son and two daughters.

Although divorced, Driggers and his clueless ex-spouse continued to live under the same roof as man and wife. In September 2005, after pleading guilty to hitting one of his daughters with a belt, the judge sentenced Paul Driggers to 180 days in jail. Shortly after his release, Driggers threatened Janice with a handgun. Because he was an ex-felon, the mere possession of the weapon was a crime. Driggers denied the allegation, and the prosecutor dropped the charges.

In February 2006, after Janice learned from a social worker that she and the man she was living with had been divorced for a year, threw him out of the house. Because they had engaged in sex under the false pretense of marriage, she filed charges of rape. A judge eventually dismissed that case.

Driggers, in an effort to recover some of his possessions that included a wall plaque that read: "Families are Forever" sued his ex-wife. He also filed a report with a county child protection agency accusing her of physically abusing their children. The agency responded by taking the children out of the home. With the children temporarily out of the house, Driggers made his big move. He asked a man he had met in prison if he knew of someone who would kill his ex-wife.

Early in April 2006, acting on his former prison associate's recommendation, Driggers called a man in Hayward, California named Matt Robinson and offered him $10,000 for the hit. Driggers said he would deposit $1,000 in Robinson's bank account to pay for his trip to northern Idaho where they would plan and carry out the contract murder. Robinson, having left Driggers with the impression he would be thinking over the offer, reported the solicitation to the Hayward police who hooked him up with the FBI. After meeting with FBI agents, Robinson agreed to help the feds by traveling to Idaho as an undercover murder-for-hire operative.

On April 25, 2006, Driggers and Robinson met in a restaurant in Coeur d'Alene. They discussed, in addition to the murder, a number of criminal schemes including the manufacture of methamphetamine, and the counterfeiting of documents to be used in identify theft. Three months later, on July 21, Driggers drove his gold Jaguar onto a Lowe's parking lot in Coeur d'Alene. He was there to meet Robinson who was wired for sound. Driggers handed the man he thought would murder his ex-wife another $1,000. The murder-for-hire mastermind promised to pay Robinson the balance of the hit money in $500 monthly installments. Driggers also gave Robinson a photograph of Janice and a handmade map showing how to get to her house in Priest River. The map, carefully drawn and detailed, included suggested escape routes. In order to maintain contact with his hit man as the plot unfolded, Driggers had purchased a pair of walkie-talkies. He also instructed Robinson on how to dispose of the victim's corpse. This mastermind was leaving nothing to chance.

Driggers, in explaining to Robinson that killing his ex-wife was the only way he could acquire custody of his children, anticipated that the police would suspect him of having her murdered. "They don't like me," he said. "They hate me. They'd like to put a needle in my arm...We've already made some mistakes. I don't want to get hurt on this. The first three months of the investigation is going to be intense. They're going to check everything...I'm the green light, but you're driving the car. You have a couple of options. You can keep the money and go home. You can do it and get it done, or try to do it, and if it's too difficult, you can drop it."

The following day, July 22, 2006, Driggers called Robinson and gave him the final go-ahead for the operation. Ten days later, FBI agents who had been keeping track of Driggers, arrested him on the charge of attempted murder-for-hire. When informed that his conversations with Robinson had been taped, Driggers surprised the arresting agents by insisting that he was innocent.

From his Kootenai County Jail cell a week after being taken into custody, Driggers, referring to his ex-wife as a "vindictive schizophrenic," said this to a local newspaper reporter: "I'm the one who's really being abused. There's been such a climate of fear and paranoia in my case that any action I take to try and protect my property is determined as a move toward hurting my ex-wife, to physically hurting my ex-wife." A federal grand jury, three weeks after Driggers' press interview, indicted him for using interstate commerce to facilitate a murder-for-hire scheme.

The Driggers murder trial got underway, in the federal courthouse in Coeur d'Alene, on January 3, 2007. The defendant, insisting that he was the true victim in the case, promised reporters that when jurors heard his side of the story, they would find him not guilty. But before he got the opportunity to defend himself on the stand, the jurors heard the conversation Matt Robinson had taped in the Lowe's parking lot. After playing the two-hour recording, the government rested its case.

On January 11, Driggers, wearing a raspberry colored blazer, climbed into the witness box with the intent of portraying himself as the victim. He had been so distraught over the possibility of losing custody of his children he had gone to bed every night under the influence of sleeping pills and booze. "It was hard to get out of bed in the morning because I'd always hear the voices of my children saying, 'Daddy, daddy, we want you to come home.' I lost the purpose of my life. I had no reason to live."

In addressing the issue of his murder-for-hire conversations with Matt Robinson, Driggers dismissed them as "hypothetical" discussions in which he was merely exploring possible solutions to his "predicament." "There's a difference," he said, "between a statement and an agreement. I didn't want to kill her. I was upset about many things happening in my life."

The jury, following a brief period of deliberation, found Paul Driggers guilty of attempted murder-for-hire. The verdict surprised no one. But the case wasn't over. Driggers' attorney, noting that a copy of his client's rap sheet had inadvertently found its way into the jury room, moved for a mistrial. The jurors were not supposed to know about the defendant's criminal history. Although only one juror actually looked at the document, the judge had no choice but to declare a mistrial.

The following month, Driggers was tried again on the same evidence. The second jury, also requiring little time to deliberate, found him guilty as charged. The judge sentenced Paul Driggers to the maximum penalty allowed under federal law, a $17,000 fine and ten years in prison.

The Gary Melius Case

Born in 1945 in the Jackson Heights section of Queens, New York, Gary Melius began his career as a plumber, became a builder, and eventually made his fortune in real estate. In 1984, he bought a decaying 1919 French-style chateau on Long Island's Gold Coast. The Huntington, Long Island property, called Oheka Castle, was featured in the classic film "Citizen Kane." Melius turned the 109,000-square foot chateau into a luxury hotel, catering facility, and wedding venue. He also resided there.

A close associate of former U.S. Senator Alphonse D'Amato and contributor of hundreds of thousands of dollars to republican and democrat politicians, Melius was a force in Long Island politics. In 2010, the Oheka Castle hosted the wedding of the now disgraced ex-congressman Anthony Weiner and his wife Huma Abedin, a top Hillary Clinton aide.

Like most rich and powerful men in politics, Gary Melius has cultivated enemies. In February 2014, he conferred with law enforcement officials regarding evidence he said he had of political bribery and witness tampering. Melius claimed to have proof of corruption that would send several high-ranking officials to prison.

In 2013, Melius was at the heart of a political scandal that led to the resignation of Nassau County Police Commissioner Thomas Dale.

Mr. Melius also had enemies in the business world. He has been caught up in a legal battle over control of a company called Interceptor that manufactures ignition locks designed to curb drunken driving. On February 21, 2014, at a company shareholder's meeting, Melius announced that he planned to name a new board of directors.

Melius has accused the company's founder, John Ruocco, of mismanagement and financial improprieties. Ruocco has called Melius a "political fixer." In December 2013, a judge sided with Melius by stripping Ruocco of much of his ownership of the company.

At half past noon on Monday, February 24, 2014, just after Mr. Melius sat down behind the wheel of his Mercedes in the valet parking lot at Oheka Castle, a masked gunman approached the front driver's side window of the vehicle. The assailant fired a shot that hit Melius in the forehead. As the gunman fled the scene in a get-away car, the wounded 69-year-old climbed out of the Mercedes and stumbled back into his house.

The injured man's daughter drove her father to Syosset Hospital. From there he was transferred to the North Shore-Long Island Jewish Health System in Manhasset. It was there he underwent emergency surgery. Mr. Melius is expected to survive the shooting.

In speaking to reporters shortly after the assault, Deputy Inspector Matthew C. Lewis, the Commander of the Suffolk County Police Department's Major Crimes Bureau, said, "This looks to be a targeted crime." In other words, Mr. Melius may have been the victim of an attempted assassination, and perhaps the target in a murder-for-hire plot.

As of August 2014 the authorities have not arrested a suspect in the case.

Attempted Murder-Suicide

In 2014, Ebony Wilkerson and her three children, ages 10, 9, and 3, lived with her husband, the children's father, in North Charleston, South Carolina. The 32-year old mother, pregnant with her fourth child, was losing her mind.

On Sunday, March 2, 2014, Ebony called 911 and said she had been physically assaulted by her husband of 14 years. To officers with the North Charleston Police Department, she claimed that her husband had abused her in a Myrtle Beach hotel room.

Following treatment at a local hospital, Ebony put her three children into her black Honda Odyssey and left the state en route to her sister's apartment in Dayton Beach, Florida.

The distraught mother's sister, Jessica Harrell, saw signs that Ebony was in the midst of a mental and emotional breakdown. On Monday, March 3, at Jessica's urging, Ebony Wilkerson checked herself into a nearby hospital for psychiatric treatment. But the next morning she checked herself out of the health facility.

That day, as Ebony ranted incoherently about demons, the Devil, disembodied voices, and various hallucinations, Jessica called 911 about having her committed involuntarily into a mental facility. Before Jessica got off the phone Ebony put her children in her minivan and drove off.

A short time later, a Daytona Beach patrol officer pulled Ebony over. Although the officer recognized that the woman driving the Honda carrying the kids seemed to be mentally disturbed, the police officer let her go about her business. The patrolman didn't think he had enough evidence to take Ebony into custody pursuant to a Florida law that allows manifestly mentally ill people to be detained for their own wellbeing and the safety of others. The officer found nothing specific that indicated that this woman was dangerous, or about to go off the deep end.

Two hours after the police officer stopped Wilkerson, Tim Tesseneer, driving with his wife on the sands of Daytona Beach, noticed a black minivan moving slowing through the surf in shallow water. As he ran toward the vehicle Tesseneer heard screams and saw two children waving frantically for help. "Please help us," one of the youngsters yelled. One of the kids was trying to wrestle control of the steering wheel from the driver.

When Ebony became aware of Tesseneer's presence, she calmly said, "We're okay. We're okay." Obviously she and her children were not okay.

Stacy Robinson, another man who had seen the car in the Atlantic Ocean, opened a back door and pulled out the 9 and 10-year-old. The 3-year-old child remained strapped in her car seat. A lifeguard who had joined the rescue effort dived through a front widow and unbuckled the toddler's seatbelt. As the van drifted into deeper water, he handed the terrified 3-year-old to a second lifeguard who removed the child from the bobbing vehicle. One of the other men pulled Ebony out of the Honda.

Ebony and the children were taken to the Halifax Health Medical Center for evaluation. In speaking to a police officer at the hospital, one of the Wilkerson children said, "Mom tried to kill us. Mom is crazy." According to the child, his mother told them to "close their eyes and to sleep." She had locked the doors and rolled up the windows and said they were all going to a better place.

On Friday, March 7, 2014, when a doctor released Ebony Wilkerson from the hospital, police officers booked her into the Volusia County Jail on three counts of attempted first-degree murder and three counts of aggravated child abuse. The judge set her bond at $1.2 million. In May 2014 the judge reduced her bail to $90,000.

If Ebony Wilkerson is eventually incarcerated long term over her attempted suicide-mass murder, it will probably be in a mental institution. The fact she was pregnant may make treating her illness with anti-psychotic drugs problematic. Fortunately for her children she picked a public place to try to commit murder-suicide.

The Road Menace

Jill Anjuli Hansen, a 30-year-old washed-out blonde with a figure that made a Barbie doll look bloated, aspired to become a professional surfer. The resident of Honolulu's Maunalani Heights neighborhood, Hansen also claimed to be a model and owner of a swimsuit line. But in her community, if Hansen was known for anything, it was for being a violent-prone woman who drove like a maniac.

In 2010, Hanson was convicted twice for speeding. A year later, police caught her driving without a license and car insurance. Local officers arrested her three times in 2014 for speeding, including driving 72 in a 35-MPH zone. The Maunalani Heights Neighborhood Watch Group's 500 members were alerted to Hansen and her reckless driving habit. A representative of the group was reported as saying, "We need everybody to be on the lookout for her, it's that scary. Two people were almost run over by her. One person had a head-on collision with Hansen."

On April 18, 2014, Honolulu police arrested Hansen on a charge of third-degree assault. The judge in that case reportedly ordered her to undergo mental evaluation. (According to Hansen's father, his daughter, on Facebook, had solicited someone to murder him. As a result, he obtained a restraining order against her.)

On Wednesday, May 14, 2014, in the Diamond Head section of Waikiki, 73-year-old Elizabeth Conklin got out of her BMW 328 Wagon in the parking garage to her apartment complex. As Conklin walked away from her vehicle, Jill Hansen, who had followed her into the parking area, slammed her gray Volkswagen Passat into the woman, knocking her a distance of twenty feet.

Following the impact, Hansen climbed out of her VW and walked over to the injured woman who was writhing in pain on the garage floor. Instead of calling 911, Hansen returned to her car, climbed in, and was about to take another run at the downed woman when a building employee named Chris Khory grabbed a crow bar and smashed out Hansen's back window.

Mr. Khory's timely intervention caused Hansen to exit the VW and flee the scene on foot. Paramedics rushed the victim to a nearby hospital where doctors treated Conklin for numerous cuts and bruises.

At the hospital, Elizabeth Conklin told police officers that the attack was not the result of an earlier road-rage incident. She believed her attacker had followed her home with the intent of stealing her car. "I parked in my normal parking place," she said. "I got out and all of a sudden woke up in an ambulance. She saw my car, it was the car she wanted. She followed me and was going to kill me to get the car."

An hour or so after running down Elizabeth Conklin in the Waikiki parking garage, Jill Hansen was on her computer updating her Facebook page with a photograph of the victim's BMW. She also informed her Facebook friends and readers that she had just been accepted into the Association of Surfing Professionals. "I am becoming a professional!" she wrote. "I have worked so hard to get to where I am today. I am so grateful for the support of surfers and the ASP."

Police officers arrested Hansen at her apartment seven hours after she intentionally plowed into the 73-year-old victim and fled. Officers booked the suspect into jail on the charge of attempted murder. The judge set her bail at $1 million.

A Murderous Cruise Ship Crime

Ketut Pujayasa, a 28-year-old citizen of Indonesia, worked as a room service attendant on Holland America's Nieuw Amsterdam. Following a background investigation that included a criminal history check, the cruise line hired Pujayasa in 2012. According to the cruise line, up until he went berserk and attempted to rape and murder a 31-year-old female passenger, he possessed an excellent work record.

On February 14, 2014, the Nieuw Amsterdam sat in international waters off Honduras. That morning Pujayasa delivered breakfast to the American passenger's room. When he knocked on the door, she allegedly yelled, "Wait a minute, son of a bitch!"

Taking the woman's outburst as an insult to himself and his family, Pujayasa brooded over the incident for hours. That evening, when off duty, he used his master key to enter the woman's vacant stateroom. From there he entered the room's outdoor balcony where he fell asleep.

Later that night, when Pujayasa awoke on the balcony, he realized the woman was asleep in her bed. He crept into the room, removed his trousers and underwear, and climbed on top of her. The victim resisted, and in the course of a struggle, he slammed her in the face with a laptop computer. In an attempt to choke her silent, Pujayasa wrapped a cord attached to a curling iron around her neck. She retaliated by kicking him in the genitals and trying to stab him with a corkscrew.

Fearing that someone on board would hear the commotion created by the fight and come to the passenger's aid, the smallish Indonesian tried to pull the victim out onto the balcony where he could toss her overboard. At this moment, another passenger, reacting to the screaming and sounds of a scuffle, pounded on the woman's door.

Pujayasa, still naked from the waist down, let go of the victim and stepped out onto the balcony. From there he jumped to an adjacent balcony, entered that room, and fled from the crime scene.

The victim ran out of her room with her face bruised and swollen and the curling iron dangling from her neck.

Back in his quarters, Pujayasa told his roommate that he had just killed a passenger.

The Nieuw Amsterdam, on February 15, 2014, docked at Roatan, Honduras. From there the victim was flown to a hospital in southern Florida. She is expected to survive the beating.

When the cruise ship docked at Fort Lauderdale on February 16, FBI agents took Ketut Pujayasa into custody. Before being booked into the Broward County Jail on federal charges of attempted murder and aggravated sexual abuse, the suspect confessed fully to his FBI interrogators. A federal magistrate denied Pujayasa bond.

The Would Be Monster

On June 12, 2014, Florida Department of Law Enforcement Officers arrested 29-year-old Shawn Ryan Thomas on charges of premeditated attempted homicide, attempted sexual assault, and ten counts of possession of child pornography. According to a confidential informant, Thomas planned to lure two parents and a juvenile female to a vacant house in Orlando under the charade of producing a television show. Investigators believed that Thomas intended to murder the parents with a knife then rape and kill the girl. He also planned to film the rape for a DVD he could sell.

Police officers reported that Thomas lured a father, grandfather and child to a vacant house on June 7, 2014 but the family became suspicious and left.

At the time of his arrest, Thomas possessed a bag containing a knife, sexual lubricant, a camera and tripod, and plastic sheets. The judge denied Thomas bail.

22 EXCESSIVE POLIC FORCE

Fear Mongering

Police administrators, aware that Americans tend to be wary of governmental authority, have never been above fear mongering. The "thin blue line" metaphor--the notion that a fragile barrier of uniformed cops stands between civilized society and hordes of rapists and looters--is a good example of scaring citizens into accepting and appreciating excessive police authority.

Those skeptical of the "thin blue line" concept were proven right in the early 1970s following a series of experiments in Kansas City, Missouri by the Rand Corporation. The studies revealed no correlation between police patrols and crime prevention. Government fear mongering, from the "reefer madness" era through "thin blue line" period continues. Now, in addition to the specter of a society collapsing under the weight of drug addiction and crime, the fear of terrorism has propelled the move toward a more militarized, heavy-handed form of law enforcement. Today, getting on an airplane, or entering a public school, is like visiting someone in prison. Police officers patrol many big cities the way soldiers walk the streets of Kabul, Afghanistan. Many politicians want to turn schoolteachers into armed police officers. (If I had a child in school, I'd advise him not to talk back to any teacher under stress who's packing heat.) If this trend isn't reversed, the day may come when the fear of crime and terrorism will be matched by the fear of the police.

As Winston Churchill once said, "Democracy means that when there's a knock at the door at three in the morning, it's probably the milkman." Today, in America, it's certainly not going to be the milkman, and if it's a SWAT team at your door, forget the knock.

The Mind of a Cop

When you ride around all day long and you're dealing with shootings, you're dealing with robberies, you're dealing with all this violent crime that's constantly going on, that's going to influence how you respond in certain situations. And we have to take that into account in our training. We teach our officers to try to interact with people and realize that not everybody in a given neighborhood is a thug or a criminal they're not all out to hurt you. These are important things that I think we've got to face head on.

Philadelphia Police Commissioner Charles Ramsey, 2013

Taser Madness

Tasers, which have been around since the 1970's, are handheld devices that deliver an electrical shock that temporarily stuns and disables suspects who resist authority or pose serious physical threats to arresting officers. The original five-watt stun gun, which produced a major jolt, was followed in 1994 by a seven-watt version called the Air-Taser, a product manufactured and sold by Taser International. In 1998, the company developed a higher-powered Taser designed to stop the more combative, dangerous suspect likely to fight through the lighter applications. A year or so later, Taser International came out with the M26, a 26-watt device that stunned subjects with 50,000 volts. The company began selling the X26 in 2003, a lighter, more portable version of the M26.

While representatives of Taser International insist that their non-lethal device is safe, critics of the stun gun, such as Amnesty International, claim that Tasers have killed more than a hundred people. In cases where citizens have died after being shocked by the police, forensic pathologists have found preexisting illnesses or the presence of drugs and other toxic substances. The safety debate continues in forensic medicine and in the courts. But among those who recognize and appreciate that Tasers provide a nonlethal alternative to clubs and guns, there is concern over the indiscriminant use of the device on people whose behavior doesn't call for such force. Over the past few years, police officers have used the device on children as young as six years of age; people who were mentally ill or physically disabled; and elderly women. Police officers have also stunned peaceful protestors and citizens stopped for traffic violations and other minor offenses whose actions did not justify the unpleasant experience of being jolted by 50,000 volts.

Officers in 11,000 police agencies carry Taser guns. Although there is no governmental agency that keeps a record of the frequency and consequences of Taser use, groups like Amnesty International assert that the frequency of Taser use in on the rise. [Studies have also shown that the increased use of Taser guns has not reduced the number of police involved shootings.] The large number of reported Taser incidents provides anecdotal evidence that officers are becoming less reluctant to deploy this nonlethal but extremely unpleasant type of force.

The Shock Proof Man

In the *Guinness Book of World Records* there seems to be a record for just about everything. But there is no mention of the man police used their Taser guns on 71 times within a span of thirty minutes. This had to be a world record in the category of repeatedly shocking someone who didn't die from it. The man who holds this unofficial record will simply be referred to as Bob.

Bob, a 25-year-old veteran of the Afghanistan War who suffers from post traumatic stress disorder, after being allegedly disowned by his family in Phoenix, moved in with a relative in Flagstaff, Arizona. One evening in July 2010, after taking PCP and bath salts, Bob entered a Chevron gas station and store on Highway 89 in Doney Park just north of Flagstaff. Barefoot, Bob wandered about the place leaving muddy footprints, then approached the cashier and asked to be reported to the police.

When Arizona Department of Public Safety (DPS) Officer Brian Barnes arrived at the Chevron station, he encountered Bob in the parking lot in front of the store. As the officer approached the suspect, Bob ran toward the entrance of the station with the officer in close pursuit. When Bob slammed into the closed door, he bounced back into the officer, and they both fell to the ground. Bob jumped up, this time opened the door, and ran inside. After shooting Bob with his Taser gun, Officer Barnes and a bystander managed to handcuff the out-of-control man. His hands, however, were not restrained behind his back.

Bob settled down a bit, but the moment Coronino County Deputy Sheriff Don Bartlett arrived, Bob started acting up. To hold him down, the 260 pound deputy sat on his legs, but when that didn't stop the violent thrashing and kicking, Deputy Barnes gave Bob a taste of his Taser. When that didn't help, he zapped him two more times.

As the DPS Officer and the deputy struggled with the drug-crazed man in the Chevron station, EMT and firefighters arrived at the scene, followed by Sheriff's Office Sergeant Gerrit Boeck. During the next thirty minutes, Deputy Bartlett used his Taser twenty more times on Bob with Officer Barnes helping out electronically. While shocking the hell out of the suspect he kept resisting, shocking the hell out of them.

Finally, the three police officers, with the help of several firefighters, strapped the handcuffed madman onto a gurney, but as they slid him into the ambulance, Bob managed to grab Deputy Bartlett's belt. Sergeant Boeck, thinking that Bob was trying to get ahold of the deputy's gun, started punching him in the arm. It took several officers to pry Bob's fingers from the Deputy's belt.

Once they got Bob into the ambulance, a paramedic injected him with a tranquilizer used to control animals. The drugs kicked in and Bob settled down.

At the Flagstaff Medical Center, a doctor diagnosed Bob as being in a state of excited delirium that gave him superhuman strength and rendered him impervious to pain. After a few days hospital personnel discharged Bob. The authorities decided not to charge him with resisting arrest, assaulting a police officer, or disorderly conduct. (The county prosecutor was probably concerned with the Taser overuse, and decided to let a sleeping dog lie.)

Regarding the issue of excessive force, the DPS referred the case to the county attorney's office for investigation. That Bob survived all that electricity, especially when in a state of excited delirium, is miraculous. Had he died, the medical examiner would probably have listed the cause of his death, excited delirium syndrome.

These officers were presented with an extremely difficult situation and when their Taser guns didn't work ran out of good options. Sometimes the police encounter situations they are not equipped to handle. When it became obvious that their Tasers weren't working, the officers should have stopped using them.

The officers were cleared of any wrongdoing.

Taser Used On Deaf Man

Officers from the Hawthorne Police Department in Los Angeles County, California twice used a Taser on a man who was trying to sign to them that he was deaf...The officers then beat the deaf man until he was unconscious then charged him with assault. A federal complaint has since been filed against the police department for violating Jonathan Meister's rights under the Americans with Disabilities Act. According to the complaint... the cops "shot Taser darts into Mr. Meister, administered a number of painful electric shocks, struck him with their fists and feet, and forcibly took him to the ground....

Meister was picking up a snowboard that a friend had loaned to him ahead of a skiing trip to Utah...The four officers questioned him outside his friend's house. He was dressed in snowboarding gear and was loading boxes into his car. Due to his disability, he did not hear their questions. One officer then grabbed his hand, and Meister attempted to signal to the officers that he was deaf. The officers, however, took his hand movements as "resistance"....

Grace Stafford, The Daily Caller, February 17, 2014

Out of Control Cops

Bay Area Rapid Transit police in February 2014 used a Taser on a harmless, unarmed man more than once, even as he was lying facedown and restrained on the floor of a passenger train. Horrified onlookers--who repeatedly asked the officers to stop torturing the man--recorded the incident on cell phone cameras. The unnamed black man was apparently intoxicated. Police claim that they approached him because he was harassing other passengers, although some of the eyewitnesses disputed that....

The police asked the man to get off the train. When he refused they used a Taser on him. A few minutes later, as the man was held against the floor, an officer shocked him again--this time, for five long seconds. He was eventually dragged off the train and charged with public drunkenness and resisting arrest....

Robby Soave, The Daily Caller, February 13, 2014

Secret Police

There is nothing more ludicrous than a politician, standing in front of a television camera with a straight face, telling citizens that our government is transparent. By transparent, meaning open and honest in the way it operates in our best interest. That, of course, is pure baloney. Government, on all levels and across the board, is *secretive*. It is in the nature of the beast, and for good reason. If the pubic ever fully discovered what our "public servants" were really up to, there would be much less government.

In many ways, the government functions a lot like organized crime. Government protects itself through a code of silence, whistleblower intimidation, perjury, evidence tampering, and the shielding of the leaders from criminal culpability. And like soldiers in the Mafia, most government employees are in for life. To expose the government, investigators must rely on the same tactics the FBI used to bring down the Mafia. Problem is, the FBI is part of the government.

Anyone who knows anything about policing--federal, state, and local-- knows that law enforcement agencies do not welcome public scrutiny. Police officers hate cellphone cameras, civilian review boards, oversight committees, police commissions, and other watchdog groups. Cops also hate their fellow officers assigned to internal affairs units. For decades, police administrators, working hand-in-hand with friendly politicians, have engaged in shameless fear mongering to scare the public into putting up with highly militaristic, zero tolerance, policing tactics. Because very little in law enforcement is on the level, it's in the best interest of our police authorities to keep civilians in the dark. It has been this way since the beginning of professional policing

Alex Bustamante, the Inspector General for the Los Angeles Police Department, a police watchdog group, recently presented his oversight board with a report that detailed how LAPD administrators handled use of non-lethal force cases. These police-involved incidents included body holds, punches, baton strikes, and the firing of Tasers and beanbag guns. Such cases accounted for 95 percent of the department's use of force incidents.

According to the inspector general's report, special units within the agency conducted these investigations. The less serious cases were merely reviewed by regular field supervisors. The supervisors in charge of these whitewash inquiries made certain that statements by involved officers and witnesses were not recorded. Departmental policy dictated that only a single account of a use of force incident was written up for the record. And that account was from the officer's point of view. As a result, these reports often did not present the true story of the incident under review. This, of course, was the intended result. These were essentially cover-up exercises. Public employees had become masters of the cover-up.

Inspector General Bustamante told reporters that the above LAPD internal policies and procedures had made it impossible for his group to assess the quality of these in-house investigations. Moreover, there was no way for the watchdog group to determine if LA cops were abusing their power.

Government agencies, to maintain their authority and to grow, need to operate in secret. It's a matter of institutional survival. As far as most politicians and bureaucrats are concerned, the public has *no* right to know anything. Government leaders tell us it's our job to *trust* them. In law enforcement the message to the public has always been: leave policing to the professionals. We know what we are doing, and we do not need you sticking your nose into *our* business. In other words, we don't work for you. You work for us, so shut up and go away.

Kicking Stomach in Georgia

In response to a child custody dispute, Dekalb County police officer Jerad Wheeler, at 6:30 PM on December 12, 2011, pulled up to Darrius Usher's house in Tucker, Georgia. Kiera Wade and Usher were fighting over their son, Jamal. The mother had come to the house to take the boy home, but Usher wasn't cooperating. The cursing and shouting father, instead of calming down and speaking to officer Wheeler, walked away from him toward the back of the dwelling. As a second police officer rolled up to the scene, the father's aunt entered the house, fetched the boy, and carried him to his mother's car. This infuriated Usher who stormed out of the house onto the front porch. He was carrying, in his right hand, a length of metal pipe. "You're gonna have to take me to jail," he shouted.

Reaching for his sidearm, officer Wheeler instructed Usher to drop the weapon. The angry father released the pipe then charged toward the car occupied by Kiera and his son. Wheeler fired two Taser prongs into Usher's back, causing him to collapse before reaching the vehicle.

The subduing of the out-of-control father should have ended this disturbance. But as is often the case in situations like this, a family member couldn't leave well enough alone. As the second officer placed Mr. Usher into handcuffs, the arrestee's sister, Raven Dozier, got into the act by screaming at officer Wheeler. As the big woman moved toward him, the young officer, on three occasions, told her to "get back." She ignored his commands, and when Dozier got within three feet of him, he employed a so-called front push kick to her stomach.

In Wheeler's incident report, he wrote: "The kick was a front push kick to the abdomen as I was taught to do in the [police] academy. After this, she stayed back." Dozier returned to the house.

Wheeler placed Mr. Usher into his patrol car, and accompanied by his partner, walked into the dwelling to arrest Raven Dozier. At this point, another member of the family told Wheeler that he had kicked the stomach of a woman who was more than 8 months pregnant. According to Wheeler's report: "At the time of the alteration it was very dark and Ms. Dozier had a large shirt on. I could not tell by the sight of her at the time that she was pregnant."

Complaining of stomach pains, Dozier asked to see a doctor. Officer Wheeler called for an ambulance, and followed the emergency vehicle to the hospital where a physician noted a contusion and some spotting on her abdomen. From the hospital, Wheeler transported Dozier to the Dekalb County Jail. When personnel at the lockup refused to take this prisoner into custody due to medical concerns, Wheeler informed Dozier that she would be charged with obstruction and disorderly conduct. She could expect to receive her court date in the mail. In the meantime, her brother had been booked into the Dekalb County Jail on the charge of disorderly conduct.

Shortly after the domestic disturbance, Raven Dozier filed a complaint with the police department's internal affairs office. Four of officer Wheeler's supervisors, and an internal affairs detective, reviewed the case, and concluded that Wheeler's front push kick fell within the agency's use of force policy.

Two weeks after being kicked in the stomach, Dozier, following an emergency C-section, gave birth to a healthy baby. The criminal charges against Dozier have been dropped.

In May 2012, Raven Dozier's attorney, Marr Bullman, filed a civil suit against Jared Wheeler and the Dekalb County Police Department. In speaking to a reporter, attorney Bullman said, "This officer is just another loose cannon. And I don't know how a 180-pound pregnant woman comes at you 'aggressively.'" (A description Wheeler used in his incident report.) Bullman claimed that Wheeler had arrested his client out of a need to establish justification for the stomach kick in the event something happened to the baby.

If Raven Dozier's lawsuit ever goes to trial, Wheeler's short history as a police officer might become an issue. Reportedly, in September 2011, a 53-year-old woman complained that Wheeler had twisted her arm while shoving her into a patrol car. A few months later, pursuant to a 911 call, Wheeler allegedly went to the wrong address where he shot a leashed dog.

While a nine month pregnant woman had no business confronting a police officer in a domestic dispute involving someone else, officer Wheeler should not have kicked a woman, pregnant or not, in the stomach. (If this officer lost his job or was otherwise punished for his behavior, there is no record of it.)

Four Cops Beat Innocent Man To Death

A disturbing video of a police incident in an Oklahoma parking lot shows a man who had committed no crime dying after being roughed up and violently restrained by four cops--all while his grief-stricken wife watched in horror. Luis Rodriguez, 44, died in a Moore, Oklahoma movie theater parking lot. Police were responding to a reported domestic disturbance. Rodriguez's wife admitted to slapping the couple's 19-year-old daughter in the face over a disagreement about the girl's behavior. Rodriguez, however, was not involved and had not done anything wrong....

But when police arrived, they wanted to question Rodriguez. According to the Moore Police Department, Rodriguez was not cooperative, and cops were forced to handcuff and restrain him. [Pursuant to today's highly militarized, hair-trigger form of policing, you have to be very careful around cops. There are many ways they can kill you.]

Cell phone video shows the immediate aftermath of the restraining process. Several cops can be seen pinning Rodriguez facedown on the ground. One officer kneels on his back while others hold his arms. He does not move or speak at this point, and it's unclear whether he is still alive. The officers seem unaware that anything is wrong, however, and continue to keep him pinned to the ground.

Mrs. Rodriquez shot the video. She said, "You killed my husband!" She then begins to cry....

Robby Soave, The Daily Caller, February 25, 2014

The Chidester Case

At ten on the night of May 25, 2005, the Utah County Metro SWAT team was about to break into a house on South State Street in Springville to confiscate methamphetamine, guns, and other contraband they might find in the dwelling. The Sierra Team, one of the four Utah County SWAT groups involved in the raid, pulled into the neighborhood first. The six snipers in the unit took up positions 50 yards from the target house. The Sierra snipers were in place to watch the house and report any activity at or near the dwelling to the other SWAT units as they moved into their attack positions. From this point on, any bystander who happened onto the surveillance are would be viewed through rifle-scope crosshairs.

The remaining 24 SWAT officers arrived at the scene. Alpha Team members, taking up positions 70 yards from the house, would break into the dwelling through the front entrance. Team Charlie had the side door. The Bravo squad, setting up behind a wooden fence in the back, 500 yards from the target, would enter the house through the rear door.

At 10:30, the Alpha, Charlie, and Bravo teams were supposed to reach the target at the same time, tossing flash bang grenades into the front, side, and rear of the house. Because of some kind of miscommunication, the Bravo team entered the back door ahead of the other two units that were moving toward the dwelling from 65 yards away.

Forty-year-old Larry Chidester lived in the basement quarters of his parents' place next door to the SWAT target. Awakened by the flash bang explosions coming from the other side of his house, Larry came out his side door to investigate what he thought was a car accident. Instead, he saw a group of SWAT officers charging toward his neighbor's house. Before he got back inside, Larry heard one of the officers yell, "There's one?" Alpha Team member Jason Parker, a reserve sheriff's deputy, ran up to Larry and ordered him to the ground. Each time Larry lowered his arms to help himself down, Deputy Parker, his rifle pointed at Chidester's head, yelled, "Keep you hands up!"

"I'm not resisting! I'm not resisting!" Larry pleaded as Deputy Parker tackled him to the ground and kept him there for a minute or so with his knee pressed into the middle of his back. Although not seriously injured, Chidester had the wind knocked out of him, and suffered abrasions to his forehead, nose, shoulder, back, and knees.

As Larry Chidester lay pinned to the ground under reserve deputy Parker's knee, Sergeant Deke Taylor and another Alpha Team officer stormed into the Chidester house. Deputy Taylor encountered Larry's mother, Emily, in the kitchen, and at gunpoint, ordered her to the floor. The other officer found Lawrence Chidester in the bedroom sitting on the edge of his bed putting on his trousers. This deputy grabbed Mr. Chidester by the shirt and threw him to the floor, ripping the garment off his back. Shortly after the two Alpha Team officers left the Chidesters shaking and bruised, a third deputy entered the house and apologized for the armed intrusion.

Sheriff Jim Tracy insisted that the Chidester incident did not fall into the category of a wrong-house raid. His men were merely protecting themselves by taking control of the target area. From a law enforcement point of view, the only mistake involved the deputy's on-site apology, which suggested police wrongdoing.

The Chidesters filed suit against the Utah County Sheriff's Office and deputies Jason Parker and Deke Taylor individually for violating their Fourth Amendment rights of privacy. The deputies raised the issue of qualified police immunity, arguing that they had acted in good faith. A federal district court judge, in August 2006, ruled that the Chidesters had grounds to sue the officers as individuals. The deputies appealed this decision, and in March 2008, the Tenth Circuit Court of Appeals held that Deputy Parker's actions did protect him from personal liability under the immunity doctrine. However, the appeals court judges did not bar the plaintiffs from suing Utah County and Deputy Taylor as an individual. The lawsuit, as of August 2014, remains unresolved.

Cop Pulls Gun on Speeder

With tensions apparently high following the fatal shooting of a state trooper, Michigan State Police Trooper Timothy Wagner claims he was being extra cautious when he drew his firearm and pointed it an a 18-year-old woman during a traffic stop in April 2014. The incident caught on Wagner's dash cam, sparked allegations of excessive force and a formal investigation. Though no criminal charges were filed, even St. Joseph County prosecutor John McDonough said in a statement that what he heard come out of the trooper's mouth made him "sick to my stomach."

The incident began after Wagner said he clocked the woman's red Pontiac going 77 mph in a 55 mph zone. The dash cam video showed the trooper activating his lights and siren before pulling a quick U-turn to pull over the driver. About 45 seconds after the U-turn the woman pulled off to the side of the road.

Wagner was seen getting out of his car with his handgun already drawn and pointed at the car. He slowly approached the vehicle and ordered the woman to get out. The trooper then handcuffed the woman and took her back to his cruiser.

"I chased you for two miles doing almost 80 mph after I went right by you and turned around, that's the problem," the trooper was heard telling the woman. "You really have to pay attention to what's going on."

The woman apologized and told the trooper she didn't see him immediately. She did not deny she was driving too fast. The woman claimed there was a report of a burglary at her residence and she was in a hurry to get home. Wagner confirmed the burglary report and eventually let the woman go without a ticket, though he said he "probably should take her to jail."

After reviewing the case, prosecutor McDonough decided there was not enough evidence to warrant criminal charges against the officer. However, he made his disapproval of the trooper's actions known.

Jason Howerton, theblaze.com, May 20, 2014

Cop Goes Nuts at McDonald's

A frustrated cop with a short fuse and a gun can be dangerous. Being threatened at gunpoint by an out-of-control police officer isn't any less frightening than being mugged by an armed robber. It may even be worse because if you're killed by a cop people will assume you were doing something wrong. If you're not killed, and complain, who's going to take your word over the word of a police officer? That's when it's helpful to have credible witnesses, and better yet, surveillance camera footage.

Eighteen-year-old Ryan Mash, on April 9, 2013, was in his pickup truck with two friends at a McDonald's in Forsyth County, Georgia. As he waited at the take-out window for his order, Scott Biumi, a sergeant with the Dekalb County Police Department, got out of the vehicle idling behind the pickup. Biumi approached the truck and stationed himself between Mash and the McDonald's service window. The young men in the truck noticed a police badge attached to the belt of the angry McDonald's customer yelling at Mash.

"Stop holding up the drive-thru," the officer screamed. As the stunned young men tried to comprehend what was happening, a berserk Biumi continued to chew-out Mash. At one point in the tirade, he said, "You never know who you're dealing with."

"No sir, I don't," Mash replied.

"Keep you're mouth shut!" Biumi warned.

"I'm sorry for the inconvenience," Mash replied.

The 48-year-old officer returned to his vehicle, but before the McDonald's food came out of the window, Biumi came steaming back to the driver's side of the pickup. (Mash must have felt like he was in a horror movie.) This time the officer pulled his gun and pointed it at the terrified driver. "You don't want to mess with me!" Biumi shouted. After dishing out another thirty seconds of verbal abuse, the gun-wielding cop returned to his vehicle.

Before pulling out of McDonald's (on this day not a happy place), one of Mash's passengers jotted down the license number to the gunman's car. The entire confrontation was also recorded by a McDonald's surveillance camera.

Later in the day of the McDonald's drive-thru blowup, deputies with the Forsyth County Sheriff's Office took officer Biumi into custody on the charge of aggravated assault. The following day, the Dekalb County police officer was released from jail on a $22,000 bond.

Sergeant Biumi was placed on administrative leave with pay. The incident, in addition to being investigated by the Dekalb County Internal Affairs Office, was being looked into by the Georgia Peace Officer Standards and Training Council.

The Georgia Peace Officer Standards and Training Council suspended Biumi's law enforcement certification that prohibited him from working as a police officer in the state.

In December 2013, a judge sentenced the ex-cop to ten years probation.

Shooting Family Pets

The Browns say a patrolman wielding a shotgun killed a member of their family. Cali, a gentle and loving pit bull was shot to death after jumping the backyard fence in Ardmore, Oklahoma say her owners, who have started a massive social media drive to get the officer disciplined.

Sarah Brown says a neighbor witnessed the shooting and heard the cop boasting about how "awesome" it looked when the dog's collar blew off from the blast.

592

Ardmore Police Captain Eric Hamblin said the March 2014 shooting was justified because animal control officers were unable to collect the dog after receiving phone complaints that a pit bull was acting aggressively in the neighborhood. According to Hamblin, the policeman who shot Cali has received death threats....

Brown says the neighbor told her the cop had laughed after shooting her 2-year-old dog...The dog joined the family as a puppy and had no history of bad behavior, family members said....

Deborah Hastings, *New York Daily News*, March 25, 2014

Police Beat Elderly Jaywalker

The New York Police Department is receiving widespread criticism after officers injured an 84-year-old man--who doesn't speak English and didn't understand police orders--for the crime of jaywalking. Kang Wong committed jaywalking at an Upper West Side [Manhattan] intersection in New York City around 5 PM on Sunday, January 19, 2014...He was a resident of the area.

An officer soon approached him and tried to write him a ticket. But Wong, who spoke only broken English, didn't understand what was happening, and continued walking away from the officer. When the officer tried to grab him, the old man pushed back. Several cops descended on Wong and threw him against a wall. The elderly man came away from the encounter with a bloodied face.

Wong was handcuffed and taken to the hospital and then to the police station. Later that night he was released, but will face charges of jaywalking, resisting arrest, obstructing government administration, and disorderly conduct.

Robby Soave, The Daily Caller, January 20, 2014

Deputy Shaquille O'Neal

In 2006, Michael Harmony, a lieutenant with the Bedford County Sheriff's office, commanded the battle against child pornography in south central Virginia. Lieutenant Harmony headed a high-profile regional task force called Blue Ridge Thunder. Shaquille O'Neal, the 7 foot 1, 325-pound center for the Miami Heat professional basketball team, an off-season reserve deputy with the Bedford County Sheriff's Office, was a member of the regional task force. The sheriff had enlisted the famous basketball player, also a gun-carrying reserve officer in Miami Beach, as the public face of the area's anti-child pornography campaign. O'Neal had accompanied the Blue Ridge Thunder team on several military-style child pornography raids.

In September 2006, a cyberspace undercover investigator assigned to the task force, downloaded child pornography via an Internet Provider (IP) address. Based on this information, a local magistrate subpoenaed Fairpoint Communications, the source IP, requiring the company to identify the person or persons at this IP site. The IP complied, providing the authorities with the name of A. J. Nuckols, a resident of Gretna, Virginia. The police didn't know it, but someone at Fairpoint Communications had misread the subpoena. Therefore the identification of the Nuckols family in connection with the IP address was a mistake. Without further investigation into Mr. Nuckols and his family, the police used this faulty information to acquire a warrant to search his house.

Mr. Nuckols, a 45-year-old tobacco and cattle farmer, lived with his wife, Lisa, an elementary school teacher, on a farm near Gretna. Two of their children, ages 12 and 16, lived at home. Their 21-year-old daughter attended college nearby. The family kept their computer, mostly used by the children for homework, in their living room. The parents didn't know their own email address, and rarely shopped online or downloaded information from the Internet. There was nothing in their histories, lifestyle, or associations that suggested any connection to child pornography.

Saturday morning at 10:30 A.M., September 23, 2006, two officers from the Blue Thunder Task Force knocked on the Nuckol's front door. Invited into the house by Lisa, they informed her of the warrant allowing them to search the dwelling for child pornography. "I was in shock," Lisa later told a newspaper reporter. "At first it was not just disbelief. I told them, 'We don't live that way.' "

As the police officers spoke to Lisa Nuckols, a fleet of police cars from Bedford and Pittsylvania Counties rolled up to the house. Suddenly 10 officers, dressed in black and camouflage, and wearing flak jackets, were moving about the yard carrying semiautomatic weapons. Mr. Nuckols, working near the barn, looked across the field and saw all the police vehicles. Fearing that something awful had happened to his wife, or one of his children, he jumped into his truck and sped to the house.

"What's going on?" Mr. Nuckols asked as he climbed out of the pickup. Instead of getting an answer, one of the officers dropped into a shooting position, aimed his pistol at the farmer, and said, "Turn around and put your hands on the truck." Another member of the team handcuffed Mr. Nuckols behind his back. As they led him toward the house, Lieutenant Michael Harmony reportedly said, "Had a rough day? It's about to get a whole lot worse."

Lieutenant Harmony informed Mr. Nuckols that he or someone in his family was suspected of having downloaded child pornography from 150 web sites. The police were there to search the house for evidence of this crime. Later, in a letter to the editor of the local newspaper, Mr. Nuckols expressed how he felt at that moment: "When it finally became clear what they were there for, I was just flat-out mad. They came and assaulted my family for something we had nothing to do with."

The Nuckols children came home at 2 P.M. from a high school cross-country meet. The police, still in the house, asked them if they had downloaded child pornography. The children were as stunned by the accusation as their parents. Ninety minutes later, the officers departed, taking with them the family computer, DVDs, videotapes, and other personal belongings. Before he left, Lieutenant Harmony told Mr. Nuckols that the child pornography investigation would take between six and nine months to wrap up, noting that the state crime lab was backed up.

At one point during the siege, Mr. Nuckols recognized the famous basketball player. "You're Shaquille O'Neal," he said. The big man, dressed like the others, and armed, replied that his name was Tony. Nine days later, when the Nuckols family learned that the search and seizure had been based on an erroneous IP address identification, O'Neal denied involvement in the raid. However, after the Bedford County Sheriff's Office confirmed his participation, he admitted his role.

After the raid, before they were aware of the mistake, Lisa Nuckols told neighbors and friends what happened. Worried that she might lose her job, she advised the principal and the school superintendent as well. In his letter to the newspaper editor, Mr. Nuckols wrote: "When you come into someone's home, that's an intrusion. I feel the same about the raid as I would about any assault on our home and family. A robber would be wrong, and these officers were wrong. No matter what the spin the police put on it, the public will always believe it's wrong. People can't believe this happens in this country."

In response to the criticism following the revelation that the Blue Ridge Thunder team had raided the wrong house, Lieutenant Harmony blamed the Fairpoint Company. According to him, the IP had made the mistake, not the police. Lieutenant Mike Taylor with the Pittsylvania County Sheriff's Office, though not a participant in the raid, apologized to the Nuckols family.

Shaquille O'Neal, however, took another approach by accusing Mr. Nuckols of exaggerating his account of the raid to make the police look bad. When members of the media questioned him about his role in the operation, the basketball player reportedly said, "We did everything right, went to the judge, got a warrant. You know, they [the Nuckols] made it seem like we beat them up, and that never happened."

Police Take Down a Kid

On September 26, 2013 at Baldwin South Intermediate School in Quincy, Illinois, a school official called the police to deal with a "meltdown" by an autistic 9-year-old boy named Roger Parker, Jr. Roger was sent to a specific area to calm down by school officials. When Roger decided to climb a dividing wall, instead of calling a parent to come and pick up the child, the school officials made the decision to call the police. Calling the police almost always makes situations worse.

The officer who arrived, Officer Bill Calkins, pulled Roger by his arms and legs in an attempt to physically remove him from the wall. The officer pulled him in a manner that caused Roger to hit his eye against the divider.

After causing injury to Roger's eye, the officer tried to restrain him. In response, Roger swung around and kicked the officer in his nose.

Roger was pulled to the floor, handcuffed, and taken to the police station where his mother was told that he was being fingerprinted, photographed, and booked for aggravated battery to a police officer.

Copblock, September 27, 2012

Keep Your Pets Away From Cops

A man who's dog was shot and killed by Salt Lake City police posted a video of an exchange he had with officers minutes after the shooting. Sean Kendall's 3-year-old Weimaraner, named Geist, was shot in the head on June 24, 2014 after officers entered the homeowner's house while searching for a missing child…."Which officer shot my dog? Please," Kendall asked several officers standing in his front yard when he arrived at the scene.

"We were looking for a lost child," one officer responded. A neighborhood parent had reported her 3-year-old child missing earlier in the day. The child was later found asleep in the basement of the family's home. [Why didn't they start the search in the missing boy's house?]

"And that gives you probable cause to enter a private residence without permission from the owner?" asked a livid Kendall who asked for the names and badge numbers of the officers.

"He [the shooting officer] was threatened by the dog, and he shot the dog. That's as simple as it gets," one officer said. [Cops like to keep things simple.] The officer who shot Geist was not at the scene at the time, though the officers gave Kendall his name. [The cop was probably meeting with his union rep.]

"So backing up slowly and leaving the residence was not an option?" Kendall asked, his voice growing more agitated. "I understand it wasn't you personally," Kendall said, "but you guys killed my dog. I had this dog for three years. He was my best friend, and he was shot because an officer couldn't back out of my house! Is that against policy? Is that against training?" Kendall asked....

Chuck Ross, The Daily Caller, June 26, 2014

The Police Chokehold

In 1983, following a decade of arrestee and inmate deaths in New York City caused by the use of police chokeholds, the commissioner banned this restraining technique in the city's lockups and station houses. Ten years later, Police Commissioner Raymond Kelly prohibited the use of police chokeholds all together.

On Friday, July 18, 2014, four police officers working in the Tompkinsville section of Staten Island, New York, confronted 43-year-old Eric Garner as he stood on the sidewalk in front of a store. The officers accused the father of four and grandfather of six of selling so-called "loosies," individual untaxed cigarettes. Several bystanders video-recorded the exchange between the officers and the 350-pound asthmatic.

Addressing the officers, Garner said, "Every time you see me, you're messing with me. I'm tired of it. I'm minding my own business. Please leave me alone."

When one of the officers reached out to place the suspect into custody, Garner said, "Don't touch me." At that moment a second officer, from behind, wrapped his arm around the arrestee's neck. Garner collapsed to the pavement. The second Garner hit the ground, the other three officers piled on. With his head pressed hard against the sidewalk, Garner, at least eight times, yelled, "I can't breathe!" He then slipped into unconsciousness.

Two paramedics and a pair of EMTs from Staten Island's Richmond University Medical Center, in response to the police call for medical assistance, rolled up to the scene. After the medical personnel arrived, bystanders pleaded with the medical crew to do more than just check the unresponsive man's vital signs. Ten minutes passed before the ambulance crew lifted the unconscious man onto a gurney and slid him into the emergency vehicle. At the hospital, an hour after the police encounter, Garner died of cardiac arrest.

A police supervisor placed Daniel Pantaleo, the officer seen grabbing Garner from behind, on desk duty pending an internal affairs inquiry into Garner's death. The district attorney of Staten Island announced that investigators in his office would conduct an investigation into the matter.

Officer Pantaleo was not a stranger to such incidents. Two people, in separate cases, had sued him for excessive force in the past few years. Because Garner was black and the arresting officers were white, the fatality immediately triggered accusations of police racism.

On July 19, 2014, the day after Mr. Garner's death, Richmond University Medical Center officials suspended the four-member ambulance crew without pay. A hospital spokesperson said an internal investigation was underway.

Patrick J. Lynch, the president of the Patrolman's Benevolent Association, told reporters that the union stood behind officer Pantaleo. "This was a police officer that wanted to place this person [Garner] under arrest and bring him to the sidewalk. This was not a chokehold."

A Deadly Police Chase

It took 137 bullets, 62 police, 22 minutes, 13 shooting officers and two fatalities to end the police chase of Timothy Russell and Malissa Williams. Cleveland police officers began pursuing the light blue 1979 Chevy Malibu carrying the pair at about 10:30 PM on November 29, 2012. Authorities suspected the two were involved in drug activity. At some point the car is believed to have backfired, causing several officers to think shots were fired at them. Police did not find a gun in the car and those close to the pair say they don't know why Russell didn't stop the car. In the end police shot 43-year-old Russell 23 times and passenger Malissa Williams, 30, 24 times.

Two years later, a debate ignited by the deaths of Russell and Williams is spreading across the country as violent deaths and injuries cause authorities to rethink chase strategies. In Cleveland and in cities nationwide many experts, police departments and everyday citizens are questioning how and when police officers should conduct such pursuits.

While chases have gone on for decades, mounting concerns about public safety and excessive force claims are fueling police changes in states like Florida, Kansas, and California. In 2014, the Cleveland Police Department adopted a restrictive police chase policy: officers can only chase those suspected of a violent felony or driving while intoxicated. The move is part of a growing national trend among departments to limit chases...

Yamiche Alcindor, *USA Today*, June 28, 2014

23 DOMESTIC ABUSE

Can Violence Be Deterred?

Most of the rapes and murders, and other crimes of high emotion or specific motivation...are perpetrated by people who fit one or more of the following profiles: They are emotionally out of control; they are convinced that they are so justified in the act they are committing that it is not even a crime; and/or they believe that they won't be caught.... Put more simply, they are so angry, delusional, arrogant, or lacking in moral conscience that they don't care about the punishment. They don't connect the dots between behavior and consequence until after the act is committed.

Kamala D. Harris, *Smart on Crime*, 2009

Pediatrician Water Boards His Daughter

Dr. Melvin L. Morse, after earning his medical degree in 1980 from George Washington University, interned in pediatrics at the University of California at San Francisco. Dr. Morse completed his residency in pediatrics at Children's Hospital in Seattle then set up a private practice in the city. The young doctor also held the position of Clinical Associate Professor of Pediatrics at the University of Washington.

In the late 1980s, through his nonprofit organization called The Institute for the Scientific Study of Consciousness, Dr. Morse interviewed hundreds of children who had been declared clinically dead. These interviews led him to believe that children, too young to have been indoctrinated in religion and the belief in an afterlife, experienced near-death telepathic conversations and encounters with dead friends and relatives. (A manipulating interviewer of children who has an agenda can get them to believe anything.)

Cashing in on the results of his interview results, Dr. Morse, in 1991, published his first book (co-authored with writer Paul Perry). Called *Closer to the Light*, the book made *The New York Times* bestseller's list for three months and was eventually published in 19 languages in 38 countries. An accomplished self-promoter with a good publicist, the new-age guru appeared on the Larry King and Oprah Winfrey shows.

During the height of his doctor/feel-good-author fame, the pseudoscientist appeared on ABC's "20-20," NBC's "Unsolved Mysteries," and "Dateline," as well as "Good Morning America" and the "Tom Snyder Show." Dr. Morse was also the subject of dozens of uncritical articles in major newspapers and serious magazines.

In 1992, in the midst of his fame, Dr. Morse and his co-author cranked out a follow-up book called *Transformed by the Light*. The second work didn't do nearly as well as *Closer to the Light*. The doctor and his co-author's last book, *Where God Lives: The Science of the Paranormal and How Our Brains Are Linked to the Universe*, came out in 2001. (The *science* of the Paranormal?)

In 2012, the 58-year-old new age pediatrician lived with his second wife Pauline in Sussex, Delaware with his 5 and 11-year-old daughters. (I don't know what prompted his move from the state of Washington to Delaware, or when that took place. I do know he had gone through a contentious divorce from his first wife.) A look at Dr. Morse's bizarre website ramblings about "big ideas" that had drawn people to him from all over the world suggests his own brain has broken contact with reality. (How does a highly educated pediatrician go from physician to the publisher of junk science in the first place?)

On July 12, 2012, an incident involving Dr. Morse and his 11-year-old daughter marked the end of his credibility, even among his new-age followers. After pulling into his driveway that day, the girl, for one reason or another, refused to get out of the vehicle. The doctor yanked her out of the car by the ankles and dragged her across the gravel into the house where he gave her a spanking. Later in the day, the daughter informed a neighbor of what happened to her. The neighbor reported the girl's story to the police.

The following day local police officers arrested Dr. Morse. State child protection agents took his daughters into protective custody.

On Monday, August 6, 2012, Dr. Morse's 11-year-old daughter, while being questioned by officers with the Delaware State Police at the Child Advocacy Center, accused her father of subjecting her to what he called "water boarding." On at least four occasions, beginning in May 2009, Dr. Morse held her face under running faucets in the kitchen and the bathroom causing tap water to shoot up her nose. The abuse replicated the sensation of drowning. While he tortured his daughter the girl's 40-year-old mother looked on. The accuser's 5-year-old sister reportedly informed police officers she had witnessed the water boarding.

A local prosecutor charged Dr. Melvin Morse and his wife with felony counts of reckless endangerment, endangering the welfare of a child, and conspiracy to commit assault. Police officers took them into custody on Tuesday, August 7, 2012. After brief stints in the Sussex Correctional Institution, they made bail ($14,500 each) and were released.

Attorney Joe Hurley publicly questioned the credibility of his client's 11-year-old daughter, suggesting that she might have made false accusations to get attention.

Two days after the water boarding arrests, Secretary of State Jeffrey Bullock announced that Dr. Morse presented a "clear and immediate danger to public health" if permitted to continue practicing medicine. The state official ordered the emergency suspension of his Delaware medical license.

On April 11, 2014, Superior Court Judge Richard F. Stokes sentenced Dr. Morse to three to five years in prison. The judge denied a motion by Morse to remain free on bail while his attorney appealed his case. Dr. Morse said he was under treatment for prostate cancer. The judge sentenced the doctor's wife to probation.

Hard Ball Politics and Domestic Violence

Even in Nevada where hardball politics and corruption often go hand-in-hand, state assemblyman Steven Brooks had embarrassed and frightened his fellow politicians. In November 2012, the former Las Vegas city councilman and second-term state legislator, along with a few other democrats in the lower house, tried to unseat the democratic assembly speaker, Marilyn Kirkpatrick. The speaker fought-off the challenge to her throne and Brooks, as the leader of the failed insurrection, was relegated to legislative oblivion. As long as Marilyn Kirkpatrick ran the Nevada assembly, Steven Brooks had no future in politics.

While Steven Brooks never directly threatened speaker Kirkpatrick, in speaking to others, he allegedly indicated his intent to shoot her dead. On January 19, 2013, after word of Brook's threats had reached the speaker, she reported the matter to the Las Vegas police. Visibly upset, Kirkpatrick said she was worried that an armed Brooks would find her and pull the trigger.

Shortly after talking with speaker Kirkpatrick, officers encountered Brooks in his car at a traffic stop. Brooks informed the police, who asked him to open his trunk, that as a Nevada state assemblyman he could deny them permission to search. When officers lifted the trunk lid they found, in a shoebox, a .357-revolver and 41 rounds of ammunition. In explaining his possession of the firearm and the ammunition, Brooks said he had attended a National Rifle Association seminar for legislators earlier in the day. This turned out to be a lie.

After seizing the revolver and the ammunition officers arrested assemblyman Brooks on the felony charge of intimidating a public officer with physical force. Released on $100,000 bail, Brooks hired a publicist who set-up a press conference to be held on January 22 in his capitol office in Carson City. Brook's attorney, to the dozen reporters who showed-up for the conference, announced that his client couldn't be present at the press conference because he had been hospitalized with a digestive disorder.

Three days after the press conference no-show, the Las Vegas police responded to Brook's home on a domestic disturbance call. The officers hauled the assemblyman to a nearby hospital for psychiatric evaluation. The next day, the politician returned home. Insisting that his medical problems were physical and not mental, and proclaiming his innocence to the threat charges, Brooks rejected a suggestion from the assembly leadership that he take a leave of absence.

On February 10, 2013, the Las Vegas police responded to another domestic disturbance call from the assemblyman's residence. He had allegedly assaulted a member of his family. When officers arrested Brooks outside his house he became combative and before being subdued, grabbed for an officer's gun.

Charged with domestic battery and obstructing police, officers booked Brooks into the Clark County Detention Center. The judge set his bail at $4,000.

In March 2014, ex-Nevada assemblyman Brooks pleaded no contest to evading a police officer and resisting arrest. The judge, pursuant to the plea deal, sentenced him to two years eight months in prison.

Forever a Victim

In 2012, Carie Charlesworth, after having divorced her husband who had abused her for years, lived in Spring Valley, California with her two sons, age nine and elven, and her twin seven-year-old girls. Carie's ex-husband, 41-year-old Martin Charlesworth was under a court restraining order that prohibited him from contacting his former wife. (Martin did have child visitation rights.) Carie earned $37,000 a year as a second grade teacher at the Holy Trinity Catholic School in El Cajon, a town not far from San Diego.

Carie Charlesworth's troubled life took a turn for the worse in January 2013 when Martin, in violation of the restraining order against him, came to the school's parking lot in an effort to contact his ex-wife. Alarmed school officials responded to Martin's presence by locking down the school and calling the police.

Police officers rushed to the elementary school where they arrested the ex-husband for violating his restraining order. Shortly thereafter, Martin pleaded guilty to the charge of stalking in violation of the domestic court mandate. The judge sentenced Martin to a year in jail minus time served. He was scheduled for release from the San Diego County lockup on June 28, 3013.

According to Martin Charlesworth's attorney, he had gone to the school that January day to discuss child custody issues with his ex-wife. In speaking to reporters, the attorney said, "He just wants what's best for his children and Carie." In addressing the media, Carie Charlesworth said that based on her ex-husband's past behavior, she was afraid for her safety when he showed up at her place of employment that day.

Shortly after the January lockdown, the principal of Holy Trinity placed Carie on paid administrative leave. But in June 2013, an official with the San Diego Catholic diocese informed the 39-year-old teacher that she would not be offered a teaching position for the upcoming school year. In the letter containing this devastating news, the diocese administrator justified the decision by pointing out that according to public records, Martin Charlesworth "has a 20-plus year history of violence, abuse and harassment of people--mostly women--and he has continued the pattern to the present."

Thirty Holy Trinity parents held a rally outside the school in support of the diocese's decision to discontinue Carie Charlesworth's employment. These parents felt that her presence in the school, given the nature of her relationship with her violent and unpredictable ex-husband, endangered their children.

Carie Charlesworth, in discussing her situation with a reporter, said, "I followed all the things they tell domestic abuse victims to do. Now I feel I was the one who got punished. This is why other victims do not come forward."

A Psychopathic Loser

Jerry Remy played second base for the Boston Red Sox before becoming a Boston area sportscaster. Jerry's son, Jared, a violent man who abused drugs and women, didn't succeed at anything. The only thing Jared Remy became known for was beating up his girlfriends. Between 1998 and 2005 police arrested him six times for assault and battery. The crimes usually included terroristic threats and destruction of property. Except for a man he attacked in 2001 with a beer bottle, Remy's victims were women.

Notwithstanding his arrests for violent offenses against vulnerable victims, Jared's only punishment involved relatively short periods in jail. In most instances he got off light because his victims refused to bring charges. (Perhaps they were afraid to.) And it didn't hurt that his father, as the color analyst for Red Sox games on the New England Sports Network, was well known among sports fans.

In 2009, Jared lost his job as a security guard at Fenway Park in Boston after he and another guard were implicated in a steroid scandal. (If you've seen photographs of Remy, he looks like a scary, muscled-up idiot.)

In 2013, Jared resided with his girlfriend Jennifer Martel and their 5-year-old daughter in a Waltham Massachusetts town house. The 27-year-old Martel worked as an assistant store manager while pursuing a degree in elementary education at Framingham University. On August 13, Remy smashed Martel's face into a mirror. She called the police that led to his arrest for assault and battery. The next day Remy walked out of the Middlesex County Jail after posting his bond. In light of the attack, and Remy's history of violence against women, a judge granted Martel an emergency temporary restraining order.

Just two days after assaulting his girlfriend, Remy returned to his town house in violation of the restraining order. In the outdoor patio, in front of his daughter and in view of several of his neighbors, Remy pulled a knife and stabbed Martel. One of the witnesses, a neighbor named Benjamin Ray, tried to pull the frenzied Remy off the victim. Mr. Ray had to retreat when Remy waved the bloody knife at him. Several neighbors dialed 911.

Waltham police officers arrested the blood-covered 25-year-old at the scene. Jennifer Martel died a short time later from multiple stab wounds. This time Remy would not be released on bail.

On September 24, 2013, a Middlesex County grand jury indicted Jared Remy for murder as well as several lesser offenses.

A week after Remy's indictments, a reporter for the *Boston Herald* interviewed Remy at the jail in Cambridge. Staying true to his sociopathic nature, Remy, with a straight face, denied stabbing Jennifer Martel to death. To the reporter, the serial abuser of women seemed upbeat and enthusiastic about his chances of an acquittal. On a more melancholy note, the inmate said, "I know my life is going to suck when I get out of here." (Only a hard-core sociopath, under these circumstances, would talk about how life is going to be bad for *him*.)

During the 30-minute interview, Remy complained to the reporter that having a famous father was working against him. "You know," he said, "I think we're just like normal people. But if our name was Smith, you'd never see any of this in the newspaper." (If Remy had been named Smith, he wouldn't have been free on bail to murder his girlfriend.)

Following the Martel's murder, state officials took custody of the killer's daughter. The murder suspect's parents petitioned a judge to turn their granddaughter over to them. (Jerry Remy, following the murder, took a leave of absence from his sports casting job.)

Jared Remy, in speaking about his daughter with the *Boston Herald* reporter, said, "If she choses to know me at some point and wants to see me, that's fine. If she doesn't, that's fine too. I just want her to be happy. I love her. I want her to go to high school, I want her to go to college, I want her to have everything in life she deserves." (In true narcissistic form, it was all about what Remy wanted.) "She's in a good place. She has a dog to play with, which makes *me* happy, because she loves animals. *I'm* happy she going to be a veterinarian one day."

Regarding the inmate's parents who had tried to visit him (he had declined to see them), Remy said, "I'm sure they're not thrilled with me right now." (Talk about an understatement.)

At his October 8, 2013 arraignment, Jared Remy pleaded not guilty to all charges.

In the aftermath of Jennifer brutal, and predictable murder, Middlesex County District Attorney Marian Ryan came under criticism for her handling of the case.

In May 2014, Jared Remy pleaded guilty to first-degree murder. The judge sentenced him to life without the chance of parole. Following the sentencing, Remy said, "Blame me for this, not my family."

A Marriage Made in Hell

In 2011, Ludwig "Sonny" Schumacher lived in Essex, Vermont with his wife Christina and their son and daughter. They had been married 17 years and the marriage was falling apart along with their professional lives.

After retiring from the Vermont National Guard as a Colonel and a F-16 pilot, Schumacher accepted an executive position with the Timberiane Dental Company in South Burlington, Vermont. Christina worked as a financial officer with the GE Healthcare Corporation, a company she had been with for more than twenty years.

In July 2011, Christina petitioned a family court judge for an order of protection against abuse from her husband. In support of her request, Christina claimed that their 15-year-old daughter was afraid of her father. "My daughter," she wrote, "is fearful and has said if I do not file this petition she will file her own. She is now staying with friends." According to the protection order petition, Mr. Schumacher had struck Christina in the face in front of the girl. He had also abused his wife by grabbing her arm and pulling her hair. The family court judge denied the protection request.

In 2012, after Christina's job at GE Healthcare was eliminated, she landed a position with MyWebGrocer. A few months later she quit that job. Ludwig Schumacher ran into employment problems himself that year. Officials at Timberiane Dental fired him.

In July 2013, a judge granted Christina a temporary order of protection against her husband after he tipped his 14-year-old son Gunnar's bed upside down with him in it. According to the court petition, Mr. Schumacher kept the boy pinned to the floor by pressing his knee against his back. When Gunnar broke free, the father allegedly threw him to the floor. Christina cited this and other incidents of her husband's out-of-control rage to illustrate a "pattern of abuse which causes fear" for her and her son.

Ludwig Schumacher appealed his wife's protection of abuse order and won. The family court judge ruled that the description of events in Christina's petition did not constitute domestic abuse by a parent as defined by Vermont law.

Christina, on September 3, 2013, filed for divorce on grounds that her 49-year-old husband had been unfaithful, abusive, and mentally ill. Shortly after the divorce filing, he moved out of the house and rented an apartment in Essex. In cross-filing for divorce, Mr. Schumacher described Christina as mentally ill, noting that during the summer of 2013 she had received intensive mental health treatment at the Seneca Center at the Fletcher Allen Health facility in Burlington.

Ludwig, on Tuesday, December 17, 3013, called Essex High School stating that his son Gunnar would be absent two days due to "a family situation." A day later, at two in the afternoon, a friend of Gunnar's went to the Schumacher apartment where he found Gunnar and his father dead.

The 14-year-old boy had been strangled and his father had hanged himself. Mr. Schumacher left behind a long suicide letter explaining why he had murdered his son and killed himself. (The authorities have not released the contents of the suicide note.)

On the day after the discovery of her dead husband and son, a doctor informed Christina that if she didn't check herself into a psychiatric ward at the Fletcher Allen Health Care facility in Burlington, she would be taken into custody by the authorities and put into the hospital without her consent. Because Christina had once told her sister that if anything happened to her children she would kill herself, the doctor felt he was acting in her best interest. Christina insisted that she did not need mental health treatment. All she wanted to do was grieve with her 17-year-old daughter. The doctor followed through on his threat by having Christina involuntarily committed to the mental ward.

On December 30, 2013, Christina called the *Burlington Free Press* and asked the newspaper to investigate her situation, saying that the state had no basis to hold her against her will in the mental facility. While Vermont law does not require a prompt judicial review of involuntary mental health commitments, the publicity Christina received from newspaper stories prompted a judicial hearing.

On January 22, 2014, after three hours of testimony before a Superior Court judge in Burlington, the judge said he disagreed with Christina's mental illness diagnosis and the assessment that she was a danger to herself and others. The judge ordered her release after five and a half weeks in the psychiatric ward.

Vermont Attorney General William Sorrell, whose office had argued for Christina's continued hospitalization, had no comment for the press.

Giving Birth to Addicted Babies

At nine o'clock on Thursday night, February 13, 2014, the authorities in Everett, Washington issued an Amber Alert to locate 31-year-old Roshell Marie Turner and her 17-day-old son, John Turner. The new mother, a heavy methamphetamine user, had given birth to the infant on January 27 in a motel room. This baby was her eighth child.

The five-foot-five, 190-pound meth addict had a rose tattoo on her upper right shoulder and a Hispanic boyfriend nicknamed "Guero." Detectives believed Turner's friend, Marylee Cavin, was helping her hide from the authorities that would surely take the baby from her.

Police and officials with Child Protective Services believed that because of the mother's heavy use of meth, her baby needed immediate medical attention. Moreover, based on this woman's parenting history with her other seven children, the authorities had reason to suspect the missing infant was being neglected.

On Friday, February 14, 2014, police officers found the mother and her baby in a south Everett apartment. The infant was alive and transported to a nearby hospital. Child Protection officers, acting on a court order, took custody of the baby as well as Turner's other children.

After being questioned by detectives at the Everett Police Department, officers booked Turner into the Snohomish County Jail on unrelated warrants. A local prosecutor indicated that the meth-abusing mother might be charged with child endangerment.

It seems reasonable to charge woman who used drugs like meth while pregnant with aggravated assault. There is no question that this behavior amounts to child abuse. As August 2014, Roshell Turner had not been charged with any crime related to her newest baby.

Parents on Meth

A Florida couple was arrested for allegedly abandoning their three young children in the woods...Michael and Sarah Butcher, both 30, were arrested on February 28, 2014 after illegally parking their red truck in a private RV park in Punta Gorda, Florida. Cops later found crystal meth in their vehicle's glove compartment, along with a syringe and a burnt spoon....

After the pair was taken to jail--where they repeatedly claimed to be brother and sister--the police received a call that three children were found walking in the woods, "very dirty, hungry, and cold."...They told police officers their parents were named Michael and Sarah. The children--ages 10, 8, and 6--had walked nearly two miles before they were found...They said their parents had driven them to a wooded area where they often went camping. While they played in the woods, their parents drove off in their truck.

Jaime Lutz, ABC News, March 4, 2014

A Failure to Protect

In 2014, three-year-old Kayleigh Slusher lived with her mother, Sara Krueger, 23, and Krueger's 26-year-old boyfriend, Ryan Scott Warner. The couple and the toddler resided in Unit 7 at the Royal Garden apartment complex in east Napa, California.

Over the past five years Warner had been in and out of bay area jails for a variety of crimes including assault and possession of drugs. When his former girlfriend, Ashley Owens, refused to abort their child, Warner had sent her a series of threatening text messages that read: "I hope the kid dies," "I will scalp you," and "I will bust out your teeth with a pipe." Warner was obviously a violent man who didn't like children, or women.

Since June 2012, Napa police officers had been called to the Krueger apartment more than a dozen times on reports of domestic disturbance, theft, vandalism, and unwanted persons. By any standard, Unit 7 at the Royal Garden complex was a dangerous place to raise a child. And a lot of relatives and neighbors knew this. The only people who seemed oblivious to the situation were the police and the child welfare authorities. Unfortunately, these were the only people with the power to protect Kayleigh Slusher.

On January 27, 2014, a neighbor called the Napa police and requested a welfare check at Unit 7. According to the caller, Krueger and her boyfriend were using drugs and not feeding the little girl. They were also making a commotion and fighting with each other. Police officers visited the apartment that day and didn't find drugs or evidence of narcotics use. The officers also observed Kayleigh who seemed okay. The officers did not notify child protective services. They left things as they found them.

A Krueger relative, worried about the little girl, called the authorities two days later. On January 29, police officers returned to the apartment, examined the girl, and left. This would be the last day of Kayleigh's short life.

At 11:50 AM on Saturday, February 1, 2014, a police dispatcher in the bay area city of Richmond received an anonymous call from a man who had "something to get off his chest" about Sara Kreuger and her boyfriend. According to the tipster, the boyfriend, a guy named Brian or Ryan, had done something bad to Krueger's daughter.

That day, two police officers arrived at Unit 7, knocked on the door, and didn't get a response. A neighbor informed the officers that the day before, January 31, 2014, a man and woman, presumably the occupants of the unit, left the apartment. The little girl was not with them. Using a key they had acquired from the apartment complex manager, the officers entered the dwelling.

In one of the bedrooms the officers found Kayleigh in bed covered in blankets up to her neck. Next to her body was a doll. She was dead, and cold to the touch. She also had bruises around her eyes and blood in her nostrils. (A forensic pathologist would determine the cause of death to be "multiple blunt impact injuries to the head, torso, and extremities." The pathologist also found evidence of prior child abuse and neglect. Manner of death: Homicide.)

The following day, February 2, police arrested Krueger and Warner at a BART station in El Cerrito, California. According to the murdered girl's mother, she found Kayleigh dead when she returned to the apartment on the afternoon of January 30, 2014. Krueger said she placed the body into a plastic bag and stored it for a time in a freezer before tucking the little corpse into the bed.

Sara Krueger and Ryan Warner were booked into the Napa County Jail on charges of murder and felony assault of a child causing death. If convicted as charged, they face up to 25 years to life in prison.

On February 25, 2014, at the murder suspects' arraignment before Napa Superior Court Judge Mark Boessenecker, the couple pleaded not guilty. The judge denied both suspects bail.

Infant's Nose Bitten Off

A teen father in Northern California is under arrest after police say he bit the nose off his one-month-old son because he was frustrated with the infant's crying. Fairfield police say 18-year-old Joshua Cooper was being held Friday, March 14, 2014 in the Solano County Jail on suspicion of child cruelty and aggravated mayhem.

Police received a call the day before by a distraught woman who said her baby was bleeding from his nose. Doctors later determined the child suffered a skull fracture and a brain hemorrhage. Also, one third of the child's nose had been severed. The child was in stable condition at Oakland Children Hospital. Investigators were trying to determine how the skull fracture and the baby's brain hemorrhage occurred.

Fox News, March 14, 2014

Wife Murdered While Reporting Assault

In 2014, Richard Kirk, 47, resided in Denver's Observatory Park neighborhood not far from the University of Denver. Richard and his wife Kristine purchased the upscale, Tudor style home in 2005. The couple had three soccer-playing grade school boys. Richard's friends described him as a religious, happy-go-lucky man devoted to his family.

On December 23, 1993, while living in Dallas, Texas, Richard, then single, was charged with felony assault. The prosecutor dropped the charge to a misdemeanor offense then eventually dismissed the case altogether. At the time, Kristine resided five miles away in a Dallas apartment.

In 2000, a police officer in Douglas County, Colorado arrested Richard for driving under the influence. (The disposition of this case is unknown.) These two incidents comprise the extent of Kirk's arrest record.

At 9:32 on the night of Monday, April 14, 2014, 44-year-old Kristine A. Kirk called a 911 dispatcher in Denver to report a domestic disturbance at her residence. She said her husband had been smoking marijuana and was scaring their three young sons. According to Kristine, he had also been hallucinating and talking about the end of the world. Most disturbingly, he said he wanted her to shoot him to death.

The dispatcher asked Kristine if there was a gun in the dwelling. The caller said yes, but it was locked inside a safe. The situation turned ominous when Kristine informed the dispatcher that her husband had gotten the handgun out of the safe and was holding it in his hand.

About thirteen minutes into the 911 call the dispatcher heard a scream and then a gunshot. At that point the line went dead. The dispatcher immediately upgraded the 911 call from a domestic disturbance case to a "code 10"--a possible shooting.

Two Denver police officers rolled up to the Kirk house on South St. Paul Street at 9:47 PM. Three minutes later, one of the officers called for an ambulance, and advised the 911 dispatcher that they "were going to need homicide."

An officer put Richard Kirk into handcuffs and escorted him to the patrol car. From the backseat of the police vehicle, without prompting, the suspect admitted shooting his wife to death.

The next day a local prosecutor charged Richard Kirk with first-degree murder. At his arraignment on Wednesday, April 16, 2014, the judge advised the suspect of the charge against him, assigned him a public defender, and ordered him held without bail. Kirk showed no emotion as he stood before the magistrate.

The media, as it often does in high-profile crimes, began assessing blame. In this case reporters were quick to note that since 2008, the 911-response time at the Denver Police Department had grown longer. According to a police spokesperson, budget cuts and fewer officers on patrol has adversely affected police response time to domestic calls.

Notwithstanding the 15 minute lapse between the victim's 911 call and the arrival of the officers, there was no way to know for sure if a faster police response would have saved Kristine Kirk's life.

Because marijuana was legal in Colorado the media made a big deal over the fact that before allegedly murdering his wife, Richard Kirk had smoked pot. Without toxicological testing and a psychiatric evaluation, there was no way to know if marijuana played a role in the killing.

An Abused Child Is Murdered

In November 2013, Florida's Department of Children and Families (DCF) reunited Rachel Fryer with her five children. They had been taken away on May 13, 2011 when her infant son Tavont'ae Gordon died. (A forensic pathologist determined that the baby's death was accidental.) Fryer claimed to have rolled over on the child. The medical examiner ruled the cause of death mechanical asphyxiation, a so-called "co-sleeping fatality." The DCF took the five remaining children from the house due to evidence of substance abuse. Besides drugs, the 32-year-old mother had other problems. She was depressed, abusive, and for years had been in trouble with the law. But after completing a parenting program, she got her five children back.

Fryer, a resident of Sanford, Florida, a town of 53,000 in the Orlando metropolitan area, served six months in jail in 2012 for violating the terms of her drug probation. Police in Seminole County arrested her in December 2013 for failure to appear in court. Over the past several years, she had been charged with resisting arrest, battery of a law enforcement officer, petty theft, and possession of marijuana.

On Monday morning, February 10, 2014, one of Fryer's neighbors, worried about the well being of the Fryer children, called the DCF and requested a welfare check of the Fryer home. A caseworker arrived at the house to find Rachel gone. The social worker removed four of Fryer's children from the dwelling. The fifth child, 2-year-old Tariji, Tavont'ae's twin sister, was missing. Concerned about the welfare of the toddler, the caseworker called the Sanford Police Department. Detectives launched a missing persons investigation.

That Monday night, Rachel Fryer showed up at the Sanford police station with a disturbing story. She claimed that on Thursday, February 6, when she tried to wake up her 2-year-old daughter, the toddler was unresponsive. She spent the next thirty minutes trying to revive the little girl with CPR. When that failed, and it became obvious that the child had stopped breathing, Fryer wrapped the body in a blanket. She did not call 911, the police department, or anyone else.

After placing the dead girl into a leopard-print suitcase, a friend drove Fryer and Tariji to Crescent City, Florida, a town of two thousand in Putnam County northeast of Sanford. In the front yard of a house on Madison Avenue, Fryer buried her daughter in a shallow grave.

In searching Fryer's cellphone, detectives discovered text messages that revealed the mother's state of mind in the days leading up to Tariji's death. In one message she had texted: "I'm bout to have a nervous breakdown. I can't take it no more....My child is retarded, I don't know what else to do....I need my depression medicine ASAP. This is too much, I'm about to lose it."

From Fryer's 7-year-old daughter, detectives learned that Fryer regularly hit her children with a broom handle, a mop, and shoes. The 7-year-old said her mother had beaten her the day before her younger sister disappeared.

On Tuesday, February 11, 2014, police officers in Crescent City, in the front yard of the house on Madison Avenue, saw a child's shoe sticking out of a freshly dug grave. Under the dirt officers found the corpse of a young girl wearing clothing that preliminarily identified the remains of Tariji Fryer. The leopard-print suitcase lay nearby.

After a prosecutor in Sanford charged Rachel Fryer with aggravated child neglect, she was booked into the John E. Polk Correctional Facility. The judge denied her bond. In the meantime, investigators waited for the results of the girl's autopsy.

On Tuesday, February 11, detectives questioned Tariji's father, 28-year-old Timothy Gordon. The DCF had not reunited Gordon with his children because he did not take the required parenting counseling in May 2011 following the death of Tavont'ae.

The Seminole County Medical Examiner's Office, on February 27, 2014, reported that Tariji Gordon had been killed by blunt force trauma to the head. Some of the victim's injuries included, according to a south Florida forensic dentist, bite marks linked to the suspect. The medical examiner ruled the girl's death a criminal homicide. Following that ruling, a local prosecutor charged Rachel Fryer with murder and aggravated child abuse.

At the suspect's murder arraignment, she pleaded not guilty. Prosecutors told reporters that in this case they will seek the death penalty.

On March 12, 2014, a Seminole County grand jury indicted Fryer for first-degree murder and several lesser offenses. According to detectives who interrogated the suspect, she has confessed to murdering her daughter.

Joe Biden on Domestic Abuse

In a speech delivered in Washington, D. C. on Wednesday, March 13, 2013, Vice President Joe Biden, the self-proclaimed criminal justice expert on subjects ranging from how to stop intruders by shot-gunning them through closed doors, to the problem of domestic violence, once again revealed the scope and depth of his stupidity. In profiling men who physically abuse women, Biden said, "We've learned that certain behaviors on the part of an abuser portend much more danger than other behaviors. For example, if an abuser has attempted to strangle his victim, if he's threatened to shoot her, if he's sexually assaulted her, these are tell tale signs to say this isn't your garden variety slap across the face."

Joe Biden has the unusual ability to make statements that are both puerile and offensive. While it's obvious that a man who attempts to strangle a woman is dangerous, a man who slaps a woman in the face could be just as dangerous. "Garden variety" or not, a man who has slapped a woman in the face has committed criminal assault. Moreover, slaps have a way of escalating to more severe beatings, and even murder.

Among the dumb politicians in Washington, Joe Biden had been the most eager to put his stupidity on display. He'd done it time and time again. In fact, he'd stepped in it so many times and in so many ways, people no longer took much notice. I guess every village had to have its idiot. But when that idiot could become the President of the United States, it's a cause for concern.

The Short Violent Life of an Abused Child

Jade Murray lived in Aurora, Missouri a town of 7,500 in the southwest corner of the state. On December 14, 2013, the 22-year-old took her 4-year-old son, Skylar Bradley, to a medical facility in Aurora. She told medical personnel that she had found her unresponsive son in his bedroom.

That evening he had been ill, and had refused to eat. The doctor noticed that the boy had bruises on his arms, side and back. From Aurora, the critically ill boy was transported to Mercy Hospital in Springfield, Missouri.

Shortly after arriving at the hospital in Springfield, Skylar Bradley died. According to the forensic pathologist who performed the autopsy, the boy died of a ruptured spleen. The medical examiner ruled his death a homicide.

Detectives with the Missouri State Highway Patrol, suspecting child abuse, questioned the dead boy's mother. Jade Murray denied hitting or otherwise abusing her son. Investigators asked if someone else had beaten the child. The mother insisted that he had not been physically mistreated by anybody.

From people who knew Jade Murray and the boy, the homicide detectives received a different picture. According to these interviewees, the hot-tempered young mother frequently took out her wrath on the boy. Several people had witnessed Murray strike the child with her fist, and noticed that he seemed permanently bruised. In one reported incident, Murray had allegedly spanked him so hard the paddle broke.

Detectives also learned that Murray not only used illegal drugs, she regularly gave Skylar NyQuil and even Xanax to sedate him.

On June 6, 2014, pursuant to an interrogation conducted by the state investigators, Jade Murray confessed to physically abusing her son. On the night he died, she admitted hitting him several times for not obeying. She had allegedly struck him so hard she knocked the child off his bed then ordered him to stay in his room. When she checked on the boy 45 minutes later, she found him unresponsive.

Following the confession, a Lawrence County prosecutor charged Murray with second-degree murder and second-degree domestic assault. Officers booked the suspect into the county jail. At her arraignment, the judge set her bond at $250,000.

If convicted of second-degree murder, Murray faced up to thirty years in prison. The domestic assault charge carries a maximum sentence of seven years behind bars.

A Stupid Sentence

Some call it creative ruling; some call it bench buffoonery. In 2012 Joseph Bray was accused of shoving his wife and putting his hands around her throat when she snapped at him for forgetting her birthday. Judge John Hurley decided to hand out a unique punishment: a little romance.

Not only did Judge Hurley order Bray to take his wife on a date, he also specified that it must be dinner at Red Lobster, followed by bowling, and that he must purchase flowers.

Sounds like a good sentence, right? Bray can throw his wife around all he wants, as long as he takes her out to dinner afterward.

Neil Patrick Steward, *Headlines! Headlines!* 2012

A History of Domestic Abuse

Spousal abuse is a serial crime committed by angry husbands across America's socio-economic landscape. Wives are beaten in trailer parks, upscale apartment buildings, suburban track homes, and in million-dollar houses in gated neighborhoods. Husbands seldom abuse their wives in public, or in front of friends and relatives. Because it's largely a hidden crime, no one knows how many wives are exposed to domestic violence.

Every so often we are reminded of the domestic abuse problem when a well-known, successful man is arrested for hurting his wife. If she is a celebrity as well, it's a big news event. If the alleged perpetrator and his victim are both members of the news media, it's an even bigger story.

The domestic violence arrest of a New York City anchorman married to a TV reporter was a reminder that even successful, high profile women are vulnerable to spousal abuse.

A former Marine and reporter that covered the war in Afghanistan, Rob Morrison, in 1989, began anchoring NBC television's weekday morning show, "Today in New York." He and his wife Ashley, a reporter for CBS-TV, lived in an apartment on Manhattan's upper West Side. Between 2003 and 2009, Ashley, alleging spousal abuse, called the New York City Police Department seven times. While only one of these calls resulted in her husband's arrest (the files of this case are sealed), NYPD police reports paint Rob Morrison as a hard-drinking, verbally abusive bully with a taste for Internet pornography.

In 2009, the couple purchased a million-dollar house in the upscale, suburban town of Darien, Connecticut. Ashley worked as a correspondent on the CBS news show, "MoneyWatch." Rob left NBC that year to anchor, in New York City, a CBS program called "News at Noon." During his first year at CBS, Rob wrote a column for the Huffington Post about raising his son titled, "Daddy Diaries: Confessions of a Stay-At-Home Anchorman."

Around two in the morning on Sunday, February 17, 2013, officers with the Darien Police Department rolled up at the Morrison residence. Ashley Morrison's mother, Martha Risk, had called 911 from her home in Columbia, Indiana. The mother reported that her son-in-law, during an argument with her 110 pound daughter, had grabbed her by the throat. Rob Morrison, the subject of the long-distance complaint, told the responding officers to "get the hell out of my house."

Rob Morrison's scratched and bleeding nose and swollen lip, and the red hand-marks on Ashley's neck, provided the Darien officers with enough physical evidence of domestic violence to support an arrest. According to the police report, as police officers escorted Rob Morrison from the house in handcuffs, he said that if released from custody, he'd return to the dwelling and kill his wife. (Morrison denies making that threat.) Throughout his encounter with the police, Morrison remained belligerent.

Later that Sunday, notwithstanding the alleged death threat against his wife, Morrison walked out of jail after posting a $100,000 bond. The next day he showed up for work at the TV station, and when asked about his nose and fat lip, Morrison didn't mention his arrest, or the domestic violence charges that had been filed against him. (When his arrest hit the news, the anchorman's superiors at CBS were not happy.)

On Tuesday, February 29, 2013, in a Stamford, Connecticut court, Rob Morrison was formally charged with felony strangulation, second degree threatening, and disorderly conduct. Judge Kenneth Povodator ordered the defendant out of the house in Darien, and pursuant to an order of protection, instructed him to stay 100 yards from his wife, except when they were at work. Judge Povodator, in referring to the Darien police report, said, "It not only reflects a serious incident, it reflects the likelihood of a serious history [of domestic violence]."

In speaking to reporters after the hearing, Morrison blamed his problems on his wife's mother, the source of the 911 domestic disturbance call. He said, "Don't piss-off your mother-in-law is the moral of this story."

Perhaps the moral of the story should be don't choke your wife.

On Wednesday, February 20, Rob Morrison announced that he had resigned from his $300,000-year-job at WCBS-TV. To reporters he said, "My family is my first and only priority right now, and I have informed CBS management that I need to put all of my time and energy into making sure that I do what's right for my wife and son...I did not choke my wife. I've never laid hands on my wife. I was just as surprised by that particular charge as probably everyone else."

Had Morrison not resigned, he may have been suspended, or fired. Moreover, there are people who were *not* surprised by the domestic violence charges against the anchorman. One of those persons is Morrison's mother-in-law, Martha Risk who, on February 20, told a reporter with the *New York Daily News* that Rob Morrison had been abusing Ashley for ten years. She said, "You wonder when you are going to get another call, if it's going to be [from] the hospital. How bad is she hurt this time? You have such a horrible feeling in yourself...This has gone on for too long." Risk told the reporter that when her son-in-law called her early Sunday morning, he was "drunk as a skunk." The moment he hung up she called 911.

In April 2014 the local prosecutor dropped the charges against Morrison following his completion of a domestic violence program. But in mid-June, less than two months after going through the program, Darien police arrested Morrison for domestic harassment. Within a period of three days he had allegedly called his estranged wife 121 times.

Ashley Morrison told police officers she was afraid that if she caused her estranged husband to be arrested, he would kill her. Fearing for her life, she and her son fled to Florida about the time officers took Mr. Morrison into custody.

At Morrison's arraignment, the judge issued a more restrictive protection order then set the suspect's bail at $50,000. Shortly thereafter the ex-TV man posted bail and went home.

Child Abusers Get Off Light

Douglas B. Barbour was a prosecutor in the Pennsylvania State Attorney's Office headquartered in Harrisburg, the capital of the state. The 33-year-old attorney was assigned to the district office in Pittsburgh, located in the western part of the state. He and his 30-year-old wife Kristen resided in Franklin Park, a borough of 14,000 just north of the city. In March 2012, the couple, through a religious organization called Bethany Christian Services, adopted a 5-year-old boy and an 11-month-old girl. The children were from Ethiopia.

On September 14, 2012, Dr. Rachel Berger at Children's Hospital of Pittsburgh examined the Barbour children. The 6-year-old boy had been brought to the hospital with hypothermia--his body temperature was 93.6-- rapid breathing, and skin lesions caused by prolonged exposure to urine. He weighed 47 pounds and was severely malnourished.

The girl, 18-months-old, had breathing difficulties, retinal hemorrhaging, brain injury, and healing fractures in her femur and a toe. (Kristen Barbour told Dr. Berger that the toddler had suffered several accidental falls.) As a result of the toddler's head trauma, she was blind in one eye, perhaps permanently. The little girl was also malnourished. (Tests would later reveal that the healing bone fractures were not the result of disease.)

Dr. Berger, suspecting child abuse, notified the Allegheny County Police Department. The boy was admitted to the hospital's urgent care center and the girl placed into protective custody. In the doctor's report, she wrote this about the 6-year-old boy: "[He is] the victim of significant neglect and possible emotional abuse over a prolonged period of time."

After spending six days in the hospital, the boy, having gained seven pounds, was taken to A Child's Place, a children's abuse facility at the Mercy Health Center in Pittsburgh.

On October 2, 2012, detectives with the Allegheny County Police Department questioned the boy at the Mercy Health Center. According to the child, whenever he soiled his pants, his parents made him eat his meals in the bathroom.

Two days after speaking to the 6-year-old, the police arrested Douglas and Kristen Barbour. They were charged with two counts of endangering the welfare of a child, and in the case of their 18-month-old daughter, aggravated assault a felony offense. Regarding the boy, the couple faced charges of simple assault, a misdemeanor. The state attorney general's office suspended Douglas Barbour without pay pending the outcome of the case.

Detectives searched the couple's suburban home in Franklin Park and found, in the boy's bedroom, nothing but a mattress and a sheet. There were no toys, window coverings, wall decorations, or anything else that makes a place livable.

According to an employee of the adoption service, Mrs. Barbour had complained that the boy was "rude, defiant, and very difficult." She also complained that both children ate too much.

On June 23, 2014, Douglas and Kristen Barbour pleaded no contest to two counts each of endangering children. Mr. Barbour pleaded to misdemeanor counts while his wife pleaded to felony charges. As part of his plea deal, Mr. Barbour received a probated sentence. Although his wife faced three to twelve months in jail, her attorney has asked for probation. The couple relinquished their parental rights and the children remain in foster care. In all probability Mr. Barbour will lose his license to practice law.

These child abusers, in my opinion, got off light. In the plea bargaining deal society got the worst of it.

Football Star Cold-Cocks His Girlfriend

In 2014, Baltimore Ravens running back Ray Rice lived in Reistertown, Maryland with his girlfriend, Janay Palmer. At three in the morning on Saturday, February 15, 2014, while Rice and Palmer were staying at the Revel Casino-Hotel in Atlantic City, New Jersey, he punched her unconscious in a hotel elevator.

According to the police report, in the midst of an argument, Palmer slapped the football player in the face. He responded with a punch that knocked her out. When she came to on the carpet near the elevator door, she refused to receive medical attention. She and Rice checked out of the hotel and went home.

Jim McClain, an Atlantic County prosecutor, decided not to charge the 27-year-old Rice with assault.

On February 19, 2014, TMZ Sports aired a video that showed Rice dragging his unconscious girlfriend out of the elevator. She was seen lying facedown on the hotel floor.

Officials with the National Football League (NFL) reviewed the incident pursuant to the league's personal conduct policy. Under that clause, the NFL had the authority to suspend Rice for the season or banishing him from the league. On July 24, 2014, Commissioner Roger Goodell suspended the three-time Pro Bowler from playing in the first two games of the upcoming season.

Reporters covering the case for ESPN, *USA Today,* and other media outlets criticized Goodell and the NFL for not taking domestic abuse in the league seriously.

After being knocked cold in the hotel elevator, Janay Palmer married the man who dropped her to the floor with one punch.

24 ARSON-MURDER

Set On Fire

Arson-murder cases fall into three categories. It becomes arson-murder when the victim is say, shot to death, and the killer sets a fire to cover the crime. A fire-setter who burns down a building for the insurance money and in the process kills an occupant no one knew was in the structure, commits arson-murder. And finally, using fire as the agent of death comprises arson-murder. This form of the offense is the most unusual of the three.

On Saturday, December 17, 2011, in Brooklyn, New York, a crime took place that falls into the one-of-a-kind category. It involved the cruel, cold-blooded, and sadistic murder of 73-year-old Doris Gillespie.

Shortly after four in the afternoon, as the victim returned from grocery shopping and was about to exit the elevator that stopped at her apartment floor, Gillespie encountered a man dressed like an exterminator who wore surgical gloves and a white dust mask perched atop his head the way Jackie Kennedy used to wear her sunglasses. The thin, middle-aged man held a canister with a nozzle, a Molotov cocktail, and a barbecue-style lighter. He methodically sprayed the victim and her grocery bags with a fine mist of gasoline, then ignited the rag sticking out of the flammable liquid filled bottle. As he backed out of the elevator, he tossed in the fuse-lit Molotov cocktail. The compartment filled with smoke, and the victim, engulfed in flames, burned to death as she crouched against the rear wall of the elevator. Two video cameras recorded the murder.

The following morning, 47-year-old Jerome Isaac, with burns on the left side of his face, turned himself in to the New York City Police. He said he had been hired by the victim to clean out clutter from her apartment. He said she had fired him after accusing him of theft. After Isaac harassed this woman for the $2,000 he thought she owed him, he set fire to her in the elevator.

At Isaac's Monday arraignment, the magistrate denied him bail. The police, other than the fact Isaac didn't have a criminal record, and had been seen around the neighborhood collecting bottles and cans, didn't know much about him except he's been treated for mental illness.

On January 11, 2013, a State Supreme Court judge in Brooklyn sentenced Isaac to fifty years in prison. Judge Del Gidudice called the crime the most brutal he had seen in his judicial career. "That is not something one can take from one's mind," he said.

What makes this case so disturbing, beyond the nature of the crime is that everywhere we go there are violent people. They might look and act harmless until something sets them off. There is nothing the police can do to protect us from people like this. All they can do is react, and by then it's too late.

The Arson Spree

Between December 27, 2009 and January 4, 2010, an arsonist in Northhampton, Massachusetts torched more than 40 homes. It was the biggest crime spree in the history of the town. One of the Ward 3 neighborhood fires took the lives of 81-year-old Paul Yeskie and his son Paul, Jr. who was 39. Police officers patrolling Ward 3 during the early morning hours on four of the arson-plagued nights pulled over a vehicle driven by 26-year-old Anthony P. Baye. These investigative stops did not result in Baye's arrest.

Anthony Baye was brought in for questioning on January 4, 2010 by Massachusetts State Police sergeant Paul Zipper and Trooper Michael Mazza. After he was warned of his *Miranda* rights to remain silent, and have access to an attorney, Baye asked to speak to a lawyer. The officers, instead of terminating the interrogation at that point, informed Baye that he would be better off speaking to them first. They assured him that if he took responsibility for setting the fires, the judge would go easy on him. Utilizing the age-old confession inducing technique (developed by Fred Inbau in the 1930s) of minimizing the seriousness and immorality of the crimes (referring to the arsons as "tomfoolery"), the troopers got Baye to admit setting 15 of the fires.

While Anthony Baye didn't come out and admit setting fire that killed the Yeskies, he did say he never meant to do them any harm. In soliciting the arson-murder confession, one of the interrogators misrepresented the criminal law when he assured Baye that if he hadn't *intended* to kill the Yeskies, he could not be charged with felony-murder. (Under the law in

Massachusetts, if Baye had intended to set the fire that inadvertently led to their deaths, he was guilty of criminal homicide under the felony-murder doctrine.)

Following the ten-hour, videotaped interrogation, the state troopers took Baye into custody. The local prosecutor charged him with two counts of first-degree murder, and several counts of arson. Given the seriousness of the crimes, Baye was not granted bail.

Baye's attorneys, Thomas Lesser and David Hoose, on grounds the state interrogators had violated their client's Fifth and Six Amendment rights by not discontinuing the interrogation and providing him with an attorney when he requested one, filed a motion to suppress the confession.

On September 21, 2011, Hampshire Superior Court Judge Constance B. Sweeney heard arguments on the defendant's motion to suppress. At the conclusion of the pre-trial hearing, Judge Sweeney, while expressing reservations regarding the troopers' interrogation techniques, ruled Baye's confession voluntary, and therefore admissible. The defense appealed Judge Sweeney's ruling to the Massachusetts Supreme Judicial Court that agreed to rule on the admissibility of Baye's confession before rather than after his trial.

On May 21, 2012, the Massachusetts Supreme Court Justices ruled the Baye confession involuntary, and therefore inadmissible as evidence against him. While the justices didn't specifically rule on the issue of whether continuing the interrogation after Baye requested an attorney rendered it inadmissible, the constitutional law on this issue is settled. In the Baye case, the state interrogators had clearly violated Baye's *Miranda* rights. (I'm not a fan of the *Miranda* doctrine, but that is the case law.) Under *Miranda*, a confession can be inadmissible even though it was voluntary. Once a suspect exercises his *Miranda* rights, the interrogation must stop. Anything said after this point will not be admissible evidence.

One year after the court ruled Baye's confession inadmissible, the defendant, pursuant to an agreed upon plea agreement, pleaded guilty to two counts of manslaughter. On May 15, 2013, the Hampshire Superior Court judge sentenced Anthony P. Baye to twenty years in prison and fifteen years probation.

A Botched Robbery That Turned Deadly

At 1:48 in the morning of Wednesday, October 17, 2012, a Glendale, Colorado police officer on routine patrol spotted flames coming out the back of Fero's Bar & Grill that was situated in a strip mall five miles south of downtown Denver. Firefighters, upon entering the structure to combat the blaze, discovered five corpses.

One of the four women found dead at the fire scene was 63-year-old Young Fero, the owner of the establishment. The South Korean native assumed sole proprietorship of the 28-year-old business following her divorce from its co-founder, Danny Fero. The strip mall also housed a check cashing store, a nail salon, and a tennis shop. Fero's Bar & Grill catered to regular patrons and guests staying at local hotels. The bar featured a weekly poker game, pool tables, and Japanese food. Recently it had not been a particularly busy place.

A spokesperson with the Denver Police Department, at a press conference later in the day, announced that on-site evidence indicated that the fire had been intentionally set fifteen to twenty minutes before the bar's regular 2:00 AM closing time. The bodies of the five victims showed signs of physical trauma unrelated to the blaze. As a result, investigators were operating on the theory that the victims had been murdered before someone set the place on fire. Detectives believed the murders had been committed in the commission of an armed robbery, and the arson was motivated by an effort to cover up the crime.

Besides Young Fero, the bar's owner and operator, the other victims, all patrons, were: Daria M. Pohl, 22; Kellene Fallon, 45; Ross Richter, 29; and Teressa Beesley, 45. Except the killer-arsonists, there were no other people in the bar during the robbery, murders, and fire.

On October 18, the day after the arson-murders, the Denver police arrest three men in connection with the case. Dexter Lewis, 22 and brothers Joseph Hill, 27 and Lynell Hill, 24, were each charged with five counts of murder and one count of aggravated robbery and arson.

Dexter Lewis, engaged to a woman who was seven months pregnant, had been arrested in May 2009 in Jefferson County, Colorado on several counts of assault on a police officer. He pleaded guilty to felony menacing. The other charges were dropped. That year Lewis also pleaded guilty to felony robbery, and was sentenced to three years in prison. When arrested on October 18 in connection with the Fero's Bar & Grill mass murder case, he was out on parole.

Police in Arapahoe County had arrested Lynell Hill in August 2011 on charges of misdemeanor assault, reckless endangerment, and harassment. Hill pleaded guilty to harassment involving physical force and in return received a deferred nine-month sentence that allowed him to stay out of jail as long as he stayed out of trouble.

Joseph Hill, on his Facebook page, called himself a "singer song writer" who is just a "great person to know, if you're genuine." Hill, who apparently thought a lot of himself, went on to say, "I'm very hardworking and dedicated and very ambitious as well. I'm chasing my dreams."

The Denver Medical Examiner's office ruled the manner of these five deaths as criminal homicide. All of the victims were dead before the fire started, shot to death.

The brothers pleaded guilty to the murders in December 2013. A month later the judge sentenced Joseph to five life sentences and Lynell to 70 years in prison. As part of the plea agreement, the brothers agreed to testify against Lewis. In May 2014, the prosecutor in the Lewis case announced his intention to pursue the death penalty.

The Pest Exterminator

Dr. Melissa Ketunuti, a 35-year-old pediatrician, was a second-year infectious disease fellow and researcher at the University of Pennsylvania's Perelman School of Medicine in downtown Philadelphia. The Thailand native lived in a central city town house not far from the hospital. Except for her 6-year-old pit bull/lab mix Pooch she lived alone. Dr. Ketunuti had resided at this address for three years, and was in the process of rehabilitating the dwelling.

On Monday, January 21, 2013, Dr. Ketunuti left her town house around nine in the morning to run some errands. She planned to return to her home at ten-fifty to meet with an exterminator with a pest-control company headquartered in Newtown, Pennsylvania. Dr. Ketunuti was having mice problems. When the doctor's dog walker came to the house to pick up Pooch at twelve-thirty, she smelled smoke, and upon investigation, discovered Dr. Ketunuti dead in her basement. The terrified dog walker dialed 911.

Homicide detectives and crime scene technicians arrived at the town house to find a still smoldering, badly burned corpse. The victim's face had been so severely charred by the fire it was unrecognizable. The fully dressed woman was lying facedown and had been hogtied with her wrists and ankles bound behind her back. The killer had left a length of cordage around the victim's neck suggesting that before being set on fire, she had been strangled.

Based on the dead woman's apparel and other points of identity, investigators assumed that the murdered woman in the basement was Dr. Melissa Ketunuti. Detectives found no signs of forced entry, or indications of a sexual assault. Because it didn't appear that anything had been taken from the premises, the killer had not been motivated by theft.

As investigators began tracing the victim's activities that morning, and gathering footage from neighborhood surveillance cameras, the city of Philadelphia posted a $20,000 reward for information leading to the identification and arrest of this murderer. The next day, a local community group added $15,000 to the incentive.

On Wednesday, January 23, 2013, homicide investigators were in Levittown, Pennsylvania, a sprawling suburban Bucks County community 25 miles northeast of Philadelphia. The officers were in town questioning a 37-year-old pest-control subcontractor named Jason Smith. Smith lived in a powder blue, two-story house surrounded by a white picket fence still displaying Christmas decorations. The exterminator lived there with his girlfriend, their young daughter, and the girlfriend's stepfather.

Surveillance camera footage in Ketunuti's neighborhood showed Smith, who had been scheduled for a service call at the murder victim's house that morning, walking toward the doctor's town house at ten-fifty. (The house itself was off-camera.) The tall, thin exterminator was wearing a NorthFace jacket and work gloves, and carried a satchel. Just before noon, Smith was video-recorded driving his silver Ford F-150 pickup out of the neighborhood. Before leaving, he circled the block two times. While in Levittown, officers searched Smith's house, his trash, and his truck. Investigators took a computer out of the dwelling, and from the Ford F-150, seized a jacket and a pair of work gloves.

The next day at nine o'clock in the evening, detectives returned to Levittown to arrest Jason Smith. They took him into custody as he, his girlfriend, and their daughter watched "American Idol." Charged with first-degree murder, arson, abuse of corpse, and risking a catastrophe (burning down the neighborhood), Smith was locked up and held without bail. During the arrest, the family's dog, a boxer named Tyson, charged the arresting officers and had to be shot dead.

According to a statement released by a Philadelphia law enforcement spokesperson, Smith and Ketunuti, while in the doctor's basement, got into some kind of argument. The suspect punched her to the floor, jumped on top or her, and used a length of rope to strangle her to death. In an effort to destroy physical evidence that might link him to the body, Smith set fire to the victim's clothing with his lighter. (The body contained no traces of an accelerant.)

Jason Smith, except for a 2004 DUI conviction, has no criminal record. He told his interrogators that he is addicted to prescription painkillers, and that when arguing with the pest-control customer in her basement, he "snapped." According to Smith, when the doctor "belittled" him, he flew into a murderous rage.

A friend of the suspect, in speaking to ABC News, revealed that Smith, as a child, had a difficult time controlling his anger. The friend remembers that in his childhood Smith had problems with pyromania.

In April 2013, at a preliminary hearing before Philadelphia Municipal Judge Teresa Carr Deni, homicide detective Edward Tolliver read Jason

Smith's murder confession into the record. According to Detective Henry Glenn, the victim, at the time of her violent death, was wearing riding boots. Dr. Ketunuti's hand and feet had been tied behind her with a leather strap from horse gear. Smith, in his confession, told the detectives that he had bound the victim's ankles with a riding stirrup.

After murdering Dr. Ketunuti in her home, Smith drove to another pest extermination job in New Jersey.

At the preliminary hearing, Smith's attorneys, James A. Funt and Marc Bookman, did not contest the murder charge but asked the judge to dismiss the arson count because their client had not intended to burn down the building.

On April 10, 2013, Jason Smith confessed to strangling, tying up and setting fire to the victim. As of July 2014, the Smith case had not come to trial.

A Sentence of Death

Sexually abused as a child, and addicted to methamphetamine, Rickie Lee Fowler lived a life of violence and crime. On October 25, 2003, while riding in a van driven by David Valdez, Jr., Fowler tossed burning road flares out of the moving vehicle. The 22-year-old, angry because he and his family had been evicted from their home, wanted to start fires.

During the next nine days, the twelve wildfires that swept southern California's San Bernardino foothills scorched 442 square miles of land, and burned 1,000 homes to the ground. Five people died of heart attacks while evacuating their fire-threatened dwellings.

In 2004, after being interviewed as a possible arson suspect, Fowler was sent to prison on a burglary conviction. Two years later, David Valdez, Jr., the driver of the van, was shot to death.

Fowler, while serving time on the burglary case, was convicted of repeatedly sodomizing an inmate. The judge in that case sentenced him to three terms of 25 years to life.

In 2009, after Fowler confessed to starting the October 2003 wildfires, grand jurors in San Bernardino indicted him on one count of aggravated arson and five counts of murder. The homicide indictments were based on the felony-murder doctrine. Fowler, because he had committed a felony that directly led to the killing of five people, was criminally responsible for their deaths. While Fowler had only intended to commit arson, he should have foreseen the deadly consequences of his criminal acts. In most states, convictions based on the felony-murder rule bring sentences of twenty years to life. No one convicted of an unintended homicide has ever been sentenced to death.

In August 2010, when Fowler learned that the prosecutor was seeking the death penalty in his case, he took back his confession. Two years later, a jury in San Bernardino found Rickie Fowler guilty of arson and the five counts of murder. The jurors also recommended the death penalty.

On January 28, 2013, the judge sentenced Fowler to death. This unprecedented sentence made this felony-murder case historic. Fowler's attorneys appealed his death sentence as cruel and unusual punishment in violation of the U.S. Constitution's Eighth Amendment. Because the felony in question involved intentionally causing a catastrophe, the sentence will probably be upheld on appeal.

A Dismemberment Case

Prior to his domestic assault conviction in October 2011, Donald Greenslit lived with his common-law wife Stacie Dorego and their two young children in a two-story house in Johnston, Rhode Island. Following Greenslit's conviction, probated sentence, and no-contact court order, he moved out. The couple's relationship had been a tumultuous one, marred by numerous arrests for domestic violence. He beat this woman, and beat her often.

During the early morning hours of Monday, January 22, 2012, Johnston firefighters and rescue personnel were dispatched to the Pershing Road home after receiving a call regarding smoke coming from the house. Greenslit met the responders at the front door of the smoke-filled dwelling. The 52-year-old, after assuring the firefighters that all was well, ordered them off his property. Police officers pushed Greenslit aside so the emergency personnel could extinguish the fire and check on the children.

Greenslit's children, found in their second-story bedroom, were rushed to the Hasbro Children's Hospital where they were treated for smoke inhalation. Firefighters quickly got control of the fire, but in the process, made a gruesome discovery.

In the fireplace, the emergency responders found the dismembered and smoldering remains of a woman wrapped in a blanket. At the Johnston Police Department later that morning, Greenslit admitted dismembering his wife with a power saw and setting fire to her mutilated corpse. Yes, he had stabbed Stacie Dorego to death, but in self-defense after she had attacked him with a knife.

According to Dr. Christina Stanley, the Chief Medical Examiner for Rhode Island, the 39-year-old victim had died from multiple stab wounds. The forensic pathologist ruled the death a criminal homicide.

On January 23, 2012, a Providence County prosecutor charged Greenslit with domestic murder, two counts of child abuse, the obstruction of fire officers, disorderly conduct, and the violation of a non-contact order. Two months later, a grand jury sitting in Providence indicted Greenslit on all charges. In April, at his preliminary hearing, Greenslit pleaded not guilty to domestic murder and the other offenses. He had since recanted his statement to the police that he had killed Dorego in self-defense.

The Donald Greenslit murder trial got underway on March 1, 2013 in a Providence Superior Court. Following the selection of the jury and the opening statements, the prosecution, on March 4, put two firefighters on the stand that testified that the defendant had tried to deny them entry into the smoky house. A Johnston detective climbed into the witness box and described what he had found in the basement after the fire had been extinguished. The officer recovered a piece of flesh that bore Stacie Dorego's tattoo of a butterfly.

Special Assistant Attorney General Sara Tindall-Woodman, on March 6, put a jailhouse snitch named Alex Boisclair on the stand. This witness said that he had shared a cell with the defendant, and after being cellmates for one day Greenslit confided in him that he had stabbed his common-law wife five times. According to the police informant, Greenslit said he had burned Dorego's body parts because he knew she had, upon her death, wished to be cremated. (I doubt she had envisioned her own fireplace as the cremation site.)

Defense attorney Mark Dana, on cross-examination, accused this witness of incriminating Greenslit in return for prosecutorial leniency on his own behalf. Boisclair, in denying a prosecution deal, said he was simply doing what he thought was the right thing.

On March 7, 2013, a DNA analyst testified that blood found on a circular saw recovered from the defendant's basement had come from Stacie Dorego. The DNA expert was followed to the stand by the state's chief medical examiner that said that Stacie Dorego's heart had been pierced three times by "something with a single edge." Following Dr. Christina Stanley's testimony, the prosecution rested its case. (I don't believe the prosecution introduced a murder weapon into evidence.)

On Friday, March 8, defense attorney Mark Dana rested his case without putting the defendant on the stand. (While jurors are not supposed to take this as evidence of guilt, they usually do.) Dana told the jurors that the police didn't test for DNA at the death scene because they didn't want to discover that someone else had committed the murder. He pointed out that without a confession, eyewitness, or physical evidence linking his client to the crime scene, the prosecution's case was weak, and circumstantial. The defense attorney also attacked the credibility of the jailhouse snitch.

On March 11, 2013, the jury of ten women and two men found Donald Greenslit guilty of murder. Two months later the judge sentenced Greenslit to life plus seven years.

A Degenerate Couple

Michael Philpott of Derby, England, a city of 250,000 in the central part of the country, was an eccentric, violent man who domineered and abused his women. He was also lazy, and had a taste for group sex. In December 1978, the 21-year-old, angry that his 17-year-old girlfriend planned to leave him, stabbed her 27 times. When Kim Hill's mother tried to intervene, Philpott thrust the knife into her 11 times. Prior to these attacks, Philpott had punched and slapped Kim Hill, and on one occasion had broken several of her fingers.

After the jury found Philpott guilty of two counts of attempted murder, the judge sentenced him to seven years in prison. He served only three years and two months of his sentence. In 1991, a judge sentenced Philpott to probation after he pleaded guilty to head-butting another man. Several years later Philpott pleaded guilty to a road-rage related assault.

The aging control-freak/hippie became a minor celebrity in England after appearing TV's "Jeremy Kyle Show." A year later the volatile eccentric was featured in a documentary on English television.

In 2011, the 55-year-old Philpott lived with his wife, his girlfriend, and eleven children in a 3-bedroom, two-story house in Derby. The unemployed odd ball that rarely bathed, had so far in his life, fathered 17 children with five women. Four of the children in the house had come from Philpott and his live-in mistress, Lisa Willis. (Another man was responsible for Willis' fifth child.) The remaining six children belonged to Philpott and his 45-year-old wife, Mairead.

On February 11, 2012, Lisa Willis, who had been under Philpott's thumb since she was 17, made her escape. She told Philpott that she and her kids were going swimming. The six of them left the house and didn't return. Three days later, when the 29-year-old ex-mistress came back to the house to collect clothing and other items, Philpott got physical. The police came and kept the peace while she gathered her belongings and left.

Philpott's relationship with Willis deteriorated further after she sued for custody of their four children. On May 1, 2012, he filed a false police report claiming that she had threatened his life. The revenge-seeking former lover began telling his friends that he, his wife, and one of Mairead's regular sexual partners, Paul Mosley, had concocted a plan that would get his children back. The scheme was this: they would start a small fire in the house, save the six children, then blame the arson and attempted mass murder on Lisa Willis. This plan was a harebrained and dangerous.

At 12:45 in the morning of May 11, 2012, as the children--five boys and a girl between the ages 5 and 13--slept in a bedroom on the second floor, Philpott ignited a puddle of gasoline in the hallway outside the bedroom. Outside, he climbed a ladder to the bedroom window, but couldn't smash a hole large enough to enter the house and save the children. In a state of panic, he dialed 999 (England's 911) and screamed, "I can't get in!"

By the time the children were removed from the burning house, five of them were dead. The sixth child died a few days later in the hospital.

The police, after Philpott accused Lisa Willis of setting the fire, took her into custody. They released her shortly thereafter when it became obvious she had nothing to do with the arson. Investigators quickly figured out who had started the fire and why.

Philpott and his wife moved out of their fire-damaged house and into a motel. Police bugged their motel room, and in one of the electronically intercepted conversations, Philpott told his wife to "Make sure you stick to the story."

The Michael Philpott, Mairead Philpott, and Paul Mosley manslaughter trial got underway in February 2013. Following the eight-week trial, the jury, on April 2, found all three defendants guilty as charged. The next day, at the sentence mitigation hearing, Michael Philpott's attorney, Anthony Orchard, asked the judge for the minimum sentence. The barrister said, "Despite Mr. Philpott's faults he was a very good father and loved those children. All the witnesses, even Lisa Willis, agree on this. There is no evidence at any stage that he deliberately harmed any of them." (He did, however, in an extremely reckless manner, use his children as pawns in a plot to frame his ex-mistress of a serious crime. I don't believe that qualifies him as a "very good father." That makes him, in my view, a mass murderer. In the United States these defendants would have been tried under the felony-murder doctrine rather than manslaughter.)

On April 4, 2013, Mrs. Justice Thirlwall of the Nottingham Crown Court sentenced Michael Philpott to life with a minimum term of 15 years in prison. The judge said, "I have not the slightest doubt that you, Michael Philpott, were the driving force behind this shockingly dangerous enterprise." Judge Thirlwall went on to describe this defendant as a "deliberately dangerous man," with "no moral compass." (I think he's a textbook sociopath.)

The judge sentenced Mairead Philpott and her degenerate lover Paul Mosley to 17 years in prison. These people, under the circumstances, got off light.

The Police Instructor

In 2011, 35-year-old Brett Seacat, a police instructor at the Kansas Law Enforcement Training Center, lived with his wife Vashti and their two boys, aged two and four, in Kingman, Kansas. During the early morning hours of April 30, 2011, a fire broke out in the Seacat house in the small south central Kansas town of three thousand. Brett and the boys got out of the dwelling unharmed. Vashti Seacat, found by firefighters in her bed with a bullet in her brain, did not.

According to Brett Seacat, he had been sleeping on the living room couch when, during the middle of the night, his wife called him on her cellphone from the master bedroom with instructions to get the boys out of the house. He ran upstairs to find the master bedroom on fire. When Brett lifted his wife from the bed, her body was limp, and she was bleeding from a bullet wound to her head. Because the room was breaking out in flames, Brett left his wife and rushed to save the boys.

Arson investigators determined that someone used gasoline as an accelerant to set fires at several points of origin in the Seacat master bedroom. Criminal investigators with the Kansas Bureau of Investigation (KBI) assumed that the arsonist had shot the victim in the head before torching the house. Since the Seacats were in the midst of a divorce, suspicion immediately fell upon Brett Seacat as the arson-murderer.

On May 12, 2011, two agents with the KBI interrogated Brett Seacat at the Reno County Sheriff's Office. The session lasted seven hours during which time the suspect admitted that he had purchased software to track his wife's text messages and her GPS location. He told his questioners that he had threatened to move out of the house with the boys if his wife proceeded with the divorce. The day before her death, Vashti had served her husband with the divorce papers.

During the interrogation, Seacat also conceded that on the day before his wife's sudden and violent death, he was in his office at the training center destroying computer hard drives. He said he understood why the investigators considered him a suspect in his wife's death and the arson, but insisted that she had set the fire before shooting herself in the head. According to the suspect, this was an arson-suicide case, not an arson-murder.

In describing his discovery of the fire and his wife's body, Seacat said, "I remember hearing my own voice inside my head saying, 'dead.' Then all of a sudden it sort of came to me, 'Dead. Fire. Kids.' "

In the course of the prolonged interrogation (the suspect was not under arrest), Seacat showed no emotion, and on several occasions laughed with his questioners. The KBI agents made it clear they didn't think Seacat's account of that night made any sense. Why would Vashti risk her children's lives by setting the fire, calling him on the phone, then climbing into bed, pulling up the covers, and shooting herself in the head? Moreover, Brett had no traces of soot from the fire, or blood from his wife, on his clothing. The suspect responded to this by saying: "I'm with you on that. It doesn't make sense at all."

Agents with the KBI, on Friday, May 14, 2011, arrested Brett Seacat on charges of first-degree murder, aggravated arson, and two counts of child endangerment. A magistrate set his bail at $1 million.

On May 23, 2013, the Seacat murder trial got underway at the Kingman County Court House in the town of Kingman. Following the opening statements by the attorneys on both sides of the case, the state began presenting its evidence with testimony from the medical examiner, arson investigators, and the KBI agents who had interrogated the defendant in May of 2011.

On May 30, 2013, the state put Karen Roberts on the stand. Roberts, who worked with the defendant at the Kansas Law Enforcement Training Center, testified that on the day before Vashti Seacat's death, the defendant had asked for an overhead projector to be pulled out of storage. According to the witness, Seacat spent the entire day locked into his office. (According to prosecutors, the last handwritten entry in the victim's journal, a message suggesting suicide, had been forged. Pursuant to this theory, Seacat had used the overhead projector to practice writing in his wife's hand. Seacat claimed that he needed the device in connection with a fraud investigation he was conducting.)

KBI forensic scientist Chris Riddle, on May 31, 2013, testified that he had found traces of gasoline on the defendant's trousers. A state forensic document examiner revealed that the last entry in Vashti's journal was not in her handwriting. The expert could not, however, identify the defendant as the forger.

Joy Trotnic, one of Vashti Seacat's co-workers, took the stand and said that on the day before her death, Vashti had expressed concern that her estranged husband would not move out of the house as promised. "Do you think Brett would burn down the house with me in it?" she asked.

Connie Suderman, the Seacat marriage counselor, told the jurors that the defendant had called her shortly after Vashti's death. According to this witness, he said, "I killed her. Vashti is dead and it's my fault." In describing her conversation with the defendant that day, the therapist said, "I wouldn't say in hearing his voice that I thought he was distressed in any way. He was quite calm. I didn't hear sadness. I didn't hear tearfulness or crying or expressions of surprise or horror or words of exhaustion."

According to the marriage counselor, Vashti Seacat had indicated that her husband "wasn't doing well" with the pending divorce. "She [Vashti] told me that he [the defendant] had awakened her from her sleep and told her that he had a dream that he had killed her."

On June 6, 2013, after the prosecution rested its case, defense attorney Roger Falk put his client on the stand. The defendant explained that he had melted two laptop hard drives after he had arrived at work that day to protect against identity theft. He said he had planned to sell the computers.

During his testimony, the defendant spoke with ease, and occasionally smiled at the jurors. While portraying himself as a loving husband and father, the defendant admitted that he had threatened to expose his wife's alleged affairs, wreck her career, and take away her sons if she divorced him.

An expert witness named Gene Gietzen testified for the defense that a KBI arson investigator had improperly packaged a pair of trousers the defendant wore on the day in question. As a result, this evidence could have been contaminated.

On Monday, June 10, the prosecutor and the defense attorney made their closing arguments to the jury of five men and eight women. The next day, the jury returned its verdict: guilty of all charges.

On August 5, 2013, the judge sentenced Seacat to life plus six years and three months.

The Black Forest Wildfire

A wildfire is generally defined as an uncontrolled fire in an area of combustible vegetation that occurs in the countryside or a wilderness area. Fires of this nature can be brush fires or forest fires. Wildfires are caused naturally by lightening strikes and accidentally by careless campers. Occasionally controlled fires set by government fire officials to reduce highly combustible underbrush grow out of control and burn down the entire forest. Wildfire arsonists usually set the fires for reasons that are pathological.

At two in the afternoon of Tuesday, June 11, 2013, a fire that started in the Black Forest north of Colorado Springs, Colorado, quickly raged out of control. When finally contained and extinguished on Thursday, June 20, the blaze had killed two people, destroyed 509 homes, and blackened 22 square miles of land. The Black Forest disaster is the most destructive wildfire in the history of the state.

Fire investigation specialists with the ATF, the U. S. Forestry Service, and the El Paso County Sheriff's Office had ruled out nature and accident as the cause of the Black Forest Wildfire. That left arson, and because the blaze killed two people, the case was being handled, under the felony-murder doctrine, as an arson-murder investigation.

At the suspected area of the wildfire's origin, investigators were seen crawling on their hands and knees in search of physical clues pertaining to the method of ignition, and the identity of the fire setter.

In terms of establishing the cause of a fire--locating its point of origin or origins--the debris analysis of a structural fire generally provides a more complete and clearer picture of the fire's cause. Signs of an incendiary structural fire might include heavy burning and intense heat at a spot without an ignition source, multiple points of origin, and traces of an accelerant such as gasoline. These arson indicators usually don't exist at the scene of an intentionally set wildfire.

Because wildfires begin in remote areas, there are usually no eyewitnesses to the event. In home and business arson cases, investigative leads include the standard motives of insurance fraud and the elimination of a business competitor. In fatal fires, all of the motives that go with criminal homicide are available to the investigator. These leads and pool of usual suspects are rarely available in wildfire arson cases.

As of July 2014, the authorities had not arrested a suspect in this case.

If the Black Forest arsonist is identified, it will probably be because he couldn't keep his mouth shut. Someone--a former girlfriend, an ex-wife, a cellmate, or a drinking buddy--will have to come forward with incriminating evidence. Once that occurs, there is always a good chance of a confession based upon a plea arrangement.

The Blow Torch Murder

In April 2010, 44-year-old Angela, the mother of an 11-year-old boy from a previous relationship, married David Davis. Angela's son, a red headed fifth-grader named Jonathan Foster, lived with his paternal grandmother. In November 2010 the child moved into the Huston Texas duplex with his mother and new stepfather.

When he drank, David Davis became violent. One of his assaults sent Angela to the hospital. On December 14, 2010, after he slapped his stepson in the face, Angela and Jonathan moved a hundred feet away into the apartment of a woman who had befriended Angela.

In the early afternoon of December 24, 2010, a woman who said she was Jonathan's babysitter spoke on the telephone to one of Angela's co-workers at a meat market where she was employed as a cashier. The woman said she wanted to speak to Angela. The co-worker passed the message on to Angela who said she didn't have a babysitter. Angela called the number and a woman answered the phone. Just before the line went dead, Angela heard her son's voice. She rushed home to check on Jonathan. He was not in the apartment. Fearing foul play, Angela called 911 and reported her son missing.

Detectives with the Houston Police Department, from the beginning, treated the case as a possible kidnapping. The police, suspecting Angela's estranged husband David, questioned him closely. David Davis said he had checked on Jonathan just 25 minutes before Angela came home to find him missing. At that time the boy was playing a video game. "There's no doubt in my mind that he's been snatched," the stepfather said. "I think a pedophile took him."

As investigators questioned other family members and neighbors, and volunteers handed out fliers, Angela faced a television camera and said to the abductor, "Don't hurt my baby." On the possibility that Jonathan had been kidnapped by a stranger, detectives questioned fifty registered sex offenders in the northwest Houston area.

On December 28, 2010, four days after Jonathan went missing, a Houston Police Department's K-9 unit recovery dog detected what turned out to be his badly charred remains. (He had to be identified by dental records.) The body had been dumped in a ditch five miles from his residence. The body was bound with twine. Near the corpse detectives found a welder's torch.

Surveillance camera footage from a building near Jonathan's body showed a silver Ford pickup truck pulling up to the site at six o'clock that Christmas eve. A black woman got out of the vehicle, reached into the bed, took out what appeared to be a body, and placed it into the ditch.

Detectives quickly identified the woman in the truck as 44-year-old Mona Yvette Nelson, an acquaintance of the woman who had been sharing her apartment with Angela and Jonathan. Two weeks earlier Mona had met David Davis, the boy's stepfather. According to witnesses, Mona Nelson had been seen recently in the vicinity of the murdered child's home.

As a maintenance employee, Nelson had worked with acetylene torches and various types of welding equipment. A former boxer, Nelson had been convicted in 1984 of aggravated robbery that brought her a ten-year probated sentence. She had since been arrested for various drug charges and for making terroristic threats against another woman. Nelson owned a truck that looked like the silver Ford driven by the woman seen on surveillance tapes dumping the body into the ditch.

On December 30, 2011, at a press conference, a spokesperson for the Houston Police Department announced that Mona Nelson, charged with capital murder, had been arrested for Jonathan Foster's death. Having been denied bond, the suspect was incarcerated in the Harris County Jail. In a search of her northwest Houston residence, detectives found twine similar to the cordage found on Jonathan's body. Officers also recovered an acetylene tank used in welding. Sections of Nelson's carpet had been recently burned.

According to the police spokesperson, Nelson, under police questioning, had admitted dumping Jonathan's body in the ditch. The suspect had not, however, confessed to murdering the boy.

The day after Nelson's arrest, a local television reporter interviewed her at the Harris County Jail. Nelson told the correspondent that one of Jonathan's family members, on Christmas Eve had asked her to dump the contents of a garbage container. The unnamed relative paid her twenty dollars for the job. She had been drunk on vodka and had no idea what was in the plastic container. "I didn't know what was in it until they were showing me pictures in the interrogation room. I'm not a monster," she said, "I have five grandkids and I love kids."

Houston homicide detective Mike Miller, in response to Nelson's statements to the TV reporter, pointed out that Jonathan's body had not been found in a container. In describing the murder suspect, Detective Miller said, "She is a cold soul-less murderer who showed an absolute lack of remorse in taking the life of Jonathan Foster. One or two people I've ever talked to had eyes like she did. It was really cold." Detective Miller said that all of the victim's family members, including his stepfather David Davis, had solid alibis. Mona Nelson had acted alone, he said.

On Monday, January 3, 2011, Mona Nelson appeared before a judge who asked her if she understood her rights. She said that she did. The judge appointed Nelson an attorney, informed her of the charge, and sent her back to jail. A month later, Harris County prosecutor Connie Spence presented the case to a grand jury that returned a true bill of capital murder.

The Nelson murder trial got underway on Monday, August 12, 2013 before district judge Jeannine Barr. The defendant had waived her right to a jury trial, putting her fate entirely in the hands of this judge. Nelson's attorney, Alan Tanner, before the opening statements and presentation of witnesses, asked Judge Barr to quash five recorded statements his client had made to detectives over a stretch of seventeen hours at her home and at the police station. According to the defense attorney, the interrogators continued to question Nelson after she complained a dozen times of being ill. The officers did not address Nelson's health complaints until after the interrogation. (Detectives took her to a nearby hospital where doctors found nothing wrong with her.)

On Tuesday, August 13, Mona Nelson, pursuant to the procedural law question regarding the admissibility of her police statements, testified how her interrogators had worn her down. Although she asked to consult with an attorney a dozen times, the questioning continued. Attorney Tanner argued that the interrogating officers had violated his client's Fifth Amendment right against self-incrimination. He also asserted that her statements had not been given voluntarily and were therefore inadmissible in court.

Judge Barr, later that afternoon, made her evidentiary ruling. She excluded the statements Nelson made after she had requested to see a lawyer. Since these requests came late in the interrogation session, most of her statements were admissible.

In her opening remarks before Judge Barr, prosecutor Spence admitted that the state would not be establishing a motive for Jonathan's murder.

(While a prosecutor likes to have motive evidence, it is not a legal requirement for a murder conviction. All the state has to prove is criminal intent. In law, the why is not relevant.) The prosecutor promised the judge that she would prove beyond a reasonable doubt that Mona Nelson, sometime between 2:15 and 6:08 PM on December 24, 2010, tortured and killed the 11-year-old Foster boy with a blowtorch at her home, then dumped his charred remains in a ditch. Spence said that one of the key pieces of evidence she would introduce involved Jonathan's sweat shirt found in a trashcan near the defendant's house. The garment bore traces of Nelson's blood.

Defense attorney Tanner reminded the judge that just because his client had dumped the boy's body in the ditch didn't necessary mean that she had killed him. In foreshadowing the thrust of his defense, Tanner cast suspicion on the victim's stepdad, David Davis. According to the defense attorney, the boy had come between Davis and his estranged wife that may have been the motive behind the murder. All Mona Nelson did was dispose of the contents of a garbage can that had been given to her.

The victim's mother took the stand as the state's first witness. Next, the prosecutor presented several detectives who described the physical evidence recovered from the Nelson home and how it related to the evidence found near Jonathan Foster's charred corpse. David Davis, the stepfather, took the stand and admitted that he had hit the victim's mother. He said he had never harmed the boy. Through direct examination, prosecutor Spence established the witness' whereabouts at the time of the abduction and the murder.

Lois Sims, the supervisor at the meat market who took the phone call for Angela Davis on the afternoon of December 24, 2010, described the caller as an angry, foul-mouthed woman. The caller wanted the telephone number of the woman leasing the duplex where Davis and her son were staying. "If you don't get her on the phone now, something's going to happen. He [Jonathan] won't be here for long."

Defense attorney Tanner pointed out that the two meat market supervisors had described the caller as a white woman. (The defendant was black.)

On August 19, 2013, two Houston Police Department K-9 officers testified that three cadaver dogs had reacted strongly to a box of burned carpeting at Nelson's house. One of the witnesses said, "There was a strong odor of human remains there. An arborist (tree expert) testified that leaves at the dumpsite had come from post oak trees. There were no such trees where Jonathan's body had been recovered, but around Nelson's house, there were seven trees of this kind.

The prosecutor played a videotaped statement from Nelson in which she admitted being at the place where Jonathan's body had been dumped.

She said she had emptied a garbage container at the site. She said she didn't know the contents of the plastic container.

The following day, a forensic scientist from the FBI Crime Laboratory testified that a Looney Tunes sweatshirt that belonged to Jonathan, recovered from the defendants trashcan, contained Nelson's blood and DNA. Two other DNA experts agreed with this analysis. The presence of this trace evidence on the sweatshirt suggested that the victim had put up a fight.

On Friday morning, August 23, the prosecution rested its case. Allen Tanner launched his client's defense with the testimony of a woman who gave Mona Nelson an alibi. Following the testimony of two other witnesses, the defense rested its case. Mona Nelson did not take the stand on her own behalf.

The next day, defense attorney Allen Tanner delivered his closing argument to the judge. "Mona Nelson," he said, "had absolutely no motive to kill Jonathan Foster. They searched and searched for a motive and there's no reason why she would have killed that boy." In referring to David Davis, the estranged husband, Tanner said, "He wanted to get her back and he told people at work that Jonathan is the root of all his problems....The [prosecution's] case got weaker and weaker....There are more and more unanswered questions now than there were at the beginning. The evidence is clear there could be people who committed this crime and we have no idea at this time who they are."

When it came her turn to address the judge, prosecutor Spence said, "This defendant took Jonathan Foster back to her house and killed him. We'll never know how she killed him because she burned his body to the point where you can't tell."

On Monday morning, August 26, 2013, Judge Jeannine Barr found Mona Nelson guilty as charged. She imposed the automatic sentence of life without parole. After hearing the verdict, Nelson said, "I'm innocent, and I maintain my innocence. I wouldn't harm anybody."

Defense attorney Allen Tanner told reporters he would file an appeal on the grounds of insufficient evidence. "We believe someone else kidnapped this child and someone else killed this child."

Not Fully Human

On January 1, 1999, when firefighters in the north central California town of Murphy arrived at Karl Karlsen's one-story house, the dwelling was already engulfed in flames. The fire had gotten so intense it had blown out the windows. While Karlsen's three young children were safe, his 31-year-old wife Christina did not make it out of the inferno.

Questioned about the fast-developing house fire, Karl Karlsen told fire officials and the police that when it started he had been in the garage. He managed, he said, to pull his children out of the burning structure through their bedroom windows, but he had not been able to save his wife.

An arson investigator looking into the cause and origin of the blaze, after finding what he interpreted as separate areas of deep charring on the floor (burn patterns suggesting multiple points of origin), suspected that the Karlsen fire had been set. (I don't know if the cause and origin investigator found traces of accelerants to back up his incendiary fire suspicions, or if Christina Karlsen had been autopsied to determine if she had been alive at the time of the fire.) The fire investigator, based on the fact there was no physical evidence consistent with the children having been exposed to smoke and soot, didn't believe the youngsters had been in the house when the fire started.

The speed and intensity of the fire, the multiple points of origin, the condition of the children, and the fact a vehicle Karl Karlsen owned had gone up in flames a year earlier, pointed to a possible arson-murder case. (Almost all serious car fires are intentionally set for the insurance money.) Notwithstanding suspicions of arson, the cause of the fatal house fire went into the books as undetermined. While Christina Karlsen's father, Art Alexander, suspected foul play, no charges were filed in connection with his daughter's death.

Shortly after the blaze that took his wife's life, Karl and his children moved to Seneca County, New York where he used his $200,000 fire insurance payout to buy a farm near Varick, a small town 55 miles southwest of Syracuse in the Finger Lakes region of the state.

After moving to New York State, Karl married his second wife Cindy who helped him run the farm. On November 20, 2008, Karl Karlsen's 23-year-old son Levi was in his father's garage working on a pickup truck. A graduate of the Romulus Area High School, Levi, the father of two girls, was employed as a machine operator at a glass manufacturing company in nearby Geneva. At eight o'clock that evening, Cindy Karlsen called 911 to report an accident involving Karl's son Levi. In the Karlsen garage, on the floor near the truck, emergency technicians found Levi. He was dead.

Karl Karlsen told deputies from the Seneca County Sheriff's Office that when he and Cindy left the farm to attend a family event that afternoon at four, Levi had been working beneath the jacked-up truck. When Karl returned to the garage about four hours later, he found that the vehicle had toppled off the jack. The father lifted the pickup off his son with the jack and pulled his body out from under the truck. Levi Karlsen was pronounced dead on arrival at the Geneva General Hospital.

The Seneca County Coroner's Office classified the manner of Levi Karlsen's death as accidental. As a result, there was no criminal investigation into his sudden death. (I presume Levi's body was not autopsied, and do not know if officers took photographs of the death scene. Since the body had been moved before the arrival of the deputies, I'm not sure how useful these photographs would have been anyway.)

In March 2012, more than three years after Levi Karlsen's sudden and violent death, homicide investigators with the Seneca County Sheriff's Office and the New York State Police Violent Crime Investigation Unit, became interested in the case. The piece of information that opened the criminal inquiry involved Karl Karlsen's purchase of a life insurance policy on his son just days before the young man's demise. According to that policy, Karl Karlsen was the sole beneficiary.

Three and a half years after Karl Karlsen received the life insurance money from his son's death, he must have been in financial trouble. Police arrested him in June 2012 on the charge of passing a pair of bad checks in Seneca Falls, New York. The bogus checks totaled $685.30.

On November 24, 2012, four years after Levi Karlsen died in his father's garage, Seneca County District Attorney Barry Porch charged Karl Karlsen with second-degree murder. Based on an eight-month homicide investigation conducted by state and county officers, the prosecutor believed the father had intentionally caused the truck to fall on his son. With Livi pinned beneath the vehicle, Karl took Cindy to the family event. Upon his return to the farm four hours later, the suspect "discovered" his son lying under the fallen vehicle. Karl asked his second wife to call 911. Investigators and the district attorney believed that the suspect, when he took out the life insurance on his son, planned to murder him.

In September 2013, at a pretrial hearing on the second-degree murder charge related to Levi Karlsen's death, the defendant's second wife Cindy (she was in the process of divorcing him) shed new light on the homicide investigation. In early November 2012, after learning that Karl had invested part of his son's $700,000 insurance payout to purchase a $1.2 million policy on her life, began cooperating with Seneca County investigators.

Cindy Karlsen agreed to wear a wire and meet her estranged husband in a crowded restaurant in hopes of getting him to admit that he had killed his son. She took the stand at the hearing and said, "I led him to believe our marriage had a chance if he came clean. I told him he could trust me."

At the restaurant, Karl told Cindy that he had removed the truck's front tires and raised the vehicle on a single jack before asking his son to repair the brake and transmission lines. "It was so wobbly," he said.

"Tell the truth," Cindy replied.

"It was never meant to be. It was never planned from day one to ever go that way," Karl said.

A week following the audio-recorded conversation, investigators with the Seneca County Sheriff's Office interrogated the suspect for almost ten hours during which time Karlsen denied killing Levi 75 times. Eventually, however, Karlsen signed a statement in which he acknowledged that he had knocked the truck off its jack and walked away. But in the videotaped interrogation, Karlsen insisted that he had not *intentionally* caused the truck to fall on his son. He told detectives that because he had been taking pain pills for various ailments, his memory of the incident was fuzzy. "In some ways," he said, "my mind was blank."

Immediately following the marathon interrogation, detectives took Karlsen into custody.

On November 7, 2013, the day before his trial, Karlsen confessed to crushing his son to death for the insurance money. He pleaded guilty to second-degree murder. Six weeks later, Seneca Court Judge Dennis Bender, before sentencing Karlsen to 15 years to life, told him he wasn't "fully human."

A Delayed Death

Robert Middleton, on June 28, 1998, turned eight. Early in the evening of his birthday, his 13-year-old neighbor, Don Willburn Collins, doused him with gasoline and set him on fire. Robert survived the attack, but suffered third-degree burns over most of his body. The crime took place in Splendora, Texas, a small town in the Houston metropolitan area.

Collins confessed to the police, was arrested, and spent several months in juvenile detention. He was not, however, prosecuted as a juvenile or an adult for the assault. According to the Montgomery County prosecutor in charge of the investigation, the state did not have enough evidence against Collins to go forward with the case. As a result, the authorities had no choice but to release the suspect. (I suspect some kind of procedural screw up that precluded a criminal conviction.)

Over the years, Robert Middleton underwent 100 painful surgeries and many skin grafts that still left him horribly disfigured. In 2011, after being diagnosed with skin cancer, Robert, in a videotaped deposition given shortly before his death at the age of 23, revealed that two weeks before the arson-assault, Don Collins had sexually molested him. Collins had torched the boy to prevent him from reporting the rape.

The medical examiner, finding that Middleton's burns caused his cancer, ruled his death a homicide. Following this manner of death determination, detectives with the Montgomery County Sheriff's Office conducted a seven-month cold case investigation into the 1998 sexual molestation and subsequent arson.

Three years after setting Robert Middleton on fire, a jury found Collins guilty of sexually molesting another 8-year-old boy. At the time of that rape,

Collins was fifteen. For that offense he spent four years in juvenile detention. The assault took place in San Jacinto County, Texas.

In 2012, Robert Middleton's parents won a $150 million wrongful death suit against Collins. Because the man who had set fire to their son was homeless, the plaintiffs knew they would never collect the civil judgment.

A Montgomery county judge, in 2013, transferred the Collins/Middleton case from juvenile to adult court after the district attorney charged Collins with felony murder. Under the felony-murder doctrine, a person who commits a felony is culpable for any death that occurs in the commission of that crime. In the Collins case, the underlying felony is sexual assault. While the sexual crime didn't cause Middleton's death, it did lead to the arson that in turn caused the cancer that killed the victim. (The arson-assault wouldn't work as the underlying felony because the statute of limitations on that offense had run out. The sexual assault, however, wasn't reported until 2011.)

In terms of the law, the prosecution in this case may run into a felony-murder causation problem. The prosecutor will have to directly link the arson to the sexual attack. There is also the passage of time between the rape and the victim's cancer death. In the old days when crimes were not codified, there was a common law principal related to criminal homicide called the year and a day rule. If the victim of an assault died a year and one day after the attack, too much time had passed to allow a murder charge.

Collin's attorney has challenged the transfer of his client's case into adult court. In 1998, under Texas law, a person under the age of 14 could not be charged as an adult with a capital offense. Collins was 13 when he allegedly raped then set fire to the victim. (In 1999 state legislators dropped the age to ten.)

Don Collins, 29, was placed into the San Jacinto County Jail on a felony charge related to his failure to register as a sex offender. He was held on $1 million bond.

A local prosecutor, in June 2014, charged Collins with murder in connection with Robert Long's death. Collins pleaded not guilty to the homicide charge. His murder trial is scheduled for January 5, 2015.

25 DRUG ENFORCEMENT ABUSE

Origins of the War On Drugs

The war-on-crime atmosphere of the 1930s influenced national drug policy, solidifying the belief that drugs were a criminal rather than a medical or social problem. A national panic over marijuana broke out in the 1930s. The movie *Reefer Madness*, for example, offered a sensationalized picture of marijuana's allegedly evil effects. The 1937 Marijuana Tax Act established harsh penalties for the possession and sale of marijuana. Harry Anslinger, commissioner of the Federal Bureau of Narcotics [now the DEA], imitated [J. Edgar] Hoover, whipping up public fears in order to build a bureaucratic empire. In a popular magazine article, "Marijuana: Assassin of Youth," he painted a terrifying picture of the "sweeping march" of marijuana addiction, causing murder, rape, robbery, and other "deeds of maniacal insanity."

Samuel Walker, *Popular Justice: Second Edition*, 1998

Drug War Shock Troops

American law enforcement has become zero tolerant, more violent, and militarized. Local, state, and federal teams of elite paramilitary special weapons and tactics (SWAT) teams regularly patrol big-city streets and break into homes unannounced. Officers on routine patrol carry high-powered semi and fully automatic weapons. Virtually every law enforcement agency in the country either has its own SWAT unit or has officers who are members of a multijurisdictional force. The barrier between the U.S. military and domestic law enforcement has broken down.

The police have become soldiers and military personnel now function as civilian law enforcers. Paramilitary police officers wear combat gear, are transported in army-surplus armored personnel carriers, receive special forces training, and view criminal suspects as enemy combatants. Federal, state, and local law enforcement agencies field teams of military-trained snipers. In many jurisdictions, the "occupying force" model of policing has replaced the "public servant" concept of law enforcement. The idea of community policing has become outmoded. If one didn't know any better, one would think that the nation is in the grip of an historic crime wave. Today, compared with the 1930s and the late 1960s through the 1970s, the current rate of violent crime is much lower.

Every year SWAT teams conduct forced entry, no-knock raids into 40,000 to 50,000 homes in search of illegal drugs and drug paraphernalia. In many jurisdictions all drug-related search warrant executions involve SWAT team entries. Once a law enforcement agency forms a paramilitary unit, the officers on the team must be kept busy to stay sharp. For this reason, a vast majority of SWAT raids consist of low-risk police work and are therefore unnecessary.

The predawn, no-knock SWAT raid into a private home has become the signature of the government's escalating war on drugs. Even when the raids are not in some way botched, as when officers break into the wrong house, innocent bystanders, including children, are injured, manhandled, and/or traumatized. Following these raids, residents are left with broken doors, windows, and furniture as well as ransacked rooms. Occasionally the "flash bang" grenades the raiders use to disorient occupants cause injuries and start fires. Subjects of these raids, thinking criminals are raiding their homes, pick up guns in self-defense. These people are often shot and killed. If they shoot and kill a police officer, they go to prison. In these cases it doesn't matter that the defendants didn't know who they were shooting at. Some end up on death row.

Minneapolis SWAT

Acting on information from a narcotics snitch, a Minneapolis SWAT team of eighteen officers, on the night of February 16, 2010, used a battering ram to enter the apartment rented by Rickia Russell. The 30-year-old occupant heard her front door being smashed open followed by the sound of a flash bang grenade rolling into her living room. Upon explosion, the percussion device ignited her sofa and seriously burned her leg. As Russell lay facedown on the floor with her hands cuffed behind her back, she tried to tell the officers about her charred limb. They told her to shut up.

The officers, armed with a warrant alleging that someone named David Conley was selling drugs out of this apartment, found no narcotics, drug paraphernalia, guns, or any other contraband or evidence of a crime. Rickia Russell did not know a David Conley. The SWAT team had obviously raided the wrong apartment. But instead of apologizing and offering to repair the damage they had caused, the police arrested Russell for the misdemeanor of operating a "disorderly house." The authorities, however, never followed through with a formal charge.

On December 9, 2011, the Minneapolis City Council offered Russell, who had suffered permanent injuries from the flash bang grenade, a million dollar settlement. This horribly botched police operation was not the first botched paramilitary police raid in Minneapolis

The Vang Khang Raid

Vang Khang, his wife Yee Moua, and their six children, hill people from Laos, lived in a high-crime neighborhood in northeast Minneapolis. Just before midnight on December 16, 2007, Yee Moua, while watching television, heard window glass shatter. Thinking that criminals were breaking into the house, she bolted up the stairs to where her husband and children were sleeping.

Awakened by the commotion, Mr. Khang grabbed his shotgun, and hearing heavy footsteps advancing up the stairs, fired a warning shot through his bedroom door. Khang didn't know it, but he had opened fired on officers with the Minneapolis Police Department's Violent Offender Task Force (VOTF). The paramilitary unit had broken into the wrong house in search of street-gang guns and drugs. The exchange of gunfire that erupted after Khang's warning shot included 22 bullets from VOTF officers and two more blasts from Khang's shotgun, pellets that struck the body armor of two of the officers. The moment Khang heard his children yelling, "It's the police!" Khang, who miraculously had not been shot, dropped the shotgun and raised his arms. A few seconds later, he was on the floor with a boot planted in the middle of his back.

The Minneapolis Police, quickly realizing that their informant had directed them to the wrong house, did not take Khang into custody. VOTF officers, leaving behind broken windows and bullet holes in the bedroom wall, left the house without apologizing to the family they had endangered and traumatized.

Seven months after the bungled raid, the Minneapolis police chief awarded the VOTF officers who had raided the wrong house, medals of valor for "bravery in action under fire." In December 2008, the Minneapolis City Council approved a $600,000 settlement for the Khang family.

Paramilitary policing in Minneapolis has been expensive, and a threat to public safety.

Wrong House Raid in Georgia

In Gwinnett County, Georgia, a suburban community of 700,000 within the Atlanta metropolitan area, narcotics officers had been watching a house in Lawrenceville for three months. Members of the county police department's Special Investigations Section suspected that the man living at 2934 Valley Spring Drive was selling methamphetamine. At 9:15 A.M. on December 9, 2008, 20 officers with the department's 60-member SWAT unit began making final preparations for a no-knock raid. Thirty minutes later, after a detective with the Special Investigations Section pointed out the meth suspect's house, the SWAT team moved in on the target. The officers didn't know it, but the detectives had sent them to the wrong house. The suspected drug dealer lived a few places down the street.

The day after the raid, John Louis, the 38-year-old whose house the police wrongfully entered, described the intrusion to a television reporter: "They came in here and put guns on us. The house was full of police. I never had a gun in my face before...All I see is a bunch of police, guns drawn, yelling, 'Hands in the air! Hands in the air!' "

When the SWAT officers broke down the front door, Heather Jones, John Louis's girlfriend who had been asleep with their three-month baby, stepped out of the bedroom in her nightgown. Police ordered her to the floor at gunpoint. The couple asked the police what they wanted and were told to shut up and remain still. The raid came to an abrupt halt when one of the officers, seeing the baby, realized they had broken into the wrong place. As the SWAT unit decamped to raid the suspect's house, one of the officers apologized for the intrusion and promised to have the front door repaired.

In an interview with a TV correspondent the next day, a Gwinnet Police Department spokesperson pointed out that the narcotics officers had been watching the meth suspect's house for three months. In response to this, John Louis said, "If you had this house under surveillance for three months, why did you come here? You broke in and put all our lives in danger, and all you can say is you're sorry?"

The police spokesperson, in explaining what went wrong, said, "Somehow there was an investigator that had been working closely with the case that...mistakenly pointed out the wrong house, the wrong location." When asked if the police department had any kind of policy regarding no-knock raids, the police representative replied, "We double check the address, there's a description of the location as well as an address of the house that we're looking at on the search warrant, and we always have someone double check that every time."

Three days after the raid, the commander of the Special Investigations Section, in a news release, announced that the detective who had directed the SWAT team to the wrong house had been transferred to the uniform division. Without identifying this officer, the commander characterized the incident as a "case of human error and not deliberate malfeasance on the part of the investigator."

Had Mr. Louis, thinking that criminals were invading his home picked up a gun for self-protection he would be dead. As long as the war on drugs rages on, and officer safety trumps all other considerations, SWAT teams will be deployed in low-risk situations. Non-violent criminal suspects and innocent people will continue to be traumatized, injured, and in some cases, killed.

Drug War Informants

Americans love drugs and they hate informants. But as a result of the endless war on drugs, more and more citizens are snitching on each other. Many arrested drug users are turned into informants, or "flipped" by narcotics officers. Instead of avoiding prison sentences, some of these reluctant drug informants end up dead. In the language of war, they are collateral damage.

For good or bad, informants have always played a vital role in law enforcement. Most of them can be placed into one of three groups: paid "professionals;" jailhouse snitches; and flipped drug arrestees. The professionals snitch for money, the jailhouse types do it for lighter sentences, and many of the flipped drug informants cooperate with the police out of fear and desperation. People caught in possession of small quantities of marijuana tend to be the least street-wise, and ill equipped to protect themselves against the targeted professional drug merchants. A good number of flipped informants are addicts who feel they have no choice but to put themselves in harm's way.

The Rachel Hoffman Debacle

In February 2007, a Tallahassee police officer pulled over 23-year-old Rachel Hoffman for a routine traffic violation. The Florida State University graduate consented to a search of her vehicle that resulted in the discovery of less than an ounce of marijuana. A few weeks later, narcotics officers found, in her apartment, 5 ounces of grass and 4 ecstasy pills. The prosecutor charged her with several narcotics counts that, according to her arresting officers, would send her to prison. However, if she agreed to act as a snitch/undercover operative in a bust-buy drug sting, the prosecutor would put in a good word with the judge. After some initial resistance, Hoffman agreed to buy 1,500 ecstasy pills, 2 ounces of cocaine, and a handgun from two drug dealers she had never met. The fact a gun was involved didn't seem to bother Hoffman's police handlers. This was a deal made in hell.

At seven in the evening on May 7, 2008, when Hoffman arrived at the sting site, the two suspects told her the deal would go down at another location. Surveillance officers watched as she climbed into a stolen BMW with the two drug dealers. They drove off, and Hoffman's handlers, unprepared for a last minute change of plans, lost touch with their civilian undercover operative. The drug suspects had figured out that Hoffman was a snitch, and shot her to death in the car with the firearm she was supposed to buy.

In response to public outrage over Rachel Hoffman's murder while working for the Tallahassee Police, Chief Dennis Jones publicly called her a criminal who was responsible for the botched undercover drug operation that led to her death. His mindless statement created such a firestorm of public criticism the chief was forced to apologize. (I'm sure that was sincere.) The narcotics officers were suspended with pay, and the chief had to admit that his officers had put an untrained informant in danger and bungled the job of protecting her. Rachel Hoffman's parents sued the police department and the city for the wrongful death of their daughter.

In 2010, the two men who killed Rachel Hoffman were convicted of murder and sentenced to life. Also that year, the Florida legislature passed "Rachel's Law," a statute that requires law enforcement agencies in the state to do the following two things with regard to drug informants: upon arrest, advise them they cannot promise light sentences in return for their cooperation as snitches; and instruct them they have a right to consult with an attorney before agreeing to go undercover. If the drug arrestee agrees to help catch other drug offenders, they have to receive a certain amount of training.

I doubt that the Florida law has had much impact on how many drug arrestees cops in Florida flip. The practice of using arrestees as undercover narcotic agents should be prohibited. Unarmed civilians without police training and experience should not be coerced into becoming soldiers in the drug war.

A Stupid Raid

On February 1, 2009, a British newspaper published a photograph of Michael Phelps, the star of the 2008 Olympics, smoking a marijuana pipe at a party in Columbia, South Carolina. Although the photograph had been taken three months earlier, Leon Lott, the television-friendly sheriff of Richland County, known for his aggressive approach to drug enforcement, opened a narcotics investigation of the famous gold medalist swimmer.

Sheriff Lott, in September 2008, had overseen the purchase of an Army surplus armored personnel carrier equipped with a .50-caliber belt-fed machine gun. The combat vehicle was used to transport his SWAT team to drug raids. Six days after he had launched the Phelps investigation, a 12-man Richland County SWAT team, guns drawn, broke into a Lake Murray house rented by four University of South Carolina students believed to have attended the November 2008 party. After confiscating less than a gram of marijuana, Lott's deputies arrested the students for drug possession, and grilled them about Michael Phelps. As it turned out, none of the arrestees had attended the party, and were of no help in the Phelps investigation.

From Lake Murray, Sheriff Lott's SWAT officers traveled to Columbia and raided the party house where they seized six grams of marijuana and the bong depicted in the newspaper photograph. The deputies arrested four more students, and charged them with misdemeanor possession of marijuana. Thanks to the sheriff and his SWAT team, the peace and dignity of the great state of South Carolina was being secured, one marijuana possession bust at a time.

At a news conference on February 15, 2009, Sheriff Lott announced that his officers had not gathered enough evidence to charge Michael Phelps with a crime. (This must have put fear in the hearts of the good citizens of Richland County.) "We had a photo," he said, "and we had him saying he was sorry for his inappropriate behavior. That behavior [however] could have been merely going to a party...He never said, 'I smoked marijuana.' He never confessed to that. We don't have enough we could go and arrest him."

When a reporter asked Sheriff Lott why he, in an effort to make a case out of a 3-month-old photograph of an Olympic swimmer smoking pot, had deployed his SWAT team to raid houses occupied by college students suspected of attending the party, Lott, either missing or ignoring the point, said, "As a cop, my responsibility is to enforce the law, not to create it or ignore it. Marijuana in the state of South Carolina is illegal."

In response to Sheriff Lott's assessment of his law enforcement responsibilities, two reporters for *Newsweek* wrote: "If cops chased down every kid who took a bong hit at a frat party, the jails would be full, and the lecture halls empty. Half the professors would wind up in the clink, too." But the media's principal take on the story had nothing to do with heavy-handed, militaristic law enforcement. It focused on Michael Phelps' fall from grace, and the loss of millions of dollars worth of product endorsements.

The news coverage of Sheriff Lott's idiotic SWAT raids would have been different if one of the frat boys, believing the house was being invaded by criminals, had picked up a gun.

A Near Fatal Wrong House Raid

During the early morning hours of June 27, 2006, a total of 100 federal, state, and local drug enforcement agents and officers raided 23 homes in Decatur, Huntsville, Madison, and Hartsville, Alabama. The raids culminated a two-year investigation of a Mexican-based cocaine, marijuana, and methamphetamine trafficking operation doing business in the northern part of the state. That morning, officers with the High Intensity Drug Trafficking Area Task Force arrested 29 people, including Jerome Wallace, a 28-year-old who lived on Honey Way, a dirt road in rural Limestone County. A police Officer arrested Jerome as he stood in his front yard while task force members, in search of him, broke into the wrong house down the road. The wrong house these officers raided belonged to Wallace's uncle, Jerome Jamar.

Just before daybreak, several vans rolled down Honey Way, and parked across from Kenneth Jamar's house. Agents with the DEA, ATF, FBI, and ICE, and the Alabama Bureau of Investigation, along with Alabama state troopers and SWAT teams from Huntsville and Madison County, alighted from their vehicles. A few seconds after one of the officers yelled, "Open Up! Police!" they broke into the house through the front door. Even if the 51-year-old semi-invalid with severe gout and a pacemaker had heard the officers announce themselves, he could not have made it to the door in time to let them in. Had he tried, Mr. Jamar would have walked into a flash bang grenade explosion.

Mr. Jamar, in his bedroom when he heard his front door bashed open and the stun grenade go off, picked up his pistol. SWAT team officers, when they kicked open Mr. Jamar's bedroom door, saw him standing next to his bed holding the handgun. Armed with semi-automatic rifles, the officers opened fire. One of the 16 bullets from their rifles hit Mr. Jamar in the hip, another in the groin, and a third in the foot. He went down without firing a shot.

Paramedics rushed Mr. Jamar, in critical condition, to a hospital in Huntsville where he spent two weeks in the intensive care unit. After searching his house, the police confiscated Mr. Jamar's gun collection. Perhaps because the SWAT team had broken into the wrong house, the Limestone County prosecutor chose not to charge Mr. Jamar with attempted assault.

In the days and weeks following this police involved shooting, newspaper accounts of the raid were sketchy because Mike Blakely, the sheriff of Limestone County, the official heading up the internal investigation of the incident, did not release much information to the media. According to Sheriff Blakely, the officers had to "neutralize" a man who was "aggressively resisting." When a reporter asked the sheriff to comment on the wrong house aspect of the raid, he said, "I guess you could call it a clerical error over the address, but I don't think Jamar's dwelling even has a street address." This begs the question: if Mr. Jamar's house didn't have a street address, how could there have been "a clerical error over the address?"

Because the SWAT officers who shot Kenneth Jamar were not personally responsible for the wrong house raid, and had fired their weapons in self-defense, they were cleared of criminal wrongdoing. Kenneth Jamar, in June 2008, filed a $7.5 million lawsuit in federal court claiming that the city of Huntsville, and other entities, had violated his civil rights. In April 2011, the Huntsville city council voted to settle Kenneth Jamar's suit for $500,000.

Never Say Sorry

A confidential informant told an investigator with the Rensselaer County District Attorney's Office that a number of unidentified people were selling cocaine out of three houses in Troy, New York. On June 23, 2008, a member of the county drug task force sent an undercover operative into one of the houses where he purchased cocaine from a known dealer. A few days later, a judge in Troy issued four no-knock nighttime search warrants based on nothing more than the snitch's tip, and one controlled buy.

At four in the morning on June 28, an explosion inside the house at 396 First Street awoke Ronita McColley and her 5-year-old daughter. Seconds later, officers with the Troy Emergency Response Team (ERT) and county drug police, poured into McColley's home past her splintered door. McColley would describe that moment to a local reporter this way: "The flash and then the police coming into my house, and me not having any clothes on...It was just a lot of men looking at me, and there was no female in sight." (SWAT teams are almost entirely made up of male officers.)

After breaking down Ronita McColley's front door, smashing a window with the flash bang grenade--which burned a hole in her carpet and scorched a wall--and rummaging through her personal belongings, the police found no evidence of illegal drug activity. Some of the officers thought they had accidentally raided the wrong house. But no, this was one of the addresses the snitch had identified as a cocaine site. No one got hurt that night, including McColley's 5-year-old daughter. The SWAT raiders did not apologize for the destruction and terror they had visited upon this innocent mother and her child. Moreover, no one in authority offered to replace McColley's door, the broken out window, or the carpet damaged by the percussion grenade. This wrong house SWAT raid was just another case of collateral damage in the drug war the police will never win.

In the other raids that night in Troy, the police also failed to find cocaine. Officers recovered small quantities of marijuana, but didn't take anyone into custody. The entire operation, from a drug war perspective, was a failure. Criticism of these fruitless and potentially dangerous no-knock intrusions prompted an internal police inquiry into the operation. On September 17, 2008, the *Troy Record* published excerpts from Assistant Chief of Police John Tedesco's report. According to Tedesco, "The bulk of this drug investigation was predicated upon the word of the confidential informant absent further investigation. Arguably, the reputation of proven reliable information of the CI was established. However, this fact alone does not negate the need to substantiate the CI's claims. Surveillance or controlled buys at the locations is the seemingly appropriate investigative pursuit to accomplish this function." (This is how the police write. The assistant chief could have said, "We shouldn't SWAT raid a dwelling on nothing more than the word of a snitch.")

Ronita McColley's attorney, Terry Kindlon, gave notice of his intent to file a federal lawsuit against the city of Troy. Interviewed by a *Troy Record* reporter, he said, "I sometimes think...that rather than doing thoughtful, thorough police work, they phoned it in, and ended up throwing bombs at one of the nicest, sweetest woman I have ever met." (The raid would have been just as wrong had Ronita McColley not been a nice person.)

Attorney Kindlon filed the civil rights suit in October 2008, and on March 4, 2012, the judge in a New York state U.S. District Court, ruled in favor of the city and the police.

Because this mindless police intrusion into a dwelling at night did not result in anyone being shot or seriously injured, this case did not attract much attention in the media. The fact that cases like this are not rare is the real story, a reality ignored by local media outlets uninterested in incidents that do not feature blood and guts. Had Ronita McColley, thinking that her home was being broken into by criminals, picked up a gun and shot a cop, she would have either been killed, or shipped off to prison for life. For reporters, that would have been a much better story.

Life Without Parole

In the state of Indiana, a person convicted of armed robbery will serve about six years in prison; someone convicted of rape will serve about eight; and a convicted murderer can expect to spend twenty-five years behind bars. These figures are actually higher than the nation average: eleven years and four months in prison is the typical punishment for an American found guilty of murder....

In 1990, 38-year-old Mark Young was arrested at his Indianapolis home for brokering the sale of seven hundred pounds of marijuana grown on a farm in nearby Morgan County. Young was tried and convicted under federal law. He had never before been charged with drug trafficking. He had no history of violent crime. Young's sole role in the illegal transaction had been that of a middleman--he never distributed the drugs; he simply introduced two people hoping to sell a large amount of marijuana to three people wishing to buy it. The offense occurred a year and a half before his arrest. No confiscated marijuana, money, or physical evidence of any kind linked Young to the crime. He was convicted solely on the testimony of co-conspirators who were now cooperating with the government. On February 8, 1992, Mark Young was sentenced by federal judge Sarah Evans Barker to life imprisonment without possibility of parole.

Eric Schlosser, *Reefer Madness*, 2003

An 80-Year-Old Drug War Casualty

No one is safe from raiding drug cops who are heavily armed and often mindless. A man's home is no longer his castle; it's simply a structure that can be forcefully entered by combat cops on the word of some unreliable snitch. Today, not all armed home invasions involve criminals.

Eugene Mallory, a retired engineer who had worked for Lockheed Martin forty years, resided in an unincorporated community east of Palmdale, California called Littlerock. The 80-year-old shared a home with his 48-year-old wife, Tonya Pate, and her grown son.

Drug enforcement deputies with the Los Angeles County Sheriff's office arrived at the Mallory house at 7:30 on the morning of June 25, 2013. The officers were in possession of a search warrant authorizing them to search the house for methamphetamine and the chemicals used to manufacturer it. The probable cause underlying the search was flimsy at best. Officers, from outside the house, claimed to have smelled the odor of the ingredients used to produce meth. The narcotic officers didn't have an undercover buy or even an informant. Moreover, the suspected meth factory hadn't been the subject of prolonged drug surveillance. All the cops had to go on was the smell of meth chemicals. (The fact that some rubber-stamp magistrate authorized this raid is frightening.)

After forcing their way into the dwelling without notice, deputies encountered Mr. Mallory in a bedroom at the rear of the house. It was there they shot him six times as he lay in his own bed. Officers justified the lethal force by claiming that the old man had pointed a semi-automatic handgun at them.

As it turned out, the Mallory dwelling did not contain meth or any evidence that the drug was being manufactured in the home. Deputies did come across a quantity of marijuana in Mrs. Pate's son's bedroom.

In speaking to the media about the fatal, wrong house raid, Los Angeles County spokesperson Steve Whitmore said this: "There was a drug operation that was certainly going on in this house." (Are you kidding me? The accidental finding of grass justifies the killing of an 80-year-old man in his own bed?)

On October 10, 2013, James Bergener, the attorney representing Mrs. Tonya Pate, announced that he had filed, on her behalf, a $50 million wrongful death suit against Los Angeles County. The out of control drug war not only cost Mr. Mallory his life, it will cost the taxpayers of bankrupt Los Angeles County a multi-million dollar court settlement.

In the minds of our nation's drug warriors, there will always be collateral damage. For SWAT cops war is fun and exciting. For the people being raided, it's hell.

A Wrong House Killing in Tennessee

Sixty-four-year-old John Adams and his wife Loraine lived in Lebanon, Tennessee, a town of 20,000, 14 miles east of Nashville. John, suffering from arthritis, had retired after working 37 years for the Precision Rubber Company. With his lump-sum disability payment, John had purchased a new Cadillac and a doublewide trailer on Joseph Street, a short, dead-end road on the eastern side of town. His place and the house next door were the only dwellings on the block.

At 10 o'clock Wednesday night, October 4, 2000, John and Loraine were watching television in their living room when someone pounded loudly on their front door. Loraine got out of her chair, "Who is it?" she asked. Whoever it was didn't respond. The pounding grew more intense. Realizing that someone was breaking down the door, Loraine, thinking that criminals were invading their house, yelled to John, "Baby, get your gun!"

John Adams grabbed the cane next to his easy chair and hobbled out of the room. Seconds later, five men, wearing helmets and ski masks and dressed in black combat fatigues, burst into the house. They shoved Loraine against a wall and forced her to her knees. Handcuffed and terrified, she said, "Y'all have got the wrong place! What are you looking for?"

Officers Greg Day and Kyle Shedron, rookies in their mid-twenties, encountered John standing in the hallway holding a sawed-off shotgun. Mr. Adams fired one shot, and the officers returned fire, hitting him in three places. Mr. Adams crumbled to the floor, and died four hours later on the operating table at Vanderbilt University Medical Center in Nashville.

At a news conference the following day, Lebanon chief of police Billy Weeks admitted that his officers had raided the wrong house. He acknowledged that because there were only two residences on that block, and one was a house trailer, people had a right to know how this could have happened. Chief Weeks said that the narcotics officer in charge of the case, a person he would not identify, had written the correct address on the search warrant. This address belonged to the drug suspect's house located next door to the Adams dwelling. The narcotics officer, in directing the SWAT team to the place to be entered, relied on the description of the raid target rather than the address written on the warrant. Nobody could figure out what the hell that meant.

According to Chief Weeks, the narcotics officer who had acquired the search warrant had been watching the drug suspect's house for more than a month. The judge had issued the warrant after this officer had sworn to him that an informant had purchased drugs at this house. The drug suspect's car had been parked in the Adams's driveway, which may have caused the mix-up. Although this explained how the narcotics cop might have incorrectly assigned the drug suspect's address to the Adams trailer, it also suggested that the officer had not actually witnessed the snitch enter the suspect's place to make the buy. If he had, the wrong description would not have ended up on the search warrant. Nevertheless, Chief Weeks said, "We did the best surveillance we could do, and a mistake was made. It's a very sincere mistake (what does that mean?), a costly mistake. They [Mr. and Mrs. Adams] were not the targets of our investigation. [Mr. Adams was, unfortunately, the target of the shooters.] It makes us look at our own policies and procedures to make sure this never occurs again." Mr. Adams had been shot the chief went on to say, because he fired a shotgun at officers Shedron and Day. The Tennessee Bureau of Investigation (TBI) conducted an investigation into the shooting.

Chief of Police Weeks called a second news conference on October 19 to update the media on the status of the case. Having earlier assured the public that "We did the best surveillance we could do," he now revealed that "We lost sight of our informant, and that never should occur." It seemed the head of the narcotics unit who had watched the suspect's house, and acquired the search warrant, had not actually witnessed him enter the dwelling for drugs. "What we think happened is that we have a particular [narcotics] supervisor who made a very unwise decision." The "unwise decision" presumably, was to lie to the magistrate who had issued the search warrant.

Chief Weeks placed this officer on paid administrative leave pending the outcome of the TBI investigation. "We are not trying to make excuses for what happened. But I can tell you that we did identify ourselves [before breaking into the wrong house], and maybe they [the occupants] got confused. [Mr. and Mrs. Adams were not confused. They were in the right house.] And I know we were reacting to him [Mr. Adams] shooting at us. But obviously, this wouldn't have happened if we had not been in the man's house.

John Fox, the mayor of Lebanon, also appearing before reporters that day, made the point that, wrong house or not, Mr. Adams would be alive had the SWAT team not been deployed in the first place. "We're going to back off this knocking down doors," he said. "There's going to have to be some really strong evidence that something life-threatening is actually there. I told him [Chief Weeks] to get rid of those damn black uniforms, get rid of them!" [The Lebanon SWAT team had been trained by DEA agents who recommend that officers dress in the "narco ninja" style which consists of all-black outfits and ski masks.] When we go up to knock on a door, we're going to have our suit and tie, or our [regular] police uniform, and that's it. And when they open the door, a citizen is going to be a citizen until there is actually proof of guilt."

Mayor Fox also provided information that possibly explained how the narcotics supervisor had confused the suspect's residence with the Adams trailer. According to the mayor, the confidential informant was merely an anonymous tipster. Moreover, the so-called surveillance was nothing more than a "drive-by" scan of the neighborhood. If this were true, it's hard to imagine how the narcotics officer could have acquired the search warrant without fudging the facts.

The TBI completed its investigation, and on November 3, 2000, a Wilson County grand jury indicted Lieutenant Steve Nokes, the head of the Lebanon narcotics unit. Lieutenant Nokes stood accused of criminal responsibility for reckless homicide, tampering or fabricating evidence, and aggravated perjury, all felony offenses. At his trial, Nokes pleaded not guilty, and in June 2001, the jury acquitted him of all charges.

The city of Lebanon, in May 2002, agreed to pay Loraine Adams the lump sum of $200,000. Pursuant to the court settlement, she would also receive $1,675 a month for the rest of her life. The city also paid Mr. Adams' $45,000 hospital bill, and his $5,804 funeral expenses.

Wrong House in Virginia

A Virginia grandmother still had nightmares of the wrongful police raid conducted on her apartment on the morning of April 10, 2014, at which time she was tied up and questioned in connection with an ongoing drug investigation. No drugs were recovered from the premises...Police raided the wrong residence, mistaking the elderly woman's apartment letter "E" for a "G."

Ruth Hunter, a 75-year-old who lives in Henrico, Virginia, claims she has never done anything illegal in her life...But that morning, officers with the Virginia State Police kicked in her door and tied her up with cable ties. At first she thought she was being robbed. After the officers identified themselves, they began aggressively questioning her and demanded to know where she was hiding the drugs....

"I thought it was just someone breaking in to rob me and kill me," she said. "They asked me had I ever stored drugs"....

Police eventually arrested someone else--at an apartment two doors from Hunter's home. This apartment was "G."...[Due to militarized law enforcement and sloppy policing, it's dangerous to live close to people associated with illegal drugs.]

Hunter was so disturbed by the incident she has decided to move out. She has not gotten so much as an apology from the police department and her door was still broken.

Robby Soave, The Daily Caller, April 23, 2014

DEA Overkill

In 2013, DEA agents in northern Illinois on the hunt for home marijuana growers regularly kept an eye on agricultural retailers where cannabis cultivators were known to purchase their botanical supplies. Agents would follow patrons home and the drug investigations would go from there.

On September 17, 2013, a DEA agent sitting on Midwest Hydroganics in Crest Hill, Illinois followed a woman from the store to her home in nearby Shorewood. Angela Kirking, 46, had purchased a bag of organic fertilizer she carried out of the store in a green shopping bag. She had no previous arrests for drugs or any other crimes.

The DEA agent, on suspicion Kirking was growing cannabis in her house, checked her electric bill for February through August 2013. The federal drug investigator discovered that Kirking's electric payments were higher than her neighbors' utility bills. Because people who cultivate cannabis in their homes use relatively large amounts of electricity to power their grow lights, the DEA agent became even more suspicious of Kirking.

DEA agents, on October 6, 2013, conducted a so-called "investigative garbage pull" at the suspect's house. (In most states and under federal law, a person's trash may be seized without a warrant because it's considered abandoned property that carries no expectation of privacy.) The trash-grabbing agent discovered several plant stems that smelled like cannabis.

Armed with the suspect's relatively high electric bills and the discarded marijuana stems, the DEA agent in charge of Kirking's case acquired a warrant to search her house.

On October 11, 2013, four DEA agents and five local police officers conducted a pre-dawn SWAT-style raid of Angela Kirking's home. The officers rousted the terrified woman out of bed and at gunpoint demanded to know if there were any illegal substances in the dwelling.

The heavily armed searchers found 9.3 grams of marijuana in one room and a "plant portion" on her patio. The drug cops also discovered three glass pipes, three scales, and two books on how to grow marijuana. The drug raiders also walked off with Kirking's computer and a zip drive.

Because the raid didn't produce enough evidence to warrant a federal drug charge, a Will County prosecutor charged Kirking with two state misdemeanor drug offenses.

Nine heavily armed police officers had conducted a pre-dawn, no-knock raid of a home occupied by a middle-aged woman with no history of crime. Moreover, the DEA investigator knew his suspect was not a player in an organized drug operation. In other words, the raiders knew they were not storming a drug lord's house. Predictably, the officers found no guns or a cache of drug money.

In the Kirking case, an *unarmed* DEA agent could have knocked on this woman's door in the middle of the day, showed her the search warrant, and conducted a routine, orderly search of the premises. But pursuant to today's militaristic style of policing, that approach never crossed this agent's mind. Pre-dawn SWAT raids are a lot more fun. They are also a lot more dangerous--for the civilians involved. Had Kirking picked up a gun thinking the cops were criminal home invaders, she would have been killed.

Kirking's attorney, Jeff Tomczak, argued that the DEA agent did not present enough probable cause to legally justify the issuance of the warrant. While this may or may not have been the case, the bigger policing issue involved the unnecessary and dangerous employment of SWAT tactics to enforce minor, low-risk offenses.

Another Naked Man on Cocaine

A 34-year-old…man died Sunday, June 8, 2014 after he was hospitalized following a confrontation with police early Saturday morning…Gilbert, Arizona police responded at about 3:30 AM Saturday…after callers reported that a naked man was yelling for help…Daniel Best assaulted police as they tried to detain him…It took five officers to subdue Best…Tasers were used on him several times. Police believe that Best had an altercation with his wife prior to their arrival, and that cocaine played a role in his actions….

Once in custody, Best showed signs of medical distress and the fire department transported him to a hospital, where he died….

Matthew Casey, The Republic, June 9, 2014

Are Legal Growers of Marijuana Child Abusers?

Although voters in California have legalized medical marijuana, police and prosecutors in the state continue to raid growers who they believe are illegally cultivating the cannabis for resale. (Cops also get a kick out of the raids themselves. If there were no drug war, SWAT teams would have to be disbanded, or called out in shoplifting cases.) To further criminalize pot growing, cannabis cultivators with children are being charged with child endangerment, and in some cases, abuse. In the medical marijuana community, these raids and arrests, and charges of child abuse, are considered harassment tactics by the cops and prosecutors who are against the legalization of medical marijuana. They argue that living in a house with marijuana plants is not equivalent to growing up in a crack house.

Generally, people who support marijuana decriminalization include libertarians, liberals, potheads, and the relatively small number of sick people cannabis actually helps. Opponents include social conservatives, religious groups, and the law enforcement community. Judges, caught in the middle of this social and legal debate, will have to sort it out case by case.

Daisy Bram and Jayme Walsh grew medical marijuana in their garage and on their property in Concow, California, an unincorporated community in Butte County. This remote, mountainous area in the north central part of the state is named after the Indian tribe indigenous to the region. Bram and Walsh had two children, 15-month-old Thor, and 3-week-old Zeus.

At eight in the morning of September 29, 2011, members of the Butte Interagency Narcotics Task Force, accompanied by child protection service agents, raided the Bram-Walsh house on Yellow Wood Road. They seized 96 marijuana plants, a plastic bag containing syringes and spoons, and both of the children.

Assistant District Attorney Jeff Greeson charged Daisy Bram and Jayme Walsh with a total of eight felonies that included cultivating and possessing cannabis for sale, and two counts of child abuse.

On November 30, 2011, Judge Steven Howell dismissed the child abuse charges for lack of evidence. Six weeks later, the defendants got their children back. Prosecutor Greeson, on March 8, re-filed the child abuse charges against Daisy Bram. The re-instatement of these charges upset local medical marijuana supporters who called for a grand jury investigation of the drug task force, and the child protection agency.

At the preliminary hearing on June 11, 2012 held in Oroville before Butte County Superior Court Judge Steven Howell to determine if the state had sufficient probable cause to hold Daisy Bram over for trial on the child abuse charges, prosecutor Greeson presented an expert witness.

Dr. Angela Rosas with the Sutter Medical Group testified that the psychoactive chemical in cannabis--THC--is hazardous to children. If a child eats raw marijuana plant leaves, the effect could be toxic, she said. Defense attorney Michael Levinsohn put on his own medical expert, Dr. William Courtney. Dr. Courtney, who studies the effects of marijuana on users, testified that THC isn't activated unless it's heated. He said a child would have to eat a pile of raw leaves to get sick. And not only that, the leaves have a bad taste.

On January 22, 2014, Brutte County Superior Court Judge Robert Glusman, after Daisy Bram's conviction on charges of marijuana possession and child endangerment, sentenced her to 78 days in jail and four years of probation. The judge also ordered Bram into a child abuse treatment program.

A Deadly Raid in Ohio

Eleven people were inside a mobile home near Chillicothe, Ohio when, at 10:30 PM on December 11, 2013, a dozen or so members of a local drug task force unit rolled up to the dwelling with a no-knock warrant to search for guns and drugs. One of the occupants of the trailer house was a teenage girl.

Just before breaking into the home, one of the heavily armed U.S. 23 Task Force officers tossed a flash bang grenade through a window. At the moment the device detonated officers forced their way into the house.

Following the initial chaos created by the SWAT-like raid, officers found Krystal Marie Barrows slumped on the living room couch. The 35-year-old mother of three had been shot in the head. She died shortly after being flown by helicopter to the Wexner Medical Center in Columbus.

The raiding police officers arrested two women and four men for illegally possessing pistols, assault rifles, and heroin. The task force cops also recovered stolen goods and a significant amount of cash. During the raid, none of the mobile home occupants pulled a gun or fired a shot. This meant that Krystal Barrows had been shot by one of the task force officers.

According to the results of a preliminary police inquiry into Barrows' death, Ross County sergeant Brett McKnight shot Barrows. The eleven-year veteran of the Ross County Sheriff's Office had accidentally discharged his sidearm outside the trailer when the flash bang grenade went off. The bullet pierced the trailer home's exterior wall and hit Barrows in the head.

Other than a misdemeanor drunk and disorderly conviction, Krystal Barrows did not have a criminal record. Her sons were aged 19, 14, and 9. Detectives with the Ohio Bureau of Investigation are looking into the case to determine if Sergeant McKnight had fired his gun recklessly. If that turns out to be the case, the officer could be charged with negligent homicide.

Whether officer McKnight was reckless or not, the law enforcement agencies involved in the fatal drug raid can expect to be defendants in a wrongful death suit. Taxpayers will end up paying the bill for this police involved shooting.

The War on Dogs Continues

Instead of leaving with drugs and weapons they were sent to find, a Minnesota SWAT team executing a no-knock drug raid left with the bodies of a family's two dead dogs. "The first thing I heard was "boom," Larry Lee Arman told a reporter in recalling the raid in St. Paul at seven in the morning, July 9, 2014...

Armed with a warrant for drugs and weapons, the SWAT unit barged into the house while Arman slept on a mattress with his two children. The officers shot Mello and Laylo, the family's two pit bulls. "One was running for her life, and they murdered her right here," Arman said. His sneakers were still stained with his dogs' blood. "I was laying right here and I thought I was being murdered."

Camille Perry, Arman's girlfriend and the mother of the two children, was in the bathroom when the SWAT team broke down the front door. She expressed anger that the children could have been injured. "The only thing I was thinking was my kids were going to get hit by bullets," she said...

After the shooting and a search of the house, the SWAT unit failed to find any weapons. They recovered marijuana residue, some clothing, and a bong...Neighbors were not pleased by the incident. "All of a sudden, we see the dogs thrown out like pieces of meat, like they were nothing," said a neighbor. "We cried because those dogs were real good dogs."

Chuck Ross, "SWAT Unit Kills Two Dogs," The Daily Caller, July 9, 2014

26 ASSUALT

Times Square Cookie Monster

New York City's Times Square, in the 1960s, 70s, and 80s, was one of the seediest sections of the city. The midtown Manhattan tourist attraction was inhabited by panhandlers, pickpockets, drunks passed out in their own urine, prostitutes, pimps, and guys hawking stolen and knock-off watches. Times Square was home to strip joints, hole-in-the-wall bars, peep shows, adult movie theaters, dirty bookstores, and cathouses. This was not a destination for kids or tourists in search of wholesome entertainment. This was a place to get mugged, hustled, and ripped-off.

When mayor Rudy Giuliani and his police commissioner took control of the city in the 1990s, they cleaned house in Manhattan and transformed Times Square into a Disneyesque theme park for families with young children. Toy stores, souvenir shops, clothing outlets, and fast-food restaurants replaced the adult entertainment establishments. The prostitutes, pimps, panhandlers and street hustlers were replaced by an assortment of costumed Sesame Street and comic book characters who probably think of themselves as street performers.

Instead of being accosted by whores, bums, and stolen goods merchants, Times Square tourists are hassled by a motley band of oddballs walking around the place inside Spider-Man, Superman, Wonder Woman, Elmo, Big Bird, Super Mario, and Cookie Monster outfits. (This kind of thing goes on in Los Angeles as well. Where I live, if some guy dressed up like Superman and walked around town engaging kids, he'd find himself in a police vehicle en route to jail faster than a speeding bullet.)

In Times Square, the costumed impersonators compete against each other for the attention of tourists accompanied by kids. They pose and mug it up for the children whose parents are supposed to tip them for the photo-ops. When little Lester returns to West Virginia he can impress his friends with a photograph of himself being hugged by Wonder Woman. (The street performers are not supposed to directly solicit tips. In New York City this is called "aggressive begging.")

In the scheme of things, slipping a guy in a Big Bird suit a couple of bucks for posing with your kid is harmless enough. It certainly beats having your pocket picked, or losing a couple of hundred bucks to some street corner card hustler. But occasionally, in the heat of tip-hustling competition, things get out of hand. Some of the impersonators have slipped out of character. Super Mario got in trouble for groping a woman. Spider-Man pushed a tourist, and Elmo uttered an anti-Sematic slur. Occasionally fights break out between the characters. (It would be odd seeing Big Bird knock Superman to the ground.)

On Sunday, April 7, 2013, Parmita Katkar, the former Miss India Asia Pacific beauty queen, a Bollywood actress and model, was in Times Square with her husband and two sons. From Stamford, Connecticut, the family had come to Times Square to buy a bicycle at the massive Toys-R-Us store. Around two-thirty that afternoon, Cookie Monster, AKA Osvaldo Quiroz-Lopez, set upon her and her family. The big blue furry creature grabbed up Katkar's two-year-old boy and said, "Come on, take a picture." When the mother hesitated, the Cookie Monster put the kid down, pushed him, and said, "Come on, come on! Give me the money!"

As the terrified boy's father hustled off to find cash for a tip, Quiroz-Lopez launched a verbal attack on the kid's mother. "You are a bitch," he yelled. "Your son is a bastard and your stuff is trash." (I presume the Cookie Monster was commenting on Katkar's body of work in Bollywood.)

As the shaken tourists escaped the wrath of the furious Cookie Monster, the toddler kept saying, "I don't like Cookie Monster!"

The next day, the 33-year-old Cookie Monster impersonator was arraigned in a Manhattan criminal court on charges of assault, child endangerment, and aggressive begging. He posted his $1,000 bond and was released.

In February 2014, the judge agreed to dismiss the charges against Quiroz-Lopez after the Cookie Monster performed one day of community service.

Spider-Man Punches Cop

Junior Bishop, dressed as Spider-Man, told a woman who took his photograph on July 27, 2014 in Times Square that he only accepted $5, $10 or $20 bills. As the two argued, a New York City Police officer intervened. The 25-year-old Spider-Man impersonator cursed at the police officer then punched the cop when the officer tried to take him into custody. This was, of course, very non Spider-Man-like conduct.

After assaulting the police officer, Spider-Man fled the scene on foot. Had he been the real thing, his escape would have been more dramatic, and successful. A group of police officers, a few blocks away, took Bishop into custody.

A Manhattan prosecutor charged Bishop with assault, resisting arrest, criminal mischief, and disorderly conduct.

The Columbus Stabbing Spree

On March 14, 2012, one week after John Shick shot six people in the Oakland section of Pittsburgh, John Mallet embarked on a stabbing spree in Columbus, Ohio that wounded four. In the Pittsburgh assaults, one of the victims died. The police shot both of the attackers. Officers killed Shick and they wounded Mallett.

While these violent rampages defy rational explanation and are not predictable, they do not arise out of the blue. Because the targets of these attacks are random, and the violence unprovoked, cases like this shock the community and leave people feeling vulnerable. In America, spree violence of this sort has become commonplace.

As a teenager growing up in New York City, John Mallett spent time in the juvenile wing of the jail on Rikers Island. He had stabbed a boy in a fight over a girl. As a young adult, Mallett, a paranoid schizophrenic, continued to have problems with the law. He served three years in prison for robbery. Mallett's family tried to get him help through the courts and public health. They were ignored. The criminal justice system was of no help to families of violent, mentally ill people until that they committed heinous crimes. Then it was too late.

In 2002, Mallett moved to Nashville, Tennessee where his mental illness continued to lead him into trouble. In March of that year, he was convicted of resisting arrest, and in July 2010, for criminal trespass. In February 2011, just before moving to Columbus, the authorities in Nashville charged Mallett with the unlawful possession of a weapon. (That charge was later dismissed.)

In Columbus, Mallett moved in with his aunt. He became such a problem for her, she asked him to move out. This may have placed the mentally ill man under considerable stress. On March 14, 2012, while in downtown Columbus a few blocks from the state capitol, Mallett entered the 25-story Continental Centre carrying three knives, one of which came from his aunt's kitchen. The office building housed, on the first floor, a for-profit trade school (criminal justice, security, investigation, and court reporting) called Miami-Jacobs Career College. The school, owned by the Delta Career Education Corporation headquartered in Virginia Beach, Virginia, consisted of 37 campuses and 16,000 students around the country.

In the trade school's admissions office, Mallett, carrying a knife in each hand, repeatedly stabbed two employees and a criminal justice student. Back outside, he knifed an attorney who worked for the state attorney general's office, also housed in the building. Several bystanders tried but failed to disarm Mallett. One of the witnesses dialed 911.

Within minutes of the 911 call, Columbus patrol officer Deborah Ayers pulled up to the building. The 15-year veteran of the force confronted Mallett near the building's entrance. "Sir," she yelled, "you need to put the knife down. Sir, please put the knife down!" Instead of complying with the officer's command, Mallet lunged toward her with his knife. Ayers fired 11 shots at Mallet, hitting him several times. Before he collapsed to the pavement, a second officer shocked him with a stun gun. (In police involved shootings, the shooter is almost always a male officer, and if a Taser is used, it usually precedes the gunfire.)

The 37-year-old Mallett and his four victims were rushed to a local hospital. They were expected to survive their wounds. The fact Mallett lunged at the officer with the knife suggested a suicide-by-cop attempt.

On Thursday, March 15, the day after the rampage, the local prosecutor charged John Mallett with four counts of felonious assault.

A battery of psychiatrists appointed by the court to examine Mallett concluded that he suffered from severe paranoid schizophrenia. On June 10, 2013, Franklin County Judge Kimberly Cocroft found Mallett not guilty by reason of insanity.

A few weeks after the verdict, corrections officials assigned the schizophrenic to a Columbus area forensic psychiatric facility where he'll remain incarcerated until his doctors declare he is sane enough to rejoin society.

Bacon Grease Assault

A woman was wanted for allegedly throwing bacon grease on a man with whom she had been arguing. New Castle, Pennsylvania police charged Shawntay Hope Thomas, 37 in connection with the incident that happened about 10:15 PM on Thursday, June 12, 2014 at her house.

Police say they were called to Jameson Hospital regarding a man suffering from burns and redness on his face, neck, and chest. He told officers that he and Thomas had been arguing and he had gone out to the porch. A short time later, he said, she went outside carrying a cup of hot bacon grease and threw it on him...She was charged with simple assault and harassment....

New Castle News, June 18, 2014

Daycare Assaults

Anyone who follows the news will come across, almost every day, a story featuring an irresponsible, clearly unfit parent. The fact there are probably thousands upon thousands of kids in this country being raised by drug addicts, child abusers, nut cases, and immature idiots, doesn't mitigate the problem that so many children are being raised in daycare centers by people who shouldn't be anywhere near a child.

Millions of children in the United States are being partially raised (or warehoused) in 400,000 or so licensed and regulated childcare facilities. Forty-one percent of employed mothers with preschool children, place their kids in daycare for 35 or more hours a week. In America, daycare has become a big business.

Suzanne Venker, in an online *National Review* article entitled, "Will America Ever be Ready for the Truth About Daycare," points out that politicians and media journalists avoid talking about the harm daycare is doing to the nation's children. Politicians don't want to offend female voters, and women in the media rely on daycare services themselves, and are therefore not prone to publicly discuss the issue. Venker and others, consider daycare one of the greatest tragedies of modern America. They see the phenomena as a growing epidemic of parental abandonment.

In her *National Review* piece, Venker discussed a recent e-book by May Saubiek entitled *Doing Time: What it Really Means to Grow Up in Daycare.* According to the author, daycare children received very little individualized attention, and when they did, because of high daycare employee turnover, it often came from a stranger. Because daycare was a business that relied on customers who believed their children were happy, and being cared for by people who cared, parents aren't told how miserable their children really are. On the contrary, parents received rose-colored reports of how well their kids were adapting and progressing. Parents were often told that the daycare experience helped "socialize" their children. According to Saubiek, daycare life fostered aggressive behavior by forcing kids into survival mode. If a child wanted a toy, he or she learned to fight for it.

Some child facilities were obviously better than others, and conditions might not be so bleak as Saubiek describes in her book. But it seems, to some degree, that a good number of working mothers' children were paying the price for the realities of modern society. Daycare workers were not highly paid, thoroughly investigated, or well trained. And they were being drawn from a society awash in alcoholism, mental illness, drug addiction, pedophilia, and ignorance.

The Delaware Daycare Fight Club

On August 18, 2012, police officers in Dover, Delaware watched a video that showed two 3-year-old boys engaged in a fight organized and supervised by three workers at The Hands of Our Future Daycare Center. One of the Dover daycare workers recorded the combat on her cellphone. When one of the toddlers cried, "He's pinching me!" one of these fight organizers said, "No pinching, only punching."

In speaking to a reporter, Dover police captain Tim Stump said, "It's difficult to watch. One of the kids involved ran over to one of the adults for protection, but she turned him around back into the fight. They were just wailing on each other, I mean slapping, pinching, throwing each other onto tables." (The fight viewed by the police had occurred back in March 2012.)

On August 21, the police arrested 19-year-old Tianna Harris, Lisa Parker, 47, and 21-year-old Estefania Myers. Charged with assault, endangering the welfare of a child, reckless endangering, and conspiracy, these daycare workers were placed into the county jail on $10,000 bond each. All three suspects posted bail and were released from custody shortly after their arrests.

In December 2012, Myers and Parker pleaded guilty to felony assault and conspiracy. The judge sentenced both women to one year of probation. In June 2013, Harris, after pleading guilty, got off light as well with a year of probation.

Someone should ask how one daycare center had *three* abusers working at the facility at the same time. Was this facility licensed? Who in Delaware was in charge of daycare oversight? And finally, was there anyway to protect daycare children from this form of institutional abuse?

The Maternity Ward Assault

Patrol officers spend much of their time responding to late night and early morning domestic violence calls involving alcohol, drugs, abusive men, and battered women. (These young officers, mostly from middle-class backgrounds, must eventually develop an extremely low opinion of lower-class citizens.) Constant exposure to the underbelly of American culture is one of the drawbacks of police work.

On January 15, 2012, at 7:40 in the evening, police officers in Lower Merion, Pennsylvania, a suburban community outside of Philadelphia, were summoned to a domestic disturbance at an unusual place. The call had come from the maternity ward in Lower Merion's Lankenau Hospital. The victim of the assault (her name was not made public) had given birth two days earlier.

Richard Lavon Davis, Jr., while visiting his girlfriend, the mother of his child, became agitated when he and the new mother couldn't agree on the baby's name. Davis, who had been holding the infant, laid it in its crib when the argument heated up. After screaming and cursing, Davis lost complete control of himself. The enraged father kicked a rolling table toward the chair where the mother sat. When she rose to her feet, Davis punched her twice in the face, knocking her onto the hospital bed. (I guess if you're going to get assaulted, a hospital room is not a bad place to be.)

The day after the maternity ward attack, Montgomery County Assistant District Attorney Wallis Brooks charged the 23-year-old father with simple assault, a crime that carried a maximum sentence of five years.

A year after the hospital assault, Davis pleaded guilty to punching the new mother in the maternity ward. On February 15, 2013, Montgomery County Judge Joseph Smyth sentenced him to eight to twenty-three months in the county jail. The sentence included 96 hours of community service, and mandatory domestic violence counseling. (Why 96 hours instead of 100 or 84? And counseling? What kind of person needs to be told that punching the mother of your newborn child is wrong? What will keep this man from punching-out the anger management counselor?)

In speaking to the press following the sentencing hearing, prosecutor Brooks said, "...he assaulted a new mother and his conduct was outrageous...It's absurd that an argument over the name of the child would lead to this kind of physical violence against a defenseless woman who is just recovering from one of nature's most beautiful experiences, the birthing of a child."

The convicted man's attorney, Gregory Nestor, told reporters that his client was "...quite remorseful about what he did." (If there's any remorse in this case, it should be on the part of the woman this man impregnated.) The lawyer, in speaking highly of his client, said, "That by coming into court and pleading guilty and accepting the sentence...indicates his acceptance of responsibility for his actions."

The sentence in this case was a joke. If Davis was capable of hitting the mother of his 2-day-old baby, life for this mother and child could get a lot worse when he's released from jail.

A Brutal and Senseless Assault in China

On August 24, 2013, outside the Shanxi Province town of Linfen in rural northeast China, a woman grabbed 6-year-old Guo Bin as he walked along a path not far from his home. This woman lured the boy into a field where, in a shocking act of brutality, she used a sharp instrument to gouge out his eyes. Several hours later, a member of Guo Bin's family found the boy, his face covered in blood, wandering in a field on the family farm.

In China, due to a donor shortage, corneas are worth thousands of dollars on the black market. As a result, investigators considered the possibility the boy had been victimized by an organ trafficker. The authorities abandoned this theory when at the site of the attack crime scene investigators recovered the boy's eyeballs with the corneas in tact. Police officers also recovered a bloody purple shirt presumably worn by the assailant.

A witness reported seeing the boy that afternoon with an unidentified woman wearing a purple shirt. According to Guo Bin, the woman who attacked him spoke with an accent from outside the region. She also had dyed blond hair. The victim told investigators that this woman had used a sharp stick to cut out his eyeballs. Based on the nature of the boy's wounds, doctors believed he had been attacked with a knife.

According to physicians, Guo Bin, with a visual prosthesis, might someday regain partial vision. Following the attack, the boy's family received $160,000 in donations from members of the public.

Six days after the gruesome assault, 41-year-old Zhang Huiyang, the victim's aunt, killed herself by jumping into a well. While Guo Bin did not identify his aunt as the assailant, and she did not match his description of the attacker, the authorities, through DNA, linked her to the purple shirt found at the crime scene.

The boy's mother, in speaking to an Associated Press reporter, pointed out that following the assault her obviously traumatized son had been disoriented. "It is easy to understand why he wasn't clear about the situation," she said.

Since there was no rational motive behind a senseless assault like this, the Chinese authorities assume the boy's aunt suffered from some kind of mental illness.

Babysitter From Hell

In 2012, after Benjamin and Hope Jordan moved to Charleston, South Carolina, they hired 21-year-old Alexis Kahn to regularly babysit their 7-

month-old son Finn while they were away at work. Kahn had never been arrested, and came with references.

Five months after bringing Alexis Kahn into their home to care for their most precious possession, the Jordans noticed that their dog, an otherwise friendly black lab, disliked the babysitter. According to Mr. Jordan, "He [the dog] was very aggressive towards her and a few times we actually had to physically restrain him from going towards her."

Worried that the dog's behavior revealed something sinister about the babysitter, the Jordans hid an iPhone under the couch to record what went on between Kahn, the dog, and the baby in their absence. That evening, after work, the couple looked at their iPhone. They were shocked by what they had recorded. The Jordans heard Kahn tell the baby to "shut up." Next they heard the babysitter cussing followed by sounds of their baby being slapped. The baby's cries of distress became cries of pain. "I just wanted to...go back in time and just grab him up," said the father.

The Jordans fired the babysitter and reported the suspected assault to the Charleston police. Officers arrested Kahn a few weeks later. Confronted with the iPhone evidence, the suspect confessed to assaulting the Jordan baby.

On September 8, 2013, Alex Kahn pleaded guilty to one count of assault and battery in a Charleston County Circuit Court. The judge handed down a three-year sentence. The ex-babysitter will have to spend a year behind bars before being eligible for parole. And her name has been added to the state's child abuse register which means she can never work with children. (Unfortunately, this will not prevent her from *having* children.)

According to the baby's parents, Finn had no lingering effects from his abuse at the hands of this babysitter from hell. If your dog doesn't like your babysitter, keep the dog and look for a new sitter.

The High Altitude Slap

On February 8, 2013, Jessica Bennett, a passenger on a Delta Air Line flight from Minneapolis/St. Paul to Atlanta, sat in row 28, seat B next to Joe Rickey Hundley. Jonah, her black 19-month-old adopted son (she is white) sat on her lap. Hundley, the 60-year-old president of an aircraft parts manufacturing company in Hayden, Idaho had been knocking down double vodkas and made the passengers seated around him uncomfortable with his belligerent remarks and attitude. At one point Hundley, in an obnoxious fashion, told Bennett that the kid was too big to be sitting on her lap.

As the plane descended into Atlanta, the change in cabin pressure caused Jonah to cry. Aware that Hundley was becoming increasingly annoyed with the boy, Bennett did her best to calm her son down. But the child was in pain and continued to bawl. Hundley, unable to control his anger, turned to Bennett and said, "shut that [N-word] kid up!"

Stunned by what she had just heard, Bennett asked, "What did you say?"

Hundley pushed his lips next to Bennett's ear and repeated the racial slur. He then did something even more outrageous and unexpected; he slapped Jonah in the face with an open hand, cutting the child below his right eye. This did not, obviously, stop the crying.

Passengers and crew, aware of the intoxicated, loud and bellicose passenger, rushed to Bennett's aid to make sure the angry drunk didn't hit the boy again. When the executive from Idaho walked off the plane in Atlanta he was met by a couple of FBI agents. He has been charged in federal court with assaulting a child younger than 16. If convicted, Hundley faced a maximum sentence of one year in prison. According to court records, Hundley, in 2007, pleaded guilty in Virginia to the misdemeanor assault of his girlfriend.

Joe Hundley denied slapping the boy on the plane. His attorney, Marcia Shein, told reporters that she plans to plead him not guilty. Pointing out that her client was on a personal flight to visit a sick relative, Shein wants the public to know that Mr. Hundley was under a lot of stress and was distraught. "He's not a racist. I'm going to make that clear because that's what people are suggesting. There's background information people don't know about, and in time it will come out."

Attorney Shein, in her public relations effort on Hundley's behalf, mentioned that her client has been getting hate mail. "Hopefully," she said, "this situation can be resolved. Both people are probably very nice. No one should rush to judgment."

Joe Hundley has lost his job over the slap heard around the world. On February 17, 2013, the head of Hundley's parent company, AGC Aerospace and Composites Group, a corporation headquartered in Decatur, Georgia, issued a statement which read: "Reports of the recent behavior of one of our business unit executives while on personal travel are offensive and disturbing. We have taken this matter very seriously and worked diligently to examine it since learning of the matter. As of Sunday [February 17] the executive is no longer employed with the company."

The slapped boy's father, Josh Bennett, told a reporter that, "We want to see this guy do some time."

In October 2013, Mr. Hundley pleaded guilty to assault after the Assistant United States Attorney indicated that he would be satisfied with a six-month prison sentence. When it came time for sentencing, however, the federal judge ignored the prosecutor's suggestion. On January 6, 2014, the judge sentenced Hundley to eight months in a federal lockup. In justifying the stiffer sentence, the judge cited the defendant's prior assault conviction.

Teacher Decks a Student

On November 8, 2013, 13-year-old Reginald Wells, a seventh grade student at Willie Ray Smith Middle School in Beaumont, Texas, got the surprise of his young life. In the hallway between classes he encountered 24-year-old substitute math teacher, Michael Fisher. Reginald, in a jovial attempt to attract the teacher's attention, made an insulting remark about Fisher's favorite professional football team, the Houston Texans.

The teacher's immediate response to the boy's innocent comment shocked everyone who witnessed it. Fisher punched the student hard in the shoulder. This act alone, at the very least, constituted grounds for dismissal. But the incident didn't end with the shoulder punch. When Reginald reacted by pushing the teacher away, Michael Fisher struck the boy twice in the face then delivered an uppercut that sent the four-foot eleven-inch eighty-pounder sprawling across the hallway floor. The teacher's big punch also knocked the boy unconscious for a few seconds.

When Reginald regained consciousness his face was numb, his lips sore and swollen, and the inside of his head pounded in pain. Someone at the scene summoned a school security police officer. The guard escorted Fisher out of the building. The officer did not, however, take the teacher into custody. Later that day the principal fired Michael Fisher.

Reginald Wells' mother, the moment she learned of the assault, filed a complaint with the Beaumont Independent School District Police Department. She assumed that school officials would in turn report the incident to the Beaumont Police Department.

At some point, an officer with the Beaumont Police Department questioned the fired teacher who said he felt remorse over his actions. The county prosecutor's office, however, did not follow up with criminal charges. Moreover, no one from law enforcement interviewed the victim of the assault. Reginald's mother had no recourse but to hire an attorney.

On December 19, 2013, six weeks after the middle school assault, attorney Kevin Laine told a reporter with a Beaumont television station that the school district had still not reported the crime to the local police. According to the lawyer, a school surveillance camera had recorded the attack on videotape. Mr. Laine said he had been unable to acquire a copy of that footage.

The lawyer also told the television correspondent that, "statutory law in Texas requires a reporting of such act to child protective services and the local police department."

Melody Chappell, an attorney with the Beaumont Independent School District, told a reporter that the district was not required by law to make the surveillance tape available to Wells' attorney or to the public. Chappell said the school district had acted correctly by notifying the boy's mother of the incident. Notifying the police was her responsibility.

If a local prosecutor has charged Michael Fisher with Reginald Wells' assault, there has been no coverage of it in the media.

The Angry Mob

At four in the afternoon of April 2, 2014, Steven Utash, a 54-year-old tree trimmer from the Detroit suburb of Roseville, struck a ten-year-old boy while driving his pickup truck home from work on a busy thoroughfare in an east side Detroit neighborhood. The boy was hit when he darted onto the street into the path of the slow moving vehicle. The accident happened near a Clark gas station, a Happy's Pizza place, and a liquor store.

Immediately after the mishap, Mr. Utash pulled over, jumped out of his truck, and ran to the screaming boy. What unfolded next was caught on a Clark gas station surveillance camera.

Ten or more men quickly surrounded Mr. Utash and began punching and kicking him. As he lay on the pavement being beaten, Mr. Utash repeatedly said he was sorry and pleaded with his attackers to stop. With his wallet, paycheck and cash gone, and his cellphone and equipment stolen from his truck, the bloodied Mr. Utash stumbled toward the gas station to get help. One man who tried to help him was himself assaulted by the mob.

Paramedics transported the ten-year-old to St. John's Hospital where a doctor treated him for scrapes, bruises, a swollen lip, and a sore foot. None of the boy's bones had been broken. Under the circumstances, his injuries were minor and he would be fine.

At the same hospital, physicians placed Mr. Utash into an induced coma. According to reports, he suffered serious brain injury that will require a prolonged period of recovery.

Outraged citizens in the Detroit area, through an Internet program called Go Fund Me, raised on Mr. Utash's behalf, $96,000 in just a few days. The campaign drew more than 2,000 donors. The hard working victim of the unprovoked vigilante attack earned a modest living, and did not have health care insurance. It was estimated that Mr. Utash's hospital costs were $20,000 a day.

On April 5, 2014, Detroit police officers arrested two teenage boys believed to have been involved in the gang assault. The unnamed suspects were 16 and 18-years-old. In the wake of the attack, Detroit police chief Mike Duggan asked residents of the east side neighborhood to remain calm, and people outraged by the assault to have patience while detectives work to identify all of the attackers and thieves.

In June 2014, one of the suspects, 18-year-old Bruce Wimbush, pleaded guilty to aggravated assault. Judge James Callahan sentenced Wimbush to three years probation and regular drug testing.

Although Mr. Utash was white and all of his attackers were black, the chief of police said the crime was not motivated by race. Many people considered that analysis nothing more than politically correct nonsense. If Mr. Utash had been black, would he have been so viciously attacked and robbed? If Mr. Utash were black and all of his attackers white, would the media race baiters be out in full force?

The Internet Hook-Up From Hell

In September 2010, Mary Kay Beckman, a 46-year-old mother of two from Las Vegas, met 50-year-old Wade Mitchell Ridley via the online dating service, Match.com. The couple had eight dates before Beckman realized there was something wrong with him and ended the relationship.

On January 21, 2011, four months after his last date with Beckman, Ridley, armed with a butcher's knife, broke into her garage where he waited for her to return home. When Beckman pulled into the garage and got out of her car, Ridley stabbed her ten times. In his attempt to murder his victim, Ridley also stomped her head and neck. Ridley left the garage that night thinking that he had killed Mary Kay Beckman.

Mary Kay survived the brutal attack, but had to undergo surgeries to repair her jaw, preserve her eyesight, and to have a section of her skull replaced by a synthetic material.

Shortly after the burglary and attempted murder, Las Vegas police arrested Ridley. While in police custody, he confessed to the Beckman assault. Ridley also informed his interrogators that a few weeks before stabbing and stomping Mary Kay Beckman, he murdered a woman in Phoenix. The suspect said he had used a butcher's knife to stab 62-year-old Anne Simenson to death in her home. Just before murdering Simenson, a woman he had met on Match.com, Ridley had stolen painkilling drugs from a pharmacist he had robbed at knifepoint.

On February 15, 2011, a prosecutor in Clark County, Nevada charged Wade Mitchell Ridley with the attempted murder of Mary Kay Beckman. In Arizona, a prosecutor charged Ridley with the murder of Anne Simenson.

In September 2011, Ridley entered an Alford pleas to attempted murder with the use of a deadly weapon and armed robbery. (In so pleading, Ridley didn't admit guilt but acknowledged the state had enough evidence to convict him.) The judge sentenced Ridley to 28 to 70 years in prison.

On May 17, 2012, a prison guard found Ridley hanging in his cell. The medical examiner ruled his death a suicide.

Mary Kay Beckman, on January 25, 2013, filed suit against Match.com in a Las Vegas federal court. Her attorney, Marc Saggese, told reporters that the basis of the $10 million civil action "...is the advertising that is utilized by Match.com, lulling women and men into a false sense of security." It is the plaintiff's contention that the dating service has a legal duty to warn its online customers that there might be people in the dating pool who are dangerous.

The lawyer representing Match.com responded to this assertion by saying the notion his client was liable for the behavior of a Match.com member was absurd. The attorney for the defendant said the plaintiff was the victim of a "sick, twisted" man.

If Match.com lost this lawsuit, owners of bars where men and women meet could be held liable for hook-ups that led to one of the parties being criminally victimized. It would make fixing-up friends a risky proposition for matchmakers. Who doesn't know that going out with a stranger met online, in a bar, or at a college fraternity party, is risky business? While Mary Kay Beckman was the victim of a terrible crime, she was not a victim of Match.com.

On May 29, 2013, a federal judge in Nevada threw out Beckman's case against the online dating service.

The Egg Decorating Assault

An Easter egg decorating party that went very wrong led a Brookline, Pennsylvania man to pelt his girlfriend with hard-boiled eggs before attempting to stab Pittsburgh police officers with a sword....

Aaron Goempel, 27, awaited his arraignment on charges of aggravated assault charges stemming from the disturbance shortly after midnight, Sunday, April 20, 2014. Police say they responded to reports of a fight inside a Wareman Avenue apartment and found a woman with a red and swollen eye. She told officers that when accusing Goempel of cheating on her, he became agitated and began hurling eggs. He barricaded himself in the bedroom with an exercise machine against the door....

Once officers got through the door, Goempel reached for a row of knives and swords atop the dresser. Police got him under control and took him to a cruiser where he started yelling racist obscenities at one of the officers. Goempel allegedly kicked another officer in the groin.

According to court records, Goempel's criminal record included guilty verdicts for disorderly conduct and public drunkenness dating to 2008. He was charged with harassment, assault and traffic violations.

Carl Prine, *Pittsburgh Tribune-Review,* April 20, 2014

27 THE FBI

J. Edgar Hoover

When Clint Eastwood's film, "J. Edgar," came out in 2011, my wife and I went to see it. Starring Leonardo Di Caprio as J. Edgar Hoover, the film interested me because of its emphasis on the Lindbergh kidnapping case, and the fact I was a street agent during Hoover's last six years in office (1966-1972). The film's version of the Lindbergh case overplayed the FBI's role in the crime scene investigation near Hopewell, New Jersey and the trial of Bruno Richard Hauptmann two and a half years later in Flemington, New Jersey. Although dotted with other factual errors that were minor, the treatment of the 1932 abduction and murder of the Lindbergh baby, was, on the whole, complete. As for J. Edgar Hoover himself, except for scenes with his dominating mother (Judi Dench) and Clyde Tolson, his right-hand man who loved him (Arnie Hammer), the film also caught the flavor and essence of Hoover's 48-year career as director of the FBI and America's most famous and powerful lawman.

Looking back on my six years as an FBI agent, I will say this without equivocation: Hoover's agents did not imagine him as presented in the film by Eastwood and screenwriter Dustin Lance Black. We did not see the director as a repressed homosexual scared to death of his mother. Agents saw him as a powerful figure who terrorized presidents and was so devoted to the bureau and his own image as an incorruptible crime fighter and a warrior against the internal communist threat, he would destroy anyone who tarnished him or the FBI. As a result, in the minds' of Hoover's street agents, crime fighting became secondary to avoiding the director's wrath.

Pursuant to Hoover's impossible standards of performance and agent comportment, every field agent, every day, couldn't help violate one or two of the director's thousands of rules and regulations. Agents who got caught breaking these rules, rules continuously promulgated by Hoover and his palace guards paid the price in the form of disciplinary transfers to undesirable field offices. (For example, no one wanted to work at the field division headquarters in Billings, Montana.) More than a few bureau rule violators were fired "with prejudice." Nobody knew exactly what "with prejudice" meant except that it was not good. When agents of the Hoover era tell war stories, their tales are usually not about their cases. Most likely they feature administrative horror stories.

J. Edgar Hoover's career can be viewed from the perspective of twentieth century history or from the field agent's point of view. What follows is my take on J. Edgar Hoover as an employer and law enforcement administrator during his last six years in office.

I had been a "new-agent" just a few days when I began to wonder what I had gotten myself into. In those days, before the magnificent FBI Academy in Quantico, Virginia, new agents attended seven weeks of classwork in the Old Post Office Building in Washington, D.C. and seven weeks of firearms training on the Marine base at Quantico, Virginia. Every day in D.C., our FBI instructors came into the classroom armed with horror stories designed to instill fear of the director. To a man, these instructors had that "I'm-dead-but-still-walking persona". One of them, a SOG (Seat of Government) agent from the D.C. administrative headquarters, a man who conjured up the image of a demented butcher, kept reminding the class that to survive in Mr. Hoover's FBI one had to have balls made of brass. I took this to mean we were in for a lot of low blows.

New agents were reminded over and over again never to embarrass the bureau. Blowing an investigation was one thing, but embarrassing the bureau was serious. By bureau, the instructors meant J. Edgar Hoover. The director did not forget, did not forgive, and took everything personally. Every infraction--a missed bureaucratic deadline, putting a scratch on a bureau car, not calling the office every two hours when not at work or at home--constituted a personal assault on Hoover's good name. It was simply un-American to embarrass the director of the FBI.

Hoover's ideal FBI agent consisted of a thin white male with high morals, a clean-cut appearance, and a law degree. Over the years the director had managed, through careful media manipulation, to make the G-man the cultural hero, and the outlaw, the villain. Physically, if a job candidate didn't fit Hoover's model of the all-American agent, it didn't matter how smart, brave, or moral he was. Hoover didn't tolerate mustaches, beards, long hair, or missing teeth. If you had a tattoo, forget it. The director didn't accept anyone who was color-blind or had less that 20-20 vision. Short, slightly overweight, and bulldog-faced, Hoover, based on looks alone, would not have hired himself. There were a handful of black men in the bureau, but no Hispanics, Asians, or women.

Once in the FBI, agents had to maintain a height/weight ratio that conformed to ideal life insurance policy standards. Most agents, as they approached middle age, had trouble keeping their weight under control, and dreaded the monthly weigh-ins held either in the chief clerk's desk or in the SAC's (Special Agent in Charge) office under the supervision of the boss's secretary. Notwithstanding the weight restrictions, there were a lot of older agents obviously over the pound limit.

Within the weight control program, as in all of Hoover's bureaucratic obsessions, cheating and false reporting with the knowledge and approval of the office brass were rampant. But according to the regulations, an agent who was more than ten pounds over the weight limit two months in a row could be transferred to another field office. The bureau's weight program gave the SAC a lot of power. If he wanted to unload an agent he didn't like, the boss could enforce the rule. So could a SOG inspector on a field office witch-hunt. The office transfer, as a means of punishment, gave Hoover a powerful and arbitrary tool that disrupted families and broke up marriages. This from a never-married man that disapproved of divorce.

Director Hoover also enforced a severe and detailed dress code. Agents had to wear blue, brown, gray or black suits. He forbade pin stripe suits and colorful buttoned-down or patterned dress shirts. Approved bureau footwear did not include suede shoes, loafers, or cowboy boots. (When I worked in west Texas, most agents wore fancy cowboy boots to fit in with the Texas Rangers and local sheriffs.) Agents playing it safe shoe-wise went the wing-tip route. As for head wear, all agents were supposed to wear those felt, narrow-brimmed business hats even though a bareheaded President Kennedy had rendered the fedora out of style.

In a dress code more detailed and complicated that the U.S. Constitution, an agent caught wearing a sports coat or a loud tie could get written-up. Unlike modern agents who wear jackets and ball caps emblazoned with the letters FBI, or walk around in combat gear, Hoover's men looked like 1950s IBM executives and insurance men.

To distinguish his agents from uniformed cops and city detectives who supposedly killed a lot of time by hanging around donut shops and diners drinking coffee, Hoover forbade his agents to drink coffee on the job. Taking clandestine coffee breaks with other agents therefore required a lot of trust (agents had to be aware of office snitches) and made a common workplace ritual an act of subversion. Agents were constantly on the lookout for safe coffee drinking hideaways. Bureau coffee drinkers couldn't get attached to a single restaurant or diner because to avoid detection, they had to keep moving.

One of Hoover's most unreasonable and counterproductive rules, a decree that reflected his lack of experience as a criminal investigator, concerned when agents could tackle the heavy paperwork burden the director had himself mandated. Between 9 AM and 5 PM, agents were only allowed to be in the field office ninety minutes. They were supposed to use this limited time to review their case files, make phone calls, and dictate reports and FD 302s (witness statements) to office stenographers. Agents were to spend the rest of the day out on the street investigating crime, tracking down fugitives, and uncovering subversion. As opposed to the image of the lazy detective hanging around the office all day drinking coffee and shooting the bull, Hoover wanted his investigators to be men of action.

The director's office-time restriction ignored the fact that in detective work, every hour of investigation can create two hours of paperwork. To meet Hoover's strict reporting deadlines, agents had to do much of their pencil pushing in parked cars, public libraries, restaurants, and for those brave enough to risk it, at home. Otherwise, if an agent saved all of his paperwork for the office after 5 PM, he'd end up preparing 302s and written reports well into the evening.

In the morning, agents were expected to sign-in for work before seven. For those who worked in big city offices, that meant getting up at five. Agents were also required to log in plenty of overtime that meant the sign-in and sign-out registers never came close to reflecting reality. For example, when an agent arrived at the office at seven, the guy just ahead of him would be logging in at five-thirty. If the agent who signed in just after this person wrote down his actual time of arrival, he had committed an act called "jumping the register," a serious violation of the agent's unwritten code of conduct. In Hoover's FBI, honesty was not always the best policy.

When I left the bureau, I felt I had escaped from prison. The only aspect of the job I missed involved the first-rate people. One of Hoover's greatest sins was the way he abused his personnel. He recruited the best then treated them like dirt. For the typical field agent of that era, that is Hoover's legacy.

The History of the FBI Crime Lab

Shortly after becoming the FBI's fourth director in 1924, J. Edgar Hoover envisioned a national crime laboratory under the control of the Federal Bureau of Investigation. Hoover had been influenced by August Vollmer, the innovative chief of the Berkeley, California Police Department and John H. Wigmore, author and professor at Northwestern University Law School. Vollmer and Wigmore had pioneered the formation of the Scientific Crime Detection Lab formed in Chicago in the wake of the 1929 St. Valentine's

Day Massacre. These practitioner scholars believed that the developing fields within forensic science, coupled with highly trained criminal investigators, would someday bring victory over crime. Hoover had already made the image of the latent fingerprint the unofficial logo of the FBI. A FBI crime laboratory would advance Hoover's goal to create the ideal crime fighter--a highly educated, well-trained scientific crime detection professional.

In April 1931, Hoover sent Special Agent Charles A. Appel, Jr. to Chicago to enroll in a short course sponsored by the Scientific Crime Detection Laboratory that at the time was a private, fee-charging lab partially funded by the university. Most of the lab's caseload consisted of forensic document examination, firearm identification (then called forensic ballistics), and research and development in the polygraph, a newly developing field of scientific lie detection. (In 1938 the Scientific Crime Detection Lab would be taken over by the Chicago Police Department.) Hoover also sent agent Appel to police departments in St. Louis (in 1906 the first police department to establish a fingerprint identification bureau), New Orleans, and Detroit, the only law enforcement agencies besides Berkeley and Los Angeles that had operated crime labs.

The FBI Technical Laboratory, with Charles Appel as its head, opened its doors on November 24, 1932 (in 1942 it was renamed the FBI Laboratory) in a nine-by-nine foot room in the Southern Railway Building at Thirteenth Street and Pennsylvania Avenue in Washington, DC. Special Agent Appel, its director and only employee, performed firearm identification work. Appel used the newly invented comparison microscope and an instrument designed for the examination of gun barrel interiors. To produce forensic exhibits of bullets, Appel utilized basic photographic equipment of the era. The FBI Lab, as advertised by Hoover, provided evidence analysis and testimony for the bureau as well as for any local law enforcement agency that requested forensic analysis. Hoover also promised research and development in the various forensic science fields. Hoover's ambitious undertaking eventually made the FBI an indispensable and highly visible cog in the nation's crime fighting machine.

By 1940, the laboratory, now located at FBI headquarters in Washington, DC, employed firearm identification experts, questioned document examiners, forensic chemists, physicists, metallurgists specializing in tool mark identification, forensic geologists (soil examinations), hair and fiber analysts, forensic serologists (blood and bodily fluids examinations), and latent fingerprint identification experts. The laboratory, employing over a hundred people, had gotten so large Hoover divided it into three sections: questioned documents; physics and chemistry; and latent fingerprint identification. At this time, only fifteen police departments, and sixteen states operated crime labs. The FBI Lab continued to grow. By 1958 it employed two hundred scientific, clerical and administrative personnel.

The FBI Laboratory, by the end of the 1980's, had grown into the busiest and most famous crime lab in the world. It had also become one of the top tourist attractions in Washington, DC. But even in its heyday, because of the quantity of forensic examinations and laboratory hiring criteria, there were problems with the *quality* of some of the work. The FBI Lab was the biggest and the most famous, but not the best. Overwhelmed by a staggering caseload, Hoover did not hire top-rate scientists. Moreover, there was not time for research and development. This led to some bad science and a problem with scientific objectivity.

The FBI lab had to compete for personnel with a growing number of city, county, and state crime labs. Because the FBI only hired lab employees who also met the criteria for the position of special agent, not all of the lab personnel had sufficient scientific backgrounds. All FBI Lab personnel (except clerical employees) were first sent into the field to work as agents for three years. Many of these agents had to be dragged kicking and screaming back to DC to work inside the lab. Many of these people had used their degrees in science to get into the FBI to become investigators, not bureau criminalists. Moreover, the close identification with law enforcement created by three years in the field worked against scientific objectivity. (The FBI has since changed its crime lab hiring criteria.)

J. Edgar Hoover died in office in May 1972. By 1990, his reputation as a pioneer and visionary had deteriorated. The mere mention of his name on a TV sitcom or a late night talk show brought instant laughter. Once a powerful and innovative man, Hoover, like so many other American historical figures--Charles Lindbergh for one--had been reduced by a tabloid culture and hack journalism into a character you might find in an underground comic book. The post-Hoover image of the FBI agent, while having lost some of its luster, had not gone down with the Hoover ship. Notwithstanding his fall from grace, Hoover's most profound contribution to the art and science of criminal investigation, the FBI Crime Laboratory, is still considered the gold standard of forensic science in America.

The Devil in the Blue Dress

If the longtime director of the Federal Bureau of Investigation thought much about his legacy, J. Edgar Hoover probably hoped to be remembered as the man who professionalized criminal investigation, and elevated the image of the FBI agent. As the man responsible for the FBI fingerprint bureau, crime laboratory, National Police Academy, and *The FBI Bulletin,* one could argue that Mr. Hoover played a positive role in the history of 20th Century American law enforcement.

Hoover's critics, and there are many of them, portrayed him as a power-hungry phony who, over four decades, abused his power. Although a dozen or so books have been published about J. Edgar Hoover and the FBI under his directorship, he probably wouldn't be remembered at all by the general public had there not been a book published in 1993 by the Irish journalist (some would say tabloid journalist) Anthony Summers.

In *Official and Confidential: The Secret Life of J. Edgar Hoover,* Mr. Summers, relying on information from the embittered wife of a Hoover crony, painted Hoover as a cross-dressing homosexual. Ronald Kessler, a former FBI agent and author of *Secrets of the FBI,* considers the cross-dressing story a fabrication by a vengeful woman who later served time for perjury. While most FBI historians agree with Mr. Kessler, the image of Hoover wearing a dress and high-heels has stuck. This is how he is remembered, or at least referred to, by people influenced by supermarket celebrity rags, and late-night TV.

Clint Eastwood's 2011 movie, "J. Edgar," had it not focused so much on the Lindbergh kidnapping case and Hoover's strange relationship with his mother and his right-hand man, Clyde Tolson, may have triggered a public debate over Hoover's place in the history of American law enforcement. Instead, the discussion was about the film itself.

Agents who worked under Hoover, many of whom belong to the Society of Former Special Agents of the FBI, were outraged by the movie.

On the other side of the debate, critics of the film accused Clint Eastwood of glossing over Hoover's abuse of power and the corrupting influence he had on the agency. In making this film Eastwood managed to offend everyone, including regular movie goers who thought the flick was too long, and worse, boring and off-putting.

As for J. Edgar Hoover and his legacy, he's not getting out of that dress any time soon.

The Historic Burglary

On a March evening in 1971, eight antiwar protesters burglarized an FBI office in Media, Pennsylvania, just outside of Philadelphia, with astonishing ease. A few weeks of elementary surveillance had shown the vulnerability of the target: There were no cameras to elude, no alarms to disconnect. Because the building contained residential apartments, the group chose the night of the Joe Frazier-Muhammad Ali heavyweight championship fight, an ideal distraction. [Frazier came from Philadelphia and was the hometown favorite.]

It turned out that the Pennsylvania office [a branch resident agency within the Philadelphia field division], like so many others across the country, had almost no physical protection. Security was largely symbolic, resting on the bureau's carefully buffed reputation for efficiency in tracking down America's "most wanted" criminals, from bank robbers to atomic spies. Put simply, no one messed with J. Edgar Hoover's FBI...

The stolen material included the secret case histories of thousands of Americans. Much of it was malicious gossip about things like sexual deviance and race mixing, two of Hoover's favorite subjects. Had this been all, the FBI very likely would have weathered the storm. Its pubic relations machine was enormous, and the officials charged with overseeing its operations were themselves wary of what lay in the files. Hoover had served for almost 50 years with eight presidents, because nobody dared fire a man who, in Richard Nixon's words, could "pull down the temple with him, including me." [Hoover died less than a year after the burglary.]

But there was more...the most important stolen document was a routine routing slip containing the word "Cointelpro." The term meant nothing to the burglars, for good reason. Cointelpro was among the FBI's most carefully guarded secrets, a huge program of dirty tricks and illegal activities designed to "expose, disrupt, and otherwise neutralize" groups deemed subversive by the director...

David Oshinsky, "Breaking In," *The New York Times Book Review*, February 2, 2014

The Crime Laboratory's Dark Years

Until the mid-1990s, all of the forensic scientists working in the FBI Crime Lab had at least three years' experience in the field as ordinary special agents. Staffing the lab with former criminal investigators (J. Edgar Hoover's idea) was supposed to make them better forensic practitioners. Critics of this policy believed it made them part of a law enforcement team instead of independent forensic scientists. Moreover, by basing the hiring criteria on agent qualifications, the FBI Lab was not attracting or being staffed by first-rate scientists.

Special Agent Michael P. Malone had earned his bachelor's and master's degrees in biology, and taught high school science for two years before he joined the FBI in 1970. After working four years in the field as a criminal investigator, Malone was assigned to the FBI Crime Lab. During his 25 years as a hair and fiber analyst, Malone testified in hundreds of criminal trials. He became popular as a prosecution expert, testifying in dozens of high profile cases where the fate of the defendant depended upon his identification of a crime scene hair or fiber. As an expert witness he was confident and hard to rattle, and he knew how to impress a jury.

In the early 1990s, Frederic Whitehurst, an FBI Lab bomb residue analyst who identified chemical components of explosive substances, alerted lab supervisors to problems in the trace evidence section of the facility. Whitehurst complained that the laboratory was so dirty the physical evidence was always in danger of being contaminated. Whitehurst was especially critical of hair and fiber analyst Michael Malone, whom he accused of allowing his loyalty to police and prosecutors to attenuate his independence and objectivity as a forensic scientist. In memos to the director of the lab, Whitehurst pointed out that hair and fiber identification was an inexact and subjective process, making this form of crime scene identification highly unreliable. The whistleblower noted that Malone's testimony had sent many defendants to prison, some of whom might have been innocent.

When Whitehurst's internal complaints fell on deaf ears, he began writing long, detailed letters to Michael Bromwich, the U. S. Department of Justice inspector general. Between 1991 and 1994, Whitehurst wrote Bromwich 237 letters. In September 1995, the inspector general launched an investigation after ABC's "Prime Time Live," having gotten hold of some of these letters, aired a story about Whitehurst's campaign to improve the FBI Lab. In April 1997, almost six years after Whitehurst began documenting problems in the nation's largest crime lab, Bromwich issued a 517-page report critical of the laboratory. Bromwich singled out seven lab employees, including Michael Malone, whom he described as having provided "false testimony." The inspector general recommended Malone for disciplinary action.

Two years later, a second Department of Justice investigation revealed that Agent Malone had made hair and fiber identification errors in four homicide cases in the Tampa Bay area. In the same report detailing these findings, Department of Justice investigators also criticized Whitehurst for overstating the forensic implications of his scientific analysis in some of his own cases. Whitehurst, who had been transferred to the paint identification unit of the lab, was suspended. After the bureau denied his petition for reinstatement, Whitehurst retired and entered private practice. To some, Whitehurst was a hero. To the FBI however, he was a traitor, a whistleblower the lowest form of bureaucratic life.

Michael Malone denied lying under oath or playing fast and loose with hair and fiber evidence. He blamed the FBI Lab scandal on jealous colleagues whom he described as incompetent. Regarding those cases in which DNA analysis had exonerated defendants whose hair he had identified as being at crime scenes, Malone blamed overzealous prosecutors who overstated the implications of his findings. Following the inspector general's investigations and recommendations, Malone was reassigned back to the field. He retired in December 1999. To the FBI, Malone wa the hero.

Today the head of the FBI Crime Lab hires civilians on the basis of their backgrounds in science. Even for crime lab civilians, maintaining scientific objectivity is not easy. But there is no question that the lab is far superior now than it was during those dark years. And as often the case in governmental scandals that result in improved conditions, it was a courageous whistleblower that made it all possible.

Historic FBI Fingerprint Misidentification

On March 11, 2004, terrorists in Madrid Spain bombed a passenger train, killing 191 people. The Spanish National Police sent the FBI digital images of eight latent prints found at the bombsite. These images were fed into the FBI's Integrated Automatic Fingerprint Identification System (IAFIS), a $640 million supercomputer housed in Clarksburg, West Virginia. The computer selected from its collection of 48 million fingerprints sets, 15 digital latent images as possible matches. Three FBI examiners matched one of the 15 possible matches to a latent from Spain that had been left on a plastic bag containing bomb detonators. The FBI experts believed this print belonged to a 37-year-old lawyer from Portland, Oregon named Brandon Mayfield.

If the FBI fingerprint experts were correct, Brandon Mayfield had been at the scene of the Madrid bombing. The fact that Mayfield, a former army lieutenant, had converted to Islam heightened the FBI's suspicion that he had been involved in the deadly bombing.

Fingerprint examiners in Spain agreed that Mayfield's print and the crime scene latent shared eight points of similarity, but the numerous dissimilarities kept them from declaring a match. The FBI responded by having a fourth bureau expert look at the evidence, and he too, declared a match. Shortly thereafter, FBI agents arrested Brandon Mayfield. In the meantime, the police in Spain announced that the crime scene latent belonged to an Algerian suspect, Ouhane Daoud.

A team of FBI fingerprint experts traveled to Madrid, and when they compared Mayfield's fingerprint to the actual latent, realized their mistake. Blaming the misidentification on the low-resolution image of the digital print, the FBI apologized to Mayfield. However, when a panel of fingerprint experts reviewed the evidence, they found that the misidentification had nothing to do with the quality of the digitized latent. The four FBI experts had simply overlooked easily observed dissimilarities between the two prints. They had allowed their eagerness to identify a terrorist override their scientific objectivity. There may also have been an element of groupthink in the misidentification.

Brandon Mayfield filed a lawsuit, and in November 2006, the federal government agreed to pay him $2 million in damages. The Justice Department augmented the settlement with an official apology, stating that misidentifications of this nature were rare. University of California at Irvine professor Simon Cole, disagreed. Responding to news of the settlement, he told a *Los Angeles Times* journalist that "this is a tip-of-the-iceberg phenomenon. The argument has always been that no two people have fingerprints exactly alike. But that's not what you need to have an error. What you need is for two people to have very similar fingerprints, and that's what happened here."

For years, when FBI experts testified in criminal trials, they claimed that in the history of the bureau there had never been a fingerprint misidentification. They can no longer make this claim which wasn't true then, and isn't true now. Moreover, in the wake of the Madrid bombing case embarrassment, the FBI fingerprint examiner proficiency test has come under attack. According to an FBI whistleblower, if the test had not been so ridiculously easy, cheating would be commonplace.

Working Undercover

Although it is not part of the career development program in the FBI, some agents volunteer for service as an undercover agent (UCA). All UCAs are volunteers, and there is no special compensation for performing these duties. Generally, UCAs must have a solid investigative background before being considered for such work and also receive the full support of their superiors. Their undercover activities may take place in the office territory to which they are assigned or another field office. Volunteers for this program are evaluated for their expertise and psychological suitability. Special training programs are also available at [the FBI training complex at Quantico, Virginia] to teach agents the tricks of pulling off an undercover assignment. [Undercover operatives have to be good actors.]

The vast majority of undercover operations are criminal in nature, but intelligence-directed undercover operations also take place. Generally, undercover assignments fall into one of two categories: Group II operations are authorized by the Special Agent in Charge of the field division with the concurrence of the local U.S. Attorney. Group IIs, as they are called, still require careful coordination and planning, but generally they are less sensitive, less dangerous, or shorter term, and less costly than other types of operations.

Group I undercover operations are the opposite. They may be dangerous, elaborate, lengthy, technically challenging, involving prominent personages, be very costly, or have foreign aspects involved. This group requires painstaking planning, substantial amounts of documentation, a lot of coordination, and minute review by a panel of senior FBI Headquarters and Department of Justice officials.

Perhaps the most legendary FBI Group I undercover operation was ABSCAM, a political corruption investigation that resulted in the conviction of members of Congress in the 1980s. Probably the most well known Group I operation was that of Special Agent Joe Pistone, who infiltrated the La Cosa Nostra (Mafia) with devastating results to the mobsters. So successful was Pistone in his role that he carried it out for years and was on the verge of becoming a "made guy" when the operation was terminated. His exploits were recounted in the book and movie that bears his undercover name, *Donnie Brasco*.

Joseph W. Koletar, *The FBI Career Guide*, 2006

Covering Up Cruise Ship Crime

Worldwide, there are 200 cruise ships owned by 26 cruise lines. The average ocean cruise consists of a huge boat carrying 2,000 passengers and a crew of 950. The biggest ships can hold more than 4,000 vacationers. These are small towns on water. In 2007, 12 million people purchased cruise line tickets. This is a big, global industry represented by an influential trade association called the Cruise Lines International Association (CLIA).

Over the years, cruise line companies have received bad publicity due to a series of high seas rapes, murders, and passenger disappearance cases. These high-profile crimes suggested the possibility that women and children on these huge vessels were vulnerable to molestation by crew and other passengers. One expert on cruise ship crime believed that a woman was twice as likely to be raped aboard one of these boats than on land.

When a U.S. citizen aboard a cruise ship anywhere in the world is raped, assaulted, or murdered, the FBI has jurisdiction. But until recently, the bureau did not make these crime statistics a matter of public record. As a result, people contemplating an ocean cruise had no way of assessing the crime risks associated with this form of recreation.

To enlighten and inform the American public of the relative crime risks that come with ocean cruises, Congress passed the Cruise Vessel Security and Safety Act of 2010. Under this federal statute as initially proposed, the FBI would make public all crimes reported to them by the cruise lines or by passengers directly, and do it in a timely manner. This data would be stored on a U.S. Coast Guard website. However, when the bill was in committee, high-ranking FBI administrators lobbied for the insertion of a qualification that essentially defeated the purpose of the law. FBI brass managed to get Congress to limit what the bureau had to make public. Under the legislation as enacted, the FBI was required only to report cruise ship cases that the bureau had *opened and closed.*

The FBI only opened 10 to 20 percent of cruise ship crimes that came to their attention, and the cases they did open were not closed for years. As a result only a fraction of cruise ship crime statistics were made public, and what was published was old information. This, of course, was exactly how the cruise ship industry wanted it. What the public didn't know hurt them but helped the cruise line business.

So, how did the cruise line industry get the FBI to thwart the intention of Congress, and the interests of the cruise-taking public? When did the bureau change from a law enforcement agency to a Washington lobby firm?

The cozy relationship between lawmakers and lobbyists for various enterprises is nothing new. Congress has always been up for sale. But what seems to be new is how an industry has been able to corrupt legislators *and* the FBI. How did the CLIA get to the bureau? Easy. The trade organization wines and dines top FBI personnel every two months at various vacation spots. And since 2007, two top-ranking FBI executives (they can retire at 50) have been given lucrative retirement jobs in the cruise industry. No one knows how many mid-level FBI administrators in D.C. have landed good security positions with cruise lines.

The effect of the FBI tampered with, cruise line-friendly federal crime reporting law is producing the results the CLIA has paid for. If you look at the U.S. Coast Guard crime data web site, you will find that in 2012, there has been only one reported case of cruise ship rape. Just one. Thanks to the FBI's sabotage of the Cruise Vessel Security and Safety Act of 2010, vacationers know nothing about the crime risks of an ocean vacation. Cruise ships are not child molester-rapist free zones.

Becoming a Criminal Profiler

Contrary to the impression given in such stories as *The Silence of the Lambs*, we don't pluck profiling candidates for the Investigative Support Unit right out of the Academy...It doesn't work that way. First, you have to get accepted into the Bureau. Once in, you have to prove yourself in the field as a first-rate, creative investigator, then we recruit you for Quantico. And then you're ready for two years of intensive, specialized training before you become a full-fledged member of the unit.

A good criminal profiler must first and foremost show imagination and creativity in investigation. He or she must be willing to take risks while still maintaining the respect and confidence of fellow agents and law enforcement officers. Our preferred candidates will show leadership, won't wait for a consensus before offering an opinion, will be persuasive in a group setting but tactful in helping to put a flawed investigation back on track. For these reasons, they must be able to work both alone and in groups.

Once we choose a person, he or she will work with experienced members of the unit almost in a way a young associate in a law firm works with a senior partner. If they're at all lacking in street experience, we send them to the New York Police Department to ride along with their best homicide detectives. If they need more death investigation, we have nationally recognized consultants...in the field offices where they develop a strong rapport with state and local departments and sheriff's offices.

The key attribute necessary to be a good profiler is judgment--a judgment based not primarily on the analysis of facts and figures but on instinct. It's difficult to define, but...we know it when we see it.

John Douglas and Mark Olshaker, *Journey Into Darkness*, 1977

The Joint Robbery Task Force

In the United States each year, in 5,000 bank robberies, robbers walk off with roughly $43 million. While in the past few years, the U.S. bank robbery rate has increased a bit, there are far less bank heists today than the years 1967-1990. In New York city there were only 26 bank robberies in 2010, a record low. Last year 44 banks were hit in the Big Apple, still an amazingly small number.

While bank robbery is both a state and federal crime, the FBI is usually the principal investigative agency in these cases. As a result, most bank robbery suspects are tried in federal court, and if found guilty, go to federal prison. Compared to crimes like burglary, street mugging, and arson, bank robbery solution rates are traditionally high. One reason for this is that bank robbers usually don't stop after their first job, and eventually get caught. Also, a lot of them are drunk, drugged up, or stupid.

In New York City, over the past 32 years, the Joint Bank Robbery Task Force staffed by FBI agents and detectives with the NYPD handled robberies in the five boroughs. The city contributed one sergeant and six investigators to the unit. Last year, the FBI only solved one-third of its New York City cases. In 2010, members of the task force solved 80 percent of the bank robberies.

In explaining the poor case solution rate, an FBI spokesperson blamed the NYPD for withdrawing from the task force in March 2011. Officials with the NYPD, while denying that the personnel shift explains the poor investigative results, say they cannot justify wasting the manpower on so few cases. These officers are needed elsewhere. When the task force was formed in 1980, hundreds of banks were being robbed in the city every year.

The behind the scenes inter-agency sniping over this issue has heightened tensions between the FBI and NYPD already in a turf war over a couple of terrorism cases. In law enforcement, it's an unfortunate reality that professional jealousy and rivalry has always existed between federal and local, city and county, and state and municipal agencies. Within the federal government, there is tension and conflict between various agencies within the Department of Homeland Security. And the FBI and CIA have never worked well together.

While inter-agency friction is understandable within a criminal justice system comprised of so many levels of government, it will continue to be a problem that can't be fixed by simply rearranging organizational charts, or adding more layers of bureaucracy.

Getting on the Top Ten List

In 1949, FBI Director J. Edgar Hoover started the bureau's top ten program as a way of involving the public in the apprehension of the nation's worst criminals. As of June 2012, 497 fugitives have made the list. Patricia Hearst was one of only eight women ever considered bad enough to make the program. (The bureau had a hell of a time catching her.) Since the inception of the program, 94 percent of top ten fugitives have been captured. A third of these apprehensions involved tips from members of the public.

Today, information that leads to the arrest of a top ten fugitive earns the tipster a $100,000 reward. (In the 1950s, the man who turned in the infamous bank robber Willie Sutton was murdered for his troubles. The tipster had ignored advice from the New York police not to go public. After that, law enforcement agencies, to encourage people to come forward, began offering rewards.)

What follows is a snapshot of the FBI's 2013 top ten most wanted:

Joe Luis Saenz

In July 1998, Saenz shot and killed two Los Angeles gang rivals. Two weeks later, he raped and murdered his girlfriend, and in October of that year, murdered a fourth person.

Glen Steward Godwin

In 1987, while serving time for murder in California's Folsom Prison, Godwin escaped. Later that year the police in Mexico arrested him for dealing in drugs. While serving time in Mexico, Godwin murdered a fellow inmate, and five months later, escaped.

Eduardo Ravelo

A Texas grand jury indicted Ravelo in 2008 for trafficking in heroin, marijuana, and cocaine. The capo with the Barrio Azieca crime enterprise had been an active interstate drug racketeer since 2003.

Semion Mogilevich

In April 2003, a federal grand jury in Pennsylvania indicted Mogilevich for his role in a stock fraud that cost investors $150 million. The public corporation, headquartered in Bucks County, collapsed in 1998.

Jason Derek Brown

In November 2004, Brown murdered an armored car guard in a robbery outside a Phoenix a movie theater.

Eric Justin Toth

Toth, a graduate of Purdue University and a former private school teacher, was indicted in 2008 on charges related to child pornography. The computer expert stood accused of producing, for the Internet, child pornography in the state of Maryland.

Alex Flores

Flores, in July 2000, kidnapped and murdered a 5-year-old Philadelphia girl. The victim's strangled and stabbed body was found three months later in a nearby apartment.

Robert William Fisher

Fisher was accused of the April 2001 murder of his wife and two young children in Scottsdale, Arizona.

Fidel Urbina

In March 1998, Urbina beat and raped a woman in Chicago. Seven months later, while free on bail, he assaulted, raped and strangled to death another woman. His last victim was found in the trunk of a burned-out car.

Victor Manuel Gerena

In 1983, Gerena, in the commission of a $7 million robbery of a Connecticut security company, took two employees hostage at gunpoint.

After placing his hostages in handcuffs, Gerena injected them with a toxic substance to further disable them.

All of the fugitives on the FBI's top ten but the swindler Mogilevich, were aged between 20 and 30 when they committed their crimes. Mogilevich was in his 50s.

Killed On Duty

In 1984, the FBI, in preparation for the Olympics in Los Angeles, formed an elite counterterrorism hostage rescue team comprised of so-called "assaulters," and snipers. Trained in scuba diving, rappelling from helicopters, and close combat tactics, the hostage rescue agents were equipped with military-style gear and assault weapons.

Unlike FBI SWAT teams that only train a few days a month, members of the hostage rescue unit prepare full-time. This highly militarized squad is more comparable to Navy Seal Team 6 and U. S. Army Delta units. The elite FBI counterterrorism team is headquartered at the FBI Academy in Quantico, Virginia.

Since its inception, agents in the rescue unit have responded to 850 incidents including the Boston Marathon Bombings. Members of this civilian combat force have also responded to situations in Iraq and Afghanistan.

On Friday night, May 17, 2013, twelve miles off the Virginia Beach coastline, two hostage team members participating in a maritime counterterrorism exercise, fell to their deaths into the Atlantic Ocean. Forty-one-year-old Christopher Lorek and forty-year-old Stephen Shaw were rappelling from a helicopter when the aircraft suddenly tilted because of a strong gust of wind. As the pilot struggled to regain control of the helicopter, the agents, loaded down with gear, lost their grips and fell.

By the time the agents were pulled out of the ocean, one of them was dead. The other hostage team member died at a hospital in Norfolk. The men were killed by blunt force trauma. Both agents were married and lived with their wives and children in the northern Virginia town of Quantico.

Since 2000, six other FBI Agents died in the line of duty. There are currently about 14,000 special agents in the bureau.

Special Agent Stephen Ivens

At eight o'clock Monday evening, July 30, 2012, a pair of hikers walking in the foothills of the Verdugo Mountains above Burbank, California came upon a foul odor. In the brush behind St. Francis of Xavier Catholic

Church, they discovered the skeletal remains of a man. The initial investigation by the Los Angeles County Coroner's Office indicates that the hikers had stumbled upon Stephen Ivens. Near his body death scene investigators recovered a handgun.

Stephen Ivens, a 35-year-old FBI agent assigned to the Los Angeles Field Division, had been missing since he walked away from his Burbank home on the morning of May 11, 2012. Bloodhounds had traced his scent to the Verdugo Mountains where a search party of FBI agents, local police, and volunteers had looked for him.

A married father of a 2-year-old son, Ivens had been an FBI agent a little more than three years. Before going into the bureau he had been a Los Angeles police officer. The white, 6-foot, 160- pound bespectacled agent had worked on counterterrorism cases. Because his FBI-issued revolver had been taken from the house, Ivens was presumed armed when he walked off that morning.

According to the agent's wife Thea, Special Agent Ivens had been depressed and distraught which led many to suspect he left the house that morning with the intent of killing himself. But the fact he was an FBI agent who worked on counterterrorism matters also led to speculation of international intrigue and foul play.

A few weeks after his disappearance, the authorities stopped looking for Ivens, and the media ignored the case. This added fuel to the possibility of foul play, and a government cover-up. After Ivens' body was found behind the church one and a half miles from his home, questions regarding the reasons behind his disappearance went unanswered. The big mystery involved whether or not Ivens' death--suicide or otherwise--was related to his counterterrorism work. According to Ivens' wife, he had been depressed to the point of a breakdown. The source of his distress, while related to his FBI job, was not caused by his counterterrorism assignment. He couldn't sleep, and before leaving for work each morning, suffered anxiety attacks. The exact source of his stress was not made public.

Ivens' wife Thea, who never gave up hope that he was alive, continued searching for him after the authorities had given up. During his 80-day disappearance, she maintained a blog and a website devoted to his return.

Because Ivens' remains were found just three-quarters of a mile from where the cadaver dogs had picked-up his scent, conspiracy theorists interpreted this fact as evidence that he had been murdered somewhere else, then placed behind the church where he could be easily found. People invested in this scenario disregarded a Burbank police officer's comment that "Every indication is that he [Ivens] has been there from the first day."

On August 6, 2012, Craig Harvey, the Chief Coroner Investigator with the Los Angeles County Coroner's Office announced that Stephen Ivens had shot himself in the head with a handgun. The death had been ruled a suicide. The authorities revealed that the FBI agent had been despondent, but didn't say why.

While FBI agents don't disappear everyday and stay missing for 80 days, the national media didn't show much interest in the Stephen Ivens case. Even the media in southern California didn't give the story a lot of attention. If Ivens had been even a minor celebrity, particularly someone in the entertainment industry, the media would have been all over his disappearance. There would have been daily press conferences, a three-page feature in *People Magazine*, headlines in the supermarket tabloids, and candlelight vigils attended by an army of fans. (Ivens' wife did stage one candlelight vigil in McCambridge Park to raise awareness of the case.) So-called celebrity investigative journalists would have dug into every corner of Ivens' life.

The mystery and controversy surrounding this case will only grow with time. The fact the media was so disinterested will add fuel to speculation of foul play.

The FBI Indexing System

One of the most important aspects of an FBI field office is not actually in the office: indexes. At one time, these were little more than 3 by 5 cards, maintained in scores, if not hundreds, of file cabinets in every FBI field office. For example, the New York Office of the FBI had over 7 million such cards before the system was automated. The FBI has long prided itself on information management, and under Director J. Edgar Hoover, the development of the index system was a notable first for the FBI. The Bureau had many complex rules about indexing, and laborious though it may be, it is one of the most important things an agent does. If, for example, an agent conducts an interview of a witness to a bank robbery, the person's name, address, and phone number are indexed. So, too, are the names and information developed during the course of that interview.

This indexing is now done on a computer system, so that all FBI field offices share the same information. If, years later, only the phone number came up in another investigation, it could be traced back to the original interview. Indeed, many cases have been made or advanced over the years through the ability of the FBI to retrieve information from its own files. [When I was in the bureau, each criminal complaint that came across an agent's desk had been "indexed." That is, all names, vehicles, and addresses mentioned in the complaint that were in the index file were noted. Often this cross-referencing provided an agent with his first lead in the case.]

Joseph W. Koletar, *The FBI Career Guide*, 2006

28 FORENSIC PATHOLOGY

Cause and Manner of Death

Forensic pathologists are physicians educated and trained to determine the cause and manner of death in cases involving violent, sudden, or unexplained fatalities. The cause of death is the medical reason the person died. One cause of death is asphyxia--lack of oxygen to the brain. It occurs as a result of drowning, suffocation, manual strangulation, strangulation by ligature (such as a rope, belt, or length of cloth) crushing, or carbon monoxide poisoning. Other causes of death include blunt force trauma, gunshot wound, stabbing, slashing, poisoning, heart attack, stroke, or a sickness such as cancer, pneumonia, or heart disease.

For the forensic pathologist, the most difficult task often involves detecting the *manner* of death--natural, accidental, suicidal, or homicidal. This is because the manner of death isn't always revealed by the physical condition of the body. For example, a death resulting from a drug overdose could be the result of homicide, suicide, or accident. Knowing exactly how the fatal drug got into the victim's system requires additional information, data that usually comes from a police investigation. A death investigator, for example, will try to find out if the overdose victim had a history of drug abuse, or if there were signs of a struggle at the scene of the death. Has this victim attempted suicide in the past? Did the victim leave a suicide note? Did someone have a compelling motive to kill this person? Is there evidence of a love triangle, life insurance fraud, hatred, or revenge? These are basic investigative leads that could help a forensic pathologist determine the manner of death.

When the circumstances of a suspicious death are not ascertained, or are sketchy, and the death was not an obvious homicide, the medical examiner might classify the manner of death as "undetermined." Drug overdose cases that are only slightly suspicious and therefore not thoroughly investigated often go into the books as either accidents or suicides. This is true of other forms of slightly suspicious death. Because a body is found dead in the water doesn't necessarily mean this person has drowned. This victim could have been murdered and then dumped into the water. Even in a death by drowning, the person could have died after being criminally thrown from a boat or off a pier.

There are more sudden, violent, and unexplained deaths in the United States than the nation's four hundred board-certified forensic pathologists can handle. This gruesome workload ideally should require at least a thousand forensic pathologists. As a result of this personnel shortage, not every death that calls for an autopsy gets one. Because there is also a shortage of qualified criminal investigators, not every death that requires an investigation gets the attention it deserves. This means we don't know exactly how many people in this country are murdered every year. And of the cases we know are criminal homicides, about half go unsolved. This is one of the biggest failures of our criminal justice system.

The Medical Examiner

Medical examiners are the only doctors whose patients are dead and therefore silent. They cannot explain why they died, so we have to find out in other ways. We are the detectives of death--we visit the scene; we examine the medical evidence and the laboratory findings and put them together with the circumstances and the patient's medical history. Through the autopsy, we make the body speak to us. Deciphering the message is an art as well as a science.

Our medical specialty is forensic pathology. We know about the three kinds of unnatural death--suicides, homicides, and accidents. We are trained to analyze traumatic injuries--gunshot and stab wounds, blunt force, and poison. Our work is different from that of the hospital pathologists who autopsy bodies to study the ravages of disease. Our methods are different from those of doctors who care for the living and whose concern is more the treatment than the cause. We want to know how the knife went in, from above or below, and where the person who wielded it was standing; which bullet hole was the entrance and which the exit and where the shot came from. Medically, these things may be irrelevant, but in a courtroom they are extremely significant in deciding the cause and manner of death and reconstructing how it happened.

Dr. Michael M. Baden, *Unnatural Death*, 1989

A Profession in Trouble

The autopsy, along with the crime-scene investigation, is the starting point, the foundation, of a homicide investigation. If something is missed or mishandled on the autopsy table, if the forensic pathologist draws the wrong conclusion from the evidence, the investigation is doomed.

Up until the 1930s, before the English forensic pathologist Dr. Bernard Spilsbury glamorized the profession through a series of high-profile murder case solutions, forensic pathology was called "the beastly science." Today, in the U.S., there are about 400 practicing forensic pathologists. For medical examiner and coroner systems to work properly, we need at least 800 of these practitioners. On average, about 35 of the 15,000 students who enroll in medical school every year graduate to become forensic pathologists. Recently, 12 of the nation's 37 forensic pathology programs had no students.

Forensic pathologists in the United States are overworked. Given the nature of the job, they are under constant pressure from politicians, prosecutors, homicide investigators, families of the deceased, and the media. The pay is relatively low, they often work in unsanitary morgue conditions, and in many jurisdictions, have run out of space to store dead bodies. Many forensic pathologists have burned out, and more than a few have had mental breakdowns.

Manner of Death Mistakes

Death cases aren't always what they appear to be. A recent *American Journal of Forensic Medicine and Pathology* article analyzed a decade's worth of death investigations in Fulton County [Atlanta], Georgia. The researchers found that death investigators and forensic pathologists disagreed on the manner of death in 12 percent of those cases. Twenty times, death investigators overlooked evidence such as strangulation marks, bullet wounds, and knife wounds and recorded those cases as natural or accidental deaths, only to have the pathologists conduct autopsies and discover that they were homicides. In one case, a driver inadvertently struck a pedestrian. The collision was tying up traffic and it was raining, so the investigator did a perfunctory examination before removing the body and classifying it as an accident. Pathologists later identified multiple gunshot wounds to the victim's head. By then, valuable time and evidence were lost.

Alternately, in twenty-one cases, death investigators reported homicides that proved to be accidents, suicides, or natural deaths.

John Temple, *Deathhouse, 2005*

The Excited Delirium Syndrome: Four Cases

When people die suddenly and unexpectedly without a clear reason, forensic pathologists, rather than classify them as deaths of undetermined causes, explain these fatalities as being caused by a syndrome. Attributing a mysterious or suspicious death to a syndrome, while it sounds scientific, isn't always forensically enlightening. Some of the more common causes of death syndromes include the Sudden Infant Death Syndrome (SIDS), the Shaken Baby Syndrome (SBS), and the more recent, Excited Delirium Syndrome (EDS). As causes of death, syndromes are based less on forensic science than on human behavior and the circumstances surrounding these deaths. These postmortem determinations often leave a lot to interpretation, and are therefore controversial, and subject to intense debate.

Forensic pathologists in the United States, Canada, England, and Wales, in situations involving agitated, violent, incoherent, and erratic male subjects who die suddenly while fighting with police officers or prison personnel trying to subdue them through physical force or Taser jolts, often attribute these deaths to EDS. Most of these men are overweight, a high percentage of them are black, and they are all high on drugs and/or alcohol. Many are also seriously mentally ill. Under intense stress, the hearts of these men race wildly, their body temperatures soar to 103-5 degrees, and they either die of cardiac or respiratory arrest. Dr. Vincent DiMaio, the former medical examiner of Bexar County, Texas, a well-known forensic pathologist and textbook author, believes these subjects die from overdoses of adrenaline.

The term "excited delirium" was coined by Dr. Deborah Mash, the neurologist who founded the Excited Delirium Education, Research and Information Center at the University of Miami where she has studied the brain tissue of 120 men she believes have died of EDS. Called a junk scientist and charlatan by her critics, Dr. Mash has appeared as an expert witness on behalf of Taser International, the stun gun company that was sued by families of men who have died after Tasers were used on them. When asked about her relationship with the firm, Dr. Mash reportedly said, "I don't care about the Taser, and I'll tell you why. Excited delirium was happening before the Taser...If it happened with pepper spray, you'd say, 'oh, it's the pepper spray that's killing them.'...We have some cases where there were no police involved, and they still died...Medical examiners have described cases where paramedics got to the scene and the room is trashed, there are ice cubes everywhere, and the subject is dead. That tells me that person was trying to cool down." (Miami-Dade County fire rescue paramedics carry excited delirium survival kits designed to cool overheated brains.)

Critics of EDS as a cause of death determination include the ACLU and other civil libertarian organizations. Noting that EDS is not recognized by the American Medical Association, these critics believe the authorities use EDS to cover-up and whitewash the real causes of death--police brutality and excessive force. They see EDS as a forensic device used to excuse and exonerate heavy-handed law enforcement.

September 5, 2006
Louisville, Kentucky
The police encountered 52-year-old Larry Noles, an ex-Marine, standing nude in the middle of the street. After failing to subdue Noles by force, officers shot him with a Taser three times. The highly agitated subject suddenly stopped breathing and died. The Jefferson County Medical Examiner attributed the death to EDS.

October 29, 2006
Jerseyville, Illinois
Roger Holyfield, 17, was walking in the middle of the street carrying a phone in one hand and a Bible in the other. He was screaming incoherently when approached by the police. After struggling with the out-of-control man officers used a Taser on him. Holyfield went into a coma and died the following day. The local medical examiner attributed the death to EDS.

December 17, 2006
Lafayette, Louisiana
High on cocaine and delirious, 29-year-old Terill Enard, with a broken bone sticking out of his leg, was creating a disturbance at a Waffle House restaurant. The police came, tried to restrain him then shocked him with a Taser. Enard collapsed and died at the scene. The coroner's office listed the death as "cocaine-induced Excited Delirium."

January 2008
Coral Gables, Florida
At two in the morning, Coral Gables police found ex-con Xavia Jones lying in the middle of a highway screaming, "God is coming to take me!" When officers approached him, Jones yelled, "Kill me, shoot me." Instead of shooting him an officer hit him with a Taser four times. When that had no effect, another officer gave Jones five more jolts. The subject sort of locked-up then died with a white liquid trickling from his mouth. The Miami-Dade County Associate Medical Examiner cited, "excited delirium syndrome, associated with cocaine use," as the cause of death.

July 22, 2011
Bangor, Maine

The Bangor police were called at 6:45 P.M. to deal with 32-year-old Ralph E. Willis, a man addicted to a hallucinogenic stimulant called MDPV, the key ingredient in bath salts. Officers found him running wildly around yelling at people on the street. When Willis resisted being taken into custody, several officers had to subdue him. In so doing, they used their nightsticks.

At the Penobscot County Jail, Willis continued to be agitated and uncooperative. He fought with jail personnel who put him into a holding cell. Thirty minutes later, when they checked on him, Willis appeared unresponsive. When deputy sheriffs entered the cell, Willis began to yell, grab his testicles, and bang his head against the wall. He then rolled onto his stomach, flailed his arms and legs, and stopped breathing. A short time later, they pronounced him dead at a local emergency room. Willis died of cardiac arrest, and at the time of his death, had a body temperature of 103 degrees.

The state's medical examiner ruled the manner of Willis' death accidental. The cause: MDPV toxicity. In her report, the forensic pathologist described Willis as having been in a state of excited delirium. As a result of the Willis case, the Penobscot County Jail no longer accepted prisoners who were under the influence of bath salts.

EDS in England and Wales

Research by the Bureau of Investigative Journalism, a not for profit organization based at City University in London, disclosed that excited delirium was first used in a British case in 1996. Since then coroners in England and Wales have relied on the syndrome to explain ten police restraint related deaths. In researching EDS, bureau journalists interviewed several forensic pathologists, and Dr. Deborah Mash who told an interviewer that "Just because you die in police custody, doesn't mean that what the police were doing at the time you died led to your death. That's why the police are called to the scene to begin with."

In Great Britain, Dr. Mash has drawn the wrath of several prominent critics in the field of forensic pathology. Dr. Derrick Pounder, a forensic pathology expert at the University of Dundee said, "Excited delirium is a theory...It has come from the United States, where the science is very politicized, without a robust enough analysis. If you write off a death as excited delirium, then you close the door to guilt being attributed, and more importantly, lessons being learned from the types of [police] restraint used."

Dr. Richard Shepherd, another English forensic pathologist who spoke to journalists with the Bureau of Investigative Journalism, said this: "We know there are a group of people who exhibit this very bizarre behavior. Whether they strictly fall into this group called 'excited delirium' or not, I think will become clearer as more research is done...I think it is a term that should be used with great care...."

Like its cause of death counterparts, SIDS and SBS, EDS will attract supporters and critics, and remain controversial until it is either totally rejected in the medical community, or accepted as valid forensic science.

Establishing Time of Death

Throughout the long annals of true crime lore, countless murder convictions and acquittals have come down to this: When did the killer strike? When did the victims breathe their last? In the absence of credible witnesses, the lack of an easy answer has bedeviled our criminal justice system since its inception....

Murder investigators found themselves desperate for clues as to time of death, and not just for evidence of guilt at trial. Knowing when a victim died could speed the earliest stages of an inquest by ruling out suspects with confirmed alibis and focusing scrutiny on those who did not. The *postmortem interval,* or time since death, proved even more critical in cases where a corpse turned up decomposed beyond recognition. Even an approximate time of death gave investigators a framework in which to connect the remains to a suspicious disappearance.

Yet for all its importance, determining the time of death has defied the detective's magnifying glass and the pathologist's scalpel for over 2,000 years. Even today, despite crime labs crammed with high-tech equipment for DNA analysis, toxicology, serology, and the detection of rarefied chemical vapors, we remain nearly as blind as the ancient Greeks with their belief in maggots sprouting fully formed and spontaneous from the flesh of the newly dead. [They did not realize that maggots were fly eggs.]

Nonetheless, it still startles most people to learn that a prudent medical examiner can rarely, if ever, accurately measure the interval between death and a body's discovery....

The myth of the medical expert's ability to nail down time of death has endured. No doubt this stems in part from the many pathologists who continue to offer more precision in court than their science can rightfully claim. That they do so is understandable enough, given the relentless pressure [put on them by detectives, prosecutors, and the public].

Jessica Snyder Sachs, *Corpse,* 2001

Munchausen Syndrome by Proxy

In 1977, a pediatrician from England published the results of an investigation he had conducted into the cases of 81 infants whose deaths had been classified either as Sudden Infant Death Syndrome (SIDS) or natural death. The study, by Dr. Roy Meadow of St. James University Hospital in Leeds, covered a period of 18 years. His article, "Munchausen Syndrome by Proxy: The Hinterlands of Child Abuse," which appeared in the journal *Lancet*, was shocking in its implications. Dr. Meadow claimed that these 81 babies had, in fact, been murdered, and that the forensic pathologists who had performed the autopsies had ignored obvious signs of physical abuse in the form of broken bones, scars, objects lodged in air passages, and toxic substances in their blood and urine. He came close to accusing some of these pathologists of helping patients, mostly mothers, of getting away with murder.

The Munchausen Syndrome, a psychological disorder identified in 1951 by Richard Asher, described patients who injured themselves, or made themselves sick, to attract sympathy and attention. Asher named the syndrome after Baron von Munchausen, a man known for telling tale tales. Dr. Meadow added "by proxy" because the people gaining sympathy and attention from illnesses and injuries were not hurting themselves. They were getting sympathy and attention by injuring and sickening their infants and children.

In his landmark article in *Lancet*, Dr. Meadow profiled some of the pediatric cases that had puzzled him in the early 1970s. For example, he was treating a young boy who had extremely high salt levels in his blood that were adversely affecting his kidneys. Because there was no way the boy could have eaten this much salt, Dr. Meadow came to suspect that the mother, a nurse, was force-feeding salt into the child through a nasal tube. When Dr. Meadow voiced his hypothesis to his colleagues at the hospital, they ridiculed him. In this case, however, the boy's mother confessed to exactly what Dr. Meadow had suspected. Her intent had not been to kill her child, but to use him as a way to attract attention at the hospital, an environment she found exciting and romantic.

After the publication of Dr. Meadow's shocking article, physicians all over the world sent him accounts of cases similar to the ones he had described in his *Lancet* piece. Even Dr. Meadow was shocked by some of these stories--cases that involved punctured eardrums, and induced blindness, as well as inflicted respiratory problems, stomach ailments, and allergy attacks. Years later, Dr. Meadow would design a controversial experiment involving hidden cameras in hospital rooms where suspected MSBP victims were being treated. Of the 39 children under surveillance, the cameras caught 33 parents creating breathing problems by putting their hands, bodies, or pillows over the victim's faces. Staff members monitoring nearby television screens quickly entered the hospital rooms, causing the abusers to discontinue their assaults. In England and the United States, some of these videotaped episodes were later shown on commercial television. After that exposure, MSBP was no longer an obscure psychological disorder.

In the years that followed Dr. Meadow's initial research into these child abuse and infant death cases, he came to believe that the vast majority of MSBP perpetrators were women, and that one-third of them were either nurses, or women who worked in some other capacity within the health care industry. His research also suggested that many of these mothers were married to men who were cold and indifferent, and that at least part of the motive behind making their children ill was an attempt to emotionally energize their spouses. According to Dr. Meadow, many MSBP women also enjoyed the attention and sympathy they received from physicians and nurses.

Because of his groundbreaking work on behalf of helpless and endangered children, Dr. Meadow received a lot of attention himself. He was in great demand as an MSBP consultant, was asked to give speeches and presentations all over the world, and testified as an expert witness in dozens of high-profile murder trials. In England, he received a knighthood in recognition of his contribution to the fields of medicine and forensic science. As a result of his testimony in homicide trials involving multiple SIDS deaths in the same family, his comment that "one [SIDS death] in a family is a tragedy, two is suspicious, and three is murder," became widely known as Meadow's Law. (In the United States it's referred to as "the rule of three.")

In Great Britain, in a handful of homicide trials between 1996 and 1999, the defendants challenged Dr. Meadow's theory that three SIDS cases in one family equaled murder. As a result, Meadow's Law is no longer a court-recognized doctrine in England. (Munchausen Syndrome by Proxy in Great Britain is now called, "fabricated illness.")

In the United States, a new version of this personality disorder had emerged. Called Munchausen Syndrome by Internet, mothers seek sympathy and attention by faking their own illnesses--mainly cancer--online in support groups and other social networks. At present the American Psychiatric Association does not recognize this version of the syndrome. While there is no known cure for the Munchausen Syndrome generally, the virtual form of this disorder does not involve actual self-harm, or the abuse of children.

SIDS is Not a Cause of Death

Until 1959, whenever a presumably healthy baby died in its bed for no apparent reason, forensic pathologists called it "crib death" or "cot death." These terms described where, not how, the baby died, and didn't sound very scientific. But "sudden infant death syndrome," a purely descriptive term coined by a pediatrician named J. Bruce Beckwith, sounded more technical and more ominous.

By describing the suddenness of the death instead of the place where it occurred, the term Sudden Infant Death Syndrome carries an implication of violence and foul play. While breaking new ground rhetorically, the introduction of the letters SIDS into the vocabulary of forensic pathology and criminal investigation added nothing but confusion. The time would come when SIDS, in essence, meant *suspicious* infant death syndrome, a designation that sounds more than vaguely criminal.

Stab Wounds

Estimating the length of a knife from the depth of the wound it makes can be tricky, because different parts of the body have different degrees of elasticity or give. Abdominal tissue, for instance, is soft, so that a three-inch knife plunged into the gut can be driven all the way back to the spine, producing a six-inch-deep stab wound.

At most autopsies, a trained forensic eye will take tissue flexibility into consideration and compensate appropriately in estimating puncture depth. On occasion, however, medical examiners forget to take account of this variable and as a result overestimate the length of the killing instrument, sometimes by several inches....

Stab wounds delivered to the chest do not usually cause such miscalculations. Owing to the hardness of the ribs and the sternum, this area tends not to cave in when struck, even by the point of a dagger. In some cases a rib cage will collapse under the pressure of a powerful jabbing thrust. I see this most often on the soft bones of children and the brittle bones of the elderly. But in a robust, healthy adult, the durable plating of the rib cage and sternum acts as a suit of armor, cracking and scarring but usually not breaking against the force of the lance.

Frederick Zugibe and David Carroll, *Dissecting Death*, 2006

Shaken Baby Syndrome

When a presumably healthy baby dies in its crib for no apparent reason, and there is no evidence of foul play, rather than classifying the cause of death as "unknown," or "undetermined," a coroner or medical examiner will usually call the fatality a "sudden infant death syndrome" (SIDS) case. Although this is the same as ruling the death as "undetermined," it sounds more scientific. At one time, the parents of SIDS babies found themselves under clouds of suspicion. Today, as a result of scientific study of these cases, forensic pathologists are attributing natural death causes in infant deaths that earlier would have been classified as SIDS cases.

The shaken baby syndrome (SBS) refers to signs of physical trauma found in children under six who have been violently shaken. When a baby or toddler is shaken too hard, the victim's brain is jarred against the skull, causing it to bleed and swell. Most pediatricians and forensic pathologists believe that to diagnose SBS, they must find, at minimum, evidence of subdural hematoma (brain hemorrhaging), retinal bleeding (broken veins in the eyes), and cerebral edema (liquid on the brain that causes it to swell). The conventional wisdom has been that a child with these injuries who had not been in a car accident or fallen from a two-story window had been violently shaken. Supportive evidence of SBS might include trauma to the neck and spine, bruises on the arms and torso, and broken ribs.

In the late 1990s, a handful of pediatric researchers began to question the science behind the standard SBS diagnosis. Could cerebral edema and blood in the eyes and brain have other causes, for example, vitamin deficiency, disease, or reactions to vaccines and drugs? Diseases thought to cause symptoms of SBS included hypohosphatasia, brittle bone disease; Alagilles's syndrome, a liver ailment; Bylers disease, a liver disorder common among the Amish; and glutaric acidura, acid buildup in infants that causes paralysis and retinal bleeding. Some experts believe that a relatively short fall to a hard surface, say from three feet, can cause damage to the brain similar to that found in SBS victims.

Because there is no agreement among pediatricians and forensic pathologists what physical evidence of SBS consists of, homicide trials involving defendants accused of shaking infants to death often involve dueling expert witnesses.

In 1997, a jury in Van Nuys, California convicted Shirley Ree Smith of shaking her 7-week-old grandson to death. The prosecutor convinced the jury that Smith had shaken the baby to stop him from crying. The medical examiner, in explaining why there wasn't as much cerebral bleeding as one might expect in a SBS case, said the baby had been shaken so violently the blood vessels in the brain stem suffered "shearing," causing instantaneous death without bleeding due to the fact the baby's heart had stopped beating.

The autopsy had failed to produce evidence of brain swelling or retinal bleeding.

The Smith defense put two forensic pathologists on the stand who classified the death as a SIDS case, noting that the baby had jaundice, an irregular heart beat, and low birth weight. The jury accepted the prosecution's version of the facts and found Shirley Ree Smith guilty. She received a sentence of fifteen years to life.

A state court of appeals upheld the conviction. The Ninth Circuit federal court of appeals, however, in 2006, reversed the conviction and ordered Smith released from prison on the grounds the jury had miss classified the baby's death as a SBS case. The state prosecutor appealed the reversal to the United States Supreme Court.

On October 31, 2011, the Supreme Court, in a 6 to 3 decision, reinstated Shirley Ree Smith's homicide conviction. That meant she would have to return to prison. The six justices upheld a longstanding legal principle that an appeals court cannot substitute its judgment for a jury's. The high court, recognizing the jury in the Smith case may have relied on the wrong forensic pathologists, reminded the Ninth Circuit Court that judges, in jury trials do not decide the law and the facts. If Shirley Ree Smith had a remedy in law, it would have to be in the form of executive clemency.

The Life of a Corpse

Climate and terrain have a great impact on the speed with which a body decomposes. If a body is deposited in a wooded area in upstate New York in the dead of winter, it's going to decompose much more slowly than one dumped in Florida woods in the summer. One reason is that flies and bacteria, the two main factors in turning a corpse into a skeleton, aren't active outdoors in cold weather. Research shows that bodies placed outside in the winter don't bloat as much as those in the summer, and many of them turn what we refer to as "Halloween colors"--orange and black.

Although not every case holds true, bodies usually go through several predictable stages: fresh, bloated, and dry. At this last stage, the decomposition process has ceased, maggots have finished feeding, and, unless rodents and larger carnivores eat it, the corpse will change very little even over a period of years. If there is any flesh left covering the skeleton, it will harden so that it will someday resemble leather or parchment paper.

During the early stages of decomposition, internal gases bloat the abdomen, the skin stretches like plastic wrap, and the veins fill with bacteria, turning them green and black so they look like thin highways or the graining on marble--hence the term "marbling."

Sometimes, in as little time as two weeks, the face, chin, throat, groin, and abdomen become the first areas to skeletonize. The less meaty and, to maggots, less desirable areas, such as the arms and legs, often decompose last. When you lift a body to look under it, those areas of the body in contact with the ground often resemble Swiss cheese or wormwood; this is where maggots have left the body and burrowed into the ground. Contrary to common belief, hair and nails don't keep growing after death; it's the shrinkage of the tissue that gives this illusion. Skin and hair are dead cells; they were dead before the individual died.

Rober Mann and Miryam Williamson, *Forensic Detective*, 2006

Murder Or Suicide

Levi Chavez, a 26-year-old officer with the Albuquerque, New Mexico Police Department, at nine o'clock on the night of October 21, 2007, called 911 to report that his wife had committed suicide with his department-issued Glock 9 pistol. Responding officers with the APD found, at the Chavez home in Los Lunas, 26-year-old Tera Chavez in the master bedroom with a massive exit bullet wound at the base of her skull. Next to her body officers saw the 9 mm Glock that still had a round in its chamber. Nearby lay the fatal bullet's spent shell casing and, detached from the handgun, its clip or magazine. It appeared that the barrel of the gun had been inserted into the dead woman's mouth.

Officer Chavez informed his fellow officers that he and his wife had been having marital problems for years, and that on countless occasions the mother of two, who worked at a beauty salon as a hairdresser, had threatened to kill herself.

Because it was apparent that Tera Chavez had been dead for several hours, the crime scene officers wanted to know the circumstances under which Levi had discovered his wife's corpse. In response to that question, Chavez said he last saw his wife on Friday morning, October 19 before going on duty at the APD. That night, he decided to stay over at his girlfriend Deborah Romero's house. Romero was also a member of the Albuquerque Police Department.

According to Levi Chavez, on Saturday, October 20, Tera called him 176 times. He ignored her calls by turning off his cellphone. Chavez said he spent Saturday night with Romero, and the next day, when Tera didn't call him, he began to worry. Later that Sunday evening, Levi said his mother told him that Tera had not shown up for work that day at the beauty salon. At that point he rushed home to find that his wife had committed suicide.

In 2007, the Albuquerque Police Department, due to a series of questionable police-involved shootings, and allegations of institutional corruption and departmental cover-ups of officer wrongdoing, was under investigation by the FBI. Shortly after Tera Chavez's sudden and violent death, critics of the APD accused the department of helping officer Chavez cover up the murder of his wife by destroying crime scene evidence. Because the police department had such a bad reputation, and a police officer's wife had died under suspicious circumstances, Detective Aaron Jones of the Valencia County Sheriff's Office took charge of the homicide investigation.

Detective Jones, who suspected that Levi Chavez had murdered his wife eighteen to twenty hours before he called 911, had to back off when Dr. Patricia McFeeley, the state medical examiner, ruled Tera's manner of death a suicide. In November 2007, Detective Jones showed Dr. McFeeley crime scene photographs that caused her to change Tera Chavez's manner of death to "undetermined." Despite Jone's efforts, the homicide investigation eventually died on the vine.

In April 2011, three and a half years after Tera Chavez's death, following a cold-case murder investigation, Dr. McFeeley changed the manner of death in the case to criminal homicide. Assistant Sandoval County District Attorney Bryan McKay charged Levi Chavez, who was no longer on the police force, with first-degree murder in his wife's death.

The Chavez murder trial got underway on June 3, 2013 before Sandoval District Court Judge George Eichwald. In his opening remarks to the jury, lead prosecutor McKay presented the state's theory that the defendant had murdered his wife sometime between late Saturday night October 20, 2007 and the early morning hours of Sunday, October 21. After shooting his wife in the mouth with the Glock 9 pistol, the defendant staged a suicide by placing the gun, the shell casing, and the clip next to her body.

Levi Chavez's trial attorney, David Sema, a lawyer well known in New Mexico for representing several high-profile criminal defendants, told the jurors that his client's wife had committed suicide over her husband's extramarital affairs.

Detective Aaron Jones took the stand for the prosecution. According to the Valencia County homicide detective, the Glock magazine found next to the victim's body was "unseated." By that, the witness meant it wasn't locked into the butt of the gun. This suggested that after the weapon had been discharged, the shooter had pressed a button to release the clip.

DNA expert Alanna Williams, who in 2007 worked for the New Mexico Crime Laboratory, but was now employed by the APD, testified that she had tested the Glock and a pair of sweatpants found in the Chavez home washing machine for DNA. Williams said she had found blood on the muzzle of the pistol that contained the victim's DNA. On the handgun's grip, the forensic scientist found a mixture of Tera's and the defendant's DNA. The sweatpants, believed to have been worn by the defendant, contained DNA from the victim.

Dr. Patricia McFeeley, now the former medical examiner, testified that the death scene Glock had been inserted at least one inch into Tera Chavez's mouth. The fatal bullet had vaporized the victim's brainstem. The forensic pathologist explained that the victim, after being shot, couldn't have pressed the button that released the magazine from the butt of the pistol.

One of the defendant's mistresses, APD officer Regina Sanchez, took the stand. In September 2006 she and Levi began an intimate relationship. A month later, Sanchez, believing that Chavez was in the process of divorcing Tera, allowed him to move in with her. After the witness received an angry call from Tera Chavez, he moved out.

Rose Slama, another of the defendant's girlfriends, testified that he told her that when Tera shot herself, he was in the house taking a shower.

After the prosecution rested its case on June 26, 2013, defense attorney David Sema put Dr. Alan Berman, a suicide expert who lived in Washington, D. C., on the stand. Based on Tera Chavez's diary entries, text messages, medical history, and two notes in her hand found at the death scene, Dr. Berman said he believed that she suffered from low self-esteem and self-hate due to her emotionally abusive relationship with her philandering husband. She had been, in the witness' opinion, depressed as well. According to the psychologist, these factors combined to create what he called "acute risk factors for suicide."

Dr. Berman read several text messages Tera had sent to her husband between August and October 2006. In one such message she had written: "I am a loser. I've failed at everything, especially you. I want to die." In another text she had said, "I'm tired of being your dumb wife. You treat me like shit...please respect me...I have a job."

Prosecutor McKay, on cross-examination, asked the "suicideologist" to read Tera Chavez's last diary entry, dated July 12, 2007, which read: "...so goodbye to the person I used to be. Welcome a new day. Happiness!" Dr. Berman testified that he did not believe this statement was inconsistent with a suicidal mindset.

On July 1, 2013, a crime scene reconstruction expert took the stand for the defense. In the course of demonstrating to the jury how Tera Chavez, after shooting herself in the mouth with the Glock, had pressed the button that released the magazine, failed to eject the magazine pursuant to his theory of what happened. In other words, the demonstration failed.

Defense attorney Sema, on July 9, 2013, presented his star witness. Dr. Charles V. Wetli, the former medical examiner of Suffolk County, New York, had testified for the defense in dozens of high-profile murder cases.

According to the forensic pathologist, had the defendant shoved the pistol into his wife's mouth, he would have broken some of her teeth. According to Dr. Wetli, Tera Chavez, in killing herself, had turned the gun upside down and used her thumb to pull the trigger.

Prosecutor McKay's associate, Assistant District Attorney Anne Keener, on cross-examination, showed Dr. Wetli a death scene photograph that appeared to show that one of Tera's lower teeth had been chipped. When asked if one of the dead woman's teeth had been broken, the forensic pathologist said, "It's possible." Prosecutor Keener asked Dr. Wetli if he had visited the death scene or personally examined Tera Chavez's corpse. He said that he had not.

The second major defense witness, the defendant himself, took the stand on July 11, 2013. In describing his discovery of his dead wife on the night of October 21, 2007, Levi Chavez said, "I turned on the light and it was like terror. I couldn't believe what I was seeing." The defendant told the jury that he blamed himself for Tera's suicide, and felt that God was saying to him: "This is all your fault." Chavez assured the jurors that he had found religion, and had not cheated on his second wife. At several points during his direct examination by attorney Sema, the defendant broke down in tears.

On cross-examination, prosecutor Bryan McKay asked the former police officer whey he had left his loaded department-issued gun "with a woman who was depressed and talked about possibly hurting herself. You had small children in the house."

"We had," the defendant replied, "an attempted break-in. A truck was stolen right out of our driveway when she was there. And yes, I had small children in the home, but this is exactly why I left the gun in the house. (Regarding the theft of Levi's 2004 Ford F-250 truck, Tera allegedly told her fellow beauty salon workers that he and his "cop buddies" had staged the theft as part of an insurance scam. Prosecutor McKay had attempted to get this information before the jury, but Judge Eichwald had suppressed it.)

On July 16, 2013, the jury, after ten hours of deliberation, found the defendant not guilty.

The Legal Definition of Death

Andrew Lyons shot a man in the head in September 1973 and left him brain-dead. When Lyon's attorneys found out the victim's family had donated his heart for transplantation, they tried to use this in Lyon's defense: If the heart was still beating at the time of surgery, they maintained, then how could it be that Lyons had killed him the day before?

They tried to convince the jury that, technically speaking, Andrew Lyons hadn't murdered the man, the organ surgeon had....

The judge would have none of it...In the end, Lyons was convicted of murder. Based on the outcome of the case, California passed legislation making brain death the legal definition of death. Other states quickly followed suit....

Mary Roach, *Stiff*, 2003

Kendrick Johnson

Kendrick Johnson attended Lowndes High School in Valdosta, Georgia. The thin, muscular 17-year-old played on the football and basketball teams. After attending his fourth period class on Thursday, January 10, 2013, Kendrick went missing. The next morning someone discovered the student's body stuffed upside-down inside a rolled-up wrestling mat that stood on its end in the school gymnasium. He was dead.

Lowndes County Sheriff Chris Prine, in charge of the death scene investigation, quickly concluded that the high school student's death had been accidental. According to Sheriff Prine, Kendrick must have gone into the mat headfirst to retrieve a shoe or some other item. The sheriff theorized that Kendrick got stuck inside the mat and suffocated.

On January 25, 2013, the head of the Valdosta-Lowndes Regional Crime Laboratory where a forensic pathologist had performed the autopsy ten days earlier, informed members of the media that Johnson's body had "showed no signs of blunt force trauma." Sheriff Prine assured reporters there were no other signs of a struggle on Johnson's body.

Kendrick's parents, Kenneth and Jackie Johnson, took issue with the manner of death determination and complained that officials with the sheriff's office and the Georgia Bureau of Investigation were not talking to them about their son's death.

In mid-April 2013, Lowndes County Coroner Bill Watson told a reporter with the *Valdosta Daily Times* that Kendrick Johnson's body had been moved before he arrived at the gym. According to the coroner, the sheriff had waited six hours before informing him of the gruesome discovery. (Under Georgia law, the local coroner's office must be notified *immediately* in cases of sudden, violent, or unexplained death.) Regarding the delay in notification and the moving of the body, Coroner Watson said, "Well it compromises my investigation one-hundred percent. I don't know what the county [sheriff's office personnel] did when they got on the scene...The [death] scene, in my opinion, had been compromised."

On May 4, 2013, the authorities finally provided the media with a copy of the autopsy report. According to the forensic pathologist who performed Kendrick's autopsy, the young man had died from "positional asphyxia." Lowndes County Coroner Bill Watson, based upon this cause of death determination, had no choice but to rule that Kendrick Johnson had died as a result of a freak accident.

Kenneth and Jackie Johnson, convinced that their son had been murdered, and that the authorities were involved in a cover-up, asked a judge to authorize an exhumation. In May 2013 the judge granted the request that led to a second autopsy. Dr. William R. Anderson, a forensic pathologist with the private firm Forensic Dimensions, a company located in Heathrow, Florida performed that postmortem examination. The Johnson's paid for Dr. Anderson's postmortem review.

The dead boy's parents were also pressing for a federal investigation into the closed case. In support of this request, the Johnson couple alleged that crime scene evidence had either been destroyed or tampered with. The sheriff's office had also denied the parents the opportunity to view high school surveillance camera footage of their son during the hours before he went missing. The parents also claimed that postmortem photographs of Kendrick revealed lacerations on his face and body.

On May 23, 2013, Kenneth and Jackie Johnson released copies of two reports that had been written by a pair of paramedics with the South Georgia Medical Center Mobile Healthcare Service. According to the paramedics, Kendrick's body showed obvious signs of a struggle. Moreover, they found the student's body in a pool of blood and vomit. One of the paramedics wrote that he considered the high school gym the scene of a criminal homicide. The sheriff, however, insisted that morning that Kendrick Johnson's death had been a tragic accident.

The results of the second autopsy performed by Dr. William R. Anderson were released in early September 2013. In his report, Dr. Anderson concluded that Kendrick Johnson had died from "unexplained, apparent *non-accidental* blunt force trauma to his right neck and soft tissues."

The attorney representing the Johnson family told reporters that she was sending a copy of Dr. Anderson's autopsy report to the civil rights division of the U. S. Department of Justice. The cause and manner of Kendrick Johnson's death has not been changed. Officially, he died of a freak accident.

On October 10, 2013, Kendrick Johnson's parents revealed that when their son's body was exhumed for a second autopsy, Dr. Anderson discovered that the boy's internal organs were missing. "I feel outraged about them stuffing my son's body with newspaper," Jacquelyn Johnson said. The parents have told reporters that they believe the missing organs are further evidence of foul play and a cover-up in their son's death.

Michael Moore, the United States Attorney for the Middle District of Georgia announced on October 31, 2013 that the FBI planned to investigate the circumstances surrounding Kendrick Johnson's death. "We're happy," Jacquelyn Johnson said. "The only thing we ever wanted was the truth."

In December 2013, FBI agents questioned several of Johnson's Lowndes High School classmates as well as Lowndes County coroner Bill Watson. Agents also spent time with the deceased boy's parents. The parents, in February 2014, filed a lawsuit against the funeral home that handled their son's remains. According to the plaintiffs, funeral home personnel intentionally destroyed his internal organs in an attempt to interfere with the investigation into their son's murder.

On March 13, 2014, in Macon, Georgia, four of Johnson's classmates as well as students from nearby Valdosta High School appeared before the federal grand jury looking into the death.

CNN reporters, on March 17, 2014, announced that they had acquired, through the Georgia Open Records Act, an anonymous email dated January 27, 2014. According to the police tipster, one of Johnson's classmates confessed to killing the young man. This person had not, however, confessed directly to the email sender. In an effort to identify the tipster, a Lowndes County assistant district attorney has ordered a communications company to hand over its internet records pertaining to this email.

As of August 2014, no one had been arrested in connection with Johnson's death.

The Body Bag

A good body bag gives up no clues. Little about what it contains should not be detected by any of the five senses of the observer. And nothing should be presumed--not even the length of what's inside. Death, after all, changes everything. And unnatural death changes everything absolutely.

The Office of the New York City Medical Examiner orders about 8,000 body bags each year; Philadelphia's M.E., about 3,000; and Milwaukee's about 2,000. Massachusetts' offices prefer shrouds, which are more like plastic envelopes folded and welded at the ends. They order 5,000.

The same polyvinyl chloride used to make pipes can be woven into flexible fabric of varying degrees of strength. Some body bags will be dragged over long distances of rugged underbrush; others will be hoisted on the rocker legs of helicopters. Bags may need to be nothing more than short-term storage compartments, or nothing less than unconditionally leak proof vessels of somber transport. Zippers can swoop around the edges of the bag or run right down the middle. Handles, rivets and locks are optional.

These days most body bags are white. That way you don't miss much--the red carpet fiber, the black hair, a chartreuse fleck of paint. You can see a lot, if you know how to look.

Michael Badin and Marion Roach, *Dead Reckoning*, 2001

Forensic Hired Guns

In a court of law, a phony, or hired gun forensic scientist can be more persuasive than his more qualified or ethical counterpart. This is possible because jurors make judgments based on how expert witnesses look, act, and speak. They do not analyze their resumes. A courtroom charlatan acting the part can be more believable than a real expert. Phonies like Dr. Ralph Erdmann, Dr. Louise Robbins, Dr. Pamela Fish, Dr. Michael West, and Fred Zain, to name a few, testified in hundreds of cases before they were exposed and defrocked. There are hundreds of private sector hired guns whose expert testimony is for sale for any side that will pay them. Crime lab personnel working in the various levels of government are often incompetent, or tailor their findings to the needs of police and prosecutors. In general, the field of forensic science has not lived up to its potential, and to an alarming degree, is either useless or downright corrupt. The dueling expert problem is one of the symptoms of this reality.

Vanderbilt law professor Rebecca Haw, in a 2013 article about dueling experts, discusses the "99 to 1 problem." Haw writes: "One out of 100 available experts testifies that the earth is round, and that one out of 100 who disagrees testifies that the earth is flat. To jurors, it appears that scientific consensus on the subject is divided roughly 50-50."

As the author of two books on the Lindbergh kidnapping case, I've encountered something like the 99 to 1 problem in connection with hack true crime writers who make the case that Bruno Richard Hauptmann, the man executed for the 1932 murder of the Lindbergh baby, was innocent. More than a dozen highly qualified questioned document examiners had identified Hauptmann as the writer of all the ransom letters. Since the 1935 trial, several modern handwriting experts have analyzed the evidence and drawn the same conclusion. While only one recognized forensic document examiner has expressed doubt regarding these findings, those who believe that Hauptmann was innocent, claim that the handwriting evidence in the case is in dispute. In reality, the question of who wrote the Lindbergh case ransom letters has been settled for a long time.

In researching my 2008 book, *Forensics Under Fire*, I noticed that forensic pathologists often testify against each other in shaken baby syndrome and sudden infant death cases. Coroners and medical examiners also face off against opposing forensic pathologists in suicide versus homicide cases, and trials featuring the issue of whether a victim was intentionally poisoned, or died of an overdose. Forgery and disputed will cases almost always involve opposing handwriting experts, a forensic science of the verge of being destroyed by phony practitioners. (The JonBenet Ramsey case caused a serious rift among qualified forensic document examiners.) Experts regularly disagree over the crime scene identification of footwear and tire impressions, blood spatter analysis, bite mark identification, and the cause and origin of suspicious structural fires. Even government fingerprint examiners are now being challenged in court. Ten years ago, this was unheard of.

The fact that two expert witnesses are on opposite sides of a forensic science issue doesn't necessarily mean that one of them is either a phony or in the tank. But it does mean that one of them is wrong. When jurors find the scientist who is wrong more credible than the expert who is right, criminal justice has been subverted. Forensic science is supposed to be the solution, not the problem.

Dueling Forensic Pathologists

On January 30, 2003, 19-year-old Rosa Olvera Jimenez, and the boy she regularly babysat, were alone in the 21-months-old baby's Austin, Texas home. Around noon, Bryan Gutierrez turned blue, and collapsed. Although paramedics pulled a wad of 5 paper towels out of the boy's throat, he had slipped into a vegetative state. Four months later, he died.

Jimenez, suspected of murdering the child from the onset, said she had inadvertently left a roll of paper towels in the living room while she prepared lunch in the kitchen. Bryan, his face blue, staggered into the kitchen and pointed to his throat. A few minutes later he collapsed.

Charged with murder, Jimenez went on trial on August 25, 2005 at the Travis County district court in Austin. The prosecutor put two physicians and a medical examiner on the stand. The three experts testified that it would have been physically impossible for Bryan to have accidentally swallowed all of that paper. His gag reflex would have prevented that from happening. The fact the towels were stained with blood, according to these expert witnesses, supported the theory that the obstructive mass had been pushed into his throat by force.

The Jimenez defense put Dr. Ira Kanfer, a forensic pathologist, on the stand. Dr. Kanfer testified that the victim could have accidentally choked himself with the paper towels. According to this forensic pathologist, the blood on the towels did not come from the inside of the victim's mouth, but from his lungs.

On August 31, 2005, after eight hours of deliberation, the jury found Jimenez guilty of murder. The judge sentenced her to 99 years in prison.

Defense attorneys filed a motion for a new trial on the grounds the state had not given the defense team enough money to hire a battery of experts to counter the prosecution's expert witnesses. Since the trial, two physicians who are pediatric airway specialists, and a forensic pathologist who specializes in the deaths of children, studied the case. All three of these experts believe that despite the gag reflex, Bryan Gutierrez could have accidentally choked on the paper towels.

To counter the post-conviction findings of these new defense witnesses, the prosecutor presented the analysis of an expert who agreed with the three doctors who had testified for the prosecution at the trial.

In November 2005, the Travis County district judge who had presided over the case denied the defense motion for a new trial. Jimenez's attorneys appealed this ruling. Several months later, a Texas appeals court reversed the district judge, and ordered a new trial based on the new evidence. The Travis County prosecutor appealed this decision to the state's highest court, and in April 2012, that court, in an 8 to 1 decision, denied Jimenez a new trial. According to the justices, the new scientific evidence was not enough evidence to legally reverse the trial jury's finding of guilt.

In the Jimenez murder case, forensic science failed to establish how Bryan Gutierrez had died. It didn't matter to him, but it meant everything to his babysitter who will probably die in prison. We will never know for sure if justice was done in this case.

Rigor Mortis

Rigor mortis, the stiffening of muscles after death, is due to a chemical reaction directly dependent on the temperature surrounding a body (the colder the temperature, the slower rigor develops.) Beginning several hours after all vital signs cease, it is noted first in the facial area then proceeds to the upper and lower extremities. After twelve hours it is usually complete. Finally, after twenty-four to thirty-six hours, the body passes out of rigor, this time in the reverse sequence, from the bottom of the body to the top.

Generally speaking, the more physical exertion or struggle that takes place before death, the sooner rigor begins. Moreover, the sooner rigor begins, the sooner it passes.

Frederick Zugibe and David L. Carroll, *Dissecting Death*, 2005

29 CRIME LABS

A Short History of American Forensic Science

By 1935, crime laboratories were up and running in New York City, Chicago, Detroit, Boston, Los Angeles and Philadelphia. The FBI Lab had opened its doors in 1933. The bureau's national fingerprint repository had been operating in Washington, D.C. since 1924, the year J. Edgar Hoover, an early advocate of scientific crime detection, became the agency's fourth director. August Vollmer, the progressive police administrator from Berkeley, California, and Dean John Wigmore of Northwestern University Law School, had been tireless crusaders for forensic science and physical evidence as an alternative to coerced confessions, eyewitness testimony, and jailhouse informants. Wigmore and Vollmer were the main forces behind the formation, in Chicago, of the Scientific Crime Detection Laboratory in 1930. In 1938 the private lab became part of the Chicago Police Department.

In the 1930s a pair of private practice forensic chemists and crime scene reconstruction analysts in the northwest, Oscar Heinrich and Luke May, were grabbing headlines by solving high-profile murder cases. Stories involving crimes solved through the scientific analysis of physical evidence had become commonplace features in the fact-crime magazines so popular at the time. Numerous textbooks and manuals had been published on the subjects of fingerprint identification, forensic ballistics, questioned documents, trace evidence analysis, forensic serology, forensic medicine, scientific lie detection (polygraph), and forensic anthropology, the identification and analysis of skeletal remains.

Criminal investigation textbooks of this era contained detailed instructions on how to protect crime scenes, render crime scene sketches, photograph clues, mark and package physical evidence, dust for latent fingerprints, make plaster-of-Paris casts of tire tracks and footwear impressions, and in the case of sudden, unexplained, or violent death, look for signs of criminal homicide. By the mid-thirties, virtually every court in the country accepted the expert opinions of practitioners in the major forensic fields, and jurors recognized the advantages of expert physical evidence interpretation over the more direct testimony of jailhouse snitches and eyewitnesses.

Today, notwithstanding DNA science and computerized fingerprint identification and retrieval capabilities, crime solution percentages in the United States have not improved since the mid-thirties when the FBI started collecting crime statistics. The emphasis on street policing (order maintenance), the escalating war on drugs, and the threat of domestic terrorism has diminished the role of criminal investigation and forensic science in the administration of justice. At a time when DNA technology has advanced far beyond the imaginations of the pioneers of forensic serology (Dr. Paul Kirk and others), rapists, pedophiles, and serial killers are escaping detection and arrest due to DNA analysis backlogs created by a shortage of funds and experts. Ironically, one of the byproducts of DNA science has been the release of hundreds of innocent people who have been convicted on the strength of coerced confessions, unreliable eyewitnesses, and the testimony of jailhouse informants. In the small percentage of trials involving the analysis of physical evidence, jurors are commonly exposed to conflicting scientific testimony. When faced with opposing experts, jurors tend to disregard the science altogether. The forensic pioneers of the twenties and thirties would be appalled by this hired-gun phenomena and the low productivity of today's investigative services.

During the first decade of the 21st Century, due to forensic misidentifications caused by substandard lab conditions and incompetent personnel, crime laboratories in, among other places, Houston, Chicago, Philadelphia, Detroit, and Boston, had to be temporarily closed. During this period, for the first time in the history of the science, there were numerous high-profile fingerprint misidentifications. Moreover, modern forensic science has seen the infusion of pseudo-science and bogus expertise into the nation's courtrooms.

In March 2009, the National Academy of Sciences, an organization within the National Institute of Justice, after an eighteen-month study, published a report criticizing the state of forensic science in America. The writers of the widely publicized report recommended that Congress create a federal agency to insure a firewall between forensic science and law enforcement; finance more research and personnel training; and promote universal standards of excellence in the troubled fields of DNA profiling, forensic firearms identification, fingerprint analysis, forensic document examination, and forensic pathology. From this, one might reasonably conclude that modern forensic science, weighed against the hopes and dreams of its pioneers, has not lived up to its potential.

Sherlock Holmes

The birth of the modern crime lab can be traced directly to fiction. Sir Arthur Conan Doyle was a physician and keen observer of his patients' abnormalities. He was a splendid writer, as well, and when he created Sherlock Holmes, he also imprinted on popular culture the idea that when the elements of science are coupled with applied logic, crimes can be solved. Doyle also knew that the way to brand the concept in the public's hearts and minds was to package the science in the form of a uniquely fascinating man. After all, it had worked before, in Charles Dickens' *Bleak House,* published in 1853. In that novel, Inspector Bucket personified all that amazed the public about Scotland Yard.

By the time Doyle was writing, in the 1880s, London had had a police force for fifty years and the detectives of Scotland Yard since 1842. Starting in the 1860s, those detectives had added crime scene analysis to their toolbox of skills, and the forensic sciences took a great leap forward. But when Doyle captured it all in the form of Holmes, he did more than just sell books. One avid fan was Edmund Locard, who was influenced by the writing and went on to build the world's first forensic laboratory in Lyons, France in 1910. [The so-called Locard Principle: the criminal, at least in theory, will leave part of himself at the crime scene and take part of it with him.]

The idea of crime labs spread throughout the world. In 1932, the Federal Bureau of Investigation opened its lab under Director J. Edgar Hoover. [Philadelphia, Los Angeles and Detroit formed crime labs in the 1920s.]

Michael Baden and Marion Roach, *Dead Reckoning,* 2001

Problems in Forensic Science

The nature of science itself, and the fact that forensic science is a service mainly delivered by the government, makes solving its problems a real challenge. Science is complex, constantly in flux, and often subject to disagreement. Government is slow, resistant to change, and difficult to hold accountable. The difficulty in dealing with the government generally is exacerbated by the convoluted structure of our criminal justice system, and the adversarial nature of the trial process. Today, trials are more about winning and losing than achieving truth and justice.

Most problems in forensic science can be placed into one of three categories: personnel, jurisprudence (courts and law), and science itself. Many of these problems--cuts in governmental funding, the quality of law enforcement personnel, and what legislators and judges do and don't do-- are beyond the control of forensic scientists. For these and other reasons, forensic science in America will continue to perform well below its potential. This arm of the criminal justice system therefore represents a failed promise. The gap between reality, and what television viewers see on the CSI shows, is widening.

The Houston Crime Lab

The stratified nature of our criminal justice system--federal, state, county, and local levels of law enforcement--and the adversarial nature of the trial process, exacerbates the difficulties of improving crime lab services. Most problems in forensic science can be placed into three general categories: personnel, jurisprudence (courts and law), and science itself. The principal source of the problems within the Houston Police Department's crime laboratory involved personnel.

Since 2003, the Houston Crime Laboratory has been a disgrace to forensic science. At times the lab's services had been so subpar the entire operation was shut down. Physical evidence had been lost, tampered with, and contaminated. Convictions were overturned due to discredited forensic analysis. Lab personnel had resigned, been suspended, and indicted. Because of a decade of scandal, corruption, and incompetence, innocent defendants had been convicted, and guilty persons set free.

Forensic science is supposed to improve the quality of criminal justice, not make it worse. If you want to know what can go bad in forensic science, study the recent history of the Houston Crime Laboratory. It's a textbook case of failure.

In the field of DNA analysis, the backbone of any major forensic science operation, the work of the Houston lab had been particularly atrocious. In 2008, plagued by backlogs, evidence contamination, and inaccurate test results, the DNA unit had to be closed. There have also been persistent problems in the latent fingerprint, firearms identification, and toxicology sections of the lab. In 2010, an audit disclosed 7,000 untested rape kits sitting in the evidence room. That year a lab supervisor quit over the number in inaccurate blood-alcohol test results.

On June 6, 2012, the Houston City Council voted 15-2 to hand control of the crime lab to an independent 9-member board. Only time will tell if taking control of the crime lab from the Houston Police Department will end a decade of forensic science disgrace. Separating lab personnel from the direct influence of law enforcement should make these scientists more objective. Perhaps the reorganization will mark the start of a new era of forensic science in Houston.

San Francisco

If you had to get caught dealing drugs, San Francisco was the place to be in 2010, especially if the evidence against you went to criminalist Deborah Madden. That's when Madden was accused of pilfering small amounts of cocaine from the lab for personal use. An internal review turned up significant shortages of drug evidence in several cases she handled. But Madden said she was not surprised because weight discrepancies occurred frequently at the lab. The San Francisco district attorney's office first said six cases might be compromised then dropped hundreds of cases. Later, the investigation of the lab expanded to look at the potential involvement of other crime lab employees, and the DA's office had to analyze 1,400 pending felony narcotics cases they might be forced to drop. Madden retired and no charges were filed.

A Miscellany of Murder, The Monday Murder Club, 2011

St. Paul

In St. Paul, Minnesota the police department operated the crime laboratory. Between 2007 and 2011, the laboratory handled more than 16,000 cases involving 200,000 pieces of physical evidence. In the spring of 2011, a pair of Dakota County public defenders, Lauri Traub and Christine Funk, raised questions regarding the reliability of results coming out of the lab's drug testing unit. Members of the Dakota County Drug Task Force had also expressed concerns over the quality of the lab's drug analysis.

The lab in St. Paul was one of 18 in the state of Minnesota that had not been accredited by the American Society of Crime Lab Directors, a process of authentication that could take up to two years. After public defenders Traub and Funk visited the lab in March 2012, they asked a Dakota County judge to hold a special hearing to determine if the findings of the drug testing operation can be trusted.

On July 17, at the special crime lab hearing, attorney Traub questioned Sergeant Jay Siegel, the director of the lab. Siegel, a former patrol officer who once worked as a latent fingerprint examiner, testified that he had no formal education in science. Attorney Traub presented the lab director with a list of 51 scientific protocols that must be adhered to before a crime lab meets the minimum standards of proficiency and credibility. Sergeant Siegel was forced to admit that the St. Paul Lab had been ignoring all but two of the 51 protocols. He testified that three of the criminalists who tested narcotics seized by the police had little formal training in drug analysis. The lab director also acknowledged that the facility had not been keeping proper records, and that personnel regularly misused the drug testing equipment. In Siegel's opinion, results coming out of this unit could not be trusted.

At the conclusion of the forensic science court hearing, Police Chief Thomas Smith suspended the lab's drug testing operation, and appointed a police commander to take over the administration of the facility. The chief reassigned Sergeant Siegel to another police job. Chief Thomas also ordered an internal review of the beleaguered operation.

As long the police department ran the crime lab, and it remained unaccredited, there would be problems. Because almost all criminal justice resources are earmarked for uniformed policing, and crime labs are extremely expensive to operate, the future of the St. Paul facility looked bleak.

Problems in Pensacola, Florida

Officials are investigating a crime lab chemist based in Pensacola, Florida, saying he allegedly swapped prescription drug pain pills seized as evidence with over-the-counter medication. A Florida Department of Law Enforcement spokesperson on February 1, 2014 said officials are now looking into 2,600 cases handled by the chemist since 2006.

The investigation started when the State Attorney's Office and police asked for assistance into inquiries of missing prescription pills from the Escambia County Sheriff's Office. They discovered the drugs had been replaced with the over-the-counter medication.

FDLE teams will be deployed to all agencies impacted in order to inspect evidence handled by the chemist. Members will work to confirm cases that have been potentially compromised...No charges have been filed yet, but officials said they anticipate an arrest. The suspect has been removed from his job.

ABC News, February 2, 2014

Crime Lab Rogues in Massachusetts

In August 2012, authorities in Massachusetts shut down the state crime lab in Jamaica Plain. A month later, state police officers arrested Annie Dookhan on charges related to the forensic chemist's deliberate mishandling of drug evidence, and her failure to follow lab protocols. During her tenure at the Jamaica Plain lab, Dookhan had handled more than 50,000 drug samples involving some 34,000 defendants. Now all of these cases are in jeopardy.

On January 20, 2013, Massachusetts Attorney General Martha Coakley announced that state police officers had arrested forensic chemist Sonja Farak. The 35-year-old had been a drug analyst at the state lab in Amherst. The officers arrested Farak at her home in Northampton on charges she had stolen cocaine and heroin from evidence she had certified. The forensic chemist had replaced the stolen contraband with counterfeit substances. Farak, a state chemist since 2002, was held on $75,000 bail pending her arraignment.

Two weeks before Farak's arrest, federal inspectors had given the Amherst lab a clean bill of health. After the closing of the Jamaica Plain and Amherst facilities, police and prosecutors in Massachusetts are left with the crime lab in Sudbury, the only laboratory still open in the state.

In November 2013, Dookhan pleaded guilty to faking drug tests to look more productive. The judge sentenced her to three years in prison.

Farak, in January 2014, pleaded guilty to stealing drugs from the crime lab. The judge sentenced her to two and a half years in prison with 18 months to serve and the rest suspended during a five-year probation.

The crime lab scandals in Massachusetts illustrate how much damage a couple of rogue forensic practitioners can inflict on a criminal justice system overwhelmed by the government's massive war on drugs.

State Labs in Michigan

Crime laboratories in the United States are underfunded and understaffed. This has produced serious backlogs, sloppy work, and bad forensic science. Defense attorneys across the country are routinely challenging the scientific reliability of crime lab results. Convictions have been overturned based on bad forensic science. Several crime lab units have been temporarily shut down, and denied accreditation.

The seven crime labs in the state of Michigan under the control of the Michigan State Police were at risk of losing their accreditation by the Laboratory Accreditation Board of the American Society of Crime Laboratory Directors. If that happened, the Michigan crime lab system would lose its scientific credibility, and could even be shut down.

In December 2011, the Laboratory Accreditation Board examined seven laboratories. The board issued 118 "Corrective Action Requests." (This information would not have been made public had *The Detroit News* not filed a Freedom of Information Act suit.) The crime labs had been slow or unable to address the problems. As a result, the board has given the state three extensions, the last and final extension granted in April 2011. If the problems were not fixed, the entire Michigan crime lab operation, and the state's criminal justice system, would be in trouble. If this happened, Michigan's crime lab work might have to be farmed out to other labs, including the FBI laboratory that was itself overwhelmed and struggling with backlogs.

While Michigan state police administrators insisted the problems in the crime labs are more clerical than substantive, many of the shortcomings involved issues of quality control. The accreditation inspectors found that some of the facilities were improperly storing hazardous chemicals. In the lab in Grand Rapids, food was being kept in a refrigerator that contained chemical supplies. There were also problems with measures to prevent lab contamination and evidence tampering. Inspectors saw unescorted visitors roaming the laboratories.

Most of the lab inadequacies involved various forms of record keeping and lab result reporting, problems that reflect sloppy work, lack of supervision, and understaffing. In the Michigan Forensic Science Division, there was a backlog of 10,000 cases.

Improvements in Michigan's crime lab operation kept the system from being closed down. But problems remain.

Criminal investigators and prosecutors, to function effectively, need prompt crime lab results, especially in the fields of DNA and toxicology. Backlogs slow down an investigation, and in some cases, accrue to the benefit of suspects and defendants.

The rates of violent crime across the country are dropping, but the rates of drug abuse are rising, cases that require crime lab analysis. Moreover, prosecutors, to meet jury expectations, are telling detectives to gather as much physical evidence as possible. Crime labs are having a difficult time keeping up with these demands.

30 EXPERTS FROM HELL

Is Forensic Science Real Science?

The problem with much of forensic science theory is that it is largely inductive, and has never been subject to rigorous tests that specifically attempt to falsify it. It has been said that forensic scientists in general have failed to consistently appreciate the implications of the scientific method. The progression through the stages of research, formulation of a hypothesis, testing, analyzing results, and then modifying the hypothesis where necessary has the advantage of built-in evaluators, such as the calculation of error rates, as part of the process, in addition to other benefits, including impartiality. Testing allows the generation of error rates and approximations, and good quality research is generally published, thereby being subject to peer review. Standardization of techniques and theories becomes necessary so as to ensure their validity and applicability in the hands of different researchers, scientists, and practitioners. Eventually, when a theory gains overwhelming support, it may even enter the realm of "general acceptance"; however, this by itself is no substitute for these first stages of scientific endeavor.

While academics note a tension between "science" and "forensic science," there are some who disagree that the traditional "scientific method" is appropriate for forensic science to follow, due to its unique position of straddling the disciplines of both science and law...As one author has written, forensic science operates outside the carefully controlled environment that the traditional sciences endure...Claiming that forensic science does not enjoy the pristine conditions of experimental science, and thus is not directly comparable, avoids a reality that has plagued all scientific research--a reality that has already been managed by experimental scientists through careful and deliberate hypothesis testing, but dismissed by forensic scientists by simply claiming irrelevance to their own practice. [The forensic sciences that have not undergone this rigorous scientific methodology include forensic document examination, blood spatter analysis, fingerprint identification, and human bite mark identification.]

C. Michael Bowers, *Forensic Testimony*, 2013

Courtroom Charlatan

In 1908, Albert Hamilton self-published a brochure about himself called *That Man From Auburn*. In this piece of self-advertisement, the druggist from Auburn, New York presented himself as an expert in chemistry, microscopy, handwriting identification, ink analysis, photography, fingerprints, and forensic toxicology. He also claimed expertise in the fields of gunshot wounds, bullet identification, cause of death determination, anatomy, embalming, and toxicology. To match his impressive qualifications, he awarded himself a medical degree, and from then on was known as Dr. Hamilton.

Hamilton came into prominence in 1915 when he testified for the prosecution as a firearms identification expert in a rural New York murder case. The defendant, Charlie Stielow, an illiterate farmhand who stood accused of shooting to death the elderly couple who owned the farm where he worked, was facing the death sentence. The jury found Stielow guilty of first-degree murder on the strength of a coerced confession, and the testimony of Albert Hamilton who identified a defect inside the barrel of the defendant's .22-caliber revolver as having left its individualistic mark on one of the fatal bullets. Having earned $50 a day for his work on the case, Hamilton impressed the jury with his enlarged photographs of the murder bullet. It all looked quite scientific.

In reality, Hamilton's testimony was pure hokum. The science of firearms identification, as it came to be practiced in the mid-30s, did not exist in 1915. The comparison microscope, an instrument essential to the comparison and analysis of firearms evidence, was invented in 1926. Nevertheless, Hamilton assured the jurors that the fatal bullet had been fired from the defendant's handgun. His findings went unchallenged by the defense, and no one seemed to notice that he hadn't even test-fired the so-called murder weapon. The judge sentenced Stielow to death.

Two years later, a pair of felons confessed to the murder, and the governor of New York formed a commission to review the case. The governor appointed Charles Waite, an investigator in the New York State Attorney General's office, to lead the inquiry. Waite took Stielow's revolver to a New York City police detective who knew about guns. An examination of the weapon convinced the officer that the revolver had not been fired in at least four years. Moreover, a naked eye examination of the bullets the New York police officer test-fired from the .22-caliber revolver, showed vastly different barrel marks than those on the murder slugs.

As a result of these and other post-conviction findings, the governor granted Charlie Stielow, and another defendant in the case, full pardons. Charles Waite, having been introduced to the possibilities of forensic firearms identification, went on to become a prominent practitioner in the field. In 1922, he formed the Bureau of Forensic Ballistics in New York City. In 1926 Dr. Calvin Goddard took over the bureau, the first lab of its kind. An Army surgeon and ordinance officer from Baltimore, Goddard became the most important and qualified firearms identification expert in the world.

In 1923, two Italian-American anarchists, Nicola Sacco and Bartolemo Vanzetti, were convicted of shooting a factory paymaster and his bodyguard to death in South Braintree, Massachusetts. The defendants' attorneys were seeking grounds for a new trial, and called upon the services of Albert Hamilton. Since the Sacco-Vanzetti case had been grabbing headlines for months, Hamilton eagerly got involved in the case.

Nicola Sacco's conviction was based chiefly on the testimony of three firearms identification witnesses who said the bullet that killed the guard had been fired from his Colt .32-caliber handgun. The experts also believed that the gun the police found on Vanzetti had belonged to the slain guard.

After examining the firearms evidence, Hamilton reported that the fatal bullet had not been fired from Sacco's gun, and the weapon that had been in Vanzetti's possession was not the weapon that had once belonged to the bodyguard. Relying on Albert Hamilton's report, the Sacco-Vanzetti defense team filed a motion for a new trial. To counter the motion, the prosecution acquired the services of two experts who had not testified at the trial.

In November 1933, during the hearing on the motion for the new trial, Hamilton conducted an in-court demonstration involving two new Colt revolvers, and Sacco's handgun. The two Colt .32-caliber demonstration revolvers belonged to Hamilton. In front of the judge, and lawyers for both sides, Hamilton disassembled all three revolvers and placed their parts in three piles on the defense table. He then explained the functions of each part, and demonstrated how they were interchangeable. After reassembling the handguns, Hamilton placed the two new weapons back into his pocket, and handed Sacco's Colt to the court clerk. Before he left the courtroom, the judge asked Hamilton to leave his two guns behind.

Several months later, when the judge asked one of the prosecution firearms experts to inspect Sacco's revolver, the expert discovered that the barrel to Sacco's gun was brand new. Following an inquiry, Albert Hamilton admitted that the new barrel on Sacco's Colt had come from one of his revolvers. Although it was obvious to everyone that Hamilton had made the switch, presumably with a mistrial in mind, he denied any wrongdoing. Hamilton continued his association with the Sacco-Vanzetti defense, but he no longer played an important role in the case. He had destroyed his credibility as a firearms expert and witness.

The Sacco-Vanzetti motion for a new trial was denied, and in 1927, the two men died in the electric chair. Prior to their deaths, Dr. Calvin Goddard, the most qualified firearms identification expert in the world, stated that Sacco's gun had in fact been the murder weapon. (Several modern firearms identification experts have examined the ballistics evidence in the case, and agree with Dr. Goddard's findings.)

The barrel-switching incident in the Sacco-Vanzetti case apparently had little effect on Hamilton's phony career as a forensic scientist. Eight years after the Sacco-Vanzetti debacle, he testified for the defense in a New York murder case. In 1932, Stephen Witherell murdered his father, Charles. The defendant admitted shooting his father at point blank range with a Remington rifle he had stolen from his cousin. An expert with the New York City Police Department identified this rifle as the murder weapon.

By the time the trial rolled around, Stephen Witherell had recanted his confession. He took the stand on his on behalf and denied shooting anyone. In fact, he denied the body in question was even his father's. (Decomposition and the massive gunshot wound to the victim's head had made the corpse unrecognizable.) Albert Hamilton took the stand, and testified that there were two gunshot wounds on the body: the head wound caused by a rifle, and a wound on the victim's hand, made by a handgun. Actually, there was no hand wound at all, the victim had lost two fingers in an industrial accident. Once again, Hamilton had proven that he was incompetent, and a charlatan.

In 1934, Hamilton tried to insert himself in the Lindbergh kidnapping case by identifying a man named Manny Strewl as the writer of the ransom letters. Hamilton was not a qualified questioned document expert, and the writer of the extortion notes turned out to be Bruno Richard Hauptmann. The carpenter from the Bronx, an illegal alien from Germany with a criminal history in his home country, was executed in 1936 for the murder of the Lindbergh baby.

Albert Hamilton continued to disgrace himself as an expert witness in several forensic fields for another ten years, making him one of the most notorious forensic charlatans in American history. If there is anything to learn from this man's career, it is that the woods are full of phony experts, and if judges let down their guards, we will have charlatans in our courtrooms, and baloney in our verdicts.

Dr. Ralph Erdmann

Most forensic pathologists are hardworking, well intentioned, and competent. Even the best of them make honest mistakes. But over the years there have been several high-profile embarrassments to the profession. These forensic pathologists, because they were careless, incompetent, corrupt, or weak, did great harm to criminal defendants, victims of crime, and forensic science. Dr. Ralph Erdmann, a run-amok forensic pathologist who worked many years in west Texas represents the worst of the worst.

In 1981, 25 years after acquiring a medical degree in Mexico, Dr. Erdmann moved to Childress in Lubbock County, Texas. He began, on a private contract basis, doing autopsies for five small hospitals in the county. He moved to Amarillo in 1983 and began performing autopsies for hire throughout the Texas panhandle region. Over the next decade, Dr. Erdmann conducted more than 3,000 autopsies in 41 jurisdictions. In 1990, at the height of his activity, he performed 480 autopsies. The following year he did 310, most of which were performed in Lubbock County. For his work in Lubbock County, Dr. Erdmann received an annual fee of $140,000. In the smaller counties Dr. Erdmann charged $650 per autopsy. The forensic pathologist had a large territory to cover and was constantly on the move, performing autopsies on the run.

Because he covered a rural area Dr. Erdmann did not always work under ideal conditions. In cases of decomposing bodies, many of the smaller hospitals denied him access to autopsy space because of the stink. As a result he performed autopsies in funeral home garages, hospital loading docks, parking lots, and abandoned houses. Dr. Erdmann once performed an autopsy on a door laid across two 55-gallon drums.

It wasn't just his take-charge work ethic that made Dr. Erdmann so popular with detectives and county prosecutors. What they especially liked about this pathologist was his unabashed eagerness to tailor his autopsy findings to their law enforcement needs. If the prosecution needed a victim or suspect to have alcohol in his or her blood that was not a problem. It didn't matter that no blood-alcohol test had been administered in the case. If a certain time of death became necessary to incriminate a defendant, Dr. Erdmann would provide it, even if such a precise estimation violated the rules of science.

Because Dr. Erdmann made their jobs so easy, many detectives and prosecutors turned a blind eye to his personal weirdness, sloppy work habits, questionable science, embarrassing omissions, and patent dishonesty. Even with the support of the law enforcement community, Dr. Erdmann was so obviously unfit for the job he was eventually drummed out of the profession.

By 1992, after a number of defense attorneys began challenging and exposing Dr. Erdmann's methods and findings, the outlandish nature of his malpractice began to catch up to him. That year he was forced to surrender his Texas medical license to the State Board of Medical Examiners. He also pleaded guilty to charging several counties for autopsies he had not conducted. The judge sentenced Erdmann to 10 years of probation and 200 hours of community service. He also had to pay $17,000 in restitution. The following year Dr. Erdmann left Texas for the state of Washington.

A review of Dr. Erdmann's work explains how he had been able to perform so many autopsies. He cut corners. For example, he didn't bother to weigh the internal organs he removed. And in many cases, he didn't even bother to cut them out of the corpse. He simply estimated their weights. Dr. Erdmann got caught doing this when the family of a man he had autopsied noticed, in the autopsy report, the weight of the dead man's spleen. Years before his death this man's spleen had been surgically removed.

Even in situations where the cause of death was obviously murder, Dr. Erdmann didn't always get it right. In the case of a body found in a dumpster, Dr. Erdmann reported the cause of death as pneumonia. The police later arrested the suspect who had stolen the dead man's car, shot him in the head, then disposed of his body in that dumpster. Perhaps this man had pneumonia when he was shot to death, but it was the bullet that killed him. In another body-in-the-dumpster case, Dr. Erdmann lost the dead man's head, the body part containing the fatal bullet that would have connected the shooter to the murder. Without the head or the bullet, the suspect could not be prosecuted.

In a fatal hit-and-run case, Dr. Erdmann testified that the victim had died instantly of a broken neck. He based this finding on his examination of the 14-year-old victim's brain. But when the body was exhumed, another forensic pathologist found that Erdmann had not even bothered to open the boy's skull.

In the case of an infant who died in a bathtub, Dr. Erdmann determined that someone had killed the baby with a blow to the stomach. This led to the arrest of the man who was in the house when the infant died. After a second forensic pathologist examined the body, the prosecutor had to drop the murder charge. The baby had drowned accidentally. The cause of death: asphyxia.

As reported in the *ABA Journal*, as a result of Ralph Erdmann's bungled and incomplete autopsies, the defendants in 20 murder cases had grounds to appeal their convictions. The panel of experts who looked at 300 of his autopsy reports--a relatively small sampling--found that 1/3 of the bodies had not even been cut open. When confronted with this evidence, Dr. Erdmann explained it away as clerical errors. He never admitted wrongdoing and would continue to insist that he was not dishonest or incompetent. Yes, he had made a few mistakes, but he had been forced to work under unfavorable conditions. The forensic pathologist accused his critics of being revenge-minded defense attorneys and characterized the investigation of his work and career as a witch-hunt.

Eventually lawsuits and public pressure drove Dr. Erdmann out of the profession. He slipped into obscurity and has largely been forgotten.

The Fingerprint Expert

During the first ninety years of fingerprint history, defense attorneys who had clients whose latent fingerprints were found as the scenes of crimes had one option--plead them guilty in return for a lighter sentence. No one considered questioning the credibility or competence of a fingerprint expert, and no one dared challenge the scientific reliability of fingerprint identification. Fingerprints either matched or they didn't. There was nothing to challenge.

Those days are over. Since 2000, there have been numerous cases of latent fingerprint misidentification in the United States and Europe. As it turns out, many fingerprint experts in the United States are undertrained, dishonest, and biased in favor of the police. Most of the nation's competent examiners are overworked due to crime lab budget cuts. Today, it is not unusual for a criminal trial to feature dueling fingerprint experts. This is not good for forensic science, or the criminal justice system.

Earmark Identification

In the early morning hours of December 16, 1994, near Vancouver, Washington, an intruder entered James McCann's bedroom and bludgeoned him to death. In another bedroom, the burglar fractured the skull of McCann's son who managed to crawl outside where he was discovered by a passerby. Questioned at the hospital, the boy told the police he hadn't gotten a good look at the attacker whom he described at 25 to 35 years old, dark complexioned, about six feet tall, and of medium build. George Miller, a fingerprint examiner with the Washington State Crime Lab, lifted a latent ear-print off the surface of James McCann's bedroom door. The killer had apparently pressed his head against the door listening for signs of activity before entering the room. Miller processed the house for fingerprints as well, but they all turned out to belong to occupants of the dwelling.

Although he had red hair and didn't otherwise fit the general description of the killer, the police suspected David Wayne Kunze, the 45-year-old ex-husband of the woman James McCann was about to marry. When Kunze had learned of the upcoming marriage four days before the murder, he had become upset. This led investigators to suspect Kunze had attacked the victims out of jealousy and rage. The intruder had stolen McCann's television set, VCR, stereo speakers, and wallet, an aspect of the case detectives explained away by theorizing that Kunze had taken these things to throw them off his trail. Convinced that the scene had been staged to look like a burglary, the police made no effort to identify a homicidal intruder through the missing property. David Kunze consented to a search of his truck, boat, storage locker, and safety deposit box. Detectives found nothing that connected him to the home invasion and murder.

Three months passed without further developments in the investigation. Then Michael Grubb, a criminalist with the Washington State Crime Lab, compared the partial ear-print latent with photographs of Kunze's left ear and concluded that it "could have been made by David Kunze." Six months later, on September 21, 1995, Kunze voluntarily agreed to have fingerprint examiner George Miller and Michael Grubb take seven exemplar prints of his left ear. The criminalists applied hand lotion to the suspect's ear then placed panes of glass against it, using various degrees of pressure. Following that procedure, the criminalists dusted the glass with fingerprint powder, and lifted the prints with transparent tape.

Michael Grubb compared the seven exemplars with the crime scene ear latent and concluded, "David Kunze is the likely source for the ear-print and cheek-print which were lifted from the outside of the bedroom door at the homicide scene." George Miller, the crime lab fingerprint analyst, declined to offer an opinion regarding the identification of the crime scene ear latent. He said he identified fingerprints, not earmarks. In June 1996, a year and a half after the murder, and eight months after Michael Grubb identified the crime scene ear-print, the Clark County prosecutor charged Kunze with aggravated murder, assault, robbery, and burglary.

In a pretrial motion to exclude the ear-print identification, Kunze's attorney petitioned the judge for so-called *Frye* hearing. In 1923, a U. S. District Court in Washington D. C. held that lie detection technology had not been accepted in the general scientific community as a legitimate science. As a result, lie detection results did not constitute admissible evidence. This ruling became known as the "general acceptance test." To determine if latent ear-print identification was an accepted function within the forensic science community, the prosecutor and defense attorney in the Kunze case offered expert witness on both sides of the issue in a *Frye* hearing held in December 1996. This would be the most thorough, in-depth judicial/scientific review of ear-print identification in legal and forensic science history.

On the issue of latent ear-print identification as a legitimate forensic science, the prosecution presented three advocates against the defense's twelve witnesses, who, in varying degrees, were not enthusiastic about this form of pattern analysis. Michael Grubb, the manager of the Washington State Crime Lab in Seattle who had identified the crime scene ear-print as probably Kunze's, testified that comparing an earmark to a known ear print was not unlike other forms of impression identification. A criminalist who specialized in bullet-striation and tool-mark identification, Grubb said that if you can analyze patterns made by tires, shoes, fingers, gun barrels, and tools, you can render an opinion on the source of an earmark.

The next prosecution witness, Alfred V. Iannarelli, said he had studied the evidence in the McCann murder case and was certain that the crime scene earmark was an "exact" match to Kunze's left ear. Iannarelli had never worked in a crime lab, had not been to college, and had testified only once as an expert witness. He had been a deputy sheriff with the Alameda County Sheriff's Office, and the chief of campus security at California State University at Hayward. From 1948 to 1962, Iannarelli had photographed 7,000 ears; from this database he had come to the conclusion that no two ears are the same. He had also devised an ear classification system based upon twelve "anthropometric measurements," a system featured in his 1964 book, *The Iannarelli System of Ear Identification*. In 1989 Iannarelli self-published a second edition of this text, titled *Ear Identification* that included a section on latent earmark analysis. He was unable, however, to cite any ear-print studies other than his own, which explained why his books didn't contain bibliographies.

In ear-print identification, it became clear there were no texts other than Iannarelli's, no community of experts, not one section within any crime lab that specialized in this kind of work, and no professional organizations or certifying bodies. Besides Iannarelli, there was one other analyst devoted solely to this form of identification. If anyone could claim to be an internationally known ear-print expert, it was a police officer from Amsterdam named Cornelius Van der Lugt. It was therefore not surprising that Van der Lugt had examined the McCann murder scene evidence, and was the third prosecution expert at the *Frye* hearing. Van der Lugt had become interested in the ear-print identification field after reading Iannarelli's books in the early 1990s, and since had analyzed ear-print evidence in 200 cases in the Netherlands, United Kingdom, and Western Europe. He had testified as an expert in six trials, all of which were in Holland, where judges, not juries, determine a defendant's guilt or innocence.

According to Cornelius Van der Lugt, many suspects, when presented with his expert ear-print analysis, had confessed and pleaded guilty. In one case, a suspect admitted putting his ear to the door, but denied breaking in to the structure. Van der Lugt had never worked in a crime laboratory, attended college, or received any kind of formal training in science. He was certain, however, that David Kunze was the source of the McCann murder latent ear-print. As part of his *Frye* testimony, Van der Lugt praised the work done by Michael Grubb and George Miller in obtaining the seven ear-print exemplars, noting how they had varied the amount of pressure against the ear until the known and crime scene prints looked alike. When asked if ear-print identification, as a forensic science, was accepted around the world, Van der Lugt said that it was.

While the Kunze prosecution could not have put on a stronger case for ear-print identification, it was arguably not enough to meet the *Frye* standards. In other words, at least in theory, Kunze's defense attorney could have won the *Frye* debate without mounting an anti-ear-print case. But leaving nothing to chance, the defense hit back with a dozen impressive witnesses, leading off with Dr. Ellis Kerley, a physical anthropologist, and former president of the American Academy of Forensic Sciences and the American Board of Forensic Anthropology. Dr. Kerley said it was reasonable to assume that no two ears were the same, but he wasn't sure this uniqueness would always reveal itself in a crime scene earmark. He didn't consider Iannarelli's books works of science, and didn't approve of Van der Lugt's technique of getting an exemplar to match a crime scene latent by varying the pressure against the suspect's ear. "We don't do that in science...because we're not trying to make them look alike," he said. In Dr. Kerley's opinion, ear-print identification had not achieved general acceptance in the forensic science community.

Andre Moenssens, a law professor at the University of Missouri at Kansas City, the author of articles and law school texts on forensic science, and a former fingerprint expert in Belgium, testified that the "forensic sciences...do not recognize, as a separate discipline, the identification of ear impressions. There are people in the forensic science community, the broader forensic science community, who feel that it can be done. But if we are talking about a general acceptance by scientists, there is no such general acceptance...To my knowledge, there has been no investigation in the possible rate of error that comparisons between known and unknown ear samples might produce."

Following the *Frye* testimony of ten other recognized forensic scientists who did not consider latent ear-print identification a true science, the judge ruled that ear-print identification had in fact gained general acceptance in the scientific community. The decision was stunning in that it was so out of sync with the weight of the expert testimony. It was certainly bad news for David Kunze, because the prosecution would have had no case if the ear-print evidence had been excluded on the grounds it didn't meet the *Frye* test. Now the state could go forward against him.

The case went to trial on June 25, 1997. The prosecutor chose not to put Alfred Iannarelli on the stand, but the jury heard the testimony of state criminalist Michael Grubb, and the ear-print guru Cornelius Van der Lugt. A jailhouse informant followed the prosecution ear-print analysts to the stand. The snitch claimed that Kunze had confessed to him while in custody. The prosecution rested its case without identifying the murder weapon, connecting the defendant to the crime scene through DNA or fingerprints, or linking him to any of the items taken from house.

For some reason, the defense did not call upon the testimony of Dr. Ellis Kerley, Professor Andre Moenssens, or any of the other anti-ear-print *Frye* witnesses. As a result, the jury found David Kunze guilty of aggravated murder, burglary, and robbery. The judge sentenced him to life without parole.

Kunze appealed his conviction, and in 1999, a three-judge panel ruled that "the trial court erred by allowing Michael Grubb and Cornelius Van der Lugt to testify that Kunze was the likely or probable source of the ear latent, and that a new trial is therefore required." The appellate court instructed the prosecutor in the second trial not to prejudice the defense by referring to the first trial, and the resulting conviction. The appellate judges didn't want the second jury to know that Kunze had been found guilty on the strength of ear-print identification.

In March 2001, ten days into the second trial, the prosecutor made reference to the earlier conviction, and the presiding judge had no choice but to declare a mistrial. The prosecutor, after several jurors announced that had the case gone to them, they would have acquitted the defendant, announced that a third trial would not be scheduled.

DNA Expert From Hell

In 1990, prosecutors in Cook County, Illinois charged John Willis with several counts of rape in connection with a series of sexual assaults committed in the late 1980s on Chicago's South Side. Willis, a petty thief, and illiterate, denied raping the women even though several of the victims had picked him out of a lineup.

The only physical evidence in the Willis case was a scrap of toilet paper containing traces of semen. Police took this evidence to the Chicago Police Lab where Dr. Pamela Fish examined the evidence. Dr. Fish had come to the lab in 1979 with bachelors and master's degrees in biology from Loyola University. Ten years later, after taking courses at night, she earned a Ph.D. in biology from Illinois Institute of Technology. According to her handwritten lab notes, Dr. Fish determined that the secretor of the semen had type A blood. John Willis had type B blood thereby excluding him as the rapist. Dr. Fish reported, however, in contradiction to her lab notes, that the semen on the tissue possessed type B blood. She testified to this at Willis' 1991 trial. The jury, in addition to believing in Dr. Fish, believed eleven prosecution rape victim/eyewitnesses that identified the defendant as the rapist. The jury found Willis guilty and the judge sentenced him to 100 years in prison.

Eight years later, a south Chicago rapist confessed to these sexual assaults after being linked to the crimes through DNA analysis. An appeals judge set aside the Willis conviction and he was set free. On the day of his release, Dr. Fish, now the head of the biochemistry unit at the state crime lab, spoke at a DNA seminar for judges. (The Chicago Police Lab had been incorporated into the Illinois crime lab system in 1996.)

The Willis reversal led to a 2001 review of Dr. Fish's cases by the renowned DNA expert from Berkeley, California, Dr. Edward Blake. Dr. Blake studied nine cases in which Dr. Fish had testified that her blood-typing tests had produced inconclusive results. Dr. Blake found that Dr. Fish's test results had actually exonerated the defendants involved and that she had given false testimony at those trials. Dr. Blake characterized Dr. Fish's work as "scientific fraud."

In the summer of 2001, a state representative at a legislative hearing on prosecutorial misconduct suggested to the head of the Illinois State Police that Dr. Fish be transferred out of the crime lab into a position where she could do less harm. (In the public sector this is considered harsh employee discipline.) The police administrator ignored the recommendation.

In 2002, DNA exonerated three more Illinois men who were in prison for rape. These prisoners had been behind bars since 1987. Dr. Fish had testified for the prosecution in all three cases. Two years later, after the state paid John Willis a large settlement for his wrongful prosecution and incarceration, the state refused to renew Dr. Fish's employment contract. Rather than firing Dr. Fish, the state reluctantly refused to rehire her. (I would image that Dr. Fish's forensic misbehavior did not keep her from enjoying her government retirement benefits.)

In 2008, Marlon Pendleton, two years after his release from an Illinois prison where he'd been wrongfully incarcerated thirteen years on a rape conviction, sued the Chicago Police Department and Dr. Fish. The plaintiff accused a pair of detectives of manufacturing an identification made at a lineup. (These cops were notorious for this kind of behavior.) He charged Dr. Fish with perjury in connection with her DNA testimony at the trial, testimony that convinced the jury he had raped the victim. As of July 2014, Pendleton's civil suit has not been resolved.

The Celebrity Expert

Dr. Henry Lee is as close to being a household name as any forensic scientist in U.S. history. He achieved fame in a profession whose practitioners generally operate behind the scenes. In the criminal justice field, it's usually the defense attorneys who get the headlines, and in forensic science, it's often forensic pathologists like Dr. Michael Baden and Dr. Cyril Wecht.

Dr. Henry Lee, because he rose to fame in the era of true crime television, enjoyed a level of celebrity more intense and intimate than his well-known predecessors. He made hundreds of television appearances, and hosted a show on Court TV called *Trace Evidence: The Case Files of Dr. Henry Lee*. Dr. Lee's personality, demeanor, and life story helped make him a bigger-than-life character. Like sports stars and major film and television actors, he tended to be vain and dramatic. On the witness stand, he informed jurors and, as a charismatic courtroom showman, entertained them. When Dr. Lee testified for the prosecution, he became the defense attorney's worst nightmare. When he appeared on behalf of the defense, it was not good news for the prosecutor. In either case, the media loved it, and so did the jurors.

Dr. Henry Chang-Yu Lee was born in Rugao City, China on November 22, 1938. When Henry was four, the Chinese communists murdered his father. Two years later, his family fled to Taiwan to avoid the communist revolution. After graduating from the Taiwan Central Police College in 1960 with a degree in police science, Henry jointed the Taipei Police Department. Six years later, after rising to the rank of captain, he came to the United States where, in 1972, he graduated from New York City's John Jay College of criminal justice with a bachelor degree in science. In 1974, he earned a master's degree in biochemistry from New York University. A year later, he was awarded a Ph.D. in biochemistry.

In 1979, Dr. Lee became the director of the Connecticut State Police Forensic Laboratory where he also held the title of chief criminalist. Following his retirement from the lab in 2000, Dr. Lee began teaching at the University of New Haven where he founded the Henry C. Lee Forensic Institute. According to his resume, Dr. Lee has been awarded several honorary degrees, written more than 20 books (most with co-authors), published numerous scientific articles, given hundreds of speeches, investigated 4,000 homicide cases (not possible), and consulted with more than 300 law enforcement agencies.

The Wood Chipper Case

Dr. Lee vaulted onto the national stage in 1986 when an airline pilot named Richard Crafts went on trial in Connecticut for murdering his wife, Halle. Having incurred her husband's wrath by announcing her plans to divorce him, Halle Crafts had covertly audiotaped his threats to kill her. Perhaps even more incriminating, Richard Crafts was seen by a motorist, on the night of Halle's disappearance, operating a commercial-grade wood chipper in the midst of a blizzard along the bank of the Housatonic River. The audiotape and the wood chipper sighting led the police to suspect Crafts of murdering his wife. But investigators had a serious problem: they didn't have a corpse. Faced with one of those maddening cases of a good suspect, but no physical evidence, the homicide detectives called on Dr. Lee

In the couple's bedroom, Dr. Lee found traces of the victim's blood. When he examined a chainsaw that had been in the suspect's possession, Dr. Lee discovered hair follicles, traces of blood, and tissue that he identified as the victim's. In the rented wood chipper, Lee recovered the same, and at the spot where Richard Crafts had been seen operating the equipment, Dr. Lee found fragments of the victim's teeth and bones, along with follicles of her hair. It wasn't much, but it was enough to establish that Halle Crafts had been murdered. From this evidence, Dr. Lee was able to reconstruct the crime, theorizing that the defendant had bludgeoned his wife to death in their bedroom, frozen her body in a home freezer, cut her into pieces with the chainsaw, then shoved the body parts into the wood chipper which sprayed her remains into the river.

The Crafts trial jury, obviously impressed with Dr. Lee and his evidence, found the defendant guilty of first-degree murder. A few years later, while serving his life sentence, Richard Crafts confessed to murdering his wife. Featuring blood and gore, an attractive victim, a suburban killer, a dramatic trial, and scientific investigation in the mold of Sherlock Holmes, the wood chipper case turned Dr. Henry Lee into a celebrity forensic scientist.

William Kennedy Smith Case

Five years after his famous Crafts murder trial testimony, Dr. Lee took the stand on behalf of a defendant named William Kennedy Smith who was on trail for an alleged 1991 date rape that dominated the news because of the Kennedy family connection. According to the accused, following a night of drinking in Palm Beach, Florida with his accuser, the two had engaged in consensual sex on the lawn of the Kennedy family estate. Dr. Lee, to help prove that the defendant's partner had consented to sex, testified that he had found no grass stains on the woman's pantyhose, evidence one would expect to find had there been a struggle. To illustrate this point, Dr. Lee produced a grass-stained handkerchief he had rubbed against the grass in his own yard. The jury found William Kennedy Smith not guilty.

Dr. Lee's testimony in the Kennedy case drew criticism from John Hicks, the director of the FBI Laboratory, who called it "outrageous." Hicks characterized Dr. Lee's handkerchief experiment as unscientific, and labeled the conclusions drawn from it speculative. The crime lab director pointed out that the handkerchief was not made of the same fabric as the pantyhose, and the conditions that had created the handkerchief stains did not necessarily replicate the environment at the alleged crime site. Criticism of this type--that Dr. Lee's testimony is more theater than science--has followed him throughout his career.

The O. J. Simpson Case

Dr. Lee's testimony on behalf of O. J. Simpson in 1995 did not endear him to many of his forensic science colleagues. In general, Dr. Lee's testimony in that case helped the Simpson defense in five ways. It depicted Los Angeles police detectives and crime scene technicians as incompetent; it suggested that blood evidence had been contaminated; it supported the theory that evidence against the defendant had been planted; it pushed the time of the crime forward 45 minutes which accommodated Simpson's alibi; and it laid the groundwork for the theory than Nicole Simpson and Ronald Goldman had been murdered by more than one person.

On the last point, Dr. Lee's testimony contradicted the testimony of the FBI's renowned footwear identification expert, William Bodziak. Dr. Lee identified a bloody stain on an envelope and scrap of paper found in Nicole Simpson's house as a shoe print that didn't match the footwear--the Bruno Magli Italian designer shoes--prosecutors believed the defendant was wearing when he committed the murders. Mr. Bodziak testified that a shoe had not made this bloody print. Douglas Deedrich, also from the FBI Crime Lab, testified that the bloody pattern was in fact a fabric print.

At the Simpson trial, Dr. Lee also raised the possibility that a bloodstain on Ronald Goldman's blue jeans had been made by a shoe that was not a Bruno Magli. On cross-examination, when pressed about this blood print identification, Dr. Lee said that *if* these patterns were footwear marks, they were not made by the Bruno Magli brand.

Critics of Dr. Lee's testimony in the O. J. Simpson case called it an example of "blowing smoke"--a term referring to the giving of vague defense testimony intended to muddy the water in an effort to create reasonable doubt.

Since his testimony in the O. J. Simpson case, Dr. Lee has been involved in dozens of celebrated cases that include the JonBenet Ramsey murder, the Scott Peterson case, and the Phil Spector murder case where he was accused of removing a piece of crime scene evidence that might have incriminated the defendant.

Dr. Lee's participation at various levels in so many cases involving such a variety of evidence and analysis is unusual for a forensic scientist. In the field, he is almost a one-of-a-kind practitioner. At the core of his expertise, he is a forensic serologist, one who examines crime scene biological stains to determine their identify and origin. As a crime scene reconstruction expert, one who determines what happened at the crime site by taking into consideration all of the physical clues, Dr. Lee is also a blood-spatter analyst. As one who studies physical evidence to figure out, after the fact, what occurred at the scene of the crime, Dr. Lee analyzes all kinds of physical evidence, including hair follicles, fibers, bite marks, bone fragments, brain matter, tissue, gunshot powder residue, soil, dust, pollen, and other forms of trace evidence.

Dr. Lee also studied latent footwear and fingerprint patterns, and analyzed bullet trajectories. He was a generalist in a field of narrowly defined specialists. This had its appeal, and explained why he had been able to insert himself into so many celebrated cases.

Forensic Hair Identification

Forensic analysts who microscopically compare crime scene hair follicles with samples from a suspect's head or other part of the body note similarities or differences in hair length, thickness, texture, curl, color, and appearance of the medulla, the cells that runs up the center of the hair shaft. A follicle, however, cannot be individualized like a fingerprint. A hair identification expert can declare, for example, that the defendant's hair looks like a crime scene follicle, or is consistent in appearance with the questioned evidence, but they are not supposed to testify that a follicle at the scene of a crime could have come from the defendant and no one else. What nobody knows about forensic hair identification is this: if two follicles look alike in all respects, what are the chances they have come from the same person? Just how strong is such as match as incriminating evidence?

Hair identification experts also analyze crime scene strands of fiber and compare them with samples of clothing, carpets, blankets, and other fabrics associated with the defendant. Fibers can be distinguished by material, shape and color--there are 7,000 dyes used in the United States. A fiber expert can testify, for example, that a fiber on a murder victim's body is *consistent* in appearance with carpet fibers from the trunk of the defendant's vehicle. He cannot, however, say unequivocally that the follicle on the corpse came from the defendant's trunk.

Up until the mid-1990s, hair and fiber experts were routinely pushing the scientific envelope by identifying crime scene follicles and fibers the way an expert would identify a latent fingerprint. In hundreds, if not thousands of cases, defendants went to prison on the strength of this form of expert testimony. When DNA came on the scene, abuses in hair and fiber identification were exposed, and the scientific unreliability of these matches was dramatically revealed.

In Texas alone, between 1995 and 2002, DNA analysis exonerated 30 men who had been convicted solely on crime scene hair identification. Dr. Edward Blake, the Berkeley, California DNA pioneer, put forensic hair identification in perspective: "They did it because they could get away with it. A defendant in Idaho and another in Florida were sent to death row in cases where the only evidence against them were jailhouse informants and crime scene hair identifications."

Human Bite Mark Identification

The identification of a series of bruises or abrasions, usually in the shape of two semi-circles or brackets, as a human bite mark made by a particular set of teeth is a function of forensic dentistry referred to as bite mark identification. This form of impression identification, also called forensic odontology, is based on the assumption that no two people in the world have front teeth that are identical in thickness, shape, relationship to each other, and patterns of wear.

The process of comparing a bite mark to a known set of teeth is not unlike the identification of latent fingerprints, footwear, and tire track impressions. Bite mark wounds are found on victims of murder, rape, and child molestation. This type of crime scene evidence is preserved by life-size photography, tooth mark tracings onto transparent sheets, and dental casts of the impressions themselves. A suspect might be asked to bite down on a pliable surface for an impression sample, have a cast made of his teeth, or both. Usually, connecting a suspect to a victim through expert bite mark testimony will be enough evidence, by itself, to sustain a criminal conviction.

The field of bite mark identification exploded in the 1980s, and hundreds, if not thousands of defendants between 1983 and 2002 were sent to prison on the strength of bite mark testimony. Although bite mark identification had been a recognized branch of forensic science since 1970, it was the 1979 trial of serial killer Ted Bundy in south Florida that put this form of identification on the map the way the O. J. Simpson case, in the mid-1990s, popularized DNA profiling.

At the peak of bite mark evidence credibility among forensic scientists, detectives, prosecutors, and judges, this form of impression identification was put on the level with the matching of fingerprints. However, by 2003, forensic scientists were seriously questioning the assumption that bite marks were as unique and identifiable as latent fingerprints.

Over the years several leaders in the bite mark field oversold the reliability of this form of identification. For example, in 1977, Dr. Lowell J. Levine, a forensic dentistry consultant to the New York City Medical Examiner's Office, wrote: "Since every person's teeth are unique in respect to spacing, twisting, turning, shapes, tipping toward the tongue or lips, wear patterns, breakage, fillings, caps, loss and the like, all of which occur in limitless combinations, it is possible for them to leave a pattern which for identification purposes is as good as a fingerprint."

In 1996, Dr. C. Michael Bowers, a prominent southern California forensic dentist, was one of the first forensic scientists to raise doubts about the credibility of bite make identification when he wrote: "Physical matching of bite marks is a non-science which was developed with little testing and no published error rate....An opinion is worth nothing unless the supportive data is clearly describable and can be demonstrated in court. How does one weight the importance of a single rotated tooth in a bite mark when the suspect has a similar tooth? The value judgments range widely on the value of this feature. This is not science. Instead, statistical levels of confidence must be included in the process."

In a bite mark identification exercise Dr. Bowers conducted in a workshop at the 1999 American Academy of Forensic Science conference, 63 percent of the practitioners who participated made an incorrect identification, findings that displeased many in the field when Dr. Bowers published the results of his experiment. In an article published in 2003 in the *British Dental Journal*, Dr. D. K. Whittaker, a forensic dentistry professor at the University of Wales, explained why bite mark evidence is so difficult to identify, particularly bite marks on skin:

"Human bites on skin are difficult to interpret because skin is not good 'impression' material. Moreover, victims may struggle and movement will distort the image of the bite. Skin surfaces are not flat and visual distortion may be present, often heightened by photographic distortion caused by inadequate imaging techniques. Human dentitions, whilst possibly being unique in the small nuances of tooth size, shape, angulation and texture may not inflict unique bite marks that can only record gross and not fine detail. If the victim survives, the injury may change due to infection or subsequent healing and if the victim is deceased, putrefaction may introduce distortion."

Before forensic dentists in Great Britain can testify in court as bite mark experts, they must have made a minimum of twenty such identifications in other cases. In the United States, after two bite mark identifications, the American Board of Forensic Odontology certifies the practitioner as a forensic dentist. As a result, being certified in this forensic field in the United States doesn't carry much weight. (In fact, two of America's most notorious charlatans in the field were both board certified bite mark experts.)

In 2004, as part of a journalistic series on forensic science, the *Chicago Tribune* examined 154 state and federal trials involving bite mark identification testimony. In more than a quarter of these cases the prosecution and the defense forensic witnesses presented expert opinions that were diametrically opposed. If bite mark identification is an exact science practiced by highly qualified experts, this many experts should not have been testifying against each other.

The Clarence Dean Case

In 2007, 33-year-old Kristine Yitref was found beaten and strangled to death under a bed in a hotel near New York City's Times Square. Detectives arrested a 41-year-old fugitive sex offender from Alabama named Clarence Brian Dean. According to the suspect, he had killed Yitref in self-defense after she had lured him to the hotel room for sex. Dean claimed that this woman and a male friend of hers had tried to rob him. (This alleged assailant has not been identified.)

Clarence Dean is still waiting to be tried in the case. The delay has been caused by numerous challenges to the findings of a forensic dentist who has matched Dean's teeth to a bite mark on Yitref's body. In 2012, at a hearing to resolve the issue of the admissibility of bite mark identification evidence, Dr. David Senn, a San Antonio forensic dentist, testified that bite mark analysis is valid when limited to a closed population of suspects. Dr. Senn said that all of the past bite mark mistakes and misidentifications cannot be blamed on individual dentists but on the science itself.

Dr. Mary Bush, a researcher at the University of Buffalo also testified at the pre-trial hearing challenging bite mark identification. Her research, published in the *Journal of Forensic Sciences*, has found that human dentition is not unique and cannot be accurately transferred to skin.

On September 5, 2013, Manhattan State Supreme Court Justice Maxwell Wiley ruled that the bite mark testimony must be allowed at Clarence Dean's upcoming murder trial. A representative of New York's Innocent Project told reporters that Judge Wiley's decision was "contrary to the overwhelming consensus of the scientific community."

Expert Versus Expert

In 1994, police found the body of 25-year-old Melissa Padilla in a concrete pipe along Route 1 near Woodbridge, New Jersey. Naked from the waist down, she had been beaten and sexually assaulted. The killer had bitten her on the chin and left breast. Padilla had been abducted the night before from a nearby convenience store in the Avenel section of Woodbridge. The police had no suspects, and the investigation quickly died on the vine.

In April 1995, the state police in Maine contacted the Padilla case investigators with a lead. They had arrested 31-year-old Steven Fortin for the sexual assault of a female state police officer who had been bitten on the chin and left breast. Fortin was also living in Woodbridge at the time of Padilla's murder. Although the suspect denied involvement in the New Jersey homicide, he pleaded guilty, in November 1995, to the assault in Maine. The judge sentenced him to 20 years.

Five years after entering prison in Maine, the authorities in New Jersey put Fortin on trial for the murder of Melissa Padilla. The prosecution's key witness, FBI criminal profiler Robert Hazelwood, connected the defendant to the Padilla murder by noting similarities in its criminal MO to the sexual assault in Maine. The jury in New Jersey, on the strength of this testimony, found Fortin guilty. In February 2004, the New Jersey Supreme Court overturned the conviction on the grounds it was not supported by sufficient evidence.

New Jersey prosecutors retried Steven Fortin in 2007. This time they had physical evidence connecting him to the victim. A DNA analyst testified that the defendant could not be excluded as the primary source of the saliva recovered from the Marlboro cigarette butt found near Padilla's body. According to this expert, only one out of 3,500 people could be linked to this evidence. Moreover, the defendant could not be excluded as the DNA source of the blood and tissue traces found under the victim's fingernails.

Dr. Lowell J. Levine, one of the pioneers in the field of crime scene bite mark identification, a forensic dentist from upstate New York, had compared photographs of the victim's bite mark wounds (These photographs did not include a ruler measuring the marks because the photographer didn't recognize the bruises as teeth marks.) with photographs of the defendant's front teeth. Dr. Levine noticed a space between Fortin's lower front incisors that corresponded to a space in the mark on the victim's left breast. Dr. Levine testified that although he could not say to a scientific certainty that the defendant had bitten the victim, he could not exclude him as the biter.

Dr. Adam Freeman, a forensic dentist from Westport, Connecticut, testified that in his study of 259 bite mark cases, the largest study of its kind, he found only 5 cases in which the attackers had bitten their victims on the chin and the breast. Dr. Freeman's testimony helped link the defendant, circumstantially, to the sexual assault in Maine for which he had pleaded guilty.

Steven Fortin's defense team countered Dr. Levine with another world-renowned forensic scientist, Dr. Norman Sperber, the chief forensic dentist with the California Department of Justice. Sperber had testified for the defense at the first trial, but the jury had disregarded his testimony. Dr. Sperber, like Dr. Levine, had testified for the prosecution in the 1979 trial of serial killer Ted Bundy. Since then, Dr. Sperber had appeared as an expert witness in 215 trials. According to his analysis, Steven Fortin could not have made the bite marks on Melissa Padilla's body. According to Dr. Sperber: "The tracing of his [Fortin's] teeth doesn't even come close to the crime scene bite marks." The witness went on to say that bite mark analysis has limitations as a form of crime scene associative evidence. It is not as reliable, he said, as DNA and fingerprint identification. "Skin is a serious limitation for bite mark analysis because it rebounds and is movable," he said. "Bite mark evidence is not a true science."

On December 4, 2007, the jury of nine men and three women, after deliberating nine hours, found Steven Fortin guilty of first-degree murder, and first-degree sexual assault. The judge sentenced him to life plus twenty years.

A Bogus Identification

At ten-thirty in the morning of Thanksgiving Day 1997, a medical assistant found 41-year-old Dr. Margo Prade slumped behind the wheel of her van in the doctor's office parking lot. The Akron, Ohio physician, shot six times with a handgun at close range, had fought with her murderer. Physical evidence of this struggle included buttons ripped from Dr. Prade's lab coat, a bite mark on her left inner arm, and traces of blood and tissue under her fingernails.

A few months after the murder, Akron police arrested the victim's husband, Douglas Evans Prade. Captain Prade, a 29-year veteran of the Akron Police Department, denied shooting his wife to death. He insisted that at the time of the killing he was in the workout room of the couple's Copley Township condominium complex.

In 1997, DNA science, compared to today, was quite primitive. As a result, DNA tests of trace evidence from the bite mark and the blood and tissue under the victim's fingernails, was inconclusive. DNA analysts were unable to include or exclude Captain Prade as the source of this crime scene evidence.

Video footage from a security camera at a car dealership next to the murder scene revealed the shadowy figure of a man climbing into Dr. Prade's van at 9:10 in the morning of her death. An hour and a half later, the man exited the murder vehicle and was seen driving off the parking lot in a light-colored car. Homicide detectives never identified this man who could not have been taller than five-nine. The suspect stood over six-foot-three. Had investigators focused their efforts on identifying the man in the surveillance video, they would have solved the case. But detectives set their minds set on the victim's husband and ignored all evidence and leads that pointed in a different direction.

To make their case against Captain Douglas Prade, detectives asked a retired Akron dentist named Dr. Thomas Marshall to compare a photograph of the death scene bite mark to a dental impression of the suspect's lower front teeth. According to Dr. Marshall, the only person who could have bitten Dr. Pride was her husband. The suspect's known dental impressions, according to the dentist, matched the crime scene evidence perfectly. At the time, before advanced DNA technology exposed bite mark identification analysis as junk science, Dr. Marshall's identification carried great weight.

In September 1998, following a two-week trial in a Summit county court, the jury, after only deliberating four hours, found Douglas Parade guilty of murdering his wife. The only evidence the prosecution had pointing to the defendant's guilt was Dr. Thomas Marshall's bite mark identification. Without the dentist's testimony, there wouldn't have been enough evidence against Douglas Prade to justify his arrest.

Following the guilty verdict, the defendant stood up, turned to face the courtroom spectators, and said, "I didn't do this. I am an innocent convicted person. God, myself, Margo, and the person who killed Margo all know I'm innocent." Common Pleas Judge Mary Spicer sentenced Douglas Prade to life without the chance of parole until he served 26 years. Shortly thereafter, the prisoner began serving his sentence at the state prison in Madison, Ohio. At that point he expected to die behind bars.

In 2004, attorneys with the Jones Day law firm in Akron, and the Ohio Innocence Project, took up Douglas Prade's case. After years of motions, petitions, reports, and hearings, an Ohio judge ordered DNA tests of the saliva traces from the bite wound, scrapings from the victim's lab coat, and scrapings from under Dr. Prade's fingernails.

In August 2012, DNA analysis of the crime scene trace evidence revealed that none of the associative evidence came from Douglas Prade. (The DNA work was performed by the DNA Lab Diagnostic Center in Fairfield, Ohio.) Summit County Judge Judy Hunter, on January 29, 2013, ordered the release of the 66-year-old prisoner.

On March 19, 2014, an Ohio appeals court decided that the new DNA evidence did not prove that Prade didn't murder his wife. The appellate judge said that Prade's release from prison was a mistake, and that he should be taken back into custody. The morning after that decision, Mr. Prade found himself back behind bars.

But later that day, after the Ohio Supreme Court reversed the appeals court re-incarceration order, Prade was released from jail. He will remain free while the state's highest court reviews the case.

Douglas Prade, an innocent man, spent 15 years in prison on the bogus bite mark testimony of a junk forensic scientist. Over the past two decades, there have been dozens of wrongful convictions based on bite mark identification.

31 CRIME INVESTIGATION

The Father of the Third Degree

The history of American criminal investigation does not begin with thinking detectives inspired by the fictitious Sherlock Holmes, but with a police detective who achieved fame and success by acquiring confessions through rubber hose brutality referred to as the "third degree." Although Thomas J. Byrnes is not as familiar today as the nineteenth century private investigator, Allan Pinkerton, it was Byrnes who set the stage for decades of institutionalized police brutality in the United States. It was Byrnes who practiced interrogation techniques that decades later produced the U. S. Supreme Court's *Miranda* decision. (*Miranda v. Arizona,* 1966)

A Civil War veteran living in New York City, Byrnes joined the police department in 1863. Following a brief stint as a patrolman, the smart and ambitious young man got promoted into the newly formed detective bureau where he quickly made a name for himself. In 1880, two years after grabbing headlines for solving a $3 million Manhattan bank burglary, Byrnes, now a captain took charge of the detective bureau made up of two sergeants and fourteen investigators. With thirty thousand professional thieves and 2,000 gambling dens, New York, one-third the size of London, had three times the crime. Businessmen in the Wall Street district, overrun by sneak thieves, forgers, pickpockets, and burglars, turned to Byrnes for help. The police captain responded by putting out the word, through a network of paid informants and other law enforcement contacts, that any thief caught south of his infamous Dead Line would be sent to Blackwell's Island for a severe beating; a threat Byrnes carried out with precision and joy until the thieves, having received the message, stayed out of the financial district. The tycoons of Wall Street showed their gratitude by making Captain Byrnes one of the wealthiest police detectives in history.

Byrnes, as much a businessman as police detective, found other sources of income. During his tenure as Captain of Detectives, he followed the standard policing practice of ignoring, for a price, the city's gambling establishments, whorehouses, and opium dens. One the New York's most notorious madams paid $30,000 a year in police bribes.

As an investigator, Byrnes, in addition to employing a stable of paid, confidential informants, would let lesser criminals off the hook in return for evidence against the bigger fish. He taught his detectives how to identify criminals, particularly safe-crackers and other signature offenders, through their individualistic crime scene techniques--their so-called methods-of-operation, or M.O. The use of informants, criminal intelligence, and M.O. were tactics pioneered by Allan Pinkerton, the only investigator in the country more famous than Byrnes.

It is not surprising that Byrnes, as an ambitious, publicity-seeking detective working in a era before judicial restraints on police behavior, adapted, as his principal investigative technique, the coerced confession. From a brutally pragmatic point of view, the beauty of the third degree is that it is not necessary, in the acquisition of a confession, to be interrogating the guilty party. By being the first to publicize the fact he would do whatever it took to get a confession, Byrnes established police brutality as a standard operating procedure, making himself the unofficial father of the third degree. For the next fifty some years, until the U. S. Supreme Court in1936 specifically excluded confessions extracted from physically abused prisoners, the third degree became the staple of criminal investigation in America. While *Brown v. Mississippi* didn't end police brutality, it marked the start of a new era in criminal investigation. However, Byrnes' ghost would inhabit, in varying degrees, interrogation rooms across the country throughout the Twentieth Century.

Although he worked in the era before the advent of crime statistics--annual crime rates, case clearance percentages and such--Byrnes used statistics, figures no less reliable than their modern counterparts, as indices of success. At one point in his career, Byrnes claimed responsibility for 3,300 arrests leading to an accumulated ten thousand year prison sentence. Statistically, there is no telling what percentage of the men he put behind bars were innocent of the crimes charged. Aware that the investigative reputation of Scotland Yard exceeded that of his own department, Byrnes, in the wake of the 1888 serial killings of five prostitutes in East London, challenged Jack-the-Ripper to ply his trade in New York. When a gutted female corpse washed up on the New York side of the Hudson River shortly after Byrnes' burst of bravado, there was serious concern that the ripper had taken up his challenge.

Thomas Byrnes reached the peak of his fame in 1886 with the publication of a book, under his name, called *Professional Criminals of America*.

The massive work contained the mug shots and detailed criminal histories of four hundred of the city's most active house burglars, safecrackers, pickpockets, check forgers, and con artists. Reprinted for the first time in 1969, it is considered a classic work in the history of property crime in America.

In 1892, a crusading Presbyterian minister in New York City named Dr. Charles H. Parkhurst, launched a religious crusade to clean up vice in the city, and to expose the police corruption that allowed it to exist. The crusade led to political hearings headed by a New York state senator named Lexow. In 1894 Byrnes, now a police superintendent was called before the Lexow Committee to explain how he, a public servant, had become so wealthy. As a result of the highly publicized hearings, the mayor resigned and a handful of patrolmen were indicted on charges of bribery. Byrnes, and several other police bigwigs were simply forced to resign.

After leaving the force in 1895, the 54-year-old father of the third degree took a high paying job as general manager of an insurance company. The Lexow politicians, having enjoyed the limelight, left town, and the moment they did, the corruption and vice returned.

In America, the ward and watch system of policing evolved into a better-organized, more efficient system of bribe giving and receiving. For the next sixty to seventy years, American law enforcement would be plagued by corruption and brutality. In the late 1800s, D. J. Cook, the superintendent of the Rocky Mountain Detective Association who had been a sheriff and a deputy U.S. marshal, issued words of wisdom applicable to his time and a generation of future cops: "Never hit a prisoner over the head with your pistol, because you may afterwards want to use your weapon and find it disabled."

In 1910, the week before he died at age 69, Thomas Byrnes transferred to his wife a Fifth Avenue building worth a half-million dollars. Two years later, the lawyer-writer Arthur Train, in his best-selling book, *Courts and Criminals,* described the status of criminal investigation some seventy years following the formation of the New York City Police Department: "The detective business swarms with men of doubtful honesty and morals...who are accustomed to exaggeration if not to perjury, and who have neither the inclination nor the ability to do competent work."

Qualities of a Great Investigator

The creator of Sherlock Holmes, Sir Arthur Conan Doyle, said that a first-class investigator had to have a good mind, exact knowledge, and the powers of observation and deduction. That's true, as far as it goes, but Dr.

Doyle forgot to mention persistence, audacity, objectivity, and above all, integrity. And a little luck never hurt anyone.

Identifying Criminal Types by Appearance

For the first five thousand years or so, mankind's detective work was incredibly shoddy. A criminal investigation prior to the 1800s generally meant little more than a hasty search for eyewitnesses and motives and, above all, the coercion of the accused into confessing.

That began to change in the mid-to late 1800s, as schools of forensic medicine opened up, as detectives turned to fingerprints and police departments began to collect mug shots. French chemists refined blood analysis.

By the 1890s, criminologists appeared to be on the verge of a startling breakthrough: identifying criminal body types or markers.

Internationally acclaimed Italian scientist, Cesare Lombroso, claimed that by carefully examining the physical characteristics of a suspect, every nook and cranny of the body, he could help determine guilt or innocence. [Actually, Lombroso claimed the ability to identify criminal *types* by analyzing their faces and general builds. For example, short, stocky men with low foreheads were often criminals.]

Imagine the implications. Say someone was accused of rape, but the eyewitness identification was a bit shaky. What if Lombroso could inspect the man's body or skull and find definitive markers revealing the man to be a rapist? Would it be the suspect's ear? His tongue? No body part was off-limits to these scientific pioneers.

Richard Zacks, *An Underground Education*, 1997

Policing Versus Criminal Investigation

Successful criminal investigators are intelligent, analytical people who like to solve problems and figure things out. They are also curious, competitive, and well organized. They are unafraid of complexity, pay great attention to detail, are articulate, and can express themselves well on paper.

Dedicated criminal investigators are life-long students, people who embrace new challenges and tough assignments. They are not only intelligent; they have trained themselves to think clearly, draw relevant conclusions, and keep bias out of their calculations. They are not afraid of difficult, emotionally draining work. Result oriented, they are not spinning their wheels until they are old enough to retire.

People who make first-class detectives are often not suited for general police work, and a good street cop will not necessarily turn into even a merely competent investigator. The fields of law enforcement (peace keeping and order maintenance) and criminal investigation are vastly different functions that appeal to different kinds of people.

The uniformed police officer, often having to act quickly and decisively, instead of thoughtful discretion, is more likely to act pursuant to a detailed code or rules and regulations which have been committed to memory. Training a police officer is therefore nothing like preparing someone for criminal investigation. For that reason, criminal investigators should be recruited from an entirely different pool of job candidates. For example, there is no reason to require trainee investigators to be as physically fit as uniformed officers, or to learn how to deal with drunks, drug addicts, and domestic disturbances. It would be also a waste of time to school future detectives in traffic enforcement.

Detective trainees are not only drawn from the wrong well, instructors often improperly train them. Detective training often focuses on investigative techniques designed to resolve cases quickly rather than correctly. The emphasis is quite often on the acquisition of direct evidence in the form of eyewitness identification, and the confession, rather than the more time consuming and complex gathering and interpretation of physical evidence, an endeavor that requires special training and more complex thinking. Perhaps this is why so many crime scenes are either ignored or improperly processed. This also explains why there are so many false confessions, and people sent to prison on the strength of questionable line-up and mug shot identifications. Another common method of getting a case off the books involves the use of unreliable jailhouse informants who testify against defendants in return for police or prosecution favors.

Because most detectives are not accustomed to digging deeply into a case--that is peeling away layers and layers of leads--they are often stumped when merely scratching the surface of a case fails to reveal the perpetrator. There is also the problem of the so-called "veteran rookie", the uniformed cop who after fifteen years on patrol finally makes the detective squad. These officers are not only investigative rookies they are quite often burned-out bureaucrats waiting until they are old enough to retire. It's not that old dogs can't learn new tricks, they don't want to.

Eyewitness Misidentification

Advances in the social sciences and technology have cast a new light on eyewitness identification. Hundreds of studies on eyewitness identification have been published in professional and academic journals. One study by the University of Virginia Law School Professor Brandon L. Garett found that eyewitness misidentifications contributed to 76 percent of the cases overturned by DNA evidence.

Matthew Mangino, mattmangino.com, August 3, 2013

Forensic Hypnosis

Advocates of forensic hypnosis claim that crime victims and witnesses, under a hypnotic state, can remember events they have forgotten, and sharpen memories that are still with them. Forensic hypnotists are often brought into cases to help, for example, a witness or victim recall a license plate number, or an odometer reading. Investigators also use the technique to retrieve more detailed descriptions of suspects. Supporters of forensic hypnosis point to cases where its use has solve crimes. Detractors (myself included) can point to instances where hypnotically induced information turned out to be inaccurate, and even harmful.

In the 1970s I was tangentially involved in an arson-murder case where a forensically hypnotized witness/victim identified an innocent man as the fire setter. In one of my own cold case murder investigations, a witness I had someone forensically hypnotize, produced information that led me on a wild goose chase. In Pennsylvania and several other states, hypnotically induced testimony, because it is unreliable, is inadmissible in court.

A lot can go wrong when a victim or a witness is questioned while in a hypnotic state. The hypnotist can unwittingly suggest information to the subject that taints the results. Under hypnosis, the personal beliefs and prejudices of the interviewee can seep into remembered accounts and descriptions.

Researchers have found that people under hypnosis are fully capable of lying, and the process can bring to the surface a subject's false beliefs. Because of these and other problems with this investigative technique, I am not a fan of forensic hypnosis, particularly when practiced by psychologists who make their livings putting clients under to help them stop smoking, lose weight, stop taking drugs, or get off booze. In my opinion, composite sketches based on the memories of hypnotized eyewitnesses are, at best, useless. In the practice of criminal investigation, I place forensic hypnotists in the same category as astrologists and psychic detectives.

Catching Serial Killers

The identification of a serial murderer frequently occurs through happenstance or a fluke.... A serial murderer may be apprehended for driving a stolen vehicle, and very quickly the police learn they are dealing with a much more violent crime, as was the case when Ted Bundy was pursued in a stolen car in Pensacola, Florida. Following his arrest, the Pensacola police soon learned that they had more than a car thief in their jail.

Another example of routine police work and an unrelated crime leading to the arrest of a serial murderer and a serial murder investigation occurred on June 28, 1993, in Long Island, New York. In the early morning hours two state troopers spotted a tan 1984 Mazda pickup with no license plates driving on the Southern State Parkway. The driver refused to pull over and the officers pursued the pickup. The chase ended 25 minutes later when the Mazda slammed into a utility pole. The driver was unhurt and was arrested. Following the arrest, the officers noticed a very strong smell coming from the bed of the truck where the officers found the badly decomposed body of Tiffany Bresciani, a 22-year-old woman from Manhattan. The driver, Joel Rifkin, would within hours confess to the killing of 16 other women.

Steven A. Egger, *The Killers Among Us*, 1998

The Polygraph as an Interrogation Tool

Several years ago, a story went around about an ingenious small town cop who hooked a young thief up to a copy machine the kid thought was a lie detector. When the suspect gave an answer the interrogator didn't like, he hit the print button causing a sheet of paper to come out of the copier that read, "Not True." The suspect, convinced a sophisticated lie detection instrument had incriminated him, confessed. Whenever I told this story in class, I said it happened in West Virginia, and that the judge, offended by the cop's clever dishonesty, threw the confession out.

The copy machine-as-polygraph story probably didn't happen in West Virginia, or anywhere else. But it illustrates an important point about scientific lie detection. Polygraph examiners can use the polygraph to coax confessions out of guilty suspects. The debate over polygraph accuracy, in this context, is not relevant. What does matter is this: most suspects believe the polygraph works. In the right hands, it can be an effective interrogation tool. In 2012, the Georgia Bureau of Investigation made public a videotape of a murder suspect's polygraph examination and follow-up interrogation.

The transcript of this session reveals how a professional polygraph examiner/interrogator can acquire a confession.

On Friday, December 2, 2010, 7-year-old Jorelys Rivera, a resident of the River Ridge Apartment complex in Canton, Georgia outside of Atlanta, went missing. Three days later, police found her body in a dumpster not far from where she had been abducted. Ryan Brunn, a 20-year-old newly hired maintenance man had lured the girl into a vacant apartment where he had raped and murdered her.

On the day following the discovery of the murdered girl's body, Keith Sitton, a special agent with the Georgia Bureau of Investigation, gave the suspect a polygraph test. What follows is the word-for-word account of that session:

SITTON: Regarding that girl, do you intend to answer the [polygraph] questions truthfully?

BRUNN: Yes.

SITTON: Did you participate in any way in causing the death of that girl?

BRUNN: No.

SITTON: Do you know for sure who caused the death of that girl?

BRUNN: No.

In discussing the results of the polygraph test with Brunn, Sitton said, "I can see you're not doing good on this test. Those [last two] questions are really bothering me."

"I promise you. I'll take the test again," Brunn replied. His voice was weak, and he was obviously nervous.

"There's something on this that you're not telling us, something that you're keeping to yourself. What is it you're holding back? We're going to solve this thing. It's just written all over you. Something's bothering you."

"I'm not bothered at all."

"You haven't told the complete truth about everything."

"I have," Brunn replied.

The GBI agent asked Brunn about having been accused of sexually fondling a young girl in Virginia: "You know what I'm talking about," he said.

"I don't."

"Remember, I said you had to be 100 percent truthful. I asked you [on the polygraph] if anyone made accusations. So what you have done is told me a lie.

"They put things in that child's head. I'm a good person. I didn't do anything to that little Spanish girl, and I didn't do nothing to the other girl [the one in Virginia]."

The next day, Sutton questioned Brunn again. He informed the suspect that according to the polygraph he had lied. To this, Brunn said, "I should have told the truth straight up. But I didn't. I was scared." At this point, Brunn made a full confession. He said he had raped the girl, cut her throat, wrapped her in a garbage bag, and dumped her body in the trash compactor.

On January 17, 2011, Ryan Brunn pleaded guilty to murdering Jorelys Rivera. The judge sentenced him to life without parole. A year later, while serving his time at the Georgia State Prison, Brunn used his sweatshirt to hang himself.

Can You Beat the Polygraph?

In order for a polygraph (lie detection) test result to be accurate, the instrument must be in good working order. The polygraph examiner must be properly trained and experienced in question formation and line chart interpretation. The subject of the test--the examinee--must be a willing participant in the process. Not everyone is suited for polygraph testing. People who are ill, on drugs, under the influence of alcohol, extremely obese, retarded, or mentally unbalanced do not make good polygraph subjects. Criminal suspects who are emotionally exhausted from a police interrogation should not be tested. Children and old people should not be placed on the lie detector.

The polygraph instrument measures and records the examinee's involuntary, physiological (bodily) responses to answers to a set of ten yes or no questions. The examinee should know in advance what questions the examiner plans to ask him. Based upon changes in the examinee's blood pressure, heart rate, breathing patterns, and galvanic skin response, the examiner will draw conclusions on whether the subject has told the truth or lied. Polygraph examiners are not recognized in the criminal court system as expert witnesses, therefore polygraph results are not admissible as evidence of guilt in criminal cases.

Congress passed a federal law in 1988 that prohibits the use of the polygraph as a private sector pre-employment screening measure. It is widely used, however, in law enforcement as an investigative tool, and as a way to screen job applicants.

Over the years, more and more local, state and federal law enforcement agencies have required job applicants to submit to polygraph tests. These law enforcement job candidates are typically asked if they've ever sold drugs, stolen significant amounts of money or merchandise from their employers, or are seriously in debt. Employment candidates may also be asked if they have omitted anything important from their resumes or job applications.

In 2013, 73,000 Americans were either given polygraph tests as part of the federal job application process, or were tested to determine if they should be allowed to keep their jobs. Federal agencies involved in national security such as the National Security Administration, the FBI, and the CIA, periodically polygraph employees to make sure they haven't gone rogue. Other federal agencies that require periodic screening tests include the DEA, ICE, the Secret Service, ATF, and the Postal Inspection Service.

Not everyone is a fan of the polygraph technique. Generally, there are two kinds of polygraph critic. There are the anti-polygraph people who object to this form of lie detection because they believe the instrument and the technique is junk science and therefore no more reliable than a flip of a coin. The other group objects to polygraph use because they believe the instrument is utilized to violate the privacy of those tested. Critics in this camp accuse polygraph examiners, and the people who hire them, of abusing the process by digging for dirt that is unrelated to the job application process.

Over the years there have been numerous high-profile examples of FBI and CIA spies who avoided detection for years even though they were subjected to regular polygraph testing. Aldrich Ames, the counterintelligence CIA officer convicted of spying in 1994, must have found a way to beat polygraph screening. (I do not believe that suspects in specific criminal cases can lie to competent examiners and get away with it.) This was also true of FBI agent Robert Hanssen who was convicted of thirteen counts of espionage in 2001.

According to Russell Tice, the National Security Administration whistleblower that was one of the first to leak evidence of the NSA's spying on U. S. citizens has revealed that during his 20-year career in counterintelligence, he beat the polygraph a dozen times. Mr. Tice believes that due to political correctness and lawsuits, polygraph tests have become easier to manipulate. He says that beating the job screening polygraph examination has actually become easy. Over the years Mr. Tice and others have published, in print and online, instructions on how to beat the polygraph.

Polygraph examiners ask what they term relevant, irrelevant, and control questions. Irrelevant questions such as "Have you ever eaten pasta?" are intended to set the baseline of a truthful response. Control questions are designed to create a baseline or point of reference for deceptive responses. To do that, polygraph examiners ask subjects questions likely to produce deceptive answers. In other words they want the subject to lie. For example: "Have you ever lied to your parents?" or "Have you ever cheated on a test?" Most subjects, when they answer "no" to these questions, are lying. Relevant questions are ones that directly address the point of the polygraph examination. In national security screening, an employee with access to classified information might be asked if he has leaked classified documents to a journalist. To determine if the subject is telling the truth about not leaking information, the polygraph examiner compares his physiological responses to the relevant query with his responses to the control and irrelevant questions.

According to those who have made it their mission to teach people how to beat the polygraph, manipulation techniques, or so-called "countermeasures," deal with how the examinee should respond to the control and relevant questions. In answering a control question designed to produce a deceitful physiological baseline, the subject, while telling the expected lie, should bite his tongue. The idea here is to cause the polygraph instrument to record a strong physiological reaction to the subject's lying. When asked a relevant question the answer to which will be a lie, the subject is instructed to find a way to distance himself from the question by daydreaming, counting backward, or slowing down his breathing.

If this countermeasure works, the relatively mild responses to the relevant questions, when compared to the wild reactions to the control questions, will lead the examiner to conclude that the subject has told the truth.

Law enforcement job applicants are better off telling the truth and hoping for the best. Very few people have the presence of mind and discipline to successfully employ these polygraph manipulation tricks. As for national security employees who are either spies or future whistleblowers, they have nothing to lose by trying these techniques. Notwithstanding Aldrich Ames, Robert Hanssen, and Russell Tice, fooling a competent polygraph examiner is a lot easier said than done.

Indicators of Interrogation Room Deception

Any suspect who is overly polite, even to the point of repeatedly calling the interrogator "sir" may be attempting to flatter the interrogator to gain his confidence. The suspect who, after being accused says, "No offense to you, sir, but I didn't do it," "I know you are just doing your job," or "I understand what you are saying" is evidencing his lying about the matter under investigation. A truthful suspect has no need to make such apologetic statements, or even to explain that he understands the interrogator's accusatory statements. To the contrary, the truthful suspect may very well react aggressively with a direct denial or by using strong language indicating anger over even an implied accusation.

A suspect who "swears to God" or offers to "swear on a stack of Bibles," or utters other oaths to support his answers, is, in many instances, not telling the truth. Typical examples of expressions used by lying suspects who try to make their statements believable are: "I swear to God, sir," or "With God as my witness." The suspect may even go so far as to state "on my poor dead mother's grave, sir." On the other hand, truthful suspects are confident of their truthfulness and do not need such props. The interrogator should bear in mind, however, that within some cultural surroundings, swearing and similar expressions may be rather commonplace, and do not necessarily mean that the suspect is lying.

Fred E. Inbau, *Criminal Interrogation and Confessions,* 1986

A False Confession

In 1990, following a botched robbery of a diamond courier in Brooklyn, New York, the robbers carjacked and murdered Rabbi Chaskel Werzberger, a survivor of the Holocaust. A few days after the highly publicize murder, police officers picked up a 35-year-old unemployed drug addict named David Ranta.

Following his interrogation by NYPD detective Louis Scarcella, Ranta signed a confession in which he admitted helping plot the diamond robbery. A boy that witnessed the crime picked Ranta out of a police line-up.

A few months later, a Brooklyn jury, relying on the defendant's confession, and the line-up identification, found David Ranta guilty of murdering the Rabbi. The judge sentenced him to 35 years in prison.

The Conviction Integrity Unit of the Brooklyn District Attorney's Office took up the old Werzberger murder case after it became apparent that the evidence against Ranta had been unreliable. Years after the conviction, the young eyewitness of the diamond robbery informed investigators that detectives had coached him into picking Ranta out of the line-up. Evidence also surfaced that cast serious doubt on the reliability of the confession.

On March 21, 2013, David Ranta walked free after serving 23 years behind bars. He was 58.

Louis Scarcella, the retired NYPD detective who was in charge of the case, told an Associated Press reporter that Brooklyn prosecutors had pressured him to bring the Rabbi's killer to justice quickly. (I have no doubt that is true.) "I caught a lot of cases and I got confessions," Scarcella said. "I was called in and I did my job and I got confessions." (A detective's job is to get the truth.) Scarcella denies coaching the boy into the line-up identification, and says he continues to stand behind his role in the case.

There was no evidence to suggest that Detective Scarcella intentionally framed an innocent man. Moreover, the prosecutor in the case also bore responsibility in this wrongful conviction. But because of public pressure to catch the killer of a Holocaust surviving Rabbi, the prosecutor went ahead with the case and put the burden of determining the guilt or innocence of this defendant on the jury. And he did it with unreliable evidence. Many jurors assume, even in weak cases, that because the defendant is being prosecuted, he must be guilty. It appeared that neither the detective nor the prosecutor were interested in digging deeper into the case. If they had, Ranta would have been exonerated and the real perpetrators brought to justice.

Two days after he walked out of prison, David Ranta suffered a massive heart attack and died.

Can Interrogators Lie?

Courts have long upheld the rights of interrogators to lie to suspects, with a single exception, which stems from a 1997 Supreme Court decision. In that case, *Bram v. United States,* the court held that a confession was not admissible if it came from threats or "direct or implied promises," such as an assurance that a suspect would be treated more leniently if he confessed, or more harshly if he did not. Despite the restriction on both "direct" and "implied" promises, in the years since 1997, courts have tended only to reject confessions when there was evidence of an explicit threat or promise.

Since then, the practices of interrogators have grown more nuanced, to include threats and promises that are merely and subtly implied, and therefore more often accepted in courtrooms as legitimate. Even when an explicit threat or promise is made, it can be difficult for an interrogation suspect to prove that coercive techniques were used, as most interrogations are not recorded in their entirely, and a detective's word can carry more weight with a jury than that of the accused.

Sarah Burns, *The Central Park Five,* 2011

Human License Plates

A mother in Georgia recently got into trouble for taking her 10-year-old son to a tattoo shop where he got tattooed in honor of his dead brother. The local prosecutor's office charged the woman with child cruelty. Under Georgia law, only physicians and osteopaths can tattoo people under 18. (Why would a doctor ink a kid in the first place?) This story got me thinking about tattoos, and the role they play, and have played, in the identification of criminals and their victims.

Not too long ago, people most likely to get a tattoo were enlisted military personnel, prison inmates, and members of street gangs. Truman Capote, the author of *In Cold Blood* once told a journalist that of the dozens of mass murderers and serial killers he had interviewed, all of them had tattoos. Today, that would surprise no one. In 2006, according to a Pew Research Center survey, more than 36 percent of people between the ages 18 and 40 have at least one tattoo. This percentage is probably much higher now. (It seems that 90 percent of college and professional football and basketball players are tattooed. And as a boxing fan, I have noticed that more and more prizefighters are heavily tattooed.)

Tattoos, along with clothing, personal belongings, fingerprints, scars, moles, and teeth, are helpful in the identification of corpses that have been dumped in the water, in fields and in the woods. In 1935, two fishermen caught a shark off the coast of Sydney, Australia. They took the live fish to a local aquarium where it disgorged a human arm that had been severed by a knife. The arm also bore a distinctive tattoo that led to the identification of a murder victim named James Smith. Smith had been an ex-boxer with a history of crime. The case became known as the Shark Arm Murder.

The police routinely ask crime victims and eyewitnesses if the suspect had any tattoos. Former prison inmates and members of street gangs assist law enforcement by identifying themselves as such through inked individualized body markings. In England in the late 1800s, before criminal identification bureaus adopted fingerprints, ID clerks took note of arrestees' tattoos and their locations, data classified and filed for future retrieval. Today, in California, the CALGANG database consists of a collection of gang tattoos. In Florida, the authorities created a database that featured 372,000 tattoos of people who have been arrested in that state.

In 2010, Michigan State University licensed tattoo-matching technology to Morpho Trak, the world's leading provider of biometric (eye, hand, signature, and voice ID) identification systems. Corrections and law enforcement officers use the tattoo database to identify criminal suspects and homicide victims.

Dr. Nina Jablonski, head of the anthropology department at Penn State said that, "Tattoos are part of an ancient and universal tradition of human self-declaration and expression." In some cases, these tattoos express anti-social attitudes, and declare that their owners have histories of crime.

The Eyewitness

Before a witness can recall a complex incident, the incident must be accurately perceived at the onset; it must be stored in memory. Before it can be stored, it must be within a witness's perceptual range, which means that it must be loud enough and close enough so the ordinary senses pick it up. If visual details are to be perceived, the situation must be reasonably well illuminated. Before some information can be recalled, a witness must have paid attention to it. But even though an event is bright enough, loud enough, and close enough, and even though attention is being paid, we can still find significant errors in a witness's recollection of the event, and it is common for two witnesses to the same event to recall it very differently.

Elizabeth Loftus, *Eyewitness Testimony*, 1979

Eyewitness Identification Experts

Pennsylvania criminal defendants are able to offer expert testimony about the unreliability of eyewitness identification following a decision by a divided state Supreme Court that overturned a 20-year prohibition against such evidence. [In the past, the judge could inform jurors of the dangers of eyewitness testimony in the jury instruction phase of the trial.]

Pennsylvania will join the great majority of states and federal courts when it comes to letting an expert tell jurors about research into eyewitness testimony...[Since more that thirty years ago, hundreds of studies have shown just how unreliable this kind of evidence can be. A countless number of rape and robbery defendants have been sent to prison on the strength of false line-up identifications. Today, in almost all jurisdictions, eyewitness testimony alone will not, by law, sustain a conviction.]

Associated Press, May 29, 2014

Police Rewards

In response to crimes that create public outrage and/or fear--abducted children, missing women found dead, venerated objects vandalized or stolen, acts of terrorism, serial killings, and highly publicized murders--law enforcement agencies almost always post monetary rewards for information leading to the capture and successful prosecution of the perpetrators. The highest rewards come from the federal government. The U.S. State Department put up $25 million for the head of Osama Bin Laden, and $2 million for the capture of James "Whitey" Bulger, the Boston mobster suspected of 18 murders. For years, both of these fugitives lived normal lives in public view. Bin Laden was killed last May, and Bulger, on the lam since 1995, was caught last year in California.

Although the federal government pays out more than $100 million a year in rewards, and claims this money is well-spent, there is no concrete evidence that monetary incentives play a significant role in bringing criminals and terrorists to justice. Reward offerings may not only be ineffective, they may actually have an adverse effect on the administration of justice.

In cases where rewards have been posted, there is no data that indicates the percentage of instances in which the monetary incentive produced a positive result. Moreover, in those cases where reward seekers did come forward with important information, we don't know if those cases would have been eventually solved anyway. There is a real possibility that the police are substituting rewards for old-fashioned shoe leather. The question is: do rewards serve the public, or are they merely public relations gimmicks for lazy investigators?

The overuse of rewards encourages citizens not to cooperate with the police unless they are paid. In many high profile murder cases, the first thing the police do is post a reward. I think this sends the following message to the perpetrators: "We don't have a clue, and we are desperate for a lead."

The principal objection to law enforcement rewards, particularly in nationally publicized cases, involves the extra investigative hours it takes to run down all of the false leads created by tipsters hoping for a piece of the reward money. The publicity alone draws out of the woodwork all manner of false confessors, phony eyewitnesses, visionaries, psychics, psychotics, and people bored and lonely. Adding a reward incentive to this mix exacerbates the problem.

Whether they help or hinder, and we will never know for sure, rewards are here to stay. Law enforcement administrators love them, and the public has come to expect them. I think rewards comprise a criminal investigative placebo.

32 CRIME, THE MEDIA & POPULAR CULTURE

True Detective Magazines: The Golden Era

In 1988, on my way to Chicago to interview Fred E. Inbau, the John Henry Wigmore Professor of Law at Northwestern University, I stopped in Beloit, Wisconsin to visit Chester Rose. Mr. Rose, a worker in a Rockport shoe factory, had sent me a long letter following the publication of my book, *The Lindbergh Case*. Since then we had corresponded regularly with the most informative letters coming from him. Chet was a true crime buff with an encyclopedic knowledge of murder cases he had read about in thousands of fact-crime magazines published in the 1920s, 30s, and 40s. By the 1970s, Chet had amassed a huge collection of true detective magazines he stored in his detached garage. His wife, tired of his true crime obsession, burned the garage to the ground. A few years later they were divorced. (Her mysterious disappearance would have made a better story.)

While never a fan of true detective magazines, I became interested in the golden era of this form of nonfiction crime publishing. Aimed at the adult male reader, the pulp art covers--often featuring sexy women in distress-- promised stories of salacious violence and mayhem. (Today, the vast majority of true crime readers are women.) Unlike many writers for crime fiction periodicals such as *Black Mask* who went on to become famous authors of mystery novels, the literary contributors to the fact-crime magazines remained relatively unknown. Exceptions include writers Dashiell Hammett, Jim Thompson, and Alan Hynd.

True crime magazines usually featured ten murder cases per issue. (Occasionally there were accounts starring con men, counterfeiters, safe crackers, forgers, pickpockets, and extortionists.) Because true crime readers were armchair detectives, good investigative work comprised a major element of each story. Editors liked cases solved by the emerging forensic sciences of latent fingerprint identification, blood stain analysis, tire impression evidence, biological time of death estimation, handwriting identification, and forensic ballistics. It also helped if the homicides were exceptionally gruesome such as one cover story that featured a woman tied to a tree to be eaten alive by hyenas.

True crime magazines in the golden era reflected the history of crime in America. In the 1920s and 30s the magazines featured depression era bank robbers like John Dillinger, "Pretty Boy" Floyd, "Baby Face" Nelson, and Ma Barker and her degenerate son Fred. Bonnie and Clyde, Al Capone, Alvin Karpis and "Machine Gun" Kelly all made regular appearances between the covers of fact-crime publications. In 1931, *True Detective Mysteries* started a regular feature called "Line Up." Police departments across the country sent in mug shots and descriptions of fugitives on the run. Readers who recognized these criminals and turned them in received small cash rewards. By 1944 "Line Up" had been responsible for the apprehension of more than 300 fugitives. The magazine also ran an ongoing piece called "Crime Doesn't Pay" consisting of photographs of bad guys who had been recently brought to justice. (Crime did pay for *True Detective Mysteries*.) Many of the men shown in this feature were destined for the electric chair.

In 1933, *True Detective Mysteries* started a series of articles by the famous Seattle criminalist, Luke S. May. All of these pieces involved criminals who had been outfoxed by scientific crime detection. By 1940, Luke May was also writing a regular question and answer column about forensic science. May also authored several books featuring his most interesting cases.

True Detective Mysteries, first published by Bernard Macfadden in 1924, is considered the first fact-crime magazine. Within a few years Macfadden would be publishing several true crime periodicals including *Master Detective*. At his peak, Macfadden was selling two million magazines a month. In the 1930s, a true crime buff could choose between 100 magazines with titles like, *Front Page Detective, Official Detective, Baffling Detective, True Gangster, Detective Yarns, Spicy Detective, Current Detective,* and *Detective World.*

By the end of World War II, the golden era of the true detective magazine came to an end. Mass-market paperbacks and television would finish off the last of the true crime magazines. Macfadden Publications, in 1971, sold off *True Detective Mysteries* to a British firm. In the summer of 1995, the company ceased publication altogether. In the 1960s, Macfadden managing editor Marc Gerald said, "...our readership of blue-hairs, shut-ins, Greyhound bus riders, cops, and axe murderers are old and dying fast."

Today, true crime buffs have access to mass-market paperbacks, cable television, and the Internet. Patterson Smith, the antiquarian bookseller doing business in New Jersey, has a database of 30,000 articles out of 2,000 fact-crime magazines. To request a search of this repository, the crime researcher can submit the name of the crime victim, the name of the perpetrator, the location of the crime, the year it took place, or a brief account of the case. In researching my book *Fall Guys*, I read a couple of 1950s true detective magazine articles about the axe murder of Helen Zubryd. I found these pieces quite inaccurate.

The Fascination With True Crime

People seem to have an insatiable appetite for reading about true crime...Many in the cast of true crime characters are professionals, or semi-professionals whose lives revolve around matters of crime. Lay people too have a role--as jurors, for example. There is also, of course, the story of a much larger cohort of laymen and women: people accused of breaking the law; and their victims. Their stories are not, in the main, pleasant or uplifting; the lives caught up in these webs are so often ruined and wasted lives; through these pages parade example after example of foolishness, vice, self destruction, selfishness, evil, and greed. They are stories with few, if any heroes, and few, if any happy endings. But these stories are important to the country; and they exert a weird fascination.

Lawrence M. Friedman, *Crime and Punishment in American History*, 1993

TV Forensic Science

The various "CSI" television shows depicting forensic scientists who are each versed in forensic pathology, firearms identification, fingerprint identification, toxicology, blood spatter analysis, DNA profiling, forensic anthropology, odontology, and document examination, and who also process crime scenes, conduct homicide investigations, and make arrests, inspire thousands of high school graduates every year to enroll in criminal justice programs offered by at least two thousand colleges and universities. When asked why they have chosen criminal justice as a major, many of these students say "forensics." When asked what they mean by "forensics," CJ majors express hopes of some day doing what the stars of the "CSI" shows do every week on television.

Eventually these students find out that the "CSI" people do not exist in reality. A small percentage of these forensic hopefuls actually earn degrees in science and get jobs in crime labs. A handful of them attend medical school and became forensic pathologists. A few join police departments as patrol officers and work their way up to the position of criminal investigator.

Most of the criminal justice students who initially express an interest in "forensics" do not want to be stuck all day in a crime lab. They avoided science courses in high school, and want no part of science in college. Most of these CJ majors end up working in the corrections system as prison guards, parole agents, or as social workers.

In a November 4, 2011 article in *The New York Times*, Christopher Drew reported that colleges and universities are not graduating nearly enough people holding degrees in science, technology, engineering, and math (STEM). Studies have found that between 40 and 60 percent of STEM majors either switch to other subjects or fail to graduate. These students were either unprepared for college-level science or quit because they weren't willing to put in the hard work these studies require. Kevin Rask, a professor at Wake Forest conducted a study in 2010 that showed the lowest grades on campus were issued in the introductory math and science courses. The chemistry department's grades averaged 2.78 out of a possible 4.0. Math students earned an average of 2.90. Education, language and English courses recorded the highest averages ranging from 3.33 to 3.36.

Violent Crime as Entertainment

American culture as a whole has cultivated a taste for violence that seems to be insatiable. We are a people obsessed with violence, and consequently, our entertainment industry is driven by such violence. The violence of our popular culture reflected in movies, TV programs, magazines, and fact or fiction books in the latter part of the twentieth century has made the shocking realism of this violence a routine task that we all face. Our own sense of humanity is anesthetized to the point of losing consciousness. [The trend has continued into the twenty-first century. A recent study showed that movies rated R in the 1990s are much milder than their modern counterparts. Moreover, the Internet is a venue for people who enjoy the aftermath of criminal deviance and raw violence.]

Steven A. Egger, *The Killers Among Us*, 1998

Types of Fascinating Murder Cases

Most crimes, even serious ones, make the nightly news or the local newspaper once or twice then slip into media oblivion. A few attract local or regional public interest for a period of time. Only a handful of cases become national news stories, and even fewer rise to what could be called celebrity crime status. Celebrated crimes of the twentieth century would include the Lindbergh kidnapping, the O. J. Simpson murder, and the John F. Kennedy assassination. I don't think the twenty-first century has seen its first truly celebrated crime. But there have been quite a few fascinating murder cases over the past fourteen years.

Twenty-Four Types of Newsworthy Murder Cases

1. Murder cases featuring strong suspects with no eyewitnesses or physical clues.
2. Serial murders with plenty of physical clues but no suspects.
3. Dismemberment cases involving innocent and unlikely victims.
4. Carefully planned murders by physicians, priests, university professors, and other unlikely suspects.
5. Black widow poisoning cases involving several dead husbands.
6. Angel of death hospital poisoning cases involving several patients.
7. Murder investigations that feature either brilliant or bungled police work.
8. Murder-for-hire cases involving unlikely masterminds.
9. Murders that produce trials featuring conflicting expert forensic testimony.
10. Sudden and suspicious death cases involving dueling cause and manner of death testimony.
11. Murders involving dueling blood spatter, ballistic, and human bite mark evidence.
12. Murder trials involving obvious suspects but missing bodies. (So-called no-body cases.)
13. Murders involving evil kids.
14. Love triangle murder cases involving prominent people and plenty of sex.
15. Murders involving celebrity defendants.
16. Major mafia hits.
17. Domestic bombing cases involving many victims.
18. Mass school shootings.
19. Murders with unusual motives.
20. Murders involving unusual murder weapons.
21. Murderous armored truck heists.
22. Murder trials involving the acquittal of obviously guilty defendants.
23. Murder cases featuring the conviction of innocent defendants.
24. Cold case murders solved by modern forensic science.

The Stars of Criminal Trials

It is a fact of life that victims get lost in murder trials as the focus of attention shifts to the defendant in the courtroom. It is also a fact that the defendant becomes a sympathetic figure in many people's eyes. The charismatic star O. J. Simpson dominated the proceedings the moment he made his entrance into the courtroom each morning, totally aware of the effect his presence made. His cadre of lawyers, as well as one of the deputies who guarded him, were deferential. His every reaction, from his frequent exasperation to his occasional laughter, captivated the attention of the room. When photographs of the slashed victims, Nicole Brown Simpson and Ronald Goldman, lying in grotesque positions in gallons of blood, were flashed on the large screen in the courtroom, observers no longer recoiled in horror. They had become used to them.

Dominick Dunne, *Justice,* 2001

The JonBenet Ramsey Case

A 5:52 AM emergency call that a child had been kidnapped brought a pair of Boulder, Colorado police officers to John and Patsy Ramsey's 3-story house on December 26, 1996. Patsy Ramsey said she had found a handwritten ransom note inside on the stairs. Fearing that her 6-year-old daughter, JonBenet, had been kidnapped for ransom, she had called 911. After a cursory sweep of the 15-room dwelling, the patrolmen called for assistance.

During the next two hours, amid friends and relatives who had come to console the family, police set up wiretap and recording equipment to monitor negotiations with the kidnappers. At one in the afternoon, Boulder detective Linda Arndt asked John Ramsey to look around the house for "anything unusual." Thirty minutes later, he and one of his friends discovered JonBenet's body in a small basement room. Her mouth had been sealed with duct tape, and she had lengths of white rope coiled around her neck and right wrist. The rope around her neck was tied to what looked like the handle of a paintbrush. Breaking all the rules of crime scene investigation, John Ramsey removed the tape, carried his daughter up the basement steps, and laid her body on the living room floor. Detective Arndt picked up the child, placed her body next to the Christmas tree, and covered it with a sweat shirt. Because the police had not conducted a thorough and timely search of the house, there would be no crime scene photographs.

In the months following the murder, the police, prosecutors, media, and most Americans believed that someone in the family had killed JonBenet Ramsey. But if this were the case, then who had written the two and a half page ransom note? Forensic document examiners eliminated John Ramsey as the ransom note writer, and all but one handwriting expert concluded that Patsy had probably *not* authored the document. Also, evidence surfaced that an intruder could have come into the house through a broken window in the basement.

After a 13-year battle with ovarian cancer, Patsy Ramsey died on June 14, 2006. She was 49. The media that had helped police and prosecutors portray the Ramseys as child murderers treated the death as a one-day news event, giving it less attention than the passing of a supporting actor on an old TV sitcom. In April 2006, two months before her death, the Ramseys flew from their home in Michigan back to Boulder where they met with district attorney Mary Keenan (now Lacy), who asked them if they had ever heard of a man named John Mark Karr. They Ramseys said they had not-- neither the name nor the description of this man rang a bell. What did he have to do with the case?

Karr, a 41-year-old itinerate elementary school teacher, an American living in Bangkok, Thailand, since 2002 had been corresponding with Michael Tracey, a journalism professor at the University of Colorado. Karr's interest in the JonBenet murder had drawn him to the Boulder professor who had produced three television documentaries favorable to the theory the crime had been committed by an intruder. The emails from Karr, sent under the pseudonym Daxis, had recently become quite bizarre, reflecting more than just a morbid interest in the case. After receiving a series of disturbing phone calls from this man, Professor Tracey alerted the district attorney's office. The calls were traced to John Mark Karr in Bangkok.

After Daxis had confessed to Tracey that he had accidentally killed JonBenet while inducing asphyxia for his sexual gratification, he became a suspect in the murder. Karr had revealed over the phone that when he couldn't revive Jon Benet, he had struck her in the head with a blunt object. He told the professor that he had engaged in oral sex with the victim, but had not performed sexual penetration. Aware that Tracey was writing a book on the Ramsey case, Karr offered the author the inside story from the killer's point of view. In the event the book became a movie, Karr wanted to be played by Johnny Depp.

Having taken over the Ramsey case investigation from the Boulder Police Department, the district attorney's office began investigating John Mark Karr. District attorney investigators spoke to the authorities in Bangkok, and read hundreds of the emails Karr had sent to the professor. One of the messages suggested that Karr had a general knowledge of forensic science, and had made all of this up: "The DNA might not match, but you can't trust the test."

As Ramsey case investigators gathered details of Karr's life and background, it became clear that he was not an ordinary man, and that his strangeness was not inconsistent with the profile of a person who might commit a Ramsey-type crime. After Karr's parents divorced when he was 9, he went to live with his grandparents in Hamilton, Alabama. In 1983, one year after graduating from Hamilton High School, Karr, then 20, married a 13-year-old girl. The marriage ended 9 months later in an annulment. In 1989, Karr married 16-year-old Lara Marie Knutson. In 4 years, he and his wife had three sons. While pursuing a teaching degree through an online teacher's college, Karr opened a licensed day-care center in his home. Although he didn't have a teaching degree, he also worked as a substitute teacher at Hamilton High School. He acquired a college degree in 1999, and that year closed his day-care business. A year later, Karr and his family were residing in Petaluma, California where he taught as a substitute in six schools in the Sonoma Valley Unified School District.

One year after arriving in Petaluma, while teaching at the Pueblo Vista Elementary School, Karr was arrested by investigators from the Sonoma County Sheriff's Office. They had found child pornography on Karr's computer, and arrested him on 5 misdemeanor counts of possessing such material. Karr's bail was reduced after he spent 6 months in the county lockup awaiting trial, and he was released on October 2001. While in custody, Karr had written a letter to Richard Allen Davis who had been convicted on kidnapping and murdering Polly Klaas in Petaluma. When Karr failed to show for a court appearance in the pornography case, the judge issued a bench warrant for his arrest, making him a California fugitive from justice.

During the child pornography investigation, detectives in Sonoma County came across writings and notes Karr had made pertaining to the murder of JonBenet Ramsey. In these musings, Karr had speculated on the killer's thoughts as he committed the crime. Although these were not confessions, the Sonoma detectives took the writings seriously enough to notify the authorities in Boulder. There were follow-up discussions between investigators in California and Colorado, but nothing came of the discovery.

Karr was now divorced. His children and former wife had moved back to Hamilton, Alabama, and following his release from the Sonoma County Jail, Karr fled the country. He taught in Honduras and Costa Rica, and worked as a children's nanny in Germany, the Netherlands, and South Korea. In December 2005, Karr arrived in Bangkok where he had landed a grade-school teaching position.

On August 11, 2006, 4 months after district attorney Mary Lacy learned that the Ramsey email writer and telephone confessor was John Mark Karr, police and immigration authorities in Thailand informed her that Karr was living in a downtown Bangkok apartment. In less than a week, Karr would be starting a new teaching job at the New Sathorn International School in the city. Because the authorities didn't want this man interacting with young girls at this school, the Thai police planned to arrest and deport Karr within the next five days. This development presented Lacy with a dilemma. If she did nothing, a man who had confessed to killing JonBenet Ramsey would slip away upon his return to the United States. If she filed charges against Karr, and had him extradited back to Colorado, the probable cause supporting the arrest warrant would be based entirely on his emails and his telephone confessions. Lacy's investigators had not linked Karr to the ransom note through his handwriting, could not place him in Colorado on or about December 26, 1996, and had not matched his DNA to a pair of foreign bloodstains on JonBenet's underwear.

Operating on the theory that John Mark Karr was *not* a false confessor, and that his DNA would eventually connect him to the victim, Lacy presented her case to a Boulder judge who issued a warrant for Karr's arrest on charges of first-degree murder, kidnapping, and sexual assault. The district attorney also dispatched one of her investigators to Bangkok.

After watching Karr's apartment building for 5 days, police and immigration officials took him into custody on August 16, 2006. In response to a Thai police officer that informed Karr that he had been charged with first-degree murder in Boulder Karr declared that his killing of JonBenet had been accidental, and therefore the charge should more appropriately be second-degree murder. He had confessed again.

After being flown to Los Angeles from Bangkok, Karr arrived in Colorado on August 24 where he was incarcerated in the Boulder County Jail. Four days later, the John Mark Karr phase of the Ramsey case came to an abrupt end when Mary Lacy announced that because Karr's DNA didn't match the crime scene evidence, the charges against him would be dropped. Moreover, he had not written the ransom note. The case quickly fell out of the news, and John Mark Karr slipped back into obscurity.

The JonBenet Ramsey case shot back into the news in October 2013 when a Colorado judge ordered the release of indictments returned against the Ramseys in 1999. The Boulder County Grand Jury alleged that each parent "did permit a child to be unreasonably placed in a situation which posed a threat of injury to the child's life or health which resulted in the death of JonBenet Ramsey." The grand jurors also alleged that the Ramseys "did render assistance to a person, with intent to hinder, delay and prevent the discovery, detention, apprehension, prosecution and punishment of said person for the commission of a crime, knowing the person being assisted has committed and was suspected of the crime of murder in the first degree and child abuse resulting in death."

Boulder district attorney Alex Hunter refused to sign off on the indictments because the charges were not supported by sufficient evidence to support a conviction.

In speaking to reporters, the Ramsey family attorney L. Lin Wood called the indictments "nonsensical." According to Wood, "they reveal nothing about the evidence reviewed by the grand jury and are clearly the result of a confused and compromised process."

Regarding the old indictments, CNN legal analyst Jeffrey Tobin, in pointing out the indictments merely showed that a majority of the grand jurors felt there was probable cause to charge the parents--a lower standard than proving guilt beyond a reasonable doubt--said, "it doesn't precisely say that the grand jury thought the parents killed JonBenet. It's not precisely clear what they thought."

While it is not being investigated, the JonBenet Ramsey murder case remains unsolved.

Famous True Crime Automobiles

The invention and popularity of the automobile changed and defined the nature of criminal behavior in America and around the world. The motorized vehicle became the instrument, and the fruit of crime. Cars, in the old days referred to as "machines," provided a degree of mobility that changed the nature of law enforcement as well. By 1920, police departments across the country were entirely motorized, and soon after that, they were equipped with two-way radios. In 1926, the U.S. Supreme Court, in *U.S. v. Carroll*, held that an automobile could be searched without a warrant if there was probable cause to believe the vehicle was being used in the commission of a crime. In those days, the offense often involved the transportation of contraband liquor. A motorized America, and the resultant mobility of the criminal, contributed to the federalization of American law enforcement. By the 1930s, bank robbery, kidnapping, interstate car theft, and transporting prostitutes across state lines (White Slave Traffic Act) became federal offenses investigated by the FBI. By 1947, the FBI Crime Lab featured a reference collection of tire treads against which crime scene impression could be compared.

Many crime and police history buffs are fascinated with vehicles owned or used by serial killers, mafia bosses, depression era bank robbers, and famous murder victims. People who collect and restore old cars are interested in this aspect of crime history as well. Police and crime museums around the country exhibit old police cars, paddy wagons, and vehicles that had been used in historic regional crimes.

The Bonnie and Clyde Death Car

On May 23, 1934, a small army of cops in southern Louisiana ambushed the depression era outlaws, Bonnie and Clyde. In a barrage of bullets, the police riddled the couple's 1934 gray Ford sedan killing them both. These folk-hero degenerates had stolen the deluxe sedan in Topeka, Kansas from a woman named Ruth Warren. (For a time the car was known as the "Warren Death Car.") When the federal government refused to release the blood-soaked, bullet-ridden Ford, Ruth Warren, realizing its value as crime memorabilia, sued the government and won.

From 1940 to 1952, the shot-up Ford was on exhibit at an amusement park in Cincinnati, Ohio. In 1952, a man with the name Ted Toddy bought the car for $14,500. During the 1980s, the Bonnie and Clyde vehicle sat on display at several casino-resorts in Nevada. I'm not sure where the car is today, but not too long ago it could be seen at Whiskey Pete's Resort and Casino in Prim, Nevada. (In January 2012, at an auction in Kansas City, Missouri, a collector bought two Bonnie and Clyde bank robbery guns. The Thompson submachine gun, and the 1897 Winchester 12-gauge shotgun, had been recovered in 1933 from the couple's hideout in Joplin. The collector paid $210,000 for the weapons.)

Al Capone's Cadillac

The vicious prohibition era gangster from Chicago, during his murderous career as a bootlegger, owned several cars. The vehicle most closely associated with Capone is a 1928 green Cadillac limousine. The armor-plated V-8, equipped with bulletproof windows sold for $621,500 at a 2010 auction in California. The fact President Franklin D. Roosevelt had used the car after Capone went to prison, added to its value.

The Lindbergh Kidnap Car

Bruno Richard Hauptmann, on the night of March 1, 1932, drove his 1930 blue Dodge sedan from the Bronx, New York to the Charles Lindbergh estate near Hopewell, New Jersey. The 36-year-old unemployed carpenter used the homemade wooden extension ladder, compressed across the back seat of his car, to climb to the Lindbergh baby's second-story nursery window. Today, in West Trenton, the New Jersey State Police Museum and Learning Center, has the ladder on display. But they don't have the car Hauptmann used to commit the "crime of the century."

In 1958, after the state of New Jersey sold Hauptmann's Dodge at auction for $800, it disappeared. If you own a 1930 4-door Dodge that was once blue, check the vehicle identification number against the VIN on record at the New Jersey museum. You might own an important piece of American crime history.

Ted Bundy's "Teaching Tool"

Crime memorabilia collector Arthur Nash, in 2010, sold the 1968 Volkswagen Beetle owned by the executed serial killer, Ted Bundy, to the privately owned National Museum of Crime and Punishment in Washington, D.C. (The museum opened in 2008.) In the 1970s, Bundy lured many of him female victims into the car where many of them were raped and murdered. Museum speakers at the vehicles unveiling, aware that critics would accuse them of using Bundy's death car to extract admission fees from true crime sickos, insisted they were using the Volkswagen as a "teaching tool." At the highly publicized unveiling, one of the museum owners said, "Specifically, we don't recommend hitchhiking to anyone. This car represents a warning sign that you have to be careful."

JFK Assassination Vehicles

Early in 2011, at an auction in Scottsdale, Arizona, a bidder paid $120,000 for the ambulance that had carried the slain president, on November 23, 1963, from Andrews Air Force Base to the Bethesda National Hospital in Maryland. There has since been a debate over the authenticity of this purchase. Some believe the ambulance is a fake.

In 2012, the same auction house will be offering for sale the 1963 Cadillac hearse used to carry President Kennedy's body from the Dallas hospital to Air Force One at Dallas Love Field.

Other Infamous Vehicles

A few other collectible crime cars include: John Dillinger's 1933 Essex-Terraplane; the 1931 black Lincoln owned by Dutch Schultz; O. J. Simpson's 1995 white Ford Bronco; and the D.C. Snipers' Chevrolet Caprice.

Extreme Crime

Media focus on the most extreme variants of criminal behavior often causes people to forget that most crime does not involve stranger abductions, sadistic torture, chopping off of body parts, or using commercial airliners as bombs. Although the real-life catalog of bizarre and extreme crimes is filled with horror, tragedy, and untold human harm and loss, it includes an even longer list of more benign offenses that most TV producers would have no interest in devoting a one-hour prime time show to.

Jacqueline B. Helfgott, *Criminal Behavior,* 2008

O. J. Innocent?

From the June 1994 day in Los Angeles when Nicole Brown Simpson and Ronald Goldman were stabbed and slashed to death outside of O.J. Simpson's ex-wife's condo, to his October 1995 acquittal, the double murder case dominated the news in the U.S. and abroad. The investigation and trial involved DNA analysis, blood spatter interpretation, and plenty of forensic medicine. Because the physical evidence pointed to Simpson's guilt, the not guilty verdict introduced the public to the concept of jury nullification.

The infamous case turned police detectives, defense attorneys, and the trial judge into instant celebrities. Several of the major players in the case landed lucrative book deals. A few of these people evolved into television personalities. The Simpson case put CNN on the map, and elevated the careers of more than a few talking heads.

In America, the combination of celebrity-worship and the fascination with violent crime has produced a dozen or so "crimes of the century." In my opinion, the 20th Century featured three crimes of the century: the Lindbergh Kidnapping (1932), The John F. Kennedy Assassination (1961), and the O.J. Simpson double murder. In the Lindbergh case, Bruno Hauptmann, after being convicted on the strength of physical evidence connecting him to the crime, was executed in April 1936. Since then, there have been a handful of books, several television documentaries, hundreds of articles, and a HBO movie devoted to the theory that Hauptmann was an innocent man framed by the New Jersey State Police. It is my view that these exonerations of Hauptmann amount to junk history.

There have been more than 500 books written about the Kennedy assassination. While not an expert on this case, I subscribe to the view that Lee Harvey Oswald was the lone assassin. Dr. John Kelly, a friend of mine who taught in the University of Delaware's criminal justice department, spent twenty years investigating the assassination. He is firmly convinced that the Warren Commission got it right.

Because the physical evidence pointing to O.J. Simpson's guilt was so plentiful and incriminating, the case hadn't moved into the revisionist stage until this year. A few months ago a book came out that purports to exonerate Simpson. It has been followed by a television documentary in which another man is identified as the Nicole Simpson/Ronald Goldman killer. The revisionist stage of the O.J. Simpson case has begun.

In his book, *O.J. Is Innocent and I Can Prove It*, true crime writer/private investigator William Dear makes the case that Simpson's then 40-year-old son Jason committed the murders. According to the author, while O.J. was present when they were murdered, he didn't wield the knife. This is convenient because it helps explain away the physical evidence linking O.J. to the death scene.

So, what evidence does this revisionist author have against Jason Simpson? Not much. In Jason's abandoned storage locker, Mr. Dear found a hunting knife that could have been the murder weapon. There was nothing on the knife connecting it to the crime. After the murders, Jason retained an attorney. The author also found a photograph of Jason Simpson in which he is wearing a knit cap similar to one recovered from the crime scene. Two months before the murders, Jason Simpson assaulted his girlfriend, and according to some crime profiler, the suspect has a homicidal personality. And finally, Jason Simpson did not have an airtight alibi. Although there is not enough here to justify a legal arrest, William Dear managed to pad this "evidence" into a book-length manuscript someone was willing to publish. When the book first came out, it attracted a little media attention then quickly faded from the news. But uncritical readers willing to believe revisionist accounts of famous cases based on nothing but speculation and faux evidence have embraced Dear's book. I am not one of them.

On November 21, 2012, the Investigation Discovery Channel aired a documentary called "My Brother the Serial Killer," a story about a convicted serial killer from Kentucky named Glen Edward Rogers. Narrated by his older brother Clay Rogers, the documentary is a well told, visually dramatic, and interesting biography of a serial killer. The 60-year-old murderer, who claims to have killed 70 women, has been on Florida's death row for fifteen years. Rogers has exhausted his appeals and could be executed within the year. To me, the documentary revealed how easy it is for serial killers to get away with their murders.

The documentary's main hook, however, is its connection to the O.J. Simpson case. According to a criminal profiler and true crime writer named Anthony Meloli, Glen Rogers revealed to him that O.J. Simpson had hired him to break into Nicole's condo. Rogers, who claims that he was working at the dwelling as a painter, was supposed to steal a set of $20,000 diamond earrings Simpson had given to his ex-wife. According to Rogers, O.J. told him, "You may have to kill her." Rogers also informed the profiler that after murdering Nicole Simpson, he took an angel pin off her body and mailed it to his mother. The killer's mom supposedly wore this piece of jewelry at one of her son's murder trials.

As the story goes, O.J., shortly after the murders, walked up the bloody sidewalk to check on Roger's work. This doesn't make sense. One would think that Simpson would take pains to distance himself from the burglary and possible murder. In so doing, he left his shoe impressions at the crime scene. (Again, how convenient.)

Ronald Goldman's sister, Kim Goldman, in speaking to a reporter after having watched "My Brother the Serial Killer," said, "I am appalled at the level of irresponsibility demonstrated by the network and the producers of the so-called documentary." A spokesperson for the LAPD said, "We have no reason to believe that Mr. Rogers was involved [in the case]. Nevertheless, in the interest of being thorough in the case, our robbery/homicide detectives will investigate [Roger's] claims." If I were in charge of the re-investigation, I would bring in an objective, highly qualified polygraph examiner and hook Rogers up to the instrument before they give him the needle. If he passes the test, the case could move forward. If he fails the lie detector, chalk up his story to a guy who just wants some attention, and a criminal profiler looking for his next book. Except for the O.J. Simpson angle, "My Brother the Serial Killer" is an outstanding true crime documentary.

Public Opinion in Big Cases

Why should trial lawyers care about public relations? Their job is to persuade judges and jurors, not the public or the pundits. But the jurors come from the same public that would be watching the preliminary hearing on television. And judges, too, are human beings, who are influenced by public opinion.

Alan M. Dershowitz, *Reasonable Doubt*, 1996

Crime Myths

In order for the momentum of a crime myth to be prolonged...myths must be accompanied by certain characterizations. Momentum is achieved if the crime problem has traits that either instill fear or threaten the vast majority of society in some appreciable way. Not unlike Greek mythology, modern crime myths must follow certain themes for success. There must be "virtuous' heroes, "innocent" victims, and "evil" villains who pose a clear and certain threat to the audience. Only then can a crime myth reach its potential. [There were two crime myths that dominated the 1980s: hundreds of serial killers running loose and an epidemic of stranger kidnappings of children. Currently there is a myth that an army of meth and bath salts zombies roam the streets of our cities.]

Victor Kappeler, *The Mythology of Crime and Criminal Justice*, 2000

True Crime Writer Joe McGuinniss

Joe McGuinniss was born in Manhattan, New York on December 9 1942. Raised by well-to-do parents in New York City and Los Angeles, he graduated in 1964 from Holy Cross University in Worcester, Massachusetts. After failing to get into Columbia University's graduate school of journalism, McGuinniss became a staff reporter for the *Worcester Telegram.*

Following stints at *The Philadelphia Bulletin* and *The Philadelphia Inquirer,* McGuinniss published his first book in 1968. *The Selling of the President,* a nonfiction account of the marketing of presidential candidate Richard Nixon, became a bestseller and remained on *The New York Times* bestseller list for six months. That book established the 26-year-old author's reputation as a serious investigative journalist and landed him a job as writer-in-residence at the *Los Angeles Harold Examiner.*

The Jeffrey MacDonald Murder Case

On February 17, 1970, Green Beret Captain and Army surgeon Jeffrey MacDonald reported a deadly invasion of his home at Fort Bragg, North Carolina. At the scene Army Criminal Investigation Division (CID) officers found MacDonald's wife Colette and his two daughters, Kimberly and Kristen, stabbed to death. MacDonald himself had superficial puncture wounds. According to MacDonald, he had struggled with the hippie intruders who had murdered his family.

Following an internal military review of the case, Captain MacDonald was cleared of wrongdoing. But in January 1975, a federal grand jury indicted him on three counts of first-degree murder. He vigorously maintained his innocence and stuck to his original version of the mass murder.

At some point after MacDonald's indictment, Joe McGuinniss entered the case as a journalist who intended to write a book exonerating the Green Beret officer. The writer acquired access into the inner circle of the MacDonald defense team by gaining MacDonald's trust as a loyal friend. In reality, the more McGuinniss learned about the case, the more convinced he became of MacDonald's guilt. The true crime writer believed that MacDonald, a sociopath who wanted to be free of his family, had murdered his wife and daughters in a homicidal frenzy aided by his abuse of diet pills.

In 1979, when the jury found MacDonald guilty as charged, McGuinniss, to maintain his position within the MacDonald defense team, feigned shock and outrage. But when McGuinniss' book on the case, *Fatal Vision,* came out in 1983, it was Jeffery MacDonald and his supporters who were shocked and outraged by the author's duplicity.

Shortly after the publication of *Fatal Vision,* a book that quickly became a runaway bestseller, Jeffery MacDonald sued the true crime writer for beach of contract.

When the first of its kind lawsuit went to trial, several well-known true crime authors such as Joseph Wambaugh and Norman Mailer testified on McGuinniss' behalf as expert witnesses. According to Wambaugh and Mailer, McGuinniss had done what any serious investigative journalist would do to get to the bottom of a case. In other words, a true crime writer has no duty to be honest with the person he's writing about. At the conclusion of the trial, some jurors bought McGuinniss' defense but others did not. This led to a hung jury.

The insurance company for the publisher of *Fatal Vision,* shocked and concerned that some of the jurors had sided with a man who had killed his wife and two children over the guy who had written the book about the mass murder, settled the suit out of court for $325,000. In the court of public opinion, McGuinniss did not come off as a likable person, and ordinary people did not approve of his journalistic trickery.

In 1989, journalist Janet Malcolm wrote a long piece about the MacDonald-McGuinniss suit in *The New Yorker.* A year later the article came out as a book called *The Journalist and the Murderer.* (It's a great read, by the way.) Malcolm's defining of the journalist/subject relationship as inherently exploitive has become a source of debate. Regarding the MacDonald/McGuinniss relationship, Malcolm famously wrote: "Every journalist who is not too stupid or full of himself to notice what is going on knows that what he does is morally indefensible."

Jerry Allen Potter and Fred Bott published a book called *Fatal Justice* that argues for MacDonald's innocence. According to these authors, McGuinniss's book is full of substantive errors and groundless speculation.

Regardless of one's take on MacDonald's guilt or innocence, *Fatal Vision* is an exceptionally well-written account of a fascinating murder case. It also popularized the concept of the sociopathic killer who appears normal on the outside but in reality is a pathologically narcissistic liar without feelings of guilt.

Joe McGuinniss followed *Fatal Vision* with two bestselling true crime books. *Blind Faith*, published in 1989, is about a New Jersey man who hired a hit man to murder his wife. *Cruel Doubt*, 1991, features teenage murderers inspired by the role-playing game Dungeons and Dragons.

The method McGuinniss used to research his last book, a biography of Sarah Palin, also stirred controversy. In 2010, he rented a house in Wasilla, Alaska next door to the former vice presidential candidate. Critics called McGuinniss a peeping Tom, and Palin accused him of stalking her and her family. *The Rogue: Searching for the Real Sarah Palin* came out in 2011. The book, failing to break new ground about a person the public had lost interest in, did not make the bestseller list.

On March 10, 2014, Joe McGuinniss died in a Worcester Massachusetts hospital from prostate cancer. At his death at age 71, he was living in Pelham with his second wife Nancy Doherty.

Fatal Vision is considered by many to be a true crime classic equal to Joseph Wambaugh's *Onion Field,* Truman Capote's *In Cold Blood,* and Norman Mailer's *Executioner's Song.*

Jeffery MacDonald remains in prison and continues to maintain his innocence.

The Wiseguy Persona

The wiseguy does not see himself as a criminal or even a bad person; he sees himself as a businessman, a shrewd hustler, one step ahead of ordinary suckers. The wiseguy lives by a vastly different set of rules than those observed by regular people, rules that were fashioned by their criminal forefathers and proven to work by generations of mobsters before them. Wiseguys exist in a bizarre parallel universe, a world where avarice and violence and corruption are the norm, and where the routines that most ordinary people hold dear--working good jobs, being with family, living an honest life--are seen as the curse of the weak and stupid. Wiseguys resemble us in many ways, but make no mistake: they might as well be from another planet, so alien and abnormal are their thoughts and habits.

Joseph D. Pistone, *The Way of the Wiseguy*, 2004

Charles Manson's Intelligence

Charles Manson scored 109 on one prison I.Q. test, when he was 16, and 121 on another a few years later. The first result is slightly above average; the second is said to be in the "high normal" range. Jeff Guinn [the author of *The Life and Times of Charles Manson*] doesn't identify which tests were given. Was Manson brilliant, as some have claimed? He probably wasn't. He cobbled together his pseudo-philosophy by studying Dale Carnegie and L. Ron Hubbard. He had no sense of how to adjust his conduct, grooming habits or conversation when dealing with the Hollywood producers who might have helped him realize his absolute goal: to become a rock star more famous than the Beatles. He had no clue how to self-censor, shooting himself in the foot over and over. Even so, he proved to be spellbinding to the vulnerable.

Ann Rule in reviewing Jeff Guinn's 2013 book for *The New York Times Book Review*

Groundbreaking Crime Films of the 1960s

In 1957, Robert Bloch published *Psycho* based on the crimes of Wisconsin serial killer and cannibal Ed Gein. Alfred Hitchcock brought the novel to the screen in 1960. That changed everything. A new bogeyman replaced vampires, werewolves and other monsters as the thing that would haunt human dreams. Thanks to Anthony Perkins' terrifying performance as the psychotic Norman Bates, the public's new nightmares featured the guy down the street and the girl next door with evil hidden in their minds and horrors buried under the floorboards or in the backyard. The perceptions that Norman Bates created are reinforced every time the news features another story of some gardener or carpenter or mailman or nurse who had killed a dozen or more people. Hitchcock also introduced the public to the fictional film version of a Ted Bundy-like killer in *Strangers on a Train*.

In 1967, the prototype of Hannibal the Cannibal, the professional as madman, was portrayed by Peter O'Toole in *Night of the Generals*. While the character of General Tanz is a Nazi, which personifies a monster already, the concept of such a brilliant serial killer character is a frightening creation. Here we have a sexual psychopath in uniform, with power and authority. Picture this same character as a police officer or some other powerful authority figure and you have the public's worst nightmare.

In 1968, the groundwork for today's genre of true crime movies was laid out with the film *The Boston Strangler*. This was the first docudrama about a real-life serial killer.

Also in 1968, Rod Steiger portrayed the perfect fictional serial killer in *No Way to Treat a Lady*. Here is a classic model of the sexual psychopath who vents his obsessional hate for his mother on his victims. The character is extremely true-to-life with all the chameleon qualities that exist in real serial killers. He is intelligent and egotistical and never changes his pattern until suitable motivation is provided.

Sean Mactire, *Malicious Intent*, 1995

Best Crime Films (fiction and nonfiction)

Fargo (1996)

Set in North Dakota and Minnesota, this dark comedy features a car salesman who arranges to have his wife kidnapped for ransom, and a pregnant, small town police chief who investigates a pair of highway murders. Any film that has one killer stuffing another into a wood chipper can't be bad. This film works on all levels.

The Informant (2009)

This is a fact-based comic drama about a pathologically lying FBI whistle-blower in the mid-1990s Archer Daniels Midland lysine price-fixing conspiracy. The film is an adaptation of journalist Kurt Eiechenwald's 2000 book of the same name. Matt Damon, the whistle blowing company embezzler, is brilliant as a nerd from Indiana with a background in science that finds himself in over his head.

Insomnia (1997)

A psychological thriller set in a small Alaskan town near the Arctic Circle, about a true crime novelist (Robin Williams) who murdered a high school girl, and the world-weary Los Angeles Detective (Al Pacino) out to arrest him. The exhausted cop (who can't sleep because the sun never sets) tries to cover-up the accidental shooting of his partner by switching ballistics evidence. A riveting small town tale set in a northern wilderness.

One-Hour Photo (2002)

This tense, leisurely paced psychological drama features a lonely and alienated box store camera film developer (Robin Williams) who develops a pathological fixation on a man, his wife and their boy who he thinks is the ideal American family. His disillusionment triggers an event that leads to his undoing. This film is more about mood and the comparative bleakness of one man's life than it is about criminal violence.

Se7ven (1995)

A gritty detective yarn featuring a pair of homicide investigators (Brad Pitt and Morgan Freeman) trying to identify and stop a serial killer whose victims have violated one of the seven sins of gluttony, envy, lust, pride, sloth, greed, and wrath. In the end, the young detective is faced with a sickening dilemma pertaining to the sin of wrath. This film is as graphic and good as it is brutal.

The Departed (2006)

Set in Boston, Massachusetts, the rise and bloody fall of Irish crime boss Francis Costello (Jack Nicholson). The film features two state cops (Leonardo Di Caprio and Matt Damon), one corrupt and the other working undercover to identify him. Loosely based on the life of the real Boston mobster, Whitey Bulger who, after years as a fugitive, was recently arrested in California. This is a great film with big stars playing big roles.

Donnie Brasco (1997)

In the 1970s FBI agent Joe D. Pistone infiltrated the Bonanno crime family in New York. The agent's (Johnny Depp) undercover stint led to the conviction of dozens of Mafia figures. The FBI pulled the agent, using the name Donnie Brasco, off the case just before his cover was blown. The film is a realistic depiction of a crime family and the type of people who become "made" men.

Goodfellas (1990)

Unlike "The Godfather" that in some ways romanticizes and glorifies the Mafia of the 1940s and 50s, the wiseguys portrayed in *Goodfellas* are realistically portrayed as violent thugs in cheesy suits. The film is based on the true story of Henry Hill (Robert De Niro), the Irish hood from Brooklyn who masterminded the 1970s multi-million-dollar Air France heist at JFK. In the end, drugs, greed and recklessness bring down this crew of fascinating degenerates. The film is an adaptation of Nicholas Pileggi's 1986 book, *Wiseguys*.

Pulp Fiction (1994)

This Quentin Taratino, Los Angeles noir classic, features a pair of philosophizing hit men (John Travolta and Robert Jackson), a boxer (Bruce Willis) on the lamb because he didn't throw a fight, and an underworld crime scene cleanup specialist (Harvey Keitel). The film, comprised of loosely connected episodes told in flashbacks and flash forwards, breaks new ground in visual storytelling.

Dead Presidents (1995)

This is a loosely fact-based film about a group of men returning to the Bronx after combat duty as Marines in Vietnam. The action comes to a head when an armored truck heist goes terribly wrong. The film transforms violence into choreographed art.

The Onion Field (1979)

This film adaptation of Joseph Wambaugh's 1973 nonfiction book of the same name (Wambaugh also wrote the screenplay), tells the story of the

1963 execution style murder of LAPD officer Ian Campbell. Gregory Powell and an accomplice abducted Campbell and his partner Karl Hettinger at gunpoint and drove them to an onion field near Bakersfield where Powell murdered Campbell. In 1972 Powell's death sentence was commuted to life. Powell, played in the movie by James Woods, has never expressed remorse for the cold-blooded murder. He is still behind bars and has terminal prostate cancer. The film, an indictment of the California criminal justice system, makes the time and effort to convict these two killers--endless defense motions, court delays, appeals and the like--a part of the story. Young moviegoers today may find the film a little slow. I think it is a classic.

Training Day (2001)

This police drama, covering a single day, follows the on-duty actions of a corrupt LA narcotics cop (Denzel Washington), his crew of dirty officers, and a trainee (Ethan Hawk). In this film, except for the trainee who has traded in his uniform for plainclothes, you can't tell the good guys from the bad guys. This is an unflattering look at Los Angeles, the drug culture, and the cops.

The Firm (1993)

A young hotshot lawyer (Tom Cruise) realizes his prestigious Memphis law firm is corrupt and behind the murders of two former law partners. The young lawyer is caught between the FBI and his murderous employer. The film also stars Gene Hackman as the new attorney's legal mentor. The film is a tense Sydney Pollack thriller.

Serpico (1973)

This is the true story of New York Police Officer Frank Serpico (Al Pacino) who blew the whistle on the culture of police corruption in the 1960s and 70s. Serpico's courage led to the Knapp Commission Hearings in 1971, and a series of police reforms. Based on the nonfiction book of the same title by Peter Maas.

Ronin (1998)

An international crime thriller set in France about former special-forces operatives and intelligent agents (Robert De Niro et. al.) whose mission involves stealing a mysterious package from a heavily guarded convoy. Some great car chase scenes.

Casino (1995)

Casino is a Martin Scorsese film about the real life Las Vegas casino manager Frank Rosenthal (Robert De Niro) who ran three casinos in the

1970s and 80s. A gripping and vivid adaptation of Nicholas Pileggi's book of the same title, the film depicts Las Vegas during its gangster era. The movie also stars Sharon Stone as De Niro's out-of-control wife. Also starring Joe Pesci as an out-of-control gangster who, like De Niro, comes to a bad end. Both men had outlived their time as Las Vegas moved out of its gangster era.

Dragnet

Although not one of those kids who wanted to grow up to be a police detective, or one who devoured mystery novels, crime-fighting comics, or Sherlock Holmes fiction, I was a big fan of the TV series "Dragnet" starring Jack Webb as Sergeant Joe Friday of the Los Angeles Police Department. The show first aired from 1951 to 1959, then came back in 1967 and ran to 1970. I can't remember why "Dragnet" appealed to me as a middle and high school student, but after watching a few episodes recently on a TV retro network, I know why I like it now. I admire the show today because the stories, based on actual police files, portray the bureaucracy, boredom, frustrations and drudgery--punctuated by bursts of danger--of real life detective work.

The crimes featured on "Dragnet," ranging from murder, armed robbery, missing persons, arson, check fraud, embezzlement, and even shoplifting, unfolded in a straightforward fashion, helped along by Jack Webb's voice-over narration in which you are informed of the time, date, and place of every scene. The acting is direct and unpretentious (stilted if you're a fan of the modern, angst-ridden I'm-going-for-an-acting-award style) and doesn't overshadow the terse, crisp, clear-eyed exposition and dialog. I like the script writing, an enjoyable blend of Ernest Hemingway and first-rate news reporting. Journalism school students should be required to watch episodes of "Dragnet" and encouraged to emulate its style.

Each "Dragnet" episode had a beginning, middle, and end. I especially enjoyed the story wrap-ups because you learned the fate of the criminal suspects who were tried and convicted in "Department 187 of the Superior Court of California, in and for the city and county of Los Angeles." First-degree murderers were "executed in the manner prescribed by law at the state penitentiary, San Quentin, California." Bam. Case closed.

Jack Webb also produced the show that was written principally by James E. Moser who peppered the scripts with police terminology such as M. O. and APB (all points bulletin). Moser realistically portrayed criminal cases solved by detectives that doggedly went through the investigative steps. Detective Joe Friday didn't have feelings in his "gut," or lay awake at night in angst over the mental and emotional strains of being a cop. He did his job in workman like fashion without all the bellyaching.

"Dragnet" was good stuff then, and, in my opinion, refreshing now.

Music and Crime

School shootings, like other mass murders and suicide clusters, reflects the culture of the times. The role of the media takes many forms in such events, but perhaps nothing rules and mirrors the culture of adolescents the way music does. Yesterday's swing and jazz, as remembered in bebop, the Lindy, the shimmy, and the Charleston, have evolved into the music that fills our world today: Rock and roll. New wave. Punk. Heavy metal. Grunge rock. Hip-Hop. Gangsta rock. Death rock. The beat, lyrics, groups and individual artists are held in high regard. Rock-star look-alikes are everywhere. And the fashion follows the music in more than clothing. Attitudes and beliefs systems are born from the messages communicated or reinforced through teen music.

Loren Coleman, *The Copycat Effect*, 2004

ABOUT THE AUTHOR

Jim Fisher is a graduate of Westminster College (Pennsylvania) and Vanderbilt University Law School. As an ex-FBI agent and former professor of criminal justice at Edinboro University of Pennsylvania, he has authored eleven books in the true crime genre. His narrative nonfiction works include the definitive account of the Lindbergh kidnapping case, the murder persecution of two juveniles, the brutal killing of an Amish woman, the crimes of a rogue literary agent, and the looting of a major archaeological site. He has been nominated twice for the Mystery Writers of America's Edgar Allan Poe award in the best fact crime category. Fisher has appeared numerous times on nationally broadcast radio and television shows. He currently publishes the popular true crime blog, jimfishertruecrime.blogspot.com.

The Massive True Crime Test
True and False

1. Forensic anthropologists perform autopsies.
2. Deputy sheriffs usually work for the state.
3. The so-called right-wrong test pertains to the insanity defense.
4. A felony is a more serious crime than a misdemeanor.
5. Manslaughter is a more serious homicide offense than second-degree murder.
6. Burglary is essentially a crime of unlawful intrusion.
7. Lying under oath as a trial witness is called perjury.
8. The Miranda Doctrine applies to cases involving Fourth Amendment issues.
9. In a trial, the prosecutor puts his case on first.
10. The jury process is open to the public.
11. In investigative jargon, M. O. stands for Missing Officer.
12. Jailhouse informant evidence is not reliable.
13. Policing has become, over the past decades, less militaristic.
14. Rigor Mortis refers to post mortem body temperature.
15. The U. S. Attorney General heads the federal department of justice.
16. Federal trials are held in U.S. District Courts.
17. There are ten justices on the U.S. Supreme Court.
18. SIDS stands for Sudden Infant Death Syndrome.
19. The term "true bill" pertains to the indictment process.
20. "Angel of Death" cases involve women who murder their husbands.
21. The identification of human bite marks on human skin is highly scientific and reliable as forensic evidence.
22. J. Edgar Hoover ran the Department of Drug Administration.
23. Marilyn Monroe died of a drug overdose.
24. The jury acquitted O. J. Simpson of double murder.
25. Normally a SWAT team does not need a search warrant to search a dwelling for drugs.
26. SWAT stands for Special Weapons and Tactics.
27. SWAT policing started in Los Angeles.
28. The death penalty has been abolished in all but five states.
29. County coroners are elected and medical examiners appointed.
30. As a trial witness an expert can give relevant opinion testimony.
31. A defendant cannot be convicted of murder if there is no body.
32. The modern polygraph was invented in Berkeley, California.
33. The term "passing the trash" generally refers to pedophile schoolteachers.

34. Embezzlement is not a nonviolent crime.
35. There are roughly 50,000 murders a year in the U.S.
36. The longer a person has been dead, the easier it is to pinpoint the time of death.
37. Rapists are almost always serial offenders.
38. Arsonists are comparatively hard to convict.
39. Robbery is a crime against the person.
40. No female has ever been executed in the electric chair.
41. A revolver is a semi-automatic handgun.
42. Crime scene fingerprints are referred to as "latents."
43. The crime of swindling is a form of theft.
44. Recently, pickpockets have become a problem in New York City.
45. Pedophiles cannot be rehabilitated.
46. Governors usually appoint county prosecutors.
47. In the U.S., the crime solution rate for murder is about 80 percent.
48. Most arsonists are over the age of thirty.
49. Since the mid-1990s, the rate of violent crime in the United States had decreased.
50. Recently, condemned prisoners have been executed with the lethal injection of a single drug.
51. The right of free speech is in the Fourth Amendment.
52. The right to remain silent is in the Fifth Amendment.
53. Not every human death calls for an autopsy.
54. It is a crime to kill oneself.
55. In most states it is a crime to patronize a prostitute.
56. There is no longer a shortage of DNA analysts in the country.
57. Hit and run cases comprise a silent crime wave in America.
58. A criminal trial held without a jury is called a bench trial.
59. All criminal defendants are presumed to be innocent and sane.
60. The so-called pigeon drop scam is a good example of a long con.
61. Dr. Henry Lee is a famous forensic pathologist.
62. The JonBenet Ramsey murder case has not been solved.
63. The term "third-degree" pertains to arson investigation.
64. Criminology is a branch of sociology.
65. Physical evidence is by definition circumstantial evidence
66. *In Cold Blood* by Truman Capote is about a 1959 murder in Kansas.
67. Poisoners like arsenic because it leaves no traces in the body.
68. One of the Miranda rights includes the right to a psychiatric examination.
69. Gun ownership is a right protected by the Second Amendment.
70. Very few medical students go on to become forensic pathologists.
71. CSI stands for Crime Suspect Interrogation.
72. APB stands for all-point-bulletin.

73. When a homemade bomb explodes, there is nothing left of the device.
74. Blood spatter analysis is a function of toxicology.
75. Many states now have anti-stalking laws.
76. Rape is one of the most underreported crimes.
77. Eyewitness identification is unreliable evidence.
78. Crime labs didn't exist in the U.S. until the mid-1950s.
79. Shoplifters unable to control the urge to steal are said to suffer from kleptomania.
80. Retail employees steal less from their employers than retail customers.
81. Serial killers like Ted Bundy are not legally insane.
82. Bank robbery is essentially an American crime.
83. Double jeopardy protects citizens from being arrested twice for the same crime.
84. President Richard Nixon launched the so-called war on drugs.
85. Grand juries indict rather than convict suspects.
86. A criminal defendant's right to an attorney comes from the Fourth Amendment.
87. Human hair follicles are as individualistic as fingerprints.
88. In murder cases, prosecutors, in order to convict, do not have to prove the defendant's motive for the crime.
89. They still execute people in Texas, Florida, Ohio, and Oklahoma.
90. In California at one time, condemned prisoners were put to death in the gas chamber.
91. Jails are designed for extended incarceration while prisons are short-term facilities.
92. Most serial killers stand out from the crowd because they look and act strangely.
93. Forensic scientists should not consider themselves as part of a law enforcement team.
94. J. Edgar Hoover was the FBI's first director.
95. Reefer madness refers to marijuana.
96. In California, corrections officials cannot parole convicted rapists and pedophiles.
97. Murder-for-hire hit men are usually highly trained professional killers.
98. A corpse in the heat will decompose faster than a body in the cold.
99. There is no such thing as a female serial killer.
100. A lot of people the police shoot are mentally ill.

Check the answers on the next page.

Answers

1.F (forensic pathologists) **2.**F (county) **3.**T **4.**T **5.**F **6.**T **7.**T **8.**F (interrogations) **9.**T **10.**T **11.**F (modus operandi) **12.**T **13.**F **14.**F (body stiffening) **15.**T **16.**T **17.**F (nine) **18.**T **19.**T **20.**F (nurses and doctors who murder patients) **21.**F **22.**F (FBI) **23.**T **24.**T **25.**F **26.**T **27.**T **28.**F (32) **29.**T **30.**T **31.**F **32.**T **33.**T **34.**F **35.**F (about 11,000) **36.**F **37.**T **38.**T **39.**T **40.**F **41.**F **42.**T **43.**T **44.**T **45.**T **46.**F (they're elected) **47.**F (about 50 percent) **48.**F **49.**T **50.**T **51.**F (First Amendment) **52.**T **53.**T **54.**F **55.**T **56.**F **57.**T **58.**T **59.**T **60.**F (short con) **61.**F (criminalist) **62.**T **63.**F (coerced confessions) **64.**T **65.**T **66.**T **67.**F **68.**F **69.**T **70.**T **71.**F (crime scene investigation) **72.**T **73.**F **74.**F **75.**T **76.**T **77.**T **78.**F (1930s) **79.**T **80.**F **81.**T **82.**T **83.**F (being convicted) **84.**T **85.**T **86.**F (Sixth Amendment) **87.**F **88.**T **89.**T **90.**T **91.**F **92.**F **93.**T **94.**F (Fourth Amendment) **95.**T **96.**F **97.**F **98.**T **99.**F **100.**T

Printed in Great Britain
by Amazon